New Perspectives on

Microsoft® Office 2007

Brief

Ann Shaffer
Patrick Carey
June Jamrich Parsons
Dan Oja
Kathleen T. Finnegan

Lisa Ruffolo
Robin M. Romer
Katherine T. Pinard
Jane E. Pedicini

Roy Ageloff
University of Rhode Island

Joseph J. Adamski
Grand Valley State University

S. Scott Zimmerman
Brigham Young University

Beverly B. Zimmerman
Brigham Young University

THOMSON
COURSE TECHNOLOGY

Australia • Canada • Mexico • Singapore • Spain • United Kingdom • United States

THOMSON
COURSE TECHNOLOGY

New Perspectives on Microsoft® Office 2007—Brief
is published by Thomson Course Technology.

Acquisitions Editor:
Kristina Matthews

Senior Product Manager:
Kathy Finnegan

Product Manager:
Erik Herman

Associate Product Manager:
Brandi Henson

Editorial Assistant:
Leigh Robbins

Senior Marketing Manager:
Joy Stark

Marketing Coordinator:
Jennifer Hankin

Developmental Editors:
Laurie Brown, Jessica Evans,
Mary Kemper, Katherine T. Pinard,
Robin M. Romer, Lisa Ruffolo

Content Project Managers:
Daphne Barbas, Danielle Chouhan,
Catherine DiMassa, Jennifer Goguen
McGrail, Matthew Hutchinson

Composition:
GEX Publishing Services

Text Designer:
Steve Deschene

Cover Designer:
Elizabeth Paquin

Cover Art:
Bill Brown

Preface

The New Perspectives Series' critical-thinking, problem-solving approach is the ideal way to prepare students to transcend point-and-click skills and take advantage of all that Microsoft Office 2007 has to offer.

In developing the New Perspectives Series for Microsoft Office 2007, our goal was to create books that give students the software concepts and practical skills they need to succeed beyond the classroom. We've updated our proven case-based pedagogy with more practical content to make learning skills more meaningful to students.

With the New Perspectives Series, students understand *why* they are learning *what* they are learning, and are fully prepared to apply their skills to real-life situations.

"I really love the Margin Tips, which add 'tricks of the trade' to students' skills package. In addition, the Reality Check exercises provide for practical application of students' knowledge. I can't wait to use them in the classroom when we adopt Office 2007."

—Terry Morse Colucci
Institute of Technology, Inc.

About This Book

This book provides essential, hands-on coverage of the new Microsoft Office 2007 suite, and includes the following:

- A new "Getting Started with Microsoft Office 2007" tutorial that familiarizes students with the new features and user interface
- Two Word 2007 tutorials that cover core skills and exciting new features, such as design themes and Live Preview
- Three Excel 2007 tutorials that present key concepts and skills, as well as new topics including table styles and conditional formatting
- Three Access 2007 tutorials that guide students through the database creation process and cover new features, such as working in Layout view and the Navigation Pane
- One PowerPoint 2007 tutorial that teaches students the fundamentals of creating well-designed presentations
- One Outlook tutorial that covers basic e–mail skills and introduces innovations such as Instant Search, the To–Do Bar, and color categories
- Coverage of Windows Vista basics and file management
- New business case scenarios throughout, which provide a rich and realistic context for students to apply the concepts and skills presented

System Requirements

This book assumes a typical installation of Microsoft Office 2007 and Microsoft Windows Vista Ultimate with the Aero feature turned off (or Windows Vista Home Premium or Business edition). Note that you can also complete the tutorials in this book using Windows XP; you will notice only minor differences if you are using Windows XP. Refer to the tutorial "Getting Started with Microsoft Office 2007" for Tips noting these differences. The browser used for any steps that require a browser is Internet Explorer 7.

The New Perspectives Approach

"I appreciate the real-world approach that the New Perspective Series takes. It enables the transference of knowledge from step-by-step instructions to a far broader application of the software tools."

—Monique Sluymers
Kaplan University

Context

Each tutorial begins with a problem presented in a "real-world" case that is meaningful to students. The case sets the scene to help students understand what they will do in the tutorial.

Hands-on Approach

Each tutorial is divided into manageable sessions that combine reading and hands-on, step-by-step work. Colorful screenshots help guide students through the steps. **Trouble?** tips anticipate common mistakes or problems to help students stay on track and continue with the tutorial.

InSight

InSight Boxes

New for Office 2007! InSight boxes offer expert advice and best practices to help students better understand how to work with the software. With the information provided in the InSight boxes, students achieve a deeper understanding of the concepts behind the software features and skills.

Tip

Margin Tips

New for Office 2007! Margin Tips provide helpful hints and shortcuts for more efficient use of the software. The Tips appear in the margin at key points throughout each tutorial, giving students extra information when and where they need it.

Reality Check

Reality Checks

New for Office 2007! Comprehensive, open-ended Reality Check exercises give students the opportunity to practice skills by creating practical, real-world documents, such as resumes and budgets, which they are likely to use in their everyday lives at school, home, or work.

Review

In New Perspectives, retention is a key component to learning. At the end of each session, a series of Quick Check questions helps students test their understanding of the concepts before moving on. Each tutorial also contains an end-of-tutorial summary and a list of key terms for further reinforcement.

Apply

Assessment

Engaging and challenging Review Assignments and Case Problems have always been a hallmark feature of the New Perspectives Series. Colorful icons and brief descriptions accompany the exercises, making it easy to understand, at a glance, both the goal and level of challenge a particular assignment holds.

Reference Window

Task Reference

Reference

While contextual learning is excellent for retention, there are times when students will want a high-level understanding of how to accomplish a task. Within each tutorial, Reference Windows appear before a set of steps to provide a succinct summary and preview of how to perform a task. In addition, a complete Task Reference at the back of the book provides quick access to information on how to carry out common tasks. Finally, each book includes a combination Glossary/Index to promote easy reference of material.

Our Complete System of Instruction

Coverage To Meet Your Needs

Whether you're looking for just a small amount of coverage or enough to fill a semester-long class, we can provide you with a textbook that meets your needs.

- Brief books typically cover the essential skills in just 2 to 4 tutorials.
- Introductory books build and expand on those skills and contain an average of 5 to 8 tutorials.
- Comprehensive books are great for a full-semester class, and contain 9 to 12+ tutorials.

So if the book you're holding does not provide the right amount of coverage for you, there's probably another offering available. Go to our Web site or contact your Thomson Course Technology sales representative to find out what else we offer.

Student Online Companion

This book has an accompanying online companion Web site designed to enhance learning. This Web site includes:

- Internet Assignments for selected tutorials
- Student Data Files
- PowerPoint presentations

CourseCasts – Learning on the Go. Always available...always relevant.

Want to keep up with the latest technology trends relevant to you? Visit our site to find a library of podcasts, CourseCasts, featuring a "CourseCast of the Week," and download them to your mp3 player at http://coursecasts.course.com.

Our fast-paced world is driven by technology. You know because you're an active participant— always on the go, always keeping up with technological trends, and always learning new ways to embrace technology to power your life.

Ken Baldauf, host of CourseCasts, is a faculty member of the Florida State University Computer Science Department where he is responsible for teaching technology classes to thousands of FSU students each year. Ken is an expert in the latest technology trends; he gathers and sorts through the most pertinent news and information for CourseCasts so your students can spend their time enjoying technology, rather than trying to figure it out. Open or close your lecture with a discussion based on the latest CourseCast.

Visit us at http://coursecasts.course.com to learn on the go!

Instructor Resources

We offer more than just a book. We have all the tools you need to enhance your lectures, check students' work, and generate exams in a new, easier-to-use and completely revised package. This book's Instructor's Manual, ExamView testbank, PowerPoint presentations, data files, solution files, figure files, and a sample syllabus are all available on a single CD-ROM or for downloading at www.course.com.

Skills Assessment and Training

SAM 2007 helps bridge the gap between the classroom and the real world by allowing students to train and test on important computer skills in an active, hands-on environment.

SAM 2007's easy-to-use system includes powerful interactive exams, training or projects on critical applications such as Word, Excel, Access, PowerPoint, Outlook, Windows, the Internet, and much more. SAM simulates the application environment, allowing students to demonstrate their knowledge and think through the skills by performing real-world tasks.

Designed to be used with the New Perspectives Series, SAM 2007 includes built-in page references so students can print helpful study guides that match the New Perspectives textbooks used in class. Powerful administrative options allow instructors to schedule exams and assignments, secure tests, and run reports with almost limitless flexibility.

Blackboard

Online Content

Blackboard is the leading distance learning solution provider and class-management platform today. Thomson Course Technology has partnered with Blackboard to bring you premium online content. Content for use with *New Perspectives on Microsoft Office 2007, Brief* is available in a Blackboard Course Cartridge and may include topic reviews, case projects, review questions, test banks, practice tests, custom syllabi, and more.

Thomson Course Technology also has solutions for several other learning management systems. Please visit http://www.course.com today to see what's available for this title.

Acknowledgments

The entire New Perspectives team would like to extend its sincere thanks to the New Perspectives Office 2007 advisory board members and textbook reviewers listed below. We are extremely grateful to all of them for their contributions in the development of this text. Their valuable insights and excellent feedback helped us to shape this text, ensuring that it will meet the needs of instructors and students both in the classroom and beyond. Thank you all!

New Perspectives Office 2007 Advisory Board

Patti J. Impink, Macon State College
Gayle E. Larson, Dakota County Technical College
Cindy J. Miller, Ivy Tech Community College, Lafayette
Terry Morse Colucci, Institute of Technology, Inc., Clovis, CA
Lucy Parakhovnik, California State University, Northridge
Monique Sluymers, Kaplan University

Textbook Reviewers

Bernice Eng, Brookdale Community College
J. Patrick Fenton, West Valley College
Glen A. Johansson, Spokane Community College
Melinda Rose, Radford University
Deborah A. Tieman, Ivy Tech Community College, Fort Wayne

Brief Contents

Table of Contents

Getting Started with Microsoft Office 2007

Word

Tutorial 1 Creating a Document

Tutorial 2 Editing and Formatting a Document
Preparing a Handout on Choosing a Design Style . . . . .WD 45

Excel

Tutorial 1 Getting Started with Excel
Creating an Order Report . . . . .EX 1

Access

PowerPoint

Outlook

Objectives

Session 1
- Start Windows Vista and tour the desktop
- Explore the Start menu
- Run software programs, switch between them, and close them
- Manipulate windows
- Identify and use the controls in menus, toolbars, and dialog boxes

Session 2
- Navigate your computer with Windows Explorer and the Computer window
- Change the view of the items in your computer
- Get help when you need it
- Shut down Windows

Exploring the Basics of Microsoft Windows Vista

Investigating the Windows Vista Operating System

Case | Back to Work

Back to Work is a nonprofit agency in Minneapolis, Minnesota, that helps people who want to develop skills for the contemporary workforce, such as retirees and parents who are returning to careers after raising a family. Back to Work creates customized plans for people preparing for full- or part-time work, particularly in the areas of retail, hospitality, administrative support, and manufacturing. Elena Varney, the director of the agency, coordinates training sessions on developing computer skills, ranging from basic introductions to computers, Windows, and the Internet, to more advanced topics such as using word-processing programs, spreadsheets, and databases. Elena recently hired you to teach some introductory computer classes. Your first class, on using the Microsoft Windows Vista operating system, meets next week. Although you frequently use computers to visit Web sites and exchange e-mail, you have only learned the essential Windows skills in passing, not in an organized, comprehensive approach. To help you prepare for your class, Elena offers to walk you through the curriculum, from starting the computer and opening and closing programs to shutting down the computer.

In this tutorial you will start Windows Vista and practice some fundamental computer skills. Then you'll learn how to navigate with the Computer window and Windows Explorer. Finally, you'll use the Windows Vista Help system.

Starting Data Files

There are no starting Data Files needed for this tutorial.

Session 1

Starting Windows Vista

Elena Varney begins helping you plan the class by first defining the operating system. She explains that the **operating system** is software that helps the computer perform essential tasks such as displaying information on the computer screen and saving data on disks. (Software refers to the **programs**, or **applications**, that a computer uses to complete tasks.) Your computer uses the **Microsoft Windows Vista** operating system—**Windows Vista** for short. Windows is the name of the operating system, and Vista indicates the version you are using. Microsoft has released many versions of Windows since 1985, and is likely to continue developing new versions.

Much of the software created for the Windows Vista operating system shares the same look and works the same way. This similarity in design means that after you learn how to use one Windows Vista program, such as Microsoft Office Word (a word-processing program), you are well on your way to understanding how to use other Windows Vista programs. Windows Vista allows you to use more than one program at a time, so you can easily switch between your word-processing program and your appointment book program, for example. Windows Vista also makes it easy to access the **Internet**, a worldwide collection of computers connected to one another to enable communication. All in all, Windows Vista makes your computer an effective and easy-to-use productivity tool.

Windows Vista starts automatically when you turn on your computer. After completing some necessary start-up tasks, Windows Vista displays a Welcome screen, which lists all the users for the computer. Before you start working with Windows Vista, you must click your user name and perhaps type a password. A **user name** is a unique name that identifies you to Windows Vista, and a **password** is text—often a confidential combination of letters and numbers—that you must enter before you can work with Windows Vista. After you provide this information, the Windows Vista desktop appears and the Welcome Center window opens, which provides information about your computer and how to set it up according to your preferences.

To begin your review of Windows Vista, Elena asks you to start Windows Vista.

To start Windows Vista:

▶ 1. Turn on your computer. After a moment, Windows Vista starts and the Welcome screen appears.

   Trouble? If you are asked to select an operating system, do not take action. Windows Vista should start automatically after a designated number of seconds. If it does not, ask your instructor or technical support person for help.

   Trouble? If this is the first time you have started your computer with Windows Vista, messages might appear on your screen informing you that Windows is setting up components of your computer.

▶ 2. On the Welcome screen, click your user name and enter your password, if necessary. By default, the Welcome Center window opens on the desktop, as shown in Figure 1. Your desktop might look different.

   Trouble? If your user name does not appear in the list of users on the Welcome screen, ask your instructor or technical support person which name you should click.

   Trouble? If you need to enter a password, type your password, and then click the Continue button or press the Enter key to continue.

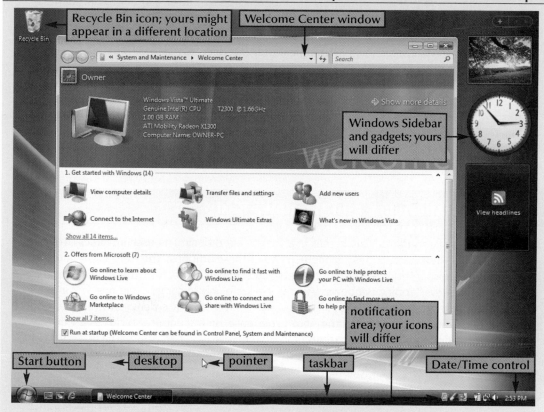

Welcome Center window open on the Windows Vista desktop ◀ Figure 1

3. Look at your desktop and locate the objects labeled in Figure 1. (Your desktop might not contain all of them.) The objects on your desktop might appear larger or smaller than those in Figure 1, depending on your monitor's settings. Figure 2 describes the purpose of each of these objects.

Elements of the Windows Vista desktop ◀ Figure 2

Element	Description
Icon	A small picture that represents an object available to your computer
Pointer	A small object, such as an arrow, that moves on the screen when you move the mouse
Desktop	Your workplace on the screen
Date/Time control	An element that shows the current date and time and lets you set the clock
Taskbar	A strip that contains buttons to give you quick access to common tools and the programs currently running
Start button	A button that provides access to Windows Vista programs, documents, and information on the Internet
Notification area	An area that displays icons corresponding to services running in the background, such as an Internet connection
Sidebar	A place on the desktop where Windows stows gadgets, which are small, handy programs such as sticky notes and clocks
Welcome Center window	A window that lists tasks first-time users can perform to quickly set up their computers

Trouble? If a blank screen or animated design replaces the Windows Vista desktop, your computer might be set to use a **screen saver**, a program that causes a monitor to go blank or to display an animated design after a specified amount of idle time. Press any key or move your mouse to restore the Windows Vista desktop.

The Windows Vista screen uses a **graphical user interface** (**GUI**, pronounced "gooey"), which displays icons that represent items stored on your computer, such as programs and files. A computer **file** is a collection of related information; typical types of files include text documents, spreadsheets, digital pictures, and songs. Your computer represents files with **icons**, which are pictures of familiar objects, such as file folders and documents. Windows Vista gets its name from the rectangular work areas, called "windows," that appear on your screen as you work, such as the Welcome Center window shown in Figure 1. You will learn more about windows later in this tutorial.

InSight	**The Aero Experience and Windows Basic**

Like Windows XP, Windows Vista comes in a variety of editions. The user interface in Windows Vista is called Aero, and is available in two of these editions. The Aero experience features a semitransparent glass design that lets you see many objects at the same time, such as two or more overlapping windows. (Aero is available only in certain versions of Windows Vista.) Aero also offers other features for viewing windows that are demonstrated later in this tutorial. To take advantage of the Aero experience, your computer requires hardware with features designed for enhanced graphics. Otherwise, you can use the basic version of Aero, called Windows Basic, which provides the same elements as the enhanced experience, including windows and icons, but not the same graphic effects. This tutorial assumes that you are using Windows Basic.

Touring the Windows Vista Desktop

In Windows terminology, the Windows Vista **desktop** is a workspace for projects and the tools that you need to manipulate your projects. When you first start a computer, it uses **default settings**, those preset by the operating system. The default desktop you see after you first install Windows Vista, for example, displays an abstract image that shades from blue to green to yellow. However, Microsoft designed Windows Vista so that you can easily change the appearance of the desktop. You can, for example, change images or add patterns and text to the desktop background.

Interacting with the Desktop

To interact with the objects on your desktop, you use a **pointing device**. The most common type is called a **mouse**, so this book uses that term. If you are using a different pointing device, such as a trackball or touchpad, substitute that device whenever you see the term "mouse."

You use a pointing device to move the mouse pointer over objects on the desktop, or to **point** to them. The pointer is usually shaped like an arrow ⃕, although it changes shape depending on the pointer's location on the screen and the tasks you are performing. As you move the mouse on a surface, such as a mouse pad, the pointer on the screen moves in a corresponding direction.

When you point to certain objects, such as the objects on the taskbar, a **ScreenTip** appears near the object to tell you the purpose or function of the object to which you are pointing.

Elena suggests that you acquaint students with the desktop by viewing a couple of ScreenTips.

To view ScreenTips:

▶ **1.** Use the mouse to point to the **Start** button ⊕ on the taskbar. After a few seconds, you see a ScreenTip indentifying the button, as shown in Figure 3.

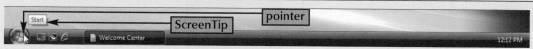

▶ **2.** Point to the time displayed at the right end of the taskbar. A ScreenTip for today's date (or the date to which your computer's time clock is set) appears.

Clicking refers to pressing a mouse button and immediately releasing it. Clicking sends a signal to your computer that you want to perform an action on the object you click. In Windows Vista, you perform most actions with the left mouse button. If you are told to click an object, position the mouse pointer on that object and click the left mouse button, unless instructed otherwise.

When you click the Start button, the Start menu opens. A **menu** is a group or list of commands, and a **menu command** is text that you can click to complete tasks. If a right-pointing arrow follows a menu command, you can point to the command to open a **submenu**, which is a list of additional choices related to the command. The **Start menu** provides access to programs, documents, and much more.

To open the Start menu:

▶ **1.** Point to the **Start** button ⊕ on the taskbar.

▶ **2.** Click the left mouse button. The Start menu opens. An arrow ▶ points to the All Programs command on the Start menu, indicating that you can view additional choices by navigating to a submenu.

▶ **3.** Click the **Start** button ⊕ on the taskbar to close the Start menu.

You need to select an object to work with it. To **select** an object in Windows Vista, you usually point to and then click that object. Sometimes, you can select menu commands by pointing to them. Windows Vista shows you which object is selected by highlighting it, usually by changing the object's color, putting a box around it, or making the object appear to be indented.

To select a menu command:

▶ **1.** Click the **Start** button ⊕ on the taskbar.

▶ **2.** Point to **All Programs** on the Start menu. The All Programs command is highlighted to indicate it is selected. After a short pause, the All Programs list opens. See Figure 4.

Figure 4 | **All Programs list**

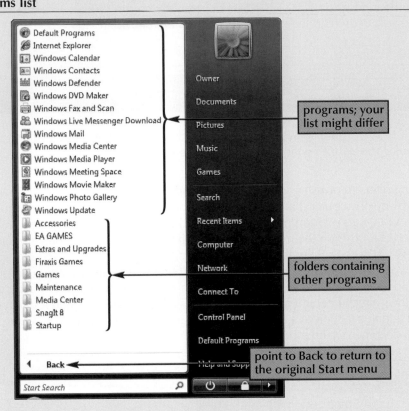

- Default Programs
- Internet Explorer
- Windows Calendar
- Windows Contacts
- Windows Defender
- Windows DVD Maker
- Windows Fax and Scan
- Windows Live Messenger Download
- Windows Mail
- Windows Media Center
- Windows Media Player
- Windows Meeting Space
- Windows Movie Maker
- Windows Photo Gallery
- Windows Update
- Accessories
- EA GAMES
- Extras and Upgrades
- Firaxis Games
- Games
- Maintenance
- Media Center
- SnagIt 8
- Startup

◄ Back

Start Search

programs; your list might differ

folders containing other programs

point to Back to return to the original Start menu

Trouble? If a submenu opens instead of the All Programs list, you pointed to the wrong command. Move the mouse so that the pointer points to All Programs.

▶ **3.** Click the **Start** button on the taskbar to close the Start menu.

In addition to clicking an object to select it, you can double-click an object to open or start the item associated with it. For example, you can double-click a folder icon to open the folder and see its contents. Or you can double-click a program icon to start the program. **Double-clicking** means to click the left mouse button twice in quick succession.

Elena suggests that you have students practice double-clicking by opening the Recycle Bin. The Recycle Bin holds deleted items such as folders until you remove them permanently.

To view the contents of the Recycle Bin:

▶ **1.** In the upper-right corner of the Welcome Center window, click the **Close** button [X] to close the window.

▶ **2.** Click the desktop, and then point to the **Recycle Bin** icon on the desktop. A ScreenTip appears that describes the Recycle Bin.

▶ **3.** Click the left mouse button twice quickly to double-click the **Recycle Bin** icon. The Recycle Bin window opens, as shown in Figure 5.

Contents of the Recycle Bin | **Figure** 5

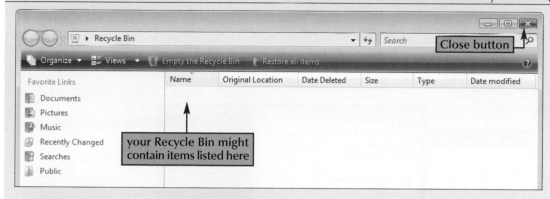

Trouble? If the Recycle Bin window does not open, and you see only the Recycle Bin name highlighted below the icon, you double-clicked too slowly. Double-click the icon again more quickly.

4. Click the **Close** button ⊠ in the upper-right corner of the Recycle Bin window.

You'll learn more about opening and closing windows later in this session.

Your mouse has more than one button—in addition to the left button, the mouse has a right button that you can use for performing certain actions in Windows Vista. However, the term "clicking" continues to refer to the left button; clicking an object with the *right* button is called **right-clicking**.

In Windows Vista, right-clicking selects an object and opens its **shortcut menu**, which lists actions you can take with that object. You can right-click practically any object—the Start button, a desktop icon, the taskbar, and even the desktop itself—to view commands associated with that object. Elena reminds you that you clicked the Start button with the left mouse button to open the Start menu. Now you can right-click the Start button to open the shortcut menu for the Start button.

To right-click an object:

1. Position the pointer over the **Start** button 🪟 on the taskbar.

2. Right-click the **Start** button 🪟 to open its shortcut menu. This menu offers a list of actions you can take with the Start button. See Figure 6.

Start button shortcut menu | **Figure** 6

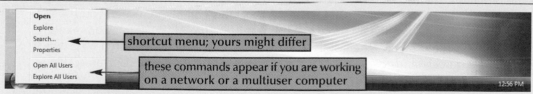

Trouble? If the shortcut menu does not open and you are using a trackball or a mouse with three buttons or a wheel, make sure you click the button on the far right, not the one in the middle.

Trouble? If your menu looks slightly different from the one in Figure 6, it is still the correct Start button shortcut menu. Its commands often vary by computer.

3. Press the **Esc** key to close the shortcut menu. You return to the desktop.

Exploring the Start Menu

Recall that the Start menu is the central point for accessing programs, documents, and other resources on your computer. The Start menu is organized into two panes, as shown in Figure 7, and each pane lists items you can point to or click.

Figure 7 | **Start menu**

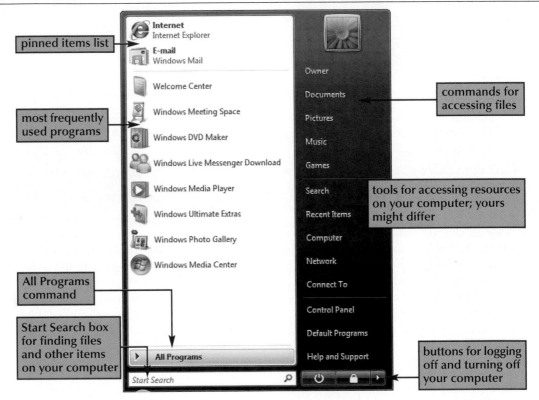

pinned items list

most frequently used programs

All Programs command

Start Search box for finding files and other items on your computer

commands for accessing files

tools for accessing resources on your computer; yours might differ

buttons for logging off and turning off your computer

Tip

To pin a program to the Start menu, right-click the program icon, and then click Pin to Start Menu on the shortcut menu.

The left pane organizes programs for easy access. The area at the top of the left pane is called the **pinned items list**. Pinned items stay on the Start menu until you remove them. By default, Windows Vista lists the Web browser and e-mail program on your computer in the pinned items list. You can pin other items to this list. When you use a program, Windows Vista adds it to the **most frequently used programs list**, which appears below the pinned items list. Windows Vista can list only a certain number of frequently used programs—after that, the programs you have not opened recently are replaced by the programs you used last.

Near the bottom of the left pane is the All Programs command, which you have already used to display the All Programs list. You'll use the All Programs command shortly to start a program. The last item in the left pane is the **Start Search box**, which helps you quickly find anything stored on your computer, including programs, documents, pictures, and music.

From the right pane of the Start menu, you can access common locations and tools on your computer. For example, the **Documents** folder is your personal folder, a convenient place to store documents, graphics, and other work. The **Computer** window is a tool that you use to view, organize, and access the programs, files, and drives on your computer.

From the lower section of the right pane, you can open windows that help you work effectively with Windows Vista, including **Control Panel**, which contains specialized tools that help you change the way Windows Vista looks and behaves, and **Help and Support**, which provides articles, demonstrations, and steps for performing tasks in Windows Vista. (You'll explore Windows Help and Support later in this tutorial.) Finally, you also log off and turn off your computer from the Start menu. When you **log off**, you end your session with Windows Vista but leave the computer turned on.

> **Tip**
>
> Point to an item in the left or right pane of the Start menu to display a Screen-Tip describing the item.

Log Off or Turn Off? | InSight

If more than one person uses your computer, you should generally log off Windows rather than shutting down the computer. That way, the computer is ready for someone else to use. In either case, it's a good idea to log off (or shut down) when you're finished working, to prevent an unauthorized person from accessing and changing your work.

Now that you've explored the Start menu, you're ready to use it to start a program.

Starting a Program | Reference Window

- Click the Start button on the taskbar, and then point to All Programs.
- If necessary, click the folder that contains the program you want to start
- Click the name of the program you want to start.

or

- Click the name or icon of the program you want to start in the pinned items list or the most frequently used programs list on the Start menu.

Elena mentions that Windows Vista includes an easy-to-use word-processing program called WordPad, which you can start to write a letter or report. You open Windows Vista programs from the Start menu. Programs are usually located on the All Programs list or in one of its folders. A **folder** is a container that helps to organize the contents of your computer. To start WordPad, you navigate to the Accessories folder in the All Programs list.

To start the WordPad program from the Start menu:

▶ **1.** Click the **Start** button 🌐 on the taskbar to open the Start menu.

▶ **2.** Point to **All Programs**, and then click **Accessories**. The Accessories folder opens. See Figure 8.

Figure 8 | **Start menu and related submenus**

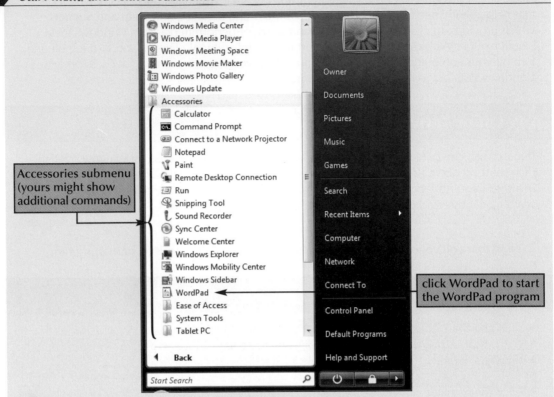

Trouble? If a different folder opens, point to Back to return to the initial Start menu, point to All Programs, and then click Accessories.

▸ **3.** Click **WordPad**. The WordPad program window opens, as shown in Figure 9.

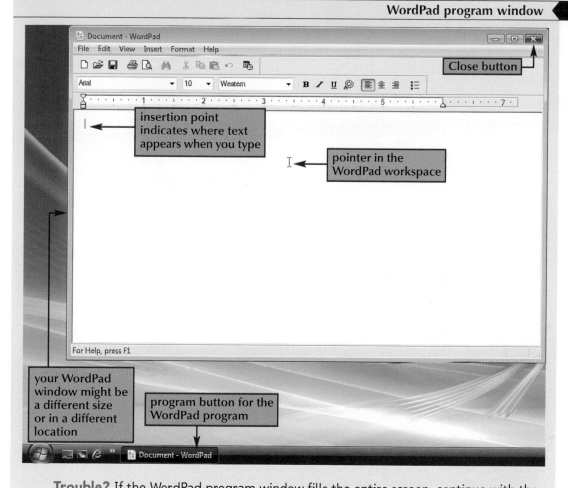

WordPad program window ◀ **Figure 9**

Trouble? If the WordPad program window fills the entire screen, continue with the next step. You will learn how to manipulate windows shortly.

When a program is started, it is said to be open or running. A **program button** appears on the taskbar for each open program. You click a program button to switch between open programs. When you are finished using a program, you can click the Close button located in the upper-right corner of the program window to **exit**, or close, that program.

To exit the WordPad program:

▶ 1. Click the **Close** button ▨ on the WordPad title bar. The WordPad program closes and you return to the desktop.

Running Multiple Programs

One of the most useful features of Windows Vista is **multitasking**, which allows you to work on more than one task at a time. To demonstrate, Elena suggests that you start WordPad and leave it running while you start the Paint program.

To run WordPad and Paint at the same time:

▶ 1. Start WordPad again.

▶ 2. Click the **Start** button 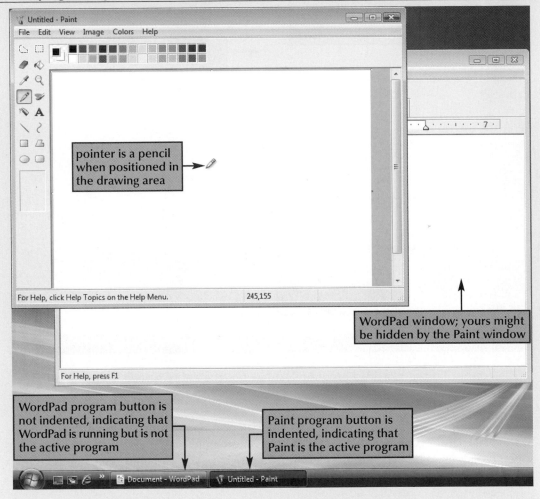 on the taskbar, point to **All Programs**, click **Accessories**, and then click **Paint**. The Paint program window opens, as shown in Figure 10. Now two programs are running at the same time.

Figure 10 ▶ **Two programs open**

pointer is a pencil when positioned in the drawing area

WordPad window; yours might be hidden by the Paint window

WordPad program button is not indented, indicating that WordPad is running but is not the active program

Paint program button is indented, indicating that Paint is the active program

Trouble? If the Paint program fills the entire screen, continue with the next set of steps. You will learn how to manipulate windows shortly.

The **active program** is the one you are currently using—Windows Vista applies your next keystroke or command to the active program. Paint is the active program because it is the one in which you are currently working. The WordPad program button is still on the taskbar, indicating that WordPad is still running even if you can't see its program window.

Switching Between Programs

Because only one program is active at a time, you need to switch between programs if you want to work in one or the other. The easiest way to switch between programs is to use the program buttons on the taskbar.

Tip

When more than one window is open, the active program appears on top of all other open windows.

To switch between WordPad and Paint:

▶ **1.** Click the program button labeled **Document - WordPad** on the taskbar. The Word-Pad program window moves to the front, and now the Document - WordPad button appears indented, indicating that WordPad is the active program.

▶ **2.** Click the program button labeled **Untitled - Paint** on the taskbar to switch to the Paint program. The Paint program is again the active program.

In addition to using the taskbar to switch between open programs, you can also close programs from the taskbar.

Closing Programs from the Taskbar

You should always close a program when you are finished using it. Each program uses computer resources, such as memory, so Windows Vista works more efficiently when only the programs you need are open. Elena reminds you that you've already closed an open program using the Close button on the title bar of the program window. You can also close a program, whether active or inactive, by using the shortcut menu associated with the program button on the taskbar.

To close WordPad and Paint using the program button shortcut menus:

▶ **1.** Right-click the **Untitled - Paint** button on the taskbar. The shortcut menu for the Paint program button opens. See Figure 11.

Program button shortcut menu ◀ **Figure 11**

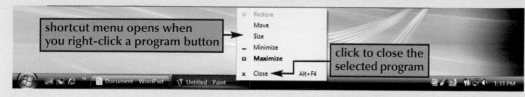

▶ **2.** Click **Close** on the shortcut menu. The Paint program closes and the program button labeled "Untitled - Paint" no longer appears on the taskbar.

▶ **3.** Right-click the **Document - WordPad** button on the taskbar, and then click **Close** on the shortcut menu. The WordPad program closes and its program button no longer appears on the taskbar.

Using Windows and Dialog Boxes

When you run a program in Windows Vista, the program appears in a **window**, a rectangular area of the screen that contains a program, text, or other data. A window also contains **controls**, which are graphical or textual objects used for manipulating the window and for using the program. Figure 12 describes the controls you see in most windows.

Figure 12 ▶ Window controls

Figure 12 ▶ Window controls

Control	Description
Menu bar	Contains the titles of menus, such as File, Edit, and Help
Sizing button	Lets you enlarge, shrink, or close a window
Status bar	Displays information or messages about the task you are performing
Title bar	Contains the window title and basic window control buttons
Toolbar	Contains buttons that provide you with shortcuts to common menu commands
Window title	Identifies the program and document contained in the window
Workspace	Includes the part of the window where you manipulate your work—enter text, draw pictures, and set up calculations, for example

Elena suggests that you start WordPad and identify its window controls.

To look at the window controls in WordPad:

▶ **1.** Start WordPad. On your screen, identify the controls that are labeled in Figure 13.

Figure 13 ▶ WordPad window controls

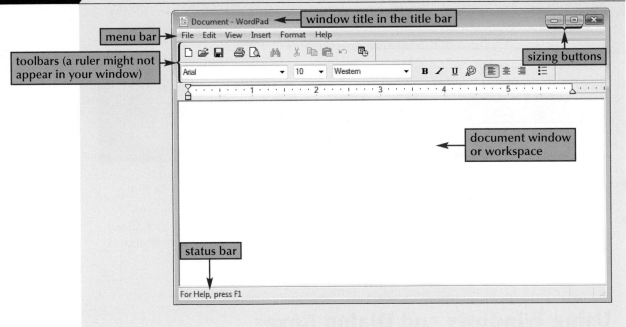

Manipulating Windows

In most windows, three buttons appear on the right side of the title bar. The first button is the Minimize button, which hides a window so that only its program button is visible on the taskbar. Depending on the status of the window, the middle button either maximizes the window or restores it to a predefined size. You are already familiar with the last button—the Close button.

You can use the Minimize button when you want to temporarily hide a window but keep the program running.

To minimize the WordPad window:

▶ **1.** Click the **Minimize** button ⬚ on the WordPad title bar. The WordPad window shrinks so that only the Document - WordPad button on the taskbar is visible.

   Trouble? If the WordPad program window closed, you accidentally clicked the Close button. Use the Start button to start WordPad again, and then repeat Step 1. If you accidentally clicked the Maximize or Restore Down button, repeat Step 1.

You can redisplay a minimized window by clicking the program's button on the taskbar. When you redisplay a window, it becomes the active window.

To redisplay the WordPad window:

▶ **1.** Click the **Document - WordPad** button on the taskbar. The WordPad window is restored to its previous size.

   The taskbar button provides another way to switch a window between its minimized and active states.

▶ **2.** Click the **Document - WordPad** button on the taskbar again to minimize the window.

▶ **3.** Click the **Document - WordPad** button once more to redisplay the window.

The Maximize button enlarges a window so that it fills the entire screen. Use maximized windows when you need to see more of the program and your data.

To maximize the WordPad window:

▶ **1.** Click the **Maximize** button ⬚ on the WordPad title bar.

   Trouble? If the window is already maximized, it fills the entire screen, and the Maximize button does not appear. Instead, you see the Restore Down button. Skip this step.

The Restore Down button reduces the window so that it is smaller than the entire screen. This feature is useful if you want to see more than one window at a time, move the window to another location on the screen, or change the dimensions of the window.

To restore a window:

▶ **1.** Click the **Restore Down** button ⬚ on the WordPad title bar. After a window is restored, the Restore Down button ⬚ changes to the Maximize button ⬚ .

You can use the mouse to move a window to a new position on the screen. When you click an object and then press and hold down the mouse button while moving the mouse, you are **dragging** the object. You can move objects on the screen by dragging them to a new location. If you want to move a window, you drag the window by its title bar. You cannot move a maximized window.

To drag the restored WordPad window to a new location:

▶ **1.** Position the mouse pointer on the WordPad title bar.

▶ **2.** Press and hold down the left mouse button, and then move the mouse up or down a little to drag the window. The window moves as you move the mouse.

3. Position the window anywhere on the desktop, and then release the left mouse button. The WordPad window stays in the new location.

4. Drag the WordPad window to the upper-left corner of the desktop.

You can also use the mouse to change the size of a window. When you point to an edge or corner of a window, the pointer changes to a double-headed arrow, similar to ⬉. You can use this resize pointer to drag an edge or lower corner of the window and change the size of the window.

To change the size of the WordPad window:

1. Position the pointer over the lower-right corner of the WordPad window. The pointer changes to ⬉. See Figure 14.

Figure 14 | Preparing to resize a window

resize pointer

2. Press and hold down the mouse button, and then drag the corner down and to the right.

3. Release the mouse button. Now the window is larger.

You can also use the resize pointer to drag the lower-left corner of the window and change its size. To change a window's size in any one direction, drag the left, right, top, or bottom window borders left, right, up, or down.

Selecting Options from a Menu

Many Windows Vista programs use menus to organize the program's features and available functions. The menu bar is typically located at the top of the program window, immediately below the title bar, and shows the names of the menus, such as File, Edit, and Help.

When you click a menu name, the choices for that menu appear below the menu bar. Like choices on the Start menu, these choices are called menu commands. To select a menu command, you click it. For example, the File menu is a standard feature in some Windows Vista programs and contains the commands typically related to working with a file: creating, opening, saving, and printing. Menu commands that are followed by an ellipsis (...) open a dialog box. A **dialog box** is a special kind of window where you enter or choose settings for how you want to perform a task. For example, you use the Page Setup dialog box to set margins and some printing options.

Because the Page Setup dialog box contains many typical controls, Elena suggests you use the Page Setup command on the WordPad File menu to open that dialog box.

Tip

If you open a menu, and then decide not to select a command, you can close the menu by clicking its name again or by pressing the Esc key.

To select the Page Setup menu command from the File menu:

1. Click **File** on the WordPad menu bar to open the File menu.

2. Click **Page Setup** to open the Page Setup dialog box.

3. After examining the dialog box, click the **Cancel** button to close the Page Setup dialog box.

If you selected options in the Page Setup dialog box that you want to retain, you click the OK button instead of the Cancel button.

Not all menu items and commands immediately carry out an action—some show sub-menus or ask you for more information about what you want to do. The menu gives you visual hints about what to expect when you select an item. These hints are sometimes referred to as **menu conventions**. Figure 15 shows examples of these menu conventions.

Examples of menu conventions ◄ **Figure 15**

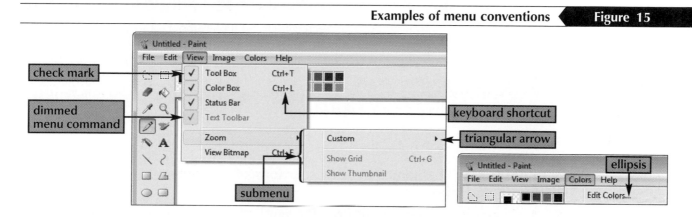

Figure 16 describes the Windows Vista menu conventions.

Menu conventions ◄ **Figure 16**

Convention	Description
Check mark	Indicates a toggle, or "on-off" switch (like a light switch), that is either checked (turned on) or not checked (turned off).
Ellipsis	Three dots that indicate you can make additional selections after you select that command. Commands without dots do not require additional choices—they take effect as soon as you click them. If a command is followed by an ellipsis, a dialog box opens where you can enter details about how you want a task carried out.
Triangular arrow	Indicates the presence of a submenu. When you point to a menu option that has a triangular arrow, a submenu appears.
Dimmed command	Command that is not currently available.
Keyboard shortcut	Key or combination of keys that you can press to select the menu command without actually opening the menu.

Using Toolbars

Many Windows Vista programs include one or more toolbars, which are typically displayed near the top of the program window. A toolbar is a row, column, or block of buttons or icons that gives you one-click access to frequently used menu commands. Just as menu commands are grouped on menus according to task, the buttons on a toolbar are also grouped and organized by task.

You can explore the WordPad toolbar buttons by looking at their ScreenTips.

InSight	**Toolbars, Menus, and Ribbons**

Some Windows Vista programs such as Microsoft Office 2007 combine the toolbars and menu bar into a single component called the Ribbon. The Ribbon organizes commands into logical groups that are displayed on a tab. Each tab is designed for a particular activity, such as writing or designing a page. Many buttons on the Ribbon are similar to the buttons on a toolbar—they perform a command with one click. Buttons with arrows work like menus—you click a button to display a menu of related options.

To determine the names and descriptions of the buttons on the WordPad toolbar:

▶ **1.** Position the pointer over the **Print Preview** button 🔍 on the WordPad toolbar. After a short pause, the ScreenTip for the button appears below the button, and a description of the button appears in the status bar.

Trouble? If you closed WordPad after the previous set of steps, restart the program.

▶ **2.** Move the pointer to each button on the toolbar to display its name and purpose.

You select a toolbar button by clicking it, which performs the button's command. One of the buttons you pointed to on the WordPad toolbar is called the Undo button. Clicking the Undo button reverses the effects of your last action. Elena says you can see how this works by typing some text, and then clicking the Undo button to remove that text.

To use the Undo button on the WordPad toolbar:

▶ **1.** Type your name in the WordPad window.

▶ **2.** Click the **Undo** button ↶ on the WordPad toolbar. WordPad reverses your last action by removing your name from the WordPad window.

Besides menus and toolbars, windows can contain list boxes and scroll bars, which you'll learn about next.

Using List Boxes and Scroll Bars

As you might guess from the name, a **list box** displays a list of available choices from which you can select one item. In WordPad, the Date and Time dialog box includes a list box that contains formats for displaying the date and time. You can choose a date and time format from the Available formats list box in the Date and Time dialog box. List box controls usually include arrow buttons, a scroll bar, and a scroll box. A scroll bar appears when the list of available options is too long or wide to fit in the list box. You use the arrows and scroll box to move through the complete list.

To use the Date and Time list box:

1. Click the **Date/Time** button 🔣 on the WordPad toolbar to open the Date and Time dialog box, which lists the current date in many formats. See Figure 17.

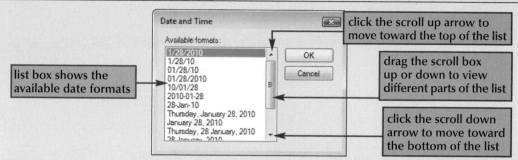

list box shows the available date formats

click the scroll up arrow to move toward the top of the list

drag the scroll box up or down to view different parts of the list

click the scroll down arrow to move toward the bottom of the list

2. To scroll down the list, click the **scroll down arrow** button on the scroll bar three times.

3. Drag the **scroll box** to the top of the scroll bar by pointing to the scroll box, pressing and holding down the left mouse button, dragging the scroll box up, and then releasing the left mouse button. The list scrolls back to the beginning.

4. Find a date format similar to "January 28, 2010" in the Available formats list box, and then click that date format to select it.

5. Click the **OK** button to close the Date and Time dialog box. The current date is inserted into your document.

A list box is helpful because it includes only options that are appropriate for your current task. For example, you can select only dates and times in the available formats from the list box in the Date and Time dialog box—no matter which format you choose, WordPad will recognize it. Sometimes a list might not include every possible option, so you can type the option you want to select. In this case, the list box includes an arrow on its right side. You can click the arrow to view options and then select one or type appropriate text.

Buttons can also have arrows. The arrow indicates that the button has more than one option. Rather than crowding the window with a lot of buttons, one for each possible option, including an arrow on a button organizes its options logically and compactly into a list. Toolbars often include list boxes and buttons with arrows. For example, the Font Size button list box on the WordPad toolbar includes an arrow. To select an option other than the one shown in the list box or on the button, you click the arrow, and then click the option that you want to use.

To select a new font size from the Font Size button list box:

1. Click the **Font Size button arrow** 10 ▾ on the WordPad toolbar.

2. Click **18**. The Font Size list closes, and the font size you selected appears in the list box.

3. Type a few characters to test the new font size.

4. Click the **Font Size button arrow** 18 ▾ on the WordPad toolbar again.

5. Click **12**.

> **6.** Type a few characters to test this type size. The text appears in the smaller font size.

Dialog boxes also contain scroll bars and list boxes. You'll examine a typical dialog box next.

Working with Dialog Boxes

Recall that when you select a menu command or item followed by an ellipsis, a dialog box opens that allows you to provide more information about how a program should carry out a task. Some dialog boxes organize different kinds of information into bordered rectangular areas called groups. Within these groups, you usually find tabs, option buttons, check boxes, and other controls that the program uses to collect information about how you want it to perform a task. Figure 18 displays examples of common dialog box controls.

| Figure 18 | Examples of dialog box controls |

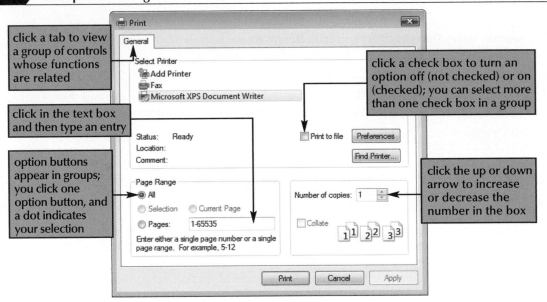

Elena says a good way to learn how dialog box controls work is to open a typical Windows Vista dialog box. You can use the WordPad Options dialog box to determine how text fits in the WordPad window and which toolbars appear. You'll remove the check mark from a check box and select an option button, and then see how these settings affect the WordPad window. Note that by default the status bar appears at the bottom of the WordPad window and that the ruler uses inches.

To work with a typical Windows Vista dialog box:

> **1.** Click **View** on the WordPad menu bar, and then click **Options**. The Options dialog box opens, by default, to the Rich Text tab.
>
> **Trouble?** If the Options dialog box does not display the Rich Text options, click the Rich Text tab.

> **2.** Click the **Status bar** check box to remove the check mark.

> **3.** Click the **Options** tab to select the measurement units that the WordPad ruler uses.

> **4.** Click the **Centimeters** option button.

5. Click the **OK** button. WordPad accepts your changes and closes the Options dialog box.

Examine the WordPad window and note that the ruler now uses centimeters instead of inches and the status bar no longer appears at the bottom of the window. You can use the Options dialog box again to restore the WordPad window to its original condition.

To restore the WordPad window:

1. Click **View** on the WordPad menu bar, and then click **Options**. The Options dialog box opens.

2. On the Rich Text tab, click the **Status bar** check box to insert a check mark.

3. Click the **Options** tab, and then click the **Inches** option button.

4. Click the **OK** button. The WordPad window now includes a status bar and a ruler that uses inches as its measurement unit.

5. Click the **Close** button ❎ on the WordPad title bar to close WordPad.

6. When you see the message "Do you want to save changes to Document?" click the **Don't Save** button.

> **Tip**
>
> You can also close a window by clicking File on the menu bar, and then clicking Close or Exit.

In this session, you started Windows Vista and toured the desktop, learning how to interact with the items on the desktop and on the Start menu. You also started two Windows programs, manipulated windows, and learned how to select options from a menu, toolbar, and dialog box.

Session 1 Quick Check | Review

1. What does the operating system do for your computer?
2. A(n) _____ is a group or list of commands.
3. Name two ways to change the size of a window.
4. In Windows Vista, right-clicking selects an object and opens its
   _____ .
5. How can you access the programs listed on the All Programs list?
6. Even if you can't see an open program on your desktop, the program might be running. How can you tell if a program is running?
7. Why should you close each program when you are finished using it?

Session 2

Exploring Your Computer

To discover the contents and resources on your computer, you explore, or navigate, it. **Navigating**, in this context, means to move from one location to another on your computer, such as from one window to another. Windows Vista provides two ways to navigate, view, and work with the contents and resources on your computer—the Computer window and Windows Explorer.

Navigating with the Computer Window

The Computer window represents your computer, its storage devices, and other objects. The icons for each of these objects appear in the right pane of the Computer window. See Figure 19. The Computer window also has a left pane, called the Navigation pane, which shows icons and links to other resources. This window also contains a toolbar with buttons that let you perform common tasks, and a Details pane at the bottom of the window that displays the characteristics of an object you select in the Computer window.

Figure 19 ▶ **Relationship between your computer and the Computer window**

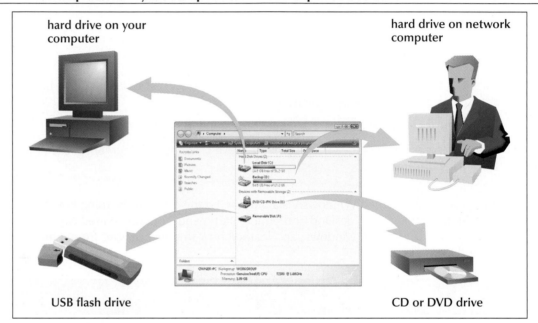

hard drive on your computer

hard drive on network computer

USB flash drive

CD or DVD drive

Each storage device you can access on your computer is associated with a letter. In older computers with one or more floppy drives, the first one is drive A and the second one is drive B. The first hard drive is usually drive C (if you add other hard drives, they are usually designated D, E, and so on). If you have a CD or DVD drive or plug a USB flash drive into a USB port, it usually has the next letter in the alphabetic sequence. If you can access hard drives on other computers in a network, those drives sometimes (although not always) have letters associated with them as well. In the example shown in Figure 19, the network drive has the drive letter D.

You can use the Computer window to keep track of where you store your files and how you organize your files. In this session, you will explore the contents of your hard disk, which is assumed to be drive C. If you use a different drive on your computer, such as drive E, substitute its letter for "C" throughout this session.

Now, you'll open the Computer window and explore the contents of your computer.

To explore the contents of your computer using the Computer window:

▶ **1.** If you took a break after the previous session, make sure that your computer is on and Windows Vista is running.

▶ **2.** Click the **Start** button 🪟 on the taskbar, and then click **Computer** in the right pane. The Computer window opens. See Figure 20. Your window might look different.

Computer window ◄ Figure 20

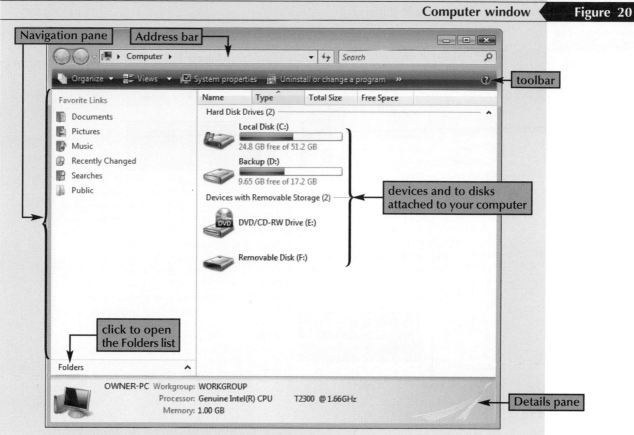

3. In the Navigation pane, click the **Music** folder. The right pane displays the contents of that folder. See Figure 21.

Figure 21 Contents of the Music folder

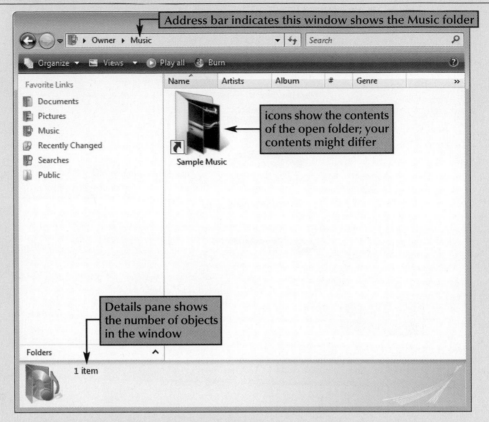

The Music folder is a convenient location for storing your music files. Many digital music players use this location by default when you rip, download, play, and burn music. Note that in Figure 21, the Sample Music icon represents a **shortcut**, a special type of file that serves as a direct link to another location that your computer can access, such as a folder, document, program, Windows tool, or Web site.

Trouble? If your window looks different from Figure 21, you can still perform the rest of the steps. For example, your window might contain a different number of folders and files.

▶ **4.** Double-click the **Sample Music** icon to open the Sample Music folder. The right pane of the window shows the contents of the folder you double-clicked. You can learn more about the contents of a folder by selecting one or more of its files.

▶ **5.** Click the first file listed in the Sample Music folder to select it. See Figure 22. (Your files might appear in a different order.)

Viewing files in a folder   **Figure 22**

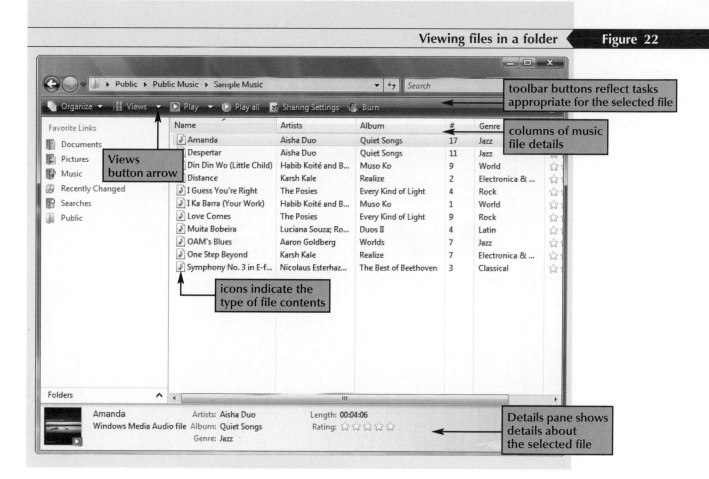

As you open folders and navigate with the Computer window, the contents of the toolbar change so that they are appropriate for your current task—in Figure 22, the toolbar lists actions to take with the selected music file, such as Play all and Burn.

Next, you'll change the view of the Computer window.

Changing the View

Windows Vista provides at least seven ways to view the contents of a disk—Extra Large Icons, Large Icons, Medium Icons, Small Icons, List, Details, and Tiles. The default view is Details view, which displays a small icon and lists details about each file. The icon provides a visual cue to the type of file. Although only Details view lists all file details, such as the file size and the date it was modified, you can see these details in any other view by pointing to an icon to display a ScreenTip.

To practice switching from one view to another, Elena says you can display the contents of the Sample Music folder in Large Icons view. To do so, you'll use the Views button on the toolbar.

To view files in Large Icons view:

▶ **1.** In the Sample Music folder, click the **Views button arrow** on the toolbar. See Figure 23. Your files might differ.

Trouble? If you click the Views button instead of the arrow, you cycle through the views. Click the Views button arrow, and then continue with Step 2.

Figure 23 | **Preparing to change views**

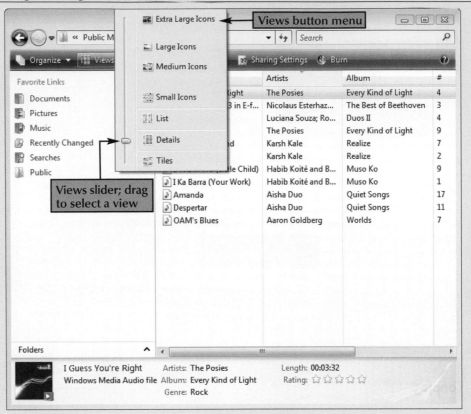

▶ **2.** Click **Large Icons**. The window shows the same files, but with larger icons than in Details view.

▶ **3.** Click the **Views button arrow** on the toolbar, and then click **Details** to return to Details view.

No matter which view you use, you can sort the file list by filename or other detail, such as, size, type, or date. This helps if you're looking for a particular file in a long file listing. For example, suppose you want to listen to a song by a certain artist, but can't remember the song title. You can sort the music file list in alphabetic order by artist to find the song you want.

To sort the music file list by artist:

▶ **1.** Click the **Artists** button at the top of the list of files. The up-pointing arrow on the Artists button indicates that the files are sorted in ascending (A–Z) alphabetic order by artist name.

▶ **2.** Click the **Artists** button again. The down-pointing arrow on the Artists button indicates that the sort order is reversed, with the artists listed in descending (Z–A) alphabetic order.

▶ **3.** Click the **Close** button [X] to close the Sample Music window.

Now you can compare the Computer window to Windows Explorer, another navigation tool.

Navigating with Windows Explorer

Like the Computer window, Windows Explorer also lets you easily navigate the resources on your computer. Most of the techniques you use with the Computer window apply to Windows Explorer—and vice versa. Both let you display and work with files and folders. By default, however, Windows Explorer also lets you see the hierarchy of all the folders on your computer. Viewing this hierarchy makes it easier to navigate your computer, especially if it contains many files and folders.

Elena suggests that you have students compare navigation tools by using Windows Explorer to open the same folders you opened in the Computer window. As with other Windows Vista programs, you start Windows Explorer using the Start menu.

To start Windows Explorer:

▶ 1. Click the **Start** button 🔘 on the taskbar, point to **All Programs**, click **Accessories**, and then click **Windows Explorer**. The Windows Explorer window opens, as shown in Figure 24. By default, this window shows the contents of the Documents folder when you first open it.

Windows Explorer window ◀ **Figure 24**

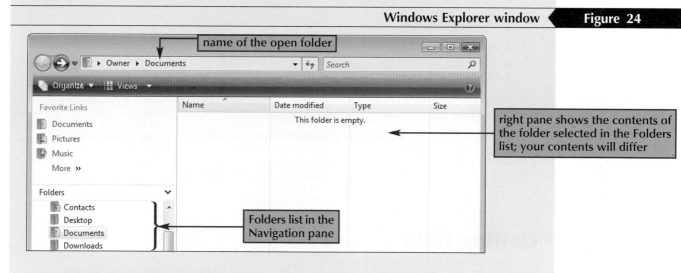

Trouble? If your Windows Explorer window looks slightly different from the one displayed in Figure 24, the configuration of your computer probably differs from the computer used to take this figure. Continue with Step 2.

▶ 2. If the Windows Explorer window is not maximized, click the **Maximize** button 🔲 on the Windows Explorer title bar.

Windows Explorer has the same tools and features you used in the Computer window: the Navigation pane, toolbar, Details pane, and file list in the right pane. However, the default Navigation pane in Windows Explorer includes a Folders list, which displays the folders on your computer. In the Folders list, you can click any folder to navigate directly to it.

The Folders list organizes your files and folders based on their location in the hierarchy of objects on your computer. Initially, the Folders list shows the main objects you can access from your desktop, including the Documents folder. If your desktop contains other folders or objects, those are displayed as well. The right pane of the Windows Explorer window displays the contents of the object selected in the Folders list. When you point to the Folders list, triangles appear next to some icons. An open triangle ▷ indicates that a folder contains other folders that are not currently displayed in the Folders list. Click the triangle to open the folder and display its subfolders. A filled triangle ◢ indicates the folder is open, and its subfolders are listed below the folder name. To display the contents of a folder or object in the right pane of Windows Explorer, click the name of the folder or object.

InSight | **Navigating with Windows Explorer and the Computer Window**

Navigating with Windows Explorer usually involves clicking triangles in the Folders list to open objects and find the folder you want, and then clicking that folder to display its contents in the right pane. In contrast, navigating with the Computer window usually involves double-clicking folders in the right pane to open them and find the file you want. In general, it's easier to navigate your computer using the Folders list because it shows the hierachy of folders on your computer.

To compare Windows Explorer to the Computer window, Elena suggests that you open the same folder you opened before using the Computer window.

To open a folder:

► 1. Click the **Music** folder in the Folders list. The contents of the Music folder appear in the right pane of the Windows Explorer window, and the folder you opened is selected in the left pane.

   Trouble? If the Music folder does not appear in the Folders list, click the open triangle icon next to your personal folder (the one with your name).

► 2. In the right pane, double-click **Sample Music**. The same music files you displayed earlier appear in the window.

► 3. Click the **Close** button ❌ on the title bar to close the window.

Getting Help

Tip

For Help with a program such as WordPad, first start the program, and then click Help on the program's menu bar.

Windows Vista Help and Support provides on-screen information about the program you are using. Help for the Windows Vista operating system is available by clicking the Start button and then clicking Help and Support on the Start menu.

When you start Help for Windows Vista, a Windows Help and Support window opens, which gives you access to Help files stored on your computer as well as Help information stored on the Microsoft Web site. If you are not connected to the Web, you only have access to the Help files stored on your computer.

Next you will start Windows Vista Help, and then explore the information provided in the Windows Help and Support window.

To start Windows Vista Help:

► 1. Click the **Start** button 🟦 on the taskbar.

► 2. Click **Help and Support**. The home page of Windows Help and Support opens. See Figure 25. The contents of the home page differ depending on whether you are connected to the Internet.

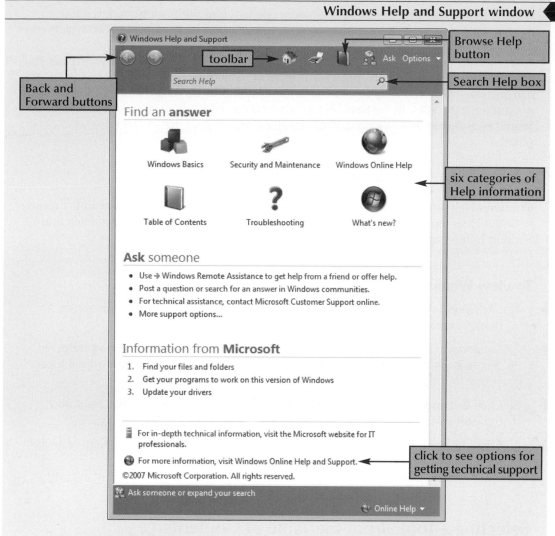

Windows Help and Support window | **Figure 25**

Trouble? If the Help and Support window does not display the information you see in Figure 25, click the Browse Help icon on the toolbar at the top of the window to view Help contents.

The home page in Windows Help and Support organizes help and support information into six categories: Windows Basics, Security and Maintenance, Windows Online Help, Table of Contents, Troubleshooting, and What's new? The Windows Basics topics are designed for novice Windows users, and What's new? is for users who are familiar with earlier versions but who are new to Windows Vista. You are more likely to use Windows Online Help and the Table of Contents when you are more experienced and are looking for an answer to a particular question. (You need an Internet connection to use Windows Online Help.) Security and Maintenance provides articles about keeping your computer and Windows Vista in top condition, and Troubleshooting guides you step by step through procedures to help you solve problems.

To view the topics in a category, you click a category icon in the Find an answer section of the Windows Help and Support home page. Click a topic to open an article providing detailed information about that topic or instructions for performing a task. You can also use the toolbar to navigate Windows Help and Support. For example, click the Home button to return to the Windows Help and Support home page. In addition to buttons providing quick access to pages in Windows Help and Support, the toolbar contains

Tip

You can also start Windows Vista Help and Support from a folder window by clicking the Help button (a circled question mark) on the toolbar.

two other navigation buttons—the Back button and the Forward button. You use these buttons to navigate the pages you've already opened. Use the Back button to return to the previous page you viewed. After you do, you activate the Forward button, which you can click to go to the next page of those you've opened.

If you can't find the topic you want listed in any of the Help categories, the word that you are using for a feature or topic might be different from the word that Windows Vista uses. You can also use the Search Help box to search for all keywords contained in the Help pages, not just the topic titles. In the Search Help box, you can type any word or phrase, click the Search Help button, and Windows Vista lists all the Help topics that contain that word or phrase.

Viewing Windows Basics Help Topics

Windows Help and Support includes instructions on using Help itself. You can learn how to find a Help topic by using the Windows Basics category on the Windows Help and Support home page.

To view Windows Basics topics:

▶ 1. Click **Windows Basics**. A list of topics related to using Windows Vista appears in the Windows Help and Support window.

▶ 2. Scroll down to the "Help and support" heading, and then click **Getting help**. An article explaining how to get help appears, with the headings in the article listed in the "In this article" section.

▶ 3. Click **Getting help with dialog boxes and windows**. The Windows Help and Support window scrolls to that heading in the article.

▶ 4. Click the **Back** button ⬅ on the toolbar. You return to the previous page you visited, which is the Windows Basics: all topics page.

Selecting a Topic from the Table of Contents

The Table of Contents logically organizes all of the topics in Windows Help and Support into books and pages. In the Table of Contents, you click a book to display the titles of its pages. Click a page to get help about a particular topic. For example, you can use the Table of Contents to learn more about files and folders.

To find a Help topic using the Table of Contents:

Tip

You can display the Contents page whenever you are working in Windows Help and Support by clicking the Browse Help icon on the toolbar.

▶ 1. Click the **Help and Support home** button 🏠 on the Windows Help and Support toolbar.

▶ 2. Click **Table of Contents** on the home page. The Contents page opens, listing books of Windows Help and Support topics.

▶ 3. Click **Files and folders** to display the list of pages included in the Files and folders book.

▶ 4. Click the topic **Working with files and folders**. The page you selected opens in the Windows Help and Support window.

▶ 5. In the first line below the "What are files and folders" heading, click the word **file**, which is green by default. A ScreenTip shows the definition of file.

6. Click a blank area of the Windows Help and Support window to close the ScreenTip.

Another Help tool is the Search Help box, a popular way to find answers to your Windows Vista questions.

Searching the Help Pages

If you can't find the topic you need by using the Home or Table of Contents pages, or if you want to quickly find Help pages related to a particular topic, you can use the Search Help box. Elena provides a typical example. Suppose you want to know how to exit Windows Vista, but you don't know if Windows refers to this as exiting, quitting, closing, or shutting down. You can search the Help pages to find just the right topic.

To search the Help pages for information on exiting Windows Vista:

1. Click in the Search Help box. A blinking insertion point appears.

2. Type **shutdown** and then click the **Search Help** button 🔎 . A list of Help pages containing the word "shutdown" appears in the Windows Help and Support window. See Figure 26.

Search Help results ◀ **Figure 26**

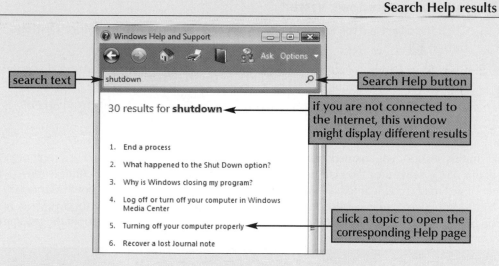

3. Click the **Turning off your computer properly** topic. The article appears in the Windows Help and Support window.

   If this article did not answer your question, you could click the **Ask someone or expand your search** link at the bottom of the Windows Help and Support window. Doing so opens a page listing other ways to get Help information.

4. Click the **Close** button ✕ on the title bar to close the Windows Help and Support window.

If you are connected to the Internet, you can use Windows Online Help to find up-to-date information about Windows Vista on the Microsoft Web site. From the Help and Support home page, you can also contact Microsoft support or get in touch with other users of Windows Vista.

Now that you know how Windows Vista Help works, Elena reminds you to use it when you need to perform a new task or when you forget how to complete a procedure.

Shutting Down Windows Vista

You should always shut down Windows Vista before you turn off your computer. Doing so saves energy, preserves your data and settings, and makes sure your computer starts quickly the next time you use it.

The commands for shutting down your computer are included on the More Options button menu. The More Options button ▶ is located at the bottom of the right pane of the Start menu. Typically, you use the Shut Down command on the More Options button menu when you want to turn off your computer. However, your school might prefer that you select the Log Off command on the More Options button menu. This command logs you off of Windows Vista but leaves the computer turned on, allowing another user to log on without restarting the computer. Check with your instructor or technical support person for the preferred method at your lab.

In addition to the Shut Down, Restart, and Log Off commands, your More Options button menu might include the Sleep command. When you select Sleep, Windows Vista saves all of your work and desktop settings so that when you wake your computer, your work session is restored quickly. You can also put your PC to sleep by clicking the Power button ⏻ on the Start menu. If you are working with a desktop PC, wake your computer by moving the mouse or pressing a key. If you are working with a mobile PC, wake your computer by pressing the hardware power button.

> **Tip**
>
> When you use the Shut Down command, Windows Vista saves any Windows settings that you changed and saves any information in memory to your hard disk.

To shut down Windows Vista:

▶ 1. Click the **Start** button 🔵 on the taskbar, and then point to the **More Options** button ▶.

▶ 2. Click **Shut Down**. Windows Vista displays a message that it is shutting down, and then turns off your computer.

Trouble? If you are supposed to log off rather than shut down, click Log Off instead and follow your school's logoff procedure.

In this session, you learned how to start and close programs and how to use multiple programs at the same time. You learned how to work with windows and the controls they employ. Finally, you learned how to get help when you need it and shut down Windows Vista. With Elena's help, you should feel comfortable with the basics of Windows Vista, and be prepared to teach Back to Work clients the fundamentals of using this operating system.

Review | Session 2 Quick Check

1. The _____ window represents your computer, its storage devices, printers, and other objects.
2. Explain how to open a folder in the Folders list and display its subfolders.
3. When you navigate from the Computer window displaying the drives on your computer to the Sample Music folder, what happens to the toolbar in the Computer window?
4. How can you view file details such as size or date modified in Large Icons view?
5. In the Windows Explorer window, what appears in the right pane when you click a folder icon in the left pane?
6. In Windows Help and Support, the _____ page organizes a vast amount of help and support information into six categories.

7. How can you quickly find Help pages related to a particular topic in the Windows Help and Support window?

8. You should always _____ Windows Vista before you turn off your computer.

Tutorial Summary | Review

In this tutorial, you learned the basics of Windows Vista. You toured the desktop and learned how to open objects on the desktop. You explored the Start menu and opened its submenus. You started programs from the Start menu, and then switched between multiple programs. You worked with windows by manipulating them. You selected options from a menu and buttons on a toolbar. You also examined typical dialog boxes and their controls. Then you explored your computer with the Computer window and Windows Explorer, learned how to get help when you need it, and finally shut down Windows Vista.

Key Terms

active program
application
click
Computer
control
Control Panel
default settings
desktop
dialog box
Documents
double-click
drag
exit
file
folder
graphical user
    interface (GUI)

Help and Support
icon
Internet
list box
log off
menu
menu command
menu convention
Microsoft Windows Vista
most frequently used
    programs list
mouse
multitask
navigate
operating system
password
pinned items list

point
pointing device
program
program button
right-click
screen saver
ScreenTip
select
shortcut
shortcut menu
Start menu
Start Search box
submenu
user name
window
Windows Vista

Practice | Review Assignments

Practice the skills you learned in the tutorial.

There are no Data Files needed for the Review Assignments.

The day before your first class teaching Back to Work clients the basics of using Windows Vista, Elena Varney offers to help you design a class syllabus and to observe your tour of the operating system. You'll start working on the Windows Vista desktop, with no windows opened or minimized. Complete the following steps, recording your answers to any questions according to your instructor's preferences:

1. Start Windows Vista and log on, if necessary.
2. Use the mouse to point to each object on your desktop. Record the names and descriptions of each object as they appear in the ScreenTips.
3. Click the Start button. How many menu items or commands are on the Start menu?
4. Start WordPad. How many program buttons are now on the taskbar? (Don't count toolbar buttons or items in the notification area.)
5. Start Paint and maximize the Paint window. How many programs are running now?
6. Switch to WordPad. What are two visual clues that tell you that WordPad is the active program?
7. Close WordPad, and then restore the Paint window.
8. Open the Recycle Bin window. Record the number of items it contains.
9. Drag the Recycle Bin window so that you can see it and the Paint window.
10. Close the Paint window from the taskbar.
11. Click the Organize button on the toolbar in the Recycle Bin window. Write down the commands on the menu. Point to Layout, and then click Menu Bar to display the menu bar.
12. Use any menu on the Recycle Bin menu bar to open a dialog box. What steps did you perform? What dialog box did you open? For what do you think you use this dialog box? Click Cancel to close the dialog box.
13. Close the Recycle Bin window.
14. Open the Computer window, and then open the Public folder from the Navigation pane. (*Hint*: If the Folders list is open, scroll the top part of the Navigation pane to see all of the folders in the Navigation pane.)
15. Open any folder in the Public folder that interests you. List the name and contents of that folder.
16. Close all open windows.
17. Start Windows Explorer. Use the Folders list to navigate to the same folder you opened in Step 14. What steps did you perform?
18. Change the view of the icons in the right pane of the Windows Explorer window. What view did you select? Describe the icons in the Windows Explorer window.
19. Close the Windows Explorer window, and then open Windows Help and Support.
20. Use the What's new? topics to learn something new about the Windows Vista desktop. What did you learn? How did you find this topic?
21. Use the Table of Contents to find information about the topic of mobile PCs, an enhanced feature in Windows Vista. How many topics are listed? What is their primary subject matter?
22. Use the Search Help box to find information about the topic of mobile PCs. How many topics are listed?
23. Close Help, and then shut down or log off Windows.
24. Submit your answers to the preceding questions to your instructor, either in printed or electronic form, as requested.

Apply		**Case Problem 1**

Use the skills you learned in the tutorial to explore the contents of a computer for a small electronics business.

There are no Data Files needed for this Case Problem.

First Call Electronics First Call Electronics is a small business in Atlanta, Georgia, that provides training and repair services for electronic devices, including computers, cell phones, cameras, and portable music players. Antoine Guillaume runs the training department, and has hired you to conduct one-on-one training sessions with new computer users. You are preparing for a visit to a client who wants to determine the contents of his new Windows Vista computer, including sample media files and related programs already provided in folders or menus.

Some of the following steps instruct you to list the contents of windows. Refer to the instructions in the Reality Check exercise at the end of this tutorial if you want to print images of these windows instead. Complete the following steps:

1. Start Windows Vista and log on, if necessary.
2. From the desktop or the Start menu, open the Computer window.
3. List the names of the drives on the computer.
4. Click the Documents link in the Navigation pane. Does the Documents folder contain any subfolders? If so, what are the names of the subfolders? If your Documents folder does not contain subfolders, click the Pictures and Music links in the Navigation pane and identify the contents of one of those folders.
5. Display the Folders list in the Computer window. (*Hint:* Click the Folders button near the bottom of the Navigation pane.) Where is the Documents folder located in the folder structure of your computer?
6. Open the Pictures folder, and then open a folder containing images, if necessary. View the files as Extra Large Icons.
7. Navigate to a folder that contains graphics, music, or other media files, such as videos or recorded TV. Point to a file to open the ScreenTip. What type of file did you select? What details are provided in the ScreenTip?
8. Close the Computer window and then start Windows Explorer. In the Folders list, navigate to the Public folder.
9. Open the Public Pictures folder in the Public folder. Describe the contents of this folder. (If you cannot access the Public Pictures folder, return to the Pictures folder.) Open a subfolder, and then double-click a file icon. Describe what happens.
10. Close all open windows, and then use the Start menu to open a program that you could use with picture files. What program did you start?
11. Open Windows Help and Support, and then find and read topics that explain how to use a program you started in a previous step.
12. Close all open windows.
13. Submit your answers to the preceding questions to your instructor, either in printed or electronic form, as requested.

| Apply | | Case Problem 2 |

Use the skills you learned in the tutorial to work with Windows Vista installed on a computer for a catering business.

There are no Data Files needed for this Case Problem.

East End Catering   After completing culinary school and working as a sous chef for restaurants in Santa Fe, New Mexico, Felicia Makos started a catering company specializing in dishes that contain organic, locally grown ingredients. So that she can concentrate on cooking and marketing, she hired you to help her perform office tasks as her business grows. She asks you to start by teaching her the basics of using her computer, which runs Windows Vista. She especially wants to know which programs are installed on her computer and what they do.

Some of the following steps instruct you to list the contents of windows and menus. Refer to the instructions in the Reality Check exercise at the end of this tutorial if you want to print images of these windows instead. Complete the following steps:

1. Open the Start menu and write down the programs on the pinned items list.
2. Start one of the programs on the pinned items list and then describe what it does. Close the program.
3. Open the Start menu and write down the programs on the most frequently used programs list.
4. Start one of the programs on the most frequently used programs list and then describe what it does. Close the program.
5. Open the Accessories folder from the All Programs list, and examine the programs in the Accessories folder and its subfolders.
6. Use Windows Help and Support to research one of the programs you examined in the previous step, such as Calculator or Notepad. Determine the purpose of the program and how to perform a task using that program.
7. Use the Search Help box in Windows Help and Support to list all the Help topics related to the program you researched in the previous step.

✛ **EXPLORE**   8. Start the program you researched. Click Help on the program's menu bar (or click the Help button) and then click each command on the Help menu to explore the Help topics. Compare these topics to the ones included in Windows Help and Support.

✛ **EXPLORE**   9. Open and read a Help topic in the program. Find a similar topic in Windows Help and Support, and then read that topic. Compare the topics, if they are different, to determine when you would be likely to use Windows Help and Support, and when you'd use the program's Help.

10. Close all open windows.
11. Submit your answers to the preceding questions to your instructor, either in printed or electronic form, as requested.

Challenge | Case Problem 3

Extend what you've learned to customize the Windows Explorer window for an alternative energy company.

There are no Data Files needed for this Case Problem.

Friedman Alternatives Warren Friedman recently started his own small firm called Friedman Alternatives, which analyzes and recommends sources of alternative energy for various manufacturing businesses. Most of these businesses want to cut their expenses related to energy, and are interested in helping to conserve fuel and preserve the environment. Warren typically uses the Windows Explorer window to work with his files, but suspects he is not taking full advantage of its features. As his new special-projects employee, he asks you to show him around the Windows Explorer window and demonstrate how to customize its appearance. Complete the following steps:

1. Start Windows Explorer. Click the Organize button on the Windows Explorer toolbar, and write down any commands that seem related to changing the appearance of the window.

⊕ **EXPLORE** 2. Select a command that lays out the Windows Explorer window so that it displays a single pane for viewing files. Then restore the window to its original condition.

3. Navigate to a folder containing graphic files, such as the Pictures folder. Double-click the Sample Pictures folder to open it. (If your computer does not contain a Sample Pictures folder, open any folder that displays pictures.) Display the icons using Large Icons view.

4. Change the view to Details view. Describe the difference between Large Icons and Details view.

⊕ **EXPLORE** 5. Click the Slide Show button on the toolbar. Describe what happens, and then press the Esc key.

6. With the Details pane open, click a picture file. Describe the contents of the Details pane.

⊕ **EXPLORE** 7. Repeatedly click the Views button to cycle from one view to another. Describe the changes in the window.

8. Display the window in Details view.

⊕ **EXPLORE** 9. Close the Folders list. (*Hint*: Click the Folders button.) On the Organize button menu, click Folder and Search Options to open the Folder Options dialog box. Select the option that uses Windows classic folders, and then click the OK button. Describe the changes in the Sample Pictures window.

⊕ **EXPLORE** 10. Open the Folder Options dialog box again, click the Restore Defaults button, and then click the OK button.

11. Open the Windows Help and Support window and search for information about folder options. Find a topic explaining how to show or hide file extensions for known file types. Record your findings.

12. Close all open windows.

13. Submit the results of the preceding steps to your instructor, either in printed or electronic form, as requested.

Research | Case Problem 4

Work with the skills you've learned, and use the Internet, to provide information to an import/export company.

There are no Data Files needed for this Case Problem.

Majolica Imports   After moving from southern France to New York City, Marie and Bruno Tattinger decided to start a company importing hand-painted French and Italian ceramics. Both travel frequently, and use laptop computers running Windows Vista to run their business when they are on the move. They have hired you as a consultant to help them use and maintain their computers. Marie asks you to help her research wireless networks so she can set up a wireless network at home and in their office. You suggest starting with Help and Support, and then expanding to the Internet to search for the latest information. Complete the following steps:

1. In Windows Help and Support, find information about the hardware Marie needs to set up a wireless network.
2. On the Windows Help and Support home page, use the Windows Online Help link to visit the Microsoft Web site containing Windows Vista information.
3. Use the Search text box on the Microsoft Web site to search for information on Microsoft.com about setting up a wireless network.
4. Choose a topic that describes how to set up a wireless network for a home or small office, and then read the topic thoroughly.
5. Write one to two pages for Marie explaining what she needs to set up a wireless network at home, and the steps she should perform.
6. Submit the results of the preceding steps to your instructor, either in printed or electronic form, as requested.

Assess | SAM Assessment and Training

If you have a SAM user profile, you may have access to hands-on instruction, practice, and assessment of the skills covered in this tutorial. Log in to your SAM account (**http://sam2007.course.com**) to launch any assigned training activities or exams that relate to the skills covered in this tutorial.

Review | **Quick Check Answers**

Session 1

1. The operating system is software that helps the computer perform essential tasks such as displaying information on the computer screen and saving data on disks.
2. menu
3. Drag a border or corner of the window, or restore or maximize the window.
4. shortcut menu
5. Click the Start button, and then point to the All Programs command.
6. Its button appears on the taskbar.
7. to conserve computer resources such as memory

Session 2

1. Computer
2. Point to the Folders list, and then click an open triangle next to a folder.
3. Some buttons change to let you perform tasks appropriate for music files, such as Play all and Burn.
4. Point to the file and view its ScreenTip, or click the file and view the Details pane.
5. the contents of the folder you clicked
6. home
7. use the Search Help box
8. shut down

Ending Data Files

There are no ending Data Files needed for this tutorial.

Reality Check

Even if you are familiar with some features of Windows Vista or regularly use your computer for certain tasks, such as accessing Web sites or exchanging e-mail, take some time to explore the basics of Windows Vista on your computer. As you work through this Reality Check exercise, you will record settings on your computer. To so do, you can capture and print images of the desktop and windows you open. If you experience problems with your computer later or want to restore these settings, you can refer to these printed images. You can also use the printed images to get acquainted with new programs and windows.

To print screen images:

1. Start Paint and then minimize the program window.
2. Open the window you want to preserve or arrange the desktop as you want it. If you want to capture a window, make sure that window is the active window.
3. Hold down the Alt key and press the Print Screen key. (On some keyboards, this appears as the PrtScn key or uses another similar abbreviation.) This temporarily saves an image of the active window. To capture an image of everything shown on the screen, press the Print Screen key without holding down the Alt key.
4. Restore the Paint program window, click Edit on the Paint menu bar, and then click Paste. (You can also press Ctrl+V to paste the image in the Paint program window.)
5. Click File on the menu bar, click Print to open the Print dialog box, and then click the Print button to print the image.
6. To clear the window and prepare for the next screen image, click Image on the menu bar, and then click Clear Image.

Now you can explore Windows Vista on your computer and preserve screen images as directed.

1. Start Windows Vista and log on, if necessary.
2. Should you ever need to restore your computer, print images of your current desktop, the Start menu, the Computer window showing the drives on your computer, and your Documents folder.
3. Open a folder in the Documents folder that you are likely to use often. Make sure the Folders list shows the location of this folder on your computer. Print an image of this window.
4. To get acquainted with programs that are included with Windows Vista, start at least two accessory programs that are new to you. Open the File menu or click tabs in each program, and then capture and print the image of each screen.
5. Using the menu bar, toolbar, or tabs in the new programs, find a dialog box in each program that you are likely to use. Print an image of the dialog boxes.
6. Use Windows Help and Support to find information about a feature or technique covered in this tutorial. Choose a topic that you want to know more about. Print an image of the Windows Help and Support window displaying information about this topic.
7. Close all open windows, and then shut down or log off Windows.

Objectives

- Develop file management strategies
- Explore files and folders
- Create, name, copy, move, and delete folders
- Name, copy, move, and delete files
- Work with compressed files

Managing Your Files

Creating and Working with Files and Folders in Windows Vista

Case | Distance Learning Company

The Distance Learning Company specializes in distance-learning courses for people who want to participate in college-level classes to work toward a degree or for personal enrichment. Distance learning is formalized education that typically takes place using a computer and the Internet, replacing normal classroom interaction with modern communications technology. The company's goal is to help students gain new skills and stay competitive in the job market. The head of the Customer Service Department, Shannon Connell, interacts with the Distance Learning Company's clients on the phone and from her computer. Shannon, like all other employees, is required to learn the basics of managing files on her computer.

In this tutorial, you'll work with Shannon to devise a strategy for managing files. You'll learn how Windows Vista organizes files and folders, and you'll examine Windows Vista file management tools. You'll create folders and organize files within them. You'll also explore options for working with compressed files.

Starting Data Files

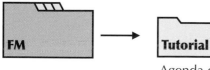

FM → Tutorial	Review	Case1
Agenda.docx	Billing.xlsx	Inv Feb.xlsx
Holiday.bmp	Car Plan.xlsx	Inv Jan.xlsx
Members.htm	Commissions.xlsx	Inv March.xlsx
New Logo.bmp	Contracts.xlsx	Painting-Agenda.docx
Proposal.docx	Customers.xlsx	Painting-Eval.docx
Resume.docx	Loan.docx	Painting-Manual.docx
Stationery.bmp	Photos.pptx	Paris.jpg
Vinca.jpg	Speech.wav	Still Life.jpg
	Water lilies.jpg	

Organizing Files and Folders

Knowing how to save, locate, and organize computer files makes you more productive when you are working with a computer. A **file**, often referred to as a **document**, is a collection of data that has a name and is stored on a computer. After you create a file, you can open it, edit its contents, print it, and save it again—usually using the same program you used to create it. You organize files by storing them in **folders**, which are containers for your files. You need to organize files so that you can find them easily and work efficiently.

A file cabinet is a common metaphor for computer file organization. A computer is like a file cabinet that has two or more drawers—each drawer is a storage device, or **disk**. Each disk contains folders that hold documents, or files. To make it easy to retrieve files, you arrange them logically into folders. For example, one folder might contain financial data, another might contain your creative work, and another could contain information you're collecting for an upcoming vacation.

A computer can store folders and files on different types of disks, ranging from removable media—such as **USB drives** (also called USB flash drives), **compact discs (CDs)**, and **digital video discs (DVDs)**—to **hard disks**, or fixed disks, which are permanently stored on a computer. Hard disks are the most popular type of computer storage because they can contain many gigabytes of data and are economical.

To have your computer access a removable disk, you must insert the disk into a **drive**, which is a computer device that can retrieve and sometimes record data on a disk. See Figure 1. A hard disk is already contained in a drive, so you don't need to insert it each time you use the computer.

Figure 1 ▶ **Comparing drives and disks**

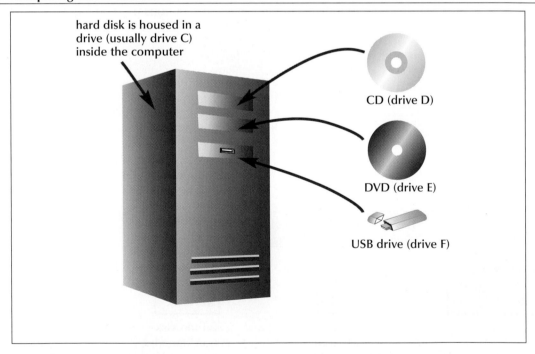

A computer distinguishes one drive from another by assigning each a drive letter. The hard disk is usually assigned to drive C. The remaining drives can have any other letters, but are usually assigned in the order that the drives were installed on the computer—so your USB drive might be drive D or drive F. Most contemporary computers have ports for more than one USB drive.

Understanding the Need for Organizing Files and Folders

Windows Vista stores thousands of files in many folders on the hard disk of your computer. These are system files that Windows Vista needs to display the desktop, use drives, and perform other operating system tasks. To ensure system stability and find files quickly, Windows Vista organizes the folders and files in a hierarchy, or **file system**. At the top of the hierarchy, Windows Vista stores folders and important files that it needs when you turn on the computer. This location is called the **root directory**, and is usually drive C (the hard disk). The term "root" refers to another popular metaphor for visualizing a file system—an upside-down tree, which reflects the file hierarchy that Windows Vista uses. In Figure 2, the tree trunk corresponds to the root directory, the branches to the folders, and the leaves to the files.

Windows file hierarchy   Figure 2

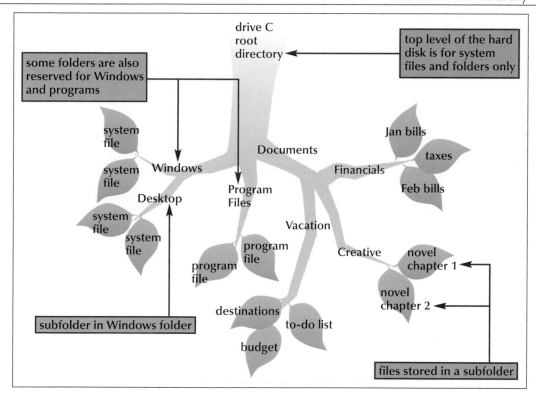

Note that some folders contain other folders. An effectively organized computer contains a few folders in the root directory, and those folders contain other folders, also called **subfolders**.

The root directory, or top level, of the hard disk is for system files and folders only—you should not store your own work here because it could interfere with Windows or a program. (If you are working in a computer lab, you might not be allowed to access the root directory.)

Do not delete or move any files or folders from the root directory of the hard disk—doing so could mean that you cannot run or start the computer. In fact, you should not reorganize or change any folder that contains installed software because Windows Vista expects to find the files for specific programs within certain folders. If you reorganize or change these folders, Windows Vista cannot locate and start the programs stored in that folder. Likewise, you should not make changes to the folder that contains the Windows Vista operating system (usually named Windows or Winnt).

Because the top level of the hard disk is off-limits for your files—the ones that you create, open, and save on the hard disk—you must store your files in subfolders. If you are working on your own computer, you should store your files within the Documents folder. If you are working in a computer lab, you will probably use a different location that your instructor specifies. If you simply store all your files in one folder, however, you will soon have trouble finding the files you want. Instead, you should create folders within a main folder to separate files in a way that makes sense for you.

Likewise, if you store most of your files on removable media, such as USB drives, you need to organize those files into folders and subfolders. Before you start creating folders, whether on a hard disk or removable disk, you should plan the organization you will use.

Developing Strategies for Organizing Files and Folders

The type of disk you use to store files determines how you organize those files. Figure 3 shows how you could organize your files on a hard disk if you were taking a full semester of distance-learning classes. To duplicate this organization, you would open the main folder for your documents, create four folders—one each for the Basic Accounting, Computer Concepts, Management Skills II, and Professional Writing courses—and then store the writing assignments you complete in the Professional Writing folder.

Figure 3 **Organizing folders and files on a hard disk**

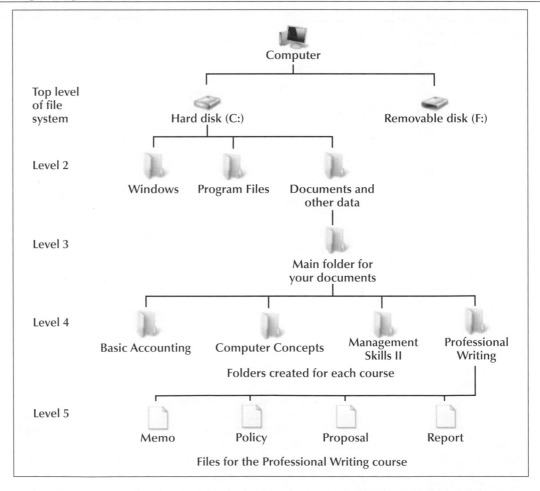

If you store your files on removable media, such as a USB drive or rewritable CD, you can use a simpler organization because you do not have to account for system files. In general, the larger the medium, the more levels of folders you should use because large media can store more files, and, therefore, need better organization. For example, you could organize your files on a 128-MB USB drive. In the top level of the USB drive, you could create folders for each general category of documents you store—one each for Courses, Creative, Financials, and Vacation. The Courses folder could then include one folder for each course, and each of those folders could contain the appropriate files.

If you work on two computers, such as one computer at an office or school and another computer at home, you can duplicate the folders you use on both computers to simplify transferring files from one computer to another. For example, if you have four folders in your Documents folder on your work computer, you would create these same four folders on your removable media as well as in the Documents folder of your home computer. If you change a file on the hard disk of your home computer, you can copy the most recent version of the file to the corresponding folder on your removable media so that it is available when you are at work. You also then have a **backup**, or duplicate copy, of important files that you need.

Planning Your Organization

Now that you've explored the basics of organizing files on a computer, you can plan the organization of your files for this book by writing in your answers to the following questions:

1. How do you obtain the files for this book (on a USB drive from your instructor, for example)?_____
   _____

2. On what drive do you store your files for this book (drive A, C, D, for example)?
   _____

3. Do you use a particular folder on this drive? If so, which folder do you use?_____
   _____

4. Is this folder contained within another folder? If so, what is the name of that main folder?_____

5. On what type of disk or drive do you save your files for this book (hard disk, USB drive, CD, or network drive, for example)?_____

If you cannot answer any of these questions, ask your instructor for help.

Exploring Files and Folders

Windows Vista provides two tools for exploring the files and folders on your computer—Windows Explorer and the Computer window. Both display the contents of your computer, using icons to represent drives, folders, and files. However, by default, each presents a slightly different view of your computer. **Windows Explorer** shows the files, folders, and drives on your computer, making it easy to navigate, or move from one location to another within the file hierarchy. The **Computer** window shows the drives on your computer and makes it easy to perform system tasks, such as viewing system information. Most of the time, you use one of these tools to open a **folder window** that displays the files and subfolders in a folder.

The Windows Explorer and Computer windows are divided into two sections, called **panes**. The left pane is the **Navigation pane**. It contains a **Favorite Links list**, which can provide quick access to the folders you use often, and a **Folders list**, which shows the hierarchy of the folders and other locations on your computer. The right pane lists the contents of these folders and other locations. If you select a folder in the left pane, for example, the files stored in that folder appear in the right pane.

> **Tip**
>
> The term "folder window" refers to any window that displays the contents of a folder, including the Computer, Windows Explorer, and Recycle Bin windows. In all of these windows, you can use the same techniques to display folders and their contents, navigate your computer, and work with files.

If the Folders list showed all the folders on your computer at once, it could be a very long list. Instead, you open drives and folders only when you want to see what they contain. If a folder contains subfolders, an expand icon ▷ appears to the left of the folder icon. (The same is true for drives.) To view the folders contained in an object, you click the expand icon. A collapse icon ◢ then appears next to the folder icon; click the collapse icon to hide the folder's subfolders. To view the files contained in a folder, you click the folder icon, and the files appear in the right pane. See Figure 4.

Figure 4 ▶ **Viewing folder contents in Windows Explorer**

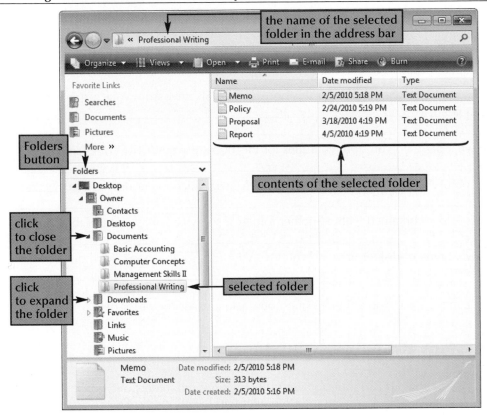

Using the Folders list helps you navigate your computer and orients you to your current location. As you move, copy, delete, and perform other tasks with the files in the right pane of a folder window, you can refer to the Folders list to see how your changes affect the overall organization.

Both Windows Explorer and the Computer window let you view, organize, and access the drives, folders, and files on your computer. In addition to using the Folders list, you can navigate your computer in other ways:

- **Opening drives and folders in the right pane**: To view the contents of a drive or folder, double-click the drive or folder icon in the right pane of a folder window.
- **Using the Address bar**: Use the Address bar to navigate to a different folder. The Address bar displays your current folder as a series of locations separated by arrows. Click a folder name or an arrow button to navigate to a different location.

Tip

To display or hide the Folders list in a folder window, click the Folders button in the Navigation pane.

- **Clicking the Back, Forward, and Recent Pages buttons**: Use the Back, Forward, and Recent Pages buttons to navigate to other folders you have already opened. After you change folders, use the Back button to return to the original folder or click the Recent Pages button to navigate to a location you've visited recently.
- **Using the Search box**: To find a file or folder stored in the current folder or its subfolders, type a word or phrase in the Search box. The search begins as soon as you start typing. Windows finds files based on text in the filename, text within the file, and other characteristics of the file, such as tags (descriptive words or phrases you add to your files) or the author.

These navigation controls are available in Windows Explorer, Computer, and other folder windows, including many dialog boxes. In fact, all of these folder windows share common tools. By default, when you first open Computer, it shows all the drives available on your computer, whereas Windows Explorer shows the folders on your computer. However, by changing a single setting, you can make the two windows interchangeable. If you open the Folders list in Computer, you have the same setup as Windows Explorer. Likewise, if you close the Folders list in the Windows Explorer window, you have the same setup as in the Computer window.

Shannon prefers to use Windows Explorer to manage her files. You'll use Windows Explorer to manage files in the rest of this tutorial.

Using Windows Explorer

Windows Vista also provides a folder for your documents—your **personal folder**, which is designed to store the files and folders you work with regularly and is labeled with the name you use to log on to Windows Vista, such as Shannon. On your own computer, this is where you can keep your data files—the memos, videos, graphics, music, and other files that you create, edit, and manipulate in a program. Windows Vista provides a few built-in folders in your personal folder, including Music (for songs and other music files), Pictures (for photos and other image files), and Documents (for text, spreadsheets, presentations, and other files you create). If you are working in a computer lab, you might not have a personal folder or be able to access the Documents folder, or you might have a personal folder or be able to store files there only temporarily because that folder is emptied every night. Instead, you might permanently store your Data Files on removable media or in a different folder on your computer or network.

When you start Windows Explorer from the All Programs menu, it opens to the Documents folder by default. If you cannot access the Documents folder, the screens you see as you perform the following steps will differ. However, you can still perform the steps accurately.

To examine the organization of your computer using Windows Explorer:

▶ 1. Click the **Start** button 🔘 on the taskbar, click **All Programs**, click **Accessories**, and then click **Windows Explorer**. The Windows Explorer window opens.

▶ 2. Scroll the Folders list, point to the **Folders list**, and then click the **expand** icon ▷ next to the Computer icon. The drives and other useful locations on your computer appear under the Computer icon, as shown in Figure 5. The contents of your computer will differ.

Figure 5 ▶ **Viewing the contents of your computer**

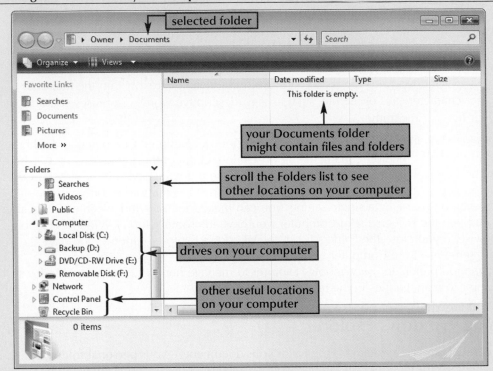

3. Click the **expand** icon ▷ next to the Local Disk (C:) icon. The contents of your hard disk appear under the Local Disk (C:) icon.

   Trouble? If you do not have permission to access drive C, skip Step 3 and read but do not perform the remaining steps.

   Documents is still the selected folder. To view the contents of an object in the right pane, you can click the object's icon in the Folders list.

4. If necessary, scroll up the list, and then click the **Public** folder in the Folders list. Its contents appear in the right pane. Public is a built-in Windows Vista folder that contains folders any user can access on this computer.

Navigating to Your Data Files

The **file path** is a notation that indicates a file's location on your computer. The file path leads you through the Windows file system to your file. For example, the Holiday file is stored in the Tutorial subfolder of the FM folder. If you are working on a USB drive, for example, the path to this file might be as follows:

F:\FM\Tutorial\Holiday.bmp

   This path has four parts, and each part is separated by a backslash (\ ):

- **F**: The drive name; for example, drive F might be the name for the USB drive. If this file were stored on the hard disk, the drive name would be C.
- **FM**: The top-level folder on drive F.
- **Tutorial**: A subfolder in the FM folder.
- **Holiday.bmp**: The full filename with the file extension.

If someone tells you to find the file F:\FM\Tutorial\Holiday.bmp, you know you must navigate to your USB drive, open the FM folder, and then open the Tutorial folder to find the Holiday file. By default, the Address bar includes arrow buttons instead of back-slashes when displaying a path. To navigate to a different folder in the FM folder, for example, you can click the arrow button to right of FM in the Address bar, and then click the folder name.

You can use Windows Explorer to navigate to the Data Files you need for the rest of this tutorial. Refer to the information you provided in the "Planning Your Organization" section and note the drive on your system that contains your Data Files. In the following steps, this is drive F, a USB drive. If necessary, substitute the appropriate drive on your system when you perform the steps.

To navigate to your Data Files:

▶ **1.** Make sure your computer can access your Data Files for this tutorial. For example, if you are using a USB drive, insert the drive into the USB port.

Trouble? If you don't have the Data Files, you need to get them before you can proceed. Your instructor will either give you the Data Files or ask you to obtain them from a specified location (such as a network drive). In either case, be sure that you make a backup copy of your Data Files before you start using them, so that the original files will be available on your copied disk in case you need to start over because of an error or problem. If you have any questions about the Data Files, see your instructor or technical support person for assistance.

▶ **2.** In the Windows Explorer window, click the **expand** icon ▷ next to the drive containing your Data Files, such as Removable Disk (F:). A list of the folders on that drive appears.

▶ **3.** If the list of folders does not include the FM folder, continue clicking the **expand** icon ▷ to navigate to the folder that contains the FM folder.

▶ **4.** Click the **expand** icon ▷ next to the FM folder, and then click the **FM** folder. Its contents appear in the Folders list and in the right pane of the Windows Explorer window. The FM folder contains the Case1, Review, and Tutorial folders, as shown in Figure 6. The other folders on your system might vary.

Figure 6   Navigating to the FM folder

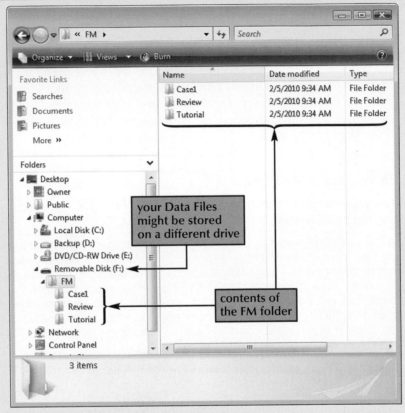

5. In the left pane, click the **Tutorial** folder. The files it contains appear in the right pane. You want to view them as a list.

6. Click the **Views button arrow** on the toolbar, and then click **List**. The files appear in List view in the Windows Explorer window. See Figure 7.

Figure 7   Files in the Tutorial folder in List view

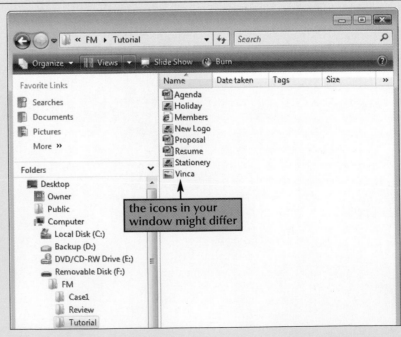

The file icons in your window depend on the programs installed on your computer, so they might be different from the ones shown in Figure 7.

Working with Folders and Files

After you devise a plan for storing your files, you are ready to get organized by creating folders that will hold your files. For this tutorial, you create folders in the Tutorial folder. When you are working on your own computer, you usually create folders within the Documents folder in your personal folder.

Examine the files shown in Figure 7 again and determine which files seem to belong together. Holiday, New Logo, and Vinca are all graphics files containing pictures or photos. The Resume and Stationery files were created for a summer job hunt. The other files were created for a neighborhood association to update a playground.

One way to organize these files is to create three folders—one for graphics, one for the job hunt files, and another for the playground files. When you create a folder, you give it a name, preferably one that describes its contents. A folder name can have up to 255 characters, except / \ : * ? " < > or |. Considering these conventions, you could create three folders as follows:

- **Graphics folder**: Holiday, New Logo, and Vinca files
- **Job Hunt folder**: Resume and Stationery files
- **Playground folder**: Agenda, Proposal, and Members files

Guidelines for Creating Folders | InSight

- **Keep folder names short and familiar**: Long filenames can be cut off in a folder window, so use names that are short but clear. Choose names that will be meaningful later, such as project names or course numbers.
- **Develop standards for naming folders**: Use a consistent naming scheme that is clear to you, such as one that uses a project name as the name of the main folder, and includes step numbers in each subfolder name, such as 01Plan, 02Approvals, 03Prelim, and so on.
- **Create subfolders to organize files**: If a file listing in a folder window is so long that you must scroll the window, consider organizing those files into subfolders.

Creating Folders

You've already seen folder icons in the windows you've examined. Now, you'll create folders in the Tutorial folder using the Windows Explorer toolbar.

Creating a Folder | Reference Window

- In the left pane, click the drive or folder where you want to create a folder.
- Click the Organize button on the toolbar, and then click New Folder (*or* right-click a blank area in the folder window, point to New, and then click Folder).
- Type a name for the folder, and then press the Enter key.

Next you will create three folders in your Tutorial folder. The Windows Explorer window should show the contents of the Tutorial folder in List view.

To create folders in a folder window:

▶ **1.** Click the **Organize** button on the toolbar, and then click **New Folder**. A folder icon with the label "New Folder" appears in the right pane. See Figure 8.

Figure 8

Creating a folder in the Tutorial folder

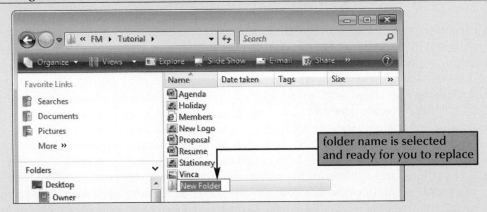

Trouble? If the "New Folder" name is not selected, right-click the new folder, click Rename, and then continue with Step 2.

Windows Vista uses "New Folder" as a placeholder, and selects the text so that you can replace it with the name you want.

▶ **2.** Type **Graphics** as the folder name, and then press the **Enter** key. The new folder is named "Graphics" and is the selected item in the right pane.

You are ready to create a second folder. This time, you'll use a shortcut menu to create a folder.

▶ **3.** Right-click a blank area near the Graphics folder, point to **New** on the shortcut menu, and then click **Folder**. A folder icon with the label "New Folder" appears in the right pane with the "New Folder" text selected.

▶ **4.** Type **Job Hunt** as the name of the new folder, and then press the **Enter** key.

▶ **5.** Using the toolbar or the shortcut menu, create a folder named **Playground**. The Tutorial folder contains three new subfolders.

Moving and Copying Files and Folders

If you want to place a file into a folder from another location, you can either move the file or copy it. **Moving** a file removes it from its current location and places it in a new location you specify. **Copying** places the file in both locations. Windows Vista provides several techniques for moving and copying files. The same principles apply to folders—you can move and copy folders using a variety of methods.

Reference Window | **Moving a File or Folder**

- Right-click and drag the file or folder you want to move to the destination folder.
- Click Move Here on the shortcut menu.

or

- Right-click the file or folder you want to move, and then click Cut on the shortcut menu.
- Navigate to and right-click the destination folder, and then click Paste on the shortcut menu.

Next, you'll move the Agenda, Proposal, and Members files to the Playground folder.

To move a file using the right mouse button:

1. Point to the **Agenda** file in the right pane, and then press and hold the *right* mouse button.

2. With the right mouse button still pressed down, drag the **Agenda** file to the **Playground** folder. When a "Move to Playground" ScreenTip appears, release the button. A shortcut menu opens.

3. With the left mouse button, click **Move Here** on the shortcut menu. The Agenda file is removed from the main Tutorial folder and stored in the Playground subfolder.

   Trouble? If you release the mouse button before dragging the Agenda file to the Playground folder, the shortcut menu opens, letting you move the file to a different folder. Press the Esc key to close the shortcut menu without moving the file, and then repeat Steps 1 through 3.

4. In the right pane, double-click the **Playground** folder. The Agenda file is in the Playground folder.

5. In the left pane, click the **Tutorial** folder to see its contents. The Tutorial folder no longer contains the Agenda file.

The advantage of moving a file or folder by dragging with the right mouse button is that you can efficiently complete your work with one action. However, this technique requires polished mouse skills so that you can drag the file comfortably. Another way to move files and folders is to use the **Clipboard**, a temporary storage area for files and information that you have copied or moved from one place and plan to use somewhere else. You can select a file and use the Cut or Copy commands to temporarily store the file on the Clipboard, and then use the Paste command to insert the file elsewhere. Although using the Clipboard takes more steps, some users find it easier than dragging with the right mouse button.

You'll move the Resume file to the Job Hunt folder next.

To move files using the Clipboard:

1. Right-click the **Resume** file, and then click **Cut** on the shortcut menu. Although the file icon is still displayed in the folder window, Windows Vista removes the Resume file from the Tutorial folder and stores it on the Clipboard.

2. In the Folders list, right-click the **Job Hunt** folder, and then click **Paste** on the shortcut menu. Windows Vista pastes the Resume file from the Clipboard to the Job Hunt folder. The Resume file icon no longer appears in the folder window.

3. In the Folders list, click the **Job Hunt** folder to view its contents in the right pane. The Job Hunt folder now contains the Resume file.

   You'll move the Stationery file from the Tutorial folder to the Job Hunt folder.

4. Click the **Back** button ◀ on the Address bar to return to the Tutorial folder, right-click the **Stationery** file in the folder window, and then click **Cut** on the shortcut menu.

5. Right-click the **Job Hunt** folder, and then click **Paste** on the shortcut menu.

6. Click the Back button ⊙ on the Address bar to return to view the contents of the Job Hunt folder. It now contains the Resume and Stationery files. See Figure 9.

Figure 9
Moving files

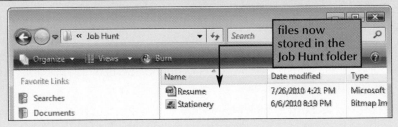

7. Click the **Forward** button ⊙ to return to the Tutorial folder.

You can also copy a file using the same techniques as when you move a file—by dragging with the right mouse button or by using the Clipboard. You can copy more than one file at the same time by selecting all the files you want to copy, and then clicking them as a group. To select files that are listed together in a window, click the first file in the list, hold down the Shift key, click the last file in the list, and then release the Shift key. To select files that are not listed together, click one file, hold down the Ctrl key, click the other files, and then release the Ctrl key.

Reference Window | **Copying a File or Folder**

- Right-click and drag the file or folder you want to copy to the destination folder.
- Click Copy Here on the shortcut menu.

or

- Right-click the file or folder you want to copy, and then click Copy on the shortcut menu.
- Navigate to the destination folder.
- Right-click a blank area of the destination folder window, and then click Paste on the shortcut menu.

You'll copy the three graphics files from the Tutorial folder to the Graphics folder now.

To copy files using the shortcut menu:

1. In the Tutorial window, click the **Holiday** file.

2. Hold down the **Ctrl** key, click the **New Logo** file, click the **Vinca** file, and then release the **Ctrl** key. Three files are selected in the Tutorial window.

3. Right-click a selected file, and then click **Copy** on the shortcut menu.

4. In the right pane, double-click the **Graphics** folder to open it.

5. Right-click a blank area in the right pane, and then click **Paste** on the shortcut menu. Windows Vista copies the three files to the Graphics folder.

6. Switch to List view, if necessary.

Now that you are familiar with two ways to copy files, you can use the technique you prefer to copy the Proposal and Members files to the Playground folder.

To copy the two files:

▶ 1. In the Graphics folder window, click the **Back** button ⬅ on the toolbar to return to the Tutorial folder.

▶ 2. Use any technique you've learned to copy the **Proposal** and **Members** files from the Tutorial folder to the Playground folder.

You can move and copy folders in the same way that you move and copy files. When you do, you move or copy all the files contained in the folder.

Naming and Renaming Files

As you work with files, pay attention to **filenames**—they provide important information about the file, including its contents and purpose. A filename such as Car Sales.docx has three parts:

- **Main part of the filename**: The name you provide when you create a file, and the name you associate with a file
- **Dot**: The period (.) that separates the main part of the filename from the file extension
- **File extension**: Usually three or four characters that follow the dot in the filename

The main part of a filename can have up to 260 characters—this gives you plenty of room to name your file accurately enough so that you'll know the contents of the file just by looking at the filename. You can use spaces and certain punctuation symbols in your filenames. Like folder names, however, filenames cannot contain the symbols \ / ? : * " < > | because these characters have special meaning in Windows Vista.

A filename might display an **extension**—three or more characters following a dot—that identifies the file's type and indicates the program in which the file was created. For example, in the filename Car Sales.docx, the extension "docx" identifies the file as one created by Microsoft Office Word 2007, a word-processing program. You might also have a file called Car Sales.xlsx—the "xlsx" extension identifies the file as one created in Microsoft Office Excel 2007, a spreadsheet program. Though the main parts of these filenames are identical, their extensions distinguish them as different files. You usually do not need to add extensions to your filenames because the program that you use to create the file adds the file extension automatically. Also, although Windows Vista keeps track of extensions, not all computers are set to display them.

Be sure to give your files and folders meaningful names that help you remember their purpose and contents. You can easily rename a file or folder by using the Rename command on the file's shortcut menu.

Guidelines for Naming Files | InSight

The following are a few suggestions for naming your files:

- **Use common names**: Avoid cryptic names that might make sense now, but could cause confusion later, such as nonstandard abbreviations or imprecise names like Stuff08.
- **Don't change the file extension**: When renaming a file, don't change the file extension. If you do, Windows might not be able to find a program that can open it.
- **Find a comfortable balance between too short and too long**: Use filenames that are long enough to be meaningful, but short enough to read easily on the screen.

Next, you'll rename the Agenda file to give it a more descriptive name.

To rename the Agenda file:

 ▶ 1. In the Tutorial folder window, double-click the **Playground** folder to open it.

 ▶ 2. Right-click the **Agenda** file, and then click **Rename** on the shortcut menu. The file-name is highlighted and a box appears around it.

 ▶ 3. Type **Meeting Agenda**, and then press the **Enter** key. The file now appears with the new name.

   Trouble? If you make a mistake while typing and you haven't pressed the Enter key yet, press the Backspace key until you delete the mistake, and then complete Step 3. If you've already pressed the Enter key, repeat Steps 1 through 3 to rename the file again.

   Trouble? If your computer is set to display file extensions, a message might appear asking if you are sure you want to change the file extension. Click the No button, right-click the Agenda file, click Rename on the shortcut menu, type "Meeting Agenda.docx", and then press the Enter key.

All the files in the Tutorial folder are now stored in appropriate subfolders. You can streamline the organization of the Tutorial folder by deleting the files you no longer need.

Deleting Files and Folders

Tip

To retrieve a deleted file from the hard disk, double-click the Recycle Bin, right-click the file you want to retrieve, and then click Restore.

You should periodically delete files and folders you no longer need so that your main folders and disks don't get cluttered. In the Computer window or Windows Explorer, you delete a file or folder by deleting its icon. Be careful when you delete a folder, because you also delete all the files it contains. When you delete a file from a hard disk, Windows Vista removes the filename from the folder, but stores the file contents in the Recycle Bin. The **Recycle Bin** is an area on your hard disk that holds deleted files until you remove them permanently; an icon on the desktop allows you easy access to the Recycle Bin. If you change your mind and want to retrieve a file deleted from your hard disk, you can use the Recycle Bin to recover it or return it to its original location. However, after you empty the Recycle Bin, you can no longer recover the files that were in it.

When you delete a file from removable media, it does not go into the Recycle Bin. Instead, it is deleted as soon as its icon disappears—and you cannot recover it.

Shannon reminds you that because you copied the Holiday, New Logo, Proposal, Members, and Vinca files to the Graphics and Playground folders, you can safely delete the original files in the Tutorial folder. As with moving, copying, and renaming files and folders, you can delete a file or folder in many ways, including using a shortcut menu.

To delete files in the Tutorial folder:

 ▶ 1. Use any technique you've learned to navigate to and open the **Tutorial** folder.

 ▶ 2. Click **Holiday** (the first file in the file list), hold down the **Shift** key, click **Vinca** (the last file in the file list), and then release the **Shift** key. All the files in the Tutorial folder are now selected. None of the subfolders should be selected.

 ▶ 3. Right-click the selected files, and then click **Delete** on the shortcut menu. Windows Vista asks if you're sure you want to delete these files.

 ▶ 4. Click the **Yes** button.

So far, you've moved, copied, renamed, and deleted files, but you haven't viewed any of their contents. To view file contents, you can preview or open the file. When you double-click a file in a folder window, Windows Vista starts the appropriate program and opens the file. To preview the file contents, you can select the file in a folder window, and then open the Preview pane by clicking the Organize button, pointing to Layout, and then clicking Preview Pane.

Working with Compressed Files

If you transfer files from one location to another, such as from your hard disk to a removable disk or vice versa, or from one computer to another via e-mail, you can store the files in a **compressed (zipped) folder** so that they take up less disk space. You can then transfer the files more quickly. When you create a compressed folder, Windows Vista displays a zipper on the folder icon.

You compress a folder so that the files it contains use less space on the disk. Compare two folders—a folder named Pictures that contains about 8.6 MB of files and a compressed folder containing the same files, but requiring only 6.5 MB of disk space. In this case, the compressed files use about 25 percent less disk space than the uncompressed files.

You can create a compressed folder using the Compressed (zipped) Folder command on the New submenu of the shortcut menu in a folder window. Then, you can compress files or other folders by dragging them into the compressed folder. You can open files directly from a compressed folder, although you cannot modify the file. To edit and save a compressed file, you must extract it first. When you **extract** a file, you create an uncompressed copy of the file and folder in a folder you specify. The original file remains in the compressed folder.

If a different compression program has been installed on your computer, such as WinZip or PKZIP, the Compressed (zipped) Folder command might not appear on the New submenu. Instead, it might be replaced by the name of your compression program. In this case, refer to your compression program's Help system for instructions on working with compressed files.

Shannon suggests you compress the files and folders in the Tutorial folder so that you can more quickly transfer them to another location.

To compress the folders and files in the Tutorial folder:

▶ **1.** If necessary, navigate to the Tutorial folder.

▶ **2.** Right-click a blank area of the right pane, point to **New** on the shortcut menu, and then click **Compressed (zipped) Folder**. A new compressed folder with a zipper icon appears in the Tutorial window. See Figure 10. Your window might appear in a different view.

Creating a compressed folder ◀ **Figure 10**

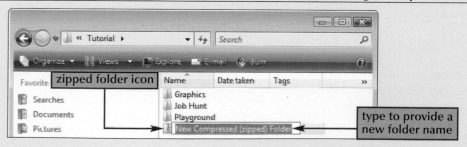

Trouble? If the Compressed (zipped) Folder command does not appear on the New submenu, a different compression program is probably installed on your computer. Click a blank area of the Tutorial window to close the shortcut menu, and then read but do not perform the remaining steps.

▶ **3.** Type **Final Files**, and then press the **Enter** key. Windows Vista names the compressed folder in the Tutorial folder.

▶ **4.** Click the **Graphics** folder, hold down the **Shift** key, click the **Playground** folder in the right pane, and then release the **Shift** key. Three folders are selected in the Tutorial window.

▶ **5.** Drag the three folders to the **Final Files** compressed folder. Windows Vista copies the files to the folder, compressing them to save space.

You open a compressed folder by double-clicking it. You can then move and copy files and folders in a compressed folder, although you cannot rename them. When you extract files, Windows Vista uncompresses and copies them to a location that you specify, preserving the files in their folders as appropriate.

To extract the compressed files:

▶ **1.** Right-click the **Final Files** compressed folder, and then click **Extract All** on the shortcut menu. The Extract Compressed (Zipped) Folders dialog box opens.

▶ **2.** Press the **End** key to deselect the path in the text box, press the **Backspace** key as many times as necessary to delete "Final Files," and then type **Extracted**. The final three parts of the path in the text box should be "\FM\Tutorial\Extracted." See Figure 11.

Figure 11 ▶ **Extracting compressed files**

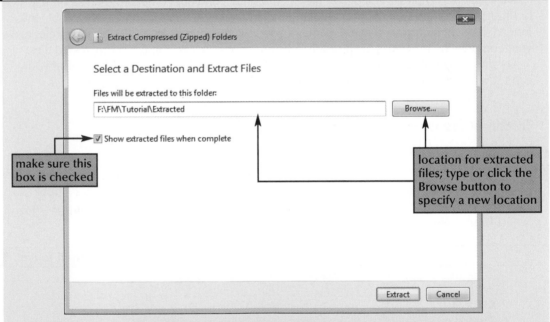

▶ **3.** Make sure the **Show extracted files when complete** check box is checked, and then click the **Extract** button. The Extracted folder opens, showing the Graphics, Job Hunt, and Playground folders.

▶ **4.** Open each folder to make sure it contains the files you worked with in this tutorial.

▶ **5.** Close all open windows.

Quick Check | Review

1. What do you call a named collection of data stored on a disk?
2. Name two types of removable media for storing files.
3. The letter C is typically used for the _____ drive of a computer.
4. What are the two tools that Windows Vista provides for exploring the files and folders on your computer?
5. What is the notation you can use to indicate a file's location on your computer?
6. True or False: The advantage of moving a file or folder by dragging with the right mouse button is that you can efficiently complete your work with one action.
7. What part of a filename indicates the file type and program that created it?
8. Is a file deleted from a compressed folder when you extract it?

Tutorial Summary | Review

In this tutorial, you examined Windows Vista file organization, noting that you need to organize files and folders to work efficiently. You learned about typical file management strategies, including how to organize files and folders by creating folders, moving and copying files, and renaming and deleting files. You also learned how to copy files to a compressed (zipped) folder, and then extract files from a compressed folder.

Key Terms

backup	extract	move
Clipboard	Favorite Links list	Navigation pane
compact disc (CD)	file	pane
compressed (zipped) folder	file path	personal folder
Computer	file system	Recycle Bin
copy	filename	root directory
disk	folder	subfolder
document	folder window	USB drive
drive	Folders list	Windows Explorer
extension	hard disk	

Practice	**Review Assignments**

Practice the skills you learned in the tutorial.

Data Files needed for the Review Assignments: Billing.xlsx, Car Plan.xlsx, Commissions.xlsx, Contracts.xlsx, Customers.xlsx, Loan.docx, Photos.pptx, Speech.wav, Water lilies.jpg

Complete the following steps, recording your answers to any questions:

1. Use the Computer window or Windows Explorer as necessary to record the following information:
    - Where are you supposed to store the files you use in the Review Assignments for this tutorial?
    - Describe the method you will use to navigate to the location where you save your files for this book.
    - Do you need to follow any special guidelines or conventions when naming the files you save for this book? For example, should all the filenames start with your course number or tutorial number? If so, describe the conventions.
    - When you are instructed to open a file for this book, what location are you supposed to use?
    - Describe the method you will use to navigate to this location.

2. Use the Computer window or Windows Explorer to navigate to and open the FM\Review folder provided with your Data Files.

3. Examine the nine files in the Review folder included with your Data Files, and then answer the following questions:
    - How will you organize these files?
    - What folders will you create?
    - Which files will you store in these folders?
    - Will you use any built-in Windows folders? If so, which ones? For which files?

4. In the Review folder, create three folders: Business, Finances, and Project.

5. Move the **Billing**, **Commissions**, **Contracts**, and **Customers** files from the Review folder to the Business folder.

6. Move the **Car Plan** and **Loan** files to the Finances folder.

7. Copy the remaining files to the Project folder.

8. Delete the files in the Review folder (do *not* delete any folders).

9. Rename the **Speech** file in the Project folder to **Ask Not**.

10. Create a compressed (zipped) folder in the Review folder named **Final Review** that contains all the files and folders in the Review folder.

11. Extract the contents of the Final Review files folder to a new folder named **Extracted**. (*Hint:* The file path will end with "\FM\Review\Extracted.")

12. Locate all copies of the **Loan** file in the subfolders of the Review folder. In which locations did you find this file?

13. Close all open windows.

14. Submit the results of the preceding steps to your instructor, either in printed or electronic form, as requested.

Apply	**Case Problem 1**

Use the skills you learned in the tutorial to manage files and folders for an arts organization.

Data Files needed for this Case Problem: Inv Feb.xlsx, Inv Jan.xlsx, Inv March.xlsx, Painting–Agenda.docx, Painting–Eval.docx, Painting–Manual.docx, Paris.jpg, Still Life.jpg

Jefferson Street Fine Arts Center   Rae Wysnewski owns the Jefferson Street Fine Arts Center (JSFAC) in Pittsburgh, and offers classes and gallery, studio, and practice space for aspiring and fledgling artists, musicians, and dancers. Rae opened JSFAC two years ago, and this year the center has a record enrollment in its classes. She hires you to teach a painting class and to show her how to manage her files on her new Windows Vista computer. Complete the following steps:

1. In the FM\Case1 folder in your Data Files, create two folders: Invoices and Painting Class.
2. Move the **Inv Jan**, **Inv Feb**, and **Inv March** files from the Case1 folder to the Invoices folder.
3. Rename the three files in the Invoices folder to remove "Inv" from each name.
4. Move the three text documents from the Case1 folder to the Painting Class folder. Rename the three documents, using shorter but still descriptive names.
5. Copy the remaining files to the Painting Class folder.
6. Switch to Details view, if necessary, and then answer the following questions:
   a.   What is the largest file in the Painting Class folder?
   b.   How many files in the Painting Class folder are JPEG images?
7. Delete the **Paris** and **Still Life** files from the Case1 folder.
8. Open the Recycle Bin folder by double-clicking the Recycle Bin icon on the desktop. Do the Paris and Still Life files appear in the Recycle Bin folder? Explain why or why not. Close the Recycle Bin window.
9. Copy the Painting Class folder to the Case1 folder. The duplicate folder appears as "Painting Class – Copy." Rename the Painting Class – Copy folder as **Graphics**.
10. Delete the text files from the Graphics folder.
11. Delete the **Paris** and **Still Life** files from the Painting Class folder.
12. Close all open windows, and then submit the results of the preceding steps to your instructor, either in printed or electronic form, as requested.

Challenge	**Case Problem 2**

Extend what you've learned to discover other methods of managing files for a social service organization.

There are no Data Files needed for this Case Problem.

First Call Outreach   Victor Crillo is the director of a social service organization named First Call Outreach in Toledo, Ohio. Its mission is to connect people who need help from local and state agencies to the appropriate service. Victor has a dedicated staff, but they are all relatively new to Windows Vista. In particular, they have trouble finding files that they have saved on their hard disks. He asks you to demonstrate how to find files in Windows Vista. Complete the following:

⊕ EXPLORE

1. Windows Vista Help and Support includes topics that explain how to search for files on a disk without looking through all the folders. Click the Start button, click Help and Support, and then use one of the following methods to locate topics on searching for files.
   • In the Windows Help and Support window, click the Windows Basics icon. Click the Working with files and folders link. In the "In this article" list, clicking Finding your files.

- In the Windows Help and Support window, click the Table of Contents icon. (If necessary, click the Home icon first, and then click the Table of Contents icon.) the Files and folders link, and then click Working with files and folders. In the "In this article" list, click Finding your files.
- In the Search Help box, type **searching for files**, and then press the Enter key. Click the Find a file or folder link. In the article, click the Show all link.

✦ EXPLORE 2. Read the topic and click any See also or For more information links in the topic, if necessary, to provide the following information:
    a. Where is the Search box located?
    b. Do you need to type the entire filename to find the file?
    c. Name three file characteristics you can use as search options.

✦ EXPLORE 3. Use the Windows Vista Help and Support window to locate topics related to managing files and folders. Write out two procedures for working with files and folders that were not covered in the tutorial.

4. Submit the results of the preceding steps to your instructor, either in printed or electronic form, as requested.

Assess | **SAM Assessment and Training**

If you have a SAM user profile, you may have access to hands-on instruction, practice, and assessment of the skills covered in this tutorial. Log in to your SAM account (**http://sam2007.course.com**) to launch any assigned training activities or exams that relate to the skills covered in this tutorial.

Review | **Quick Check Answers**

    1. file
    2. USB drives, CDs, and DVDs
    3. hard disk
    4. Windows Explorer and the Computer window
    5. file path
    6. True
    7. extension
    8. No

Ending Data Files

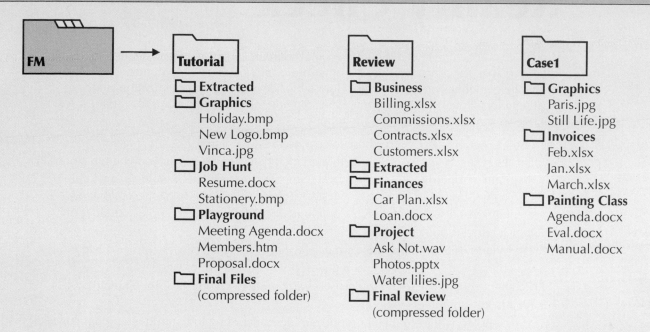

FM

Tutorial
- **Extracted**
- **Graphics**
  - Holiday.bmp
  - New Logo.bmp
  - Vinca.jpg
- **Job Hunt**
  - Resume.docx
  - Stationery.bmp
- **Playground**
  - Meeting Agenda.docx
  - Members.htm
  - Proposal.docx
- **Final Files**
  - (compressed folder)

Review
- **Business**
  - Billing.xlsx
  - Commissions.xlsx
  - Contracts.xlsx
  - Customers.xlsx
- **Extracted**
- **Finances**
  - Car Plan.xlsx
  - Loan.docx
- **Project**
  - Ask Not.wav
  - Photos.pptx
  - Water lilies.jpg
- **Final Review**
  - (compressed folder)

Case1
- **Graphics**
  - Paris.jpg
  - Still Life.jpg
- **Invoices**
  - Feb.xlsx
  - Jan.xlsx
  - March.xlsx
- **Painting Class**
  - Agenda.docx
  - Eval.docx
  - Manual.docx

Reality Check

Now that you have reviewed the fundamentals of managing files, organize the files and folders you use for course work or for other projects on your own computer. Be sure to follow the guidelines presented in this tutorial for developing an organization strategy, creating folders, naming files, and moving, copying, deleting, and compressing files. To manage your own files, complete the following tasks:

1. Use a program such as Word or Notepad to create a plan for organizing your files. List the types of files you work with, and then determine whether you want to store them on your hard disk or on removable media. Then sketch the folders and subfolders you will use to manage these files. If you choose a hard disk as your storage medium, make sure you plan to store your work files and folders in a subfolder of the Documents folder.

2. Use Windows Explorer or the Computer window to navigate to your files. Determine which tool you prefer for managing files, if you have a preference.

3. Create or rename the main folders you want to use for your files. Then create or rename the subfolders you will use.

4. Move and copy files to the appropriate folders according to your plan, and rename and delete files as necessary.

5. Create a backup copy of your work files by creating a compressed file and then copying the compressed file to a removable disk, such as a USB flash drive.

6. Submit your finished plan to your instructor, either in printed or electronic form, as requested.

Objectives

- Explore the programs that comprise Microsoft Office
- Start programs and switch between them
- Explore common window elements
- Minimize, maximize, and restore windows
- Use the Ribbon, tabs, and buttons
- Use the contextual tabs, Mini toolbar, and shortcut menus
- Save, close, and open a file
- Use the Help system
- Print a file
- Exit programs

Getting Started with Microsoft Office 2007

Preparing a Meeting Agenda

Case | Recycled Palette

Recycled Palette, a company in Oregon founded by Ean Nogella in 2006, sells 100 percent recycled latex paint to both individuals and businesses in the area. The high-quality recycled paint is filtered to industry standards and tested for performance and environmental safety. The paint is available in both 1 gallon cans and 5 gallon pails, and comes in colors ranging from white to shades of brown, blue, green, and red. The demand for affordable recycled paint has been growing each year. Ean and all his employees use Microsoft Office 2007, which provides everyone in the company with the power and flexibility to store a variety of information, create consistent files, and share data. In this tutorial, you'll review how the company's employees use Microsoft Office 2007.

Starting Data Files

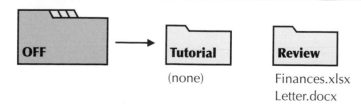

OFF → Tutorial

(none)

Review

Finances.xlsx
Letter.docx

Exploring Microsoft Office 2007

Microsoft Office 2007, or **Office**, is a collection of Microsoft programs. Office is available in many suites, each of which contains a different combination of these programs. For example, the Professional suite includes Word, Excel, PowerPoint, Access, Outlook, and Publisher. Other suites are available and can include more or fewer programs (for additional information about the available suites, go to the Microsoft Web site). Each Office program contains valuable tools to help you accomplish many tasks, such as composing reports, analyzing data, preparing presentations, compiling information, sending e-mail, and planning schedules.

Microsoft Office Word 2007, or **Word**, is a computer program you use to enter, edit, and format text. The files you create in Word are called **documents**, although many people use the term *document* to refer to any file created on a computer. Word, often called a word processing program, offers many special features that help you compose and update all types of documents, ranging from letters and newsletters to reports, brochures, faxes, and even books—all in attractive and readable formats. You can also use Word to create, insert, and position figures, tables, and other graphics to enhance the look of your documents. For example, the Recycled Palette employees create business letters using Word.

Microsoft Office Excel 2007, or **Excel**, is a computer program you use to enter, calculate, analyze, and present numerical data. You can do some of this in Word with tables, but Excel provides many more tools for recording and formatting numbers as well as performing calculations. The graphics capabilities in Excel also enable you to display data visually. You might, for example, generate a pie chart or a bar chart to help people quickly see the significance of and the connections between information. The files you create in Excel are called **workbooks** (commonly referred to as spreadsheets), and Excel is often called a spreadsheet program. The Recycled Palette accounting department uses a line chart in an Excel workbook to visually track the company's financial performance.

Microsoft Office Access 2007, or **Access**, is a computer program used to enter, maintain, and retrieve related information (or data) in a format known as a database. The files you create in Access are called **databases**, and Access is often referred to as a database or relational database program. With Access, you can create forms to make data entry easier, and you can create professional reports to improve the readability of your data. The Recycled Palette operations department tracks the company's inventory in a table in an Access database.

Microsoft Office PowerPoint 2007, or **PowerPoint**, is a computer program you use to create a collection of slides that can contain text, charts, pictures, sound, movies, multimedia, and so on. The files you create in PowerPoint are called **presentations**, and PowerPoint is often called a presentation graphics program. You can show these presentations on your computer monitor, project them onto a screen as a slide show, print them, share them over the Internet, or display them on the World Wide Web. You can also use PowerPoint to generate presentation-related documents such as audience handouts, outlines, and speakers' notes. The Recycled Palette marketing department has created an effective slide presentation with PowerPoint to promote its paints to a wider audience.

Microsoft Office Outlook 2007, or **Outlook**, is a computer program you use to send, receive, and organize e-mail; plan your schedule; arrange meetings; organize contacts; create a to-do list; and jot down notes. You can also use Outlook to print schedules, task lists, phone directories, and other documents. Outlook is often referred to as an information management program. The Recycled Palette staff use Outlook to send and receive e-mail, plan their schedules, and create to-do lists.

Although each Office program individually is a strong tool, their potential is even greater when used together.

Integrating Office Programs

One of the main advantages of Office is **integration**, the ability to share information between programs. Integration ensures consistency and accuracy, and it saves time because you don't have to reenter the same information in several Office programs. The staff at Recycled Palette uses the integration features of Office daily, including the following examples:

- The accounting department created an Excel bar chart on the previous two years' fourth-quarter results, which they inserted into the quarterly financial report created in Word. They included a hyperlink in the Word report that employees can click to open the Excel workbook and view the original data.
- The operations department included an Excel pie chart of sales percentages by paint colors on a PowerPoint slide, which is part of a presentation to stockholders.
- The marketing department produced a mailing to promote its recycled paints to local contractors and designers by combining a form letter created in Word with an Access database that stores the names and addresses of these potential customers.
- A sales representative wrote a letter in Word about an upcoming promotion for new customers and merged the letter with an Outlook contact list containing the names and addresses of prospective customers.

These are just a few examples of how you can take information from one Office program and integrate it with another.

Starting Office Programs

You can start any Office program by clicking the Start button on the Windows taskbar, and then selecting the program you want from the All Programs menu. As soon as the program starts, you can immediately begin to create new files or work with existing ones. If an Office program appears in the most frequently used programs list on the left side of the Start menu, you can click the program name to start the program.

Starting Office Programs | Reference Window

- Click the Start button on the taskbar.
- Click All Programs.
- Click Microsoft Office.
- Click the name of the program you want to start.

or

- Click the name of the program you want to start in the most frequently used programs list on the left side of the Start menu.

You'll start Excel using the Start button.

To start Excel and open a new, blank workbook:

1. Make sure your computer is on and the Windows desktop appears on your screen.

   Trouble? If your screen varies slightly from those shown in the figures, your computer might be set up differently. The figures in this book were created while running Windows Vista with the Aero feature turned off, but how your screen looks depends on the version of Windows you are using, the background settings, and so forth.

Windows XP Tip

The Start button is the green button with the word "start" on it, located at the bottom left of the taskbar.

2. Click the **Start** button on the taskbar, and then click **All Programs** to display the All Programs menu.

3. Click **Microsoft Office** on the All Programs list, and then point to **Microsoft Office Excel 2007**. Depending on how your computer is set up, your desktop and menu might contain different icons and commands.

   Trouble? If you don't see Microsoft Office on the All Programs list, click Microsoft Office Excel 2007 on the All Programs list. If you still don't see Microsoft Office Excel 2007, ask your instructor or technical support person for help.

4. Click **Microsoft Office Excel 2007**. Excel starts, and a new, blank workbook opens. See Figure 1.

| Figure 1 | New, blank Excel workbook |

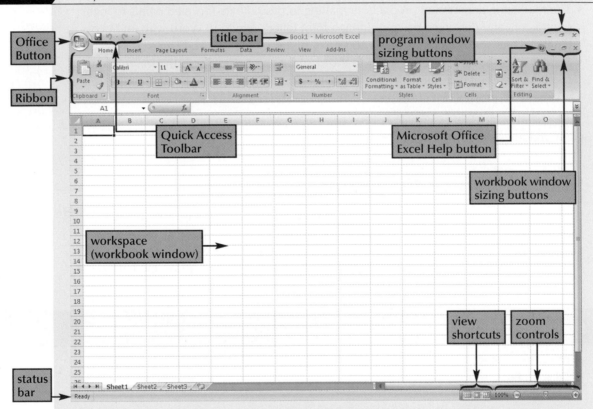

Trouble? If the Excel window doesn't fill your entire screen, the window is not maximized, or expanded to its full size. You'll maximize the window shortly.

You can have more than one Office program open at once. You'll use this same method to start Word and open a new, blank document.

To start Word and open a new, blank document:

1. Click the **Start** button on the taskbar, click **All Programs** to display the All Programs list, and then click **Microsoft Office**.

   Trouble? If you don't see Microsoft Office on the All Programs list, click Microsoft Office Word 2007 on the All Programs list. If you still don't see Microsoft Office Word 2007, ask your instructor or technical support person for help.

2. Click **Microsoft Office Word 2007**. Word starts, and a new, blank document opens. See Figure 2.

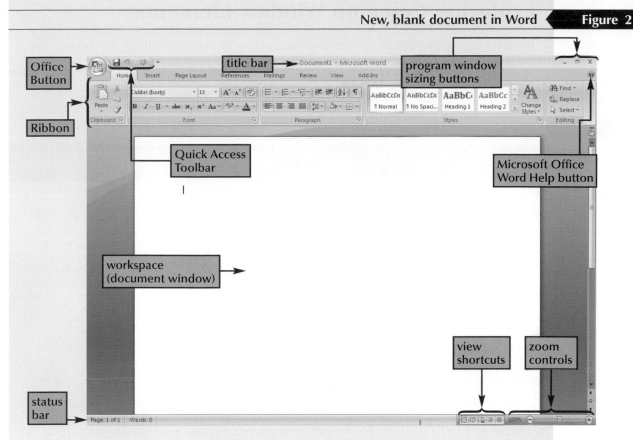

New, blank document in Word | Figure 2

Trouble? If the Word window doesn't fill your entire screen, the window is not maximized. You'll maximize the window shortly.

Switching Between Open Programs and Files

Two programs are running at the same time—Excel and Word. The taskbar contains buttons for both programs. When you have two or more programs running or two files within the same program open, you can use the taskbar buttons to switch from one program or file to another. The button for the active program or file is darker. The employees at Recycled Palette often work in several programs at once.

To switch between Word and Excel files:

▶ 1. Click the **Microsoft Excel – Book1** button on the taskbar. The active program switches from Word to Excel. See Figure 3.

Excel and Word programs opened simultaneously | Figure 3

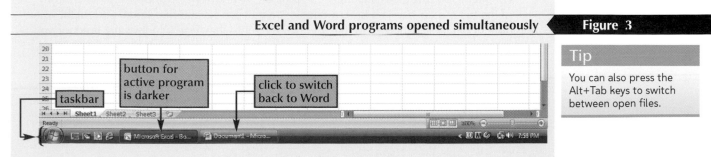

Tip

You can also press the Alt+Tab keys to switch between open files.

▶ 2. Click the **Document1 – Microsoft Word** button on the taskbar to return to Word.

Exploring Common Window Elements

The Office programs consist of windows that have many similar features. As you can see in Figures 1 and 2, many of the elements in both the Excel program window and the Word program window are the same. In fact, all the Office programs have these same elements. Figure 4 describes some of the most common window elements.

Figure 4   Common window elements

Element	Description
Office Button	Provides access to document-level features and program settings
Quick Access Toolbar	Provides one-click access to commonly used commands, such as Save, Undo, and Repeat
Title bar	Contains the name of the open file, the program name, and the sizing buttons
Sizing buttons	Resize and close the program window or the workspace
Ribbon	Provides access to the main set of commands organized by task into tabs and groups
Microsoft Office Help button	Opens the Help window for that program
Workspace	Displays the file you are working on (Word document, Excel workbook, Access database, or PowerPoint slide)
Status bar	Provides information about the program, open file, or current task as well as the view shortcuts and zoom controls
View shortcuts	Change how a file is displayed in the workspace
Zoom controls	Magnify or shrink the content displayed in the workspace

Because these elements are the same in each program, after you've learned one program, it's easy to learn the others. The next sections explore these common features.

Resizing the Program Window and Workspace

There are three different sizing buttons. The Minimize button ▬ , which is the left button, hides a window so that only its program button is visible on the taskbar. The middle button changes name and function depending on the status of the window—the Maximize button ▢ expands the window to the full screen size or to the program window size, and the Restore Down button ▣ returns the window to a predefined size. The Close button ✕ , on the right, exits the program or closes the file. Excel has two sets of sizing buttons. The top set controls the program window and the lower set controls the workspace. The workspace sizing buttons look and function in exactly the same way as the program window sizing buttons, except the button names change to Minimize Window and Restore Window when the workspace is maximized.

Most often, you'll want to maximize the program window and workspace to take advantage of the full screen size you have available. If you have several files open, you might want to restore down their windows so that you can see more than one window at a time, or you might want to minimize programs or files you are not working on at the moment. You'll try minimizing, maximizing, and restoring down windows and workspaces now.

To resize windows and workspaces:

▶ **1.** Click the **Minimize** button ▭ on the Word title bar. The Word program window reduces to a taskbar button. The Excel program window is visible again.

▶ **2.** If necessary, click the **Maximize** button ▭ on the Excel title bar. The Excel program window expands to fill the screen.

▶ **3.** Click the **Restore Window** button ▭ in the lower set of Excel sizing buttons. The workspace is resized and is now smaller than the full program window. See Figure 5.

Resized Excel window and workspace ◀ **Figure 5**

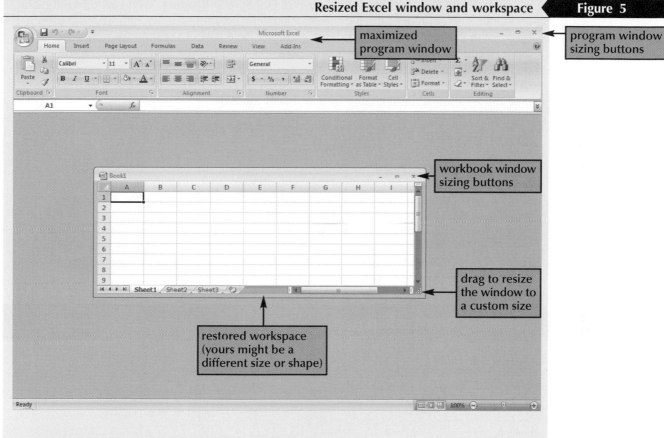

- maximized program window
- program window sizing buttons
- workbook window sizing buttons
- drag to resize the window to a custom size
- restored workspace (yours might be a different size or shape)

▶ **4.** Click the **Maximize** button ▭ on the Excel workbook window title bar. The Excel workspace expands to fill the program window.

▶ **5.** Click the **Document1 - Microsoft Word** button on the taskbar. The Word program window returns to its previous size.

▶ **6.** If necessary, click the **Maximize** button ▭ on the Word title bar. The Word program window expands to fill the screen.

The sizing buttons give you the flexibility to arrange the program and file windows on your screen to best fit your needs.

Getting Information from the Status Bar

The **status bar** at the bottom of the program window provides information about the open file and current task or selection. It also has buttons and other controls for working with the file and its content. The status bar buttons and information displays are specific to the individual programs. For example, the Excel status bar displays summary information about a selected range of numbers (such as their sum or average), whereas the Word status bar shows the current page number and total number of words in a document. The right side of the status bar includes buttons that enable you to switch the workspace view in Word, Excel, PowerPoint, and Access as well as zoom the workspace in Word, Excel, and PowerPoint. You can customize the status bar to display other information or hide the **default** (original or preset) information.

Switching Views

Each program has a variety of views, or ways to display the file in the workspace. For example, Word has five views: Print Layout, Full Screen Reading, Web Layout, Outline, and Draft. The content of the file doesn't change from view to view, although the presentation of the content will. In Word, for example, Page Layout view shows how a document would appear as the printed page, whereas Web Layout view shows how the document would appear as a Web page. You can quickly switch between views using the shortcuts at the right side of the status bar. You can also change the view from the View tab on the Ribbon. You'll change views in later tutorials.

Zooming the Workspace

Zooming is a way to magnify or shrink the file content displayed in the workspace. You can zoom in to get a closer look at the content of an open document, worksheet, or slide, or you can zoom out to see more of the content at a smaller size. There are several ways to change the zoom percentage. You can use the Zoom slider at the right of the status bar to quickly change the zoom percentage. You can click the Zoom level button to the left of the Zoom slider in the status bar to open the Zoom dialog box and select a specific zoom percentage or size based on your file. You can also change the zoom settings using the Zoom group in the View tab on the Ribbon.

Reference Window | Zooming the Workspace

- Click the Zoom Out or Zoom In button on the status bar (or drag the Zoom slider button left or right) to the desired zoom percentage.

or

- Click the Zoom level button on the status bar.
- Select the appropriate zoom setting, and then click the OK button.

or

- Click the View tab on the Ribbon, and then in the Zoom group, click the zoom setting you want.

The figures shown in these tutorials are zoomed to enhance readability. You'll zoom the Word and Excel workspaces.

To zoom the Word and Excel workspaces:

▶ **1.** On the Zoom slider on the Word status bar, drag the **slider button** to the left until the Zoom percentage is **10%**. The document reduces to its smallest size, which makes the entire page visible but unreadable. See Figure 6.

Word document zoomed to 10% | Figure 6

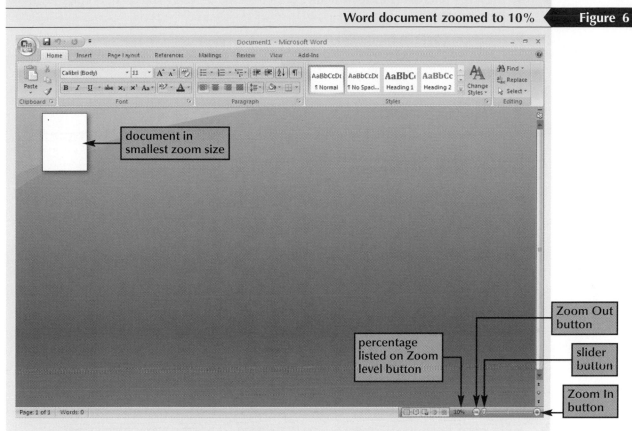

document in smallest zoom size

Zoom Out button

percentage listed on Zoom level button

slider button

Zoom In button

You'll zoom the document so its page width fills the workspace.

2. Click the **Zoom level** button `10%` on the Word status bar. The Zoom dialog box opens. See Figure 7.

Zoom dialog box | Figure 7

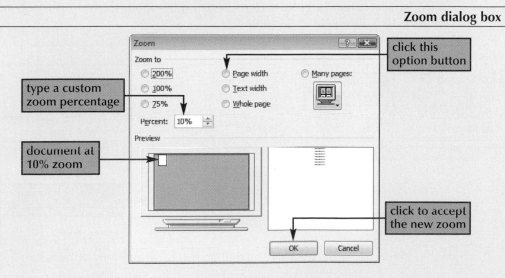

click this option button

type a custom zoom percentage

document at 10% zoom

click to accept the new zoom

3. Click the **Page width** option button, and then click the **OK** button. The Word document magnifies to its page width to match the rest of the Word figures shown in these tutorials.

Now, you'll zoom the workbook to 120%.

4. Click the **Microsoft Excel – Book1** button on the taskbar. The Excel program window is displayed.

5. Click the **Zoom In** button on the status bar two times. The workspace magnifies to 120%. This is the zoom percentage that matches the rest of the Excel figures shown in these tutorials.

6. Click the **Document1 – Microsoft Word** button on the taskbar. The Word program window is displayed.

Using the Ribbon

The **Ribbon** at the top of the program window just below the title bar is the main set of commands that you click to execute tasks. The Ribbon is organized into tabs. Each **tab** has commands related to particular activities. For example, in Word, the Insert tab on the Ribbon provides access to all the commands for adding objects such as shapes, pages, tables, illustrations, text, and symbols to a document. Although the tabs differ from program to program, the first tab in each program, called the Home tab, contains the commands for the most frequently performed activities, including cutting and pasting, changing fonts, and using editing tools. In addition, the Insert, Review, View, and Add-Ins tabs appear on the Ribbon in all the Office programs except Access, although the commands they include might differ from program to program. Other tabs are program specific, such as the Design tab in PowerPoint and the Datasheet tab in Access.

To use the Ribbon tabs:

1. In Word, point to the **Insert** tab on the Ribbon. The Insert tab is highlighted, though the Home tab with the options for using the Clipboard and formatting text remains visible.

2. Click the **Insert** tab. The Ribbon displays the Insert tab, which provides access to all the options for adding objects such as shapes, pages, tables, illustrations, text, and symbols to a document. See Figure 8.

Figure 8 ▶ **Insert tab on the Ribbon**

3. Click the **Home** tab on the Ribbon. The Ribbon displays the Home options.

Clicking Button Icons

Each **button**, or icon, on the tabs provides one-click access to a command. Most buttons are labeled so that you can easily find the command you need. For the most part, when you click a button, something happens in your file. If you want to repeat that action, you click the button again. Buttons for related commands are organized on a tab in **groups**. For example, the Clipboard group on the Home tab includes the Cut, Copy, Paste, and Format Painter buttons—the commands for moving or copying text, objects, and formatting.

Buttons can be toggle switches: one click turns on the feature and the next click turns off the feature. While the feature is on, the button remains colored or highlighted to remind you that it is active. For example, in Word, the Show/Hide button on the Home tab in the Paragraph group displays the nonprinting screen characters when toggled on and hides them when toggled off.

Some buttons have two parts: a button that accesses a command and an arrow that opens a menu of all the commands available for that task. For example, the Paste button on the Home tab includes the default Paste command and an arrow that opens the menu of all the Paste commands—Paste, Paste Special, and Paste as Hyperlink. To select a command on the menu, you click the button arrow and then click the command on the menu.

The buttons and groups change based on your monitor size, your screen resolution, and the size of the program window. With smaller monitors, lower screen resolutions, and reduced program windows, buttons can appear as icons without labels and a group can be condensed into a button that you click to display the group options. The figures in these tutorials were created using a screen resolution of 1024 × 768 and, unless otherwise specified, the program and workspace windows are maximized. If you are using a different screen resolution or window size, the button icons on the Ribbon might show more or fewer button names, and some groups might be condensed into buttons.

You'll type text in the Word document, and then use the buttons on the Ribbon.

To use buttons on the Ribbon:

▶ **1.** Type **Recycled Palette**, and then press the **Enter** key. The text appears in the first line of the document and the insertion point moves to the second line.

Trouble? If you make a typing error, press the Backspace key to delete the incorrect letters, and then retype the text.

▶ **2.** In the Paragraph group on the Home tab, click the **Show/Hide** button ¶ . The nonprinting screen characters appear in the document, and the Show/Hide button remains toggled on. See Figure 9.

Trouble? If the nonprinting characters are removed from your screen, the Show/Hide button ¶ was already selected. Repeat Step 2 to show the nonprinting screen characters.

Button toggled on | **Figure 9**

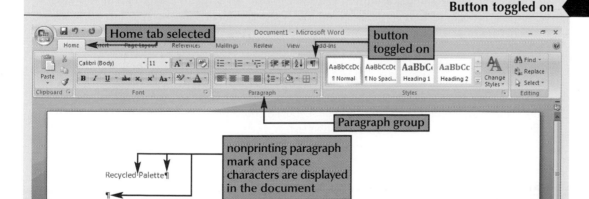

▶ **3.** Drag to select all the text in the first line of the document (but not the paragraph mark).

▶ **4.** In the Clipboard group on the Home tab, click the **Copy** button 🗎. The selected text is copied to the Clipboard.

▶ **5.** Press the ↓ key. The text is deselected and the insertion point moves to the second line in the document.

▶ **6.** In the Clipboard group on the Home tab, point to the top part of the **Paste** button. Both parts of the Paste button are highlighted, but the icon at top is darker to indicate it will be clicked if you press the mouse button.

▶ **7.** Point to the **Paste button arrow**. The button arrow is now darker.

▶ **8.** Click the **Paste button arrow**. A menu of paste commands opens. See Figure 10. To select one of the commands on the list, you click it.

Figure 10	Two-part Paste button

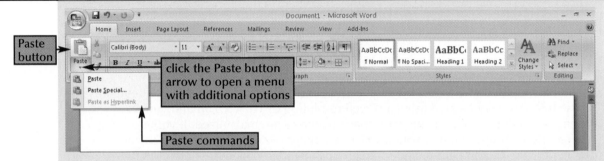

▶ **9.** Click **Paste**. The menu closes, and the text is duplicated in the second line of the document.

As you can see, you can quickly access commands and turn features on and off with the buttons on the Ribbon.

InSight | Using Keyboard Shortcuts and Key Tips

Keyboard shortcuts can help you work faster and more efficiently. A **keyboard shortcut** is a key or combination of keys you press to access a tool or perform a command. To quickly access options on the Ribbon, the Quick Access Toolbar, and the Office Button without removing your hands from the keyboard:

1. Press the Alt key. Key Tips appear that list the keyboard shortcut for each Ribbon tab, each Quick Access Toolbar button, and the Office Button.
2. Press the key for the tab or button you want to use. An action is performed or Key Tips appear for the buttons on the selected tab or the commands for the selected button.
3. Continue to press the appropriate key listed in the Key Tip until the action you want is performed.

You can also use keyboard shortcuts to perform specific commands. For example, Ctrl+S is the keyboard shortcut for the Save command (you hold down the Ctrl key while you press the S key). This type of keyboard shortcut appears in ScreenTips next to the command's name. Not all commands have this type of keyboard shortcut. Identical commands in each Office program use the same keyboard shortcut.

Using Galleries and Live Preview

A button can also open a **gallery**, which is a grid or menu that shows a visual representation of the options available for that command. For example, the Bullet Library gallery in Word shows an icon of each bullet style you can select. Some galleries include a More button that you click to expand the gallery to see all the options in it. When you hover the pointer over an option in a gallery, **Live Preview** shows the results you would achieve in your file if you clicked that option. To continue the bullets example, when you hover over a bullet style in the Bullet Library gallery, the current paragraph or selected text previews that bullet style. By moving the pointer from option to option, you can quickly see the text set with different bullet styles; you can then select the style that works best for your needs.

To use a gallery and Live Preview:

▶ **1.** In the Paragraph group on the Home tab, click the **Bullets button arrow** ⊟⏷ . The Bullet Library gallery opens.

▶ **2.** Point to the **check mark bullet** style. Live Preview shows the selected bullet style in your document, so you can determine if you like that bullet style. See Figure 11.

Live Preview of bullet style ◀ **Figure 11**

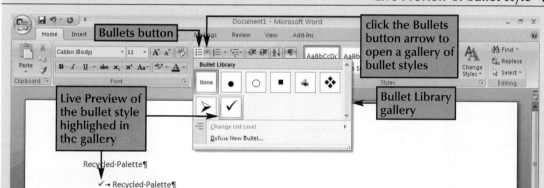

▶ **3.** Place the pointer over each of the remaining bullet styles and preview them in your document.

You don't want to add bullets to your document right now, so you'll close the Bullet Library gallery and deselect the Bullets button.

▶ **4.** Press the **Esc** key on the keyboard. The Bullet Library gallery closes and the Bullets button is deselected.

▶ **5.** Press the **Backspace** key on the keyboard to delete the text "Recycled Palette" on the second line.

Galleries and Live Preview let you quickly see how your file will be affected by a selection.

Opening Dialog Boxes and Task Panes

The button to the right of the group names is the **Dialog Box Launcher**, which you click to open a task pane or dialog box that provides more advanced functionality for that group of tasks. A **task pane** is a window that helps you navigate through a complex task or feature. For example, the Clipboard task pane allows you to paste some or all of the items that have been cut or copied from any Office program during the current work session and the Research task pane allows you to search a variety of reference resources from within a file. A **dialog box** is a window from which you enter or choose settings for how you want to perform a task. For example, the Page Setup dialog box in Word contains options for how you want a document to look. Some dialog boxes organize related information into tabs, and related options and settings are organized into groups, just as they are on the Ribbon. You select settings in a dialog box using option buttons, check boxes, text boxes, lists, and other controls to collect information about how you want to perform a task.

In Excel, you'll use the Dialog Box Launcher for the Page Setup group to open the Page Setup dialog box.

To open the Page Setup dialog box using the Dialog Box Launcher:

▶ **1.** Click the **Microsoft Excel – Book1** button on the taskbar to switch from Word to Excel.

▶ **2.** Click the **Page Layout** tab on the Ribbon.

▶ **3.** In the Page Setup group, click the **Dialog Box Launcher**, which is the small button to the right of the Page Setup group name. The Page Setup dialog box opens with the Page tab displayed. See Figure 12.

Figure 12   **Page tab in the Page Setup dialog box**

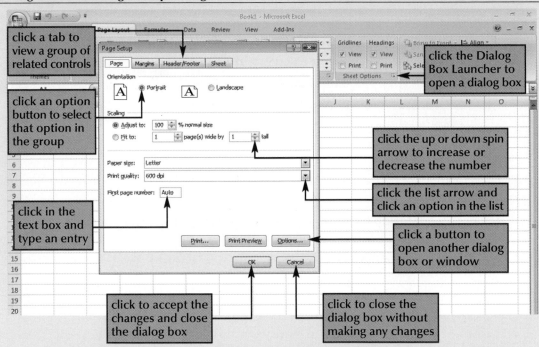

click a tab to view a group of related controls

click the Dialog Box Launcher to open a dialog box

click an option button to select that option in the group

click the up or down spin arrow to increase or decrease the number

click the list arrow and click an option in the list

click in the text box and type an entry

click a button to open another dialog box or window

click to accept the changes and close the dialog box

click to close the dialog box without making any changes

▶ **4.** Click the **Landscape** option button. The workbook's page orientation changes to a page wider than it is long.

▶ **5.** Click the **Sheet** tab. The dialog box displays options related to the worksheet. You can click a check box to turn an option on (checked) or off (unchecked). You can check more than one check box in a group, whereas you can select only one option button in a group.

▶ **6.** In the Print group, click the **Gridlines** check box and the **Row and column headings** check box. Check marks appear in both check boxes, indicating that these options are selected.

You don't want to change the page setup right now, so you'll close the dialog box.

▶ **7.** Click the **Cancel** button. The dialog box closes without making any changes to the page setup.

Using Contextual Tools

Some tabs, toolbars, and menus come into view as you work. Because these tools become available only as you might need them, the workspace on your screen remains more open and less cluttered. However, tools that appear and disappear as you work can be distracting and take some getting used to.

Displaying Contextual Tabs

Any object that you can select in a file has a related contextual tab. An **object** is anything that appears on your screen that can be selected and manipulated as a whole, such as a table, a picture, a text box, a shape, a chart, WordArt, an equation, a diagram, a header, or a footer. A **contextual tab** is a Ribbon tab that contains commands related to the selected object so you can manipulate, edit, and format that object. Contextual tabs appear to the right of the standard Ribbon tabs just below a title label. For example, Figure 13 shows the Table Tools contextual tabs that appear when you select a table in a Word document. Although the contextual tabs appear only when you select an object, they function in the same way as standard tabs on the Ribbon. Contextual tabs disappear when you click elsewhere on the screen and deselect the object. Contextual tabs can also appear as you switch views. You'll use contextual tabs in later tutorials.

Table Tools contextual tabs  Figure 13

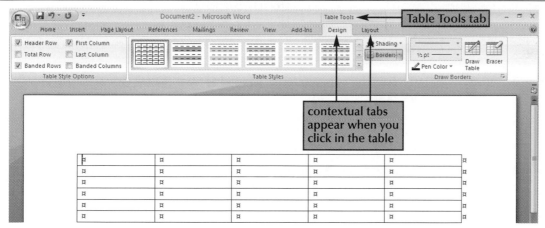

Accessing the Mini Toolbar

The **Mini toolbar** is a toolbar that appears next to the pointer whenever you select text, and it contains buttons for the most commonly used formatting commands, such as font, font size, styles, color, alignment, and indents that may appear in different groups or tabs on the Ribbon. The Mini toolbar buttons differ in each program. A transparent version of the Mini toolbar appears immediately after you select text. When you move the pointer over the Mini toolbar, it comes into full view so you can click the appropriate formatting button or buttons. The Mini toolbar disappears if you move the pointer away from the toolbar, press a key, or press a mouse button. The Mini toolbar can help you format your text faster, but initially you might find that the toolbar disappears unexpectedly. All the commands on the Mini toolbar are also available on the Ribbon. Be aware that Live Preview of selected styles does not work in the Mini toolbar.

You'll use the Mini toolbar to format text you enter in the workbook.

To use the Mini toolbar to format text:

1. If necessary, click cell **A1** (the rectangle in the upper-left corner of the worksheet).

2. Type **Budget**. The text appears in the cell.

3. Press the **Enter** key. The text is entered in cell A1 and cell A2 is selected.

4. Type **2008**, and then press the **Enter** key. The year is entered in cell A2 and cell A3 is selected.

   You'll use the Mini toolbar to make the word in cell A1 boldface.

5. Double-click cell **A1** to place the insertion point in the cell. Now you can select the text you typed.

6. Double-click **Budget** in cell A1. The selected text appears white in a black background, and the transparent Mini toolbar appears directly above the selected text. See Figure 14.

Figure 14 | Transparent Mini toolbar

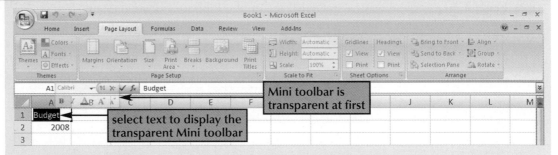

7. Move the pointer over the Mini toolbar. The Mini toolbar is now completely visible, and you can click buttons.

   Trouble? If the Mini toolbar disappears, you probably moved the pointer to another area of the worksheet. To redisplay the Mini toolbar, repeat Steps 5 through 7, being careful to move the pointer directly over the Mini toolbar in Step 7.

8. Click the **Bold** button **B** on the Mini toolbar. The text in cell A1 is bold and the Mini toolbar remains visible so you can continue formatting the selected text. See Figure 15.

Tip

You can redisplay the Mini toolbar if it disappears by right-clicking the selected text.

Figure 15 | Mini toolbar with the Bold button selected

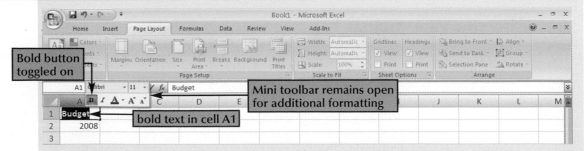

You don't want to make any other changes, so you'll close the Mini toolbar.

9. Press the **Enter** key. The Mini toolbar disappears and cell A2 is selected.

Opening Shortcut Menus

A **shortcut menu** is a list of commands related to a selection that opens when you click the right mouse button. Each shortcut menu provides access to the commands you'll most likely want to use with the object or selection you right-click. The shortcut menu includes commands that perform actions, commands that open dialog boxes, and galleries of options that provide Live Preview. The Mini toolbar also opens when you right-click. If you click a button on the Mini toolbar, the rest of the shortcut menu closes while the Mini toolbar remains open so you can continue formatting the selection. Using a shortcut menu provides quick access to the commands you need without having to access the tabs on the Ribbon. For example, you can right-click selected text to open a shortcut menu with a Mini toolbar, text-related commands, such as Cut, Copy, and Paste, as well as other program-specific commands.

You'll use a shortcut menu in Excel to delete the content you entered in cell A1.

To use a shortcut menu to delete content:

▶ 1. Right-click cell **A1**. A shortcut menu opens, listing commands related to common tasks you'd perform in a cell, along with a Mini toolbar. See Figure 16.

Shortcut menu with Mini toolbar ◄ **Figure 16**

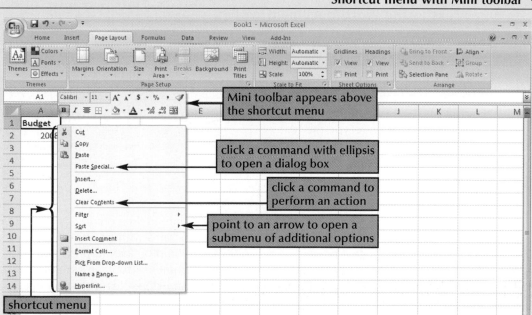

You'll use the Clear Contents command to delete the bold text from cell A1.

▶ 2. Click **Clear Contents** on the shortcut menu. The shortcut menu closes, the Mini toolbar disappears, and the formatted text is removed from cell A1.

You'll use the Clear Contents command again to delete the year from cell A2.

▶ 3. Right-click cell **A2**, and then click **Clear Contents** on the shortcut menu. The year is removed from cell A2.

> **Tip**
>
> Press the Esc key to close an open menu, shortcut menu, list, gallery, and so forth without selecting an option.

Shortcut menus enable you to quickly access commands that you're most likely to need in the context of the task you're performing.

Working with Files

The most common tasks you perform in any Office program are to create, open, save, and close files. The processes for these tasks are basically the same in all the Office programs. In addition, there are several methods for performing most tasks in Office. This flexibility enables you to use Office in a way that best fits how you like to work.

The **Office Button** provides access to document-level features, such as creating new files, opening existing files, saving files, printing files, and closing files, as well as the most common program options, called **application settings**. The **Quick Access Toolbar** is a collection of buttons that provide one-click access to commonly used commands, such as Save, Undo, and Repeat.

To begin working in a program, you need to create a new file or open an existing file. When you start Word, Excel, or PowerPoint, the program opens along with a blank file—ready for you to begin working on a new document, workbook, or presentation. When you start Access, the Getting Started with Microsoft Access window opens, displaying options for creating a new database or opening an existing one.

Ean has asked you to continue working on the agenda for the stockholder meeting. You already started typing in the document that opened when you started Word. Next, you will enter more text in the Word document.

To enter text in the Word document:

▶ 1. Click the **Document1 – Microsoft Word** button on the taskbar to activate the Word program window.

▶ 2. Type **Meeting Agenda** on the second line of the document, and then press the **Enter** key. The text you typed appears in the document.

   Trouble? If you make a typing error, press the Backspace key to delete the incorrect letters, and then retype the text.

Saving a File

As you create and modify Office files, your work is stored only in the computer's temporary memory, not on a hard disk. If you were to exit the programs without saving, turn off your computer, or experience a power failure, your work would be lost. To prevent losing work, save your file to a disk frequently—at least every 10 minutes. You can save files to the hard disk located inside your computer, a floppy disk, an external hard drive, a network storage drive, or a portable storage disk, such as a USB flash drive.

Reference Window | **Saving a File**

To save a file the first time or with a new name or location:
- Click the Office Button, and then click Save As (or for an unnamed file, click the Save button on the Quick Access Toolbar or click the Office Button, and then click Save).
- In the Save As dialog box, navigate to the location where you want to save the file.
- Type a descriptive title in the File name box, and then click the Save button.

To resave a named file to the same location:
- Click the Save button on the Quick Access Toolbar (or click the Office Button, and then click Save).

The first time you save a file, you need to name it. This **filename** includes a descriptive title you select and a file extension assigned by Office. You should choose a descriptive title that accurately reflects the content of the document, workbook, presentation, or database, such as "Shipping Options Letter" or "Fourth Quarter Financial Analysis." Your descriptive title can include uppercase and lowercase letters, numbers, hyphens, and spaces in any combination, but not the following special characters: ? " / \ < > * | and :. Each filename ends with a **file extension**, a period followed by several characters that Office adds to your descriptive title to identify the program in which that file was created. The default file extensions for Office 2007 are .docx for Word, .xlsx for Excel, .pptx for PowerPoint, and .accdb for Access. Filenames (the descriptive title and the file extension) can include a maximum of 255 characters. You might see file extensions depending on how Windows is set up on your computer. The figures in these tutorials do not show file extensions.

You also need to decide where to save the file—on which disk and in what folder. A **folder** is a container for your files. Just as you organize paper documents within folders stored in a filing cabinet, you can organize your files within folders stored on your computer's hard disk or a removable disk, such as a USB flash drive. Store each file in a logical location that you will remember whenever you want to use the file again. The default storage location for Office files is the Documents folder; you can create additional storage folders within that folder or navigate to a new storage location.

You can navigate the Save As dialog box by clicking a folder or location on your computer in the Navigation pane along the left side of the dialog box, and then double-clicking folders in the file list until you display the storage location you want. You can also navigate to a storage location with the Address bar, which displays the current file path. Each location in the file path has a corresponding arrow that you can click to quickly select a folder within that location. For example, you can click the Documents arrow in the Address bar to open a list of all the folders in the Documents folder, and then click the folder you want to open. If you want to return to a specific spot in the file hierarchy, you click that folder name in the Address bar. The Back and Forward buttons let you quickly move between folders.

Tip

Office adds the correct file extension when you save a file. Do not type one in the descriptive title, or you will create a duplicate (such as Meeting Agenda. docx.docx).

Windows XP Tip

The default storage location for Office files is the My Documents folder.

Saving and Using Files with Earlier Versions of Office | InSight

The default file types in Office 2007 are different from those used in earlier versions. This means that someone using Office 2003 or earlier cannot open files created in Office 2007. Files you want to share with earlier Office users must be saved in the earlier formats, which use the following extensions: .doc for Word, .xls for Excel, .mdb for Access, and .ppt for PowerPoint. To save a file in an earlier format, open the Save As dialog box, click the Save as type list arrow, and then click the appropriate 97-2003 format. A compatibility checker reports which Office 2007 features or elements are not supported by the earlier version of Office, and you can choose to remove them before saving. You can use Office 2007 to open and work with files created in earlier versions of Office. You can then save the file in its current format or update it to the Office 2007 format.

The lines of text you typed are not yet saved on disk. You'll do that now.

To save a file for the first time:

Windows XP Tip

To navigate to a location in the Save As dialog box, you use the Save in arrow.

▶ **1.** Click the **Save** button 🖫 on the Quick Access Toolbar. The Save As dialog box opens because you have not yet saved the file and need to specify a storage location and filename. The default location is set to the Documents folder, and the first few words of the first line appear in the File name box as a suggested title.

▶ **2.** In the Navigation pane, click the link for the location that contains your Data Files, if necessary.

Trouble? If you don't have the starting Data Files, you need to get them before you can proceed. Your instructor will either give you the Data Files or ask you to obtain them from a specified location (such as a network drive). In either case, make a backup copy of the Data Files before you start so that you will have the original files available in case you need to start over. If you have any questions about the Data Files, see your instructor or technical support person for assistance.

▶ **3.** Double-click the **OFF** folder in the file list, and then double-click the **Tutorial** folder. This is the location where you want to save the document.

Next, you'll enter a more descriptive title for the filename.

▶ **4.** Type **Meeting Agenda** in the File name box. See Figure 17.

Figure 17 ▶ **Completed Save As dialog box**

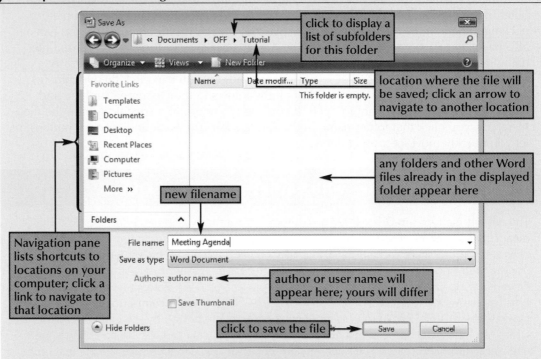

Trouble? If the .docx file extension appears after the filename, your computer is configured to show file extensions. Continue with Step 5.

▶ **5.** Click the **Save** button. The Save As dialog box closes, and the name of your file appears in the title bar.

The saved file includes everything in the document at the time you last saved it. Any new edits or additions you make to the document exist only in the computer's memory and are not saved in the file on the disk. As you work, remember to save frequently so that the file is updated to reflect the latest content of the document.

Because you already named the document and selected a storage location, the Save As dialog box doesn't open whenever you save the document again. If you want to save a copy of the file with a different filename or to a different location, you reopen the Save As dialog box by clicking the Office Button, and then clicking Save As. The previous version of the file remains on your disk as well.

You need to add your name to the agenda. Then, you'll save your changes.

To modify and save the Word document:

▶ **1.** Type your name, and then press the **Enter** key. The text you typed appears on the next line.

▶ **2.** Click the **Save** button 🖫 on the Quick Access Toolbar to save your changes.

Closing a File

Although you can keep multiple files open at one time, you should close any file you are no longer working on to conserve system resources as well as to ensure that you don't inadvertently make changes to the file. You can close a file by clicking the Office Button and then clicking the Close command. If that's the only file open for the program, the program window remains open and no file appears in the window. You can also close a file by clicking the Close button in the upper-right corner of the title bar or double-clicking the Office Button. If that's the only file open for the program, the program also closes.

As a standard practice, you should save your file before closing it. However, Office has an added safeguard: If you attempt to close a file without saving your changes, a dialog box opens, asking whether you want to save the file. Click the Yes button to save the changes to the file before closing the file and program. Click the No button to close the file and program without saving changes. Click the Cancel button to return to the program window without saving changes or closing the file and program. This feature helps to ensure that you always save the most current version of any file.

You'll add the date to the agenda. Then, you'll attempt to close it without saving.

To modify and close the Word document:

▶ **1.** Type today's date, and then press the **Enter** key. The text you typed appears below your name in the document.

▶ **2.** In the upper-left corner of the program window, click the **Office Button** 🖽. A menu opens with commands for creating new files, opening existing files, saving files, printing files, and closing files.

▶ **3.** Click **Close**. A dialog box opens, asking whether you want to save the changes you made to the document.

▶ **4.** Click the **Yes** button. The current version of the document is saved to the file, and then the document closes. Word is still running.

After you have a program open, you can create additional new files for the open program or you can open previously created and saved files.

Opening a File

When you want to open a blank document, workbook, presentation, or database, you create a new file. When you want to work on a previously created file, you must first open it. Opening a file transfers a copy of the file from the storage disk (either a hard disk or a portable disk) to the computer's memory and displays it on your screen. The file is then in your computer's memory and on the disk.

Reference Window | **Opening an Existing File or Creating a New File**

- Click the Office Button, and then click Open.
- In the Open dialog box, navigate to the storage location of the file you want to open.
- Click the filename of the file you want to open.
- Click the Open button.

or

- Click the Office Button, and then click a filename in the Recent Documents list.

or

- Click the Office Button, and then click New.
- In the New dialog box, click Blank Document, Blank Workbook, Blank Presentation, or Blank Database (depending on the program).
- Click the Create button.

Ean asks you to print the agenda. To do that, you'll reopen the file.

To open the existing Word document:

> **1.** Click the **Office Button** 🔘, and then click **Open**. The Open dialog box, which works similarly to the Save As dialog box, opens.

> **2.** Use the Navigation pane or the Address bar to navigate to the **OFF\Tutorial** folder included with your Data Files. This is the location where you saved the agenda document.

> **3.** Click **Meeting Agenda** in the file list. See Figure 18.

Figure 18 ▶ **Open dialog box**

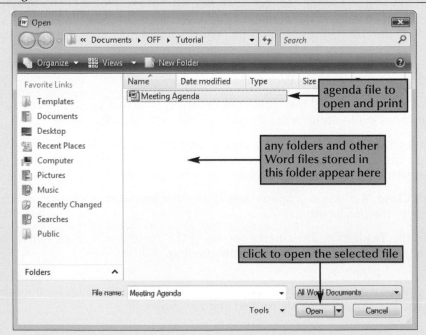

> **4.** Click the **Open** button. The agenda file opens in the Word program window.

Next, you'll use Help to get information about printing files in Word.

Getting Help

If you don't know how to perform a task or want more information about a feature, you can turn to Office itself for information on how to use it. This information, referred to simply as **Help**, is like a huge encyclopedia available from your desktop. You can get Help in ScreenTips, from the Help window, and in Microsoft Office Online.

Viewing ScreenTips

ScreenTips are a fast and simple method you can use to get help about objects you see on the screen. A **ScreenTip** is a box with the button's name, its keyboard shortcut if it has one, a description of the command's function, and, in some cases, a link to more information. Just position the mouse pointer over a button or object to view its ScreenTip. If a link to more information appears in the ScreenTip, press the F1 key while the Screen-Tip is displayed to open the Help window with the appropriate topic displayed.

To view ScreenTips:

▶ **1.** Point to the **Microsoft Office Word Help** button 🔘. The ScreenTip shows the button's name, its keyboard shortcut, and a brief explanation of the button. See Figure 19.

ScreenTip for the Help button ◀ **Figure 19**

▶ **2.** Point to other buttons on the Ribbon to display their ScreenTips.

Using the Help Window

For more detailed information, you can use the **Help window** to access all the Help topics, templates, and training installed on your computer with Office and available on Microsoft Office Online. **Microsoft Office Online** is a Web site maintained by Microsoft that provides access to the latest information and additional Help resources. For example, you can access current Help topics, templates of predesigned files, and training for Office. To connect to Microsoft Office Online, you need Internet access on your computer. Otherwise, you see only those topics stored locally.

Reference Window | **Getting Help**

- Click the Microsoft Office Help button (the button name depends on the Office program).
- Type a keyword or phrase in the "Type words to search for" box, and then click the Search button.
- Click a Help topic in the search results list.
- Read the information in the Help window. For more information, click other topics or links.
- Click the Close button on the Help window title bar.

You open the Help window by clicking the Microsoft Office Help button ⓦ located below the sizing buttons in every Office program. Each program has its own Help window from which you can find information about all the Office commands and features as well as step-by-step instructions for using them. You can search for information in the Help window using the "Type words to search for" box and the Table of Contents pane.

The "Type words to search for" box enables you to search the Help system using keywords or phrases. You type a specific word or phrase about a task you want to perform or a topic you need help with, and then click the Search button to search the Help system. A list of Help topics related to the keyword or phrase you entered appears in the Help window. If your computer is connected to the Internet, your search results come from Microsoft Office Online rather than only the Help topics stored locally on your computer. You can click a link to open a Help topic with step-by-step instructions that will guide you through a specific procedure and/or provide explanations of difficult concepts in clear, easy-to-understand language. For example, if you type "format cell" in the Excel Help window, a list of Help topics related to the words you typed appears in the Help window. You can navigate through the topics you've viewed using the buttons on the Help window toolbar. These buttons—including Back, Forward, Stop, Refresh, Home, and Print—are the same as those in the Microsoft Internet Explorer Web browser.

You'll use the "Type words to search for" box in the Help window to obtain more information about printing a document in Word.

To use the "Type words to search for" box:

▶ 1. Click the **Microsoft Office Word Help** button ⓦ . The Word Help window opens.

▶ 2. Click the **Type words to search for** box, if necessary, and then type **print document**. You can set where you want to search.

▶ 3. Click the **Search button arrow**. The Search menu shows the online and local content available.

4. If your computer is connected to the Internet, click **All Word** in the Content from Office Online list. If your computer is not connected to the Internet, click **Word Help** in the Content from this computer list.

5. Click the **Search** button. The Help window displays a list of topics related to your keywords. See Figure 20.

Search results displaying Help topics ◀ **Figure 20**

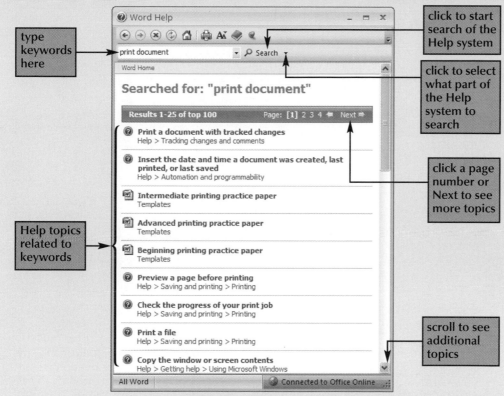

Trouble? If your search results list differs from the one shown in Figure 20, your computer is not connected to the Internet or Microsoft has updated the list of available Help topics since this book was published. Continue with Step 6.

6. Scroll through the list to review the Help topics.

7. Click **Print a file**. The Help topic is displayed in the Help window so you can learn more about how to print a document. See Figure 21.

Figure 21   **Print a file Help topic**

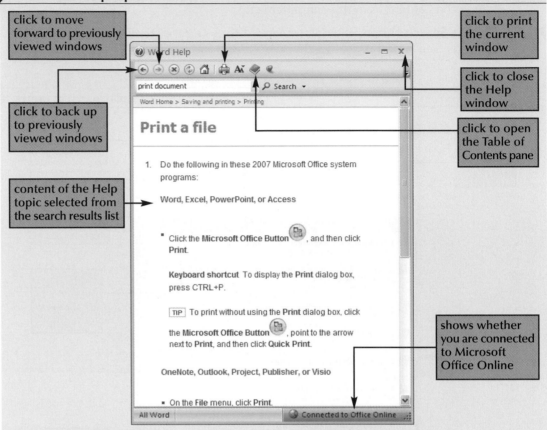

click to move forward to previously viewed windows

click to print the current window

click to back up to previously viewed windows

click to close the Help window

click to open the Table of Contents pane

content of the Help topic selected from the search results list

shows whether you are connected to Microsoft Office Online

Trouble? If you don't see the Print a file Help topic on page 1, its current location might be on another page. Click the Next link to move to the next page, and then scroll down to find the Print a file topic, repeating to search additional pages until you locate the topic.

▶ **8.** Read the information.

Another way to find information in the Help system is to use the Table of Contents pane. The Show Table of Contents button on the Help window toolbar opens a pane that displays a list of the Help system content organized by subjects and topics, similar to a book's table of contents. You click main subject links to display related topic links. You click a topic link to display that Help topic in the Help window. You'll use the Table of Contents to find information about getting help in Office.

To use the Help window table of contents:

▶ **1.** Click the **Show Table of Contents** button 📖 on the Help window toolbar. The Table of Contents pane opens on the left side of the Help window.

▶ **2.** Click **Getting help** in the Table of Contents pane, scrolling up if necessary. The Getting help "book" opens, listing the topics related to that subject.

▶ **3.** Click the **Work with the Help window** topic, and then click the **Maximize** button 🗖 on the title bar. The Help topic is displayed in the maximized Help window, and you can read the text to learn more about the various ways to obtain help in Word. See Figure 22.

Table of Contents pane in the Help window **Figure 22**

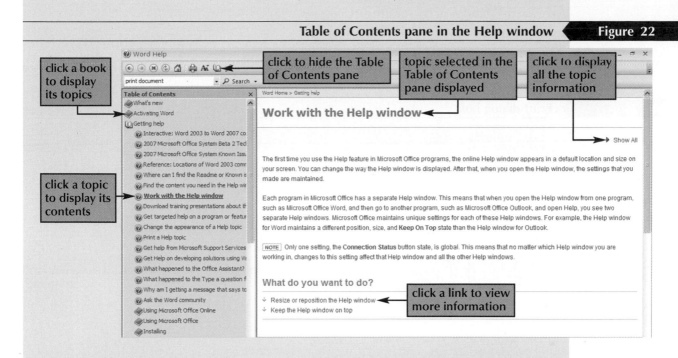

Trouble? If your search results list differs from the one shown in Figure 22, your computer is not connected to the Internet or Microsoft has updated the list of available Help topics since this book was published. Continue with Step 4.

4. Click **Using Microsoft Office Online** in the Table of Contents pane, click the **Get online Help, templates, training, and additional content** topic to display information about that topic, and then read the information.

5. Click the links within this topic and read the information.

6. Click the **Close** button ☒ on the Help window title bar to close the window.

Printing a File

At times, you'll want a paper copy of your Office file. The first time you print during each session at the computer, you should use the Print command to open the Print dialog box so you can verify or adjust the printing settings. You can select a printer, the number of copies to print, the portion of the file to print, and so forth; the printing settings vary slightly from program to program. If you want to use the same default settings for subsequent print jobs, you can use the Quick Print button to print without opening the dialog box.

Printing a File	Reference Window

- Click the Office Button, and then click Print.
- Verify the print settings in the Print dialog box.
- Click the OK button.
or
- Click the Office Button, point to Print, and then click Quick Print.

Now that you know how to print, you'll print the agenda for Ean.

To print the Word document:

▶ **1.** Make sure your printer is turned on and contains paper.

▶ **2.** Click the **Office Button** 🔘, and then click **Print**. The Print dialog box opens. See Figure 23.

Figure 23 | Print dialog box

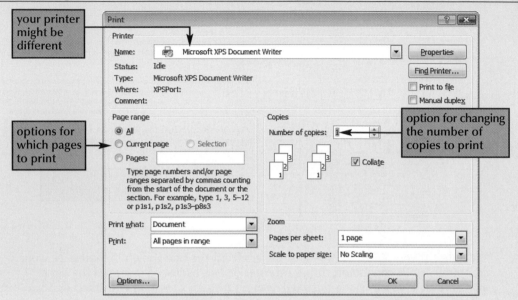

your printer might be different

options for which pages to print

option for changing the number of copies to print

Trouble? If a menu of Print commands opens, you clicked the Print button arrow on the two-part Print button. Click Print on the menu to open the Print dialog box.

▶ **3.** Verify that the correct printer appears in the Name box in the Printer group. If necessary, click the **Name** arrow, and then click the correct printer from the list of available printers.

▶ **4.** Verify that **1** appears in the Number of copies box.

▶ **5.** Click the **OK** button to print the document.

Trouble? If the document does not print, see your instructor or technical support person for help.

Exiting Programs

When you finish working with a program, you should exit it. As with many other aspects of Office, you can exit programs with a button or a command. You'll use both methods to exit Word and Excel. You can use the Exit command to exit a program and close an open file in one step. If you haven't saved the final version of the open file, a dialog box opens, asking whether you want to save your changes. Clicking the Yes button saves the open file, closes the file, and then exits the program.

To exit the Word and Excel programs:

▶ **1.** Click the **Close** button ☒ on the Word title bar to exit Word. The Word document closes and the Word program exits. The Excel window is visible again.

> **Trouble?** If a dialog box opens, asking if you want to save the document, you might have inadvertently made a change to the document. Click the No button.
>
> ▶ **2.** Click the **Office Button** 🔘, and then click **Exit Excel**. A dialog box opens, asking whether you want to save the changes you made to the workbook. If you click the Yes button, the Save As dialog box opens and Excel exits after you finish saving the workbook. This time, you don't want to save the workbook.
>
> ▶ **3.** Click the **No** button. The workbook closes without saving a copy, and the Excel program exits.

Exiting programs after you are done using them keeps your Windows desktop uncluttered for the next person using the computer, frees up your system's resources, and prevents data from being lost accidentally.

Quick Check | Review

1. What Office program would be best to use to create a budget?
2. How do you start an Office program?
3. Explain the difference between Save and Save As.
4. How do you open an existing Office file?
5. What happens if you open a file, make edits, and then attempt to close the file or exit the program without saving the current version of the file?
6. What are two ways to get Help in Office?

Tutorial Summary | Review

You have learned how to use features common to all the programs included in Microsoft Office 2007, including starting and exiting programs; resizing windows; using the Ribbon, dialog boxes, shortcut menus, and the Mini toolbar; opening, closing, and printing files; and getting Help.

Key Terms

Access	Help window	Office Button
application settings	integration	Outlook
button	keyboard shortcut	PowerPoint
contextual tab	Live Preview	presentation
database	Microsoft Office 2007	Quick Access Toolbar
default	Microsoft Office Access 2007	Ribbon
dialog box	Microsoft Office Excel 2007	ScreenTip
Dialog Box Launcher	Microsoft Office Online	shortcut menu
document	Microsoft Office	status bar
Excel	Outlook 2007	tab
file extension	Microsoft Office	task pane
filename	PowerPoint 2007	Word
folder	Microsoft Office Word 2007	workbook
gallery	Mini toolbar	zoom
group	object	
Help	Office	

| Practice | **Review Assignments** |

Practice the skills you learned in the tutorial.

Data Files needed for the Review Assignments: Finances.xlsx, Letter.docx

You need to prepare for an upcoming meeting at Recycled Palette. You'll open and print documents for the presentation. Complete the following:

1. Start PowerPoint.
2. Use the Help window to search Office Online for the PowerPoint demo "Demo: Up to Speed with PowerPoint 2007." (*Hint*: Use "demo" as the keyword to search for, and make sure you search All PowerPoint in the Content from Office Online list. If you are not connected to the Internet, continue with Step 3.) Open the Demo topic, and then click the Play Demo link to view it. Close Internet Explorer and the Help window when you're done.
3. Start Excel.
4. Switch to the PowerPoint window using the taskbar, and then close the presentation but leave open the PowerPoint program. (*Hint:* Click the Office Button and then click Close.)
5. Open a new, blank PowerPoint presentation from the New Presentation dialog box.
6. Close the PowerPoint presentation and program using the Close button on the PowerPoint title bar; do not save changes if asked.
7. Open the **Finances** workbook located in the OFF\Review folder included with your Data Files.
8. Use the Save As command to save the workbook as **Recycled Palette Finances** in the OFF\Review folder.
9. Type your name, press the Enter key to insert your name at the top of the worksheet, and then save the workbook.
10. Print one copy of the worksheet using the Print button on the Office Button menu.
11. Exit Excel using the Office Button.
12. Start Word, and then open the **Letter** document located in the OFF\Review folder included with your Data Files.
13. Use the Save As command to save the document with the filename **Recycled Palette Letter** in the OFF\Review folder.
14. Press and hold the Ctrl key, press the End key, and then release both keys to move the insertion point to the end of the letter, and then type your name.
15. Use the Save button on the Quick Access Toolbar to save the change to the Recycled Palette Letter document.
16. Print one copy of the document, and then close the document.
17. Exit the Word program using the Close button on the title bar.

| Assess | SAM Assessment and Training |

If you have a SAM user profile, you may have access to hands-on instruction, practice, and assessment of the skills covered in this tutorial. Log in to your SAM account (**http://sam2007.course.com**) to launch any assigned training activities or exams that relate to the skills covered in this tutorial.

| Review | **Quick Check Answers** |

1. Excel
2. Click the Start button on the taskbar, click All Programs, click Microsoft Office, and then click the name of the program you want to open.
3. Save updates a file to reflect its latest contents using its current filename and location. Save As enables you to change the filename and storage location of a file.
4. Click the Office Button, and then click Open.
5. A dialog box opens asking whether you want to save the changes to the file.
6. Two of the following: ScreenTips, Help window, Microsoft Office Online

Ending Data Files

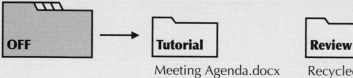

Meeting Agenda.docx

Recycled Palette Finances.xlsx
Recycled Palette Letter.docx

Reality Check

At home, school, or work, you probably complete many types of tasks, such as writing letters and balancing a checkbook, on a regular basis. You can use Microsoft Office to streamline many of these tasks.

Note: Please be sure *not* to include any personal information of a sensitive nature in the documents you create to be submitted to your instructor for this exercise. Later on, you can update the documents with such information for your own personal use.

1. Start Word, and open a new document, if necessary.
2. In the document, type a list of all the personal, work, and/or school tasks you do on a regular basis.
3. For each task, identify the type of Office file (document, workbook, presentation, or database) you would create to complete that task. For example, you would create a Word document to write a letter.
4. For each file, identify the Office program you would use to create that file, and explain why you would use that program. For example, Word is the best program to use to create a document for a letter.
5. Save the document with an appropriate filename in an appropriate folder location.
6. Use a Web browser to visit the Microsoft Web site at *www.microsoft.com* and research the different Office 2007 suites available. Determine which suite includes all the programs you need to complete the tasks on your list.
7. At the end of the task list you created in your Word document, type which Office suite you decided on and a brief explanation of why you chose that suite. Then save the document.
8. Double-click the Home tab on the Ribbon to minimize the Ribbon to show only the tab names and extend the workspace area. At the end of the Word document, type your opinion of whether minimizing the Ribbon is a helpful feature. When you're done, double-click the Home tab to display the full Ribbon.
9. Print the finished document, and then submit it to your instructor.

Objectives

Session 1.1
- Plan a document
- Identify the components of the Word window
- Set up the Word window
- Create a new document

Session 1.2
- Scroll a document and move the insertion point
- Correct errors and undo and redo changes
- Enter the date with AutoComplete
- Change a document's line and paragraph spacing
- Save, preview, and print a document
- Create an envelope

Creating a Document

Writing a Business Letter

Case | Carlyle University Press

Carlyle University Press is a nonprofit book publisher associated with Carlyle State University in Albany, New York. The Press, as it is referred to by both editors and authors, publishes scholarly books, with an emphasis on history and literature. When a new author signs a contract for a book, he or she receives the *Author's Guide*, a handbook describing the process of creating a manuscript. In this tutorial, you will help one of the editors, Andrew Suri, create a cover letter to accompany a copy of the *Author's Guide*.

You will create the letter using **Microsoft Office Word 2007** (or simply **Word**), a popular word-processing program. Before you begin typing the letter, you will learn how to start the Word program, identify and use the elements of the Word window, and adjust some Word settings. Next, you will create a new Word document, type the text of the cover letter, save the letter, and then print the letter. In the process of entering the text, you'll learn several ways to correct typing errors. Finally, you will create an envelope for the letter.

Starting Data Files

There are no starting Data Files needed for this tutorial.

Session 1.1

Four Steps to a Professional Document

With Word, you can create polished, professional documents in a minimal amount of time. You can type a document in Word, adjust margins and spacing, create columns and tables, add graphics, and then quickly make revisions and corrections. The most efficient way to produce a document is to follow these four steps: (1) planning, (2) creating and editing, (3) formatting, and (4) printing or distributing online.

In the long run, planning saves time and effort. First, you should determine what you want to say. State your purpose clearly and include enough information to achieve that purpose without overwhelming or boring your reader. Be sure to organize your ideas logically. Decide how you want your document to look as well. In this case, your letter will take the form of a standard business letter, in the block style.

Figure 1-1 shows what the completed, block style letter will look like when it is printed on Carlyle University Press letterhead. You will create the letter in this tutorial by following detailed steps. Throughout the tutorial, you might want to refer back to Figure 1-1 for help locating the various parts of a block style letter.

Figure 1-1 ▶ **Completed block style letter**

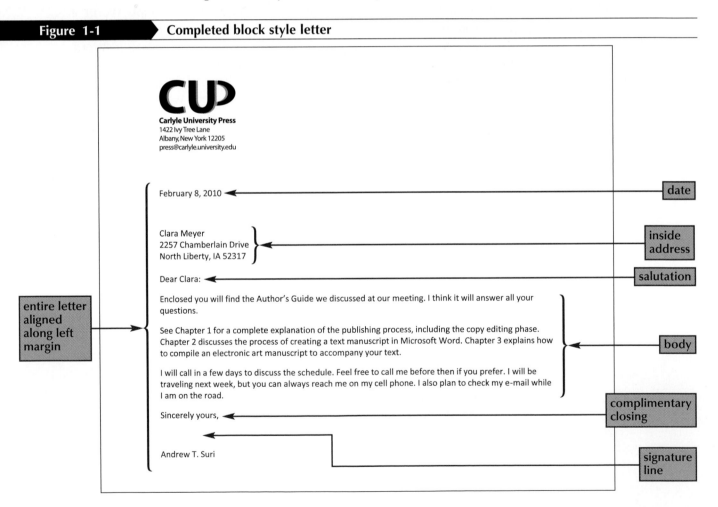

Writing a Business Letter | InSight

There are several accepted styles for business letters. The main differences among them have to do with how parts of the letter are indented from the left margin. In the block style, which you will use to create the letter in this tutorial, each line of text starts at the left margin. In other words, nothing is indented. Another style is to indent the first line of each paragraph. The choice of style is largely a matter of personal preference, or it can be determined by the standards used in a particular business or organization.

After you plan your document, you can create and edit it using Word. Creating the document generally means typing the text of your document. Editing consists of reading the document you've created; correcting, adding, deleting, or moving text to make the document easy to read; and finally, correcting your errors.

To make your document visually appealing, you need to format it. Formatting—for example, adjusting margins, setting line spacing, and using bold and italic—can help make your document easier to read.

Finally, you will usually want to print your document so that you can give it to other people, or you might want to distribute it via e-mail. Whether you print the document yourself or e-mail it to others, it is important to preview it first to make sure it is suitable for printing.

Exploring the Word Window

Before you can apply these four steps to produce a letter in Word, you need to start Word and learn about the general organization of the Word window. You'll do that now.

To start Microsoft Word:

▶ **1.** Click the **Start** button 🔵 on the taskbar, click **All Programs**, click **Microsoft Office**, and then click **Microsoft Office Word 2007**. The Word window opens. See Figure 1-2.

Figure 1-2 **Maximized Word window**

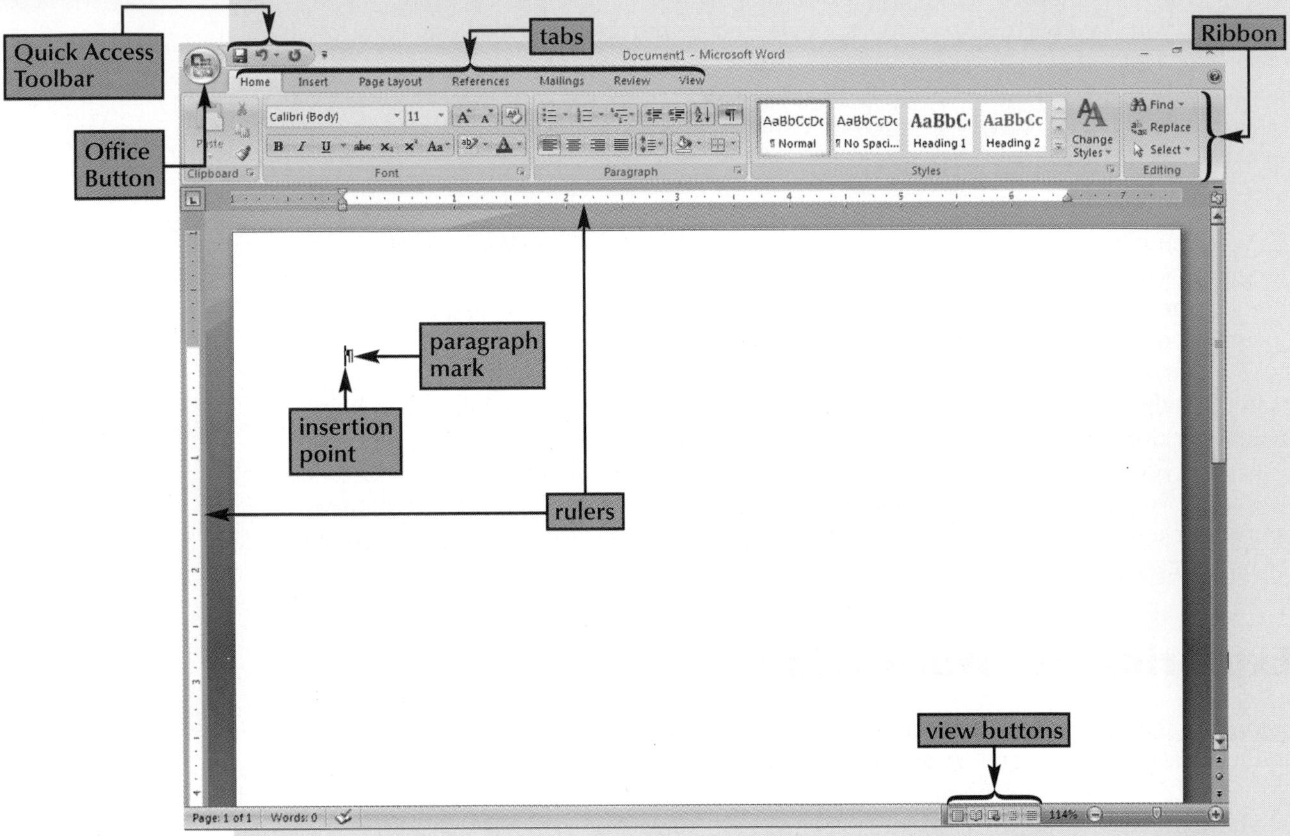

Quick Access Toolbar

tabs

Ribbon

Office Button

paragraph mark

insertion point

rulers

view buttons

Trouble? If you don't see the Microsoft Office Word 2007 option on the Microsoft Office submenu, look for it in a different submenu or as an option on the All Programs menu. If you still can't find the Microsoft Office Word 2007 option, ask your instructor or technical support person for help.

▶ 2. If the Word window does not fill the entire screen, click the **Maximize** button 🔲 in the upper-right corner of the Word window. Your screen should now resemble Figure 1-2.

Trouble? If your screen looks slightly different from Figure 1-2, just continue with the steps. You will learn how to change the appearance of the Word window shortly.

Word is now running and ready to use. Don't be concerned if you don't see everything shown in Figure 1-2. You'll learn how to adjust the appearance of the Word window soon.

The Word window is made up of a number of elements, which are described in Figure 1-3. You might be familiar with some of these elements, such as the Office Button and the Ribbon, because they are common to all Microsoft Office 2007 programs.

Parts of the Word window   Figure 1-3

Window Element	Description
Office Button	Provides access to the Word Options dialog box and to commands that control what you can do with a document that you have created, such as saving, printing, and so on
Ribbon	Provides access to commands that are grouped according to the tasks you perform in Word
Tabs	Provide one-click access to the groups of commands on the Ribbon; the tabs you see change depending on the task you are currently performing
Quick Access Toolbar	Provides access to common commands you use frequently, such as Save
Rulers	Show page margins, tab stops, row heights, and column widths
Insertion point	Shows where characters will appear when you start typing
Paragraph mark	Marks the end of a paragraph
View buttons	Allow you to change the way the document is displayed

If at any time you would like to learn more about an item on the Ribbon, position your mouse pointer over the item without clicking anything. A **ScreenTip**, a small box with information about the item, will appear.

Opening a New Document

You'll begin by opening a new blank document (in case you accidentally typed something in the current page while you were examining the Word window).

To open a new document:

▶ 1. Click the **Office Button** 🔘 in the upper-left corner of the Word window and view the menu of commands that opens. These commands are all related to working with Word documents. See Figure 1-4.

Microsoft Office menu   Figure 1-4

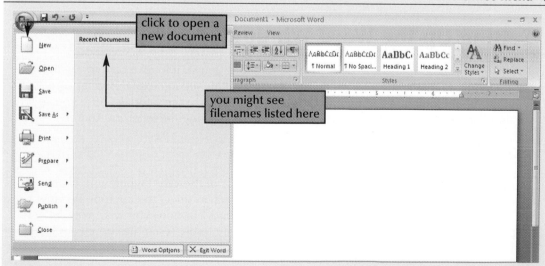

▶ **2.** Click **New**. The New Document dialog box opens. See Figure 1-5. In this dialog box, you can choose from several different types of documents. In this case, you simply want a new, blank document, which is already selected for you, as in Figure 1-5.

Figure 1-5   **New Document dialog box**

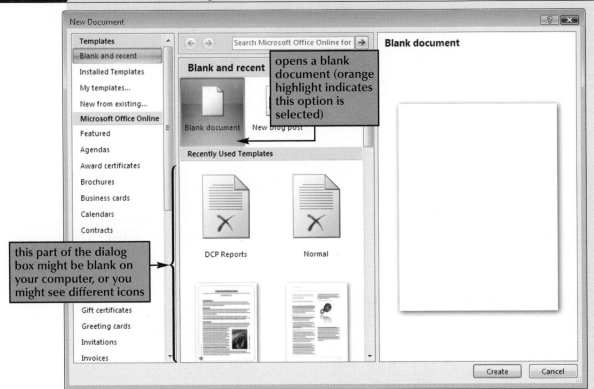

▶ **3.** Verify that the **Blank document** option is selected (that is, highlighted in orange), and then click the **Create** button at the bottom of the dialog box. The New Document dialog box closes and a new document (named Document2) opens. Later in this tutorial, you'll choose a more descriptive name for this document.

Setting Up the Word Window

To make it easier to follow the steps in these tutorials, you should take care to arrange your window to match the tutorial figures. The rest of this section explains what your window should look like and how to make it match those in the tutorials. After you've set up your window to match the figures, you'll begin writing the letter for Andrew.

Selecting Print Layout View

You can use the View buttons in the lower-right corner of the Word window to change the way your document is displayed. You will learn how to select the appropriate view for a document as you gain more experience with Word. For now, you want your letter displayed in Print Layout view because this view most closely resembles how your letter will look when you print it.

To make sure Print Layout view is selected:

▶ **1.** Click the **Print Layout** button 🔲 , as shown in Figure 1-6. If your window was not in Print Layout view, it changes to Print Layout view now. The Print Layout button is now highlighted in orange, indicating that it is selected. See Figure 1-6.

Selecting Print Layout view | Figure 1-6

Print Layout button is orange to show it is selected

other view buttons

Page: 1 of 1 | Words: 0 | 114%

Displaying the Rulers and Selecting the Home Tab

Depending on the choices made by the last person to use your computer, you might not see the rulers. The options controlling the rulers are located on the Ribbon's View tab. When Word opens, the Home tab is typically displayed, so to display the rulers, you need to switch to the View tab. Even if the rulers are currently displayed on your computer, perform the following steps to get some practice moving among the tabs on the Ribbon.

Displaying the Rulers | Reference Window

- Click the View tab.
- In the Show/Hide group, click the Ruler check box to display a check mark.

To display the rulers:

▶ **1.** At the top of the Word window, click the **View** tab. This tab contains buttons and commands related to displaying the document.

▶ **2.** In the Show/Hide group on the View tab, locate the Ruler check box. If it already contains a check mark, the rulers are already displayed on your screen. If the Ruler check box is empty, click it to insert a check mark. You should now see a vertical ruler on the left side of the document and a horizontal ruler below the Ribbon. See Figure 1-7.

Figure 1-7 ▶ Displaying the rulers

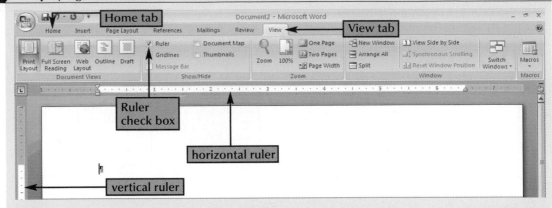

> **3.** Click the **Home** tab. The Ribbon changes to show Word's basic text-editing options, as shown earlier in Figure 1-2.

Displaying Nonprinting Characters

Tip

The Show/Hide ¶ button is an example of a toggle button. Clicking it toggles the nonprinting characters on or off, just as flipping a toggle light switch turns a lamp on or off.

Nonprinting characters are symbols that appear on the screen but are not visible on the printed page; they help you see details that you might otherwise miss. For example, one nonprinting character (¶) marks the end of a paragraph, and another (•) marks the space between words. It is helpful to display nonprinting characters so you can see whether you've typed an extra space, ended a paragraph, and so on.

Depending on how your computer is set up, nonprinting characters might be displayed automatically when you start Word. In Figure 1-8, you can see the paragraph symbol (¶) in the blank document window. Also, the Show/Hide ¶ button is highlighted on the Ribbon. Both of these indicate that nonprinting characters are displayed. If they are not displayed on your screen, you need to perform the following step.

To display nonprinting characters:

> **1.** In the Paragraph group on the Home tab, click the **Show/Hide ¶** button ¶ if it is not already selected. A paragraph mark (¶) appears at the top of the document window. Your screen should match Figure 1-8.

Figure 1-8 ▶ Nonprinting characters displayed

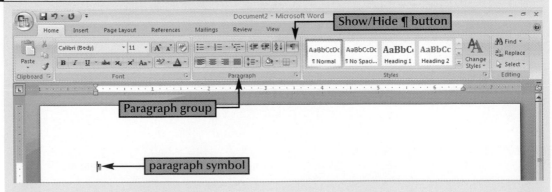

Trouble? If the Show/Hide ¶ button was already highlighted before you clicked it, you turned off nonprinting characters instead of turning them on. Click the Show/Hide ¶ button a second time to select it.

Checking the Font and Font Size

Next, you need to make sure the correct font and font size are selected. The term **font** refers to the shape of the characters in a document. **Font size** refers to the size of the characters. You'll learn more about fonts in Tutorial 2. For now, you just need to make sure that the font and font size selected on your computer match those selected in the figures in this book. The figures in this book were created using the default font and font size. (The term **default** refers to settings that are automatically selected.)

To verify that the correct font is selected:

▶ **1.** In the Font group on the Home tab, locate the **Font** and **Font Size** boxes. See Figure 1-9.

Font settings   **Figure 1-9**

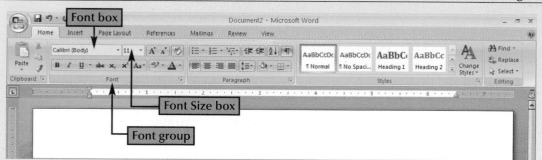

The setting in the Font box should read "Calibri (Body)" as in Figure 1-9. If you see something else in your Font box, click the **Font** list arrow, and then click **Calibri (Body)**.

Trouble ? If you see just "Calibri" in your font box instead of "Calibri (Body)" you should still perform Step 1.

▶ **2.** The setting in your Font Size box should read "11." If you see something else in your Font size box, click the **Font Size** list arrow, and then click **11**.

Checking the Zoom Setting

Next, you'll take care of the document **Zoom level**, which controls the document's on-screen magnification. A Zoom level of 100% shows the document as if it were printed on paper. It is often helpful to increase the Zoom level to more than 100% (zoom in) to make the text easier to read. Other times, you may want to decrease the Zoom level to less than 100% (zoom out) so that you can see more of the document at a glance. To make your screen match the figures in this tutorial, you need to set the Zoom level to **Page width**, a setting that shows the entire width of the document on your screen. You can change the Zoom level by using the Zoom buttons in the lower-right corner of the Word window.

Tip

Changing the zoom affects only the way the document is displayed on the screen; it does not affect the document itself.

To check your Zoom setting:

▶ **1.** In the lower-right corner of the Word window, locate the current Zoom level, the Zoom Out button, the Zoom In button, and the Zoom slider. In Figure 1-10, the current Zoom setting is 114%, but yours might be higher or lower. In the next two steps you'll practice zooming in and zooming out. Then you will select the Page width setting.

| Figure 1-10 | Options for changing the Zoom setting |

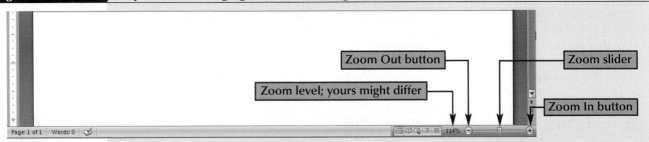

▶ **2.** Click the **Zoom In** button ⊕ several times to increase the document magnification. The Zoom level increases and the Zoom slider moves to the right.

▶ **3.** Click the **Zoom Out** button ⊖ several times to decrease the document magnification. The Zoom level decreases and the Zoom slider button moves to the left.

▶ **4.** Click the **Zoom level**. The Zoom dialog box opens. The Zoom level in the Zoom dialog box matches the Zoom level shown in the lower-right corner of the Word window. In Figure 1-11, the current Zoom setting is 110%, but yours might be different.

| Figure 1-11 | Zoom dialog box |

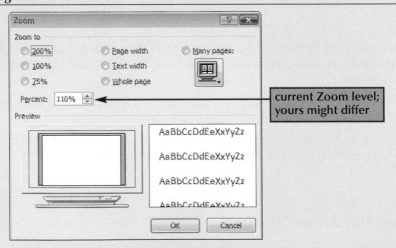

▶ **5.** Click the **Page width** option button to select it, and then click the **OK** button. The Zoom dialog box closes and the Zoom level adjusts to display the full width of the document page. The exact Zoom level on your computer will depend on the size of your monitor. On a 15-inch monitor, the Zoom level is probably 114%.

To make sure your window always matches the figures in these tutorials, remember to complete the checklist in Figure 1-12 each time you are working in this book.

Window Element	Setting
Document view	Print Layout
Nonprinting characters	Displayed
Rulers	Displayed
Word window	Maximized
Zoom	Page width
Font	Identical to setting shown in figures
Font size	Identical to setting shown in figures

Now that you have planned your letter, opened Word, identified screen elements, and adjusted settings, you are ready to begin your letter to Clara Meyer, Carlyle Press's new author.

Beginning a Letter

Before you begin writing, you should insert some blank lines to ensure that you leave enough room for the Carlyle University Press letterhead. The amount of space you leave at the top of a letter depends on the size of the letterhead. In this case, pressing Enter four times should add enough space.

Adjusting Margins vs. Inserting Blank Lines | | InSight

As you gain experience with Word, you'll learn how to adjust a document's margin to add blank space at the beginning of a document. (The term **margin** refers to the blank space around the top, bottom, and sides of document.) Adjusting margins is a better method than inserting blank lines, because it ensures that you won't accidentally delete a blank line as you edit the document. However, until you learn more about margins, inserting blank lines is a useful shortcut that enables you to jump right into the task of typing your letter.

To insert blank lines in the document:

▶ **1.** Press the **Enter** key four times. Each time you press the Enter key, a nonprinting paragraph mark appears, and the insertion point moves down to the next line. By default, Word inserts some space between each paragraph mark. You'll learn how to change this setting later in this tutorial. For now, you can ignore this space. On the vertical ruler, you can see that the insertion point is about 1.5 inches from the top margin. Although you might find it hard to see on the ruler, the top margin itself is 1 inch. This means the insertion point is now located a total of 2.5 inches from the top of the page. See Figure 1-13.

Figure 1-13 **Document window after inserting blank lines**

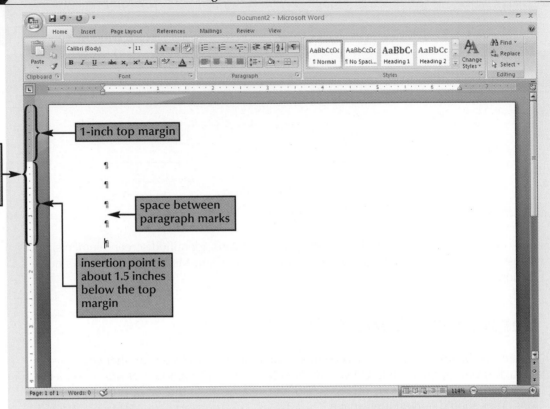

insertion point is a total of 2.5 inches below the top of the page

1-inch top margin

space between paragraph marks

insertion point is about 1.5 inches below the top margin

Trouble? If your insertion point is higher or lower on the vertical ruler than in Figure 1-13, don't worry. Different monitors produce slightly different measurements when you press the Enter key.

The insertion point is now low enough in your document to allow room for the letterhead when you print the document. You are ready to start typing.

Entering Text

Normally, you begin a letter by typing the date followed by the inside address. However, typing these two items involves using some specialized Word features. To give you some experience with simply typing text, you'll start with the salutation and the body of the letter. Then you'll go back later to add the date and the inside address.

You'll start by typing the salutation (the "Dear Clara:" text, shown earlier in Figure 1-1). If you make a mistake while typing, press the Backspace key to delete the incorrect character and then type the correct character.

To type the salutation:

▶ 1. Type **Dear Clara:** and then pause to notice the nonprinting character (•) that appears to indicate a space between the two words.

> **2.** Press the **Enter** key to start a new paragraph for the body of the letter. If you have typed a block style business letter before, you might be accustomed to pressing Enter twice between paragraphs. However, because Word is set up to insert extra space between paragraphs by default, you need to press the Enter key only once to start a new paragraph. See Figure 1-14.

Letter with salutation | **Figure 1-14**

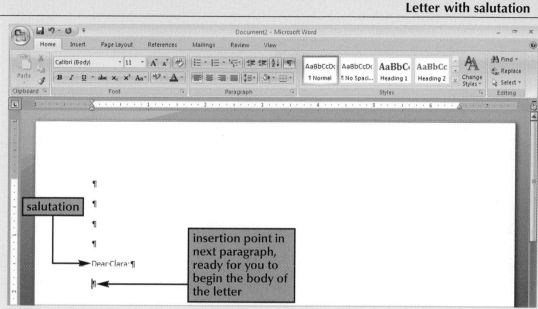

Now you are ready to begin typing the body of the letter (shown earlier in Figure 1-1). As you do, notice that when you reach the end of a line, you can keep typing; the insertion point just moves down to the next line. Depending on the length of the word you are typing when you reach the end of the line, the word will either stay on that line, or if it is long, it will move to the next line. This automatic line breaking is called **word wrap**. You'll see how word wrap works as you begin typing the body of the letter.

To begin typing the body of the letter:

> **1.** Type the following sentence, including the period: **Enclosed you will find the Author's Guide we discussed at our meeting.**

> **2.** Press the **spacebar**.

> **3.** Type the following sentence: **I think it will answer all your questions.**
>
> Notice how Word moves the insertion point to a new line when the preceding line is full.

> **4.** Press the **Enter** key to end the first paragraph. When you are finished, your screen should look similar to Figure 1-15. Notice that, in addition to inserting space between paragraphs, Word also inserts a smaller amount of space between lines within a paragraph.

Figure 1-15 Completed first main paragraph

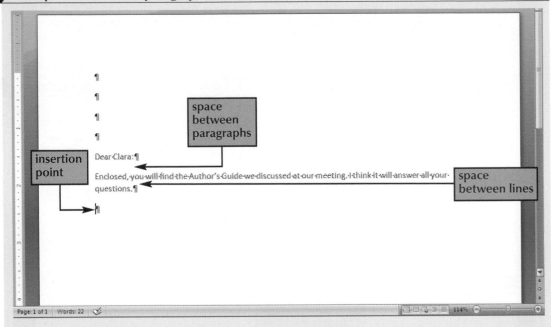

Before you continue with the rest of the letter, you should save what you have typed
so far.

Reference Window | **Saving a Document for the First Time**

- Click the Save button on the Quick Access Toolbar.
- Type a name in the File name text box.
- Select the location where you want to save the file.
- Click the Save button at the bottom of the Save As dialog box.

To save the document:

1. On the Quick Access Toolbar, click the **Save** button 🔲 . The Save As dialog box
   opens. Note that Word suggests using the first line you typed ("Dear Clara") as the
   filename. You will replace the suggested filename with something more
   descriptive.

2. Type **Meyer Letter** in the File name text box, replacing the suggested filename.

   Next, you need to tell Word where you want to save the document. In this case,
   you want to use the Tutorial subfolder in the Tutorial.01 folder provided with your
   Data Files.

   Trouble? The Tutorial.01 folder is included with the Data Files for this text. If you
   don't have the Word Data Files, you need to get them before you can proceed. Your
   instructor will either give you the Data Files or ask you to obtain them from a
   specified location (such as a network drive). In either case, be sure that you make a
   backup copy of your Data Files before you start using them, so that the original
   files will be available on your copied disk in case you need to start over because of
   an error or problem. If you have any questions about the Data Files, see your
   instructor or technical support person for assistance.

3. Use the options in the Save As dialog box to select the Tutorial subfolder within the Tutorial.01 folder. See Figure 1-16.

Save As dialog box ◄ Figure 1-16

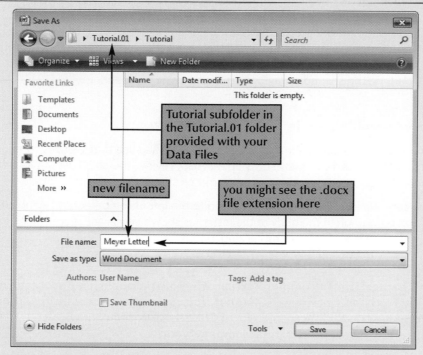

Trouble? If Word adds the .docx extension to your filename, your computer is configured to show file extensions. Just continue with the tutorial.

4. Click the **Save** button in the Save As dialog box. The dialog box closes, and you return to the document window. The new document name (Meyer Letter) appears in the title bar.

Note that Word adds the .docx extension to document filenames to identify them as Microsoft Word 2007 documents, whether your computer is set up to display them or not. These tutorials assume that file extensions are hidden, but it is okay if they are displayed.

You've made a good start on the letter, and you've saved your work so far. In the next session, you'll finish typing the letter, and then you'll print it.

Session 1.1 Quick Check | Review

1. In your own words, explain the importance of planning a document.
2. On what tab is the Ruler check box located?
3. Explain how to change the document view to Print Layout.
4. True or False: Nonprinting characters are symbols that can appear on the screen but are not visible on the printed page.
5. True or False: Pressing the Enter key is the only way to insert blank space at the top of a document.
6. What is the file extension for Microsoft Word 2007 documents?

Session 1.2

Scrolling a Document

At this point, unless you are working on a large monitor, your screen probably looks as if it doesn't have enough room to type the rest of Andrew's letter—but of course there is room. As you continue to add text to your document, the text at the top will **scroll** (or shift up) and disappear from the top of the document window. You'll see how scrolling works as you type the second paragraph in the body of the letter.

To observe scrolling while you're typing text:

1. If you took a break after the previous session, make sure that Word is running and that the Meyer Letter document is open. Also, review the checklist in Figure 1-12 and verify that your screen is set up to match the figures in this tutorial.

2. Make sure the insertion point is positioned to the left of the paragraph symbol below the first paragraph in the body of the letter (as shown earlier in Figure 1-15). If it is not, move the insertion point by clicking in that location now.

3. Type the following two paragraphs:

   See Chapter 1 for a complete explanation of the publishing process, including the copy editing phase. Chapter 2 discusses the process of creating a text manuscript in Microsoft Word. Chapter 3 explains how to compile an electronic art manuscript to accompany your text.

   I will call in a few days to discuss the schedule. Feel free to call me before then if you prefer. I will be traveling next week, but you can always reach me on my cell phone. I also plan to check my e-mail while I am on the road.

   Trouble? If you make a mistake while typing, press the Backspace key or the Delete key to delete any incorrect characters, and then type the correct characters.

4. Press the **Enter** key.

5. Type **Sincerely yours,** (including the comma) to enter the complimentary closing.

6. Press the **Enter** key 10 times so you can see the document scroll up to accommodate the blank paragraphs. You're doing this only to demonstrate how a document scrolls up. You'll delete the extra blank paragraphs shortly.

   As you pressed the Enter key repeatedly, the upper part of the document probably scrolled off the top of the document window. Exactly when this happens depends on the size of your monitor. See Figure 1-17.

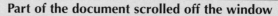

Part of the document scrolled off the window

Figure 1-17

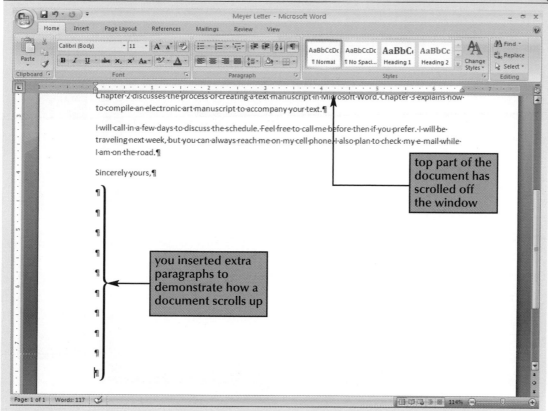

You don't really want all those blank paragraph marks after the complimentary closing, so you need to delete them.

7. Press the **Backspace** key eight times. When you finish, you should see two paragraph marks below the complimentary closing, with the insertion point blinking to the left of the bottom one. This allows enough space for a signature.

8. Type **Andrew Suri**, and then press the **Enter** key. A wavy red line appears below "Suri." In Word, such lines indicate possible spelling errors. Because Andrew's last name is not in the Word dictionary, Word suggests that it might be spelled incorrectly. You'll learn more about Word's error-checking features in a moment. For now, you can ignore the wavy red line.

You've completed most of the letter, so you should save your work.

9. On the Quick Access Toolbar, click the **Save** button. Word saves your letter with the same name and in the same location you specified earlier. Don't be concerned about any typing errors. You'll learn how to correct them later in this tutorial.

In the previous set of steps, you watched paragraph marks and text at the top of your document move off the window. Anytime you need to see the beginning of the letter, you can scroll this hidden text back into view. When you do, the text at the bottom of the window will scroll out of view. There are three ways to scroll the document window: click the up or down arrows in the vertical scroll bar, click anywhere in the vertical scroll bar, or drag the scroll box. See Figure 1-18.

Figure 1-18 ▶ **Scrolling the document window**

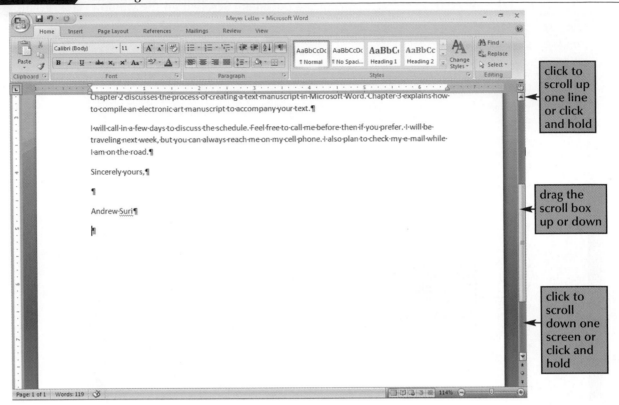

To practice scrolling the document using the vertical scroll bar:

▶ **1.** Position the mouse pointer over the arrow at the top of the vertical scroll bar. Press and hold the mouse button to scroll the text. When the text stops scrolling, you have reached the top of the document and can see the beginning of the letter. Note that scrolling does not change the location of the insertion point in the document.

▶ **2.** Click the down arrow on the vertical scroll bar several times. The document scrolls down one line at a time.

▶ **3.** Click anywhere in the vertical scroll bar below the scroll box. The document scrolls down one full screen.

▶ **4.** Drag the scroll box up to the top of the scroll bar, so you can see the beginning of the letter.

▶ **5.** Continue practicing these steps until you feel comfortable scrolling up and down. When you are finished, scroll the document so you can see the complimentary closing at the end of the letter.

Andrew asks you to include his middle initial in the signature line. Performing this task will give you a chance to practice moving the insertion point around the document.

Moving the Insertion Point Around a Document

When you scroll a document, you change the part of the document that is displayed on the screen. But to change the location in the document where new text will appear when you type, you need to move the insertion point. One way to move the insertion point is to scroll up or down and then click where you want to insert new text. However, it is often more efficient to use the keyboard so you don't have to move your hand to the mouse, move the insertion point, and then move your hand back to the keyboard to type. You can use the arrow keys, ←, ↑, →, and ↓, to move the insertion point one character at a time to the left or right or one line at a time up or down. In addition, you can press a variety of key combinations to move the insertion point from one paragraph to another, to the beginning or end of the document, and so on. As you become more experienced with Word, you'll learn which methods you prefer.

Before you add Andrew's middle initial to the signature line, you'll take some time to practice moving the insertion point around the document.

To move the insertion point with keystrokes:

▶ 1. Press the **Ctrl+Home** keys (that is, press the Ctrl key and hold it down while you press the Home key). The insertion point moves to the beginning of the document.

▶ 2. Press the **Page Down** key to move the insertion point down to the next screen.

▶ 3. Press the ↑ key several times to move the insertion point up one line at a time, and then press the → key several times to move the insertion point to the right one character at a time.

▶ 4. Press the **Ctrl+End** keys. The insertion point moves to the end of the document.

▶ 5. Use the arrow keys to position the insertion point to the right of the "w" in "Andrew." Now you can add Andrew's middle initial.

▶ 6. Press the **spacebar**, and then type the letter **T** followed by a period so that the signature line reads "Andrew T. Suri."

Figure 1-19 summarizes the keystrokes you can use to move the insertion point around a document.

Keystrokes for moving the insertion point | **Figure 1-19**

To move the insertion point	Press
Left or right one character at a time	← or →
Up or down one line at a time	↑ or ↓
Left or right one word at a time	Ctrl+ ← or Ctrl+ →
Up or down one paragraph at a time	Ctrl+ ↑ or Ctrl+ ↓
To the beginning or to the end of the current line	Home or End
To the beginning or to the end of the document	Ctrl+Home or Ctrl+End
To the previous screen or to the next screen	Page Up or Page Down
To the top or to the bottom of the document window	Alt+Ctrl+Page Up or Alt+Ctrl+Page Down

Using the Undo and Redo Commands

To undo (or reverse) the last thing you did in a document, you can click the **Undo button** on the Quick Access Toolbar. If you want to restore your original change, the **Redo button** reverses the action of the Undo button (or redoes the undo). To undo more than your last action, you can click the Undo button arrow on the Quick Access Toolbar. A list will open that shows your most recent actions.

Andrew asks you to undo the addition of his middle initial, to see how the signature line looks without it.

To undo the addition of the "T.":

▶ **1.** On the Quick Access Toolbar, place the mouse pointer over the **Undo** button [icon], but don't click it. The ScreenTip "Undo Typing (Ctrl + Z)" appears, indicating that your most recent action involved typing. The item in parentheses is the keyboard shortcut for the Undo command. See Figure 1-20.

Figure 1-20 ▶ **Using the Undo button**

▶ **2.** Click the **Undo** button [icon] on the Quick Access Toolbar. The letter "T," the period, and the space you typed earlier are deleted.

Trouble? If something else changes, you probably made another edit or change to the document between the addition of Andrew's middle initial and the undo action. Click the Undo button on the Quick Access Toolbar until the letter "T," the period, and the space following it are deleted. If a list of possible changes appears under the Undo button, you clicked the arrow next to the Undo button rather than the Undo button itself. Press the Esc key to close the list.

Andrew decides that he does want to include his middle initial after all. Instead of retyping it, you'll redo the undo.

▶ **3.** On the Quick Access Toolbar, place the mouse pointer over the **Redo** button and observe the "Redo Typing (Ctrl + Y)" ScreenTip.

▶ **4.** Click the **Redo** button [icon] on the Quick Access Toolbar. Andrew's middle initial (along with the period and an additional space) are reinserted into the signature line.

▶ **5.** Click the **Save** button [icon] on the Quick Access Toolbar to save your changes to the document.

Correcting Errors

If you notice a typing error as soon as you make it, you can press the Backspace key, which deletes the characters and spaces to the left of the insertion point one at a time. Backspacing erases both printing and nonprinting characters. After you erase the error, you can type the correct character(s). You can also press the Delete key, which deletes characters to the right of the insertion point one at a time.

In many cases, however, Word's **AutoCorrect** feature will do the work for you. Among other things, AutoCorrect automatically corrects common typing errors, such as typing "adn" for "and." For example, you might have noticed AutoCorrect at work if you forgot to capitalize the first letter in a sentence as you typed the letter. AutoCorrect can automatically correct this error as you type the rest of the sentence. You'll learn more about using AutoCorrect as you become a more experienced Word user. For now, just keep in mind that AutoCorrect corrects certain typing errors automatically. Depending on how your computer is set up, some or all AutoCorrect features might be turned off. You'll learn how to turn AutoCorrect on in the following steps.

Whether or not AutoCorrect is turned on, you can always rely on Word's **spelling checker**. By default, this feature continually checks your document against Word's built-in dictionary. If you type a word that doesn't match the correct spelling in Word's dictionary, or if a word is not in the dictionary at all (as is the case with Andrew's last name, Suri), a wavy red line appears beneath the word. A wavy red line also appears if you type duplicate words (such as "the the"). Word also includes a grammar checker, which is turned off by default. You will learn how to use the grammar checker in Tutorial 2.

Before you can practice using AutoCorrect and the spelling checker, you need to verify that you have the correct settings in the Word Options dialog box.

To verify the spelling checker and AutoCorrect settings:

▶ **1.** Click the **Office Button** 🔘 , and then (at the bottom of the Office menu) click the **Word Options** button. The Word Options dialog box opens.

▶ **2.** In the left pane, click **Proofing**. Options related to proofing a document are displayed in the right pane.

▶ **3.** Verify that the **Check spelling as you type** check box contains a check mark.

▶ **4.** Verify that the **Mark grammar errors as you type** check box does *not* contain a check mark. (This option is typically turned off by default.)

▶ **5.** Near the top of the right pane, click the **AutoCorrect Options** button. The AutoCorrect: English (United States) dialog box opens.

▶ **6.** Locate the **Capitalize first letter of sentences** check box and the **Replace text as you type** check box. If they are not already checked, click them to insert check marks now. (It is okay if other check boxes have check marks.) See Figure 1-21.

Figure 1-21 ▶ Selecting AutoCorrect options

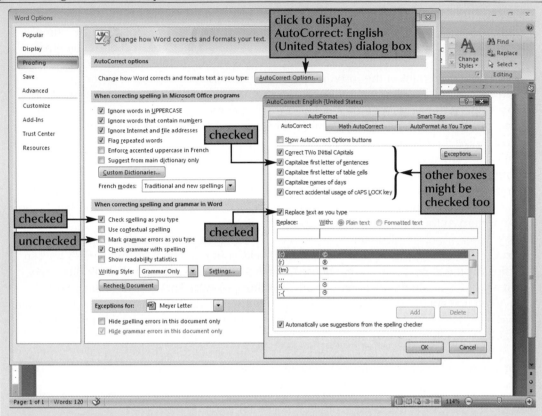

▶ **7.** Click the **OK** button to close the AutoCorrect English (United States) dialog box, and then click the **OK** button again to close the Word Options dialog box.

The easiest way to see how these features work is to make some intentional typing errors.

To correct intentional typing errors:

▶ **1.** Use the arrow keys to move the insertion point to the left of the last paragraph mark in the document.

▶ **2.** Carefully and slowly type the following sentence exactly as it is shown, including the spelling errors: **notice how microsoft Word corects teh commen typing misTakes you make**. See Figure 1-22.

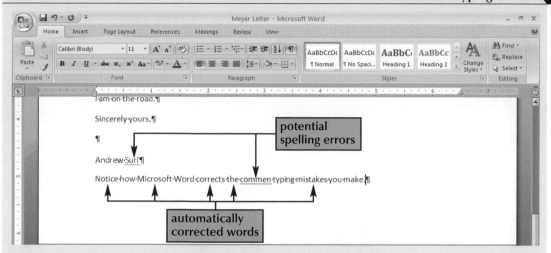

Trouble? If you see wavy green underlines, the grammar checker is turned on and you made a mistake not included in Step 2. Delete the text you just typed, repeat Steps 1–4 in the preceding set of steps to turn the grammar checker off, click the OK button to close the Word Options dialog box, and then begin these steps again with Step 1.

When you pressed the spacebar after the word "commen," a wavy red line appeared beneath it, indicating that the word might be misspelled. Also, Word automatically capitalized the word "Notice" (because it is the first word in the sentence) and "Microsoft" (because it is a proper noun). And, when you pressed the spacebar after the words "corects," "teh," and "misTakes," Word automatically corrected the typing errors.

Correcting Spelling Errors

After you verify that AutoCorrect made the changes you want, you should review your document for red wavy underlines, which indicate potential spelling errors. In the following steps, you will learn a quick way to correct such errors.

To correct spelling and grammar errors:

▶ 1. Position the I-beam pointer over the word "commen," and then click the right mouse button. A shortcut menu appears with suggested spellings. You also see the Mini toolbar, which provides easy access to some of the most commonly used options in the Home tab for the object you've right-clicked. You'll learn more about the Mini toolbar as you gain more experience with Word. See Figure 1-23.

Figure 1-23 | **Shortcut menu with suggested spellings**

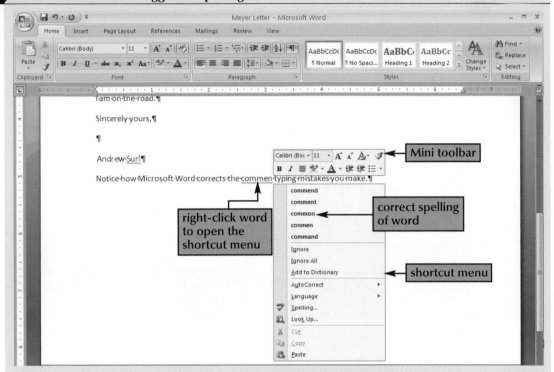

Trouble? If the shortcut menu doesn't appear, repeat Step 1, making sure you click the right mouse button, not the left one. If you see a different menu from the one shown in Figure 1-23, you didn't right-click exactly on the word "commen." Press the Esc key to close the menu, and then repeat Step 1.

▶ **2.** Click **common** in the shortcut menu. The menu closes (along with the Mini toolbar), and the correct spelling appears in your document. Notice that the wavy red line disappears after you correct the error.

Proofreading the Letter

You can see how quick and easy it is to correct common typing errors with AutoCorrect and the spelling checker. Remember, however, to proofread each document you create thoroughly. AutoCorrect will not catch words that are spelled correctly but used improperly (such as "your" for "you're"). Before you can proofread your letter, you need to delete the practice sentence.

To delete the practice sentence:

▶ **1.** Make sure the insertion point is to the right of "common" in the sentence you just typed, and then press the **Delete** key repeatedly to delete any spaces and characters to the right of the insertion point.

▶ **2.** Press the **Backspace** key repeatedly until the insertion point is located just left of the paragraph mark below Andrew's name. There should only be one paragraph mark below his name. If you accidentally delete part of the letter, retype it, using Figure 1-1 as a guide.

Now you can proofread the letter for any typos. You can also get rid of the wavy red underline below Andrew's last name.

To proofread the document:

▶ 1. Be sure the signature line is visible. Because Word doesn't recognize "Suri" as a word, it is marked as a potential error. You need to tell Word to ignore this name wherever it occurs in the letter.

▶ 2. Right-click **Suri**. A shortcut menu and the Mini toolbar open.

▶ 3. Click **Ignore All** on the shortcut menu. This tells Word to ignore the word "Suri" each time it occurs in this document. The wavy red underline disappears from below Andrew's last name.

▶ 4. Scroll up to the beginning of the letter and proofread it for typing errors. If a word has a wavy red underline, right-click it and choose an option on the shortcut menu. To correct other errors, click to the right or left of the error, use the Backspace or Delete key to remove it, and then type a correction.

▶ 5. On the Quick Access Toolbar, click the **Save** button ⊞ . Word saves your letter with the same name and to the same location you specified earlier.

Next, you need to return to the beginning of the document and insert the date. In the process, you'll learn how to use Word's AutoComplete feature.

Inserting a Date with AutoComplete

The advantage of using a word-processing program such as Microsoft Word is that you can easily make changes to text you have already typed. In this case, you need to insert the current date at the beginning of the letter. Andrew tells you that he wants to send the *Author's Guide* to Clara Meyer on February 8, so you need to insert that date into the letter now.

Before you can enter the date, you need to move the insertion point to the correct location.

To move the insertion point and add some blank lines:

▶ 1. Scroll up to display the top of the document.

▶ 2. Click to the left of the "D" in "Dear Clara" in the salutation, press the **Enter** key twice, then press the ↑ key twice to move the insertion point up to two paragraphs above the salutation. There are now six blank paragraphs before the salutation. The insertion point is located in the second blank paragraph above the salutation. The vertical ruler tells you that the insertion point is located about 1.5 inches from the top margin (that is, the insertion point is now located where the salutation used to be). As you'll recall, the top margin is one inch deep, so the insertion point is now approximately 2.5 inches from the top of the page. This is where you will insert the date. See Figure 1-24.

Figure 1-24 | **Insertion point positioned for adding date**

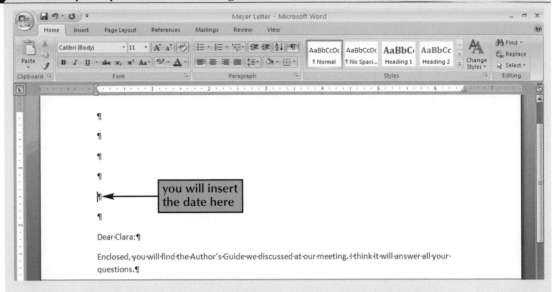

To insert the date, you can take advantage of Word's **AutoComplete** feature, which automatically inserts dates and other regularly used items for you. In this case, you can type the first few characters of the month, and let Word insert the rest.

To insert the date:

▶ 1. Type **Febr** (the first four letters of February). A rectangular box appears above the line, as shown in Figure 1-25. If you wanted to type something other than February, you could continue typing to complete the word. In this case, though, you want to accept the AutoComplete suggestion.

Figure 1-25 | **AutoComplete suggestion**

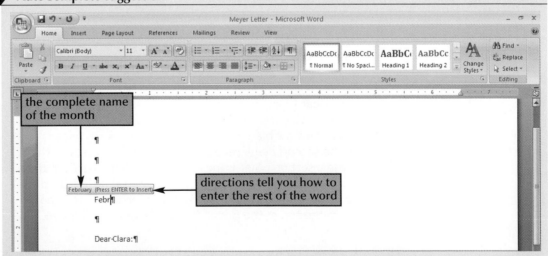

▶ 2. Press the **Enter** key. The rest of the word "February" is inserted in the document.

3. Press the **spacebar**, type **8, 2010**, and then press the **Enter** key twice. The date is finished, and the insertion point is now located where you want to begin typing the inside address.

Trouble? If February happens to be the current month, you will see a second AutoComplete suggestion displaying the current date after you press the spacebar. To ignore that AutoComplete suggestion, continue typing the rest of the date as instructed in Step 3.

You're ready to type the inside address. But first, you need to learn a little more about paragraph and line spacing in Microsoft Word.

Understanding Line and Paragraph Spacing

In Word, any text that ends with a paragraph mark symbol (¶) is a paragraph. A **paragraph** can be a group of words that is many lines long, a single word, or even a blank line, in which case you see a paragraph mark alone on a single line. (Recall that the letter to Clara Meyer includes several blank paragraphs at the beginning of the document.) As you work with paragraphs in a document, you need to be concerned with two types of spacing—line spacing and paragraph spacing.

Line spacing determines the amount of space between lines of text within a paragraph. Lines that are closely positioned one on top of another are said to be single spaced. Technically speaking, single spacing allows for the tallest character in a line of text. All other line spacing options are measured as multiples of single spacing. For example, 1.5 line spacing allows for one and one-half times the space of single spacing. Likewise, double spacing allows for twice the space of single spacing. By default, the line spacing in Word 2007 documents is set to 1.15 times the space allowed in single spacing. This allows for the largest character in a particular line as well as a small amount of extra space.

The other type of spacing you need to be concerned with, **paragraph spacing**, determines the amount of space before and after a paragraph. Paragraph spacing is measured in points; a **point** is approximately $1/72$ of an inch. The default setting for paragraph spacing in Word is 0 points before each paragraph and 10 points after each paragraph.

Although line spacing and paragraph spacing are two different things, it is common to refer to paragraph spacing with the same terms used to refer to line spacing. So, paragraphs that appear very close together, with no space for text in between, are often referred to as single spaced. Paragraphs that have space enough for a single line of text between them are said to be double spaced. The default paragraph spacing in Word (10 points after each paragraph) is designed to look like double spacing (although it is slightly tighter than true double spacing). Figure 1-26 shows the Meyer Letter document zoomed to 90%, so you can see its spacing at a glance.

Figure 1-26 Line and paragraph spacing in the letter to Clara Meyer

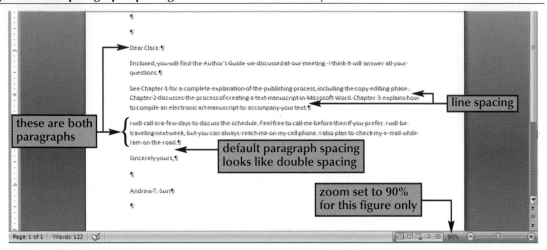

In a block style letter, the inside address (shown earlier in Figure 1-1) should be single spaced. However, with Word's default paragraph spacing, when you press the Enter key to move from the name line in the inside address, to the street address line, and then to the city and state line, Word inserts extra space after each paragraph. This results in an inside address that is double spaced. You'll see how this works in the following steps. Then you'll learn how to correct the problem.

To type the inside address:

1. Type the following: **Clara Meyer**, press the **Enter** key, type **2257 Chamberlain Drive**, press the **Enter** key, and then type **North Liberty, IA 52317**. Do not press the Enter key after typing the zip code; you should already see one blank paragraph before and after the inside address. See Figure 1-27.

Letter with inside address | Figure 1-27

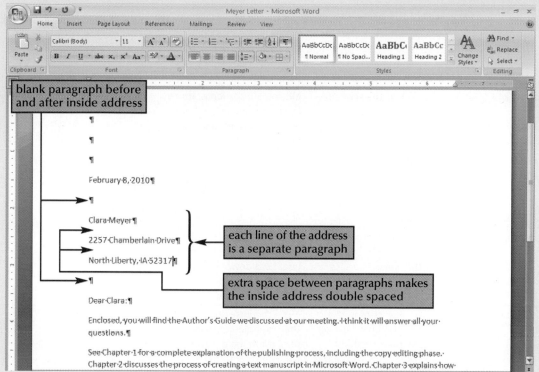

Remember that each line of the inside address is actually a separate paragraph. As you can see in Figure 1-27, the extra space Word inserted between these separate paragraphs results in an inside address that appears to be double spaced.

To correct this problem, you need to **select**, or highlight, the inside address and then change the paragraph spacing. Andrew is also concerned about the document's line spacing. He doesn't really like the extra space between lines, so he asks you to remove it. To change this, you need to select the entire document and then change the line spacing.

Selecting Parts of a Document

You can select one or more paragraphs, one or more words, any other part of a document, or even the entire document, by using the mouse or the keyboard. However, most people find that the mouse is easier and more efficient to use. With the mouse you can quickly select a line or paragraph by clicking the **selection bar** (the blank space in the left margin area of the document window). You can also select text using various combinations of keys. Figure 1-28 summarizes methods for selecting text with the mouse and the keyboard. A notation such as "Ctrl+Shift" means you press and hold the two keys at the same time.

Figure 1-28 ▶ **Methods for selecting text**

To Select	Mouse	Keyboard	Mouse and Keyboard
A word	Double-click the word	Move the insertion point to the beginning of the word, hold down Ctrl+Shift, and then press →	
A line	Click in the selection bar next to the line	Move the insertion point to the beginning of the line, hold down Shift, and then press ↓	
A sentence	Click at the beginning of the sentence, then drag the pointer until the sentence is selected		Press and hold down Ctrl, and then click within the sentence
Multiple lines	Click and drag in the selection bar next to the lines	Move the insertion point to the beginning of the first line, hold down Shift, and then press ↓ until all the lines are selected	
A paragraph	Double-click in the selection bar next to the paragraph, or triple-click within the paragraph	Move the insertion point to the beginning of the paragraph, hold down Ctrl+Shift, and then press ↓	
Multiple paragraphs	Click in the selection bar next to the first paragraph in the group, and then drag in the selection bar to select the paragraphs	Move the insertion point to the beginning of the first paragraph, hold down Ctrl+Shift, and then press ↓ until all the paragraphs are selected	
An entire document	Triple-click in the selection bar	Press Ctrl+A	Press and hold down Ctrl, and then click in the selection bar
A block of text	Click at the beginning of the block, and then drag the pointer until the entire block is selected		Click at the beginning of the block, press and hold down Shift, and then click at the end of the block
Nonadjacent blocks of text	Press and hold down Ctrl, and then drag the mouse pointer to select multiple blocks of nonadjacent text		

You'll practice many of these selection methods in Tutorial 2. For now, you will focus on selecting the multiple paragraphs of the inside address and the entire document. You'll start by selecting the inside address.

To select the inside address:

▶ 1. Click to the left of the "C" in "Clara Meyer" in the inside address, and then drag the mouse right and down until the entire inside address is selected. Make sure the paragraph mark to the right of the zip code is also selected. See Figure 1-29.

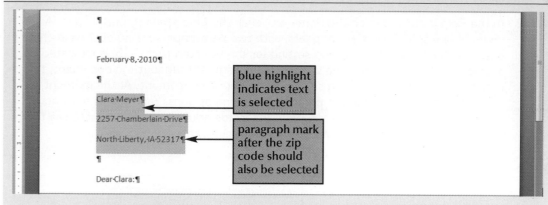

Trouble? If you selected only part of the inside address, or selected a different part of the document, click anywhere in the document to remove the blue high-light, and then begin again with Step 1.

Trouble? Don't be concerned if you see the Mini toolbar hovering over the selected text.

Now that the inside address is selected, you are ready to remove the extra space after each paragraph. You'll also adjust the line spacing, as Andrew requested.

Adjusting Paragraph and Line Spacing

There are several ways to adjust paragraph and line spacing in Word. The quickest method, which you'll use in this tutorial, is to click the Line spacing button in the Paragraph group on the Home tab. (In Tutorial 2, you'll learn another technique that offers more options.)

Clicking the Line spacing button opens a menu with some commonly used line spac-ing options: single spacing (listed on the Line spacing menu as 1.0), double spacing (listed as 2.0), and so on. The paragraph spacing options offered by the Line spacing but-ton are more streamlined: you can choose to add or remove a default amount of extra space before or after each paragraph. You cannot specify a particular amount of space.

Understanding Spacing Between Paragraphs		InSight

To many people, "to single space between paragraphs" means pressing the Enter key once after each paragraph. Likewise, "to double space between paragraphs" means pressing the Enter key twice after each paragraph. With the default paragraph spacing in Word 2007, however, you only need to press the Enter key once to insert a double space after a paragraph. Keep this in mind if you're used to pressing the Enter key twice; otherwise, you could end up with more space than you want between paragraphs.

Andrew asks you to remove the extra space between the lines within paragraphs. This means you need to change the line spacing from 1.15 to 1.0 (that is, to single spacing). You'll start by adjusting the paragraph spacing in the inside address, and then turn your attention to the line spacing for the entire document.

To adjust the paragraph spacing in the inside address:

▶ **1.** Verify that the inside address is still selected.

▶ **2.** In the Paragraph group on the Home tab, click the **Line spacing** button ⬓⬓▾ . A menu of line spacing options appears, with two paragraph spacing options at the bottom. The current line spacing setting for the selected text (1.15) is indicated by a check mark. Because the line spacing is the same throughout the document, this is also the current line spacing setting for the entire document. At the moment, you are more interested in the paragraph spacing options. Your goal is to remove the extra space after each paragraph in the inside address, so you need to use the last option on the menu, Remove Space After Paragraph. See Figure 1-30.

Figure 1-30 ▶ **Line and paragraph spacing options**

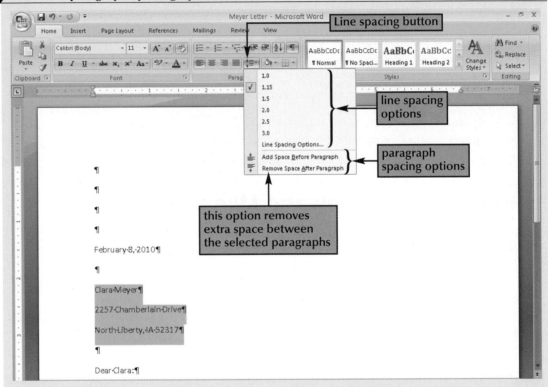

▶ **3.** Click **Remove Space After Paragraph**. The menu closes, and the extra space after each of the three paragraphs of the inside address is removed. The paragraphs are now closer together.

▶ **4.** Click anywhere in the document to deselect the inside address. Notice that the change in paragraph spacing in the inside address did not affect the rest of the document because you had selected only the inside address. The paragraphs in the body of the letter are still separated by extra space, so that they appear to be double spaced.

The three paragraphs of the inside address are closer together, but they don't exactly look single spaced. That's because the default line spacing setting (which you'll recall adds a small amount of space below each line) remains in effect, adding a small amount of extra space below the single line of text in each of the three inside address paragraphs. When you change the line spacing for the entire document to single spaced in the next set of steps, the inside address will finally look single spaced.

To adjust the line spacing for the entire document:

▶ 1. Press the **Ctrl + A** keys. The entire document is selected, as indicated by the blue highlight.

▶ 2. In the Paragraph group on the Home tab, click the **Line spacing** button 🔳. The Line spacing menu opens. As you saw earlier, the default line spacing setting of 1.15 is currently selected, as indicated by the check mark. You want to change the setting to single spacing, or 1.0.

▶ 3. Click **1.0**. The Line spacing menu closes.

▶ 4. Click anywhere in the document to deselect it. The lines of the entire document move closer together, and the inside address is now single spaced. The lines within the paragraphs in the rest of the document are also single spaced. The double spacing between paragraphs everywhere in the letter except the inside address remains unchanged. See Figure 1-31.

Tip

A line spacing setting of 1.15 is fine for most documents. However, some people prefer a setting of 1.0.

New line spacing in the document ◀ **Figure 1-31**

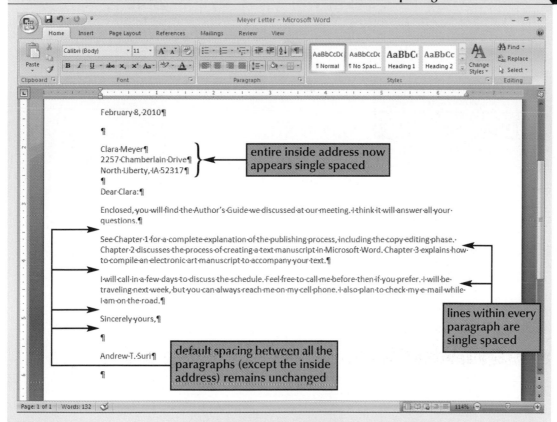

Previewing and Printing a Document

Do you think the letter is ready to print? If you print too soon, you risk wasting paper and printer time. For example, if you failed to insert enough space for the company letterhead, you would have to add more space, and then print the letter again. To avoid wasting paper and time, you should first display the document in the **Print Preview window**. By default, the Print Preview window shows you the full page; there's no need to scroll through the document.

To preview the document:

▶ **1.** Proof the document one last time and correct any new errors. Always remember to proof your document immediately before printing it.

▶ **2.** Click to the left of the last paragraph mark in the document (just below Andrew's name), press the **Enter** key and type your first, middle, and last initials in lowercase. In a block style letter, it is customary for the typist to include his or her initials below the signature line. In this case, adding your initials also ensures that you will be able to identify your copy of the letter when you retrieve it from the printer.

▶ **3.** Click the **Office Button** , point to **Print**, and then click **Print Preview**. The Print Preview window opens and displays a full-page version of your letter, as shown in Figure 1-32. This shows how the letter will fit on the printed page. The Ribbon in Print Preview includes a number of useful options for changing the way the printed page will look.

| Figure 1-32 | Full page displayed in the Print Preview window |

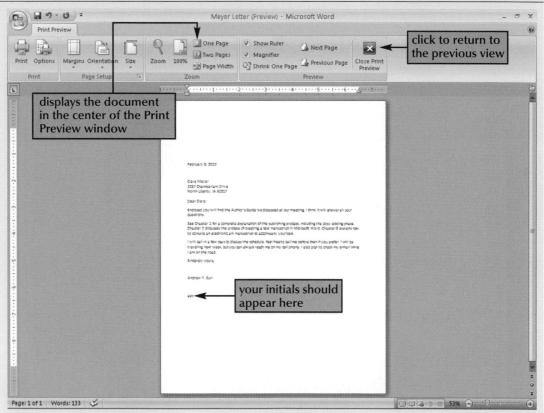

Trouble? If your letter is not centered in the Print Preview window, click the One Page button in the Zoom group on the Print Preview tab.

Trouble? If you don't see a ruler above the document, click the Show Ruler check box in the Preview group on the Print Preview tab to insert a check mark and display the ruler.

> **4.** Review your document and make sure its overall layout matches the document in Figure 1-32. If you notice a problem with paragraph breaks or spacing, click the Close Print Preview button in the Preview group on the Print Preview tab, edit the document, and then open the Print Preview window again and check your work.
>
> **5.** In the Preview group on the Print Preview tab, click the **Close Print Preview** button to return to Print Layout view.
>
> **6.** Click the **Save** button 🖫 on the Quick Access Toolbar to save the letter with your newly added initials.

In Andrew's letter, the text looks well spaced, and the letterhead will fit at the top of the page. You are ready to print the letter.

To print a document, click the Office Button, and then click Print. This opens the Print dialog box, where you can adjust various printer settings. Or, if you prefer, you can click the Office Button, point to Print, and then click Quick Print. This prints the document using default settings, without opening a dialog box. In these tutorials, the first time you print, you should check the settings in the Print dialog box and make sure the number of copies is set to 1. After that, you can use the Quick Print command.

To print the letter document:

> **1.** Make sure your printer is turned on and contains paper.
>
> **2.** Click the **Office Button** (🔘), and then click **Print**. The Print dialog box opens.
>
> **3.** Make sure the Printer section of the dialog box shows the correct printer. Also, make sure the number of copies is set to 1.
>
> **Trouble?** If the Name list box in the Print dialog box shows the wrong printer, click the Name list arrow, and then select the correct printer from the list of available printers. If you're not sure what the correct printer is, check with your instructor or technical support person.
>
> **4.** Click the **OK** button. Assuming your computer is attached to a printer, the letter prints.

Your printed letter should look similar to Figure 1-1, but without the Carlyle University letterhead. Also, your initials should appear below Andrew's name, on the last line of the letter.

| **Printing Documents on a Shared Printer** | InSight |

If your computer is connected to a network, be sure to print only those documents that you need in hard copy format. You should avoid tying up a shared printer with unnecessary printing.

Creating an Envelope

After you print the letter, Andrew asks you to create an envelope in which to mail the *Author's Guide*. Creating an envelope is a simple process because Word automatically uses the inside address from the letter as the address on the envelope. By default, Word does not add extra space between the paragraphs on an envelope, and the line spacing is set to 1.0. As a result, addresses on an envelope are single spaced.

- Click the Mailings tab on the Ribbon.
- In the Create group, click the Envelopes button to open the Envelopes and Labels dialog box.
- Verify that the Delivery address box contains the correct address. If necessary, type a new address or edit the existing one.
- If necessary, type a return address. If you are using preprinted stationery that already includes a return address, click the Omit check box to insert a check mark.
- To print the envelope immediately, insert an envelope in your printer, and then click the Print button.
- To store the envelope along with the rest of the document, click the Add to Document button.
- To print the envelope after you have added it to the document, insert an envelope in your printer, open the Print dialog box, and print the page containing the envelope.

Andrew tells you that your printer is not currently stocked with envelopes. He asks you to create the envelope and add it to the document. Then he will print the envelope later, when he is ready to mail the *Author's Guide* to Clara.

To create an envelope:

▶ 1. Click the **Mailings** tab on the Ribbon.

▶ 2. In the Create group on the Mailings tab, click the **Envelopes** button. The Envelopes and Labels dialog box opens, as shown in Figure 1-33. By default, Word uses the inside address from the letter as the delivery address. Depending on how your computer is set up, you might see an address in the Return address box. Because Andrew will be using his company's printed envelopes, you don't need to print a return address on this envelope.

Figure 1-33 ▶ **Envelopes and Labels dialog box**

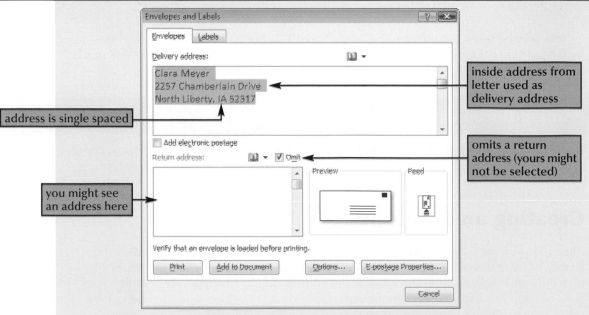

inside address from letter used as delivery address

address is single spaced

omits a return address (yours might not be selected)

you might see an address here

▶ 3. If necessary, click the **Omit** check box to insert a check mark.

4. Click the **Add to Document** button. The dialog box closes, and you return to the document window. The envelope is inserted at the top of the document, with the address single spaced. The double line with the words "Section Break (Next Page)" indicate how the envelope is formatted, and will not be visible when you print the envelope. The envelope will print in the standard business envelope format. (You'll have a chance to print an envelope in the exercises at the end of this tutorial.)

5. Save your changes to the document. You are finished with the letter and the envelope, so you can close the document.

6. Click the **Close** button ⊠ on the Word program title bar. The Meyer Letter document closes. If you have no other documents open, Word closes also.

   Trouble? If you see a dialog box with the message "Do you want to save the changes to 'Meyer Letter?'" click the Yes button.

Congratulations on creating your first letter in Microsoft Word 2007. You'll be able to use the skills you learned in this tutorial to create a variety of professional documents.

Session 1.2 Quick Check | Review

1. True or False: The spelling checker is turned off by default.
2. True or False: To accept an AutoComplete suggestion, such as the name of a month, you need to click a button on the Ribbon.
3. Explain how to correct a misspelled word using a shortcut menu.
4. What's the difference between paragraph spacing and line spacing?
5. Explain how to preview a document before you print it.
6. What tab on the Ribbon do you use to create an envelope?

Tutorial Summary | Review

In this tutorial, you learned how to set up your Word window to match the figures in this book, create a new document from scratch, and type a professional-looking letter. You practiced correcting errors and moving the insertion point around a document. You learned how to undo and redo changes and how to insert a date with AutoComplete. You adjusted paragraph and line spacing, and then you previewed and printed a document. Finally, you created an envelope.

Key Terms

AutoComplete	nonprinting characters	scroll
AutoCorrect	Page width	select
default	paragraph	selection bar
font	paragraph spacing	spelling checker
font size	point	Undo button
line spacing	Print Preview window	Word
margin	Redo button	word wrap
Microsoft Office Word	ScreenTip	Zoom level

Practice	**Review Assignments**

Practice the skills you learned in the tutorial using the same case scenario.

There are no Data Files needed for the Review Assignments.

Andrew asks you to write a letter to a local author, Philippa Gallatin, inviting her to an upcoming convention. He also asks you to create an envelope for the letter. You'll create the letter and envelope by completing the following steps. (Note: Text you need to type is shown in bold for ease of reference only; do not bold the text unless otherwise instructed.)

1. Open a new blank document.
2. Compare your screen to the checklist in Figure 1-12, and change any settings if necessary. In particular, make sure that nonprinting characters are displayed.
3. Press the Enter key four times to insert enough space for the company letterhead.
4. Type the date **November 25, 2010** using AutoComplete for "November."
5. Press the Enter key twice, then type the following inside address, using the default paragraph spacing for now:
   Philippa Gallatin
   787 First Street
   Albany, NY 12205
6. Press the Enter key twice, then type the letter's salutation, body, complimentary closing, and signature line, as shown in Figure 1-34. Accept any relevant AutoCorrect suggestions. Use the default line and paragraph spacing; do not insert any extra blank paragraphs.

Figure 1-34

Dear Philippa:

The Albany Visitors Bureau will be hosting the 2011 convention for the National Editorial Association. The convention is scheduled for the first week in March. As a major publishing force in the Albany area, we'd like to make a strong showing at the convention. In particular, we'd like to invite you to attend the opening banquet as our guest. Our own editor-in-chief, Sally Ann Hamilton, will be the keynote speaker.

The complete convention schedule will be posted on the National Editorial Association's Web site after the New Year. I'll e-mail you shortly afterward to confirm your reservation for the opening banquet. At that time, you can tell me if you'll be available to attend any of the afternoon seminars.

Sincerely,

Andrew T. Suri

7. Save your work as **Gallatin Letter** in the Tutorial.01\Review folder provided with your Data Files.
8. Practice using the keyboard to move the insertion point around the document. Use the arrow keys so the insertion point is positioned immediately to the right of the "a" in "Philippa" in the inside address.

9. Press the spacebar and then type **M.**, so the first line of the inside address reads "Philippa M. Gallatin." (Don't forget the period after the middle initial.)
10. Undo the change and then redo it.
11. Scroll to the beginning of the document and proofread your work.
12. Correct any misspelled words marked by wavy red lines. If the correct spelling of a word does not appear in the shortcut menu, close the list, and then make the correction yourself. Remove any red wavy lines below words that are spelled correctly.
13. Click at the end of Andrew's name in the signature line, press the Enter key twice, and type your initials in lowercase.
14. Select the inside address and remove the extra paragraph spacing from the selected paragraphs.
15. Select the entire document and change the line spacing to single spacing.
16. Save your changes to the letter, and then preview and print it.
17. Add an envelope to the document. Use your own address as the delivery address. Do not include a return address.
18. Save your changes and close the document.

| Apply | **Case Problem 1** |

Apply the skills you learned to create a letter about a health-care lecture.

There are no Data Files needed for this Case Problem.

Wingra Family Practice Clinic   You are a nurse at Wingra Family Practice Clinic. You have organized a lunchtime lecture series for the clinic staff in which regional medical professionals will discuss topics related to pediatric health care. You have hired your first speaker and need to write a letter confirming your agreement and asking a few questions. Create the letter by completing the following steps. As you type the document, accept the default paragraph and line spacing until you are asked to change them. Because the clinic is currently out of letterhead, you will start the letter by typing a return address. (Note: Text you need to type is shown in bold for ease of reference only; do not bold the text unless otherwise instructed.)

1. Open a new blank document. Compare your screen to the checklist in Figure 1-12, and change any settings if necessary. In particular, make sure that nonprinting characters are displayed.
2. Type your name, press the Enter key, and then type the following return address:
   Wingra Family Practice Clinic
   2278 Norwood Place
   Middleton, WI 52247
3. Press the Enter key twice, and then type **May 8, 2010** as the date.
4. Press the Enter key twice, and then type this inside address:
   Dr. Susanna Trevay
   James Madison Medical Center
   56 Ingersoll Drive
   Madison, WI 53788
5. Press the Enter key twice, type the salutation **Dear Dr. Trevay:** (don't forget the colon), and then press the Enter key once.
6. Type the following paragraph: **Thank you so much for agreeing to lecture about early childhood vaccinations on Friday, May 21. Before I can publicize your talk, I need some information. Please call by Tuesday with your answers to these questions:**

7. Press the Enter key, and then type the following questions as separate paragraphs, using the default paragraph spacing:
   Which vaccines will you cover in detail?
   Will you discuss common immune responses to vaccine antigens?
   Will you provide hand-outs with suggested vaccination schedules?

8. Save the document as **Lecture Series Letter** in the Tutorial.01\Case1 folder provided with your Data Files.

9. Move the insertion point to the beginning of the third question (which begins "Will you provide..."). Insert a new paragraph, and add the following as the new third question in the list: **Would you be willing to take questions from the audience?**

10. Correct any spelling errors indicated by red wavy lines. Because "Wingra" is spelled correctly, use the shortcut menu to remove the wavy red line under the word "Wingra" and prevent Word from marking the word as a misspelling. Repeat this to ignore "Trevay," "Ingersoll," and any other words that are spelled correctly but are marked as misspellings.

11. Insert a new paragraph after the last question, and then type the complimentary closing **Sincerely,** (including the comma).

12. Press the Enter key twice to leave room for your signature, and then type your full name. Press the Enter key and type **Wingra Family Practice Clinic**. Notice that "Wingra" is not marked as a spelling error this time.

13. Select the return address and remove the extra paragraph spacing. Do the same for the inside address. Do not attempt to change them both at the same time by selecting the return address, the date, and the inside address all at once, or you will end up with too little space before and after the date.

14. Select the entire document and change the line spacing to single spacing.

15. Save the document, preview and print it, and then close it.

| Apply | **Case Problem 2** |

Apply the skills you learned to create a letter informing a client about a new investment program.

There are no Data Files needed for this Case Problem.

Pear Tree Investment Services As a financial planner at Pear Tree Investment Services, you are responsible for keeping your clients informed about new investment options. You have just learned about a program called HigherEdVest, which encourages parents to save for their children's college educations. You'll write a letter to Joseph Robbins, a client of yours, in which you introduce the program and ask him to call for more information. Create the letter by completing the following steps. (Note: Text you need to type is shown in bold for ease of reference only; do not bold the text unless otherwise instructed.)

1. Open a new blank document. Compare your screen to the checklist in Figure 1-12, and change any settings if necessary. In particular, make sure that nonprinting characters are displayed.

2. To leave room for the company letterhead, press the Enter key until the insertion point is positioned about three inches from the top of the page. (Remember that you can see the exact position of the insertion point, in inches, on the vertical ruler.)

⊕ EXPLORE

3. Type the current date, accepting any AutoComplete suggestions that appear.

4. Press the Enter key twice and type the inside address: **Joseph Robbins, 5788 Rugby Road, Hillsborough, CO 80732**.

5. Press the Enter key twice, type the salutation **Dear Joseph:**, and then press the Enter key once.

6. Write one paragraph introducing the HigherEdVest program, explaining that you think the client might be interested, and asking him to call your office at (555) 555-5555 for more details.

7. In the next paragraph, type the complimentary closing **Sincerely,**.

8. Press the Enter key twice to leave room for your signature, and then type your name and title.

9. Save the letter as **EdVest Letter** in the Tutorial.01\Case2 folder provided with your Data Files.

10. Reread your letter carefully and correct any errors. Use the keyboard to move the insertion point as necessary.

11. Remove the extra paragraph spacing in the inside address, and then change the entire document to single spacing.

12. Save your changes, and then preview and print the letter.

⊕ EXPLORE

13. Create an envelope for the letter. Click the Omit check box to deselect it (if necessary), and then, for the return address, type your own address. Add the envelope to the document. If you are asked if you want to save the return address as the new default return address, answer No. If your computer is connected to a printer that is stocked with envelopes, click the Office Button, click Print, click the Pages option button, type **1** in the Pages text box, and then click the OK button.

14. Save and close the document.

Create	**Case Problem 3**

Use your skills to create the letter of recommendation shown in Figure 1-35.

There are no Data Files needed for this Case Problem.

Monterrey Mountain Bike Tours   You are the owner of Monterrey Mountain Bike Tours, located in Eugene, Oregon. One of your tour guides, Melissa Coia, has decided to move to the Midwest to be closer to her family. She has applied for a job as a tour guide at Horicon Marsh in Wisconsin, and has asked you to write a letter of recommendation. To create the letter, complete the following steps:

1. Open a new blank document. Compare your screen to the checklist in Figure 1-12, and change any settings if necessary. In particular, make sure that nonprinting characters are displayed.

2. Type the letter shown in Figure 1-35. Assume that you will print the letter on the company's letterhead, with the date positioned about 2.5 inches from the top of the page. Replace "Your Name" with your first and last name.

Figure 1-35

June 27, 2010

Peter Roundtree
Horicon Marsh Ranger Station
9875 Scales Bend Road
Horicon, Wisconsin 57338

Dear Mr. Roundtree:

I am writing on behalf of Melissa Coia, who has applied for a job as a tour guide at Horicon Marsh. I highly recommend that you hire Melissa. She is enthusiastic, energetic, and extremely well organized.

I would be glad to tell you more about Melissa over the phone. You can reach me during business hours at (555) 555-5555.

Sincerely,

Your Name

3. Save the document as **Melissa** in the Tutorial.01\Case3 folder provided with your Data Files.
4. Correct any typing errors.
5. Change the paragraph and line spacing so that the entire letter is single spaced, including the inside address.
6. Preview and print the letter.
7. Create an envelope for the letter. Click the Omit check box to deselect it (if necessary), and then, for the return address, type your own address. Add the envelope to the document. If you are asked if you want to save the return address as the new default return address, answer No. If your computer is connected to a printer that is stocked with envelopes, click the Office Button, click Print, click the Pages option button, type **1** in the Pages text box, and then click the OK button.
8. Save the document and close it.

| Challenge | **Case Problem 4** |

Go beyond what you've learned to write a fax coversheet for a small engineering company.

There are no Data Files needed for this Case Problem.

Gladstone Engineering As the office manager for Gladstone Engineering, you are responsible for faxing technical drawings to clients. Along with each set of drawings, you need to include a coversheet that explains what you are faxing, lists the total number of pages, and provides the name and cell phone number of the engineer who created the drawings. The fastest way to create a professional-looking coversheet is to use a template—a special Word document that comes with predefined headings, line and paragraph spacing, and other types of formatting. To create the fax coversheet, perform the following steps. (Note: Text you need to type is shown in bold for ease of reference only; do not bold the text unless otherwise instructed.)

⊕ EXPLORE

1. Click the Microsoft Office Button, and then click New. The New Document dialog box opens. In the Template list (on the left), click Installed Templates.

⊕ **EXPLORE**   2. In the Installed Templates pane (on the right), click Equity Fax, and then click Create. A fax template opens, containing generic text called placeholders that you replace with your own information. (You should always take care to remove any placeholders you don't replace with other text.)

3. Compare your screen to the checklist in Figure 1-12 and change any settings if necessary. In particular, make sure that nonprinting characters are displayed.

⊕ **EXPLORE**   4. Click the text "[Type the recipient name]." The placeholder text appears in a blue box with blue highlighting. The box containing the highlighted text (with the small rectangle attached) is called a document control, or a content control. You can enter text in this document control just as you enter text in a dialog box. You'll learn more about document controls in Tutorial 3.

5. Type **Robert Mason**, and then press the Tab key twice. A document control is now visible to the right of the word "From." If you see a name here, click in the document control (if necessary) and delete the name.

6. Type your first and last name in the document control, and then press the Tab key to highlight the placeholder text "[Type the recipient fax number]."

7. Type **(555) 555-5555**, and then continue using the Tab key as necessary to enter **4** as the number of pages and **(333) 333-3333** as the phone number. If you press the Tab key too many times and skip past a document control, you can click the document control to highlight it. If you make a typing mistake, use the Undo button to reverse the error.

⊕ **EXPLORE**   8. Use the Tab key to select the placeholder text "[Pick the date]," click the list arrow on the document control, click the right facing arrow above the calendar as necessary until you see the calendar for December 2010, and then click 10 in the calendar. The date 12.10.2010 appears in the Date document control.

9. Use the Tab key to select the placeholder text in the "Re:" section, and then press the Delete key to delete the placeholder text. Delete the "CC:" placeholder text as well.

10. Click the box to the left of "Please Reply," and then type an uppercase **X**.

11. Click the placeholder text "[Type comments]," and then type the following message: **Here are the latest drawings, created for you by Matt Xio. After you review them, please call Matt on his cell phone to discuss the next phase of this project. Thank you very much**.

12. Save the coversheet as **Mason Fax** in the Tutorial.01\Case4 folder provided with your Data Files.

⊕ **EXPLORE**   13. Zoom the document out until you can see the entire page on the screen. When you are finished reviewing the document, zoom the document until it returns to its original zoom setting.

14. Review the coversheet and correct any typos. Save the coversheet again, preview it, and then print it.

15. Close the document.

| **Research** | **Internet Assignments** ✎ |

Go to the Web to find information you can use to create documents.

The purpose of the Internet Assignments is to challenge you to find information on the Internet that you can use to work effectively with this software. The actual assignments are updated and maintained on the Course Technology Web site. Log on to the Internet and use your Web browser to go to the Student Online Companion for New Perspectives Office 2007 at **www.course.com/np/office2007**. Then navigate to the Internet Assignments for this tutorial.

Review	**Quick Check Answers**

Session 1.1

1. Planning a document saves time and effort. It ensures that you include enough information to achieve the document's purpose without overwhelming or boring the reader. It also ensures that the document is organized logically and has the appearance you want.
2. View tab
3. Click the Print Layout button on the bottom-right area of the window.
4. True
5. False
6. .docx

Session 1.2

1. False
2. False
3. Right-click the word, and then click the correct spelling in the shortcut menu.
4. Paragraph spacing controls the amount of space inserted between paragraphs. Line spacing controls the amount of space inserted between lines within a paragraph.
5. Click the Office Button, point to Print, and then click Print Preview. In the Preview group on the Print Preview tab, click the Close Print Preview button to return to the previous view.
6. Mailings tab

Ending Data Files

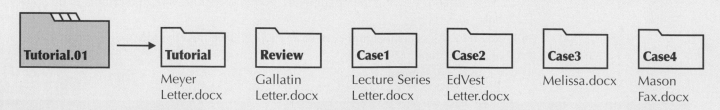

Tutorial.01 →

Tutorial
Meyer
Letter.docx

Review
Gallatin
Letter.docx

Case1
Lecture Series
Letter.docx

Case2
EdVest
Letter.docx

Case3
Melissa.docx

Case4
Mason
Fax.docx

Objectives

Session 2.1
- Check spelling and grammar
- Select and delete text
- Move text within a document
- Find and replace text

Session 2.2
- Change margins
- Change alignment and paragraph indents
- Copy formatting with the Format Painter
- Emphasize points with bullets, numbering, bold, and italic
- Change fonts and adjust font sizes
- Change the document theme
- Preview and print a document

Editing and Formatting a Document

Preparing a Handout on Choosing a Design Style

Case | Pemberly Furniture and Interiors

Natalie Lanci is the lead designer at Pemberly Furniture and Interiors, a design and furniture firm. Over the years, she has found that new customers are often intimidated by the prospect of decorating their homes. To make things easier, she has decided to create a series of handouts about interior styles and furniture. She's just finished a draft of her first handout, "Getting the Look You Want." She has marked up a printed copy of the document with notes about what she wants changed. As her assistant, it's your job to make the necessary changes and reprint the document.

In this tutorial, you will edit the handout according to Natalie's comments. You will open a draft of the document, save it with a different name, and then make the changes Natalie requested. First, you will check the document's grammar and spelling, and then you'll move text using two different methods. You will also use Word's Find and Replace feature to replace one version of the company name with another.

Next, you will change the overall look of the document by changing margins, indenting and justifying paragraphs, and copying the formatting from one paragraph to another. You'll create two bulleted lists and one numbered list. Then you'll make the title and subtitle more prominent by centering them, changing their font, and enlarging them. You'll also change the font of the company name in the body of the document, and you'll add bold to the headings to set them off from the rest of the text. You will experiment with changing the document's theme, and finally, you will preview and print the formatted document.

Starting Data Files

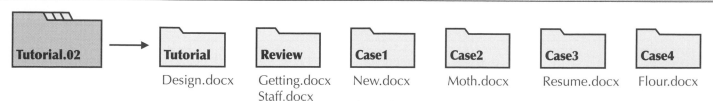

Tutorial.02 → Tutorial   Review   Case1   Case2   Case3   Case4

Design.docx   Getting.docx   New.docx   Moth.docx   Resume.docx   Flour.docx
               Staff.docx

Session 2.1

Reviewing the Document

You'll begin by opening Natalie's first draft of the document, which has the filename Design.

To open the document:

▶ 1. Start Word.

▶ 2. On the Quick Access Toolbar, click the **Office Button** (🔘), and then click **Open**. The Open dialog box opens.

▶ 3. Use the options in the Open dialog box to open the **Tutorial** subfolder within the **Tutorial.02** folder included with your Data Files.

▶ 4. Click **Design** to select the file, if necessary. The name of the selected file appears in the File name text box. See Figure 2-1.

Figure 2-1   Open dialog box

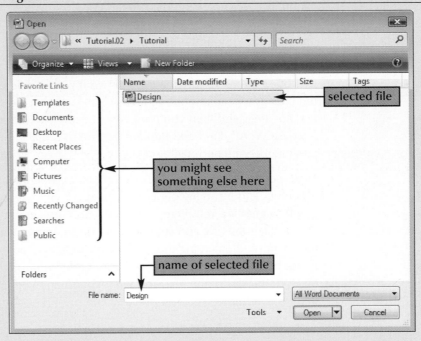

Trouble? If you see "Design.docx" in the folder, it's okay; click Design.docx and continue with Step 5. This just means that Windows is configured to display file extensions. If you can't find the file with or without the file extension, make sure you're looking in the Tutorial subfolder within the Tutorial.02 folder included with your Data Files, and check to make sure the list box next to the File name text box displays All Word Documents or All Files. If you still can't locate the file, ask your instructor or technical support person for help.

▶ 5. Click the **Open** button. The document opens with the insertion point at the beginning.

Before revising a document for someone else, it's a good idea to familiarize yourself with its overall structure. You'll do that now, and in the process make sure the document is displayed in a way that makes editing it as easy as possible.

To review the document:

▶ **1.** Verify that the document is displayed in Print Layout view, and if necessary, in the Paragraph group, click the **Show/Hide ¶** button ¶ to display nonprinting characters. If the rulers are not visible, switch to the **View** tab, and then click the **Ruler** check box to display the rulers.

▶ **2.** Take a moment to read the document. It consists of a series of headings, with explanatory text below each heading. Right now, the headings (such as "Ask Yourself Some Questions" and "Pick a Style") are hard to spot because they don't look any different from the surrounding text. You'll change that when you format the document. The document also includes some lists; you will format these later in this tutorial to make them easier to read. Natalie used the default font size, 11-point, and the default font, Calibri (Body), for the entire document. She relied on Word's default paragraph spacing to provide a visual separation between paragraphs.

▶ **3.** Scroll down until you can see the line "Stay True to Your Style." The white space after this line is the page's bottom margin. The blue space below the margin indicates a page break. This tells you that the line "Stay True to Your Style" appears on the last line of the first page. Word starts a new page whenever your text fills up a page. The Page box in the lower-left corner of the document window tells you the total number of pages in the document and which page currently contains the insertion point.

Figure 2-2 shows the page break, along with other important elements of the document. Note that in Figure 2-2 the Word window has been zoomed to 80%; this is to make it easy to see several parts of the document at once. At this point, your Zoom setting is probably 100%. To make sure you can see the entire width of the page, you'll select Page width in the Zoom dialog box in the next step.

Document with two pages ◀ **Figure 2-2**

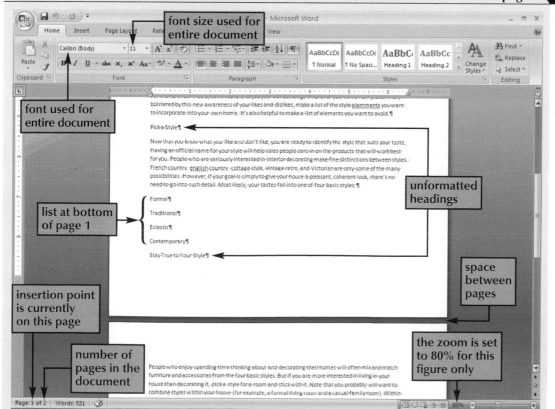

Tip

To hide the blue space between pages, double-click the blue space. To redisplay the blue space, double-click the black line.

▶ **4.** In the bottom-right corner of the Word window, click the current Zoom setting to open the Zoom dialog box, click **Page width**, and then click the **OK** button to close the Zoom dialog box. Word displays the full width of the document.

Now that you are familiar with Natalie's document, you can turn your attention to the edits she has requested. Natalie's editing marks and notes on the first draft are shown in Figure 2-3.

Figure 2-3 ▶ **Draft of handout with Natalie's edits (page 1)**

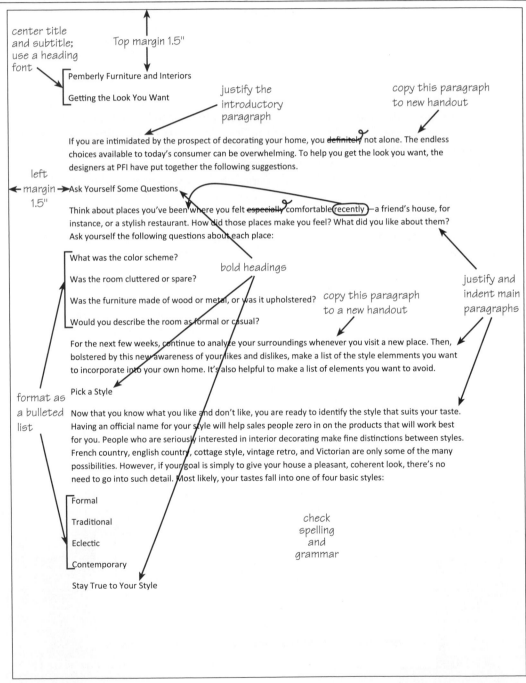

Draft of handout with Natalie's edits (page 2) | **Figure 2-3 (cont.)**

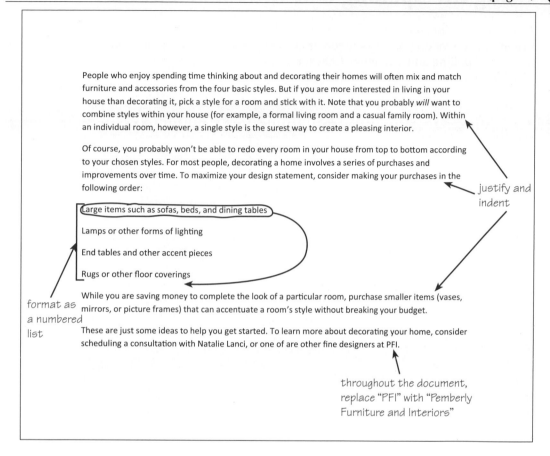

People who enjoy spending time thinking about and decorating their homes will often mix and match furniture and accessories from the four basic styles. But if you are more interested in living in your house than decorating it, pick a style for a room and stick with it. Note that you probably *will* want to combine styles within your house (for example, a formal living room and a casual family room). Within an individual room, however, a single style is the surest way to create a pleasing interior.

Of course, you probably won't be able to redo every room in your house from top to bottom according to your chosen styles. For most people, decorating a home involves a series of purchases and improvements over time. To maximize your design statement, consider making your purchases in the following order:

justify and indent

Large items such as sofas, beds, and dining tables

Lamps or other forms of lighting

End tables and other accent pieces

Rugs or other floor coverings

format as a numbered list

While you are saving money to complete the look of a particular room, purchase smaller items (vases, mirrors, or picture frames) that can accentuate a room's style without breaking your budget.

These are just some ideas to help you get started. To learn more about decorating your home, consider scheduling a consultation with Natalie Lanci, or one of are other fine designers at PFI.

throughout the document, replace "PFI" with "Pemberly Furniture and Interiors"

Before you begin editing the document, you should save it with a new name. Saving the document with a different filename creates a copy of the file and leaves the original file unchanged in case you want to work through the tutorial again.

To save the document with a new name:

▶ 1. Click the **Office Button** 🔘, and then click **Save As**. The Save As dialog box opens with the current filename highlighted in the File name text box. You could type an entirely new filename, or you could edit the current one.

▶ 2. Click to the right of the current filename to place the insertion point after the "n" in "Design."

▶ 3. Press the **spacebar**, and then type **Handout** so that the filename is "Design Handout."

▶ 4. Verify that the **Tutorial** folder is selected as the location for saving the file.

▶ 5. Click the **Save** button. The document is saved with the new filename "Design Handout" in the Tutorial folder, and the original Design file closes, remaining unchanged.

Now you're ready to begin working with the document. First, you will check it for spelling and grammatical errors.

Using the Spelling and Grammar Checker

As you type a document, Word marks possible spelling errors with a red wavy underline. When you're working on a document that someone else typed, it's a good idea to start by using the **Spelling and Grammar Checker**, a feature that checks a document word by word for a variety of errors.

Reference Window | **Checking a Document for Spelling and Grammar Errors**

- Move the insertion point to the beginning of the document, click the Review tab on the Ribbon, and then, in the Proofing group, click the Spelling & Grammar button.
- In the Spelling and Grammar dialog box, review any items highlighted in color. Possible grammatical errors appear in green; possible spelling errors appear in red. Review the suggested corrections in the Suggestions list box.
- To accept a suggested correction, click on it in the Suggestions list box, click the Change button to make the correction, and then continue searching the document for errors.
- To skip the current instance of the highlighted text and continue searching the document for errors, click the Ignore Once button.
- Click the Ignore All button to skip all instances of the highlighted text and continue searching the document for errors. Click the Ignore Rule button to skip all instances of a highlighted grammatical error.
- To type your correction directly in the document, click outside the Spelling and Grammar dialog box, make the correction, and then click the Resume button in the Spelling and Grammar dialog box.
- To add an unrecognized word to the dictionary, click the Add to Dictionary button.
- When you see a dialog box informing you that the spelling and grammar check is complete, click the OK button.

You'll see how the Spelling and Grammar Checker works as you check the Design Handout document for mistakes.

To check the Design Handout document for spelling and grammatical errors:

▶ 1. Press the **Ctrl+Home** keys to verify that the insertion point is located at the beginning of the document, to the left of the "P" in "Pemberly Furniture and Interiors."

▶ 2. Click the **Review** tab on the Ribbon, and then, in the Proofing group, click the **Spelling & Grammar** button. The Spelling and Grammar: English (United States) dialog box opens with the word "Pemberly" displayed in red, indicating a possible spelling error. In the document, "Pemberly" is highlighted in blue. Typically, the Suggestions box would contain one or more possible corrections for you to choose from, but in this case, Word doesn't recognize the name of Natalie's company because it is not included in the main dictionary. This isn't really an error. See Figure 2-4.

3. Click the **Ignore All** button. This tells Word to ignore all instances of "Pemberly" throughout the document. Now the first sentence of the document appears in green in the dialog box and in a blue highlight in the document. The Suggestions box tells you that the highlighted text is a sentence fragment. The last part of the sentence should read "you definitely are not alone," but the word "are" is missing. You can fix this problem by clicking outside the Spelling and Grammar dialog box and typing the change directly in the document.

4. Click the blue highlighted sentence outside the Spelling and Grammar dialog box. The blue highlight disappears, and the insertion point appears at the end of the sentence.

   Trouble? If you can't see the entire highlighted sentence, move the mouse pointer over the title bar of the Spelling and Grammar dialog box, press and hold the left mouse button, drag the mouse pointer until the dialog box is out of the way, and then release the mouse button.

5. Click to the left of the "n" in "not," type **are**, and then press the **spacebar**. Verify that the last part of the sentence now reads "you definitely are not alone." (You might notice that the word "definitely" makes the sentence awkward; you will delete this word in the next section.)

You've edited the document to correct the error. Now you need to return to the Spelling and Grammar dialog box to continue checking the document.

To continue checking the document:

1. Click the **Resume** button in the Spelling and Grammar dialog box to continue checking the rest of the document. The misspelled word "elemments" is highlighted in the Spelling and Grammar dialog box and in the document. The correct spelling, "elements," appears in the Suggestions box.

2. Verify that "elements" is highlighted in the Suggestions box, and then click the **Change** button. "Elements" is inserted into the document, and the word "english" is highlighted in the document. This should be "English," with an uppercase "E," instead.

3. Verify that "English" is selected in the Suggestions box, and then click the **Change** button. The word "English" is inserted in the document. A message box opens indicating that the spelling and grammar check is complete.

4. Click the **OK** button. The Spelling and Grammar dialog box closes. You return to the Design Handout document.

5. Click the **Home** tab to display the options related to editing a document again. You'll need to use these options as you continue the tutorial.

Although the Spelling and Grammar Checker is a useful tool, there is no substitute for careful proofreading. Always take the time to read through your document to check for errors the Spelling and Grammar Checker might have missed. Keep in mind that the Spelling and Grammar checker cannot pinpoint phrases that are inaccurate. You'll have to find those yourself. To produce a professional document, you must read it carefully several times. It's a good idea to ask a coworker to read your documents, too.

To proofread the Design Handout document:

1. Scroll to the beginning of the document and proofread the document. In the last sentence of the document, notice that the word "are" is used instead of the word "our." You will correct this error in the next section.

2. Finish proofreading the Design Handout document, and then click the **Save** button 🖫 on the Quick Access Toolbar to save the changes you've made so far.

Your next job is to delete some text (as shown earlier in Figure 2-3).

Deleting Text

You already have experience using the Backspace and Delete keys to delete a few characters. To delete an entire word or multiple words, it's faster to select the text first. Then you can either replace it with something else by typing over it, or you can delete it by pressing the Delete key. Right now, you need to change the word "are" to "our."

To replace "are" with "our":

1. Press the **Ctrl+End** keys. The insertion point moves to the end of the document.

2. In the last line of the document, double-click the word **are** (in the phrase "are other fine designers...").

3. Type **our**. The selected word is replaced with the correction. The phrase now correctly reads: "...our other fine designers...."

Next, Natalie wants you to delete the word "definitely" in the introductory paragraph at the beginning of the document and the word "especially" in the paragraph below the heading "Ask Yourself Some Questions." You can do this quickly by selecting multiple items and then pressing the Delete key.

To select and delete multiple items:

1. Press the **Ctrl+Home** keys. The insertion point is now located at the beginning of the document.

► **2.** In the introductory paragraph, which begins "If you are intimidated by...," double-click the word **definitely**. The word and the space following it are selected.

► **3.** Press and hold the **Ctrl** key, double-click the word **especially** in the paragraph below the heading "Ask Yourself Some Questions," and then release the **Ctrl** key. At this point the words "definitely" and "especially" should be selected. See Figure 2-5.

Text to be deleted | **Figure 2-5**

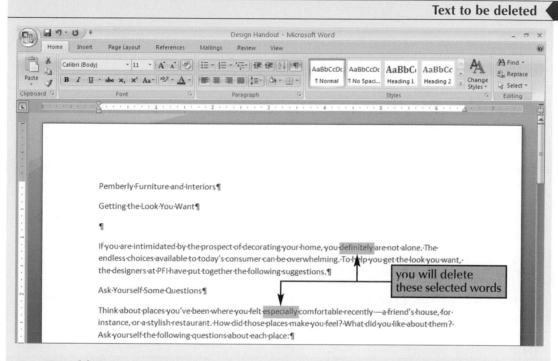

Trouble? If you don't get Step 3 right the first time, click anywhere in the document, and then repeat Steps 2 and 3.

► **4.** Press the **Delete** key. The selected items are deleted, and the words around them move in to fill the space. See Figure 2-6.

Paragraphs after deleting text | **Figure 2-6**

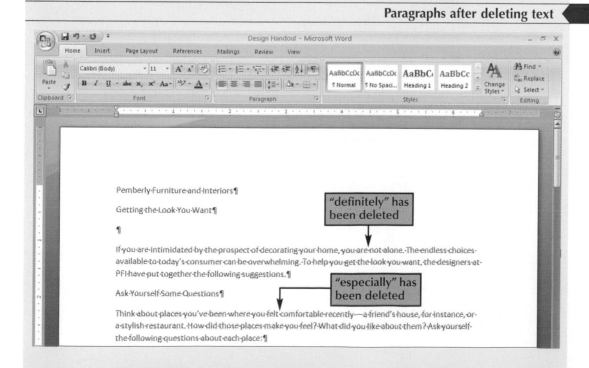

Trouble? If you deleted the wrong text, click the Undo button on the Quick Access Toolbar to reverse your mistake, and then begin again with Step 2.

▶ **5.** Scroll down to display the last line of the document, drag the mouse pointer to select "Natalie Lanci," press the **Delete** key, press the **spacebar** if necessary, and then type your first and last name. This change will make it easier for you to find your document if you print it on a network printer used by other students.

▶ **6.** Save the document.

You have edited the document by replacing "are" with "our" and by removing the text that Natalie marked for deletion. Now you are ready to make the rest of the edits she suggested.

Moving Text in a Document

One of the most useful features of a word-processing program is the ability to move text. For example, Natalie wants to reorder the four points in the section "Stay True to Your Style" on page 2. You could reorder the list by deleting an item and then retyping it at a new location, but it's easier to select and then move the text. Word provides several ways to move text: drag and drop, cut and paste, and copy and paste.

Dragging and Dropping Text

To move text with **drag and drop**, you select the text you want to move, press and hold down the mouse button while you drag the selected text to a new location, and then release the mouse button.

Reference Window | **Dragging and Dropping Text**

- Select the text you want to move.
- Press and hold down the mouse button until the drag-and-drop pointer appears, and then drag the selected text to its new location.
- Use the dotted insertion point as a guide to determine exactly where the text should be inserted.
- Release the mouse button to "drop" the text at the insertion point.

Natalie wants you to change the order of the items in the list on page 2 of the document. You'll use the drag-and-drop method to reorder these items. Because you need to select text before you can move it, you'll get practice using the selection bar (the white space in the left margin) to highlight a line of text as you do these steps.

To move text using drag and drop:

▶ **1.** Scroll up slightly until you see the list of suggested purchases, which begins "Large items such as sofas, beds, and dining tables." Natalie wants you to move the first item to the bottom of the list.

2. Move the pointer to the selection bar to the left of the line "Large items such as sofas, beds, and dining tables." The pointer changes to a right-facing arrow ⤢.

3. Click in the selection bar to the left of the line "Large items such as sofas, beds, and dining tables." The line is selected. Notice that the paragraph mark at the end of the line is also selected. See Figure 2-7.

Selected text to drag and drop ◆ **Figure 2-7**

to·your·chosen·styles.·For·most·people,·decorating·a·home·involves·a·series·of·purchases·and· improvements·over·time.·To·maximize·your·design·statement,·consider·making·your·purchases·in·the· following·order:¶

pointer in selection bar

Large·items·such·as·sofas,·beds,·and·dining·tables¶ ← **selected text to be moved**

Lamps·or·other·forms·of·lighting¶

End·tables·and·other·accent·pieces¶ **new location for selected text**

Rugs·or·other·floor·coverings¶

While·you·are·saving·money·to·complete·the·look·of·a·particular·room,·purchase·smaller·items·(vases,· mirrors,·or·picture·frames)·that·can·accentuate·a·room's·style·without·breaking·your·budget.·¶

These·are·just·some·ideas·to·help·you·get·started.·To·learn·more·about·decorating·your·home,·consider· scheduling·a·consultation·with·Natalie·Lanci,·or·one·of·our·other·fine·designers·at·PFI.¶

you should have replaced Natalie's name with yours

4. Position the pointer over the selected text. The pointer changes from a right-facing arrow ⤢ to a left-facing arrow ⤡.

5. Press and hold down the mouse button until the drag-and-drop pointer ⤡ appears. Note that a dotted insertion point appears within the selected text. (You may have to move the mouse pointer slightly left or right to see the drag-and-drop pointer or the dotted insertion point.)

6. Without releasing the mouse button, drag the selected text down until the dotted insertion point is positioned to the left of the first paragraph below the list (to the left of the "W" in "While you are saving..."). Make sure you use the dotted insertion point, rather than the mouse pointer, to guide the text to its new location. The dotted insertion point indicates exactly where the text will appear when you release the mouse button. See Figure 2-8.

Figure 2-8 **Moving text with drag-and-drop pointer**

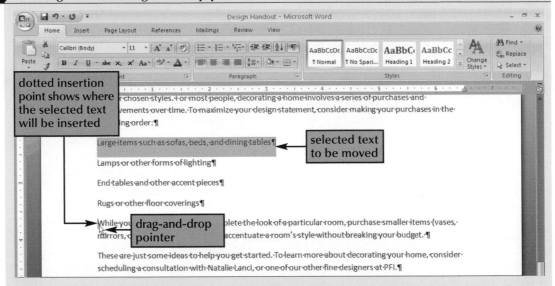

7. Release the mouse button. The selected text moves to its new location at the end of the list, as shown in Figure 2-9. Near the newly inserted text you might see the Paste Options button, which gives you access to more advanced options related to pasting text. You don't need to use the Paste Options button right now, so you can ignore it. It will disappear when you start performing another task.

Figure 2-9 **Text in new location**

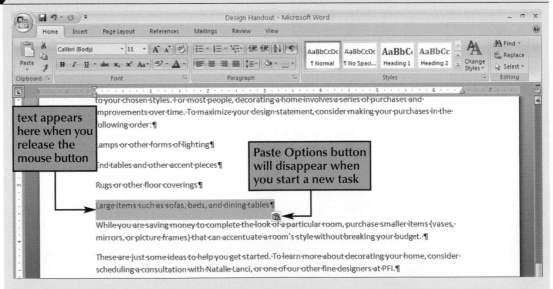

Trouble? If the selected text moves to the wrong location, click the Undo button on the Quick Access Toolbar, and then repeat Steps 2 through 7. Remember to hold down the mouse button until the dotted insertion point appears to the left of the paragraph just below the list.

8. Deselect the highlighted text by clicking anywhere in the document, and then save the document.

Dragging and dropping works well if you're moving text a short distance in a document. For moving text longer distances, another method, called cut and paste, works better. You can also use cut and paste to move text short distances, if you find that you prefer it over drag and drop.

Cutting or Copying and Pasting Text

The key to cutting and pasting is the **Clipboard**, a temporary storage area on your computer that holds text or graphics until you need them. To **cut** means to remove something from a document and place it on the Clipboard. Once you've cut something, you can paste it somewhere else. To **paste** means to place a copy of whatever is on the Clipboard into the document; it gets pasted at the insertion point.

To **cut and paste**, you select the text you want to cut (or remove) from the document, click the Cut button, and then use the Paste button to paste (or insert) it into the document in a new location. If you don't want to remove the text from its original location, you can copy it (rather than cutting it), and then paste the copy in a new location. To **copy** means to copy text (or other material, such as pictures) to the Clipboard, leaving the material in its original location.

Note that when you paste an item from the Clipboard into a document, the item also remains on the Clipboard so you can paste it again somewhere else if you want.

Cutting (or Copying) and Pasting Text | Reference Window

- Select the text or graphics you want to cut or copy.
- To remove the text or graphics, click the Cut button in the Clipboard group on the Home tab, or to copy, click the Copy button in the Clipboard group on the Home tab.
- Move the insertion point to the target location in the document.
- Click the Paste button in the Clipboard group on the Home tab.

If you need to keep track of multiple pieces of cut or copied text, it's helpful to open the **Clipboard task pane**, a special part of the Word window that displays the contents of the Clipboard. You open the Clipboard task pane by clicking the Clipboard button on the Home tab. When the Clipboard task pane is not displayed, the Clipboard can hold only one item at a time. (Each newly copied item replaces the current contents of the Clipboard.) However, when the Clipboard task pane is displayed, the Clipboard can store up to 24 items. The last item cut or copied to the Clipboard is the first item listed in the Clipboard task pane.

As indicated in Figure 2-3, Natalie suggested moving the word "recently" (in the paragraph under the heading "Ask Yourself Some Questions") to a new location. You'll use cut and paste to move this word.

To move text using cut and paste:

▶ **1.** Scroll up until you can see the paragraph below the heading "Ask Yourself Some Questions" on page 1.

▶ **2.** Double-click the word **recently**. As you can see in Figure 2-10, you need to move this word to after the phrase "places you've been."

Figure 2-10 ▶ **Text to move using cut and paste**

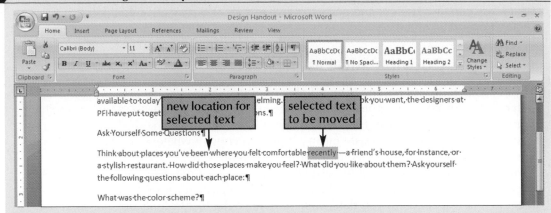

3. In the Clipboard group on the Home tab, click the **Cut** button [cut icon]. The selected text is removed from the document.

Trouble? If the Clipboard task pane opens, your computer is set up to have it open by default when you click the Cut or Copy buttons. Click its Close button for now. You'll have a chance to use the Clipboard task pane shortly.

Trouble? If you don't see the Cut button in the Clipboard group, you may have forgotten to switch back to the Home tab earlier. Click the Home tab on the Ribbon and repeat Step 3.

4. In the same line, click to the left of the "w" in "where." The insertion point is now located between the "w" and the blank space after the word "been."

5. In the Clipboard group, click the **Paste** button. The word "recently" appears in its new location. Note that Word also included a space after the word "recently," so that the sentence reads "...places you've been recently where you felt...." See Figure 2-11.

Trouble? If a menu opens below the Paste button, you clicked the Paste button arrow instead of the Paste button. Press the Esc key to close the menu, and then begin again with Step 5, taking care not to click the arrow below the Paste button.

Figure 2-11 ▶ **The word "recently" pasted in new location**

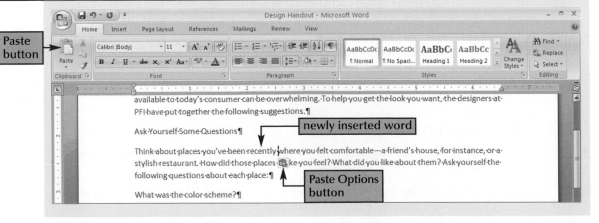

Natalie mentions that she'll be using two paragraphs from the Design Handout document as the basis for a new handout entitled "Formal Designs." She asks you to copy that information and paste it in a new document. You can do this using copy and paste. In the process, you'll have a chance to use the Clipboard task pane.

To copy and paste text into a new document:

▶ **1.** In the Clipboard group, click the **Dialog Box Launcher**. The Clipboard task pane opens on the left side of the document window. It contains the word "recently," which you copied to the Clipboard in the last set of steps. The document zooms out so that you can still see the full width of the page, even though the Clipboard task pane is open. See Figure 2-12. To minimize the clutter on the Clipboard, you will delete its current contents in the next step.

Clipboard task pane | Figure 2-12

▶ **2.** Click the **Clear All** button near the top of the task pane. The current contents of the Clipboard are deleted, and you see the following message on the Clipboard task pane: "Clipboard empty. Copy or cut to collect items."

▶ **3.** Move the mouse pointer to the selection bar and double-click in the margin next to the paragraph that begins "If you are intimidated by the prospect...." The entire paragraph is selected.

▶ **4.** In the Clipboard group, click the **Copy** button 🔲. The first part of the paragraph appears in the Clipboard task pane, but a copy of all the text you selected—the whole paragraph—is now stored on the Clipboard.

▶ **5.** If necessary, scroll down until you can see the paragraph below the list of questions, which begins "For the next few weeks, continue...."

▶ **6.** Select the paragraph that begins "For the next few weeks, continue...."

▶ **7.** Click the **Copy** button. The first part of the paragraph appears in the Clipboard task pane, as shown in Figure 2-13.

Tip

To have the Clipboard task pane open each time you cut or copy an item, click Options at the bottom of the Clipboard task pane, and then select Show Office Clipboard Automatically.

Figure 2-13 **Items in the Clipboard task pane**

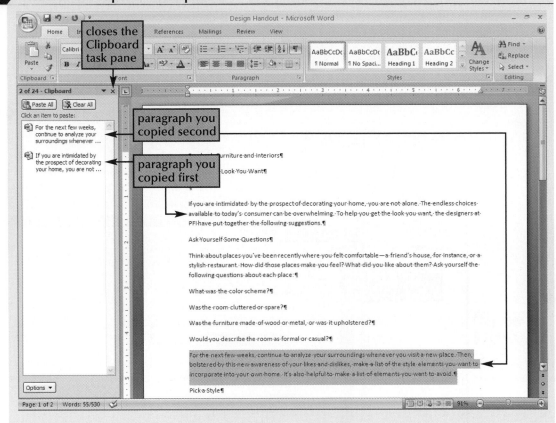

Now you can use the Clipboard task pane to insert the copied text into a new document. You'll start by opening a new, blank document.

To insert the copied text into the new document:

▶ 1. Click the **Office Button**, click **New**, verify that **Blank document** is selected, and then click the **Create** button. A new, blank document opens.

▶ 2. If the Clipboard task pane is not open, click the **Dialog Box Launcher** in the Clipboard group to open it.

▶ 3. In the Clipboard task pane, click the item that begins "**For the next few weeks**...." The text is inserted in the document.

▶ 4. Click the item that begins "**If you are intimidated by**...." The text is inserted as the second paragraph in the document.

▶ 5. Save the document as **Formal Designs** in the Tutorial.02\Tutorial folder.

▶ 6. Close the Formal Designs document. Natalie will be using this document later. You return to the Design Handout document, where the Clipboard task pane is still open. You are finished using the Clipboard task pane. In the next step you will clear the Clipboard so that you can start with an empty Clipboard when you begin work on the Review Assignments and Case Problems at the end of this tutorial.

7. Click the **Clear All** button on the Clipboard task pane. The copied items are removed from the Clipboard.

8. Click the **Close** button ⊠ on the Clipboard task pane. The Clipboard task pane closes.

9. Click anywhere in the document to deselect the highlighted paragraph, and then save the document.

Tip

The Clipboard can hold a total of 24 items. Unless you clear the Clipboard, the items you copy to it will remain there until you close Word.

Finding and Replacing Text

When you're working with a longer document, the quickest and easiest way to locate a particular character, word, or phrase is to use the **Find and Replace dialog box**. This dialog box contains three tabs:

• Find, for finding a word or phrase in a document (for example, you need to know where you referred to "textiles" in a document on interior design)

• Replace, for finding a word or phrase in a document and replacing it with something else (for example, you want to replace "formal design" with "formal style" throughout a document)

• Go To, for moving the cursor directly to a specific part of a document (for example, you want to go directly to page 29)

To open the Find and Replace dialog box, click the Find button or the Replace button (in the Editing group on the Home tab), depending on what you want to do. For example, to find a word or phrase, click the Find button, type the text you want to find in the Find what text box, and then click the Find Next button. The text you type in the Find what text box is known as the **search text**. After you click the Find Next button, Word finds and highlights the first instance of the search text. You continue clicking Find Next to find more occurrences of the search text in your document.

To replace text with something else, click the Replace button, and then type your search text in the Find what text box and the text you want to substitute in the Replace with text box. As with the Find feature, you click the Find Next button to find the next occurrence of the search text; Word stops and highlights each occurrence, allowing you to determine whether or not to substitute the replacement text. If you want to substitute the highlighted occurrence, click the Replace button. If you want to substitute every occurrence of the search text with the replacement text, without locating and reviewing each occurrence, you can click the Replace All button.

Finding and Replacing the Right Words | InSight

When using the Replace All button with single words, keep in mind that the search text might be found within other words. To prevent Word from making incorrect substitutions in such cases, it's a good idea to select the Find whole words only check box. (If you don't see this check box, click the More button to display additional options.) For example, suppose you want to replace the word "figure" with "illustration." Unless you select the Find whole words only check box, Word replaces "figure" in "configure" with "illustration" so the word becomes "conillustration."

Finding and Replacing Text

- Click either the Find button or the Replace button on the Home tab.
- Click the More button to expand the dialog box to display additional options, including the Find whole words only option. If you see the Less button, the additional options are already displayed.
- In the Search list box, select Down if you want to search from the insertion point to the end of the document, select Up if you want to search from the insertion point to the beginning of the document, or select All to search the entire document.
- Type the characters you want to find in the Find what text box.
- If you are replacing text, type the replacement text in the Replace with text box.
- Click the Find whole words only check box to search for complete words.
- Click the Match case check box to insert the replacement text with the same case (upper or lower) as in the Replace with text box. For example, if the Replace with text box contained the words "Pemberly Interiors," this would ensure that Word inserted the text with a capital (uppercase) "P" and a capital (uppercase) "I."
- Click the Find Next button.
- Click the Replace button to substitute the found text with the replacement text and find the next occurrence.
- Click the Replace All button to substitute all occurrences of the found text with the replacement text, without reviewing each occurence.

Throughout the document, Natalie wants to replace the initials "PFI" with the full company name, "Pemberly Furniture and Interiors." You'll use the Replace feature to make this change quickly and easily.

To replace "PFI" with "Pemberly Furniture and Interiors":

▶ **1.** Press the **Ctrl+Home** keys to move the insertion point to the beginning of the document.

▶ **2.** In the Editing group on the Home tab, click the **Replace** button. The Find and Replace dialog box opens, with the Replace tab displayed.

▶ **3.** If you see a **More** button in the lower-left corner of the dialog box, click it to display the additional search options. (If you see a Less button, the additional options are already displayed.) Verify that **All** is selected in the Search list box, so Word will search the entire document.

▶ **4.** Click the **Find what** text box if necessary, type **PFI**, press the **Tab** key, and then, in the Replace with text box, type **Pemberly Furniture and Interiors**.

   Trouble? If you already see the text "PFI" and "Pemberly Furniture and Interiors" in your Find and Replace dialog box, someone has recently performed these steps on your computer without closing Word afterward. Skip Step 4 and continue with Step 5.

▶ **5.** Click the **Match case** check box to insert a check. This ensures that Word will search only for "PFI" and not "pfi" in the document.

▶ **6.** Click the **Find whole words only** check box to insert a check. Your Find and Replace dialog box should look like Figure 2-14.

Find and Replace dialog box | Figure 2-14

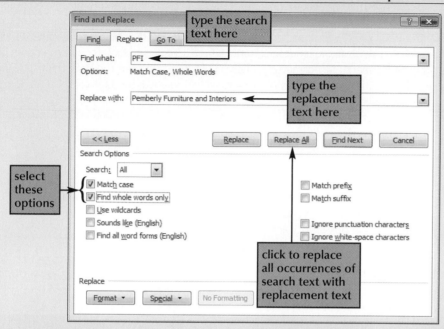

7. Click the **Replace All** button to replace all occurrences of the search text with the replacement text. When Word finishes making the replacements, you see a message box telling you that two replacements were made.

8. Click the **OK** button to close the message box, and then click the **Close** button in the Find and Replace dialog box to return to the document. The full company name has been inserted near the beginning of the document, as shown in Figure 2-15. If you scroll down to the end of the document, you'll see that it was also inserted in the last sentence.

Document with "Pemberly Furniture and Interiors" inserted | Figure 2-15

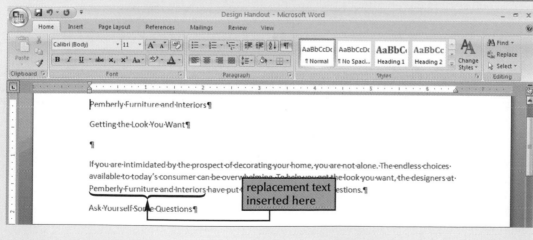

9. Save the document.

InSight | **Searching for Formatting**

You can search for formatting, such as bold or italics, using the Find and Replace dialog box in the same way that you can find text. For example, you might want to check a document to see where you used bold. Or you might need to find where you used a certain font, font size, or style. This is especially useful in long documents where scrolling to look for something would take a long time. To search for formatting, click the Format button at the bottom of the Find and Replace dialog box, click the category of formatting that you want to look for (such as Font, Paragraph, Style, and so on), and then select the formatting you want to find. You can also use the Replace tab to replace formatting in the same way you use it to replace text. To replace formatting, click the Replace tab, and then repeat the previous steps to specify the formatting that should replace the other formatting. Whether you are replacing formatting or not, note that you can look for formatting that occurs only on specific text, or you can look for formatting that occurs anywhere in a document. If you're looking for formatting on certain text (such as all instances of "Contemporary Furniture" that are bold), enter the text in the Find what text box and then specify the formatting you're looking for. To find formatting on any text in a document, leave the Find what text box empty and then specify the formatting.

You have completed the content changes Natalie requested. In the next session, you will make changes that affect the document's appearance.

Review | **Session 2.1 Quick Check**

1. True or False: You should move the insertion point to the beginning of the document before starting the Spelling and Grammar checker.
2. True or False: You need to select text before you can move it.
3. Explain how to drag and drop text.
4. Explain how to cut and paste text.
5. Suppose you want to find a word in a document. How do you open the Find and Replace dialog box?
6. How can you ensure that Word will insert "ZIP code" instead of "zip code" when you use the Find and Replace dialog box?

Session 2.2

Changing Margins

When you **format** a document, you make changes that affect the way the document looks. You'll start formatting Natalie's handout by adjusting the document's margins. By default, the margins for a Word document are one inch on the top, bottom, and sides.

When adjusting a document's margins, you'll find that the rulers are essential. They show you the current margin settings, as well as the amount that individual paragraphs are indented from the margin. On the horizontal ruler, the right edge of the left margin serves as the zero point, with the numbers to the right measuring the distance to the right edge of the page, and the numbers on the left measuring the distance to the left edge of the page. This allows you to see the exact width of the left margin at a glance. See Figure 2-16. The measurements on the vertical ruler work similarly, with the bottom edge of the top margin serving as the zero point from which all other vertical distances are measured.

Using the horizontal ruler to view margins | Figure 2-16

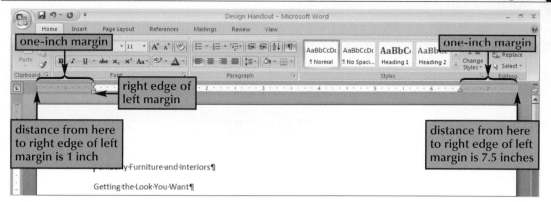

Tip

The Zoom setting affects how much of the margin you can see on the screen. If you zoom in to make the text larger and easier to read, you see less of the margin. If you zoom out, you see more of the margin.

As you'll see in the upcoming steps, you can change the page margins in the Page Setup dialog box. You can also quickly adjust a document's margins in Print Layout view by clicking an option in the Margins menu. You'll have a chance to practice these techniques in the Case Problems at the end of this tutorial.

Changing Margins for a Document | Reference Window

- Make sure no text is selected, and then, in the Page Setup group on the Page Layout tab, click the Dialog Box Launcher. If necessary, click the Margins tab to display the margin settings.
- Use the arrows to change the settings in the Top, Bottom, Left, or Right text boxes, or type a new margin value in each text box.
- Make sure the Apply to list box displays Whole document.
- Click the OK button.
- To choose from groups of predefined margin settings, click the Margins button in the Page Setup group on the Page Layout tab. In the Margins menu, click the group of margin settings that is appropriate for your document.

You need to change the top and left margins of the Design Handout document to 1.5 inches, per Natalie's note in Figure 2-3. The left margin needs to be wider than the right to allow space for holes so that the document can be inserted in a three-ring binder. Also, the top margin needs to be wider than the bottom margin so the document can be printed on the company letterhead. In the next set of steps, you'll change the margins using the Page Setup dialog box.

To change the margins in the Design Handout document:

1. Click anywhere in the document to make sure no text is selected.

2. Click the **Page Layout** tab on the Ribbon, and then, in the Page Setup group, click the **Margins** button. The Margins menu appears, displaying some common margin settings. The Normal option contains the default margin settings. You can always click Normal to return a document to the default margin settings. The item at the top of the menu, Last Custom Setting, reflects the last margin settings selected in the Page Setup dialog box. See Figure 2-17.

Figure 2-17 | Margins menu

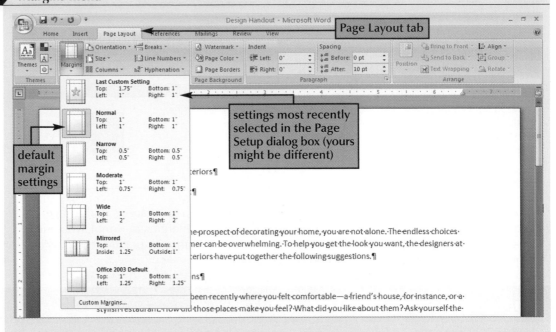

It's possible that the Last Custom Setting option matches the margin settings you want to use in the Design Handout document, but if so, ignore it. Instead, you'll open the Page Setup dialog box in the next step, so you can practice using it. You can open the Page Setup dialog box via the Custom Margins option at the bottom of the Margins menu, or you can use the Dialog Box Launcher in the Page Setup group on the Page Layout tab. You'll try the Custom Margins option now.

3. At the bottom of the Margins menu, click **Custom Margins**. The Page Setup dialog box opens.

4. Click the **Margins** tab, if it is not already selected, to display the margin settings. The Top margin setting is selected. See Figure 2-18. As you complete the following steps, keep an eye on the Preview in the bottom-left part of the dialog box, which changes to reflect changes you make to the margins.

Page Setup dialog box | Figure 2-18

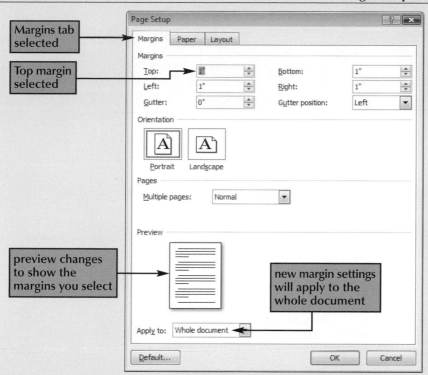

Margins tab selected

Top margin selected

preview changes to show the margins you select

new margin settings will apply to the whole document

▶ **5.** Type **1.5** to change the Top margin setting. (You do not have to type the inches symbol.)

▶ **6.** Press the **Tab** key twice to select the Left text box and highlight the current margin setting. The text area in the Preview box moves down to reflect the larger top margin.

▶ **7.** Verify that the insertion point is in the Left text box, type **1.5**, and then press the **Tab** key. The left margin in the Preview box increases.

▶ **8.** In the Apply to list box, make sure **Whole document** is selected, and then click the **OK** button to return to your document. Notice that the ruler has changed to reflect the new margin settings and the resulting reduced page area. The document text is now 6 inches wide. See Figure 2-19.

Figure 2-19 ▶ **Rulers after setting top and left margins to 1.5 inches**

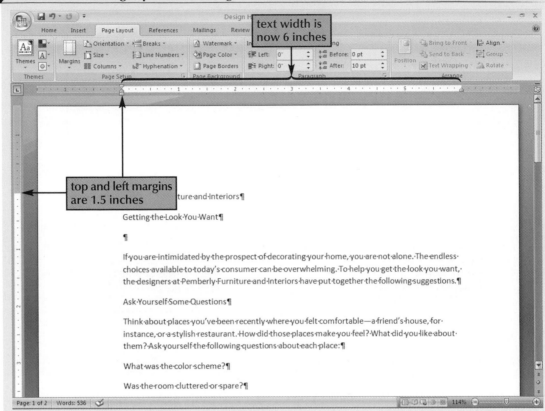

Trouble? If a double-dotted line and the words "Section Break" appear in your document, Whole document wasn't selected in the Apply to list box. If this occurs, click the Undo button 🄴 on the Quick Access Toolbar and repeat Steps 1 through 8, making sure you select the Whole document option in the Apply to list box.

▶ **9.** Save the document and then click the **Home** tab.

InSight | **Using Margins to Insert Space**

Recall that in Tutorial 1 you inserted a series of blank paragraphs at the beginning of a document in order to allow room for the company letterhead. Now that you know how to change margins, you should use this method to insert extra space in a document rather than inserting blank paragraphs. Adjusting margins allows you to be more precise, because you can specify an exact amount. Also, if you know you will usually need to use a particular margin setting for your documents, you can click the Default button on the Margins tab of the Page Setup dialog box to make your settings the default for all new documents.

In the next section, you will make some changes that will affect the way certain paragraphs are positioned between the left and right margins.

Aligning Text

The term **alignment** refers to the way a paragraph lines up horizontally between the margins. By default, text is aligned along the left margin and is **ragged**, or uneven, along the right margin. This is called **left alignment**. With **right alignment**, the text is aligned along the right margin and is ragged along the left margin. With **center alignment**, text is centered between the left and right margins and is ragged along both the left and right margins. With **justified alignment**, full lines of text are spaced between both the left and the right margins, and the text is not ragged. Text in newspaper columns is often justified. See Figure 2-20.

Varieties of text alignment   **Figure 2-20**

left alignment If you are intimidated by the prospect of decorating your home, you are not alone. The endless choices available to today's consumer can be overwhelming. To help you get the look you want, the designers at Pemberly Furniture and Interiors have put together the following suggestions.	**right alignment** If you are intimidated by the prospect of decorating your home, you are not alone. The endless choices available to today's consumer can be overwhelming. To help you get the look you want, the designers at Pemberly Furniture and Interiors have put together the following suggestions.
center alignment If you are intimidated by the prospect of decorating your home, you are not alone. The endless choices available to today's consumer can be overwhelming.	**justified alignment** If you are intimidated by the prospect of decorating your home, you are not alone. The endless choices available to today's consumer can be overwhelming. To help you get the look you want, the designers at Pemberly Furniture and Interiors have put together the following suggestions.

The Paragraph group on the Home tab includes a button for each of the four major types of alignment. The Mini toolbar, which appears when you select text in a document, includes just the Center button, which is commonly used to center titles in a document.

To align a single paragraph, click anywhere in that paragraph and then click the appropriate alignment button. To align multiple paragraphs, select the paragraphs first, and then click an alignment button.

Figure 2-3 indicates that the title and subtitle of the Design Handout should be centered and that the main paragraphs should be justified. First, you'll center the title and subtitle using the Center button on the Mini toolbar.

To center-align the title:

▶ **1.** Click and drag in the selection bar to select the title ("Pemberly Furniture and Interiors") and the subtitle ("Getting the Look You Want"). A faint image of the Mini toolbar appears near the selected text. To fully display the Mini toolbar, you need to move the mouse pointer over it.

   2. Move the mouse pointer near the Mini toolbar. The Mini toolbar is now fully visible and remains visible until you move the mouse pointer away from it. It contains one alignment button, the Center button. The Align Text Left button on the Home tab is highlighted in orange, indicating that the selected text is currently left-aligned. See Figure 2-21.

Figure 2-21   **Mini toolbar visible over selected text**

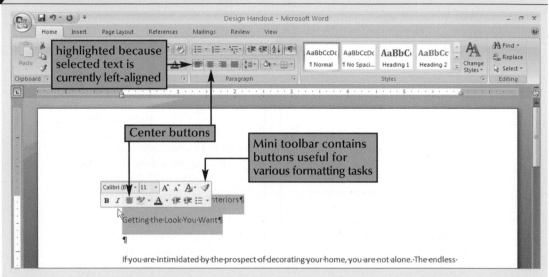

   3. On the Mini toolbar, click the **Center** button ≣. The text is centered between the left and right margins. Both Center buttons are now highlighted in orange, indicating that the selected text is centered. The Mini toolbar remains visible until you move the mouse pointer away from it.

      Trouble? If the Mini toolbar disappears before you click the Center button, click anywhere in the document to deselect the text, and then repeat Steps 1 through 3.

Next, you'll justify the text in the first two main paragraphs.

To justify the first two main paragraphs:

   1. Click anywhere in the paragraph that begins "If you are intimidated by...." If the Mini toolbar was still visible, it disappears and the insertion point is now located in the paragraph you want to align. The Align Text Left button in the Paragraph group is highlighted in orange, indicating that the paragraph containing the insertion point is left-aligned.

   2. In the Paragraph group, click the **Justify** button ≣. The paragraph text spreads out so that it lines up evenly along the left and right margins.

   3. Scroll down if necessary and click in the paragraph that begins "Think about places you've been recently.... "

   4. Click the **Justify** button ≣ in the Paragraph group again. The text is evenly spaced between the left and right margins. See Figure 2-22.

Justified paragraphs ◄ **Figure 2-22**

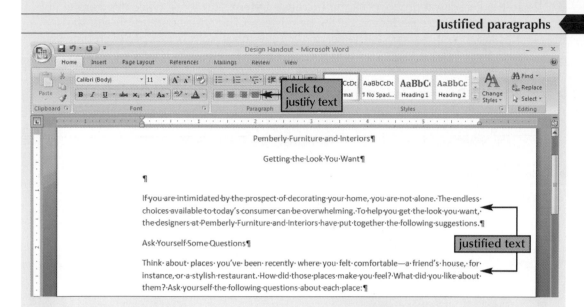

You'll justify the other paragraphs later. But first, you turn your attention to indenting a paragraph.

Indenting a Paragraph

When you **indent** a paragraph, you move the entire paragraph to the right. You can use the indent buttons on the Home tab to increase or decrease paragraph indenting in increments of 0.5 inches. The **indent markers** on the horizontal ruler allow you to see at a glance a paragraph's current indent settings. See Figure 2-23.

Indent markers on horizontal ruler ◄ **Figure 2-23**

By dragging the indent markers individually, you can create specialized indents, such as a **hanging indent** (where all lines except the first line of the paragraph are indented from the left margin) or a **right indent** (where all lines of the paragraph are indented from the right margin). You'll have a chance to try some of these specialized indents in the Case Problems at the end of this tutorial. In this document, though, you only need to indent the main paragraphs 0.5 inches. When you do a simple indent like this, the three indent markers, shown stacked on top of one another in Figure 2-23, move as a unit along with the paragraphs you are indenting.

To indent a paragraph using the Increase Indent button:

► **1.** Verify that the insertion point is still located within the paragraph that begins "Think about places you've been...."

2. In the Paragraph group, click the **Increase Indent** button ▤ twice. (Be careful not to click the Decrease Indent button by mistake.) The entire paragraph and the stacked indent markers in the horizontal ruler move right 0.5 inches each time you click the Increase Indent button. The paragraph is indented 1 inch, which is 0.5 inches more than Natalie wants.

3. Click the **Decrease Indent** button ▤ in the Paragraph group to move the paragraph left 0.5 inches. The paragraph is now indented 0.5 inches from the left margin. Don't be concerned about the list of questions. You will indent this list later, when you format it as a bulleted list. See Figure 2-24.

Figure 2-24 **Indented paragraph**

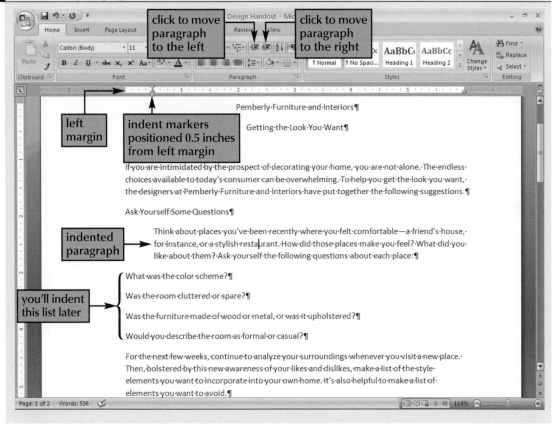

You could continue to indent and then justify each paragraph. However, it's faster to use the Format Painter button. With the Format Painter, you can easily copy both the indentation and alignment changes to the remaining paragraphs in the document.

Using the Format Painter

The **Format Painter** makes it easy to copy all the formatting features of one paragraph to other paragraphs (or from one heading to other headings, or from one word to other words). You can use this button to copy formatting to just one item or to multiple items.

Using the Format Painter

- Select the text whose formatting you want to copy. If you are trying to copy the formatting of an entire paragraph, you can just click anywhere in the paragraph.
- To copy formatting to one item, click the Format Painter button in the Clipboard group on the Home tab, and then select the text you want to format, or click anywhere in the paragraph you want to format.
- To copy formatting to multiple items, double-click the Format Painter button in the Clipboard group on the Home tab, and then select, one by one, each text item you want to format, or click anywhere in each paragraph you want to format. When you are finished, click the Format Painter button again to deselect it.

You'll use the Format Painter now to copy the formatting of the second paragraph to the other main paragraphs. The first step is to move the insertion point to the paragraph whose formatting you want to copy.

To copy paragraph formatting with the Format Painter:

▶ **1.** Verify that the insertion point is located in the paragraph that begins "Think about places you've been...."

▶ **2.** In the Clipboard group, double-click the **Format Painter** button ![icon]. When you double-click the Format Painter button, it stays selected until you click it again; you can paste the copied formatting as many times as you wish. Also, notice that when you move the pointer over text, the pointer changes to ![icon] to indicate that the format of the paragraph containing the insertion point can be "painted" (or copied) onto another paragraph.

▶ **3.** Scroll down, and then click anywhere in the paragraph that begins "For the next few weeks...." The format of this paragraph changes to match the format of the indented and justified paragraph above it. See Figure 2-25. Two paragraphs are now indented and justified. The Format Painter pointer is still visible, indicating that you can continue formatting paragraphs with it.

Formatting copied with Format Painter ◀ **Figure 2-25**

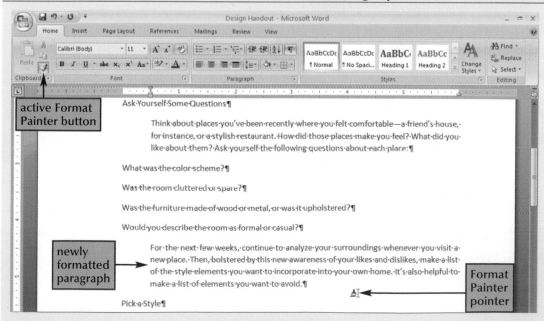

Now you need to continue copying the indented and justified formatting to the main paragraphs of text. You do not want to copy this formatting to the document headings or to the several lists. (You'll format these elements later in this tutorial.)

▶ **4.** Scroll down and click in the paragraph below the "Pick a Style" subheading, which begins "Now that you know what you like...." Also, click the paragraphs that begin "People who enjoy spending time..." and "Of course you probably won't be able...." Finally, click the paragraph that begins "While you are saving money...." Do not click the document title or subtitle, the lists, or the last paragraph of text.

Trouble? If you click a paragraph and the formatting doesn't change to match the indented and justified paragraphs, you single-clicked the Format Painter button rather than double-clicked it. Move the insertion point to a paragraph that has the desired format, double-click the Format Painter button, and then repeat Step 4.

Trouble? If you accidentally click a heading or one line of a list, click the Undo button on the Quick Access Toolbar to return the line to its original formatting. Then select a paragraph that has the desired format, double-click the Format Painter button, and repeat Step 4 to finish copying the format to the desired paragraphs.

▶ **5.** After you are finished formatting paragraphs with the Format Painter pointer, click the **Format Painter** button ⟨image⟩ to turn off the feature.

▶ **6.** Save the document.

You've saved considerable time using the Format Painter to format all the main paragraphs in your document with the correct indentation and alignment. Your next job is to make the lists easier to read by adding bullets and numbers.

Adding Bullets and Numbers

You can emphasize a list of items by adding a heavy dot, or **bullet**, before each item in the list. Bulleted lists are usually much easier to read and follow than lists that do not have bullets. For a list of items that have a particular order (such as steps in a procedure), you can use numbers instead of bullets. Natalie's printout requests that you add bullets to the list of questions on page 1 to make them stand out. She also wants you to add bullets to the list of four basic styles on page 1.

To apply bullets to a list of questions:

▶ **1.** Scroll up until you see the list of questions on page 1, which begins "What was the color scheme?"

▶ **2.** Select the four questions in the list.

▶ **3.** In the Paragraph group, click the **Bullets** button ⟨image⟩. Black circles called bullets appear before each item in the list. Also, the list is indented and the paragraph spacing between the items is reduced. After reviewing the default, circular bullet style in the document, Natalie decides she would prefer square bullets.

Trouble? If no bullets are applied and a menu opens instead, you clicked the Bullets button arrow instead of the Bullets button. Press the Esc key to close the menu, and then repeat Step 3, taking care to click the Bullets button.

▶ **4.** In the Paragraph group, click the **Bullets button arrow** ⟨image⟩ (make sure to click the arrow, not just the button). A gallery of bullet styles opens.

At the top of the gallery of bullet styles is the Recently Used Bullets section; these are the bullet styles that have been used since you started Word. You'll probably see just the round black bullets, which were applied by default when you clicked the Bullets button. However, if you had used several different bullet styles, you would see them here. Below the Recently Used Bullets section is the **Bullet Library**, which offers a variety of bullet styles. For the Design Handout, you want to use a black square, which is an option in the Bullet Library. See Figure 2-26.

Bullets gallery ◀ Figure 2-26

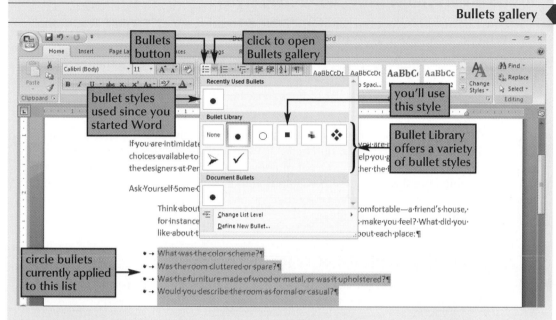

5. Move the mouse pointer over the options in the Bullet Library and observe a live preview of the bullet styles in the document. The blue highlight disappears from the selected list in the document so you can clearly see the live preview.

6. Click the **black square** in the Bullet Library. The round bullets are replaced with square bullets.

7. To align the bullets with the first paragraph, make sure the list is still selected, and then, in the Paragraph group, click the **Increase Indent** button. The bulleted list moves to the right. Figure 2-27 shows the indented bulleted list.

Indented bulleted list ◀ Figure 2-27

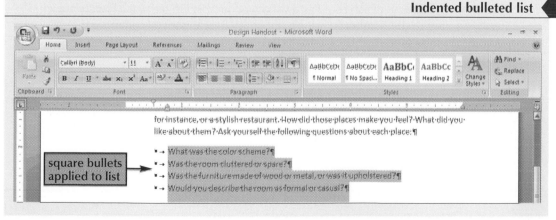

Next, you need to format the list of decorating styles on page 1 with square bullets. When you first start Word, the Bullets button applies the round bullets you saw earlier. But after you select a new bullet style, the Bullets button applies that last bullet style you used. So, to add square bullets to the decorating styles list, you just have to select the list and click the Bullets button.

To add bullets to the list of decorating styles:

▶ **1.** Scroll down and select the list of four basic decorating styles (**Formal**, **Traditional**, **Eclectic**, **Contemporary**) at the bottom of page 1.

▶ **2.** In the Paragraph group, click the **Bullets** button [icon], and then click the **Increase Indent** button [icon]. The list is now formatted with square black bullets. The list is also indented, similar to the list of questions shown earlier in Figure 2-27.

Your next step is to format the list of suggested purchases on page 2. Natalie wants you to format this information as a numbered list because it specifies purchases in a sequential order. Adding numbers to a list of items is a quick task thanks to the Numbering button, which numbers selected paragraphs with consecutive numbers. If you insert a new paragraph, delete a paragraph, or reorder the paragraphs, Word adjusts the numbers to make sure they remain consecutive.

To apply numbers to the list of suggested purchases:

▶ **1.** Scroll down and select the list that begins with **Lamps or other forms of lighting** and ends with **Large items such as sofas, beds, and dining tables**.

▶ **2.** In the Paragraph group, click the **Numbering** button [icon]. Consecutive numbers appear in front of each item in the list, with a period after each number. As you'll see in the next step, you can choose from more options by clicking the Numbering button arrow instead.

Trouble? If you see a gallery of numbering options, you clicked the Numbering button arrow instead of the Numbering button. Press the Esc key to close the gallery, and then click the Numbering button.

▶ **3.** Make sure the list is still selected in the document, and then click the **Numbering button arrow** [icon]. A gallery of numbering formats opens. Recently used numbering formats appear at the top of the list. Below the recently used formats you see the **Numbering Library**, which contains a variety of numbering formats. The style currently applied to the numbered list is highlighted in orange. You can move the mouse pointer over the options in the Numbering Library to see a live preview of the other formats in the document. See Figure 2-28.

Numbering Gallery | **Figure** 2-28

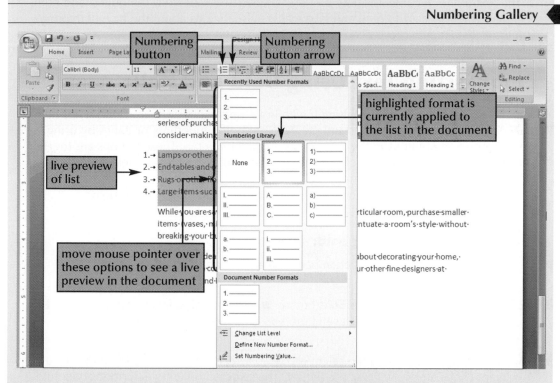

4. Move the mouse pointer over the options in the Numbering Library to display the live preview in the document. The blue highlight disappears from the selected list in the document so you can clearly see the live preview.

5. In the first row of the Numbering Library, click the far-right option, which shows numbers with a parenthesis after each number. The Numbering Gallery closes and each number is now followed by a parenthesis.

6. Make sure the list is still selected, and then in the Paragraph group, click the **Increase Indent** button. The list moves to the right so that the numbers align with the paragraph of text above it.

7. Click anywhere in the document to deselect the text. Figure 2-29 shows the indented and numbered list.

Indented numbered list | **Figure** 2-29

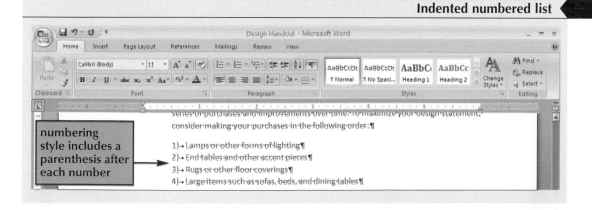

The text of the document is now properly aligned and indented. The bullets and numbers make the lists easy to read and give readers visual clues about the type of information they contain. Next, you need to adjust the formatting of individual words.

Emphasizing Text Using Bold and Italic

You can emphasize text by formatting it with bold, underline, or italic. These styles help make specific words or phrases stand out. You add bold, underline, or italics by using the corresponding buttons in the Font group on the Home tab. These buttons are **toggle buttons**, which means you can click them once to format the selected text, and click again to remove the formatting from the selected text.

Natalie wants to draw attention to the headings by formatting them in bold.

To format the headings in bold:

1. On page 1, click in the selection bar to select the heading **Ask Yourself Some Questions**.

2. In the Font group, click the **Bold** button **B**. The heading is formatted in bold. In the next step, you'll learn a useful method for repeating the task you just performed.

3. Scroll down and click in the selection bar to select the next heading in the document ("Pick a Style"). Press the **F4** key. The selected heading is formatted in bold. The F4 key repeats your most recent action. It is especially helpful when formatting parts of a document.

4. Select the last heading, **Stay True to Your Style** (at the bottom of page 1), and then press the **F4** key.

5. Click anywhere in the document to deselect the text, and then scroll up to return to the beginning of the document. The three headings appear in bold. Two of them are shown in Figure 2-30.

Figure 2-30 ▶ **Formatting headings with bold**

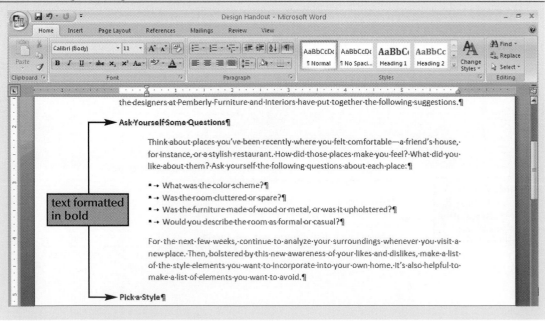

Now that it is formatted in bold, it's easy to see that the last heading, "Stay True to Your Style," is stranded at the bottom of page 1. The handout would look better if the heading was at the top of page 2, just above the first paragraph of the "Stay True to Your Style" section. To fix this problem, you need to tell Word to keep one paragraph (the heading paragraph) on the same page as the next paragraph.

To keep one paragraph with another:

1. Scroll down and click anywhere in the heading **Stay True to Your Style**.

2. In the Paragraph group, click the **Dialog Box Launcher**, and then, in the Paragraph dialog box, click the **Line and Page Breaks** tab.

3. Click the **Keep with next** check box to insert a check mark, and then click the **OK** button. The Paragraph dialog box closes, and the "Stay True to Your Style" heading moves to the top of page 2.

The Underline and Italic buttons on the Home tab work in the same way as the Bold button. You'll try formatting the title and subtitle in italics now, to see how they look.

To format the title and subtitle in italics:

1. On page 1, select the title **Pemberly Furniture and Interiors** and the subtitle **Getting the Look You Want**.

2. In the Font group, click the **Italic** button I. The title and subtitle are italicized, meaning they lean slightly to the right. The Italic button is selected, indicating that the selected text is italicized. See Figure 2-31.

Formatting headings with italics   **Figure 2-31**

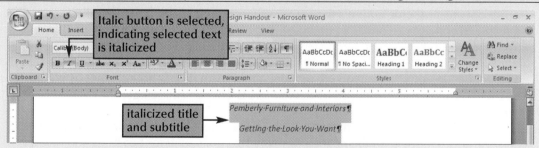

3. After reviewing the change, Natalie decides she doesn't care for the italics and asks you to remove them.

4. Click the **Italic** button I. The italic formatting toggles off. The selected text looks the way it did before you italicized it.

5. Save the document, leaving the title and subtitle selected.

Helpful Keyboard Shortcuts

For common tasks, such as applying bold and italics, it's often faster to use a **keyboard shortcut** (a combination of keys pressed at the same time) instead of clicking buttons with the mouse. For each of the keyboard shortcuts listed below, press and hold the Ctrl key, press the indicated number or letter key, and then release both keys.

• Bold selected text: Ctrl+B
• Italicize selected text: Ctrl+I

- Underline selected text: Ctrl+U
- Single-space lines within paragraph that currently contains the insertion point: Ctrl+1
- Double-space lines within paragraph that currently contains the insertion point: Ctrl+2
- Select entire document: Ctrl+A
- Cut selected text: Ctrl+X
- Copy selected text to Clipboard: Ctrl+C
- Paste most recently copied item at location of insertion point: Ctrl+V
- Undo your most recent action: Ctrl+Z

You can also save time by using **KeyTips**, sometimes called access keys, to select buttons and commands. To use KeyTips, press the Alt key and notice the letters that are displayed over each tab. Press the letter for the tab that contains the feature you want. For example, "P" is the KeyTip for the Page Layout tab; pressing it displays the Page Layout tab, with KeyTips showing for each feature on that tab. Press the KeyTip for the feature you want (for example, "B" for the Breaks button), and then notice the KeyTips that appear in the menu or gallery that opens. Press the KeyTip for the option you want. The change you select is applied to your document, and the KeyTips are hidden. You can press the Alt key to display them again for your next task. To hide KeyTips without using them, press the Esc key.

Working with Themes and Fonts

In addition to drawing attention to text with bold, italics, or underlining, you can change the shape and size of the individual letters by changing the font and font size. (As you learned in Tutorial 1, the term "font" refers to the shape of the characters in a document, and "font size" refers to the size of the characters.) You'll learn how to change the font in the Design Handout document soon, but first you need to take a few moments to learn about a related topic, document themes.

The document **theme** controls the variety of fonts, colors, and other visual effects available to you as you format a document. Twenty different themes are included in Word, with each offering a coordinated assortment of fonts, colors, and visual effects. By default, the Office theme is selected in each new Word document, including the Design Handout document you are working on now. You'll learn more about themes as you gain experience with Word. For now, you need to focus only on the relationship between themes and fonts.

One secret to creating a harmonious-looking document is to use no more than two fonts. For this reason, each theme includes only two fonts: one for headings and one for body text (that is, anything that is not a heading). In the Office theme, the heading font is Cambria, and the body font is Calibri. These two fonts were designed specifically for easy reading onscreen as well as on the printed page. A long list of other fonts is available. You can experiment with them and use them in your documents, but take care not to use too many fonts. This will create a document with a cluttered, disjointed appearance.

Applying a New Font and Font Size

To apply a font, select the text you want to format, then in the Font group on the Home tab, click the Font arrow, and click the font you want. The heading and body font for a document's theme are listed first, at the top of the font list.

To select a font size, make sure the text you want to format is selected, then in the Font group, click the Font Size arrow, and click the font size you want. Both the Font and Font Size lists allow you to see a live preview of selections by moving the mouse pointer over a font name or font size.

Natalie typed the entire Design Handout document in the Calibri font, which is intended primarily for body text, and the font size for the entire document is 11-point. She wants you to format the title and the subtitle in Cambria, which is the heading font for the Office theme. She also wants you to increase the size of the title and subtitle to 14-point.

To apply the Cambria heading font to the Design Handout document:

▶ 1. On page 1, verify that the title **Pemberly Furniture and Interiors** and the subtitle **Getting the Look You Want** are selected.

▶ 2. In the Font group, click the **Font** arrow. A list of available fonts appears. The heading and body font for the Office theme (Cambria and Calibri) appear at the top of the list. The intended use of these two fonts (Headings or Body) is specified after each font name. Calibri (Body) is highlighted in orange, indicating that this font is currently applied to the selected text. (Calibri also appears in the Font box, above the list, for the same reason.) Below the heading and body fonts is a list of fonts that have been used recently on your computer, followed by a complete alphabetical list of all available fonts. (You need to scroll the list to see all the fonts.) Each name in the list is formatted with the relevant font. For example, "Cambria" appears in the Cambria font, and "Calibri" appears in the Calibri font. See Figure 2-32.

Font list   Figure 2-32

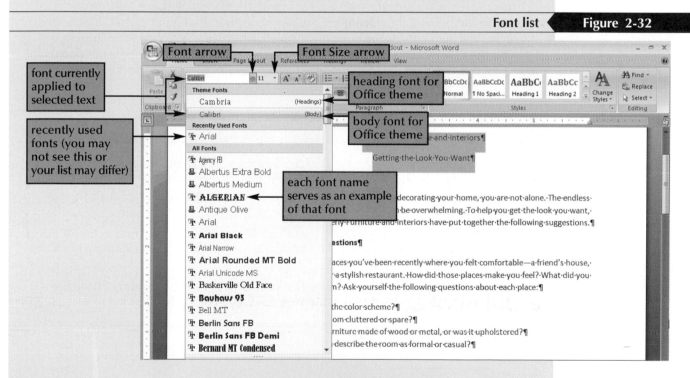

▶ 3. Without clicking, move the mouse pointer over a dramatic-looking font in the font list, such as Algerian or Arial Black, and then drag the pointer over another font. The selected text in the document shows a live preview of the font, changing again to a new font when you drag the mouse pointer to a different font name.

▶ 4. At the top of the list, click **Cambria (Headings)**. Take care to select Cambria (Headings) at the top of the list. Do not click Cambria where it appears farther down, in the alphabetical list of fonts. (The reason for this will become clear in the next section, when you learn more about document themes.) The selected title and subtitle are now formatted in Cambria, and the font list closes. "Cambria (Headings)" appears in the Font box, indicating the font currently applied to the selected text. Next, you need to increase the font size of the selected text from 11 point to 14 point.

Trouble? If you see "Cambria" in the font box rather than "Cambria (Headings)," you selected Cambria where it appears in the alphabetical list of fonts rather than at the top of the list. Begin again with Step 2, taking care to select Cambria (Headings) at the top of the list.

5. Verify that the title and subtitle are still selected, and then in the Font group click the **Font Size** arrow (shown earlier in Figure 2-32). A list of font sizes appears, with the currently selected font size (11) displayed in the Font Size box. Like the Font box, the Font Size box allows you to preview options before selecting one.

6. Drag the mouse pointer over a few font sizes, and notice how the size of the selected text changes accordingly.

7. Click **14**. The Font Size list closes and the selected text increases from 11-point to 14-point Cambria. Click within the title to deselect the text.

You've finished formatting the document's title and subtitle in the Cambria font, the preferred heading font for the Office theme. You could also apply the Cambria font to the headings within the document (such as the heading "Ask Yourself Some Questions"). However, Natalie thinks the bold you applied earlier emphasizes them enough, so you'll leave the headings as they are.

The only remaining font change has to do with the company name. Wherever it appears in the body of the document, Natalie wants to format it in the Arial font, so that it matches the sign outside the company's storefront. Arial is not one of the suggested fonts for the Office theme, and using it breaks the general rule of two fonts per document, but this is a small change that won't affect the overall look of the document.

To format the company name in the Arial font:

1. At the end of the introductory paragraph, select **Pemberly Furniture and Interiors**.

2. In the Font group click the **Font** arrow, and then click **Arial** in either in the Recently used Fonts section of the list or in the All Fonts section. The font for the company name changes from Calibri to Arial. Arial appears in the Font box, indicating that the selected text is formatted in this font.

   Trouble? If you don't see Arial in your font list, choose another font in the All Fonts section that is easy to distinguish from Calibri or Cambria but still looks suitable for a business document.

3. Scroll down to the last paragraph of the document, select **Pemberly Furniture and Interiors**, and format it in the Arial font. See Figure 2-33.

Figure 2-33   **Company name formatted in Arial**

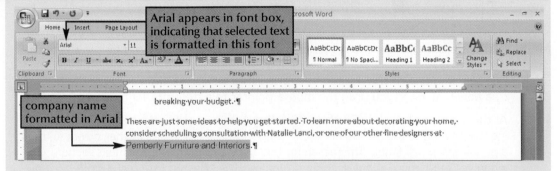

4. Deselect the company name, and then save the document.

You are finished changing the document fonts. In the next section, you'll select a new theme for the document and observe how this affects your font choices.

Changing the Document's Theme

Each document theme is designed to convey a specific look and feel. For example, the Office theme is designed to be appropriate for standard business documents. By contrast, some of the other themes are designed to give documents a more informal look, such as sleek for a new product announcement or earthy for a flyer on environmental news.

The advantage of sticking with a theme's suggested heading and body fonts (the two fonts at the top of the font list) is that if you switch to a different theme, the fonts in the document automatically change to the body and heading fonts for that theme. If you select any fonts on the font list other than the two heading and body fonts at the top of the list, they will remain unchanged in the document as you switch from one theme to another.

Natalie is considering using a different theme for future handouts. She asks you to apply the Metro theme to the Design Handout document to see how it looks.

To change the document's theme:

▶ **1.** Make sure that you saved the document using the current name (Design Handout) at the end of the last section. If you aren't sure, save the document again.

▶ **2.** Save the document as **Design Handout Metro** in the Tutorial folder.

▶ **3.** Press the **Ctrl+Home** keys to move the insertion point up to the headings at the beginning of the document. With the title and subtitle visible, you will more easily be able to see what happens when you change the document's theme.

▶ **4.** Click the **Page Layout** tab, and then click the **Themes** button. The Themes gallery opens. You might have to wait a moment until the various themes appear in the gallery. See Figure 2-34.

Themes gallery ◀ Figure 2-34

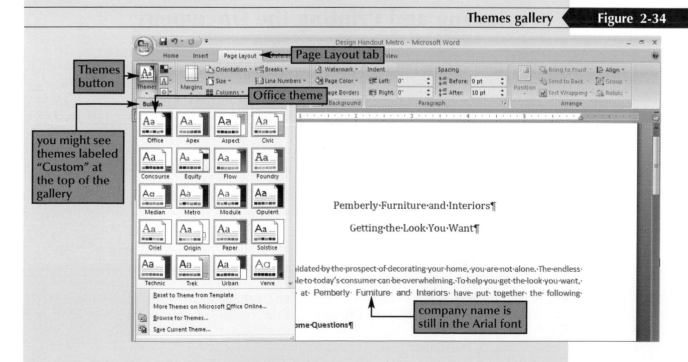

▶ 5. Without clicking, hold the mouse over the various themes in the gallery, and observe the live preview of each theme in the document. The heading and body fonts change to reflect the fonts associated with the various themes.

▶ 6. Click **Metro**. Except for the two instances of the company name (which you formatted earlier in Arial), the text in the Design Handout Metro document changes to the body and heading fonts of the Metro theme. To see exactly what the Metro theme fonts are, you can point to the Theme Fonts button in the Themes group.

▶ 7. Point to the **Theme Fonts** button ⒜ᐧ in the Themes group. A ScreenTip appears, listing the currently selected theme (Metro), the heading font (Consolas), and the body font (Corbel).

   Trouble? If a menu appears, you clicked the Theme Fonts button instead of pointing to it. Press the Esc key, and then repeat Step 7.

▶ 8. Save the document and then close it. You can give the Design Handout Metro file to Natalie later, so she can decide whether or not to use the Metro theme for future handouts. Because you saved the Design Handout document before changing the theme, you can reopen it now and continue with the tutorial.

▶ 9. Reopen the Design Handout document, which is formatted with the Office theme.

Tip

To quickly open a document you were recently working on in Word, click the Office Button and then click the document you want in the Recent Documents list.

InSight | **Changing Fonts by Changing Themes**

The two fonts at the top of the font list are not actually specific fonts; they are instructions that tell Word to use the heading and body fonts for the currently selected theme. By contrast, the other fonts in the Font list (such as Arial or Calibri where they appear in the alphabetical list of fonts) are more straightforward. When you apply one of these fonts to text in a document, it doesn't change when you change the document theme. The same is true for other kinds of formatting, such as bold, italics, or font size changes. These types of formatting remain unchanged no matter what theme you choose.

Previewing and Printing the Document

You have made all the editing and formatting changes that Natalie requested for the Design Handout document. It's helpful to preview a document after formatting it. The Print Preview window makes it easy to spot things you need to change before printing, such as text that is not aligned correctly.

To preview and print the document:

▶ 1. Click the **Office Button** ⒝, point to **Print**, and then click **Print Preview**. The document is displayed in Print Preview.

▶ 2. In the Zoom section, click the **Two Pages** button. You see both pages of the document side by side. Review the document's formatting.

   Trouble? If you notice any alignment or indentation errors, click the Close Print Preview button, correct the errors in Print Layout view, save your changes, and then return to the Print Preview window.

▶ 3. On the Print Preview tab in the Print group, click the **Print** button, check the print settings, and then click the **OK** button. After a pause, the document prints.

▶ **4.** Click the **Close Print Preview** button. You return to Print Layout view.

▶ **5.** Save the document if necessary and then close it.

You now have a printed copy of the final Design Handout document, as shown in Figure 2-35.

Final version of Design Handout document ◀ **Figure 2-35**

Session 2.2 Quick Check | Review

1. The term _____ refers to the way a paragraph lines up horizontally between the margins.
2. Explain how to indent a paragraph 1 inch or more from the left margin.
3. Explain how to copy formatting to multiple paragraphs.
4. What is the Numbering Library?
5. Explain the effect a theme has on the overall look of a document.
6. Explain how to change a paragraph's font.
7. Explain the relationship between the two items at the top of the Font list and the document's theme.

Tutorial Summary | Review

In this tutorial, you learned how to use the Spelling and Grammar checker, select parts of a document, delete text, and move text within a document. You also learned how to find and replace text. Next, you focused on formatting a document, including changing margins, aligning text, indenting paragraphs, using the Format Painter, and emphasizing text with bold and italics. Finally, you learned how to change the font and font size for selected text and you explored the relationship between fonts and themes.

Key Terms

alignment	format	ragged
bullet	Format Painter	right alignment
Bullet Library	hanging indent	right indent
center alignment	indent	search text
Clipboard	indent markers	Spelling and Grammar
Clipboard task pane	justified alignment	checker
copy	keyboard shortcut	theme
cut	Key Tips	toggle buttons
cut and paste	left alignment	
drag and drop	Numbering Library	
Find and Replace	paste	
dialog box		

Practice	**Review Assignments**

Apply the skills you learned in the tutorial using the same case scenario.

Data Files needed for the Review Assignments: Getting.docx, Staff.docx

Natalie asks you to work on a document that explains how to get started working with the designers at Pemberly Furniture and Interiors. The document starts by introducing the entire Pemberly design staff and then lists the steps involved in a major home renovation. Natalie also asks you to create a document listing the names of the firm's interior designers and interior decorators.

1. Open the file **Getting** located in the Tutorial.02\Review folder included with your Data Files, and then check your screen to make sure your settings match those in the tutorial.

2. Save the document as **Getting Started** in the same folder.

3. Use the Spelling and Grammar checker to correct any errors in the document. Assume that all names in the document and the term "Feng Shui" are spelled correctly.

4. Proofread the document carefully to check for any additional errors. Look for and correct errors in the last two paragraphs of the document that were not reported when you used the Spelling and Grammar checker.

5. Change the left and top margins to 1.5 inches using the Page Setup dialog box. Make sure to apply the change to the whole document.

6. In the list on the second page of the document, select the paragraph that begins "Interview potential construction..." and move it so that it follows the paragraph that reads "Review the final design plan."

7. Format the heading and subheading in the suggested heading font for the Office theme. Change the font size to 16 point.

8. Make all edits and formatting changes shown in Figure 2-36, and then save your work.

Figure 2-36

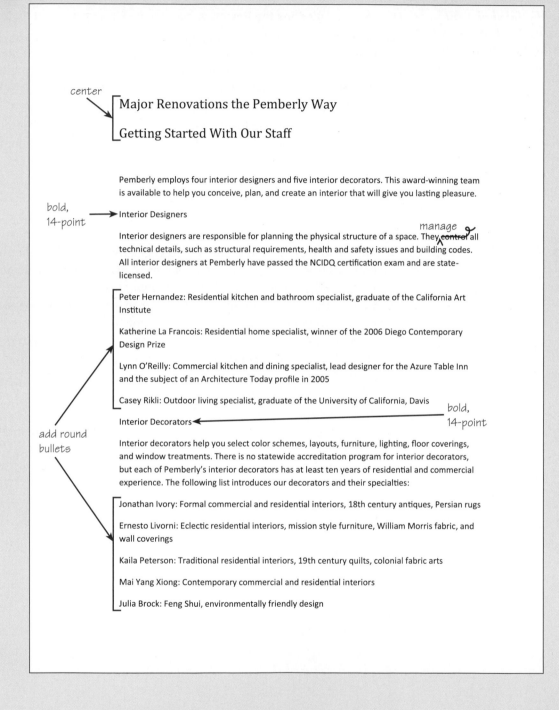

center

Major Renovations the Pemberly Way

Getting Started With Our Staff

Pemberly employs four interior designers and five interior decorators. This award-winning team is available to help you conceive, plan, and create an interior that will give you lasting pleasure.

bold, 14-point → Interior Designers

manage

Interior designers are responsible for planning the physical structure of a space. They ~~control~~ all technical details, such as structural requirements, health and safety issues and building codes. All interior designers at Pemberly have passed the NCIDQ certification exam and are state-licensed.

Peter Hernandez: Residential kitchen and bathroom specialist, graduate of the California Art Institute

Katherine La Francois: Residential home specialist, winner of the 2006 Diego Contemporary Design Prize

Lynn O'Reilly: Commercial kitchen and dining specialist, lead designer for the Azure Table Inn and the subject of an Architecture Today profile in 2005

Casey Rikli: Outdoor living specialist, graduate of the University of California, Davis

add round bullets

Interior Decorators ← *bold, 14-point*

Interior decorators help you select color schemes, layouts, furniture, lighting, floor coverings, and window treatments. There is no statewide accreditation program for interior decorators, but each of Pemberly's interior decorators has at least ten years of residential and commercial experience. The following list introduces our decorators and their specialties:

Jonathan Ivory: Formal commercial and residential interiors, 18th century antiques, Persian rugs

Ernesto Livorni: Eclectic residential interiors, mission style furniture, William Morris fabric, and wall coverings

Kaila Peterson: Traditional residential interiors, 19th century quilts, colonial fabric arts

Mai Yang Xiong: Contemporary commercial and residential interiors

Julia Brock: Feng Shui, environmentally friendly design

Figure 2-36 (cont.)

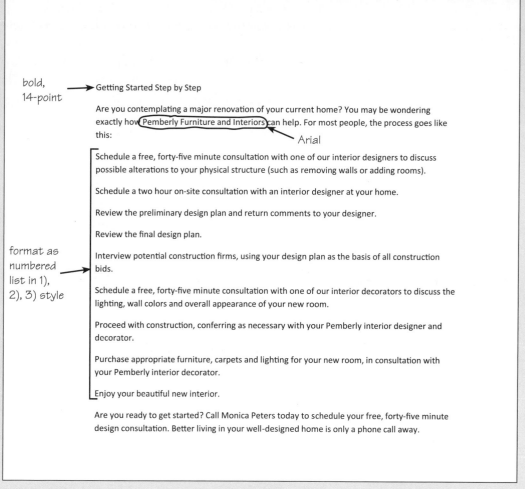

bold,
14-point

→ Getting Started Step by Step

Are you contemplating a major renovation of your current home? You may be wondering exactly how Pemberly Furniture and Interiors can help. For most people, the process goes like this:

Arial

Schedule a free, forty-five minute consultation with one of our interior designers to discuss possible alterations to your physical structure (such as removing walls or adding rooms).

Schedule a two hour on-site consultation with an interior designer at your home.

Review the preliminary design plan and return comments to your designer.

Review the final design plan.

format as
numbered
list in 1),
2), 3) style

Interview potential construction firms, using your design plan as the basis of all construction bids.

Schedule a free, forty-five minute consultation with one of our interior decorators to discuss the lighting, wall colors and overall appearance of your new room.

Proceed with construction, conferring as necessary with your Pemberly interior designer and decorator.

Purchase appropriate furniture, carpets and lighting for your new room, in consultation with your Pemberly interior decorator.

Enjoy your beautiful new interior.

Are you ready to get started? Call Monica Peters today to schedule your free, forty-five minute design consultation. Better living in your well-designed home is only a phone call away.

9. In the last paragraph of the document, replace "Monica Peters" with your first and last name.

10. Below the heading "Interior Designers," justify the paragraph that begins "Interior designers are responsible for...." Click the Increase Indent button once. Note that Word indents the justified paragraph slightly to match the bulleted list below it. Click the Increase Indent button again to indent the paragraph a full 0.5 inch. Similarly, justify and indent the paragraph below the heading "Interior Decorators" and the paragraph below the heading "Getting Started Step by Step." Finally, justify and indent the last paragraph in the document, and then indent the two bulleted lists and the numbered list to match the other indented paragraphs. When you are finished, the text and lists below the three boldface headings should all be indented by 0.5 inch. Save the document.

11. If necessary, move the heading "Getting Started Step by Step" to the top of page 2.

12. Display the Clipboard task pane. Copy the list of interior designers and their specialties (starting with Peter Hernandez and ending with Casey Rikli) to the Clipboard. Also copy the list of interior decorators and their specialties (beginning with Jonathan Ivory and ending with Julia Brock) to the Clipboard.

13. Open the file **Staff** located in the Tutorial.02\Review folder included with your Data Files, and save the document as **Pemberly Staff** in the same folder. In the subtitle, insert your first and last name after the word "by."

14. Display the Clipboard task pane. Below the heading "Interior Designers," paste the list of interior designers, which begins "Peter Hernandez." Below the heading "Interior Decorators," paste the list of interior decorators, which begins "Jonathan Ivory." In each case, start by moving the insertion point to the blank paragraph below the heading. Notice that text inserted from the Clipboard retains its original formatting.

15. Clear the contents of the Clipboard task pane, and then print the document.

16. Save the Pemberly Staff document and close it. Close the Clipboard task pane.

17. Save the Getting Started document, deselect any selected text, preview the document, and print it.

18. Save the Getting Started document as **Verve Sample** in the same folder.

19. Select the Verve theme, and then review the newly formatted document and its list of fonts. Check the company name in the paragraph below the heading "Getting Started Step by Step" and make sure it is still formatted in Arial.

20. Save the Verve Sample document, preview it, print it, and close it. Close any other open documents. Submit the finished documents to your instructor, either in printed or electronic form, as requested.

| Apply | **Case Problem 1** |

Apply the skills you learned to create a one-page flyer.

Data File needed for this Case Problem: New.docx

Peach Tree School of the Arts Students at Peach Tree School of the Arts, in Savannah, Georgia, can choose from a wide range of after-school classes in fine arts, music, and theater. Amanda Reinhard, the school director, has created a flyer informing parents of some additional offerings. It's your job to format the flyer to make it professional looking and easy to read.

1. Open the file **New** located in the Tutorial.02\Case1 folder included with your Data Files, and save the file as **New Classes** in the same folder.

2. Correct any spelling or grammar errors. Ignore the sentence fragments highlighted by the grammar checker. These fragments will make sense once they are formatted as part of a bulleted list.

3. Proofread for other errors, such as words that are spelled correctly but used incorrectly. Use the Replace command to replace "P.M." with "p.m." throughout the document.

4. Replace "Marcus Cody" with your name.

5. Change the top, left, right, and bottom margins to 1.5 inches, and then save your work.

6. Format everything in the document except the title and subtitle in 12-point Times New Roman font. Format the title and subtitle in Arial, 16 point, bold.

7. Format the list of new classes (which begins "Advanced Drawing") as a bulleted list, using the square bullet style.

8. Move the third bulleted item (which begins "Jazz Dance...") up to make it the first bulleted item in the list.

9. Format the four-step check list near the end of the document as a numbered list, using the default numbering style.

10. Save your work, preview the document, switch back to Print Layout view to make any changes you think necessary, print the document, and then close it. Submit the finished document to your instructor, either in printed or electronic form, as requested.

| Apply | | **Case Problem 2** |

Use your skills to format the summary document shown in Figure 2-37.

Data File needed for this Case Problem: Moth.docx

Hamilton Polytechnic Institute Finn Hansen is an associate researcher in the Department of Entomology at Hamilton Polytechnic Institute. He is working on a nationwide program that aims to slow the spread of a devastating forest pest, the gypsy moth. He has created a one-page document that will be used as part of a campaign to inform the public about current efforts to manage gypsy moths in North America. Format the document by completing the following steps.

1. Open the file **Moth** located in the Tutorial.02\Case2 folder included with your Data Files, and then check your screen to make sure your settings match those in the tutorial.
2. Save the file as **Gypsy Moth** in the same folder.
3. Format the document as shown in Figure 2-37.

Figure 2-37

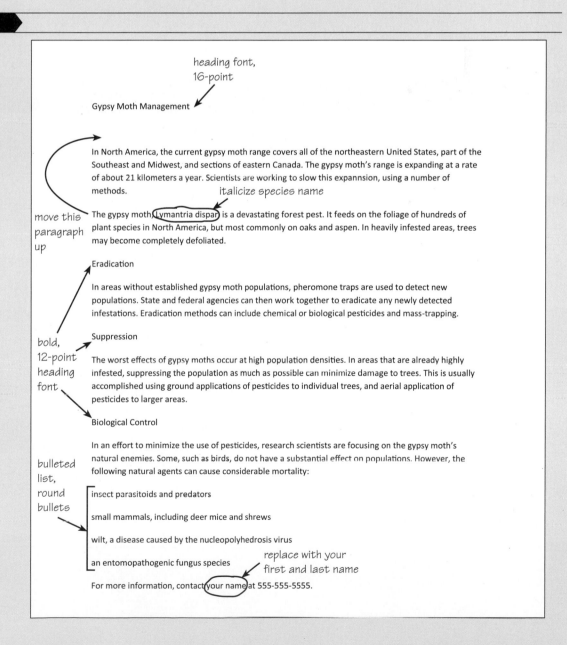

heading font, 16-point

Gypsy Moth Management

In North America, the current gypsy moth range covers all of the northeastern United States, part of the Southeast and Midwest, and sections of eastern Canada. The gypsy moth's range is expanding at a rate of about 21 kilometers a year. Scientists are working to slow this expannsion, using a number of methods.

italicize species name

move this paragraph up

The gypsy moth Lymantria dispar is a devastating forest pest. It feeds on the foliage of hundreds of plant species in North America, but most commonly on oaks and aspen. In heavily infested areas, trees may become completely defoliated.

Eradication

In areas without established gypsy moth populations, pheromone traps are used to detect new populations. State and federal agencies can then work together to eradicate any newly detected infestations. Eradication methods can include chemical or biological pesticides and mass-trapping.

bold, 12-point heading font

Suppression

The worst effects of gypsy moths occur at high population densities. In areas that are already highly infested, suppressing the population as much as possible can minimize damage to trees. This is usually accomplished using ground applications of pesticides to individual trees, and aerial application of pesticides to larger areas.

Biological Control

In an effort to minimize the use of pesticides, research scientists are focusing on the gypsy moth's natural enemies. Some, such as birds, do not have a substantial effect on populations. However, the following natural agents can cause considerable mortality:

bulleted list, round bullets

insect parasitoids and predators

small mammals, including deer mice and shrews

wilt, a disease caused by the nucleopolyhedrosis virus

an entomopathogenic fungus species

replace with your first and last name

For more information, contact your name at 555-555-5555.

⊕ EXPLORE

4. Use the ruler to indent a paragraph, as follows:

   a. Make sure the horizontal ruler is displayed and the document is in Print Layout view.

   b. Click anywhere in the paragraph below the heading "Eradication."

   c. Position the pointer on the small gray rectangle on the ruler at the left margin (the rectangle is below the two triangles). A ScreenTip with the words "Left Indent" appears.

   d. Press and hold down the mouse button. A vertical dotted line appears in the document window, indicating the current left margin. Drag the Left Indent marker right to the 0.5-inch mark on the ruler, and then release the mouse button.

5. Use the Format Painter to copy the indent to the paragraph below the heading "Suppression" and the heading "Biological Control."

6. Indent the bulleted list so it aligns below the preceding paragraph.

7. Use the Spelling and Grammar checker to make corrections as needed, proofread for additional errors, save, and preview the document.

8. Print the document, and then close it. Submit the finished document to your instructor, either in printed or electronic form, as requested.

Challenge | **Case Problem 3**

Expand your formatting skills to create a resume for an aspiring sales representative.

Data File needed for this Case Problem: Resume.docx

Educational Publishing   Elena Pelliterri has over a decade of experience in education. She worked as a writing teacher and then as a college supervisor of student teachers. Now she would like to pursue a career as a sales representative for a company that publishes textbooks and other educational materials. She has asked you to edit and format her resume. Complete the resume by completing the following steps.

1. Open the file **Resume** located in the Tutorial.02\Case3 folder included with your Data Files, and then check your screen to make sure your settings match those in the tutorial.

2. Save the file as **Elena Resume** in the same folder.

3. Search for the text "your name", and replace it with your first and last name.

4. Replace all occurrences of "Aroyo" with "Arroyo."

5. Use the Spelling and Grammar checker to correct any errors in the document. Note that this document contains lines that the Spelling and Grammar checker might consider sentence fragments but that are acceptable in a resume.

6. Delete the word "traveling" from the sentence below the "OBJECTIVE" heading.

7. Change the document theme to Metro.

8. Format the resume as described in Figure 2-38. Use the Format Painter to copy formatting as necessary.

Figure 2-38

Resume Element	Format
Name "Elena Pelliterri"	16-point, heading font, bold, with underline
Address, phone number, and e-mail address	14-point, heading font, bold
Uppercase headings (OBJECTIVE, EXPERIENCE, etc.)	11-point, heading font, bold
Two subheadings below EXPERIENCE, which begin "Rio Mesa College..." and "Middleton Public Schools..."	11-point, heading font, bold, italic
Lists of teaching experience, educational history, and so on, below the resume headings and subheadings	Bulleted list with square bullets

9. Reorder the two items under the "COMPUTER SKILLS" heading so that the second item becomes the first.

⊕ EXPLORE 10. Open a new, blank document, type some text, and experiment with the Change Case button in the Font group on the Home tab. Close the document without saving it, and then change the name "Elena Pelliterri" at the top of the resume to all uppercase.

11. Save, preview, and print the document.

⊕ EXPLORE 12. Experiment with two special paragraph alignment options: first line and hanging.

   a. Save the document as **Alignment Samples**. Make sure the horizontal ruler is displayed and the document is in Print Layout view.

   b. Select the two bulleted items under the subheading "Middleton Public Schools." Click the Bullets button to remove the bulleted list format.

   c. With the paragraphs still selected, locate the alignment markers on the left side of the horizontal ruler. Position the pointer over the bottom, triangle-shaped alignment marker. A ScreenTip with the words "Hanging Indent" appears. (If you see a different ScreenTip, such as "Left Indent," you don't have the pointer positioned properly.)

   d. Press and hold down the mouse button. A vertical dotted line appears in the document window, indicating the current left margin. Drag the Hanging Indent marker right to the 1-inch mark on the ruler, and then release the mouse button.

   e. Select the two bulleted items under the heading "Educational History" and remove the bulleted list formatting. Position the mouse pointer over the top, triangle-shaped alignment marker until you see the ScreenTip "First Line Indent." Drag the First Line Indent marker right to the 1-inch mark on the ruler, and then release the mouse button.

13. Save, preview, and print the document.

14. Close the document. Close any other open documents. Submit the finished documents to your instructor, either in printed or electronic form, as requested.

Challenge | **Case Problem 4**

Explore new ways to format an order form for a baking supply company.

Data File needed for this Case Problem: Flour.docx

McElmeel Baking Supply   Melissa Martinez is the sales manager for McElmeel Baking Supply, a wholesale distributor of gourmet baking ingredients based in Ames, Iowa. The company is currently offering a special on flour. Melissa has started work on an order form that explains the special offer. She plans to include the form with each invoice sent out next month. It's your job to format the order form to make it easy to use.

1. Open the file **Flour** located in Tutorial.02\Case4 folder included with your Data Files, and save the file as **Flour Form** in the same folder.

EXPLORE

2. When you type Web addresses or e-mail addresses in a document, Word formats them as links. When you click a Web address formatted as a link, Windows opens a Web browser (such as Microsoft Internet Explorer) and, if your computer is connected to the Internet, displays that Web page. Likewise, Word recognizes text that looks like an e-mail address, and formats such text as links as well. If you click an e-mail address formatted as a link, Windows opens a program in which you can type an e-mail message. The address you clicked is included, by default, as the recipient of the e-mail. You'll see how this works as you add a Web address and e-mail address to the order form. At the top of the document, click at the end of the company name, add a new line, and then type the address for the company's Web site: **www.McElmeelBaking.course.com**. (The company is fictitious and does not really have a Web site.) When you are finished, press the Enter key. Word formats the address in blue with an underline, marking it as a link. Move the mouse pointer over the link and read the ScreenTip.

EXPLORE

3. In the line below the Web address, type **McElmeel_Baking@course.com** and then press the Enter key. Word formats the e-mail address as a link. Press and hold the Ctrl key and then click the e-mail link. Your default e-mail program opens, displaying a window where you could type an e-mail message to McElmeel Baking Supply. (If your computer is not set up for email, close any error messages or wizard dialog boxes that open.) Close the e-mail window without saving any changes. The e-mail link is now formatted in a color other than blue, indicating that the link has been clicked.

EXPLORE

4. Right-click the Web site address, and then click Remove Hyperlink in the shortcut menu. Do the same for the e-mail address. The links are now formatted as ordinary text.

5. Delete the phrase "regular clients," and replace it with "loyal customers."

6. Use the Margins menu to change the top and bottom margins to 1 inch and the left and right margins to 2 inches.

7. Format the entire document in the Arial font.

8. At the top of the document, center and single space the company name, Web address, and e-mail address. Remove extra paragraph spacing from all three paragraphs.

9. Change the font size for the company name at the top of the document to 16 points.

10. Near the middle of the document, bold and single space the company address. Remove extra paragraph spacing from all three paragraphs.

11. Format the blank ruled lines at the bottom of the order form as a numbered list.

12. Insert your name in the form to the right of "Name:".

EXPLORE

13. Save your work and preview the document. Click the One Page button on the Print Preview tab to view the entire document on the screen at one time. Print the document and then close the Print Preview window.

✦EXPLORE 14. The Words box in the bottom, left-hand corner of the document window shows you the number of words in a document. To see more useful statistics, you can use the Word Count dialog box. Click the Words box in the lower-left corner of the document window to open the Word Count dialog box. Note the number of characters (not including spaces), paragraphs, and lines in the document, and then write these statistics in the upper-right corner of the printout. Close the Word Count dialog box.

15. Save and close the document. Submit the finished document to your instructor, either in printed or electronic form, as requested.

| Research | **Internet Assignments** |

Go to the Web to find information you can use to create documents.

The purpose of the Internet Assignments is to challenge you to find information on the Internet that you can use to work effectively with this software. The actual assignments are updated and maintained on the Course Technology Web site. Log on to the Internet and use your Web browser to go to the Student Online Companion for New Perspectives Office 2007 at **www.course.com/np/office2007**. Then navigate to the Internet Assignments for this tutorial.

| Assess | **SAM Assessment and Training** |

If you have a SAM user profile, you may have access to hands-on instruction, practice, and assessment of the skills covered in this tutorial. Log in to your SAM account (**http://sam2007.course.com**) to launch any assigned training activities or exams that relate to the skills covered in this tutorial.

| Review | **Quick Check Answers** |

Session 2.1

1. True
2. True
3. Select the text you want to move. Press and hold down the mouse button until the drag-and-drop pointer appears, and then drag the selected text to its new location. Use the dotted insertion point as a guide to determine exactly where the text will be inserted. Release the mouse button to drop the text at the insertion point.
4. Select the text you want to cut, and then click the Cut button in the Clipboard group on the Home tab. Move the insertion point to the target location in the document, and then click the Paste button in the Clipboard group on the Home tab.
5. Click the Find button in the Editing group on the Home tab.
6. Select the Match case check box.

Session 2.2

1. alignment
2. Click the Increase Indent button in the Paragraph group on the Home tab.
3. Move the insertion point to the paragraph whose formatting you want to copy, double-click the Format Painter button, and then click each paragraph you want to format. When you are finished, click the Format Painter button again to deselect it.
4. A gallery of numbered list styles. To display it (along with other numbered list options), click the Numbering button arrow in the Paragraph group on the Home tab.
5. A theme controls the variety of fonts, colors, and other visual effects available to you as you format a document. Each theme is designed to provide a coordinated, harmonious-looking document.
6. Select the text you want to change. Click the Font arrow in the Font group to display the list of fonts. Move the mouse pointer over the list of font names and observe a preview of the fonts in the selected text. Click the font you want to use.
7. They are the heading and body fonts for the document's theme. They are really instructions that tell Word to use the heading and body fonts for the currently selected theme.

Ending Data Files

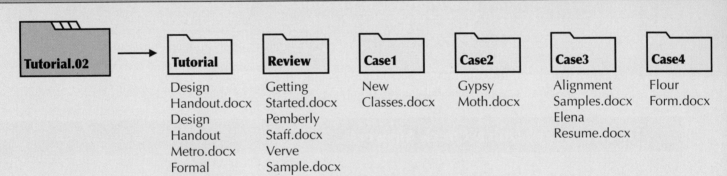

Tutorial.02 → **Tutorial**
Design Handout.docx
Design Handout Metro.docx
Formal Designs.docx

Review
Getting Started.docx
Pemberly Staff.docx
Verve Sample.docx

Case1
New Classes.docx

Case2
Gypsy Moth.docx

Case3
Alignment Samples.docx
Elena Resume.docx

Case4
Flour Form.docx

Reality Check

You've seen how Microsoft Word 2007 allows you to create polished, professional-looking documents in a variety of business settings. The word-processing skills you've learned will be useful to you in many areas of your life. For example, you could use Word's formatting features to create a flyer promoting a garage sale or a concert for a friend's band. In the following exercise, you'll create a number of useful documents of your choosing using the Word skills and features presented in Tutorials 1 and 2.

Using Templates

You can create the documents in this exercise from scratch, or you can use the templates that are available in the New documents dialog box. A **template** is a special Word document that comes with predefined headings, formatting, document controls, and graphical elements. In the New Document dialog box, click Installed Templates, and then click the template you want. To use a template after you've opened it, save it like an ordinary document, and then replace the placeholder text with your own information.

Note: Please be sure *not* to include any personal information of a sensitive nature in the documents you create to be submitted to your instructor for this exercise. Later on, you can update the documents with such Information for your own personal use.

1. Create a resume that you could use to apply for your ideal job.
2. Create a cover letter to accompany your resume and portfolio.
3. Create an envelope for your cover letter and resume.
4. Create a form that you could use to have people sign up to participate in an upcoming event or to order a product. Assume the form will be printed, and that people will fill it out using a pen or pencil. The form should be designed so that people can clearly see where they should write their names, addresses, and other pertinent information. Be sure to leave enough room for all responses. Select appropriate margins and choose an appropriate theme. Use the theme's heading font to add emphasis to some text. Use other formatting, such as bold or italics, as necessary.
5. Create a one-page flyer for an upcoming event. Use multiple fonts to add interest. Because this is an informal document, you can be as creative as you want in your use of fonts. Use bulleted lists and other formatting, such as bold and italics, to add emphasis as necessary.
6. Review all your documents carefully in Print Preview, and then submit the finished documents to your instructor, either in printed or electronic form, as requested.

Objectives

Session 1.1
- Understand the use of spreadsheets and Excel
- Learn the parts of the Excel window
- Scroll through a worksheet and navigate between worksheets
- Create and save a workbook file
- Enter text, numbers, and dates into a worksheet
- Resize, insert, and remove columns and rows

Session 1.2
- Select and move cell ranges
- Insert formulas and functions
- Insert, delete, move, and rename worksheets
- Work with editing tools
- Preview and print a workbook

Getting Started with Excel

Creating an Order Report

Case | RipCity Digital

When Amanda Dunn purchased a DVD burner a few years ago, one of her first tasks was to convert her home videos into DVDs. After she saw how simple it was, she upgraded her hardware and software and proceeded to create DVDs from home movies and slides for her parents and friends. Based on her success, Amanda decided to make a business out of her hobby and founded RipCity Digital, an online service specializing in creating DVDs from the home movies, photos, and slides sent to her from customers. Amanda wants to list the weekly orders from her customers, tracking the names and addresses of her clients, the number of DVDs that she creates, and finally the cost of creating and shipping the DVDs.

Amanda is so busy creating DVDs that she asks you to record her orders. You'll do this in **Microsoft Office Excel 2007** (or **Excel**), a computer program used to enter, analyze, and present quantitative data. You'll also enter the latest orders she received for her new business.

Starting Data Files

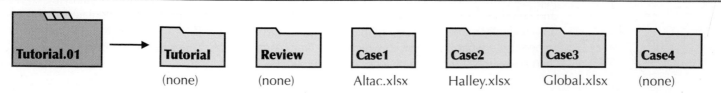

Tutorial.01	Tutorial	Review	Case1	Case2	Case3	Case4
	(none)	(none)	Altac.xlsx	Halley.xlsx	Global.xlsx	(none)

Session 1.1

Introducing Excel

Before you begin working in Excel, Amanda asks you to review some of the features, key terms, and concepts associated with spreadsheets. Understanding spreadsheets and how they work in Excel will help you as you enter RipCity Digital customer orders.

Understanding Spreadsheets

A **spreadsheet** is a collection of text and numbers laid out in a rectangular grid. Spreadsheets are often used in business for budgeting, inventory management, and decision making. They can also be used to manage personal budgets and track household assets. For example, the paper-based spreadsheet shown in Figure 1-1 shows a cash flow report. The spreadsheet records the estimated and actual cash flow for the month of January. Each line, or row, displays a different value, such as the starting cash balance or cash sales for the month. Each column displays the budgeted or actual numbers or text that describes those values. The total cash expenditures, net cash flow, and closing cash balance for the month are not entered directly, but calculated from other numbers in the spreadsheet. For example, the total cash expenditure is equal to the expenditures on advertising, wages, and supplies. For paper spreadsheets, these calculations are done using a hand calculator and then entered into the spreadsheet.

Figure 1-1	Sample paper spreadsheet

Cash Flow Comparison Budgeted vs. Actual		Jan–10
	Budgeted	Actual
Cash balance (start of month)	$4,500.00	$4,500.00
Cash receipts		
Cash sales	12,600.00	14,688.00
Cash expenditures		
Advertising	1,200.00	1,425.00
Wages	7,200.00	7,850.00
Supplies	3,600.00	4,350.00
Total cash expenditures	12,000.00	13,625.00
Net cash flow	600.00	1,063.00
Cash balance (end of month)	$5,100.00	$5,563.00

Excel is a computer program used to create electronic versions of these paper spreadsheets. Figure 1-2 shows the data from Figure 1-1 as it might appear in Excel. As with paper spreadsheets, Excel uses a rectangular grid to lay out the financial information in rows and columns. As you'll see later, values such as total cash expenditures can be calculated automatically rather than entered manually into the spreadsheet. This allows you to use Excel to perform a **what-if analysis** in which you change one or more values in a spreadsheet and then assess the effect those changes have on the calculated values.

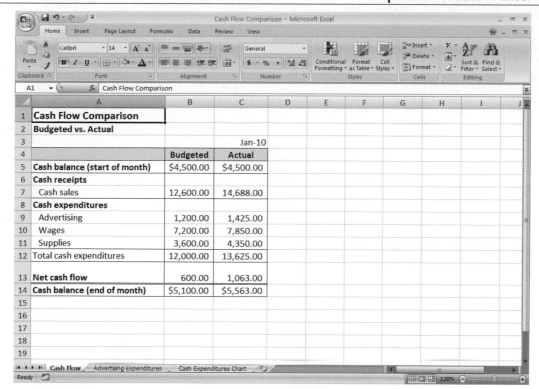

An Excel spreadsheet is more flexible than paper spreadsheets. In fact, it is no longer just an electronic substitute for paper spreadsheets. Excel is now often used for data storage, report generation, and as a tool to access data from the Internet.

Exploring the Excel Window

Before entering Amanda's data, you'll review the different parts of the Excel window. The Excel window contains many of the elements that you find in other Office 2007 programs, including a title bar, the Ribbon, scroll bars, and a status bar. The Excel window also contains features that are unique to Excel. You'll review these features after you start Excel.

To start Excel:

▶ 1. Click the **Start** button 🌐 on the Windows taskbar, click **All Programs**, click **Microsoft Office**, and then point to **Microsoft Office Excel 2007**.

  Trouble? If you don't see Microsoft Office Excel 2007 on the Microsoft Office submenu, look for it on a different submenu or on the All Programs menu. If you still cannot find Microsoft Office Excel 2007, ask your instructor or technical support person for help.

▶ 2. Click **Microsoft Office Excel 2007**. The Excel window opens.

  All the figures showing the Excel window in these tutorials are zoomed to 120% for better readability. If you want to zoom your Excel window to match the figures, complete Step 3. If you prefer to work in the default zoom of 100% or at another zoom level, continue with Step 4; you might see more or less of the worksheet on your screen, but this does not affect your work in the tutorials.

▶ 3. If you want your Excel window zoomed to match the figures, click the **Zoom In** button ⊕ on the status bar twice to increase the zoom magnification to **120%**. The worksheet is magnified to 120%, which increases the screen size of each cell, but reduces the number of worksheet cells visible in the workbook window.

▶ 4. If necessary, click the **Maximize** button 🗖 on the Excel window title bar. The Excel window fills the screen, as shown in Figure 1-3. Depending on your installation of Excel and your monitor resolution, your Excel window might look different from the one shown in Figure 1-3.

Figure 1-3 ▶ **Parts of the Excel window**

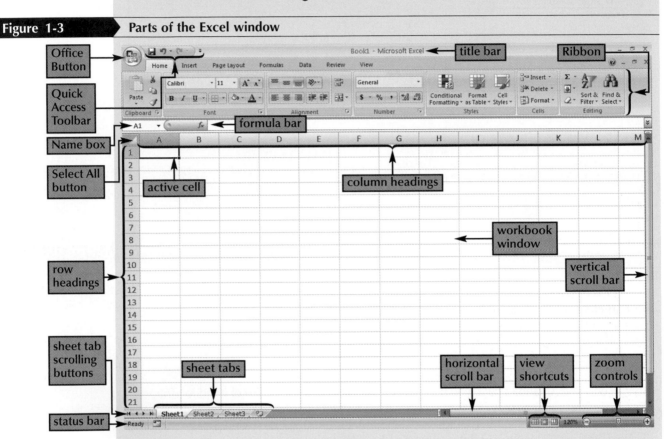

Trouble? If your screen varies slightly from those shown in the figures, your computer might be set up differently. The figures in this book were created while running Windows Vista in the Windows Vista Basic settings, but how your screen looks depends on a variety of things, including the version of Windows, background settings, and so forth.

Excel stores spreadsheets in files called **workbooks**. The contents of a workbook are shown in a **workbook window**. You can open more than one workbook window at a time to display the contents of different workbooks. You can also open multiple workbook windows for one workbook to display different views of the workbook's contents. The workbook that is currently being used is the **active workbook** and is displayed in the **active workbook window**. The name of the active workbook appears in the title bar of the Excel window. By default, Excel starts with a blank workbook named "Book1" in the workbook window, maximized to fill the entire Excel window.

Each workbook is made up of individual **sheets**, just as a notebook an accountant might use is made up of sheets of paper. Excel supports two kinds of sheets: worksheets and chart sheets. A **worksheet** contains data, laid out in rows and columns. A **chart sheet** contains an Excel chart that provides a visual representation of spreadsheet data. Charts can also be embedded within worksheets, allowing you to view both the data and charts in one sheet.

Each sheet is identified by a sheet name. The sheet names are displayed in **sheet tabs** located at the lower-left corner of the workbook window. The sheet currently displayed in the workbook window is the **active sheet**, and its sheet tab is white. In Figure 1-3, the active sheet is named "Sheet1." Other sheets included in the workbook shown in Figure 1-3, but not currently visible, are named "Sheet2" and "Sheet3." The sheet tabs for inactive sheets are gray and stacked behind the Sheet1 tab. An inactive sheet becomes active when you click its worksheet tab. By default, all new Excel workbooks are created with these three worksheets.

Each worksheet is laid out in rows and columns. **Row headings** identify each row by a different number. Row numbers range from 1 to 1,048,576. **Column headings** identify each column by a different letter. The first 26 column letters range in alphabetical order from A to Z. After Z, the next column headings are labeled AA, AB, AC, and so forth. Excel allows a maximum of 16,385 columns in a worksheet (the last column has the heading XFD).

Rows and columns intersect in a single **cell**; all the data entered in a worksheet is placed in different cells. You can have more than 17 billion cells in each worksheet. Each cell is identified by a **cell reference**, which indicates its column and row location. For example, the cell reference B6 indicates the cell located where column B intersects row 6. The column letter always appears before the row number in any cell reference. The cell in which you are working is the **active cell**. Excel distinguishes the active cell by outlining it with a thick border. In Figure 1-3, cell A1 is the active cell. The cell reference for the active cell appears in the **Name box** located in the upper-left corner of the worksheet.

Figure 1-4 describes the different parts of the Excel window, which are labeled in Figure 1-3.

Description of the Excel window elements ◄ **Figure 1-4**

Feature	Description
Office Button	A button that provides access to workbook-level features and program settings
Quick Access Toolbar	A collection of buttons that provide one-click access to commonly used commands, such as Save, Undo, and Repeat
Title bar	A bar that displays the name of the active workbook and the Excel program name
Ribbon	The main set of commands organized by task into tabs and groups
Column headings	The letters that appear along the top of the worksheet window to identify the different columns in the worksheet
Workbook window	A window that displays an Excel workbook
Vertical scroll bar	A scroll bar used to scroll vertically through the workbook window
Horizontal scroll bar	A scroll bar used to scroll horizontally through the workbook window
Zoom controls	Controls for magnifying and shrinking the content displayed in the active workbook window
View shortcuts	Buttons used to change how the worksheet content is displayed—Normal, Page Layout, or Page Break Preview view
Sheet tabs	Tabs that display the names of the worksheets in the workbook
Sheet tab scrolling buttons	Buttons to scroll the list of sheet tabs in the workbook
Row headings	The numbers that appear along the left of the worksheet window to identify the different rows in the worksheet
Select All button	A button used to select all of the cells in the active worksheet
Active cell	The cell currently selected in the active worksheet
Name box	A box that displays the cell reference of the active cell
Formula bar	A bar that displays the value or formula entered in the active cell

When Excel starts, it opens a blank workbook with Sheet1 as the active sheet and cell A1 as the active cell.

Navigating a Worksheet

Excel provides several ways to navigate a worksheet. You can use your mouse to click a cell to make it the active cell, or you can use the keyboard to move from one cell to another. Figure 1-5 describes some of the default keyboard shortcuts you can use to move between worksheet cells.

Figure 1-5 ▷ **Excel navigation keys**

Press	To move the active cell
↑, ↓, ←, →	Up, down, left, or right one cell
Home	To column A of the current row
Ctrl+Home	To cell A1
Ctrl+End	To the last cell in the worksheet that contains data
Enter	Down one row or to the start of the next row of data
Shift+Enter	Up one row
Tab	One column to the right
Shift+Tab	One column to the left
Page Up, Page Down	Up or down one screen
Ctrl+Page Up, Ctrl+Page Down	To the previous or next sheet in the workbook

You'll use both your mouse and keyboard to change the active cell in Sheet1.

To change the active cell:

▶ 1. Move your mouse pointer over cell **A5**, and then click the mouse button. The active cell moves from cell A1 to cell A5, and the cell reference in the Name box changes from A1 to A5. The column heading for column A and the row heading for row 5 are both highlighted.

▶ 2. Press the → key on your keyboard. The active cell moves one cell to the right to cell B5.

▶ 3. Press the **Page Down** key. The active cell moves down one full screen to cell B25.

   Trouble? If the active cell in your workbook is not cell B25, your monitor size and screen resolution might be different from those used for the figures in these tutorials. Continue with Step 4.

▶ 4. Press the **Page Up** key. The active cell moves up one full screen back to cell B5.

▶ 5. Press the **Ctrl+Home** keys. The active cell returns to the first cell in the worksheet, cell A1.

The mouse and keyboard provide quick ways to navigate the active worksheet. For larger worksheets that span several screens, you can move directly to a specific cell using the Go To dialog box or by typing a cell reference in the Name box. You'll try both of these methods.

To use the Go To dialog box and Name box:

▶ 1. Click the **Home** tab on the Ribbon, if necessary. The button to open the Go To dialog box is in the Editing group.

2. In the Editing group, click the **Find & Select** button. A menu of options opens.

3. Click **Go To**. The Go To dialog box opens.

4. Type **C14** in the Reference text box.

5. Click the **OK** button. Cell C14 is the active cell and its cell reference appears in the Name box. You'll use the Name box to make a different cell active.

6. Click in the **Name** box, type **A1**, and then press the **Enter** key. Cell A1 is once again the active cell.

Tip

You can also open the Go To dialog box by pressing the Ctrl+G keys.

To view more of the active worksheet, you can use the horizontal and vertical scroll bars, located at the bottom and right side of the workbook window, respectively, to move through the worksheet horizontally and vertically. Scrolling through the worksheet does not change the location of the active cell.

To scroll the worksheet:

1. Click the **down arrow** on the vertical scroll bar three times. The worksheet scrolls down three rows, but the active cell remains cell A1.

2. Click the **right arrow** on the horizontal scroll bar twice. The worksheet scrolls two columns to the right. The active cell still remains cell A1, although that cell is scrolled out of view.

   You can scroll several rows and columns by dragging the vertical and horizontal scroll boxes.

3. Drag the vertical scroll box up until you can see the first row in the worksheet.

4. Drag the horizontal scroll box to the left until you can see the first column in the worksheet.

Navigating Between Worksheets

Recall that each workbook can contain multiple worksheets and chart sheets. This enables you to better organize data and focus each worksheet on one area of data. For example, a sales report workbook might have a different worksheet for each sales region and another worksheet that summarizes the results from all the regions. A chart sheet might contain a chart that graphically compares the sales results from all of the regions. To move from one sheet to another, you click the sheet tabs at the bottom of the workbook window.

Some workbooks contain so many worksheets and chart sheets that their sheet tabs cannot all be displayed at the same time in the workbook window. For these workbooks, you can scroll through the sheet tabs using the sheet tab scrolling buttons. Similar to the horizontal and vertical scroll bars and the active cell, scrolling through the sheet tabs does not change the active sheet in the workbook window. To change the active worksheet, you must click a sheet tab.

To change the active sheet:

1. Click the **Sheet2** sheet tab. The Sheet2 worksheet, which is also blank, becomes the active worksheet. The Sheet2 tab is white, indicating that this is the active worksheet.

▶ **2.** Click the **Sheet3** sheet tab. The Sheet3 worksheet becomes the active worksheet.

▶ **3.** Click the **Sheet1** sheet tab to return to the first worksheet.

Now that you've had some experience moving around a blank workbook, you are ready to start working on Amanda's workbook.

| InSight | | **Creating Effective Workbooks** |

Effective workbooks are well planned and carefully designed. This helps you avoid errors and makes the workbook readable to others. A well-designed workbook should clearly identify its overall goal, and present information in a well-organized format. The process of developing a good workbook includes the following steps:

- Determine the workbook's purpose, content, and organization before you start entering data.
- Create a list of the sheets used in the workbook, making note of each sheet's purpose.
- Insert a documentation sheet into the workbook that describes the workbook's purpose and organization. Include the name of the workbook author, the date the workbook was created, and any additional information that will help others to track the workbook to its source.
- Enter all of the data in the workbook. Add text to indicate what the values represent and, if possible, where they originated. Other users might want to view the source of your data.
- Enter formulas for calculated items rather than entering the calculated values into the workbook. For more complicated calculations, provide documentation explaining them.
- Test the workbook with a variety of values to weed out any errors in your calculations. Edit the data and formulas to correct any errors.
- Save the workbook and create a backup copy when the project is completed. Print the workbook's contents if you need a hard-copy version for your files.

Planning a Workbook

Before you begin to enter data into a workbook, you should develop a plan. You can do this by using a **planning analysis sheet**, which includes a series of questions that help you think about the purpose of the workbook and how to achieve your desired results. In the planning analysis sheet, you answer the following questions:

- What problems do you want to solve? The answer defines the goal or purpose of the workbook.
- What data is needed to solve your problem? The answer defines the type of data that you have to collect and enter into the workbook.
- What calculations are required to solve your problem? The answer defines the formulas you need to apply to the data you've collected and entered.
- What form should the solution take? The answer defines the appearance of the workbook content and how it should be presented to others.

Amanda carefully considered these questions and developed the planning analysis sheet shown in Figure 1-6. You'll use this plan to create the workbook for Amanda.

Planning analysis sheet | Figure 1-6

Planning Analysis Sheet
Author: Amanda Dunn
Date: 4/1/2010

What problems do I want to solve?
• I need to have contact information for each RipCity Digital customer.
• I need to track how many DVDs I create for my customers.
• I need to record how much I charge my customers for my service.
• I need to determine how much revenue RipCity Digital is generating.

What data do I need?
• Each customer's name and contact information
• The date each customer order was placed
• The number of DVDs created for each customer
• The cost of creating each DVD

What calculations do I need to enter?
• The total charge for each order
• The total number of DVDs I create for all orders
• The total revenue generated from all orders

What form should my solution take?
• The customer orders should be placed in a grid with each row containing data on a different customer.
• Information about each customer should be placed in separate columns.
• The last column should contain the total charge for each customer.
• The last row should contain the total number of DVDs created and the total revenue from all customer orders.

Entering Text, Numbers, and Dates in Cells

Now that you have Amanda's plan for the workbook, your next step is to enter the data she's collected. You enter data by selecting a cell in the worksheet to make it the active cell, and then typing the content you want to enter in the active cell. When you finish typing, you can press the Enter key or the Tab key to complete the data entry and move to the next cell in the worksheet. As you enter data into the worksheet, the data entry appears in two locations: within the active cell and within the formula bar. The **formula bar** displays the content of the active cell and, as you'll see later, shows any formulas used to create calculated values.

In Excel, data falls into three general categories: text, numbers, and dates and times. **Text data** is a combination of letters, numbers, and some symbols that form words and sentences. Text data is often referred to as a **text string** because it contains a string of text characters. **Number data** is any numerical value that can be used in a mathematical calculation. **Date** and **time data** are commonly recognized formats for date and time values. For example, Excel interprets the cell entry "April 15, 2010" as a date and not as text. By default, text is left-aligned in cells, whereas numbers, dates, and times are right-aligned.

Entering Text

Tip

A documentation sheet reminds you why you created a workbook and what it contains and relays this information to others with whom you share the workbook.

Amanda wants you to enter some of the information from the planning analysis sheet into the first sheet of the workbook. The first sheet will document the purpose and content of the workbook and the sheets that follow. This documentation sheet will contain the name of the workbook, the workbook's author, the date the workbook was created, and a description of the workbook's purpose.

To enter the text for the documentation sheet:

1. Press the **Ctrl+Home** keys to make cell A1 the active cell on the Sheet1 worksheet, if necessary.

2. Type **RipCity Digital Customer Orders** in cell A1. As you type, the text appears both in cell A1 and in the formula bar.

3. Press the **Enter** key twice. Excel enters the text into cell A1 and moves the active cell down two cells to cell A3.

4. Type **Author** in cell A3, and then press the **Tab** key. The text is entered and the active cell moves one cell to the right to cell B3.

5. Type your name in cell B3, and then press the **Enter** key. The text is entered and the active cell moves one cell down and to the left to cell A4.

6. Type **Date** in cell A4, and then press the **Tab** key. The text is entered and the active cell moves one cell to the right to cell B4, where you would enter the date you created the worksheet. For now, you'll leave the cell for the date blank. You'll enter this date soon.

7. Click cell **A5** to make it the active cell, type **Purpose** in the cell, and then press the **Tab** key. The active cell moves one cell to the right to cell B5.

8. Type **To record orders from RipCity Digital customers** in cell B5, and then press the **Enter** key. Figure 1-7 shows the text entered in the Sheet1 worksheet.

Figure 1-7 ▶ **Documentation sheet**

The text you entered in cell A1 is so long that it seems to overflow into cells B1 and C1. The same is true for the text you entered in cells B3 and B5. When you enter more text than can fit in a cell, Excel displays the additional text in the adjacent cells as long as they are empty. If the adjacent cells also contain data, Excel displays only as much text as fits into the cell, cutting off, or **truncating**, the rest of the text entry. The text itself is not affected. The complete text is still entered in the cell, it's just not displayed. To display all of the text, you must increase the cell's width, which you'll learn about in the next session.

Next, you'll enter the RipCity Digital customer orders. As shown in Figure 1-8, the orders will contain the name and address of each customer, the order date, the number of DVDs created from the customer's home videos, and the price per DVD. Amanda's price per DVD decreases for larger orders.

Customer orders — **Figure 1-8**

Last	First	Address	Date	DVDs	Price per DVD
Dawes	Gregory	402 Elm St. Merrill, MI 48637	3/13/2010	7	$17.29
Garcia	Susan	1025 Drake Ave. Exeter, NH 03833	3/14/2010	25	$15.79
Torbet	Dr. Lilla	5 North Ln. Oswego, NY 13126	3/17/2010	32	$12.99
Rhoden	Tony	24 Mountain Dr. Auburn, ME 04210	3/24/2010	20	$15.79

You'll enter this data in the Sheet2 worksheet.

To enter the text labels and customer names:

1. Click the **Sheet2** sheet tab. Sheet2 becomes the active worksheet. You'll enter the column labels in cells A1, B1, C1, D1, E1, and F1.

2. Type **Last** in cell A1, and then press the **Tab** key. The label is entered in cell A1 and the active cell moves to cell B1.

3. Type **First** in cell B1, and then press the **Tab** key. The label is entered in cell B1 and the active cell moves to cell C1.

4. Type **Address** in cell C1, and then press the **Tab** key.

5. Type **Date** in cell D1, and then press the **Tab** key.

6. Type **DVDs** in cell E1, press the **Tab** key, and then type **Price per DVD** in cell F1. You've typed all the labels for the customer orders.

7. Press the **Enter** key. The active cell moves to cell A2, the start of the next row where you want to begin entering the customer data.

8. Type **Dawes** in cell A2, press the **Tab** key, type **Gregory** in cell B2, and then press the **Tab** key. You've entered the first customer's name and moved the active cell to cell C2. Figure 1-9 shows the text you've entered so far.

Text entered for the customer orders — **Figure 1-9**

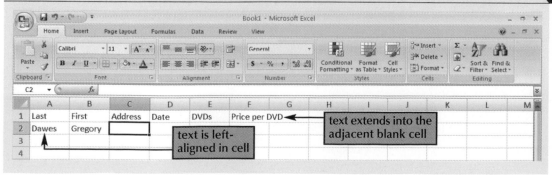

As you enter text in a worksheet, Excel tries to anticipate the text you are about to enter by displaying text that begins with the same letters as a previous entry in the same column. This feature, known as **AutoComplete**, helps make entering repetitive text easier. To accept the suggested text, press the Tab or Enter key. To override the suggested text, continue to type the text you want to enter in the cell. AutoComplete does not work with dates or numbers or when a blank cell is between the previous entry and the text you're typing.

Entering Multiple Lines of Text Within a Cell

The next cell in the Sheet2 worksheet contains the address of the first customer. Addresses are often entered on two or more separate lines. Amanda wants you to follow that convention with her customers' addresses. To place text on separate lines within the same cell, you press and hold the Alt key while you press the Enter key. This creates a line break within the cell.

Reference Window | **Entering Multiple Lines of Text Within a Cell**

- Click the cell in which you want to enter the text.
- Type the first line of text.
- For each additional line of text, press the Alt+Enter keys (that is, hold down the Alt key as you press the Enter key), and then type the text.

You'll enter the address for the first RipCity Digital customer, which will occupy two lines within the same cell.

To enter two lines of text within a cell:

▶ 1. Type **402 Elm St.** in cell C2, but do not press the Tab or Enter key. Instead, you'll insert a new line break.

▶ 2. Hold down the **Alt** key and press the **Enter** key, and then release both keys. The insertion point moves to a new line within cell C2.

▶ 3. Type **Merrill, MI 48637** on the new line, and then press the **Tab** key. The two lines of text are entered in cell C2, and cell D2 becomes the active cell. See Figure 1-10.

Figure 1-10 Two lines of text entered within a cell

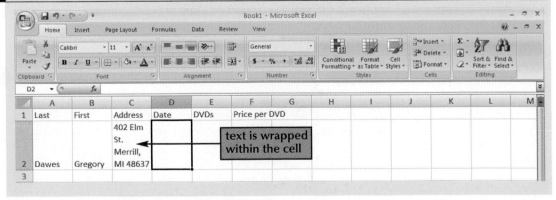

One impact of entering multiple lines of text within a cell is that it changes how text flows within the cell. Excel wraps the text within the cell, increasing the cell's height, if necessary, to show all of the text. As you can see, the text in cell C2 appears on four lines even though you entered the address on two lines. If the cell's width were increased, the text would then appear on two lines as Amanda wants. You'll do this in the next session.

Entering Dates

The next cell will contain the date of the order. You can enter dates in any of the standard formats. For example, you can enter the date April 6, 2010 in any of the following date formats (and many others) and Excel recognizes each format as representing the same date:

- 4/6/2010
- 4/6/10
- 4-6-2010
- April 6, 2010
- 6-Apr-10

In Excel, dates are actually numbers that are formatted to appear as text. This allows you to perform calculations with dates, such as determining the elapsed time between one date and another.

Sometimes Excel alters the date format you've chosen. For example, if you enter the date 4/6/10, Excel displays the date with the four-digit year value, 4/6/2010. Also, if you enter the text April 6, 2010, Excel converts the date format to 6-Apr-10. You'll enter the dates in the format *mm/dd/yyyy*, where *mm* is the month number, *dd* is the day number, and *yyyy* is the four-digit year number.

To enter the dates for the customer orders:

▶ **1.** Type **3/13/2010** in cell D2, and then press the **Tab** key to move to cell E2. The date of Gregory Dawes's order appears in cell D2 and cell E2 is the active cell.

You also need to enter the current date in the Sheet1 worksheet so you can document when you started working on this project.

▶ **2.** Click the **Sheet1** sheet tab. The Sheet1 worksheet is the active worksheet.

▶ **3.** Click cell **B4** to make it active, type today's date using the format *mm/dd/yyyy*, and then press the **Enter** key.

▶ **4.** Click the **Sheet2** sheet tab. The Sheet2 worksheet is the active worksheet, and cell E2 is still the active cell.

Entering Numbers

In the next two cells, you'll enter the number of DVDs that Amanda has created for Gregory Dawes and the price she will charge him for making each DVD. In both cases, you'll be entering numbers. In Excel, numbers can be integers such as 378, decimals such as 1.95, or negative such as −5.2. In the case of currency and percentages, you can include the currency symbol and percent sign when you enter the value. Excel treats a currency value such as $87.25 as the number 87.25 and a percentage such as 95% as the decimal number 0.95. Currency and percentages, like dates, are formatted in a convenient way for you to read. Excel right-aligns numbers within cells.

Tip

If a number exceeds its cell size, you see ###### for the truncated numeric value. You can display the entire number by increasing the column width.

You'll complete the information for Gregory Dawes's order by entering the number of DVDs Amanda created for him and the price she charged him for each DVD.

To enter the numbers for the first customer order:

▶ 1. Type **7** in cell E2, and then press the **Tab** key. The order quantity for Gregory Dawes is entered and the active cell is cell F2.

▶ 2. Type **$17.29** in cell F2, and then press the **Enter** key. The currency value is entered in cell F2, and the active cell moves to cell F3.

▶ 3. Click cell **A3**, which is where you want to enter the information for the next customer. See Figure 1-11.

Figure 1-11 ▶ First customer order completed

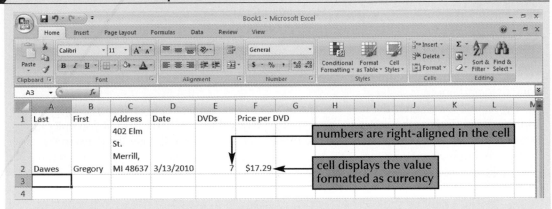

You've completed the data entry for Amanda's first customer. You still need to enter the data for three more customers into the worksheet. You'll use the same techniques you used to enter Gregory Dawes's order to enter their data.

To enter the remaining customer order data:

▶ 1. Type **Garcia** in cell A3, press the **Tab** key, type **Susan** in cell B3, and then press the **Tab** key. The second customer name is entered.

▶ 2. Type **1025 Drake Ave.** in cell C3, press the **Alt+Enter** keys, type **Exeter, NH 03833** on the next line, and then press the **Tab** key. The second customer's address is entered in the cell on two lines.

▶ 3. Type **3/14/2010** in cell D3, press the **Tab** key, type **25** in cell E3, press the **Tab** key, type **$15.79** in cell F3, and then press the **Enter** key. The rest of the second customer's data is entered.

▶ 4. Enter the following data for the remaining two customers in rows 4 and 5, making sure that you press the Alt+Enter keys to enter the addresses on two lines. See Figure 1-12.

Torbet, Dr. Lilla	**Rhoden, Tony**
5 North Ln.	**24 Mountain Dr.**
Oswego, NY 13126	**Auburn, ME 04210**
3/17/2010, 32, $12.99	**3/24/2010, 20, $15.79**

Customer data for RipCity Digital   Figure 1-12

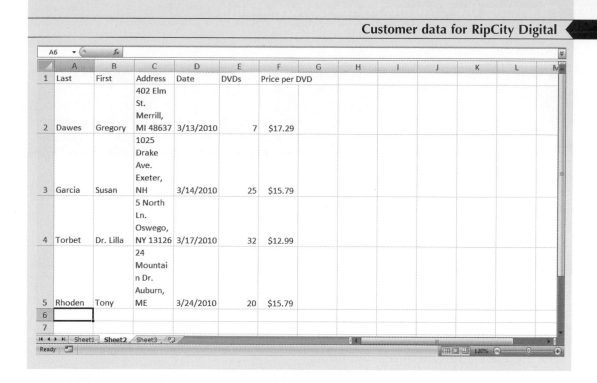

Working with Columns and Rows

Amanda has reviewed the customer order data you entered in the worksheet. She asks you to modify the worksheet to make it easier to read and include more data. To do this, you'll need to change the column widths and row heights, insert columns and rows, and delete columns and rows.

Changing Column Width and Row Height

The default sizes of the columns and rows in a worksheet might not always accommodate the information you need to enter. For example, the addresses you entered in the worksheet on two lines wrapped within the cell to display all the text. Other times, long cell content might be truncated. To make the cell content easier to read or fully visible, you can resize the columns and rows in the worksheet.

New workbooks use the default sizes for column widths and row heights. Column widths are expressed either in terms of the number of characters the column can contain or the size of the column in pixels. A **pixel** is a single point on a computer monitor or printout. The default column width is 8.38 standard-sized characters. This means that, in general, you can type about 8 or 9 characters in a cell before that entry is either truncated or overlaps the adjacent cell. Of course, if you decrease the font size of characters, you can fit more text within a given cell. Row heights are expressed in points or pixels, where a **point** is $1/72$ of an inch. The default row is 15.75 points high.

Reference Window | **Changing the Column Width or Row Height**

- Drag the right border of the column heading left to decrease the column width or right to increase the column width.
- Drag the bottom border of the row heading up to decrease the row height or down to increase the row height.

or

- Double-click the right border of a column heading or the bottom border of a row heading to AutoFit the column or row to the cell contents (or select one or more columns or rows, click the Home tab on the Ribbon, click the Format button in the Cells group, and then click AutoFit Column Width or AutoFit Row Height).

or

- Select one or more columns or rows.
- Click the Home tab on the Ribbon, click the Format button in the Cells group, and then click Column Width or Row Height.
- Enter the column width or row height you want, and then click the OK button.

Amanda suggests you increase the width of the Address column to allow the addresses to appear on two lines in the cells without additional line wrapping.

To increase the width of column C:

  1. Move the mouse pointer over the right border of the column C column heading until the pointer changes to ✛.

  2. Click and drag to the right until the width of the column heading reaches **20** characters, but do not release the mouse button. The ScreenTip shows the measurements of the new column width first as the numbers of characters and second in parentheses as pixels for the current screen resolution.

  3. Release the mouse button. The width of column C expands to 20 characters and all the addresses in column C fit on two lines with no extra line wrapping. See Figure 1-13.

Figure 1-13 | Increased column width

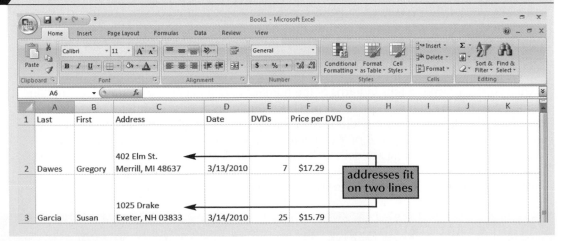

Amanda wants you to increase the widths of columns A and B to 15 characters to accommodate longer names. Rather than resizing each column separately, you can select both columns and adjust their widths at the same time. To select an entire column, you click its column heading. Likewise, to select an entire row, you click its row heading. You can drag across multiple column headings or row headings to select adjacent columns or rows. You can also press the Ctrl key as you click column or row headings to select non-adjacent columns or rows. You can select all the columns and rows in a worksheet by clicking the Select All button in the upper-left corner of the worksheet.

To increase the widths of columns A and B:

1. Click the **column A** column heading. The entire column is selected.

2. Hold down the **Ctrl** key, click the **column B** column heading, and then release the **Ctrl** key. Both columns A and B are selected.

3. Move the mouse pointer to the right border of the column B column heading until the pointer changes to ↔ .

4. Drag to the right until the column width changes to **15** characters, and then release the mouse button. Both columns are wide enough to display longer names.

The text in cell F1, "Price per DVD," overflows the cell borders. This column would look better if you increased the width of column F to 12 characters. Rather than use the mouse, you can set the column width using the Format command on the Home tab. The Format command gives you precise control in setting column widths and row heights.

To set the width of column F to 12 characters:

1. Click the **column F** column heading. The entire column is selected.

2. In the Cells group on the Home tab, click the **Format** button, and then click **Column Width**. The Column Width dialog box opens.

3. Type **12** in the Column width box, and then click the **OK** button. The width of column F changes to 12 characters, placing the text in cell F1 entirely within the borders of the cell.

The row heights didn't change after you resized the columns, which leaves a lot of blank space in the four rows of customer data. This extra blank space makes the data difficult to read and extends the content out of view. You'll reduce the heights of all these rows.

Row heights are set in the same way as column widths. You can drag the bottom border of the row or define a specific row height using the Format command on the Home tab. Another option is to autofit a column or row to its content. **Autofitting** eliminates any empty space by matching the column to the width of its longest cell entry or the row to the height of its tallest cell entry. If the column or row is blank, Excel restores the column or row to its default width or height. The simplest way to autofit a row or column is to double-click its border. You can also use the AutoFit commands.

Because you want to remove empty space from the four worksheet rows, you'll autofit the rows to their content rather than specify a particular row height.

To autofit row 2 to its content:

▶ 1. Move the mouse pointer over the bottom border of the row 2 row heading until the pointer changes to ✛.

▶ 2. Double-click the bottom border of row 2. The height of row 2 shrinks to match the content of cell C2, which is the tallest entry in the row with two lines of text.

You could continue to resize the remaining rows one at a time, but a quicker way is to select the rows you want to resize and then autofit all the selected rows simultaneously. Instead of double-clicking the row border, you'll use the AutoFit Row Height command.

To autofit the height of rows 3 through 5:

▶ 1. Drag the pointer across the row headings for rows 3, 4, and 5. The contents of rows 3 through 5 are selected.

▶ 2. In the Cells group on the Home tab, click the **Format** button. A menu of commands opens.

▶ 3. Click **AutoFit Row Height**. The height of each of the three rows autofits to its contents, and all the empty space is removed.

▶ 4. Click cell **A1** to make it the active cell. The other cells in the worksheet are deselected. Figure 1-14 shows the worksheet with the revised row heights.

| Figure 1-14 | Autofitted row heights |

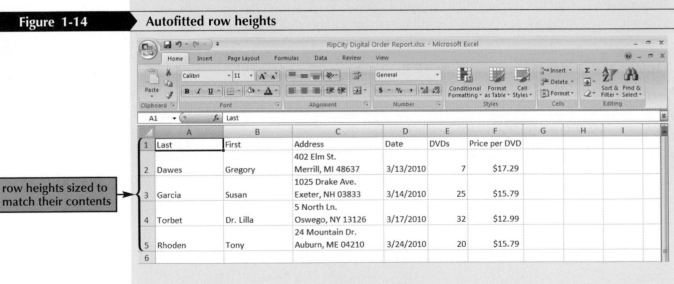

Inserting a Column or Row

Amanda notices that the worksheet doesn't include a column containing customer phone numbers. She wants you to insert a column for the customer phone numbers between the Address column and the Date column.

You can insert a new column or row anywhere within a worksheet. When you insert a new column, the existing columns are shifted to the right and the new column has the same width as the column directly to its left. When you insert a new row, the existing rows are shifted down and the new row has the same height as the row above it.

Inserting a Column or Row | Reference Window

- Select the column(s) or row(s) where you want to insert the new column(s) or row(s); Excel will insert the same number of columns or rows as you select.
- In the Cells group on the Home tab, click the Insert button (or right-click a column or row heading or selected column and row headings, and then click Insert on the shortcut menu).

You'll insert a column and enter the customer phone numbers in the new column.

To insert a new column:

▸ **1.** Click the **column D** column heading to select the entire column.

▸ **2.** In the Cells group on the Home tab, click the **Insert** button. A new column D is inserted into the worksheet and the rest of the columns shift to the right. The new column has the same width as column C.

▸ **3.** Reduce the width of column D to **15** characters.

▸ **4.** Click cell **D1** to make it the active cell, type **Phone** as the label, and then press the **Enter** key. The new column label is entered in cell D1, and cell D2 becomes the active cell.

▸ **5.** Enter the phone numbers in cells D2, D3, D4, and D5, as shown in Figure 1-15, pressing the **Enter** key after each entry.

New column inserted in the worksheet ◂ Figure 1-15

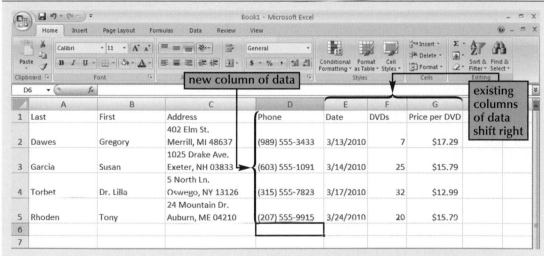

Amanda neglected to include a customer. Because the customer was RipCity Digital's first customer, he should be inserted at the top of the list. To add this new order, you need to insert a new row in the worksheet below the column labels.

To insert a new row:

▸ **1.** Click the **row 2** row heading. The entire second row is selected.

▸ **2.** In the Cells group on the Home tab, click the **Insert** button. A new row 2 is inserted, and the remaining rows shift down.

▸ **3.** Enter the new customer order shown in Figure 1-16 into row 2.

Figure 1-16 | **New row inserted in the worksheet**

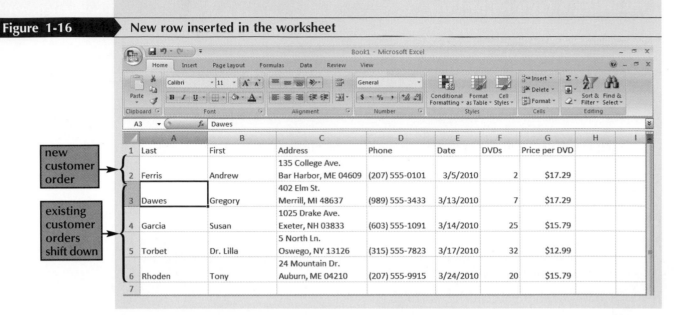

Deleting and Clearing a Row or Column

Adding new data to a workbook is common, as is removing old or erroneous data. Amanda just learned that her second customer, Gregory Dawes, canceled his order. She wants you to remove this order from the worksheet.

You can remove data in two ways: clearing and deleting. **Clearing** data from a worksheet removes the data but leaves the blank cells. **Deleting** data from the worksheet removes both the data and the cells. When you delete a column, the columns to the right shift left to fill the vacated space. Similarly, the rows below a deleted row shift up to fill the vacated space. Deleting a column or row has the opposite effect from inserting a column or row.

You'll first clear Gregory Dawes's data from the worksheet and then delete the row that contained the data. Usually, you would do this in one step by simply deleting the row, but this highlights the difference between clearing and deleting.

To clear and delete row 3:

▶ 1. Click the **row 3** row heading. The entire row 3 with Gregory Dawes's order is selected.

▶ 2. Right-click the **row 3** row heading, and then click **Clear Contents** on the shortcut menu. Excel clears the values in the third row, but leaves the blank row in that space.

▶ 3. Verify that the third row is still selected.

▶ 4. In the Cells group on the Home tab, click the **Delete** button. The third row is deleted, and the rows below it shift up. Only four customers remain in the worksheet.

Before proceeding, you'll save your workbook with the name "RipCity Digital Orders" in the default Excel workbook format.

To save the current workbook:

▶ **1.** Click the **Save** button 🔲 on the Quick Access Toolbar. Because this workbook has not yet been saved, the Save As dialog box opens.

▶ **2.** Navigate to the **Tutorial.01\Tutorial** folder included with your Data Files. You'll replace the default filename "Book1" with a more descriptive one.

Trouble? If you don't have the starting Data Files, you need to get them before you can proceed. Your instructor will either give you the Data Files or ask you to obtain them from a specified location (such as a network drive). In either case, make a backup copy of the Data Files before you start so that you will have the original files available in case you need to start over. If you have any questions about the Data Files, see your instructor or technical support person for assistance.

▶ **3.** Select **Book1** in the File name box, and then type **RipCity Digital Orders**.

▶ **4.** Verify that **Excel Workbook** appears in the Save as type box.

▶ **5.** Click the **Save** button. The Save As dialog box closes and the workbook file is saved with its descriptive filename.

Tip

You can reopen the Save As dialog box to save a workbook with a new filename, to a different location, or in another file format; click the Office Button and then click Save As.

You've entered and saved the customer order data. In the process, you worked with rows and columns. In the next session, you'll learn how to work with individual cells and groups of cells. You will also add calculations to the worksheet to determine how much revenue Amanda will generate from these orders.

Session 1.1 Quick Check | Review

1. What are the two types of sheets used in a workbook?
2. List two ways of identifying the active cell in the worksheet.
3. What is the cell reference for the cell located in the third column and fifth row of a worksheet?
4. What keyboard shortcut moves the active cell to cell A1?
5. What is text data?
6. How do you enter two lines of text within a cell?
7. Cell A4 contains "May 3, 2010"; why doesn't Excel consider this entry a text string?
8. Explain the difference between clearing a row and deleting a row.

Session 1.2

Working with Cells and Cell Ranges

A group of cells is called a **cell range** or **range**. Ranges can be either adjacent or nonadjacent. An **adjacent range** is a single rectangular block of cells. For example, all the customer order data you've entered in cell A1 through cell G5 is an adjacent range because it forms one rectangular block of cells. A **nonadjacent range** consists of two or more distinct adjacent ranges. All the last names in cell A1 through cell A5 and all the numbers in cells F1 through G5 together are a nonadjacent range because they are two distinct blocks of cells. A nonadjacent range can include as many adjacent ranges as you want.

Just as a cell reference indicates the location of an individual worksheet cell, a **range reference** indicates the location and size of a cell range. For adjacent ranges, the range reference specifies the locations of the upper-left and lower-right cells in the rectangular block separated by a colon. For example, the range reference A1:G5 refers to all the cells from cell A1 through cell G5. The range reference for nonadjacent ranges separates each adjacent range reference by a semicolon. For example, A1:A5;F1:G5 is the range reference for cells A1 through A5 and cells F1 through G5.

Selecting a Cell Range

You select adjacent and nonadjacent ranges of cells with your mouse, just as you selected individual cells. Selecting a cell range enables you to work with all of the cells in the range as a group. This means you can do things like move the cells, delete them, or clear all their contents at the same time.

Reference Window | **Selecting Cell Ranges**

To select an adjacent range:
• Click the cell in the upper-left corner of the adjacent range, drag the pointer to the cell in the lower-right corner of the adjacent range, and then release the mouse button.
or
• Click the cell in the upper-left corner of the adjacent range, press the Shift key as you click the cell in the lower-right corner of the adjacent range, and then release the Shift key.

To select a nonadjacent range of cells:
• Select a cell or an adjacent range, press the Ctrl key as you select each additional cell or adjacent range, and then release the Ctrl key.

To select all the cells in a worksheet:
• Click the Select All button located at the intersection of the row and column headings (or press the Ctrl+A keys).

You'll use the mouse pointer to select the adjacent range A1:G5, which includes all the content you entered in the worksheet so far.

To select the adjacent range A1:G5:

1. If you took a break at the end of the previous session, make sure the RipCity Digital Orders workbook is open and the Sheet2 worksheet is active.

2. Click cell **A1** to select the cell in the upper-left corner of the range A1:G5.

3. Drag the pointer to cell **G5**, which is the cell in the lower-right corner of the range A1:G5.

4. Release the mouse button. As shown in Figure 1-17, all cells in the adjacent range A1:G5 are selected. The selected cells are highlighted with color and surrounded by a black border. The first cell you selected, cell A1, is still the active cell in the worksheet.

Adjacent range A1:G5 selected | Figure 1-17

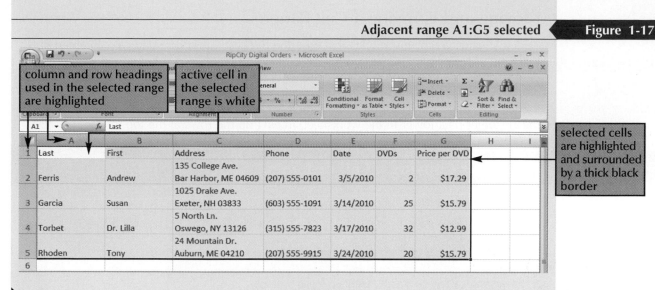

5. Click any cell in the worksheet to deselect the range.

Next, you'll select the nonadjacent range A1:A5;F1:G5.

To select the nonadjacent range A1:A5;F1:G5:

1. Select the adjacent range **A1:A5**.

2. Hold down the **Ctrl** key, and then select the adjacent range **F1:G5**.

3. Release the **Ctrl** key. As shown in Figure 1-18, all the cells in the nonadjacent range A1:A5;F1:G5 are selected.

Nonadjacent range A1:A5;F1:G5 selected | Figure 1-18

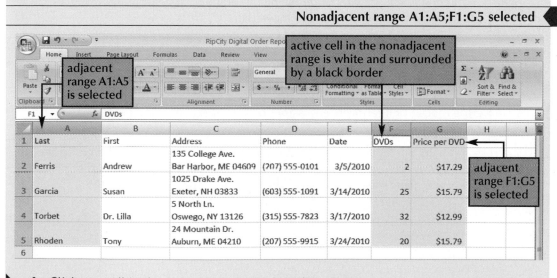

4. Click any cell in the worksheet to deselect the range.

Moving and Copying a Cell Range

Amanda wants you to insert titles that describe the customer order data you've entered. Including the company name, a descriptive title, and the date is part of good worksheet design, enabling others to quickly see the *who, what,* and *when* of the data. The current worksheet has no space to add this information. You could insert several blank rows at the top of the worksheet for this information. Another option is to select and then move the customer data lower in the worksheet, freeing up the rows at the top for the new text.

Reference Window | Moving or Copying a Cell or Range

- Select the cell or range you want to move or copy.
- Move the mouse pointer over the border of the selection until the pointer changes shape.
- To move the range, click the border and drag the selection to a new location (or to copy the range, hold down the Ctrl key and drag the selection to a new location).

or

- Select the cell or range you want to move or copy.
- In the Clipboard group on the Home tab, click the Cut button or the Copy button (or right-click the selection, and then click Cut or Copy on the shortcut menu).
- Select the cell or upper-left cell of the range where you want to move or copy the content.
- In the Clipboard group, click the Paste button (or right-click the selection, and then click Paste on the shortcut menu).

Tip

You can drag and drop to a range not currently visible. Drag the selection to the edge of the worksheet in which you want to scroll. When the new location is visible, drop the selection.

One way to move a cell or range is to select it, position the mouse pointer over the bottom border of the selection, and then drag the selection to a new location. This technique is called **drag and drop** because you are dragging the range and dropping it in a new location. You can also use the drag-and-drop technique to copy cells by pressing the Ctrl key as you drag the selected range to its new location. A copy of the original range is placed in the new location without removing the original range from the worksheet.

You'll use the drag-and-drop method to move data.

To drag and drop the customer orders:

1. Select the range **A1:G5**.
2. Move the mouse pointer over the bottom border of the selected range so that the pointer changes to ✥.
3. Press and hold the mouse button to change the pointer to ↖, and then drag the selection down four rows. Do not release the mouse button. A ScreenTip appears, indicating the new range reference of the selected cells. See Figure 1-19.

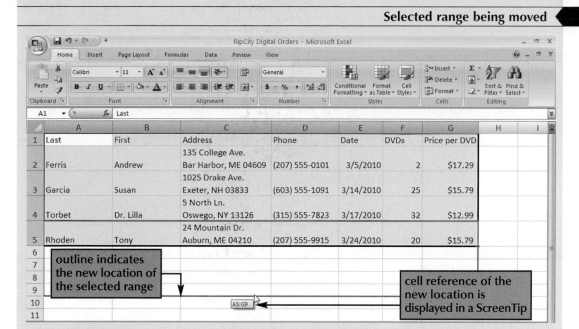

4. When the ScreenTip displays the range A5:G9, release the mouse button. The selected cells move to their new location.

5. Enter the title information shown in Figure 1-20 in the range A1:A3, pressing the **Enter** key after each entry.

	A	B	C	D	E	F	G	H
1	RipCity Digital							
2	Customer Orders							
3	3/31/2010							
4								

Some people find drag and drop a difficult and awkward way to move a selection, particularly if the worksheet is large and complex. In those situations, it's often more efficient to cut and paste the cell contents. **Cutting** places the cell contents into computer memory or on the Clipboard. The contents can then be pasted from the Clipboard into a new location in the worksheet. You'll cut and paste now.

To cut and paste cell contents:

1. With the range **A5:G9** selected, in the Clipboard group on the Home tab, click the **Cut** button. The selected range is surrounded by a blinking border, which indicates that its contents are stored on the Clipboard.

2. Click cell **A11**. This cell is the upper-left corner of the range where you want to paste the data.

▶ **3.** In the Clipboard group, click the **Paste** button. Excel pastes the contents of the range A5:G9 into the new range A11:G15. The blinking border disappears as a visual clue that the Clipboard is now empty.

▶ **4.** Select the range **A11:G15**, and then, in the Clipboard group, click the **Cut** button ✄.

▶ **5.** Click cell **A5**, and then, in the Clipboard group, click the **Paste** button. The customer order data is pasted into its original location in the range A5:G9.

Inserting and Deleting a Cell Range

Another use of selecting a range is to insert or delete cells from within the worksheet. To insert a range, select the range where you want the new cells inserted, and then click the Insert button in the Cells group on the Home tab. The existing cells shift down when the selected range is wider than it is long, and they shift right when the selected range is longer than it is wide (as illustrated in Figure 1-21). The Insert Cells command located on the Insert button menu lets you specify whether you want to shift the existing cells right or down, or whether to insert an entire row or column into the new range.

Figure 1-21 ▶ **Cells inserted within a cell range**

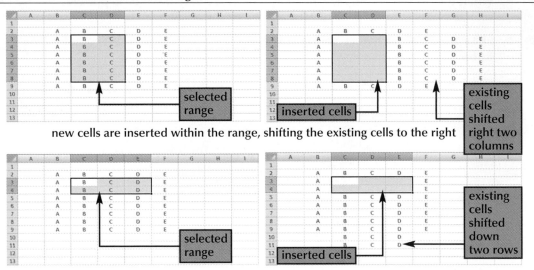

new cells are inserted within the range, shifting the existing cells to the right

new cells are inserted within the range, shifting the existing cells down

If you no longer need a specific cell or range in a worksheet, you can delete those cells and any content they contain. To delete a range, select the range, and then click the Delete button in the Cells group on the Home tab. As with deleting a row or column, cells adjacent to the deleted range either move up or left to fill in the vacancy left by the deleted cells. The Delete Cells command located on the Delete button menu lets you specify whether you want to shift the adjacent cells left or up, or whether to delete the entire column or row.

Inserting or Deleting a Cell Range

- Select a range that matches the range you want to insert or delete.
- In the Cells group on the Home tab, click the Insert button or the Delete button.

or

- Select the range that matches the range you want to insert or delete.
- In the Cells group, click the Insert button arrow and then click the Insert Cells button or click the Delete button arrow and then click the Delete Cells command (or right-click the selected range, and then click Insert or Delete on the shortcut menu).
- Click the option button for the direction in which you want to shift the cells, columns, or rows.
- Click the OK button.

You do not need to insert or delete any cells in the worksheet at this time.

Working with Formulas

Up to now you have entered only text, numbers, and dates in the worksheet. However, the main reason for using Excel is to perform calculations on data. Amanda wants the workbook to determine the number of DVDs she has to create for her customers and how much revenue will be generated by completing these orders. Such calculations are added to a worksheet using formulas and functions.

Entering a Formula

A **formula** is an expression that returns a value. In most cases, this is a number. You can also create formulas in Excel that return text strings. Every Excel formula begins with an equal sign (=) followed by an expression that describes the operation to be done. A formula is written using **operators** that combine different values, returning a single value that is then displayed in the cell. The most commonly used operators are **arithmetic operators** that perform addition, subtraction, multiplication, division, and exponentiation. For example, the following formula adds 5 and 7, returning a value of 12.

```
=5+7
```

However, formulas in Excel most often use numbers stored within cells. For example, the following formula returns the result of adding the values in cells A1 and B2.

```
=A1+B2
```

So, if the value 5 is stored in cell A1 and the value 7 is stored in cell B2, this formula would also return a value of 12. Figure 1-22 describes the different arithmetic operators and provides examples of formulas.

Figure 1-22 ▶ **Arithmetic operators**

Operation	Arithmetic Operator	Example	Description
Addition	+	=10+A1 =B1+B2+B3	Adds 10 to the value in cell A1 Adds the values in cells B1, B2, and B3
Subtraction	−	=C9−B2 =1−D2	Subtracts the value in cell B2 from the value in cell C9 Subtracts the value in cell D2 from 1
Multiplication	*	=C9*B9 =E5*0.06	Multiplies the values in cells C9 and B9 Multiplies the value in cell E5 by 0.06
Division	/	=C9/B9 =D15/12	Divides the value in cell C9 by the value in cell B9 Divides the value in cell D15 by 12
Exponentiation	^	=B5^3 =3^B5	Raises the value of cell B5 to the third power Raises 3 to the value in cell B5

If a formula contains more than one arithmetic operator, Excel performs the calculation using the same order of precedence you might have already seen in math classes. The **order of precedence** is a set of predefined rules used to determine the sequence in which operators are applied in a calculation—first exponentiation (^), second multiplication (*) and division (/), and third addition (+) and subtraction (−). For example, consider the formula below:

=3+4*5

This formula returns the value 23 because multiplication (4*5) takes precedence over addition. If a formula contains two or more operators with the same level of precedence, the operators are applied in order from left to right. Note the formula below:

=4*10/8

This formula first calculates the leftmost operation (4*10) and then divides that result of 40 by 8 to return the value 5.

To change the order of operations, you can enclose parts of the formula within parentheses. Any expression within a set of parentheses is calculated before the rest of the formula. Note the following formula:

=(3+4)*5

This formula first calculates the value of the expression (3+4) and then multiplies that total of 7 by 5 to return the value 35. Figure 1-23 shows how slight changes in a formula affect the order of precedence and the result of the formula.

Figure 1-23 ▶ **Order of precedence rules**

Formula (A1=50, B1=10, C1=5)	Order of Precedence Rule	Result
=A1+B1*C1	Multiplication before addition	100
=(A1+B1)*C1	Expression inside parentheses executed before expression outside	300
=A1/B1−C1	Division before subtraction	0
=A1/(B1−C1)	Expression inside parentheses executed before expression outside	10
=A1/B1*C1	Two operators at same precedence level, leftmost operator evaluated first	25
=A1/(B1*C1)	Expression inside parentheses executed before expression outside	1

Entering a Formula

- Click the cell in which you want the formula results to appear.
- Type = and an expression that calculates a value using cell references and arithmetic operators.
- Press the Enter key or press the Tab key to complete the formula.

Amanda wants the worksheet to include the total amount she charged for creating each customer's DVDs. The charge is equal to the number of DVDs created multiplied by the price per DVD. You've already entered this information for each customer in columns F and G. You'll enter a formula to calculate the charge for each customer in column H.

To enter the formula in column H:

▶ 1. Click cell **H5** to make it the active cell, type **Charge** for the column label, and then press the **Enter** key. The column label is entered in cell H5. Cell H6, where you want to enter the formula, is the active cell.

▶ 2. Type **=F6*G6** (the number of DVDs created multiplied by the price per DVD). As you type the formula, a list of Excel function names appears in a ScreenTip, which provides a quick method for entering functions. The list will close when you complete the formula. You'll learn more about Excel functions shortly.

▶ 3. Press the **Enter** key. The formula is entered in cell H6, which displays the value $34.58. The result is displayed as currency because cell G6 referenced in the formula contains a currency value.

After a formula has been entered into a cell, the cell displays the results of the formula and not the formula itself. If the results are not what you expect, you might have entered the formula incorrectly. You can view the formula by selecting the cell and reviewing the expression displayed in the formula bar. One challenge with formulas, particularly long formulas, is interpreting the cell references. Excel makes this simpler by color coding each cell reference in the formula and its corresponding cell in the worksheet. You'll see this when you view the formula you just entered.

To view the formula:

▶ 1. Click cell **H6** to make it the active cell. The formula you entered appears in the formula bar, whereas the value returned by the formula appears in the cell.

▶ 2. Click in the formula bar. As shown in Figure 1-24, each cell used in the formula has a different colored border that matches the color of its cell reference in the formula. This provides a visual cue to the formula, enabling you to quickly match cell references with their locations in the worksheet.

Figure 1-24

Formula references color coded

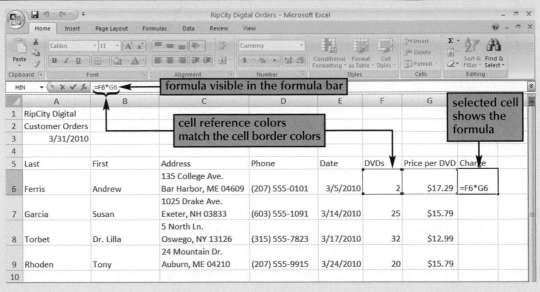

For Amanda's first customer, you entered the formula by typing each cell reference. You can also enter a cell reference by clicking the cell as you enter the formula. This technique reduces the possibility of error caused by typing an incorrect cell reference. You'll use this method to enter the formula to calculate the charge for the second customer.

To enter a cell reference in the formula using the mouse:

▶ **1.** Click cell **H7** to make it the active cell, and then type **=**. When you type the equal sign, Excel knows that you're entering a formula. Any cell that you click from now on causes Excel to insert the cell reference of the selected cell into the formula until you complete the formula by pressing the Enter or Tab key.

▶ **2.** Click cell **F7**. The cell reference is inserted into the formula on the formula bar. At this point, any cell you click changes the cell reference used in the formula. The cell reference isn't "locked" until you type an operator.

▶ **3.** Type ***** to enter the multiplication operator. The cell reference for cell F7 is "locked" in the formula, and the next cell you click will be inserted after the operator.

▶ **4.** Click cell **G7** to enter its cell reference in the formula, and then press the **Enter** key. Cell H7 displays the value $394.75, which is the total charge for the second customer.

Copying and Pasting Formulas

Sometimes, you'll need to repeat the same formula for several rows of data. Rather than retyping the formula, you can copy the formula and then paste it into the remaining rows. You'll copy the formula you just entered in cell H7 to cells H8 and H9 to calculate the charges for Amanda's two remaining customers.

To copy the formula in cell H7:

▶ **1.** Click cell **H7** to select the cell that contains the formula you want to copy.

2. In the Clipboard group on the Home tab, click the **Copy** button. The formula is copied to the Clipboard.

3. Select the range **H8:H9**, the cells in which you want to paste the formula.

4. In the Clipboard group, click the **Paste** button. Excel pastes the formula into the selected range. See Figure 1-25.

Formula copied and pasted **Figure 1-25**

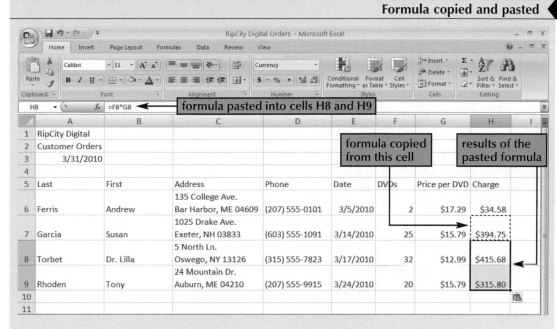

5. Click cell **H8** and verify that the formula =F8*G8 appears in the formula bar, and then click cell **H9** and verify that the formula =F9*G9 appears in the formula bar.

Pasting a formula is different from pasting a value. With the customer order data, Excel pasted the same values in a new location. With formulas, Excel adjusts the formula's cell references to reflect the new location of the formula in the worksheet. This is because you want to replicate the actions of a formula rather than duplicate the specific value the formula generates. In this case, the formula's action is to multiply the number of DVDs Amanda created for the customer by the price she charged for creating each DVD. By copying and pasting that formula, that action is replicated for every customer in the worksheet.

Introducing Functions

In addition to cell references and operators, formulas can also contain functions. A **function** is a named operation that returns a value. Functions are used to simplify formulas, reducing what might be a long expression into a compact statement. For example, to add the values in the range A1:A10, you could enter the following long formula:

```
=A1+A2+A3+A4+A5+A6+A7+A8+A9+A10
```

Or, you could use the SUM function to accomplish the same thing:

```
=SUM(A1:A10)
```

In both cases, Excel adds the values in cells A1 through A10, but the SUM function is faster and simpler to enter and less prone to a typing error. You should always use a function, if one is available, in place of a long, complex formula.

Excel supports over 300 different functions from the fields of finance, business, science, and engineering. Functions are not limited to numbers. Excel also provides functions that work with text and dates.

Entering a Function

Amanda wants to calculate the total number of DVDs she needs to create for her customers. To do that, you'll use the SUM function to add the values in the range F6:F9.

To enter the SUM function:

▶ **1.** Click cell **E10**, type **TOTAL** as the label, and then press the **Tab** key. The label is entered in cell E10, and cell F10 is the active cell.

Tip

You can also insert a range reference into a function by selecting the range with your mouse.

▶ **2.** Type **=SUM(F6:F9** in cell F10. As you begin to type the SUM function, a ScreenTip lists the names of all functions that start with the letter "S." When you type the cell references, Excel highlights all the cells in the specified range to provide a visual reminder of exactly which cells the SUM function is using. See Figure 1-26.

Figure 1-26 ▶ **SUM function being entered**

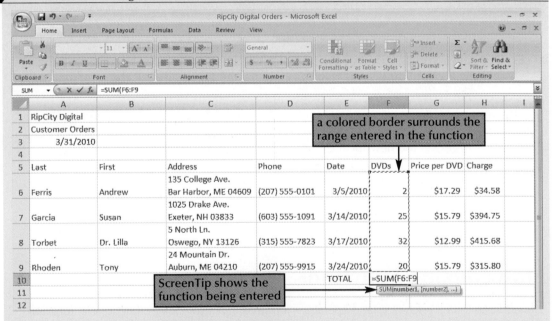

▶ **3.** Type **)** to complete the function, and then press the **Tab** key. The value of the SUM function appears in cell F10, indicating that Amanda has to create 79 DVDs to meet all of her current orders.

Entering Functions with AutoSum

A fast and convenient way to enter the SUM function is with the Sum button in the Editing group on the Home tab. The **Sum** button (also referred to as the **AutoSum** feature) quickly inserts Excel functions that summarize all the values in a column or row using a single statistic. With the Sum button, you can insert the SUM, AVERAGE, COUNT, MIN, and MAX functions to generate the following:

- Sum of the values in the column or row
- Average value in the column or row
- Total count of numeric values in the column or row
- Minimum value in the column or row
- Maximum value in the column or row

The Sum button inserts both the name of the function and the range reference to the row or column of data to which the summary function is being applied. Excel determines the range reference by examining the layout of the data and choosing what seems to be the most likely cell range. For example, if you use the Sum button in a cell that is below a column of numbers, Excel assumes that you want to summarize the values in the column. Similarly, if you use the Sum button in a cell to the right of a row of values, Excel summarizes the values in that row. When you use the Sum button, Excel highlights the range it "thinks" you want to use. You can change that range by typing a different range reference or selecting a different range with your mouse.

Understanding How the AutoSum Feature Works	InSight

Make sure to always verify the range selected by AutoSum, especially when a worksheet's column or row titles contain numbers. AutoSum cannot differentiate between numbers used as titles (such as years) and numbers used as data for the calculation.

Amanda wants to calculate the total revenue she'll generate by fulfilling her customer orders. You'll use the AutoSum feature to enter the SUM function.

To use AutoSum to calculate the total revenue:

▶ **1.** Click cell **H10** to make it the active cell.

▶ **2.** In the Editing group on the Home tab, click the **Sum button arrow** Σ ▾ . The button's menu opens and displays five common summary functions: Sum, Average, Count Numbers, Max (for maximum), and Min (for minimum).

▶ **3.** Click **Sum** to enter the SUM function. See Figure 1-27.

Figure 1-27 | SUM function entered with AutoSum

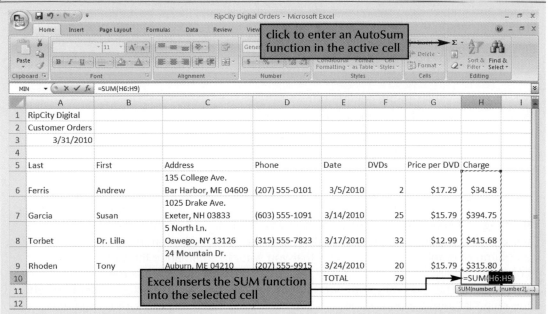

4. Verify that the range H6:H9 appears in the SUM function and is highlighted with a dotted border. The dotted border provides a visual reminder that this is where the SUM function will be applied.

5. Press the **Enter** key to accept the automatically generated formula. The total charge for all of Amanda's customers, shown in cell H10, is $1,160.81.

InSight | Creating Effective Formulas

You can use formulas to quickly perform calculations on business, science, and engineering data. To use formulas effectively:

- Do not place important data in a formula because the worksheet displays the formula result rather than the actual formula. For example, the formula =0.05*A5 calculates a 5% sales tax on a price in cell A5, but hides the 5% tax rate. Instead, enter the tax rate in another cell, such as cell A4, with an appropriate label and use the formula =A4*A5 to calculate the sales tax. Readers can see the tax rate as well as the resulting sales tax.

- Keep formulas simple. Use functions in place of long, complex formulas whenever possible. For example, use the SUM function instead of entering a formula that adds individual cells.

- Break up formulas to show intermediate results. For example, the formula =SUM(A1:A10)/SUM(B1:B10) calculates the ratio of two sums, but hides the two sum values. Instead, enter each SUM function in a separate cell, such as cells A11 and B11, and use the formula =A11/B11 to calculate the ratio. Readers can see both sums and the value of their ratio in the worksheet.

Working with Worksheets

Recall that new workbooks contain three worksheets labeled Sheet1, Sheet2, and Sheet3. You can add new worksheets to the workbook and remove unneeded ones. You can also give worksheets more descriptive and meaningful names. For Amanda's workbook, you'll remove unused worksheets from the workbook, and you'll rename the two worksheets in which you entered data.

Inserting and Deleting a Worksheet

Although each workbook includes three worksheets to start, sometimes you'll need more or fewer worksheets. You can add worksheets or delete unneeded ones. To insert a new worksheet into the workbook, right-click a sheet tab, click Insert on the shortcut menu, select a sheet type, and then click the OK button. Excel inserts the new sheet directly to the left of the active sheet. You can insert a new worksheet at the end of the workbook by clicking the Insert Worksheet tab located to the right of the last sheet tab in the workbook. The new worksheet is named with the next consecutive sheet number, such as Sheet4. You'll insert a new, blank worksheet at the end of your workbook.

To insert a new worksheet:

▶ **1.** Click the **Insert Worksheet** tab 🗐 to the right of the Sheet3 sheet tab. Excel inserts a new worksheet named "Sheet4" at the end of the workbook.

The workbook now includes two empty worksheets: Sheet3 and Sheet4. Because you don't plan to use these sheets, it's a good idea to remove them. You can delete a worksheet from a workbook in two ways. You can right-click the sheet tab of the worksheet you want to delete, and then click Delete on the shortcut menu. You can also click the Delete button arrow in the Cells group on the Home tab, and then click Delete Sheet. You'll use both of these methods to delete the Sheet3 and Sheet4 worksheets.

To delete the Sheet3 and Sheet4 worksheets:

▶ **1.** Right-click the **Sheet3** sheet tab, and then click **Delete** on the shortcut menu. Excel removes the Sheet3 worksheet.

▶ **2.** If necessary, click the **Sheet4** sheet tab to make it the active sheet.

▶ **3.** In the Cells group on the Home tab, click the **Delete button arrow**, and then click **Delete Sheet**. Excel removes Sheet4 from the workbook.

Renaming a Worksheet

The remaining worksheet names, Sheet1 and Sheet2, are not very descriptive. Amanda suggests that you rename Sheet1 as "Documentation" and rename Sheet2 as "Customer Orders." To rename a worksheet, you double-click the sheet tab to select the sheet name, type a new name for the sheet, and then press the Enter key. Sheet names cannot exceed 31 characters in length, including blank spaces. The width of the sheet tab adjusts to the length of the name you enter.

To rename the two worksheets:

▶ 1. Double-click the **Sheet2** sheet tab. The sheet name is selected in the sheet tab.

▶ 2. Type **Customer Orders**, and then press the **Enter** key. The width of the sheet tab expands to match the longer sheet name.

▶ 3. Double-click the **Sheet1** sheet tab, type **Documentation**, and then press the **Enter** key. Both sheets are renamed.

Moving and Copying a Worksheet

You can change the placement of the worksheets in a workbook. A good practice is to place the most important worksheets at the beginning of the workbook (the leftmost sheet tabs), and less important worksheets toward the end (the rightmost tabs). To reposition a worksheet, you click and drag the sheet tab to a new location relative to other worksheets in the workbook. You can use a similar method to copy a worksheet. Just press the Ctrl key as you drag and drop the sheet tab. The new copy appears where you drop the sheet tab, while the original worksheet remains in its initial position. You'll move the Documentation sheet to the end of the workbook and then return it to the beginning.

To move the Documentation worksheet:

▶ 1. If necessary, click the **Documentation** sheet tab to make that worksheet active.

▶ 2. Press and hold the mouse button so the pointer changes to ▯ and a small triangle appears in the upper-left corner of the tab.

▶ 3. Drag the pointer to the right of the Customer Orders sheet tab, and then release the mouse button. The Documentation sheet is now the second sheet in the workbook.

▶ 4. Drag the Documentation sheet back to be the first sheet in the workbook.

Editing Your Work

As you work, you might make mistakes that you want to correct or undo, or you might need to replace a value based on more current information. Amanda realizes that the price per DVD for Andrew Ferris's order should be $18.29 not $17.29 as entered in cell G6. You could simply clear the value in the cell and then type the correct value. However, sometimes you need to edit only a portion of an entry rather than change the entire contents of a cell, especially if the cell contains a large block of text or a complex formula. To edit the cell contents, you can work in **editing mode**.

> **Tip**
>
> If you make a mistake as you type in editing mode, you can press the Esc key or click the Cancel button on the formula bar to cancel all of the changes you made while in editing mode.

You can enter editing mode in several ways: (1) double-clicking the cell, (2) selecting the cell and pressing the F2 key, or (3) selecting the cell and clicking anywhere within the formula bar. When you work in editing mode, some of the keyboard shortcuts you've been using work differently because now they apply only to the text within the selected cell. For example, the Home, End, Backspace, Delete, and arrow keys now move the insertion point to different locations within the cell. The Home key moves the insertion point to the beginning of the cell's content. The End key moves the insertion point to the end of the cell's content. The left and right arrow keys move the insertion point backward and forward through the cell's content. The Backspace key deletes the character immediately to the left of the insertion point, and the Delete key deletes the character to the right of the insertion point. To exit editing mode and accept the changes you made, press the Enter key.

You'll see how keyboard commands differ when you're in editing mode as you change one digit of the value in cell G6.

To edit the value in cell G6:

▶ **1.** Click the **Customer Orders** sheet tab.

▶ **2.** Double-click cell **G6**. The mode indicator in the status bar switches from Ready to Edit to indicate that you are in editing mode.

▶ **3.** Press the **End** key. The insertion point moves to the end of the cell.

▶ **4.** Press the ← key three times. The insertion point moves to the right of the 7.

▶ **5.** Press the **Backspace** key to delete the 7, and then type **8**. The value in cell G6 changes to 18.29. See Figure 1-28.

Working in editing mode ◀ **Figure 1-28**

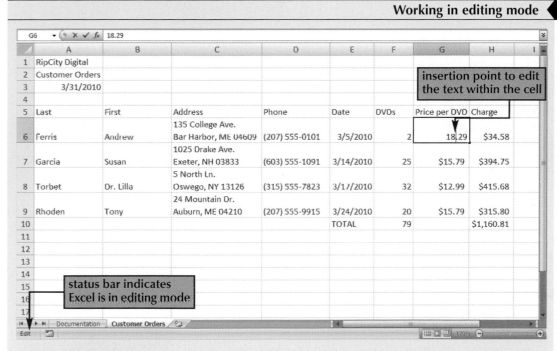

▶ **6.** Press the **Enter** key to accept the edit in cell G6. The value $18.29 appears in cell G6, the active cell is cell G7, and the mode indicator in the status bar changes from Edit to Ready to indicate that you are no longer in editing mode.

Undoing and Redoing an Action

As you revise a workbook, you might find that you need to undo one of your previous actions. To undo an action, click the Undo button on the Quick Access Toolbar. As you work, Excel maintains a list of your actions, so you can undo most of the actions you perform in a workbook during the current session. To reverse more than one action, click the Undo button arrow and click the earliest action you want to undo from the list. All actions subsequent to that action will also be undone.

You'll undo the action you just performed, removing the edit to cell G6.

To undo your last action:

▶ **1.** On the Quick Access Toolbar, click the **Undo** button 🔄.

▶ **2.** Verify that $17.29 appears again in cell G6, indicating that your last action—editing the value of this cell—has been undone.

If you find that you have gone too far in undoing previous actions, you can go forward in the action list and redo those actions. To redo an action, you click the Redo button on the Quick Access Toolbar. As with the Undo button, you can click the Redo button arrow to redo more than one action at a time. You'll use Redo to restore the value of cell G6.

To redo your last action:

▶ **1.** On the Quick Access Toolbar, click the **Redo** button 🔄.

▶ **2.** Verify that the value in cell G6 returns to $18.29.

Using Find and Replace

Amanda wants to you to replace all the street title abbreviations with their full names. Specifically, she wants you to use "Avenue" in place of "Ave.", "Lane" in place of "Ln.", and "Drive" in place of "Dr." Although you could read through the worksheet to locate each occurrence, this becomes a cumbersome process with larger workbooks. For greater speed and accuracy, you can use the **Find** command to locate numbers and text in the workbook and the **Replace** command to overwrite them. You'll replace each occurrence of a street title abbreviation.

To use the Find and Replace commands:

▶ **1.** In the Editing group on the Home tab, click the **Find & Select** button, and then click **Replace**. The Find and Replace dialog box opens.

▶ **2.** Type **Ave.** in the Find what box, press the **Tab** key, and then type **Avenue** in the Replace with box.

You can limit the search to the current worksheet or search the entire workbook. You can specify whether to match the capitalization in the Find what box and whether the search text should match the entire cell contents or part of the cell contents.

▶ **3.** Click the **Options** button to display additional Find and Replace options. See Figure 1-29.

Figure 1-29 ▶ **Find and Replace dialog box**

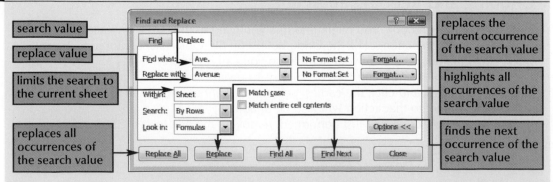

You can choose to review each occurrence of the search value and decide whether to replace it, or you can click the Replace All button to replace all occurrences at once.

4. Click the **Replace All** button. A dialog box opens, indicating that Excel has completed its search and made two replacements.

5. Click the **OK** button to close the dialog box.

6. Type **Ln.** in the Find what box, press the **Tab** key, type **Lane** in the Replace with box, click the **Replace All** button, and then click the **OK** button to close the dialog box that indicates Excel has completed its search and made one replacement.

Next, you want to replace the street abbreviation "Dr." with "Drive." Because "Dr." is also used as the abbreviation for "Doctor" for one customer, you must review each "Dr." abbreviation and make the replacement only in the addresses.

7. Type **Dr.** in the Find what box, press the **Tab** key, type **Drive** in the Replace with box, and then click the **Find Next** button. The next occurrence of "Dr." in the worksheet occurs in cell B8 with the text, "Dr. Lilla."

8. Click the **Find Next** button to ignore this occurrence. The next occurrence of "Dr." is in the mailing address for Tony Rhoden.

9. Click the **Replace** button to replace this text. You've finished finding and replacing text in the worksheet.

10. Click the **Close** button to close the Find and Replace dialog box. See Figure 1-30.

Revised customer orders | Figure 1-30

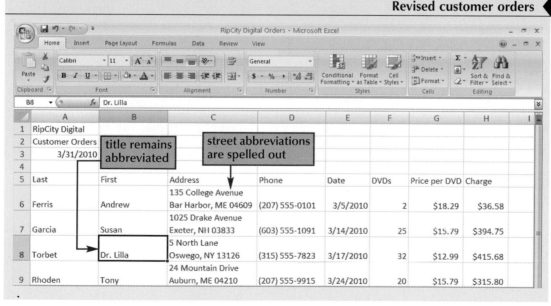

Using the Spelling Checker

Another editing tool is the spelling checker. The **spelling checker** verifies the words in the active worksheet against the program's dictionary. Although the spelling checker's dictionary includes a large number of words, as well as common first and last names and places, many words you use in workbooks might not be included. If the spelling checker finds a word not in its dictionary, the word appears in a dialog box along with a list of suggested replacements. You can replace the word with one from the list, or you can ignore the word and go to the next possible misspelling. You can also add words to the dictionary to prevent them from being flagged as misspellings in the future. Note that the spelling checker will not find a correctly spelled word used incorrectly, such as "there" instead of "their" or "your" instead of "you're." The best way to catch these types of errors is to proofread your worksheets.

Before giving the customer orders workbook to Amanda, you'll check the spelling.

To check the spelling in the worksheet:

▶ **1.** Click cell **A1**, click the **Review** tab on the Ribbon, and then, in the Proofing group, click the **Spelling** button. The Spelling dialog box opens and flags "RipCity" as a possible spelling error. Excel suggests two alternatives. See Figure 1-31.

Figure 1-31 ▶ Spelling dialog box

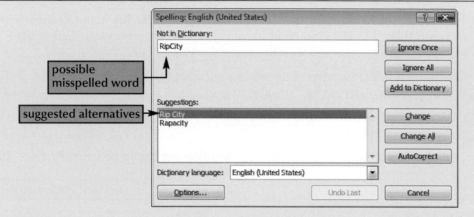

Because RipCity is the name of Amanda's company, you'll ignore all the occurrences of this spelling.

▶ **2.** Click the **Ignore All** button. The spelling checker flags "Torbet," a last name that is not in the program's dictionary.

▶ **3.** Click the **Ignore All** button to ignore the spelling of this name. The next potential spelling error is the name "Lilla" in cell B8. Amanda tells you the name should have been entered as "Lila," a first name that the spelling checker recognizes.

▶ **4.** Click **Lila** in the list of suggestions, if necessary, and then click the **Change** button. The text is changed within the cell. The spelling checker doesn't find any other errors.

Trouble? If the spelling checker finds another error, you might have another typing error in your worksheet. Use the spelling checker to find and correct any other errors in your workbook, and then continue with Step 5.

▶ **5.** Click the **OK** button to close the Spelling dialog box.

▶ **6.** Proofread the worksheet and correct any other spelling errors you find. You do not have to check the spelling in the Documentation worksheet.

Previewing and Printing a Worksheet

Now that you have finished the final edit of the workbook, you are ready to print a hard copy of the customer orders list for Amanda. However, before you print the workbook, you should preview it to ensure that it will print correctly.

Changing Worksheet Views

You can view a worksheet in three ways. **Normal view**, which you've been using throughout this tutorial, simply shows the contents of the worksheet. **Page Layout view** shows how the worksheet will appear on the page or pages sent to the printer. **Page Break Preview** displays the location of the different page breaks within the worksheet. This is particularly useful when a worksheet will span several printed pages.

You'll switch between these views to see how the Customer Orders worksheet will appear on printed pages.

To switch the worksheet views:

▶ **1.** Click the **Page Layout** button 🔲 on the status bar. Excel displays the page layout of the worksheet. You want to see the rest of the data, which extends to a second page.

▶ **2.** Reduce the zoom level to **60%**. See Figure 1-32.

Worksheet displayed in Page Layout view | **Figure 1-32**

> **Tip**
>
> You can view the workbook in the full screen space (which hides the Ribbon); in the Workbook Views group on the View tab, click Full Screen.

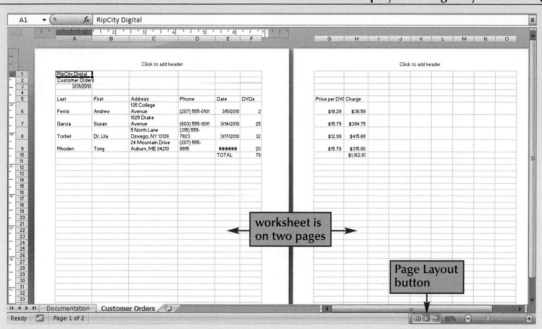

▶ **3.** Click the **Page Break Preview** button 🔲 on the status bar. The view switches to Page Break Preview, which shows only those parts of the current worksheet that will print. A dotted blue border separates one page from another.

Trouble? If the Welcome to Page Break Preview dialog box opens, this is the first time you've switched to Page Break Preview. Click the OK button to close the dialog box and continue with Step 4.

▶ **4.** Zoom the worksheet to **120%** so that you can more easily read the contents of the worksheet. See Figure 1-33.

Figure 1-33 ▶ **Worksheet displayed in Page Break Preview**

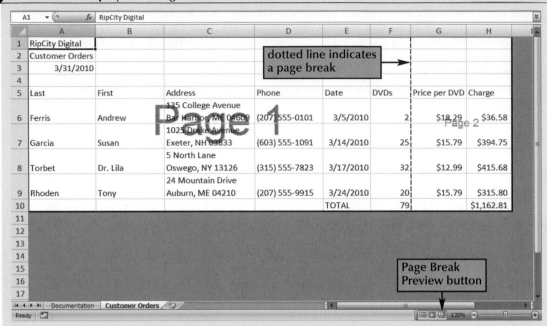

5. Click the **Normal** button ⊞ on the status bar. The worksheet returns to Normal view. A dotted black line indicates where the page break will be placed when the worksheet is printed.

Working with Portrait and Landscape Orientation

As you saw in Page Layout view and Page Break Preview, the Customer Orders worksheet will print on two pages—columns A through F will print on one page and columns G and H will print on a second page. Amanda wants the entire worksheet printed on a single page. The simplest way to accomplish this is to change the page orientation. In **portrait orientation**, the page is taller than it is wide. In **landscape orientation**, the page is wider than it is tall. By default, Excel displays pages in portrait orientation. In many cases, however, you will want to print the page in landscape orientation.

You'll change the orientation of the Customer Orders worksheet.

To change the page orientation:

▶ 1. Click the **Page Layout** tab on the Ribbon.

▶ 2. In the Page Setup group, click the **Orientation** button, and then click **Landscape**. The page orientation switches to landscape, and the Customer Orders worksheet contents fit on one page.

▶ 3. Click the **Page Layout** button ▣ on the status bar, and then verify that all the worksheet contents fit on one page.

Changing the page orientation affects only the active worksheet. The Documentation sheet remains in portrait orientation.

▶ 4. Click the **Documentation** sheet tab, and then click the **Page Layout** button 🔲. The entire contents of the Documentation worksheet fit on one page in portrait orientation.

Printing the Workbook

You can print the contents of your workbook by using the Print command on the Office Button. The Print command provides three options. You can open the Print dialog box from which you can specify the printer settings, including which printer to use, which worksheets to include in the printout, and the number of copies to print. You can perform a Quick Print using the print options currently set in the Print dialog box. Finally, you can preview the workbook before you send it to the printer to see exactly how the worksheet will look on the printer you selected with the print settings you've chosen. In general, you should always preview the printout before sending it to the printer.

You'll preview and print Amanda's workbook now.

To preview and print the workbook:

1. Click the **Office Button** 🔘, point to **Print**, and then click **Print**. The Print dialog box opens.

2. Click the **Name** box, and then click the printer to which you want to print if it is not already selected.

   Next, you need to select what to print. You can choose to print only the selected cells, the active sheet (or sheets), or all the worksheets in the workbook that contain data.

3. If necessary, click the **Entire workbook** option button to print both of the worksheets in the workbook.

4. Make sure **1** appears in the Number of copies box because you only need to print one copy of the workbook. Next, you'll preview how the worksheet will appear on the printed page with these settings.

5. Click the **Preview** button. Print Preview displays a preview of the full first page of the printout—the Documentation sheet printed in portrait orientation. The status bar shows that this is the first of two pages that will print.

6. In the Preview group on the Print Preview tab, click the **Next Page** button. Print Preview shows the second page of the printout.

   The printout will include only the data in the worksheet. The other elements in the worksheet, such as the row and column headings and the gridlines around the worksheet cells, will not print.

7. In the Print group, click the **Print** button. The workbook is sent to the printer and Print Preview closes.

Viewing and Printing Worksheet Formulas

Amanda notices that the printout displays only the worksheet values and none of the formulas. Most of the time, you will be interested in only the final results of the worksheet, not the formulas used to calculate those results. In some cases, you might want to view the formulas used to develop the workbook. This is particularly useful when you encounter unexpected results and you want to examine the underlying formulas. You can view the formulas in a workbook by switching to **formula view**, a view of the workbook contents that displays formulas instead of the resulting values. You'll switch to formula view now.

Tip

To toggle in and out of formula view, press the Ctrl+` keys. The ` grave accent symbol is usually located above the Tab key on your keyboard.

To view the worksheet formulas:

1. Click the **Customer Orders** sheet tab, if necessary, and then click the **Normal** button ⊞ on the status bar. The Customer Orders worksheet is active and displayed in Normal view.

2. Press the **Ctrl+`** keys. The worksheet changes to formula view.

3. Scroll the worksheet to the right to view the formulas in columns F and H. The column widths are wider to display the entire formula in each cell. As long as you don't resize the column widths while in formula view, they remain unchanged in other views. See Figure 1-34.

Figure 1-34 ▶ **Worksheet in formula view**

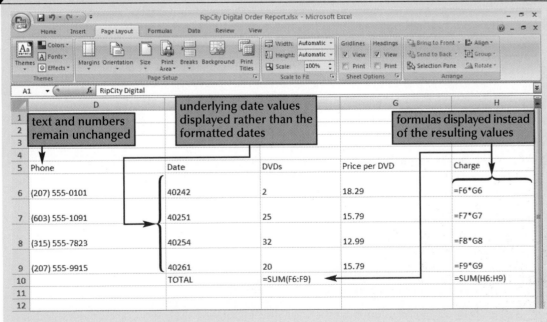

Amanda wants a printout of the formula view. The Customer Orders worksheet will not fit on one page because of the expanded column widths. You can scale the worksheet to force the contents to fit on a single page. **Scaling** a printout reduces the width and the height of the printout to fit the number of pages you specify by shrinking the text size as needed. You can also scale a printout proportionally to a percentage of its actual size. You'll scale the Customer Orders worksheet to a width and height of one page.

To scale the worksheet formulas to print on one page:

▶ **1.** In the Scale to Fit group on the Page Layout tab, click the **Width arrow**, and then click **1 page**.

▶ **2.** In the Scale to Fit group, click the **Height arrow**, and then click **1 page**. You'll verify that the worksheet formula view fits on a single page.

▶ **3.** Click the **Page Layout** button 🔲 on the status bar, and then zoom the worksheet to **50%**. The formula view of the worksheet fits on one page. See Figure 1-35.

Printout scaled to one page ◀ **Figure 1-35**

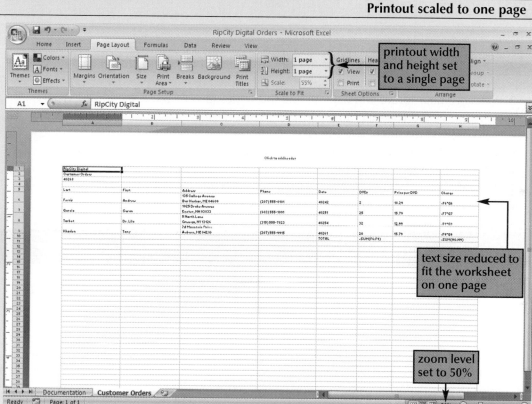

▶ **4.** Click the **Office Button** 🔴, point to **Print**, and then click **Print**. The Print dialog box opens. You'll specify that only the active worksheet will be printed.

▶ **5.** Click the **Active sheet(s)** option button to print only the Customer Orders worksheet.

▶ **6.** Click the **Preview** button. Print Preview displays a preview of the one-page printout of the Customer Orders worksheet in formula view.

▶ **7.** In the Print group on the Print Preview tab, click the **Print** button. The workbook is sent to the printer and Print Preview closes.

At this point, you've completed your work for Amanda. Before closing the workbook, you'll change the view of the workbook contents back to Normal view.

To save and close the workbook:

▶ **1.** Press the **Ctrl+`** keys to switch the worksheet back to Normal view.

▶ **2.** Save your changes to the workbook, and then close it.

Amanda is pleased with the job you've done for her. She will review the workbook you've created and let you know if she has any changes that she wants you to make.

Review | **Session 1.2 Quick Check**

1. Describe the two types of cell ranges in Excel.
2. What is the range reference for the block of cells from A3 through G5 and J3 through M5?
3. What formula would you enter to add the values in cells B4, B5, and B6? What function would you enter to achieve the same result?
4. How do you rename a worksheet?
5. Describe four ways of viewing the content of an Excel workbook.
6. Why would you scale a worksheet?
7. How do you display the formulas used in a worksheet?
8. How are page breaks indicated in Page Break Preview?

Review | **Tutorial Summary**

In this tutorial, you learned the basics of spreadsheets and Excel. After reviewing the major components of the Excel window, you navigated between and within worksheets. You entered text, dates, values, and formulas, and used the AutoSum feature to quickly insert the SUM function. You inserted and deleted rows, columns, and worksheet cells. You selected cell ranges and moved cell contents using drag and drop or cut and paste. You also created new worksheets, renamed worksheets, and moved worksheets within the workbook. You edited your work by using editing mode, finding and replacing text, and using the spelling checker to correct errors. Finally, you previewed and then printed the contents of the workbook.

Key Terms

active cell
active sheet
active workbook
active workbook window
adjacent range
arithmetic operator
AutoComplete
autofit
AutoSum
cell
cell range
cell reference
chart sheet
clear
column heading
cut
date data
delete
drag and drop

editing mode
Excel
Find
formula
formula bar
formula view
function
landscape orientation
Microsoft Office Excel 2007
Name box
nonadjacent range
Normal view
number data
operator
order of precedence
Page Break Preview
Page Layout view
pixel
planning analysis sheet

point
portrait orientation
range
range reference
Replace
row heading
scale
sheet
sheet tab
spelling checker
spreadsheet
text data
text string
time data
truncate
what-if analysis
workbook
workbook window
worksheet

| Practice | **Review Assignments** |

Practice the skills you learned in the tutorial using the same case scenario.

There are no Data Files needed for the Review Assignments.

Amanda reviewed your work on the Customer Orders worksheet, and has another set of orders she wants you to enter. The data for the new customer orders is shown in Figure 1-36. In addition to calculating the charge for creating the DVDs, Amanda also wants to include the cost of shipping in the total charged to each customer.

Figure 1-36

Date	Last	First	Address	Phone	DVDs	Price per DVD	Shipping Charge
3/27/2010	Fleming	Doris	25 Lee St. Bedford, VA 24523	(540) 555-5681	7	$18.29	$7.49
4/4/2010	Ortiz	Thomas	28 Ridge Ln. Newfane, VT 05345	(802) 555-7710	13	$16.55	$9.89
4/8/2010	Dexter	Kay	150 Main St. Greenbelt, MD 20770	(301) 555-8823	25	$15.79	$7.23
4/9/2010	Sisk	Norman	250 East Maple Ln. Cranston, RI 02910	(401) 555-3350	15	$16.55	$10.55
4/17/2010	Romano	June	207 Jackston Ave. Westport, IN 47283	(812) 555-2681	22	$15.79	$13.95

Complete the following:

1. Open a blank workbook, and then save the workbook as **Order Report** in the Tutorial.01\Review folder.
2. Rename Sheet1 as **Documentation**, and then enter the following data into the worksheet:

Cell	Data	Cell	Data
A1	**RipCity Digital**		
A3	**Author**	B3	*your name*
A4	**Date**	B4	*the current date*
A5	**Purpose**	B5	**To track customer orders for RipCity Digital**

3. Rename Sheet2 as **Customer Orders**.
4. Delete Sheet3.
5. On the Customer Orders worksheet, in cell A1, enter **RipCity Digital**. In cell A3, enter **Customer Orders Report**. In cell A4, enter **March 27 to April 17, 2010**.
6. In cells A5 through H10, enter the data from Figure 1-36. In column D, enter the address text on two lines within each cell.
7. Set the width of column A to 10 characters, columns B and C to 12 characters, column D to 20 characters, and columns E, G, and H to 16 characters.
8. Autofit all of the rows in the worksheet to the cell contents.
9. In cell I5, enter **Total**. In cell I6, insert a formula that calculates the total charge for the first customer (the number of DVDs created multiplied by the price per DVD and then added to the shipping charge). Increase the width of column I to 11 characters.
10. Copy the formula in cell I6 and paste it into the cell range I7:I10.

11. In cell E11, enter **Total**. In cell F11, use the SUM function to calculate the total number of DVDs created for all customers. In cell I11, use AutoSum to insert the SUM function to calculate the total charges for all of the customer orders.

12. Use editing mode to make the following corrections:
    - In cell D6, change the street address from 25 Lee St. to **2500 Lee St.**
    - In cell F9, change the number of DVDs from 15 to **17**.
    - In cell H8, change the shipping charge from $7.23 to **$8.23**.

13. Use the Find and Replace commands to replace all occurrences of St. with **Street**, Ln. with **Lane**, and Ave. with **Avenue**.

14. Change the page layout of the Customer Orders worksheet to print in landscape orientation on a single page.

15. Preview and print the contents of the entire workbook.

16. Change the Customer Orders worksheet to formula view, landscape orientation, and scaled to fit on a single page. Preview and print the Customer Orders worksheet.

17. Return the view of the Customer Orders worksheet to Normal view, save your changes to the Order Report workbook, and then save the current workbook as **Revised Report** in the Tutorial.01\Review folder. (*Hint:* Use the Save As command on the Office Button to save the existing workbook with a new name.)

18. Kay Dexter has canceled her order with RipCity Digital. Remove her order from the Customer Orders worksheet.

19. Add the following order directly after the order placed by June Romano: date **4/22/2010**; name **Patrick Crawford**; address **200 Valley View Road, Rome, GA 30161**; phone **(706) 555-0998**; DVDs **14**; price per DVD **$16.55**; shipping charge **$12.45**

20. Verify that Excel automatically updates the formulas and functions used in the workbook so they properly calculate the total charge for this order and for all the orders.

21. Edit the title in cell A4, changing the ending date of the report from April 17 to **April 22**.

22. Save the workbook, preview and print the contents and formulas of the revised Customer Orders worksheet, close the workbook, and then submit the finished workbook and printouts to your instructor.

| Apply | **Case Problem 1** |

Use the skills you learned to complete an income statement for a bicycle company.

Data File needed for this Case Problem: Altac.xlsx

Altac Bicycles Deborah York is a financial consultant for Altac Bicycles, an online seller of bicycles and bicycle equipment based in Silver City, New Mexico. She has entered some financial information in an Excel workbook for an income statement she is preparing for the company. She asks you to enter the remaining data and formulas.

Complete the following:

1. Open the **Altac** workbook located in the Tutorial.01\Case1 folder, and then save the workbook as **Altac Bicycles** in the same folder.

2. Insert three new rows at the top of the Sheet1 worksheet, and then enter the following text on two lines within cell A1:
   Altac Bicycles
   Income Statement*

3. In cell A2, enter **For the Years Ended December 31, 2007 through December 31, 2009**.

4. In the range C6:E7, enter the following net sales and cost of sales figures:

	2009	2008	2007
Net Sales	12,510	10,981	9,004
Cost of Sales	4,140	3,810	3,011

5. In the range C11:E14, enter the following expense figures:

	2009	2008	2007
Salaries and Wages	1,602	1,481	1,392
Sales and Marketing	2,631	2,012	1,840
Administrative	521	410	324
Research and Development	491	404	281

6. Select the nonadjacent range C18:E18;C20:E20;C24:E24, and then enter the following values for Other Income, Income Taxes, and Shares, pressing the Enter or Tab key to navigate from cell to cell in the selected range:

	2009	2008	2007
Other Income	341	302	239
Income Taxes	1,225	1,008	781
Shares	3,581	3,001	2,844

7. In the range C8:E8, enter a formula to calculate the gross margin for each year, where the gross margin is equal to the net sales minus the cost of sales.

8. In the range C15:E15, enter the SUM function to calculate the total operating expenses for each year, where the total operating expenses is the sum of the four expense categories.

9. In the range C17:E17, enter a formula to calculate the operating income for each year, where operating income is equal to the gross margin minus the total operating expenses.

10. In the range C19:E19, enter a formula to calculate the pretax income for each year, where pretax income is equal to the operating income plus other income.

11. In the range C22:E22, enter a formula to calculate the company's net income for each year, where net income is equal to the pretax income minus income taxes.

12. In the range C25:E25, enter a formula to calculate the earnings per share for each year, where earnings per share is equal to the net income divided by the number of shares outstanding.

13. Use the spelling checker to correct and replace any spelling errors in the worksheet. Ignore the spelling of Altac.

14. In cell A18, use editing mode to capitalize the word *income*.

15. Increase the width of column A to 18 characters and increase the width of column B to 25 characters. Autofit the height of row 1.

16. Rename Sheet1 as **Income Statement**; rename Sheet2 as **Documentation** and move it to the beginning of the workbook; and then delete the Sheet3 worksheet.

17. In the Documentation worksheet, enter the following text and values:

Cell	Data	Cell	Data
A1	**Altac Bicycles**		
A3	**Author**	B3	*your name*
A4	**Date**	B4	*the current date*
A5	**Purpose**	B5	**Income statement for Altac Bicycles for 2007 through 2009**

18. Save the workbook, preview the workbook and make sure each worksheet in portrait orientation fits on one page in the printout, and then print the entire workbook. Close the workbook, and then submit the finished workbook and printouts to your instructor.

Apply | **Case Problem 2**

Use the skills you learned to complete a balance sheet for a food retailer.

Data File needed for this Case Problem: Halley.xlsx

Halley Foods   Michael Li is working on the annual financial report for Halley Foods of Norman, Oklahoma. One part of the financial report will be the company's balance sheet for the previous three years. Michael has entered some of the labels for the balance sheet but wants you to finish the job by entering the actual values and formulas.

Complete the following:

1. Open the **Halley** workbook located in the Tutorial.01\Case2 folder, and then save the workbook as **Halley Foods** in the same folder.

2. Rename the Sheet1 worksheet as **Balance Sheet**, and then delete the Sheet2 and Sheet3 worksheets.

3. Insert three new rows at the top of the sheet, and then enter the following text on four lines within cell A1:

   Halley Foods
   Balance Sheet
   As of December 31
   For the Years 2007 through 2009

4. Change the width of column A to 30 characters, the width of column B to 20 characters, and the width of column C to 26 characters. Autofit the height of row 1.

5. Enter the assets and liability values shown in Figure 1-37 into the corresponding cells in the Balance Sheet worksheet for each of the last three years.

Figure 1-37

		2009	2008	2007
Current Assets	Cash and equivalents	796	589	423
	Short-term investments	1,194	1,029	738
	Accounts receivable	1,283	1,151	847
	Net inventories	683	563	463
	Deferred taxes	510	366	332
	Other current assets	162	137	103
Other Assets	Investments	7,077	5,811	4,330
	Restricted investments	910	797	681
	Property and equipment	779	696	420
	Other assets	1,178	484	485
Current Liabilities	Accounts payable	350	293	182
	Income taxes payable	608	442	342
	Accrued payroll	661	564	384
	Other accrued liabilities	1,397	1,250	775
Minority Interest		44	43	36
Shareholders' Equity	Preferred and common stock	5,557	4,821	3,515
	Retained earnings	5,666	4,007	3,401
	Other comprehensive income	289	203	187

6. Use AutoSum to calculate the total current assets, other assets, current liabilities, and shareholders' equity in the ranges D11:F11, D17:F17, D25:F25, and D33:F33, respectively, for each of the previous three years.

7. Insert a formula in the range D19:F19 to calculate the total assets (current plus other) for each year.

8. Insert a formula in the range D36:F36 to calculate the value of the total current liabilities plus the minority interest plus the total shareholders' equity for each year.

9. Use the spelling checker to correct any spelling mistakes in the Balance Sheet worksheet, and then proofread the worksheet.

10. Change the zoom level of the Balance Sheet worksheet to 70% in Normal view to view the entire contents of the sheet in the workbook window.

11. View the Balance Sheet worksheet in Page Layout view zoomed to 80%, and then scale the height and width of the worksheet to fit on one page.

12. Insert a new worksheet named **Documentation** at the beginning of the workbook.

13. In the Documentation worksheet, enter the following data:

Cell	Data	Cell	Data
A1	**Halley Foods**		
A3	**Author**	B3	*your name*
A4	**Date**	B4	*the current date*
A5	**Purpose**	B5	**Balance sheet for Halley Foods for 2007 through 2009**

14. Save, preview, and then print the entire Halley Foods Balance Sheet workbook.

15. Print the formula view of the Balance Sheet worksheet on two pages in landscape orientation. Return the Balance Sheet worksheet to Page Layout view when you're finished.

16. Save and close the workbook, and then submit the finished workbook and printouts to your instructor.

Challenge | **Case Problem 3**

Explore using Auto-Sum to calculate production statistics.

Data File needed for this Case Problem: Global.xlsx

Global Site GPS Kevin Hodge is a production assistant at Global Site GPS, a leading manufacturer of GPS devices located in Crestwood, Missouri. One of Kevin's jobs is to monitor output at the company's five regional plants. He wants to create an Excel workbook that reports the monthly production at the five sites, including the monthly average, minimum, and maximum production and total production for the previous year. He asks you to create the workbook that reports these statistics.

Complete the following:

1. Open the **Global** workbook located in the Tutorial.01\Case3 folder, and then save the workbook as **Global Site** in the same folder.

2. Rename the Sheet1 worksheet as **Production History**, and then insert 12 new rows at the top of the worksheet.

3. Increase the width of column A to 23 characters and the width of columns B through F to 14 characters.

4. In the range B7:F7, enter the titles **Plant1**, **Plant2**, **Plant3**, **Plant4**, and **Plant5**, respectively.

5. In the range A8:A11, enter **Total Units Produced**, **Average per Month**, **Maximum**, and **Minimum**, respectively.

✛EXPLORE 6. Select the range B26:F26, use AutoSum to calculate the sum of the production values for each of the five plants, and then drag and drop the selected cells to the range B8:F8.

✛EXPLORE 7. Select the range B26:F26, use AutoSum to calculate the average of the production values for each of the five plants, and then drag and drop the selected cells to the range B9:F9.

✛EXPLORE 8. Repeat Step 7 to calculate the maximum values for each of the five plants and then move those calculated values to the range B10:F10, and then repeat to calculate the minimum production values and drag and drop those calculated values to the range B11:F11.

9. In the Production History worksheet, enter the following data:

Cell	Data	Cell	Data
A1	**Global Site GPS**		
A2	**Production Report**		
A3	**Model**	B3	**MapTracker 201**
A4	**Year**	B4	**2010**
A5	**Total Units Produced**		

10. In cell B5, use the SUM function to add the values in the range B8:F8.

11. Insert a new worksheet named **Plant Directory** as the first worksheet in the workbook.

12. In cells A1 and A2, enter **Global Site GPS** and **Plant Directory**, respectively, and then enter the text shown in Figure 1-38 in the range A4:D9, making sure that the address is entered on two lines within the cell.

Figure 1-38

Plant	Plant Manager	Address	Phone
1	Karen Brookers	300 Commerce Avenue Crestwood, MO 63126	(314) 555-3881
2	Daniel Gomez	15 North Main Street Edison, NJ 08837	(732) 555-0012
3	Jody Hetrick	3572 Howard Lane Weston, FL 33326	(954) 555-4817
4	Yong Jo	900 South Street Kirkland, WA 98033	(425) 555-8775
5	Sandy Nisbett	3771 Water Street Helena, MT 59623	(406) 555-4114

13. Set the width of column B to 15 characters, the width of column C to 30 characters, and the width of column D to 16 characters. Autofit the height of each row to its content.

14. Insert a new worksheet named **Documentation** as the first worksheet in the workbook, and then enter the following data:

Cell	Data	Cell	Data
A1	**Global Site GPS**		
A3	**Author**	B3	*your name*
A4	**Date**	B4	*the current date*
A5	**Purpose**	B5	**Production report for Global Site GPS**

15. Switch the Production History worksheet to Page Layout view, change the orientation to landscape, and then verify that the worksheet fits on a single page.

16. Save your workbook, preview and print the workbook, close the workbook, and then submit the finished workbook and printouts to your instructor.

Create | **Case Problem 4**

Create an Excel workbook to record service calls for a lawn service agency.

There are no Data Files needed for this Case Problem.

Green Lawns Green Lawns provides yard service and maintenance for homes in and around Mount Vernon, Ohio. Gary Taylor manages the accounts for Green Lawns and wants to use Excel to record weekly service calls made by the company. He asks you to create the workbook for him. Gary provides you the list of service calls made in the first week of August shown in Figure 1-39.

Figure 1-39

Customer	Address	Phone	Last Service	Hours	Base Fee	Hourly Rate
David Lane	391 Country Drive Mount Vernon, OH 43050	(740) 555-4439	8/2/2010	3	$35	$15.50
Robert Gomez	151 Apple Lane Mount Vernon, OH 43051	(740) 555-0988	8/2/2010	3.5	$35	$15.50
Sandra Lee	112 Main Street Mount Vernon, OH 43050	(740) 555-3773	8/3/2010	1.5	$20	$12.50
Gregory Sands	305 Country Drive Mount Vernon, OH 43050	(740) 555-4189	8/3/2010	4	$35	$17.50
Betty Oaks	205 Second Street Mount Vernon, OH 43049	(740) 555-0088	8/3/2010	1	$20	$12.50

Complete the following:

1. Open a blank workbook, and then save it as **Green Lawns** in the Tutorial.01\Case4 folder included with your Data Files.

2. Rename Sheet1 as **Documentation**, and then enter information documenting the workbook. Include the name of the company, your name, the current date, and a brief description of the purpose of the workbook. The layout and appearance of the worksheet is up to you.

3. In Sheet2, enter the service calls shown in Figure 1-39, and then enter appropriate formulas and functions to calculate the service charge for each customer. Green Lawns charges each customer a base fee plus a working fee that is equal to the hourly rate multiplied by the number of hours worked. Also, enter a formula to calculate the total charges for all customer calls. The layout and appearance of the page is up to you.

4. Rename Sheet2 as **Service Calls**, and then delete any unused sheets in the workbook.

5. Check the spelling in the workbook, correcting any spelling errors, and then proofread the workbook.

6. Save your workbook, preview the worksheets to ensure that each fits onto a single page, and then print the entire workbook. Close the workbook, and then submit the finished workbook and printouts to your instructor.

Research | **Internet Assignments**

Use the Internet to find and work with data related to the topics presented in this tutorial.

The purpose of the Internet Assignments is to challenge you to find information on the Internet that you can use to work effectively with this software. The actual assignments are updated and maintained on the Course Technology Web site. Log on to the Internet and use your Web browser to go to the Student Online Companion for New Perspectives Office 2007 at **www.course.com/np/office2007**. Then navigate to the Internet Assignments for this tutorial.

Assess | **SAM Assessment and Training**

If you have a SAM user profile, you may have access to hands-on instruction, practice, and assessment of the skills covered in this tutorial. Log in to your SAM account (**http://sam2007.course.com**) to launch any assigned training activities or exams that relate to the skills covered in this tutorial.

Review | **Quick Check Answers**

Session 1.1

1. chart sheets and worksheets
2. The active cell is surrounded by a thick border and its cell reference appears in the Name box.
3. C5
4. the Ctrl+Home keys
5. a combination of alphanumerical characters that form words and sentences (called a text string)
6. Enter the first line of text, press the Alt+Enter keys, and then type the second line of text.
7. Because it's a date; all dates are numbers formatted to appear in standard date formats.
8. Clearing a row removes only the contents of the row, deleting a row removes the contents and the row.

Session 1.2

1. Adjacent cell ranges contain a rectangular block of cells; nonadjacent cell ranges contain a collection of adjacent cell ranges.
2. A3:G5;J3:M5
3. =B4+B5+B6; =SUM(B4:B6)
4. Double-click the sheet tab, and then type a new name on the sheet tab.
5. Normal view shows the columns and rows of the worksheet. Page Layout view shows the layout of the worksheet as it appears on a page. Page Break Preview shows the page breaks within the worksheet. Formula view shows formulas rather than the values returned by the formulas.
6. to force a worksheet to print on one page
7. Press the Ctrl+` keys to switch to formula view.
8. as dotted lines

Ending Data Files

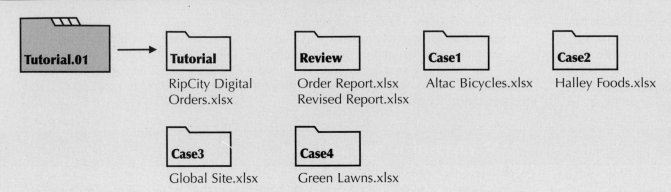

Objectives

Session 2.1
- Format text, numbers, and dates
- Change font colors and fill colors
- Merge a range into a single cell
- Apply a built-in cell style
- Select a different theme

Session 2.2
- Apply a built-in table style
- Add conditional formats to tables with highlight rules and data bars
- Hide worksheet rows
- Insert print titles, set print areas, and insert page breaks
- Enter headers and footers

Formatting a Workbook

Formatting a Financial Report

Case | ExerComp Exercise Equipment

ExerComp, based in Mason, Ohio, manufactures electronic and computer components for fitness machines and sporting goods. At the upcoming annual sales meeting, sales managers will present reports that detail the sales history of different ExerComp products. Sales manager Tom Uhen will report on the recent sales history of the X310 heart rate monitor.

Tom has already created a workbook and entered the sales figures for the past two years. He wants you to make that data more readable and informative. To do this, you will work with formatting tools to modify the appearance of the data in each cell, the cell itself, and the entire worksheet. Because much of Tom's data has been stored in tables, you will also use some special formatting tools designed for tables.

Starting Data Files

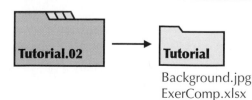

Tutorial.02 →	Tutorial	Review	Case1	Case2	Case3	Case4
	Background.jpg ExerComp.xlsx	Paper.jpg X410.xlsx	Frosti.xlsx	GrillRite.xlsx	Iowa.xlsx	Life.xlsx

Session 2.1

Formatting Workbooks

Tom already entered the data and some formulas in the worksheets, but the workbook is only a rough draft of what he wants to submit to the company. Tom's workbook has three worksheets. The Documentation sheet describes the workbook's purpose and content. The Yearly Sales sheet records the total sales of the X310 heart rate monitor for 2008 and 2009, including the total number of units sold per sales region (labeled R01 through R08) and the total revenue generated by those sales. The Monthly Sales sheet reports the number of X310 units sold in 2008 and 2009 by region and month as well as the corresponding increase in sales. You'll open the workbook and review its content.

To open the workbook:

▶ **1.** Open the **ExerComp** workbook located in the **Tutorial.02\Tutorial** folder included with your Data Files, and then save the workbook as **ExerComp Sales Report** in the same folder.

▶ **2.** In the Documentation sheet, enter your name in cell B4 and the current date in cell B5.

▶ **3.** Review the contents in the three worksheets.

In its current form, the data is difficult to read and interpret. Tom wants you to format the workbook contents to improve its readability and visual appeal. **Formatting** is the process of changing a workbook's appearance by defining the fonts, styles, colors, and decorative features. Formatting changes only the appearance of data—it does not affect the data itself.

InSight	**Formatting Workbooks Effectively**

A well-formatted workbook can be easier to read, establish a sense of professionalism, help draw attention to the points you want to make, and provide continuity between the worksheets. Too little formatting can make the data hard to understand, whereas too much formatting can overwhelm the data. Proper formatting is a balance between these two extremes. Always remember, the goal of formatting is not simply to make a "pretty workbook," but also to accentuate important trends and relationships in the data.

One goal of formatting is to maintain a consistent look within a workbook. Excel, along with all the Office 2007 programs, uses themes to do this. A **theme** is a collection of formatting that specifies the fonts, colors, and graphical effects used throughout the workbook. The Office theme is the default, although you can choose others or create your own. You can also use fonts and colors that are not part of the current theme.

As you work, **Live Preview** shows the effects of formatting options on the workbook's appearance before you apply them. This lets you see and evaluate different formats as you develop your workbook.

Formatting Text

Tom suggests that you first modify the title in the Documentation sheet. The appearance of text is determined by its **typeface**, which is the specific design used for the characters, including letters, numbers, punctuation marks, and symbols. Typefaces are organized into fonts; a **font** is a set of characters that employ the same typeface. Some commonly used fonts are Arial, Times New Roman, and Courier. **Serif fonts**, such as Times New Roman, have extra decorative strokes at the end of each character. **Sans serif fonts**, such as Arial, do not include these decorative strokes. Other fonts are purely decorative, such as a font used for specialized logos.

Fonts are organized into theme and non-theme fonts. A **theme font** is associated with a particular theme and used for headings and body text in the workbook. The Office theme uses the theme font Cambria for headings and the theme font Calibri for body text. When you don't want to associate a font with a particular design, you use a **non-theme font**. Text formatted with a non-theme font retains its appearance no matter what theme is used with the workbook.

Every font can be further formatted with a **font style**, such as *italic*, **bold**, or ***bold italic***, and special effects, such as <u>underline</u>, ~~strikethrough~~, and color to text. Finally, you can set the **font size** to increase or decrease the size of the text. Font sizes are measured in **points** where one point is approximately ¹/₇₂ of an inch.

You'll format the company name displayed at the top of each worksheet to appear in large, bold letters using the default heading font from the Office theme. Tom wants the slogan "the Intelligent path to Fitness" displayed below the company name to appear in the heading font, but in smaller, italicized letters.

To format text in the Documentation sheet:

▶ **1.** Click the **Documentation** sheet tab to make that worksheet active, and then click cell **A1** to make it active.

▶ **2.** In the Font group on the Home tab, click the **Font arrow** to display a list of fonts available on your computer. The first two fonts are the theme fonts for headings and body text—Cambria and Calibri. See Figure 2-1.

Font list ◀ **Figure 2-1**

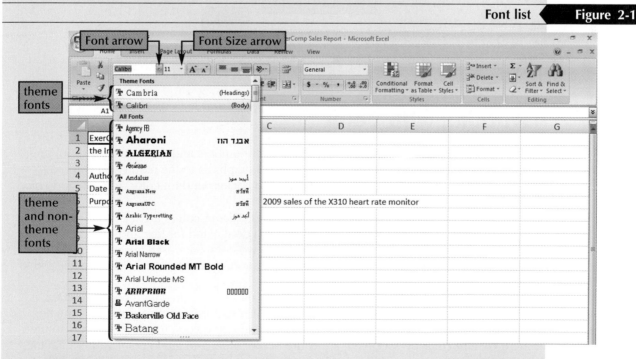

Trouble? If your screen displays more or less of the worksheet, your worksheet is at a different zoom level. If you want your worksheet zoomed to match the figures, click the Zoom In button on the status bar twice to increase the zoom magnification to 120%.

Tip

You can change the font size one point at a time. In the Font group on the Home tab, click the Increase Font Size or Decrease Font Size button.

▶ 3. Click **Cambria**. The company name in cell A1 changes to the Cambria font, the default headings font in the current theme.

▶ 4. In the Font group, click the **Font Size arrow** to display a list of font sizes, and then click **26**. The company name changes to 26 points.

▶ 5. In the Font group, click the **Bold** button **B**. The company name is boldfaced. Next, you'll format the company slogan.

▶ 6. Click cell **A2** to make it active. The slogan text is selected.

▶ 7. In the Font group, click the **Font arrow**, and then click **Cambria**. The slogan text changes to the Cambria font.

▶ 8. In the Font group, click the **Font Size arrow**, and then click **10**. The slogan text changes to 10 points.

▶ 9. In the Font group, click the **Italic** button **I**. The slogan is italicized.

▶ 10. Select the range **A4:A6**, click the **Bold** button **B** in the Font group, and then click cell **A7**. The column labels are bolded. See Figure 2-2.

Figure 2-2 ▶ **Formatted worksheet text**

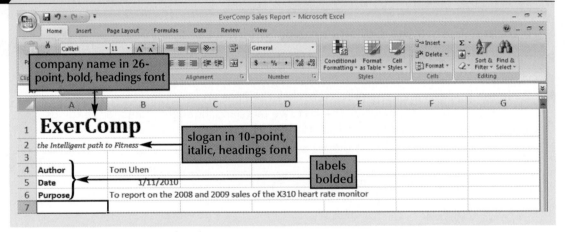

Working with Color

Color can transform a plain workbook filled with numbers and text into a powerful presentation that captures attention and adds visual emphasis to the points you want to make. By default, text is black and cells have no background fill color. You can add color to both the text and the cell background.

Colors are organized into two main categories. **Theme colors** are the 12 colors that belong to the workbook's theme. Four colors are designated for text and backgrounds, six colors are used for accents and highlights, and two colors are used for hyperlinks (followed and not followed links). These 12 colors are designed to work well together and to remain readable in all color combinations.

Ten **standard colors**—dark red, red, orange, yellow, light green, green, light blue, blue, dark blue, and purple—are always available regardless of the workbook's theme. You can also open an extended palette of 134 standard colors. In addition, you can create a **custom color** by specifying a mixture of red, blue, and green color values, making available 16.7 million custom colors—more colors than the human eye can distinguish. Some dialog boxes have an **automatic color** option that uses your Windows default text and background color values, usually black text on a white background.

Applying Font Color and Fill Color

Tom wants the labels in the Documentation sheet to stand out. You will change the ExerComp title and slogan to blue, and then you'll format the other labels in the worksheet with a blue background fill and a white font color.

To change the title and slogan font color and fill color:

1. Select the range **A1:A2**.

2. In the Font group on the Home tab, click the **Font Color button arrow** to display the available theme and standard colors. There are 10 theme colors (the two colors for hyperlinked text are not shown), and each theme color has five variations, or **accents**, in which a different tint or shading is applied to the theme color.

3. Point to the **Blue** color (the eighth color) in the Standard Colors section. The color name appears in a ScreenTip. See Figure 2-3.

Font colors   Figure 2-3

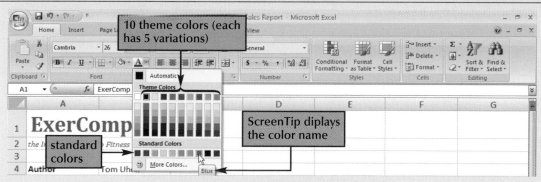

4. Click the **Blue** color. The company name and slogan change to blue.

5. Select the range **A4:A6**. You'll change both the fill and the font colors of these cells.

6. In the Font group, click the **Fill Color button arrow**, and then click the **Blue** color in the Standard Colors section. The cell backgrounds change to blue.

7. In the Font group, click the **Font Color button arrow**, and then click the **white** color (ScreenTip is White, Background1) in the Theme Colors section. The font color changes to white.

8. Click cell **A7** to deselect the range. The white text on a blue background is visible. See Figure 2-4.

Figure 2-4 Font colors and fill colors applied

Figure 2-4 Font colors and fill colors applied

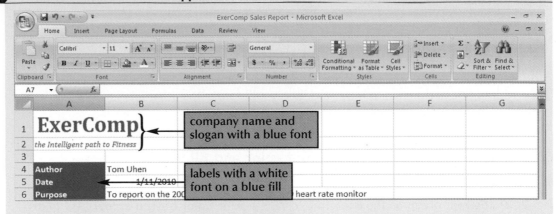

Formatting Text Selections

The ExerComp logo usually appears in two colors—"Exer" in blue and "Comp" in red. Tom asks you to make this change to the text in cell A1. You'll need to format part of the cell content one way and the rest a different way. To do this, you first select the text you want to format in editing mode, and then apply the formatting to the selection. The **Mini toolbar** appears when you select text and contains buttons for commonly used text formats. You'll use the Mini toolbar to format "Comp" in a red font.

To format the "Comp" text selection:

▶ **1.** Double-click cell **A1** to select the cell and go into editing mode, and then select **Comp**. A transparent version of the Mini toolbar appears.

▶ **2.** Click the **Font Color button arrow** [A▾] on the Mini toolbar, and then click the **Red** color (the second color) in the Standard Colors section. The text color changes and the Mini toolbar remains open for additional formatting. See Figure 2-5.

Figure 2-5 Mini toolbar used to format text

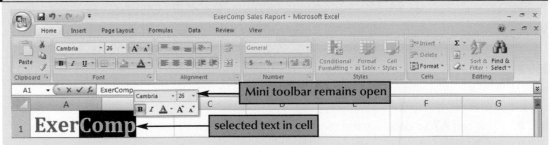

Trouble? If the Mini toolbar disappears before you can click the Font Color button arrow, you probably moved the pointer away from the Mini toolbar, pressed a key, or pressed a mouse button. Right-click the selected text to redisplay the Mini toolbar above a shortcut menu, immediately move your pointer to the Mini toolbar, and then repeat Step 2.

▶ **3.** Click cell **A7** to deselect the cell. The text "ExerComp" in cell A1 is blue and red.

Setting a Background Image

You can use a picture or image as the background for all the cells in a worksheet. An image can give the worksheet a textured appearance, like that of granite, wood, or fibered paper. The image is inserted until it fills the entire worksheet. The background image does not affect any cell's format or content. Any cells with a background color display the color on top, hiding that portion of the image. Background images do not print.

Tom has an image that resembles fibered paper that you will use as the background for the Documentation sheet.

To add a background image to the Documentation sheet:

▶ 1. Click the **Page Layout** tab on the Ribbon. The page layout options appear on the Ribbon.

▶ 2. In the Page Setup group, click the **Background** button. The Sheet Background dialog box opens.

▶ 3. Navigate to the **Tutorial.02\Tutorial** folder included with your Data Files, click the **Background.jpg** image file, and then click the **Insert** button. The image file is added to the background of the Documentation sheet.

Next, you'll change the fill color of the cells with the author's name, the date, and the workbook's purpose to white to highlight them in the worksheet.

▶ 4. Select the range **B4:B6**, and then click the **Home** tab on the Ribbon.

▶ 5. In the Font group, click the **Fill Color button arrow** 🖌▾, and then click the **white** color in the Theme Colors section.

▶ 6. Increase the width of column B to **55** characters, and then click cell **A7** to deselect the range. See Figure 2-6.

Background image added to the Documentation sheet ◀ Figure 2-6

Formatting Data

The Yearly Sales worksheet contains the annual sales figures from 2008 and 2009 for the X310 heart rate monitor. The top of the worksheet displays the number of units sold in each sales region per year, and the bottom displays the sales revenue generated by region per year. You'll add formulas to calculate the total sales for each year as well as the difference and percentage difference in sales from one year to another.

To enter formulas in the Yearly Sales worksheet:

▶ 1. Click the **Yearly Sales** sheet tab. The Yearly Sales worksheet becomes active.

▶ 2. In cells B15 and B26, enter **Total**; in cells E6 and E17, enter **Increase**; in cells F6 and F17, enter **% Increase**; and then select cell **C15**.

▶ 3. In the Editing group on the Home tab, click the **Sum** button Σ, and then press the **Enter** key. The formula =SUM(C7:C14) is entered in the cell, adding the numbers in the range C7:C14.

▶ 4. Select cell **C15**, and then, in the Clipboard group, click the **Copy** button. The formula is copied to the Clipboard.

Next, you'll paste the formula into a nonadjacent range. Remember, to select a nonadjacent range, select the first cell or range, press and hold the Ctrl key as you select other cells or ranges, and then release the Ctrl key.

▶ 5. Select the range **D15;C26:D26**, and then, in the Clipboard group, click the **Paste** button. The formula is pasted into cells D15, C26, and D26, adding the values in each column.

▶ 6. Select cell **E7**, and then enter the formula **=D7−C7** to calculate the increase in sales from 2008 to 2009 for region R01.

▶ 7. Select cell **F7**, and then enter the formula **=E7/C7** to calculate the percentage increase from 2008 to 2009.

8. Select the range **E7:F7**, and then, in the Clipboard group, click the **Copy** button.

9. Select the range **E8:F15;E18:F26**, and then, in the Clipboard group, click the **Paste** button. The formulas are copied into the selected cells.

10. Click cell **A6** to deselect the range. See Figure 2-7.

Formulas added to the Yearly Sales sheet — Figure 2-7

	A	B	C	D	E	F	G
6	Units Sold	Region	2008 Sales	2009 Sales	Increase	% Increase	
7		R01	3605	3853	248	0.068793343	
8		R02	3966	3842	-124	-0.031265759	
9		R03	3760	4035	275	0.073138298	
10		R04	3777	4063	286	0.075721472	
11		R05	3974	3725	-249	-0.062657272	
12		R06	3656	3937	281	0.076859956	
13		R07	3554	3875	321	0.090320765	
14		R08	3844	3844	0	0	
15		Total	30136	31174	1038	0.034443855	
16							
17	Revenue	Region	2008 Sales	2009 Sales	Increase	% Increase	
18		R01	104364.75	115397.35	11032.6	0.105711938	
19		R02	114815.7	115067.9	252.2	0.002196564	
20			108852	120848.25	11996.25	0.110206978	
21			109344.15	121686.85	12342.7	0.112879381	
22		R05		115047.3	111563.75	-3483.55	-0.030279285
23		R06	105841.2	117913.15	12071.95	0.114057191	
24		R07	102888.3	116056.25	13167.95	0.127982968	
25		R08	111283.8	115127.8	3844	0.034542314	
26		Total	872437.2	933661.3	61224.1	0.070175939	

formulas calculate the sales and % increases

formulas calculate the totals of the data

The sales figures are hard to read, making them difficult to interpret and understand. By default, values appear in the **General number format**, which, for the most part, displays numbers exactly as you enter them. Calculated values show as many digits after the decimal point as will fit in the cell and the last displayed digit is rounded, as you can see with the percentage increase values in column F. Only the displayed number is rounded; the actual value stored in the cell is not. Calculated values too large to fit into the cell are displayed in scientific notation.

Formatting Numbers

The Number group on the Home tab has buttons for formatting the appearance of numbers. You can select a number format, apply accounting or other currency formats, change a number to a percentage, insert a comma as a thousands separator, and increase or decrease the number of digits displayed to the right of the decimal point.

You'll add a thousands separator to the sales values to make them easier to read and remove the digits shown to the right of the decimal point because the data values for units sold will always be whole numbers. You'll format the percentage difference values as percentages with two decimal places. Tom also wants you to format the revenue values in the range C18:E26 as currency by adding dollar signs. Because applying dollar signs to large columns of numbers often makes them unreadable, standard accounting practice displays currency symbols only in the first and last rows of the range.

To format the units sold, percentage differences, and revenue numbers:

1. Select the range **C7:E15;C18:E26**, and then, in the Number group on the Home tab, click the **Comma Style** button. The numbers include a thousands separator, but still display two digits to the right of the decimal point.

> 2. Select the range **C7:E15**, and then, in the Number group, click the **Decrease Decimal** button twice. The two extra digits are removed.

> 3. Select the range **F7:F15;F18:F26**, and then, in the Number group, click the **Percent Style** button %. The values now include the percentage symbol.

> 4. In the Number group, click the **Increase Decimal** button twice. Two digits are added to the right of the decimal point.

> 5. Select the range **C18:E18;C26:E26**, and then, in the Number group, click the **Accounting Number Format** button $. The first row and the Total row display the currency symbol.

> 6. Click cell **A6** to deselect the range. See Figure 2-8.

Figure 2-8 | **Worksheet after formatting numbers**

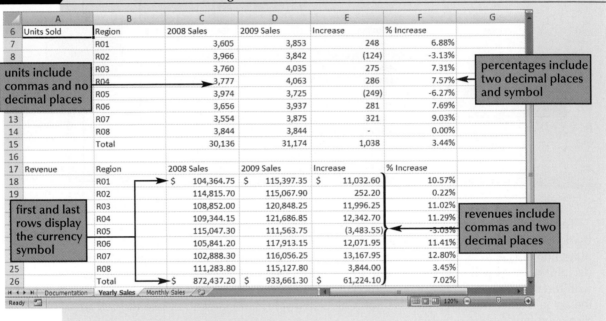

Tom examines this reformatted data and notes that the company sold 1,038 more units in 2009 than in 2008—an increase of 3.44%, which increased revenue by $61,224.10, or 7.02%. This was not uniform across all sales regions. Total sales and revenue for Region R05, for example, decreased from 2008 to 2009.

Formatting Dates and Times

Although dates and times in Excel appear as text, they are actually numbers that measure the interval between the specified date and time and January 1, 1900 at 12:00 a.m. You can then calculate date and time intervals, and you can format a date or time value. For example, you can apply a date format that displays the day of the week for any date value stored in your worksheet.

The date in the Documentation sheet is an abbreviated format, *mm/dd/yyyy*. Tom wants you to use an extended format that includes the day of the week, the full month name, the day, and the year. This Long Date format is a built-in date format.

To format the date in the Long Date format:

▶ **1.** Click the **Documentation** sheet tab to make that worksheet active, and then select cell **B5**.

▶ **2.** In the Number group on the Home tab, click the **Number Format arrow** to open a list of built-in number formats.

▶ **3.** Click **Long Date**. The date format changes to show the weekday name, month name, day, and year. See Figure 2-9.

Formatted date | Figure 2-9

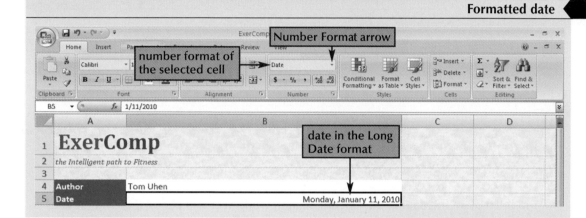

Formatting Dates for International Audiences | InSight

When your workbooks are intended for international audiences, be sure to use a date format that will be clear to everyone, such as November 10, 2010 or 10 November 2010. Many countries use a day/month/year format for dates rather than the month/day/year format commonly used in the United States. For example, the date 10/11/2010 is read as October 11, 2010 by people in the United States but as November 10, 2010 by people in most other countries.

Formatting Worksheet Cells

The date in the Documentation worksheet is formatted to display as text. Because all dates are actually numbers, they are right-aligned in the cell by default, regardless of their date format. Tom asks you to left-align the date to make it easier to read.

Aligning Cell Content

In addition to left and right alignments, you can change the vertical and horizontal alignments of cell content to make a worksheet more readable. You can also increase or decrease the space between the cell content and the cell border. In general, you should center column titles, left-align text, and right-align numbers to keep their decimal places lined up within the column. Figure 2-10 describes the alignment buttons located in the Alignment group on the Home tab.

Figure 2-10 ▶ **Alignment buttons**

Button	Description
▤	Aligns the cell content with the cell's top edge
▤	Vertically centers the cell content within the cell
▤	Aligns the cell content with the cell's bottom edge
▤	Aligns the cell content with the cell's left edge
▤	Horizontally centers the cell content within the cell
▤	Aligns the cell content with the cell's right edge
▤	Decreases the size of the indentation used in the cell
▤	Increases the size of the indentation used in the cell
▧	Rotates the cell content to an angle within the cell
▤	Forces the cell text to wrap within the cell borders
▤	Merges the selected cells into a single cell

You'll left-align the date in the Documentation worksheet and center the column titles in the Yearly Sales worksheet.

To left-align the date and center the column titles:

▶ 1. If necessary, select cell **B5**.

▶ 2. In the Alignment group on the Home tab, click the **Align Text Left** button ▤. The date shifts to the left edge of the cell.

▶ 3. Click the **Yearly Sales** sheet tab to make that worksheet active, and then select the range **C6:F6;C17:F17**.

▶ 4. In the Alignment group, click the **Center** button ▤. The column titles in columns C, D, E, and F are centered.

Indenting Cell Content

Sometimes, you want a cell's content moved a few spaces from the cell edge. This is particularly useful for entries that are considered subsections of a worksheet. For example, Tom recorded sales for eight regions and then added the totals. Each region can be considered a subsection, and Tom thinks it would look better if the region labels were indented a few spaces. You increase the indentation by roughly one character each time you click the Increase Indent button in the Alignment group on the Home tab. To decrease or remove an indentation, click the Decrease Indent button. You'll increase the indent for the region labels.

To indent the region labels:

▶ 1. Select the range **B7:B14;B18:B25**.

▶ 2. In the Alignment group on the Home tab, click the **Increase Indent** button ▤. Each region label indents one space.

▶ 3. Click cell **A6** to deselect the range. See Figure 2-11.

Centered and indented text ◀ **Figure 2-11**

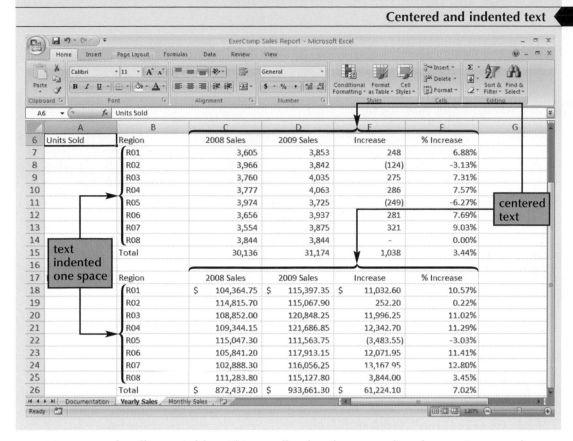

You can make all text visible within a cell rather than extending the text into an adjacent empty cell or truncating it. Just click the Wrap Text button ⊞ in the Alignment group on the Home tab. The row height increases as needed to wrap all the text within the cell.

Merging Cells

In the Yearly Sales worksheet, Tom wants the title "X310 Yearly Sales Analysis" in cell A4 centered over columns A through F. So far, you've aligned text only *within* a cell. One way to align text over several columns or rows is to **merge**, or combine, several cells into one cell. When you merge cells, only the content from the upper-left cell in the range is retained and the upper-left cell becomes the merged cell reference.

After you merge a range into a single cell, you can realign its content. The Merge button in the Alignment group on the Home tab includes a variety of merge options. Merge & Center merges the range into one cell and horizontally centers the content. Merge Across merges each of the rows in the selected range across the columns in the range. Merge Cells merges the range into a single cell, but does not horizontally center the cell content. Unmerge Cells reverses a merge, returning the merged cell back into a range of individual cells.

Tom wants you to merge and center the title in cell A4 across the range A4:F4.

To merge and center the range with the title:

▶ **1.** Select the range **A4:F4**.

▶ **2.** In the Alignment group on the Home tab, click the **Merge & Center** button. The range A4:F4 merges into one cell with a cell reference of A4 and the text is centered within the cell. See Figure 2-12.

Figure 2-12 ▶ **Merged range with centered text**

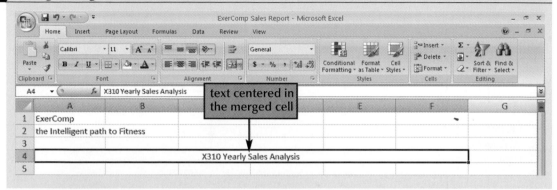

Rotating Cell Content

Text and numbers are oriented within a cell horizontally from left to right. To save space or to provide visual interest to a worksheet, you can rotate the cell contents so that they appear at any angle or orientation. These options are available on the Orientation button in the Alignment group on the Home tab.

Tom wants you to merge and center the ranges with the labels, and then rotate the labels in the merged cells A6 and A17 so they look better and take up less room.

To rotate the labels:

▶ **1.** Select the range **A6:A15**.

▶ **2.** In the Alignment group on the Home tab, click the **Merge & Center** button. The text from cell A6 is centered in the merged cell.

▶ **3.** In the Alignment group, click the **Orientation** button, and then click **Rotate Text Up**. The cell text rotates 90 degrees counterclockwise.

▶ **4.** In the Alignment group, click the **Middle Align** button. The rotated text vertically aligns within the merged cell.

▶ **5.** Select the range **A17:A26**, and then repeat Steps 2 through 4 to merge and center, rotate, and align the text.

▶ **6.** Reduce the width of column A to **5** characters. See Figure 2-13.

Merged and rotated cell text | Figure 2-13

	A	B	C	D	E	F	G	H
6		Region	2008 Sales	2009 Sales	Increase	% Increase		
7		R01	3,605	3,853	248	6.88%		
8		R02	3,966	3,842	(124)	-3.13%		
9		R03	3,760	4,035	275	7.31%		
10	Units Sold	R04	3,777	4,063	286	7.57%		
11		R05	3,974	3,725	(249)	-6.27%		
12		R06	3,656	3,937	281	7.69%		
13		R07	3,554	3,875	321	9.03%		
14		R08	3,844	3,844	-	0.00%		
15		Total	30,136	31,174	1,038	3.44%		
16								
17		Region	Sales	2009 Sales	Increase	% Increase		
18		R01	$ 104,364.75	$ 115,397.35	$ 11,032.60	10.57%		
19		R02	114,815.70	115,067.90	252.20	0.22%		
20		R03	108,852.00	120,848.25	11,996.25	11.02%		
21	Revenue	R04	109,344.15	121,686.85	12,342.70	11.29%		
22		R05	115,047.30	111,563.75	(3,483.55)	-3.03%		
23		R06	105,841.20	117,913.15	12,071.95	11.41%		
24		R07	102,888.30	116,056.25	13,167.95	12.80%		
25		R08	111,283.80	115,127.80	3,844.00	3.45%		
26		Total	$ 872,437.20	$ 933,661.30	$ 61,224.10	7.02%		

rotated labels take up less space in the merged cells

Documentation   Yearly Sales   Monthly Sales

Ready   120%

Adding Cell Borders

When a worksheet is printed, the gridlines that surround the cells are not printed by default. Sometimes you will want to include such lines to enhance the readability of the rows and columns of data. One way to do this is by adding a line, or **border**, around a cell or range. You can add borders to the left, top, right, or bottom of a cell or range, around an entire cell, or around the outside edges of a range. You can also specify the thickness of and the number of lines in the border. To create a border, use the Border button located in the Font group on the Home tab.

Tom wants you to add borders to the column titles and Total rows. Standard accounting practice is to add a single top border and a double bottom border to the Total row to clearly identify a summary row from financial data.

To add cell borders to the column labels and Total rows:

▶ 1. Select the range **B6:F6;B17:F17**. You'll add a bottom border to these column labels.

▶ 2. In the Font group on the Home tab, click the **Border button arrow** , and then click **Bottom Border**. A bottom border is added to the selected cells.

▶ 3. Select the range **B15:F15;B26:F26**. You'll add top and bottom borders to these Total rows.

▶ 4. In the Font group, click the **Border button arrow** , and then click **Top and Double Bottom Border**. The Total rows both have a single top border and a double bottom border, which is standard accounting practice.

▶ 5. Click cell **A5** to deselect the range. See Figure 2-14.

Figure 2-14 ▶ **Borders added to cells**

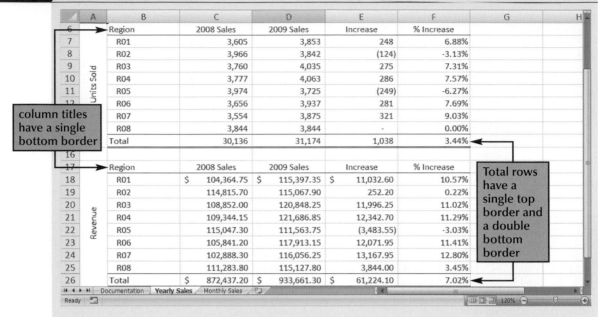

Working with the Format Cells Dialog Box

The buttons on the Home tab provide quick access to the most common formatting choices. For more options, you can use the Format Cells dialog box. For example, the numbers in cells E8 and E10 are displayed in parentheses to indicate that they are negative. Although parentheses are common in accounting to indicate negative currency values, Tom wants you to reformat the units sold numbers to display negative numbers with a minus symbol. You can do this in the Format Cells dialog box.

Tip

You can also open the Format Cells dialog box by right-clicking a cell or selected range, and then clicking Format Cells on the shortcut menu.

To open the Format Cells dialog box:

▶ 1. Select the range **C7:E15**.

▶ 2. In the Number group on the Home tab, click the **Dialog Box Launcher**. The Format Cells dialog box opens with the Number tab active.

The Format Cells dialog box has six tabs, each focusing on a different set of formatting options. You can apply the formats in this dialog box to selected worksheet cells. The six tabs are as follows:

- **Number**: Provides options for formatting the appearance of numbers, including dates and numbers treated as text (for example, telephone or Social Security numbers)
- **Alignment**: Provides options for how data is aligned within a cell
- **Font**: Provides options for selecting font types, sizes, styles, and other formatting attributes such as underlining and font colors
- **Border**: Provides options for adding cell borders
- **Fill**: Provides options for creating and applying background colors and patterns to cells
- **Protection**: Provides options for locking or hiding cells to prevent other users from modifying their contents

Although you've applied many of these formats from the Home tab, the Format Cells dialog box presents them in a different way and provides more options. You'll use the Number tab to change the number format for the selected cells. Remember, modifying the number format does not affect the value stored in the workbook.

To set the format for negative numbers of units:

1. In the Category list on the left side of the Format Cells dialog box, click **Number**.

2. Verify that **0** (zero) appears in the Decimal places box.

3. Verify that the **Use 1000 Separator (,)** check box contains a check mark.

4. In the Negative numbers list, verify that **–1,234** (the first option) is selected. See Figure 2-15.

Number tab in the Format Cells dialog box Figure 2-15

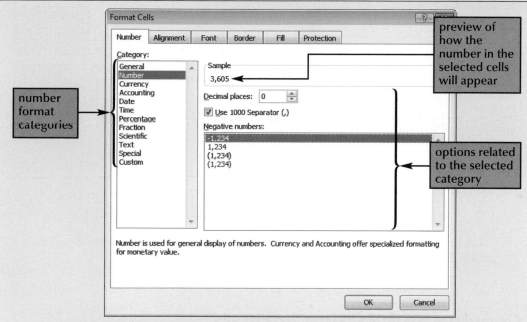

5. Click the **OK** button. The Format Cells dialog box closes and the negative numbers in the range C7:E15 appear with minus symbols, a comma as the thousands separator, and no decimal places.

Tom wants the bottom border color used for the column titles changed from black to green. You'll use the Border tab in the Format Cells dialog box to make this change.

To set the border color for the column title cells:

1. Select the range **B6:F6;B17:F17**.

2. In the Font group on the Home tab, click the **Borders button arrow** , and then click **More Borders**. The Format Cells dialog box opens with the Border tab active.

In the Border tab, you can select a line style ranging from thick to thin, choose double to dotted lines, and place these lines anywhere around the cells in the selected range. Right now, you only want to set the border line color.

▶ **3.** In the Line group, click the **Color** arrow to display the color palette, and then click **Green** (the sixth color) in the Standard Colors section.

▶ **4.** Click the bottom border of the border preview. A green bottom border is added to the preview. See Figure 2-16.

Figure 2-16 ▶ **Border tab in the Format Cells dialog box**

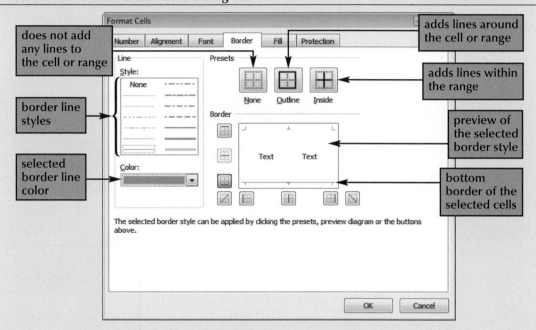

▶ **5.** Click the **OK** button. The dialog box closes and the cells with column titles have a green bottom border.

Copying and Pasting Formats

You have not yet formatted the titles in cells A1 and A2 of the Yearly Sales worksheet to match the Documentation sheet. You could repeat the same steps to format these cells, but a quicker method is to copy the formats from the Documentation worksheet into the Yearly Sales worksheet.

Copying Formats with the Format Painter

The **Format Painter** copies the formatting from one cell or range to another cell or range, without duplicating any of the data. Using the Format Painter is a fast and efficient way of maintaining a consistent look and feel throughout a workbook.

You'll use the Format Painter to copy the cell formats from the range A1:A2 in the Documentation sheet into the same range in the Yearly Sales worksheet.

To copy and paste the format:

▶ **1.** Click the **Documentation** sheet tab to make that worksheet active, and then select the range **A1:A2**.

▶ **2.** In the Clipboard group on the Home tab, click the **Format Painter** button 🗇. The formats from the selected cells are copied to the Clipboard.

▶ **3.** Click the **Yearly Sales** sheet tab to make that worksheet active, and then select the range **A1:A2**. The formatting from the Documentation sheet is removed from the Clipboard and applied to the selected cells except for the red color you applied to "Comp." Format Painter does not copy formatting applied to text selections.

▶ **4.** Double-click cell **A1** to go into editing mode, and then select **Comp** in the text string.

▶ **5.** Click the **Font Color button arrow** 🅰 ▾ on the Mini toolbar, and then click **Red** (the second color) in the Standard Colors section. The selected text changes to red.

▶ **6.** Press the **Enter** key to exit editing mode.

▶ **7.** Select the range **A1:A2** in the Yearly Sales worksheet, and then repeat Steps 2 through 6 to copy the formatting to the range A1:A2 in the Monthly Sales worksheet.

Tip

To paste a format to multiple selections, double-click the Format Painter button, select each cell or range to format, and then click the Format Painter button again to turn it off.

Copying Formats with the Paste Options Button

The Format Painter copies and pastes only formatting. When you copy and paste, you can also use the Paste Options button 🖺, which lets you choose whether to paste the formatting from a copied range along with its contents. As shown in Figure 2-17, each time you paste, the Paste Options button appears in the lower-right corner of the pasted cell or range. When you click the Paste Options button, you can choose from a list of pasting options, such as pasting only the values or only the formatting.

Using the Paste Options button ◀ **Figure 2-17**

Copying Formats with Paste Special

The Paste Special command is another way to control what you paste from the Clipboard. To use Paste Special, select and copy a range, select the range where you want to paste the Clipboard contents, click the Paste button arrow in the Clipboard group on the Home tab, and then click Paste Special to open the dialog box shown in Figure 2-18. From the Paste Special dialog box, you can specify exactly what you want to paste.

Figure 2-18   Paste Special dialog box

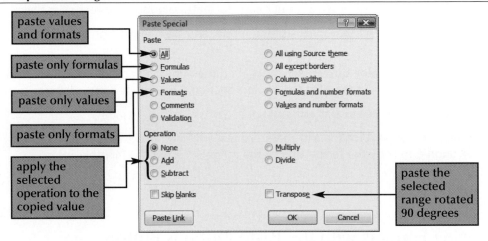

You can use the Transpose option in the Paste Special dialog box to paste a range of numbers cut from a row into a column. You can also use Paste Special to quickly modify all the values in a range. For example, you can copy the value 5 from a cell, select the range, open the Paste Special dialog box, click the Add option button in the Operation group, and then click the OK button. Excel adds 5 to every value in the selected range.

Applying Styles

A workbook often contains several cells that store the same type of data. For example, each worksheet might have a cell displaying the sheet title, or a range of financial data might have several cells containing summary totals. Using the same format on cells storing the same type of data gives your workbook a consistent look. You can do this using the Format Painter or by copying and pasting a format from one cell to another.

The Format Painter is effective, but it can also be time consuming if you have to copy the same format to many cells. Moreover, if you decide to modify the format, you must copy and paste the revised format all over again. Another way to ensure that cells displaying the same type of data use the same format is with styles. A **style** is a collection of formatting. For example, you can create a style to display sheet titles in a bold, white, 20-point Calibri font on a blue background. You can then apply that style to any sheet title in a workbook. If you later revise the style, the appearance of any cell formatted with that style is updated automatically. This saves you the time and effort of reformatting each cell individually.

Excel has a variety of built-in styles to format worksheet titles, column and row totals, and cells with emphasis. You used the built-in Currency and Percent styles when you formatted data in the Yearly Sales worksheet as currency and percentages. Some styles are connected to the workbook's current theme.

Applying Styles | Reference Window

- Select the cell or range to which you want to apply a style.
- In the Styles group on the Home tab, click the Cell Styles button.
- Point to each style in the Cell Styles gallery to see a Live Preview of that style on the selected cell or range.
- Click the style you want to apply to the selected cell or range.

Tom asks you to use some of the built-in styles to add more color and visual interest to the Yearly Sales worksheet.

To apply built-in styles to the Yearly Sales sheet:

▶ 1. Click the **Yearly Sales** sheet tab to make that worksheet active, and then select the merged cell **A4**.

▶ 2. In the Styles group on the Home tab, click the **Cell Styles** button. The Cell Styles gallery opens.

▶ 3. Point to the **Heading 1** style in the Titles and Headings section. Live Preview shows cell A4 in a 15-point, bold font with a solid blue bottom border. See Figure 2-19.

Cell Styles gallery ◀ Figure 2-19

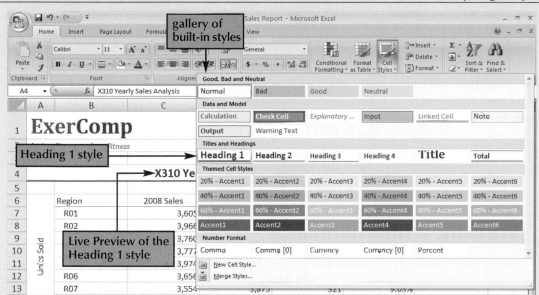

▶ 4. Move the pointer over different styles in the Cell Styles gallery to preview cell A4 with each style, and then click the **Heading 1** style. The style is applied to cell A4.

▶ 5. Select the range **B6:F6;B17:F17**, click the **Cell Styles** button, and then click the **Accent1** style in the Themed Cell Styles section. Each of the column headings is formatted.

▶ 6. Select the range **E7:F15;E18:F26**, click the **Cell Styles** button, and then click the **20% – Accent1** style in the Themed Cell Styles section. The calculated values are formatted differently from the data.

▶ 7. Click cell **F1** to deselect the range, and then zoom the worksheet to **90%**. See Figure 2-20.

Figure 2-20 Formatted yearly sales data

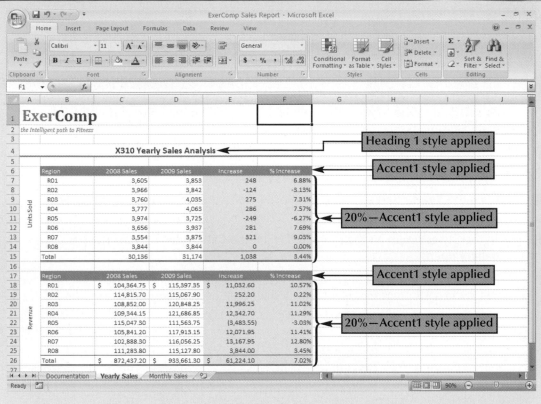

If the built-in styles don't meet your needs, you can modify an existing style or create a new one. To modify a style, right-click the style in the Cell Styles gallery, click Modify on the shortcut menu to open the Style dialog box, and then click the Format button to change the formatting for that style. Any cells formatted with that style are automatically updated. To create a new style, click New Cell Style in the Cell Styles gallery to open the Style dialog box, type a name in the Style name box, and then click the Format button to select the formatting for that style. The new cell style is added to the Cell Styles gallery.

Working with Themes

Most of the formatting you've applied so far is based on the workbook's current theme—the default Office theme. As you've seen, fonts, colors, and cell styles are organized in theme and non-theme categories. The appearance of these fonts, colors, and cell styles depends on the workbook's current theme. If you change the theme, the formatting of these elements also changes.

You'll change the workbook's theme to see its effect on the workbook's appearance.

To change the workbook's theme:

▶ **1.** Click the **Page Layout** tab on the Ribbon, and then, in the Themes group, click the **Themes** button. The Themes gallery opens. Office—the current theme—is the default.

▶ **2.** Point to each theme in the Themes gallery. Live Preview shows the impact of each theme on the appearance of the Yearly Sales worksheet.

3. Click the **Aspect** theme. The Aspect theme is applied to the workbook. See Figure 2-21.

Figure 2-21

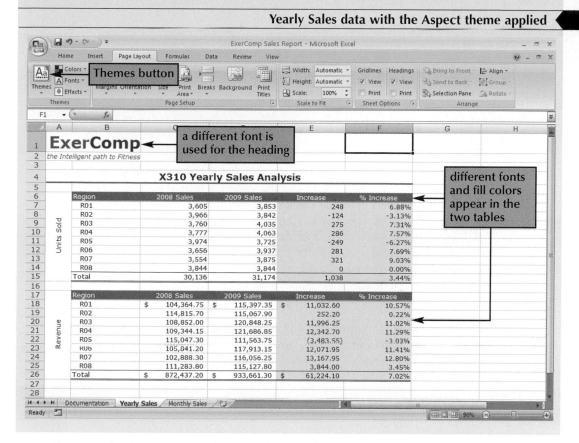

Changing the theme has made a significant difference in the worksheet's appearance. The most obvious changes are the fill colors and the fonts. Only elements directly tied to a theme change when you select a different theme. The cells you formatted with the Accent1 cell style changed because the Accent1 color is blue in the Office theme and orange in the Aspect theme. The Heading 1 style you used for the titles in cells A1 and A2 uses the Cambria typeface in the Office theme and the Verdana typeface in the Aspect theme. The Aspect theme also uses a different font for body text, which is why the rest of the text changed size and appearance.

The logo colors in cell A1 did not change because you used two standard colors, blue and red, which are not part of a theme. Changing the theme does not affect these colors.

Tom prefers the default Office theme, so you'll switch back to that theme and then save the workbook.

To select the Office theme and save the workbook:

1. In the Themes group on the Page Layout tab, click the **Themes** button, and then click the **Office** theme.

2. Save your changes to the workbook.

If you're part of a team creating files with Microsoft Office, you might want to use a common style and design theme for all your projects. The easiest way to do this is by saving the styles and themes as permanent files other members of your workgroup can use.

To copy a style from one workbook to another, open the workbook with the styles you want to copy, and then open the workbook in which you want to copy those styles. In the Styles group on the Home tab, click the Cell Styles button, and then click Merge Styles. The Merge Styles dialog box opens, listing the currently open workbooks. Select the workbook with the styles you want to copy, and then click the OK button to copy those styles into the current workbook. If you modify any styles, you must copy the styles to the other workbook; Excel does not update styles between workbooks.

You can save a workbook's theme as a file that can be used in other workbooks or Office files. Microsoft Excel, Word, and PowerPoint use the same file format for their theme files. To save a theme, in the Themes group on the Page Layout tab, click the Themes button, and then click Save Current Theme. The Save Current Theme dialog box opens. Select a save location (in a default Theme folder on your computer or another folder), type a descriptive name in the File name box, and then click the Save button. A Theme file saved in a default Theme folder appears in the Themes gallery, and any changes made to the theme are reflected in any Office file that uses that theme.

You've completed some formatting of Tom's workbook. In the process, you've formatted cells and ranges, applied built-in styles, and applied a new theme. In the next session, you'll work with table styles, conditional formatting, and page layout tools.

Review | **Session 2.1 Quick Check**

1. What is the difference between a serif font and a sans serif font?
2. What is the difference between a standard color and a theme color?
3. What is the General number format?
4. Why are dates right-aligned within a worksheet cell by default?
5. The range A1:C5 is merged into a single cell. What is the cell reference of this merged cell?
6. Where can you access all the formatting options for worksheet cells?
7. You want the range A1:A3 on all the worksheets in your workbook to be formatted the same way. Discuss two methods of applying the same format to different ranges.

Session 2.2

Formatting the Monthly Sales Worksheet

The Monthly Sales worksheet contains the sales results by month for the eight sales regions in 2008 and 2009. Tom's main goal for this data is to identify trends. He's more interested in the "big picture" than in specific numbers. He wants to know which sales regions are performing well, which are underperforming, and, in general, how the sales change throughout the year.

The top of the worksheet contains sales for 2008 and 2009. The bottom of the worksheet displays the increase in sales from 2008 to 2009 for each region and month. You need to calculate the monthly totals and do some basic formatting.

To calculate the monthly totals:

1. If you took a break after the previous session, open the ExerComp Sales Report workbook located in the Tutorial.02\Tutorial folder included with your Data Files.

2. Click the **Monthly Sales** sheet tab to make the worksheet active, and then, in cells B19, B34, B49, K6, K21, and K36, enter **Total**.

3. Select the range **K7:K18;K22:K33;K37:K48**, and then click the **Home** tab on the Ribbon.

4. In the Editing group, click the **Sum** button Σ to add the total of each row.

5. Select the range **C19:K19;C34:K34;C49:K49**, and then, in the Editing group, click the **Sum** button Σ to add the total of each column.

Next, you'll format the row and column titles.

To format the titles:

1. Select the range **A4:K4**, and then, in the Alignment group on the Home tab, click the **Merge & Center** button. The title is centered in the merged cell.

2. In the Styles group, click the **Cell Styles** button, and then click the **Heading 1** style. The Heading 1 style is applied to the title.

3. Select the range **A6:A19;A21:A34;A36:A49**, and then, in the Alignment group, click the **Merge & Center** button. The labels are centered in the merged cells.

4. In the Alignment group, click the **Orientation** button, and then click **Rotate Text Up**. The text in the three cells rotates 90 degrees.

5. In the Alignment group, click the **Middle Align** button. The text is centered both horizontally and vertically in the cells.

6. Reduce the width of column A to **5** characters.

7. Select the range **C7:K19;C22:K34;C37:K49**, and then, in the Number group, click the **Dialog Box Launcher**. The Format Cells dialog box opens with the Number tab displayed.

8. Click **Number** in the Category list, type **0** (a zero) in the Decimal places box, click the **Use 1000 Separator (,)** check box to insert a check mark, verify that the **–1,234** option is selected, and then click the **OK** button. The numbers display a thousands separator and use a minus symbol for negatives.

9. Click cell **A1** to deselect the cells. Figure 2-22 shows the formatted Monthly Sales worksheet for the first range. The other ranges are formatted similarly.

Figure 2-22 | Monthly Sales worksheet with formulas and formatting

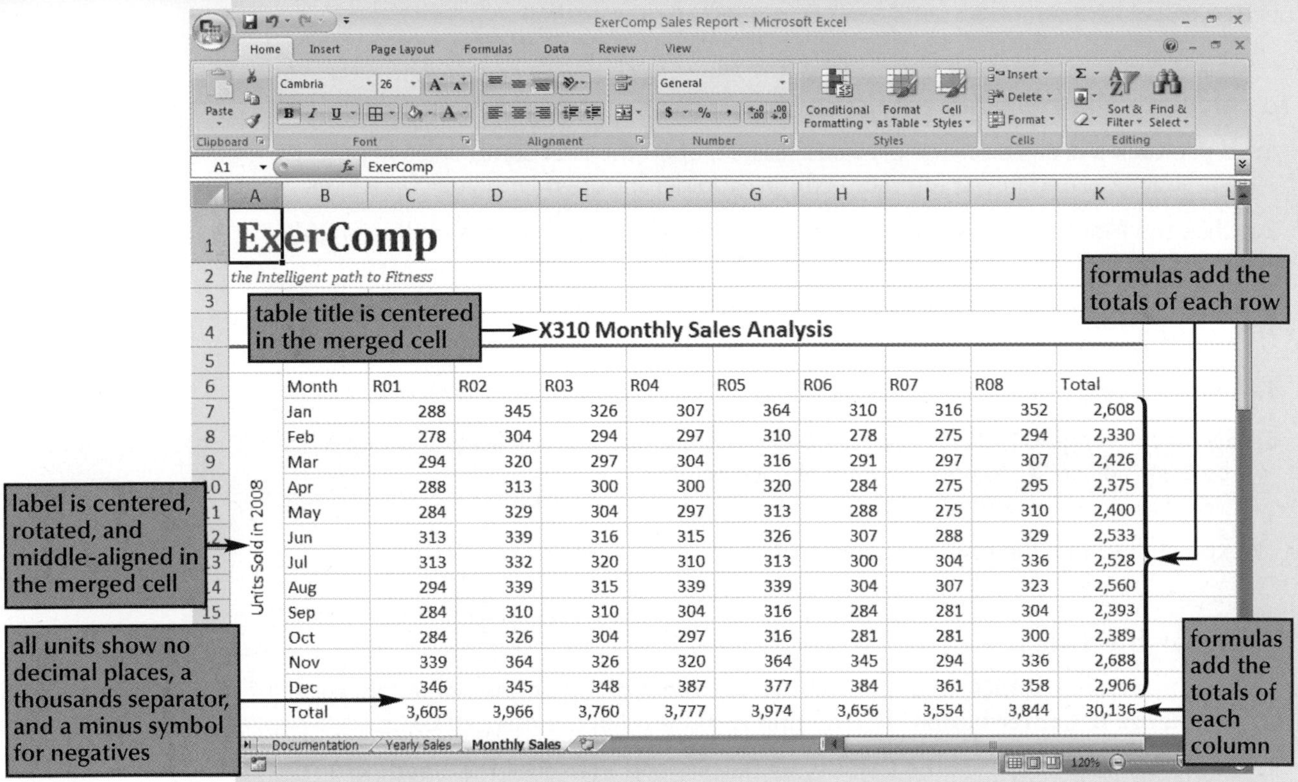

Working with Table Styles

You can treat a range of data as a distinct object in a worksheet known as an **Excel table**. After you identify a range as an Excel table, you can apply a **table style** that formats the entire table as a single unit. Excel tables can include some common elements, such as a header row that contains titles for the different columns in the table and a total row that contains formulas summarizing the values in the table's data. A table style specifies formats for each of these elements, such as font color, fill color, and so forth. Formatting an entire table with a table style is more efficient than formatting individual cells in the range.

Reference Window | **Applying a Table Style to an Existing Table**

- Select the range to which you want to apply the table style.
- In the Styles group on the Home tab, click the Format as Table button.
- Click a table style in the Table Style gallery.

A table style will update the table's formatting to reflect changes you make to the table, such as adding or deleting table rows or columns. For example, many tables display alternate rows with different fill colors. This effect, known as **banded rows**, makes the text easier to read, especially in large tables with many rows. You could create the banded rows effect by applying a cell style with a background fill to every other row in the table, but then, if you add or delete a row from the table, the banded rows effect might be lost. A table style, on the other hand, applies alternating row colors to the entire Excel table and adjusts the banded rows effect as needed if you add or delete rows. This is because a table style treats the table as a single object rather than a collection of cells. Figure 2-23 shows the banded rows effect applied both manually and with a table style.

Banded rows effect applied manually and with a table style   Figure 2-23

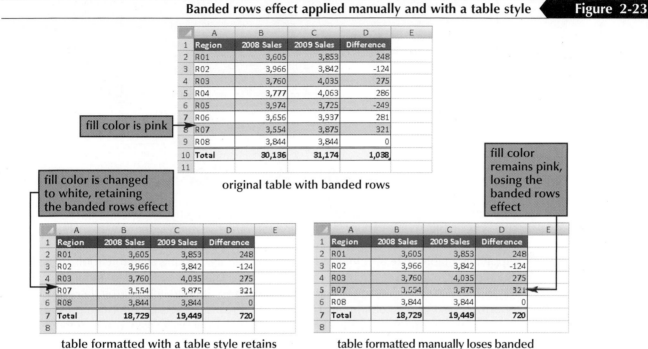

fill color is pink

original table with banded rows

fill color is changed to white, retaining the banded rows effect

fill color remains pink, losing the banded rows effect

table formatted with a table style retains banded rows after rows are deleted

table formatted manually loses banded rows after rows are deleted

Tom wants you to format the 2008, 2009, and sales increase data in the Monthly Sales worksheet as Excel tables. First, you'll apply a table style to the units sold in 2008 data.

To apply a table style to the units sold in 2008 data:

▶ **1.** Select the range **B6:K19**.

▶ **2.** In the Styles group on the Home tab, click the **Format as Table** button, and then click **Table Style Medium 2** (the second style in the first row in the Medium section). The Format as Table dialog box opens, confirming the range you selected for the table and whether the table includes header rows.

▶ **3.** Verify that the range is **=$B$6:$K$19**, verify that the **My table has headers** check box contains a check mark, and then click the **OK** button. The table style is applied.

▶ **4.** Click cell **A5** to deselect the range. See Figure 2-24.

Figure 2-24 ▶ Data formatted with a table style

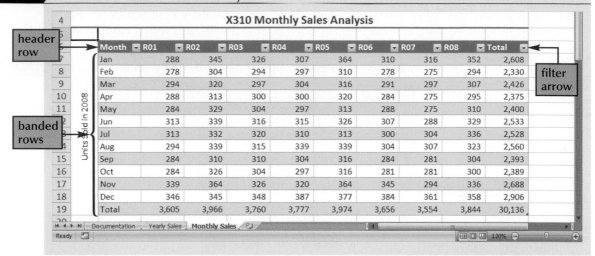

The table style treated the range as a single unit and modified its overall appearance. In this case, Table Style Medium 2 formatted the range so the header row appears in a white font on a blue fill and the remaining rows are formatted as banded rows.

Applying a table style also marks the range as a table, making available tools designed for analyzing tabular data, such as the ability to sort data, transfer data to and from an external file, and filter the data to show only those rows that match specified criteria. The filter arrows next to the column titles in the header row are used for filtering and sorting the table. Tom doesn't want to filter or sort the data right now; he asks you to remove the arrows so he can focus on the table data.

To remove the filter arrows from the table:

▶ 1. Click cell **B6** to make the table active, and then click the **Data** tab on the Ribbon.

▶ 2. In the Sort & Filter group, click the **Filter** button. The filter arrows disappear from the header row.

Selecting Table Style Options

After you apply a table style, you can choose which table elements you want included in the style. Table styles have six elements that can be turned on or off: (1) Header Row, which formats the first row of the table; (2) Total Row, which inserts a new row at the bottom of the table that adds the column values; (3) First Column, which formats the first column of the table; (4) Last Column, which formats the last column of the table; (5) Banded Rows, which formats alternating rows in different colors; and (6) Banded Columns, which formats alternating columns in different colors. For example, if you turn on the Header Row option, you can specify a format for the table's first row, which usually contains text that describes the contents of each table column. If you insert a new row at the top of the table, the new row becomes the header row and is formatted with the table style.

In the table style you just used, only the Header Row and Banded Rows options are turned on. Although the other elements are still part of the table structure, the current style does not format them. Tom wants you to format the table's last column and the header row and remove the banded rows effect.

To select the table style options:

▶ 1. If necessary, click cell **B6** to make the table active.

▶ 2. Click the **Design** tab on the Ribbon. The table design options appear on the Ribbon.

▶ 3. In the Table Style Options group, click the **Last Column** check box to insert a check mark. The last column is formatted.

▶ 4. In the Table Style Options group, click the **Banded Rows** check box to remove the check mark. The banded rows are removed from the table.

Only the Header Row and Last Column elements appear in the table. You'll use a built-in table style to format them.

▶ 5. In the Table Styles group, click the **More** button to open the Table Styles gallery, and then, in the Medium section, click **Table Style Medium 20** (the third table style in the sixth column). The table styles in the gallery show the formatting applied to the current table elements. See Figure 2-25.

Tip

To select a table style option, you can click in the table to make it active. You do not need to select the entire table.

Revised table style ◀ Figure 2-25

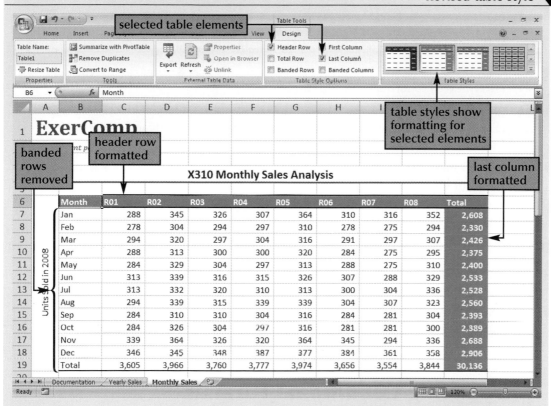

A table style might not format a table exactly the way you want. For example, Tom wants the column titles in the header row to be centered and the Total row to have a single top border and a double bottom border. Because the table style you used does not include either of these formats, you'll add these formats to the table cells. You can use cell styles and the formatting tools you've used with individual cells and ranges to format Excel tables.

To format the header row and the Total row:

▶ 1. Select the range **C6:K6**, click the **Home** tab on the Ribbon, and then, in the Alignment group, click the **Center** button ▤. The column titles are centered.

▶ 2. Select the range **B19:K19**.

▶ 3. In the Styles group, click the **Cell Styles** button, and then, in the Titles and Headings section, click **Total** (the sixth cell style).

▶ 4. Click cell **A5** to deselect the range. The Total row is formatted in bold with a single top border and a double bottom border.

Tom likes the formatting of the first table, and wants you to format the other two tables similarly. You cannot use the Format Painter to copy table formats, and you must format each range as a table separately.

To format the other two tables:

▶ 1. Select the range **B21:K34**.

▶ 2. In the Styles group on the Home tab, click the **Format as Table** button, click **Table Style Medium 6** (the sixth table style in the first row of the Medium section), and then click the **OK** button in the Format as Table dialog box.

▶ 3. Click the **Data** tab on the Ribbon, and then, in the Sort & Filter group, click the **Filter** button to turn off the filter arrows.

▶ 4. Click the **Design** tab on the Ribbon, and then, in the Table Style Options group, click the **Banded Rows** check box to remove the check mark and click the **Last Column** check box to insert a check mark.

▶ 5. In the Table Styles group, click the **More** button, and then click **Table Style Medium 20** (the sixth table style in the third row of the Medium section).

▶ 6. Select the range **C21:K21**, click the **Home** tab on the Ribbon, and then, in the Alignment group, click the **Center** button ▤.

▶ 7. Select the range **B34:K34**. You'll apply the Total cell style to this range.

▶ 8. In the Styles group, click the **Cell Styles** button, and then click **Total** (the sixth cell style in the Titles and Headings section).

▶ 9. Select the range **B36:K49** and repeat Steps 2 through 5, select the range **C36:K36** and repeat Step 6, and then select the range **B49:K49** and repeat Step 8.

Introducing Conditional Formats

So far, you have used formatting to make the workbook more readable or visually interesting. Formatting can also help you analyze data by highlighting significant numbers or trends in the data. Tom wants the sales report to highlight sales regions that have performed particularly well or done poorly in the past two years. Tom also wants to show how sales of the X310 heart rate monitor changed during the year. This information can help him plan inventory for the next year as well as project future sales and revenue.

To prepare this kind of report, you can use conditional formatting. A **conditional format** applies formatting only when a cell's value meets a specified condition. For example, a conditional format can make negative numbers red and positive numbers black. Conditional formats are dynamic, so a cell's appearance will change to reflect its current value.

Excel has four conditional formats—data bars, highlighting, color scales, and icon sets. This tutorial looks at data bars and cell highlighting.

| **Applying Conditional Formats (Data Bars and Highlights)** | Reference Window |

- Select the range or ranges to which you want to add data bars.
- In the Styles group on the Home tab, click the Conditional Formatting button, point to Data Bars, and then click a data bar color.

or

- Select the range in which you want to highlight cells that match a specified rule.
- In the Styles group, click the Conditional Formatting button, point to Highlight Cells Rules or Top/Bottom Rules, and then click the appropriate rule.
- Select the appropriate options in the dialog box, and then click the OK button.

Adding Data Bars

A **data bar** is a horizontal bar added to the background of a cell to provide a visual indicator of the cell's value. Larger values are associated with longer data bars; smaller values are associated with shorter data bars. Data bars will help Tom see how the 2008 and 2009 sales totals vary throughout the year.

To format the 2008 monthly sales with data bars:

▸ 1. Select the range **K7:K18**.

▸ 2. In the Styles group on the Home tab, click the **Conditional Formatting** button, point to **Data Bars** to open the Data Bars gallery, and then click **Purple Data Bar** (the third data bar in the second row of the Data Bars gallery). Data bars appear for the 2008 monthly sales.

▸ 3. Click cell **A3** to deselect the range. See Figure 2-26.

Data bars added to the 2008 monthly sales ◀ Figure 2-26

	Month	R01	R02	R03	R04	R05	R06	R07	R08	Total
5										
6	Month	R01	R02	R03	R04	R05	R06	R07	R08	Total
7	Jan	288	345	326	307	364	310	316	352	2,608
8	Feb	278	304	294	297	310	278	275	294	2,330
9	Mar	294	320	297	304	316	291	297	307	2,426
10	Apr	288	313	300	300	320	284	275	295	2,375
11	May	284	329	304	297	313	288	275	310	2,400
12	Jun	313	339	316	315	326	307	288	329	2,533
13	Jul	313	332	320	310	313	300	304	336	2,528
14	Aug	294	339	315	339	339	304	307	323	2,560
15	Sep	284	310	310	304	316	284	281	304	2,393
16	Oct	284	326	304	297	316	281	281	300	2,389
17	Nov	339	364	326	320	364	345	294	336	2,688
18	Dec	346	345	348	387	377	384	361	358	2,906
19	Total	3,605	3,966	3,760	3,777	3,974	3,656	3,554	3,844	30,136
20										
21	Month	R01	R02	R03	R04	R05	R06	R07		
22	Jan	352	364	345	352	336	361			
23	Feb	297	326	310	313	288	300			

Units Sold in 2008 (row label for rows 10–15)

data bar length is based on the cell value

◀ ◀ ▶ ▶ Documentation / Yearly Sales / **Monthly Sales**

Ready

120%

The data bars highlight several important facts that might not be immediately apparent from viewing the cell values. First, the highest sales occurred during the months of November, December, and January—a reflection of heavy shopping during the holiday season. Second, an increase in sales occurred during the summer months. Again, this is expected because customers are more physically active during those months and likely to purchase a heart rate monitor. Third, the periods of lowest sales occurred in the spring and fall. To find out if all of the sales regions reflect this seasonal trend, you'll add data bars to the individual sales region figures.

To add data bars for all sales regions:

▶ 1. Select the range **C7:J18**.

▶ 2. In the Styles group on the Home tab, click the **Conditional Formatting** button, point to **Data Bars**, and then click **Light Blue Data Bar** (the second data bar in the second row of the Data Bars gallery). Monthly data bars appear for all the sales regions in 2008.

▶ 3. Click cell **A3** to deselect the range. See Figure 2-27.

Figure 2-27 ▶ **Data bars added to the regional monthly sales data**

January sales for the R01 region are lower than expected

Month	R01	R02	R03	R04	R05	R06	R07	R08	Total
Jan	288	345	326	307	364	310	316	352	2,608
Feb	278	304	294	297	310	278	275	294	2,330
Mar	294	320	297	304	316	291	297	307	2,426
Apr	288	313	300	300	320	284	275	295	2,375
May	284	329	304	297	313	288	275	310	2,400
Jun	313	339	316	315	326	307	288	329	2,533
Jul	313	332	320	310	313	300	304	336	2,528
Aug	294	339	315	339	339	304	307	323	2,560
Sep	284	310	310	304	316	284	281	304	2,393
Oct	284	326	304	297	316	281	281	300	2,389
Nov	339	364	326	320	364	345	294	336	2,688
Dec	346	345	348	387	377	384	361	358	2,906
Total	3,605	3,966	3,760	3,777	3,974	3,656	3,554	3,844	30,136

Units Sold in 2008

Month	R01	R02	R03	R04	R05	R06	R07	R08	Total
Jan	352	364	345	352	336	361	325	342	2,777
Feb	297	326	310	313	288	300	297	300	2,431

Documentation | Yearly Sales | **Monthly Sales**

Ready

For the most part, the seasonal trend is reflected in all the sales regions, with some exceptions. For example, the R01 region had lower-than-expected sales during January 2008. Tom discovers that a distribution problem prevented several stores in the R01 region from receiving its stock of ExerComp heart rate monitors until near the end of January, causing the decreased sales totals. Data bars highlight this important piece of information.

Data bar lengths depend on the values in the selected range. The largest value in the range has the longest data bar; the smallest value has the shortest data bar. For example, in the Total column, the shortest data bar represents the February total of 2,330 and the longest data bar represents the December total of 2,906. You should use different colored data bars to distinguish data bars for different ranges. For example, you used blue data bars for the regional sales and purple data bars for the totals.

Because data bar lengths are based on the values in the range, changing the value of one cell in the range can affect the size of all the other cells' data bars. You'll change the units sold value in cell C7 and see how this affects the data bars.

To see the effect on data bars of changing a units sold value:

1. In cell C7, enter **588**. The lengths of all the data bars in the 2008 sales table change to reflect this increased value.

2. On the Quick Access Toolbar, click the **Undo** button ↺. The value in cell C7 returns to 288, its original value.

Clearing a Conditional Format

Tom wants you to add data bars to the 2009 sales table. You can base the data bars on the values in only the 2009 sales table, or you can base them on the values in both the 2008 and 2009 sales tables. Both approaches have advantages. Basing the data bars on only the 2009 sales allows you to focus on that data and see more detail on the seasonal and regional trends within that year. However, basing the data bars on sales results from both years makes it easier to compare sales trends from one year to another. Tom wants you to base the length of the data bars on the values from both years. First, you need to remove the data bars you created for the 2008 sales table. Then, you can add a new set of data bars based on a different selection of cells.

To clear the data bars from the 2008 sales table:

1. If necessary, click cell **C7** to select it and make the table active.

2. In the Styles group on the Home tab, click the **Conditional Formatting** button, point to **Clear Rules**, and then click **Clear Rules from This Table**. Both sets of data bars are removed from the 2008 sales table.

Next, you'll add data bars for the sales data in both the 2008 and 2009 sales tables.

To add data bars to both the 2008 and 2009 sales tables:

1. Select the range **K7:K18;K22:K33**. This selects the 2008 and 2009 monthly sales totals.

2. In the Styles group on the Home tab, click the **Conditional Formatting** button, point to **Data Bars**, and then click **Purple Data Bar** (the third data bar in the second row of the Data Bars gallery).

3. Select the range **C7:J18;C22:J33**. This selects the 2008 and 2009 monthly sales for each region.

4. In the Styles group, click the **Conditional Formatting** button, point to **Data Bars**, and then click **Light Blue Data Bar** (the second data bar in the second row of the Data Bars gallery).

5. Click cell **A20** to deselect the range. See Figure 2-28.

> **Tip**
>
> To remove all conditional formatting from a worksheet, click Clear Rules from Entire Sheet. To remove it from the selected range, click Clear Rules from Selected Cells.

Data bars added to the 2008 and 2009 sales tables

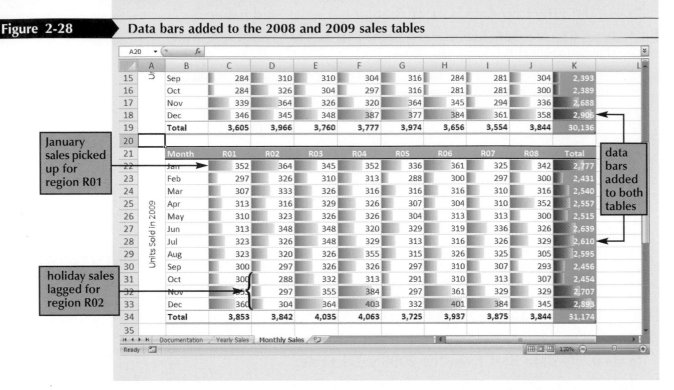

January sales picked up for region R01

holiday sales lagged for region R02

data bars added to both tables

Tom sees some of the same seasonal trends in 2009 as he saw for 2008. He notes that sales in the R01 region did not lag as they did in 2008, but sales in the R02 region were lower than expected during the holiday season. Other than that, it's hard to compare the regional and monthly sales to determine any trends from 2008 to 2009. He knows that, overall, the number of heart rate monitors sold increased in 2009, but he doesn't know if this is true for all regions and for all months. Tom wants to highlight those sales regions and months in which sales increased from 2008 to 2009.

Highlighting Cells

The third table shows the increase in sales from 2008 to 2009, which is the data that Tom wants to analyze. Because Tom wants to highlight those regions and months in 2008 in which the sales increased, you'll highlight only those cells that contain positive values. Highlighting cells based on their values is another type of conditional format. Figure 2-29 describes some of the ways that cells can be highlighted.

Figure 2-29   **Highlighting rules**

Rule	Highlights
Greater Than	Cells that are greater than a specified number
Less Than	Cells that are less than a specified number
Between	Cells that are between two specified numbers
Equal To	Cells that are equal to a specified number
Text That Contains	Cells that contain specified text
A Date Occurring	Cells that contain a specified date
Duplicate Values	Cells that contain duplicate or unique values

Tom wants you to highlight all the positive numbers in the third table to show those months and sales regions that increased sales from 2008 to 2009.

To highlight the positive sales numbers:

1. Select the range **C37:J48**. This selects the difference in sales by region and month for 2008 and 2009.

2. In the Styles group on the Home tab, click the **Conditional Formatting** button, point to **Highlight Cells Rules**, and then click **Greater Than**. The Greater Than dialog box opens. You want to highlight positive sales numbers, which are numbers greater than zero.

3. Type **0** (a zero) in the Format cells that are GREATER THAN box, click the **with** arrow, and then click **Green Fill with Dark Green Text**.

4. Click the **OK** button to apply the highlight rule.

5. Click cell **A35** to deselect the range. Cells with positive numbers are highlighted in green. See Figure 2-30.

Positive cells highlighted ◄ **Figure 2-30**

green cells indicate an increase in sales from 2008 to 2009

	Month	R01	R02	R03	R04	R05	R06	R07	R08	Total
	Jan	64	19	19	45	-28	51	9	-10	169
	Feb	19	22	16	16	-22	22	22	6	101
	Mar	13	13	29	12	0	25	13	9	114
	Apr	25	3	29	26	-13	20	35	57	182
	May	26	-6	22	29	-9	25	38	-10	115
	Jun	0	9	32	5	3	12	48	-3	106
	Jul	10	-6	28	19	0	16	22	-7	82
	Aug	29	-19	11	16	-24	22	18	-18	35
	Sep	16	-13	16	22	-19	26	26	-11	63
	Oct	16	-38	28	16	-25	29	32	7	65
	Nov	16	-67	29	64	-67	16	35	-7	19
	Dec	14	-41	16	16	-45	17	23	-13	-13
	Total	**248**	**-124**	**275**	**286**	**-249**	**281**	**321**	**0**	**1,038**

(Net Increase from 2008 to 2009)

From the highlighting, you can tell that most regions and months had increased sales in 2009. Most of the declines occurred in regions R02, R05, and R08. Tom wonders if some months or regions had particularly strong sales increases. You'll remove the current highlighting, and then highlight the top 10% in sales increases.

To highlight the top 10 percent in sales increases:

1. Select the range **C37:J48**.

2. In the Styles group on the Home tab, click the **Conditional Formatting** button, point to **Clear Rules**, and then click **Clear Rules from Selected Cells**. The current highlighting is removed.

3. In the Styles group, click the **Conditional Formatting** button, point to **Top/Bottom Rules**, and then click **Top 10 %**. The Top 10% dialog box opens.

4. Verify that **10** is entered in the % box, click the **with** arrow, and then click **Green Fill with Dark Green Text**.

5. Click the **OK** button. Cells whose sales increases for 2008 and 2009 were in the top 10% are highlighted in green.

6. Click cell **A35** to deselect the range. See Figure 2-31.

Figure 2-31 ▶ Top 10% sales increases highlighted

green cells indicate sales increases that were in the top 10%

	Month	R01	R02	R03	R04	R05	R06	R07	R08	Total
	Jan	64	19	19	45	-28	51	9	-10	169
	Feb	19	22	16	16	-22	22	22	6	101
	Mar	13	13	29	12	0	25	13	9	114
	Apr	25	3	29	26	-13	20	35	57	182
	May	26	-6	22	29	-9	25	38	-10	115
	Jun	0	9	32	5	3	12	48	-3	106
	Jul	10	-6	28	19	0	16	22	-7	82
	Aug	29	-19	11	16	-24	22	18	-18	35
	Sep	16	-13	16	22	-19	26	26	-11	63
	Oct	16	-38	28	16	-25	29	32	7	65
	Nov	16	-67	29	64	-67	16	35	-7	19
	Dec	14	-41	16	16	-45	17	23	-13	-13
	Total	**248**	**-124**	**275**	**286**	**-249**	**281**	**321**	**0**	**1,038**

Net Increase from 2008 to 2009

Documentation | Yearly Sales | **Monthly Sales**

Ready   120%

The results provide Tom with some interesting information. For example, region R08, which underperformed for most of the year, had one of the largest sales increases during April (cell J40). In fact, the increase in sales during that one month compensated for the sales declines in other months, so that by the end of the year, region R08 showed no overall decline in sales. Also, region R01 had a large increase in sales during January 2009, indicating that this region fixed the distribution problems that occurred in 2008. Finally, of the nine cells highlighted in the table, four of them come from region R07, three of those occurring during the usually slow spring months.

Tom wonders what insights he could gain from highlighting the bottom 10% of the table—the regions and months that showed the lowest sales increases in 2009.

To highlight the bottom 10 percent in sales increases:

▶ **1.** Select the range **C37:J48**.

▶ **2.** In the Styles group on the Home tab, click the **Conditional Formatting** button, point to **Top/Bottom Rules**, and then click **Bottom 10 %**. The Bottom 10% dialog box opens.

▶ **3.** Verify that **10** is entered in the % box and **Light Red Fill with Dark Red Text** is selected in the with box, and then click the **OK** button. Red cells highlight the regions and months that placed in the bottom 10% for sales increases from 2008 to 2009.

▶ **4.** Click cell **A35** to deselect the range. See Figure 2-32.

Bottom 10% of sales increases highlighted ◄ **Figure 2-32**

Month	R01	R02	R03	R04	R05	R06	R07	R08	Total
Jan	64	19	19	45	-28	51	9	-10	169
Feb	19	22	16	16	-22	22	22	6	101
Mar	13	13	29	12	0	25	13	9	114
Apr	25	3	29	26	-13	20	35	57	182
May	26	-6	22	29	-9	25	38	-10	115
Jun	0	9	32	5	3	12	48	-3	106
Jul	10	-6	28	19	0	16	22	-7	82
Aug	29	-19	11	16	-24	22	18	-18	35
Sep	16	-13	16	22	-19	26	26	-11	63
Oct	16	-38	28	16	-25	29	32	7	65
Nov	16	-67	29	64	-67	16	35	-7	19
Dec	14	-41	16	16	-45	17	23	-13	-13
Total	248	-124	275	286	-249	281	321	0	1,038

Net increase from 2008 to 2009

red cells indicate sales increases were in the bottom 10%

Tom immediately sees that the bottom 10% come from only regions R02 and R05, and that six of the nine cells highlighted occurred in the most recent months: October, November, and December. Conditional formatting has helped Tom isolate and highlight potential problem areas, which he can investigate further.

When you use conditional formatting to highlight cells in a worksheet, you should always include a **legend**, which is a key that shows each color used in the worksheet and what it means, so others know why certain cells are highlighted. Tom asks you to add a legend to the Monthly Sales worksheet.

To create a conditional formatting legend:

1. In cell D51, enter **light red**, and then click cell **D51** to select it. You'll use a highlight rule to fill this cell with the light red color used for the bottom 10% sales increases.

2. In the Styles group on the Home tab, click the **Conditional Formatting** button, point to **Highlight Cells Rules**, and then click **Text that Contains**. The Text That Contains dialog box opens.

3. Verify that **light red** appears in the Format cells that contain the text box, select **Light Red Fill with Dark Red Text** in the with box, and then click the **OK** button. Cell D51 is filled with the same light red fill color used for the bottom 10% values.

4. In cell D52, enter **light green**, and then click cell **D52** to select it. You'll use a highlight rule to fill this cell with the green color used for the top 10% sales increases.

5. In the Styles group on the Home tab, click the **Conditional Formatting** button, point to **Hightlight Cells Rules**, and then click **Text that Contains**. The Text That Contains dialog box opens.

6. Verify that **light green** appears in the Format cells that contain the text box, select **Green Fill with Dark Green Text** in the with box, and then click the **OK** button. Cell D52 is filled with the same light green fill color used for the top 10% values.

7. In cell E51, enter **Bottom 10% in terms of sales increase**, and then, in cell E52, enter **Top 10% in terms of sales increase**.

8. Select the range **E51:E52**. You'll format these cells with a cell style to distinguish them from the rest of the text in the worksheet.

9. In the Styles group, click the **Cell Styles** button, and then, in the Date and Model group, click **Explanatory** (the third cell style in the first row).

10. Click cell **A35** to deselect the range. See Figure 2-33.

Figure 2-33 | **Cell highlighting legend**

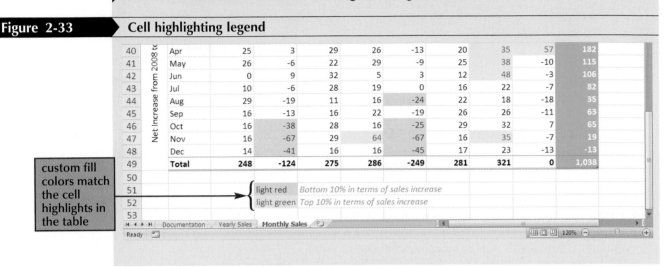

custom fill colors match the cell highlights in the table

The conditional formatting in the Monthly Sales worksheet helps Tom understand how sales of the X310 heart rate monitor changed over the past two years and helps him focus on particular sales regions for additional analysis.

InSight | Using Conditional Formatting Effectively

Conditional formatting is an excellent way to point out trends and highlight key data values, but it should be used judiciously. An overuse of conditional formatting can sometimes obscure the very data values you want to emphasize. Keep in mind the following tips:

- Document the conditional formats you use. If a bold, green font means that a sales number is in the top 10% of all sales, include that information in a legend in the worksheet.
- Don't clutter data with too much highlighting. Limit highlight rules to one or two per data set. Highlights are designed to draw attention to points of interest. If you use too many, you'll end up highlighting everything—and, therefore, nothing.
- Use color sparingly in worksheets with highlights. It's difficult to tell a highlight color from a regular fill color, especially when fill colors are used in every cell.
- Consider alternatives to conditional formats. If you want to highlight the top 10 sales regions, it might be more effective to simply sort the data with the best-selling regions at the top of the list.
- Don't let data bars overwhelm cell text. Use data bars when you're more interested in the "big picture" rather than specific cell values. If you want to show both, use a chart.

Hiding Worksheet Data

The Monthly Sales worksheet contains too much data to fit into the worksheet window without drastically reducing the zoom level. This would make the contents too small to read easily. Another way to view a large worksheet is by selectively hiding rows or columns (or even entire worksheets in a workbook). Hiding rows, columns, and worksheets is an excellent way to conceal extraneous or distracting information; but you should never hide data that is crucial to understanding a workbook.

Tom wants to view only the third table, which shows the difference in sales between 2008 and 2009, but not the other tables. You'll hide the rows that contain the first two tables and then unhide those rows after Tom has looked at the third table.

To hide and unhide worksheet rows:

▶ **1.** Select row **6** through row **35** in the Monthly Sales worksheet.

▶ **2.** In the Cells group on the Home tab, click the **Format** button, point to **Hide & Unhide**, and then click **Hide Rows**. Rows 6 to 35 are hidden, and the row numbers in the worksheet jump from row 5 to row 36. The data in the third table hasn't changed even though its formulas use data from the hidden tables.

▶ **3.** Select row **5** and row **36**, which are the rows before and after the hidden rows.

▶ **4.** In the Cells group, click the **Format** button, point to **Hide & Unhide**, and then click **Unhide Rows**. The hidden rows 6 through 35 reappear.

Formatting the Worksheet for Printing

Tom wants you to print this analysis of the monthly sales figures. In preparing the worksheet for the printer, you can select the position of the report on the page, the orientation of the page, and whether the page will include headers or footers. First, you'll look at the Monthly Sales worksheet in Page Layout view to see how it would currently print.

To view the Monthly Sales worksheet in Page Layout view:

▶ **1.** Click the **Page Layout** button 🔲 on the status bar. The worksheet switches to Page Layout view.

▶ **2.** Zoom the worksheet to **60%** to view more of the page layout. See Figure 2-34.

Page Layout view of the Monthly Sales worksheet　　　Figure 2-34

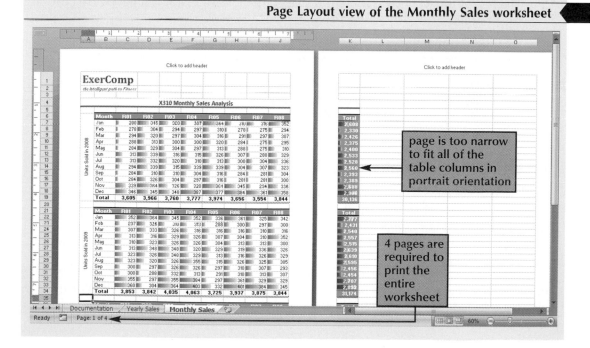

In the worksheet's current orientation, its contents do not fit on a single page and the tables break across pages. You'll change the orientation from portrait to landscape so that the page is wide enough to fit all the table columns on one page.

To change the page orientation to landscape:

▶ **1.** Click the **Page Layout** tab on the Ribbon.

▶ **2.** In the Page Setup group, click the **Orientation** button, and then click **Landscape**. The page orientation changes to landscape, making each page wide enough to display all of the columns of each table.

Defining the Print Area

By default, all parts of the active worksheet containing text, formulas, or values are printed. You can also select the cells you want to print, and then define them as a **print area**. A print area can cover an adjacent or nonadjacent range.

For his report, Tom wants to print only the first table. You'll set the print area to cover only those cells. It's generally easier to work with the print area in Page Break Preview.

To switch to Page Break Preview and define the print area:

▶ **1.** Click the **Page Break Preview** button 🔲 on the status bar, and then zoom the worksheet to **70%**.

Trouble? If the Welcome to Page Break Preview dialog box opens, click the OK button.

▶ **2.** Select the range **A1:K19**, which is the range of the first table.

▶ **3.** In the Page Setup group on the Page Layout tab, click the **Print Area** button, and then click **Set Print Area**. The print area changes to cover only the range A1:K19. The rest of the worksheet content is shaded to indicate that it will not be part of the printout.

Tom decides that he wants you to print all the content in the worksheet, so you'll clear the print area you just defined, resetting the print area to the default.

▶ **4.** In the Page Setup group, click the **Print Area** button, and then click **Clear Print Area**. The print area again covers the entire contents of the worksheet.

Inserting Page Breaks

Large worksheets often do not fit onto one page unless you scale the printout to fit, but that usually results in text that is too small to read comfortably. When a printout extends to multiple pages, Excel prints as much as fits on a page and then inserts a **page break** to continue printing the remaining worksheet content on the next page. This can result in page breaks that split worksheet content in awkward places, such as within a table.

Instead, you can insert **manual page breaks** that specify exactly where the page breaks occur. A page break is inserted directly above and to the left of a selected cell, directly above a selected row, or to the left of a selected column.

Setting and Removing Page Breaks | Reference Window

To set a page break:

- Select the first cell below the row where you want to insert a page break.
- In the Page Setup group on the Page Layout tab, click the Breaks button, and then click Insert Page Break.

To remove a page break:

- Select any cell below or to the right of the page break you want to remove.
- In the Page Setup group on the Page Layout tab, click the Breaks button, and then click Remove Page Break (or click Reset All Page Breaks to remove all the page breaks from the worksheet).

Tom wants the three tables in the Monthly Sales worksheet to print on separate pages. You'll insert page breaks to accomplish this.

To insert page breaks between the tables:

▶ **1.** Click cell **A20**.

▶ **2.** In the Page Setup group on the Page Layout tab, click the **Breaks** button, and then click **Insert Page Break**. A page break separates row 19 from row 20.

▶ **3.** Click cell **A35**, and then repeat Step 2 to insert a second page break that splits the second table from the third. The printout is now three pages. See Figure 2-35.

Worksheet in Page Break Preview ◀ Figure 2-35

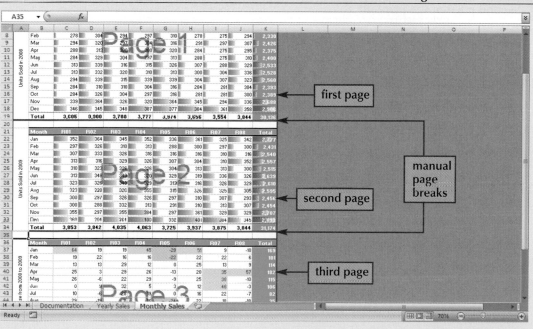

Tip

In Page Break Preview, a dashed blue line indicates an automatic page break and a solid blue line indicates a manual page break.

▶ **4.** Click the **Page Layout** button on the status bar, and then verify that each table appears on a separate page.

Adding Print Titles

The company name, the slogan, and the worksheet title all appear on the first page of the printout, but do not appear on the other two pages. This is because the range that includes that text is limited to the first page of the printout. It's a good practice to include the company name, logo, and worksheet title on each page of a printout in case a page becomes separated from the other pages. You can repeat information, such as the company name, by specifying which rows or columns in the worksheet act as **print titles**, information that prints on each page.

Tom wants the first four rows of the Monthly Sales worksheet printed on each page.

To define the print titles for the pages:

▶ **1.** In the Page Setup group on the Page Layout tab, click the **Print Titles** button. The Page Setup dialog box opens with the Sheet tab displayed.

▶ **2.** Click the **Rows to repeat at top** box, move your pointer over the worksheet, and then select the range **A1:A4**. A flashing border appears around the first four rows of the worksheet as a visual indicator that the contents of the first four rows will be repeated on each page of the printout. The cell reference $1:$4 appears in the Rows to repeat at top box.

▶ **3.** Click the **OK** button.

▶ **4.** Click the **Page Layout** button 🔲 on the status bar, and then scroll through the second and third pages of the printout in Page Layout view to verify that the company name, slogan, and worksheet title appear on each page. See Figure 2-36.

Figure 2-36	Second page of the printout

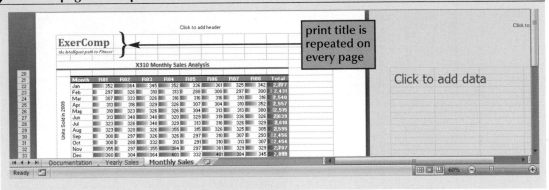

The Sheet tab in the Page Setup dialog box provides other print options, such as printing the gridlines or row and column headings. You can also print the worksheet in black and white or in draft quality. For a multiple page printout, you can specify whether the pages are ordered by first going down the worksheet and then across or across first and then down.

Adding Headers and Footers

Another way to repeat information on each page of a printout is with headers and footers. A **header** is the text printed in the top margin of each page. A **footer** is the text printed in the bottom margin of each page. A **margin** is the space between the page content and the edges of the page. Headers and footers can be used to add information to the printed page that is not found in the worksheet cells, such as the workbook's author, the date the page was printed, or the workbook filename. If the printout covers multiple pages, you can add a footer that displays the page number and the total number of pages in the printout to help ensure you and others have the entire printout.

The header and footer have three sections: a left section, a center section, and a right section. Within each section, you type the text you want to appear or insert elements such as the worksheet name or current date and time. These header and footer elements are dynamic; if you rename the worksheet, for example, the name is automatically updated in the header or footer.

Tom wants his printouts to display the workbook's filename in the header's left section and the current date in the header's right section. He wants the center footer to display the page number and the total number of pages in the printout, and the right footer to display your name as the workbook's author.

To insert the header and footer text:

1. Zoom the worksheet to **90%** in Page Layout view.

2. Scroll to the top of the worksheet, and then click the left section of the header directly above cell A1. The Header & Footer Tools contextual tab appears on the Ribbon.

3. Type **Filename:** in the left section of the header, press the **spacebar**, and then, in the Header & Footer Elements group on the Header & Footer Tools Design tab, click the **File Name** button. The code &[File], which displays the filename of the current workbook, is added into the left section of the header.

4. Press the **Tab** key twice to move to the right section of the header, and then, in the Header & Footer Elements group, click the **Current Date** button. The code &[Date] is added into the right section of the header. See Figure 2-37.

Page header   **Figure 2-37**

5. In the Navigation group, click the **Go to Footer** button. The right section of the footer is selected.

6. Click the center section of the footer, type **Page**, press the **spacebar**, and then, in the Header & Footer Elements group, click the **Page Number** button.

7. Press the **spacebar**, type **of**, press the **spacebar**, and then, in the Header & Footer Elements group, click the **Number of Pages** button. The text, "Page &[Page] of &[Pages]" appears in the center section of the footer.

8. Press the **Tab** key to move to the right section of the footer, type **Prepared by:**, press the **spacebar**, and then type your name. See Figure 2-38.

Figure 2-38   Page footer

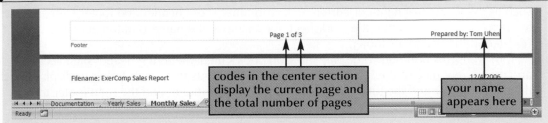

Footer

Page 1 of 3

Prepared by: Tom Uhen

Filename: ExerComp Sales Report

codes in the center section
display the current page and
the total number of pages

your name
appears here

12/4/2006

◄ ◄ ► ► Documentation Yearly Sales **Monthly Sales**

Ready

9. Click cell **A1**, and then scroll through the other two pages of the worksheet to
verify that the same header appears for each page and the center section of the
footer displays the correct page number and total number of pages.

Tom is happy with the appearance of the worksheet and the layout of the printout. He
asks you to save your work, and print the Monthly Sales worksheet.

To save the workbook and print the worksheet:

1. Click the **Normal** button ▦ on the status bar to return the Monthly Sales worksheet
to Normal view.

2. Save your changes to the workbook.

3. Print the contents of the Monthly Sales worksheet, and then close the workbook.
Each table is printed on a separate page and the headers and footers display the
filename, current date, page number and total number of pages, and your name.

Tom will analyze the finished report, and distribute it during the upcoming sales
meeting.

Review | **Session 2.2 Quick Check**

1. What is a table style?
2. What are the six table style options you can turn on and off?
3. What is conditional formatting?
4. How is the length of a data bar determined by default?
5. How would you highlight the top five values in the range A1:C20?
6. What are print titles?
7. How do you insert a page break into your worksheet?

Tutorial Summary | Review

In this tutorial, you used formatting tools to create visually appealing and informative workbooks. You formatted text, backgrounds, borders, numbers, and dates, and copied formats from one range into another. You applied built-in styles and themes to the workbook. Next, you looked at how formatting can be helpful for analyzing and interpreting data. You applied a table style to format an Excel table. Then, you used two types of conditional formatting—data bars and highlighting rules—to better understand the data entered into the workbook. Finally, you formatted the worksheet for printing by setting page breaks and page titles, and inserting headers and footers.

Key Terms

accent	Format Painter	points
automatic color	formatting	print area
banded rows	General number format	print title
border	header	sans serif font
conditional format	legend	serif font
custom color	Live Preview	standard color
data bar	manual page break	style
Excel table	margin	table style
font	merge	theme
font size	Mini toolbar	theme color
font style	non-theme font	theme font
footer	page break	typeface

Practice		Review Assignments

Practice the skills you learned in the tutorial using the same case scenario.

Data Files needed for the Review Assignments: X410.xlsx, Paper.jpg

ExerComp introduced another heart rate monitor, the X410, two years ago. Tom wants you to format a workbook that compares the sales of the X310 and X410 models during that time. The workbook has a Documentation sheet, a Model Comparison sheet comparing the total units sold for each model in the eight sales regions, and a Monthly Sales sheet reporting the number of units sold per month.

In the Model Comparison sheet, Tom wants you to highlight the sales regions that showed the greatest sales increases from 2008 to 2009. Figure 2-39 shows a preview of the formatted Model Comparison sheet.

Figure 2-39

	A	B	C	D	E	F
1	ExerComp					
2	*the Intelligent path to Fitness*					
3				highest	Highest increase in units sold	
4				highest	Highest % increase in units sold	
5						
6		Region	Units Sold (2008)	Units Sold (2009)	Increase	% Increase
7		R01	3,605	3,853	248	6.88%
8	X	R02	3,966	3,842	-124	-3.13%
9	3	R03	3,760	4,035	275	7.31%
10		R04	3,777	4,063	286	7.57%
11	1	R05	3,974	3,725	-249	-6.27%
12		R06	3,656	3,937	281	7.69%
13	0	R07	3,554	3,875	321	9.03%
14		R08	3,844	3,844	0	0.00%
15		Total	30,136	31,174	1,038	3.44%
16						
17		Region	Units Sold (2008)	Units Sold (2009)	Increase	% Increase
18		R01	2,488	4,156	1,668	67.04%
19	X	R02	2,531	4,293	1,762	69.62%
20		R03	2,231	4,292	2,061	92.38%
21	4	R04	2,613	4,851	2,238	85.65%
22	1	R05	2,512	4,308	1,796	71.50%
23		R06	2,824	4,689	1,865	66.04%
24	0	R07	2,355	4,529	2,174	92.31%
25		R08	2,412	4,140	1,728	71.64%
26		Total	19,966	35,258	15,292	76.59%

In the Monthly Sales sheet, Tom wants you to include data bars that show the monthly sales totals for both models during 2008 and 2009. Figure 2-40 shows a preview of the completed Monthly Sales sheet.

Figure 2-40

	A	B	C	D	E	F	G	H	I
1	ExerComp								
2	*the Intelligent path to Fitness*								
3									
4		**2008 Sales (Units Sold)**					**2009 Sales (Units Sold)**		
5	Month	X310	X410	All Models		Month	X310	X410	All Models
6	Jan	2,608	-	2,608		Jan	2,777	3,223	6,000
7	Feb	2,330	-	2,330		Feb	2,431	2,612	5,043
8	Mar	2,426	25	2,451		Mar	2,540	2,714	5,254
9	Apr	2,375	75	2,450		Apr	2,557	2,877	5,434
10	May	2,400	1,500	3,900		May	2,515	2,749	5,264
11	Jun	2,533	1,750	4,283		Jun	2,639	2,955	5,594
12	Jul	2,528	2,135	4,663		Jul	2,610	2,839	5,449
13	Aug	2,560	2,620	5,180		Aug	2,595	2,875	5,470
14	Sep	2,393	2,714	5,107		Sep	2,456	2,823	5,279
15	Oct	2,389	2,689	5,078		Oct	2,454	2,791	5,245
16	Nov	2,688	3,144	5,832		Nov	2,707	3,278	5,985
17	Dec	2,906	3,314	6,220		Dec	2,893	3,522	6,415
18	Total	30,136	19,966	50,102		Total	31,174	35,258	66,432

Complete the following. (*Note:* Text you need to enter is shown in bold for ease of reference only; do not bold the text unless otherwise instructed.)

1. Open the **X410** workbook located in the Tutorial.02\Review folder included with your Data Files, and then save the workbook as **X410 Sales Comparison** in the same folder. In the Documentation sheet, enter your name in cell B4 and the current date in cell B5 in the format *mm/dd/yyyy*.

2. In the Documentation sheet, set the font color of cells A1 and A2 to blue, format the text in cell A1 in a 26-point Times New Roman font, and then format the text in cell A2 in a 10-point italicized Times New Roman font. In cell A1, change the font color of the text string "Comp" to red.

3. In the range A4:A6, set the font color to white and set the fill color to blue. In the range B4:B6, set the fill color to white. In the range A4:B6, add border lines around all of the cells.

4. In cell B5, display the date with the Long Date format and left-aligned within the cell.

5. In the Documentation sheet, insert a background image, using the **Paper.jpg** image file located in the Tutorial.02\Review folder included with your Data Files.

6. Use the Format Painter to copy the format from the range A1:A2 in the Documentation sheet to the range A1:A2 in the other two sheets. In cell A1, change the font color of the text string "Comp" to red.

7. In the Model Comparison sheet, merge and center the range A6:A15, center the text vertically, and then rotate the text to a vertical orientation. (*Hint:* In the Alignment group on the Home tab, click the Orientation button, and then click Vertical Text.) Center the text in the range C6:F6, and then indent the region labels in the range B7:B14 one character.

8. In the range C7:E15, format the numbers in a Number format using a thousands separator, no decimal places, and negative numbers displayed with a minus symbol. In the range F7:F15, format the numbers in a Percentage format with two decimal places.

9. Apply the Accent1 cell style to the range B6:F6. Apply the Accent1 cell style to the merged cell A6, and then increase that cell's font size to 18 points and bold. Apply the Total cell style to the range B15:F15.

10. In the range E7:E14, apply a conditional format that adds a Top/Bottom Rule to display the highest number in the range in dark green text with a green fill. In the range F7:F14, apply a conditional format that adds a Top/Bottom Rule to display the highest number in the range in dark red text with a light red fill.

11. Use the Format Painter to copy all of the formats from the range A6:F15 to the range A17:F26.

12. In cell D3, enter **highest**, and then apply a conditional format to cell D3 that adds a Highlight Cells Rule to format the cell that contains the text "highest" with Green Fill with Dark Green Text. In cell D4, enter **highest**, and then apply a conditional format to cell D3 that adds a Highlight Cells Rule to format the cell that contains the text "highest" with Light Red Fill with Dark Red Text.

13. In cell E3, enter **Highest increase in units sold**. In cell E4, enter **Highest % increase in units sold**. Format both cells with the Explanatory Text cell style.

14. In the Monthly Sales sheet, merge and center the range A4:D4, merge and center the range F4:I4, and then apply the Heading 1 style to both merged cells. In the range B5:D5;G5:I5, center the text.

15. In the range B6:D18;G6:I18, format the numbers to show a thousands separator (,) with no decimal places to the right of the decimal point.

16. Select the range A5:D18, and then apply Table Style Light 8 (the second table style in the second row of the Light section in the Table Styles gallery). Turn off the filter arrows, and then turn on only the header row, first column, and last column table style options. In the range A18:D18, apply the Total cell style.

17. Select the range F5:I18, and then repeat Step 16, applying the Total cell style to the range F18:I18.

18. In the range D6:D17, add green data bars. In the range I6:I17, add purple data bars.

19. For the Model Comparison and Monthly Sales worksheets, set the page orientations to landscape, display your name in the center section of the header, display the sheet name in the left section of the footer, display the workbook filename in the center section of the footer, and then display the current date in the right section of the footer.

20. Save and close your workbook. Submit the finished workbook to your instructor, either in printed or electronic form, as requested.

Apply	**Case Problem 1**

Use the skills you learned to create a sales report for a winter clothing company.

Data File needed for this Case Problem: Frosti.xlsx

FrostiWear Linda Young is a sales manager for FrostiWear, a successful new store based in Hillsboro, Oregon. She's tracking the sales figures for FrostiWear's line of gloves. She created a workbook that contains the sales figures from the past year for three glove models. She wants you to help format the sales report. Figure 2-41 shows a preview of the formatted report.

Figure 2-41

		Month	Region 1	Region 2	Region 3	Region 4	Region 5	Total	
					FrostiWear				
					2009 Sales Report				
PolyFleece Mitts		Month	Region 1	Region 2	Region 3	Region 4	Region 5	Total	
		Jan	1,150	1,690	930	2,850	1,210		7,830
		Feb	1,100	2,200	680	2,340	1,100		7,420
		Mar	1,070	1,290	960	2,740	1,180		7,240
		Apr	780	1,520	720	2,170	1,180		6,370
		May	1,070	1,370	700	1,940	1,210		6,290
		Jun	670	1,300	780	3,430	1,170		7,350
		Jul	1,390	1,590	1,240	2,230	1,430		7,880
		Aug	1,310	1,730	610	2,560	960		7,170
		Sep	1,100	1,820	370	3,040	1,100		7,430
		Oct	1,350	2,010	750	2,430	1,230		7,770
		Nov	680	1,620	780	3,210	1,230		7,520
		Dec	1,120	1,170	670	1,920	1,310		6,190
		Total	12,790	19,310	9,190	30,860	14,310		86,460
ArcticBlast Gloves		Month	Region 1	Region 2	Region 3	Region 4	Region 5	Total	
		Jan	790	1,160	620	2,590	760		5,920
		Feb	1,010	1,170	610	1,950	1,010		5,750
		Mar	710	1,270	600	2,050	930		5,560
		Apr	890	1,190	750	2,030	980		5,840
		May	990	1,340	660	2,670	1,040		6,700
		Jun	990	1,280	620	2,330	800		6,020
		Jul	780	1,180	690	2,260	920		5,830
		Aug	800	1,220	560	2,460	900		5,940
		Sep	810	1,150	670	2,500	970		6,100
		Oct	760	1,070	630	2,350	1,040		5,850
		Nov	770	1,140	630	2,540	1,080		6,160
		Dec	850	1,370	590	2,490	1,060		6,360
		Total	10,150	14,540	7,630	28,220	11,490		72,030
Glomitts		Month	Region 1	Region 2	Region 3	Region 4	Region 5	Total	
		Jan	340	780	280	1,670	600		3,670
		Feb	460	810	280	1,770	480		3,800
		Mar	410	820	310	1,490	460		3,490
		Apr	490	890	330	1,610	650		3,970
		May	470	960	290	1,580	540		3,840
		Jun	480	740	340	1,780	640		3,980
		Jul	470	760	320	1,500	640		3,690
		Aug	490	690	340	1,610	600		3,730
		Sep	420	780	340	1,660	680		3,880
		Oct	460	820	350	1,800	660		4,090
		Nov	550	830	440	1,250	590		3,660
		Dec	400	790	220	1,620	540		3,570
		Total	5,440	9,670	3,840	19,340	7,080		45,370

Complete the following. (*Note:* Text you need to enter is shown in bold for ease of reference only; do not bold the text unless otherwise instructed.)

1. Open the **Frosti** workbook located in the Tutorial.02\Case1 folder included with your Data Files, and then save the workbook as **FrostiWear Sales Report** in the same folder.

2. In the Documentation sheet, enter your name in cell B3 and the date in cell B4. Set the background color for all the cells in the worksheet to standard blue, and then set the background color for the range B3:B5 to white. Add a border line around each cell in the range B3:B5.

3. Change the font of cell A1 to the Headings font of the current theme, change the font size to 36 points, change the font color to white, and then bold the text. Change the font size of the range A3:A5 to 16 points, change the font color to white, and then bold the text.

4. In the Glove Sales worksheet, merge and center the range A1:H1, apply the Title cell style, and then increase the font size to 26 points. Merge and center the range A2:H2, apply the Heading 4 cell style, and then increase the font size to 16 points.

5. Merge and center the range A3:A16, set the alignment to Middle Align, rotate the text 90° counterclockwise, apply the Accent1 cell style, increase the font size to 18 points, and then bold the text.

6. Use the Format Painter to copy the format of merged cell A3 into the range A18:A31;A33:A46.

7. Center the text in the range C3:H3. Format the range C4:H16 to include thousands separators (,) and no decimal places. Use the Format Painter to copy the formats in the range C3:H16 to the range C18:H31;C33:H46.

8. In the range B3:H16, apply the Table Style Medium 2 table style. Turn off the filter arrows, and then display the header row, first column, last column, and banded rows. In the range B16:H16, change the fill color of the Total row to standard yellow. In the range H4:H15, change the fill color of the Total column to white.

9. Repeat Step 8 for the other two tables in the worksheet.

10. Increase the width of column H to 25 characters.

11. Add blue data bars to the range H4:H15. Also add blue data bars to the ranges H19:H30 and H34:H45.

12. In the Glove Sales worksheet, set the page orientation to landscape, insert manual page breaks at cells A18 and A33, and then repeat the first two rows of the worksheet on every printed page.

13. Display your name in the center header, display the filename in the left footer, display **Page** *page number* **of** *number of pages* in the center footer, and then display the current date in the right footer.

14. Save and close your workbook. Submit the finished workbook to your instructor, either in printed or electronic form, as requested.

Create	**Case Problem 2**

Create and format a worksheet as a packing slip for GrillRite Grills.

Data File needed for this Case Problem: GrillRite.xlsx

GrillRite Grills Brian Simpko is a shipping manager at GrillRite Grills in Hammond, Indiana. He uses an Excel workbook to provide shipping and order information for customer orders and deliveries. He asks you to help create and format a worksheet that he can use to enter information for packing slips. Figure 2-42 shows the worksheet you'll create for Brian.

Figure 2-42

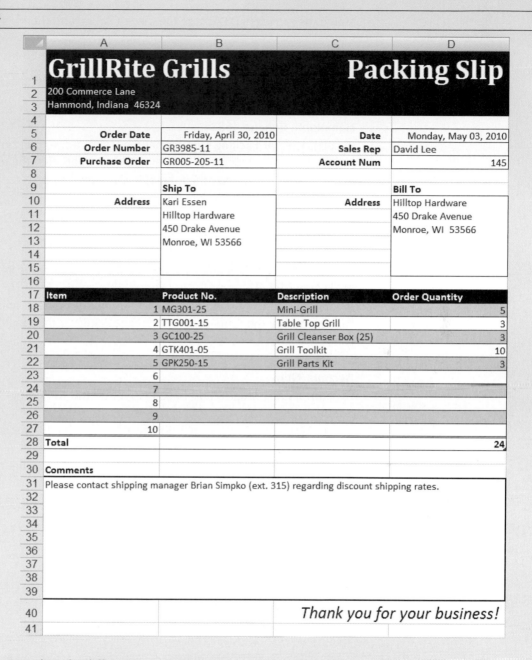

	A	B	C	D
1	**GrillRite Grills**		**Packing Slip**	
2	200 Commerce Lane			
3	Hammond, Indiana 46324			
4				
5	Order Date	Friday, April 30, 2010	Date	Monday, May 03, 2010
6	Order Number	GR3985-11	Sales Rep	David Lee
7	Purchase Order	GR005-205-11	Account Num	145
8				
9		Ship To		Bill To
10	Address	Kari Essen	Address	Hilltop Hardware
11		Hilltop Hardware		450 Drake Avenue
12		450 Drake Avenue		Monroe, WI 53566
13		Monroe, WI 53566		
14				
15				
16				
17	Item	Product No.	Description	Order Quantity
18	1	MG301-25	Mini-Grill	5
19	2	TTG001-15	Table Top Grill	3
20	3	GC100-25	Grill Cleanser Box (25)	3
21	4	GTK401-05	Grill Toolkit	10
22	5	GPK250-15	Grill Parts Kit	3
23	6			
24	7			
25	8			
26	9			
27	10			
28	Total			24
29				
30	Comments			
31	Please contact shipping manager Brian Simpko (ext. 315) regarding discount shipping rates.			
32				
33				
34				
35				
36				
37				
38				
39				
40			*Thank you for your business!*	
41				

Complete the following. (*Note:* Text you need to enter is shown in bold for ease of reference only; do not bold the text unless otherwise instructed.)

1. Open the **GrillRite** workbook located in the Tutorial.02\Case2 folder included with your Data Files, and then save the workbook as **GrillRite Grills Packing Slip** in the same folder. In the Documentation sheet, enter your name in cell B3 and the date in cell B4.

2. Insert a new worksheet at the end of the document named **Packing Slip**.

3. In the Packing Slip worksheet, select all of the cells in the worksheet. (*Hint:* Click the Select All button at the intersection of the row and column headings.) Change the font to the Body font of the current theme. For the range A1:D3, set the fill color to black and the font color to white.

4. Set the width of columns A through D to 20 characters. Set the height of the first row to 36.

5. Merge the range A1:B3, merge the range C1:D3, and then left- and top-align both merged cells.

6. In cell A1, enter the following three lines of text, and then format the first line in a 26-point bold font using the Headings font of the current theme:

    GrillRite Grills
    200 Commerce Lane
    Hammond, Indiana 46324

7. In cell C1, enter **Packing Slip**, format the text in a 26-point bold font using the Headings font of the current theme, and then right-align the text.

8. In the range A5:A7, enter the following three lines of text in a bold font, and then right-align the text and indent the text one character:

    Order Date
    Order Number
    Purchase Order

9. Format cell B5 in the Long Date format. Insert border lines around each of the cells in the range B5:B7.

10. In the range C5:C7, enter the following three lines of text, and then use the Format Painter to copy the formats from the range A5:B7 to the range C5:D7:

    Date
    Sales Rep
    Account Num

11. In cell B9, enter **Ship To** and in cell D9, enter **Bill To** and then format both in a bold font.

12. In cell A10, enter **Address** in a bold font, right-align the text, and then indent it one character.

13. Merge the cells in the range B10:B15, left- and top-align the cell contents, and then insert a border around the merged cell.

14. In cell C10, enter **Address**. Copy the format from the range A10:B15 into the range C10:D15.

15. Enter the following data into the worksheet:

Cell	Data
A17	**Item**
B17	**Product No.**
C17	**Description**
D17	**Order Quantity**
A18:A27	*the numbers from 1 to 10*

⊕ EXPLORE 16. For the range A17:D27, apply Table Style Medium 1, turn off the filter arrows, and display the header row, total row, and banded rows. In cell D28, select the SUM function from the list.

17. In cell A30, enter **Comments** in a bold font.

18. Merge the range A31:D39, left- and top-align the cell contents, and then add a thick box border around the merged cell.

19. In cell D40, enter **Thank you for your business!** in an italic, 16-point font, and then right-align the cell contents.

20. Enter the packing slip data shown in Figure 2-42.

21. Set the worksheet's page orientation to portrait, and then add a footer that displays your name in the left section, the filename in the center section, and the current date in the right section.

22. Save and close your workbook. Submit the finished workbook to your instructor, either in printed or electronic form, as requested.

Challenge | **Case Problem 3**

Explore how to use different Excel formatting features to create an election report.

Data File needed for this Case Problem: Iowa.xlsx

Lewis Reports Kay Lewis is a political columnist, commentator, and blogger. Her Web site, *Lewis Reports*, contains historical information on campaigns and elections. Recently, Kay compiled state-by-state and county-by-county voting totals for the past 15 presidential elections. She wants this information in an Excel workbook so she can analyze voting preferences and trends. Kay has created a workbook that contains the election results from the 2004 presidential election in Iowa. She asks you to format the workbook. She wants formats that quickly show which candidates won at the state and county levels as well as the margin of victory. Counties that went heavily Democratic or Republican should have formats that reflect this fact. Figure 2-43 shows a preview of the worksheet you'll format for Kay.

Figure 2-43

	A	B	C	D	E	F
1	**2004 Presidential Election**					
2						
3	**Iowa Vote Totals**					
4	State	Counties	Candidate	Votes		%
5	Iowa	99	George W. Bush (Rep)	746,600		50.46%
6			John F. Kerry (Dem)	733,102		49.54%
7			Total	1,479,702		
8						
9	**County-by-County Totals**					
10	County	Precincts	Candidate	Votes		%
11	Adair	10	Bush	2,393		56.63%
12			Kerry	1,833		43.37%
13			Total	4,226		
14	Adams	12	Bush	1,313		57.44%
15			Kerry	973		42.56%
16			Total	2,286		
17	Allamakee	23	Bush	3,523		50.62%
18			Kerry	3,437		49.38%
19			Total	6,960		

Complete the following. (*Note:* Text you need to enter is shown in bold for ease of reference only; do not bold the text unless otherwise instructed.)

1. Open the **Iowa** workbook located in the Tutorial.02\Case3 folder included with your Data Files, and then save the workbook as **Iowa Election Results** in the same folder. In the Documentation sheet, enter your name in cell B3 and the date in cell B4.
2. In the Iowa worksheet, apply the Title style to cell A1, and then apply the Heading 1 style to cells A3 and A9.
3. Apply the Accent3 style to the range A4:F4, and then center the heading text in cells D4:F4.
4. In the range D5:D7, format the numbers with a thousands separator (,) and no decimal places. In the range F5:F7, format the numbers as percentages with two decimal places.
5. Merge the range A5:A7, and then left- and top-align the cell contents. Merge the range B5:B7, and then right- and top-align the cell contents. Merge the range E5:E7.
6. Add border lines around each cell in the range A4:F7.

7. Format the range C5:D5 as white text on a standard red background. Format the range C6:D6 as white text on a standard light blue background.

8. Copy the format in the range A4:F7 to the range A10:F13.

⊕ EXPLORE   9. Add a double bottom border to the range A11:F13, and then copy the format in the range A11:F13 to the larger range A14:F307. Excel repeats the format until it fills up the larger range.

⊕ EXPLORE   10. Select the range E5;E11:E307, which shows the difference in votes between the Republican and Democratic candidates. Create a highlight rule to format cells with values greater than zero (indicating a Republican winner) in red text on a red background (thus, obscuring the text). (*Hint:* In the Greater Than dialog box, click Custom Format in the with list to open the Format Cells dialog box, and then use the Font tab and the Fill tab to select the colors.) Create a second highlight rule to format cells with values less than zero (indicating a Democratic winner) in light blue text on a light blue background. Reduce the width of column E to 3 characters.

11. Select the range F5:F7;F11:F307, which shows the vote percentages for each candidate. Apply green data bars, left-align the cells, and then increase the width of column F to 23 characters.

12. Verify the conditional formatting by entering different totals in column D and checking that the highlights and data bars are changed accurately. Restore the original values to the worksheet.

13. For the Iowa worksheet, set the page orientation to portrait, and then scale the page so that the width of the printout is one page and the height is automatic. (*Hint:* Use the buttons in the Scale To Fit group on the Page Layout tab.)

⊕ EXPLORE   14. Format the printout of the Iowa worksheet to repeat the first 10 rows of the worksheet on every page of the printout. Insert manual page breaks into the rest of the table to keep each county's vote from splitting between two pages.

15. Display your name in the center section of the header, and then display the filename in the left section of the footer, **Page** *page number* **of** *number of pages* in the center section of the footer, and the current date in the right section of the footer.

16. Save and close your workbook. Submit the finished workbook to your instructor, either in printed or electronic form, as requested.

| Create | **Case Problem 4** |

Use your creativity to format a meal-planning worksheet that highlights foods with high calorie counts and fat contents.

Data File needed for this Case Problem: Life.xlsx

Life Managers   Kate Dee is a dietician at *Life Managers*, a company in Kleinville, Michigan, that specializes in personal improvement, particularly in areas of health and fitness. Kate wants to create a meal-planning workbook for her clients who want to lose weight and improve their health. One goal of meal planning is to decrease the percentage of fat in the diet. Kate thinks it would be helpful to highlight foods that have a high percentage of fat as well as list their total fat calories. She already created an Excel workbook that contains a few sample food items and lists the number of calories and grams of fat in each item. She wants you to format this workbook.

Complete the following:

1. Open the **Life** workbook located in the Tutorial.02\Case4 folder included with your Data Files, and then save the workbook as **Life Managers Nutrition Table** in the same folder. In the Documentation sheet, enter your name in cell B3 and the date in cell B4.

2. Fat contains nine calories per gram. In the Meal Planner worksheet, add a column that calculates the calories from fat for each food item. The percentage of fat is calculated by dividing the calories from fat by the total number of calories. Enter this calculated value to the table for each food item.

3. Display all calories and grams of fat values with one decimal place. Display the fat percentages as percentages with one decimal place.

4. Design the rest of the Meal Planner worksheet as you'd like, but be sure to include at least one example of each of the following design elements:
   - A range merged into a single cell
   - Text centered and rotated within a cell
   - Cell styles applied to one or more elements
   - Border line styles applied to one or more elements

5. The FDA recommends for good health that the fat percentage should not exceed 30% of the total calories. Apply a rule to the fat percentages to highlight those food items that exceed the FDA recommendations. Include a legend to document the highlighting color you used.

6. Add data bars to the display of calories from fat values to graphically show the relative amounts of fat calories for different food items.

7. Add descriptive headers and footers to the printed document. Also insert page breaks and print titles to ensure that the printout is easily read and interpreted.

8. Save and close your workbook. Submit the finished workbook to your instructor, either in printed or electronic form, as requested.

Research | Internet Assignments

Use the Internet to find and work with data related to the topics presented in this tutorial.

The purpose of the Internet Assignments is to challenge you to find information on the Internet that you can use to work effectively with this software. The actual assignments are updated and maintained on the Course Technology Web site. Log on to the Internet and use your Web browser to go to the Student Online Companion for New Perspectives Office 2007 at **www.course.com/np/office2007**. Then navigate to the Internet Assignments for this tutorial.

Assess | SAM Assessment and Training

If you have a SAM user profile, you may have access to hands-on instruction, practice, and assessment of the skills covered in this tutorial. Log in to your SAM account (**http://sam2007.course.com**) to launch any assigned training activities or exams that relate to the skills covered in this tutorial.

Review | Quick Check Answers

Session 2.1

1. Serif fonts have extra decorative strokes at the end of each character. Sans serif fonts do not include these decorative strokes.
2. Theme colors are the colors that belong to a workbook's basic design, giving the elements in the workbook a uniform appearance. A standard color is always available to every workbook regardless of which themes might be in use.

3. the default Excel number format that displays numbers just as they're entered
4. Dates are formatted numeric values and, as such, are right-aligned in cells.
5. A1
6. Open the Format Cells dialog box.
7. You can use the Format Painter to copy and paste the format from one range into another, or you can define a style for the different ranges.

Session 2.2

1. A style applied to a table allows you to turn on table style options.
2. header row, total row, first column, last column, banded rows, and banded columns
3. A conditional format depends on the cell's value.
4. by the cell's value relative to other cells in the range for which the data bars have been defined
5. Select the range A1:C20, click the Conditional Formatting button in the Styles group on the Home tab, point to Top/Bottom Rules, and then click Top 10%. In the dialog box, enter 5 for the top items to show, and then click the OK button.
6. titles taken from worksheet rows or columns that are repeated on every page of the printed sheet
7. Select the first cell below the row at which you want to insert the page break, click the Breaks button in the Page Setup group on the Page Layout tab, and then click Insert Break.

Ending Data Files

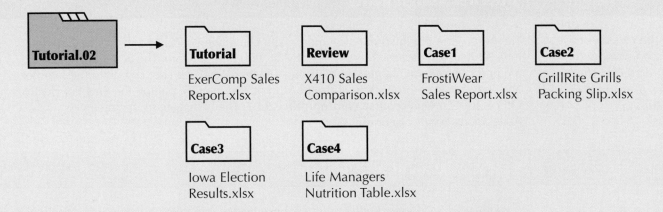

Tutorial.02 →

Tutorial
ExerComp Sales
Report.xlsx

Review
X410 Sales
Comparison.xlsx

Case1
FrostiWear
Sales Report.xlsx

Case2
GrillRite Grills
Packing Slip.xlsx

Case3
Iowa Election
Results.xlsx

Case4
Life Managers
Nutrition Table.xlsx

Objectives

Session 3.1
- Copy formulas
- Build formulas containing relative, absolute, and mixed references
- Review function syntax
- Insert a function with the Insert Function dialog box
- Search for a function
- Type a function directly in a cell

Session 3.2
- Use AutoFill to fill in a formula and complete a series
- Enter the IF logical function
- Insert the date with the TODAY function
- Calculate monthly mortgage payments with the PMT financial function

Working with Formulas and Functions

Developing a Budget

Case | Drake Family Budget

Diane and Glenn Drake, newly married, are trying to balance career, school, and family life. Diane works full-time as a legal assistant, and Glenn is in a graduate program at a nearby university where he recently was hired as a lab assistant. In the summer, he does other work that brings additional income to the family. The couple just moved into a new apartment. Although Glenn and Diane's salaries have grown in the past years, the couple seems to have less cash on hand. This financial shortage has prompted them to take a closer look at their finances and figure out how to best manage them.

Diane has set up an Excel workbook and entered the take-home pay from their two jobs. She has identified and entered expenses the family pays on a monthly basis, such as the rent and grocery bill, as well as other expenses that occur only a few times a year, such as Glenn's tuition and vacations. She wants to calculate how much money they are bringing in and how much money they are spending. She also wants to come up with a savings plan for the down payment on a house they hope to buy in a few years.

You'll help Diane complete the workbook. Diane wants you to enter formulas to perform the calculations she needs to get a better overall picture of the family's finances, which, in turn, should help the couple manage their money more effectively.

Starting Data Files

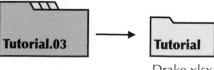

Tutorial.03 →

 Tutorial
Drake.xlsx

 Review
Timov.xlsx

 Case1
Chemistry.xlsx

Case2
Wizard.xlsx

 Case3
Loan.xlsx

 Case4
V6.xlsx

Session 3.1

Understanding Cell References When Copying Formulas

Diane has already done a lot of the work on her family budget. She used data from the past year to estimate the couple's monthly expenses for the upcoming year and she knows their monthly take-home pay. She already entered this data into an Excel workbook. You'll open this workbook now.

To open Diane's workbook:

▶ 1. Open the **Drake** workbook located in the **Tutorial.03\Tutorial** folder included with your Data Files, and then save the workbook as **Drake Family Budget** in the same folder.

▶ 2. In the Documentation sheet, enter your name in cell B3 and the date in cell B4.

▶ 3. Review the contents of the **2010 Proposed Budget** worksheet.

Diane organized the worksheet so the top displays the values that she'll use throughout her budget, such as the family's monthly take-home pay. One of the advantages of placing these values in their own cells in one location is that you can reference them in formulas throughout the worksheets. Then, rather than changing the same value in several locations, you can change it once and any formulas based on that cell are automatically updated to reflect the new value. The top of the worksheet will also include some summary calculations, such as the total take-home pay and expenses for the upcoming year as well as what Diane can expect to earn and spend on average each month. Below that section is a grid in which Diane wants to record how the family's take-home pay and expenses change month by month.

Diane points out a few things about her data. First, she has two possible values for the couple's take-home pay: one for months during the school year and one for months during the summer. Because Glenn works only part-time during the school year as a lab assistant, he earns less during that time than during the summer months. On the other hand, Diane earns the same amount throughout the year. The couple's expenses also vary throughout the year. January and August are particularly expensive months because Glenn has to pay for tuition and books for the upcoming semester. The couple is planning a trip next summer for a family reunion and expenses always seem to add up during the holiday season. With all of these factors in mind, Diane wants to make sure that they will not be caught short in any month. Glenn and Diane hope to purchase a house in about three years, so they need to follow a well-planned budget.

In the range D19:O20, Diane reserved space for entering the couple's monthly take-home pay. You'll enter their projected take-home pay for January through May, using the values at the top of the worksheet.

To insert the monthly take-home pay for January through May:

▶ 1. Click cell **D19**, type **=E5**, and then press the **Enter** key. The value 2,000, Diane's take-home pay for January, appears in cell D19.

▶ 2. In cell D20, enter the formula **=E6**. The value 950, Glenn's take-home pay for January, appears in cell D20.

3. In cell D21, enter the formula **=D19+D20**. This formula calculates the total take-home pay for the couple in the month of January.

   The couple will have the same take-home pay for the next four months as they did in January, so you can copy the formulas from January into February through May.

4. Select the range **D19:D21**, and then, in the Clipboard group on the Home tab, click the **Copy** button.

5. Select the range **E19:H21**, and then, in the Clipboard group, click the **Paste** button. Figure 3-1 shows the couple's take-home pay for January through May.

Tip

You can also use the SUM function to calculate the total take-home pay by clicking the Sum button in the Editing group on the Home tab.

Take-home pay values copied through May ◄ **Figure 3-1**

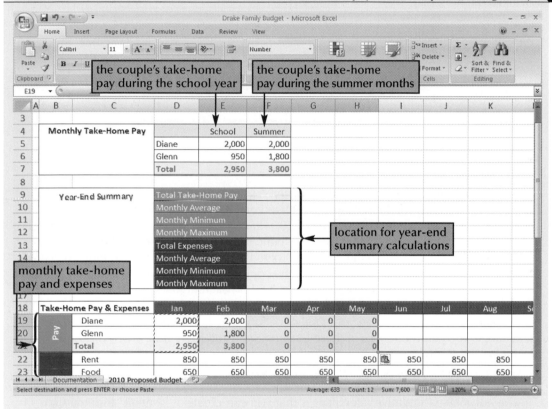

Notice that the formulas you copied and pasted from January resulted in incorrect values for February, March, April, and May. Diane's take-home pay of $2,000 is correct for January and February, but incorrectly changed to 0 for March, April, and May. Likewise, Glenn's take-home pay of $950 is correct for January, but incorrectly changed to $1,800 for February and 0 for March, April, and May. You need to investigate why you didn't get the results you expected. You'll examine how formulas change when copied to new locations in the workbook.

Using Relative References

When you enter a formula into a cell, Excel interprets cell references in the formula in relation to the cell's location. For example, the formula =A1 entered into cell A3 tells Excel to insert the value from the cell two rows above cell A3. When you copy the formula into other cells, Excel applies the same interpretation to the formula's new location, always displaying the value from the cell two rows above. Such cell references are called **relative references** because they are always interpreted in relation, or relative, to the location of the cell containing the formula. Figure 3-2 illustrates how a relative reference in a formula changes when the formula is copied to another range.

Figure 3-2   **Formula using a relative reference**

original formula with a relative reference

	A	B	C	D
1	10	20	30	
2				
3	=A1			
4				
5				

formula copied to a new range (column and row references shift based on cell location)

	A	B	C	D
1	10	20	30	
2				
3	=A1	=B1	=C1	
4				
5				

formula results

	A	B	C	D
1	10	20	30	
2				
3	10	20	30	
4				
5				

In this figure, the formula =A1 entered in cell A3 produced the result of 10, which is the value in cell A1. After the formula in cell A3 was copied to cell B3, the copied formula changed to =B1 and produced the result of 20, which is the value in cell B1. As you can see, when the formula was copied one cell to the right, the relative reference in the original formula (A1) adjusted one cell to the right to become B1. Similarly, when the formula in cell A3 was copied two cells to the right to cell C3, the copied formula changed to =C1 and produced the result of 30, which is the value in cell C1. In each instance, the formula references the cell two rows above the cell that contains the formula.

In Diane's worksheet, when you copied the formulas in the range D19:D21 into a new range, the cell references in those formulas adjusted to their new cell location. For example, the formula in cell E19 is =F5, the formula in cell F19 is =G5, and so forth. In each case, Excel references the cell that is 14 rows up and one column to the right of the current location.

The advantage of relative references is that you can create a "general" formula that you can use again and again in your worksheet. Relative references free you from having to rewrite a formula each time you copy it to a new location. For example, you can write a formula to add the values in a column of data, and then copy that formula to other columns to quickly add their values. You used this technique in the previous set of steps to calculate the couple's total take-home pay for each of the months from January to May.

Using Absolute References

Sometimes, you want references that are fixed on specific cells in the worksheet. This usually occurs when the referenced cell contains a value that needs to be repeated in different formulas throughout the workbook. In Diane's worksheet, any formulas involving take-home pay should be fixed on those cells that contain those values, which are the range E5:E6 for the school months and the range F5:F6 for the summer months.

References that are fixed are called **absolute references**. In Excel, absolute references are marked with a $ (dollar sign) before each column and row designation. For example, B8 is a relative reference to cell B8, whereas $B$8 is an absolute reference to cell B8. When you copy a formula that contains an absolute reference to a new location, the reference does not change. Figure 3-3 shows an example of how copying a formula with an absolute reference does not change the cell reference.

Formula using an absolute reference | Figure 3-3

	A	B	C	D
1	10	20	30	
2				
3	=$A$1			
4				
5				

original formula with an absolute reference

	A	B	C	D
1	10	20	30	
2				
3	=$A$1	=$A$1	=$A$1	
4				
5				

formula copied into a new range (column and row references fixed regardless of cell location)

	A	B	C	D
1	10	20	30	
2				
3	10	10	10	
4				
5				

formula results

In this figure, the formula =$A$1 entered in cell A3 produced the result of 10, which is the value in cell A1. After the formula in cell A3 was copied to cell B3, the copied formula remained unchanged and produced the result of 10, which is the value in cell A1. As you can see, when the formula was copied one cell to the right, the absolute reference in the original formula (A1) did not change. Similarly, when the formula in cell A3 was copied two cells to the right to cell C3, the copied formula and the results did not change. In each instance, the formula references the cell A1.

You'll see how absolute references work when you fix the formulas in cells D19 and D20, and then recopy the formulas.

To use absolute references in the take-home pay formulas:

▶ 1. In cell D19, enter **=$E$5**. This formula contains an absolute reference to cell E5, which contains Diane's take-home pay during the school months.

▶ 2. In cell D20, enter **=$E$6**. This formula contains an absolute reference to cell E6, which contains Glenn's take-home pay during the school months.

▶ 3. Copy the corrected formulas in the range **D19:D20**, and then paste them in the range **E19:H20**. As shown in Figure 3-4, the months of February through May now correctly show the take-home pay values that Diane has specified for the school months.

Figure 3-4

Results of formulas with absolute references

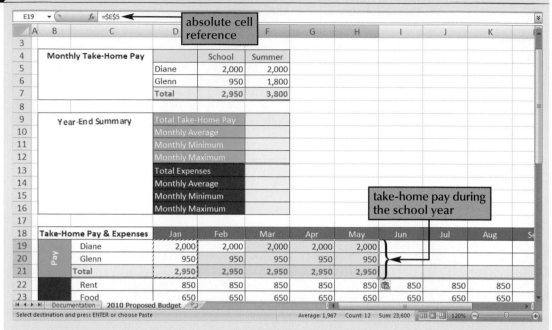

4. Click each cell in the range E19:H20 to verify that the formulas =$E$5 and =$E$6 were copied into the appropriate cells.

InSight | **Understanding Relative and Absolute References**

Part of writing effective formulas is knowing when to use relative and absolute references. Use relative references when you want to repeat the same formula with different cells. For example, in a customer order worksheet, you might need to calculate the cost of an item multiplied by the quantity being purchased. To repeat this formula for all of the items in an order, you would use relative references for the item cost and item quantity. Use absolute references when you want different formulas to refer to the same cell. For example, in a customer order worksheet, you might need to apply the same sales tax percentage to each order. You could store the sales tax percentage in a worksheet cell, and then use an absolute reference to that cell in the formula that multiples the order total with the sales tax percentage.

Using Mixed References

A formula can also contain mixed references. A **mixed reference** contains both relative and absolute references. For example, a mixed reference for cell A2 can be either $A2 or A$2. In the mixed reference $A2, the column reference is fixed on column A and the reference to row 2 is relative. In the mixed reference A$2, the column reference is relative and the row reference is fixed. In other words, a mixed reference "locks" one part of the cell reference while the other part can change. When you copy and paste a formula with a mixed reference to a new location, the absolute portion of the cell reference remains fixed and the relative portion shifts. For example, the mixed reference in the formula =$A2 in cell B2 becomes =$A3 when copied to cell B3, and the mixed reference in the formula =B$1 in cell B2 becomes =C$1 when copied to cell C2.

Figure 3-5 shows an example of using a formula with a mixed reference in which the column is relative and the row is fixed. When you copy and paste the formula from cell A3 into cells A4 and A5, the row reference remains fixed on row 1. In this instance, the column reference, which is relative, doesn't change either, because the formula was copied to the same column. However, when you copy the formula to other columns, the column reference, which is relative, shifts to reflect the new column location. The row reference remains fixed on row 1 and doesn't change no matter where you copy the formula.

Formulas using mixed references ◀ **Figure 3-5**

original formula with a mixed reference

formula copied to a new range (row reference fixed on row 1, column reference shifts based on the cell location)

formula results

As you develop formulas, you might want to switch a cell reference from relative to absolute or mixed. Rather than retyping the formula, you can switch the reference in editing mode by selecting the cell reference and pressing the **F4 key**. As you press the function key, Excel cycles through the different reference types, starting by changing a relative reference to an absolute reference, then to a mixed reference with the row absolute, then to a mixed reference with the column absolute, and then finally back to a relative reference.

Entering Relative, Absolute, and Mixed References | Reference Window

- To enter a relative reference, type the cell reference as it appears in the worksheet. For example, enter B2 for cell B2.
- To enter an absolute reference, type $ (a dollar sign) before both the row and column references. For example, enter $B$2.
- To enter a mixed reference, type $ before either the row or column reference. For example, enter $B2 or B$2.

or

- Select the cell reference you want to change.
- Press the F4 key to cycle the reference from relative to absolute to mixed and then back to relative.

You'll use the F4 key to cycle through the different types of references as you enter the remaining formulas with the take-home pay for the summer months.

To insert the remaining take-home pay formulas:

▶ 1. Click cell **I19**, type **=**, and then click cell **F5**. The formula =F5 appears in the cell, which remains in editing mode. This formula enters Diane's summer take-home pay for June.

▶ 2. Select the cell reference **F5** in the formula, and then press the **F4** key. The formula changes to =$F$5, which is an absolute reference.

▶ 3. Press the **F4** key again. The formula changes to =F$5, which is a mixed reference with a relative column reference and an absolute row reference.

▶ 4. Press the **F4** key again to change to formula to =$F5, which is a mixed cell reference with an absolute column reference and a relative row reference.

▶ 5. Press the **F4** key again to return to the formula to =F5, which is a relative reference.

▶ 6. Press the **F4** key one more time to change the formula back to =$F$5, and then press the **Enter** key to exit editing mode. You want an absolute reference to cell F5 so that the formula always references Diane's summer take-home pay.

▶ 7. In cell I20, enter the formula **=$F$6**. This formula uses an absolute reference to enter Glenn's summer take-home pay for June, and won't change when copied to the rest of the months.

▶ 8. In cell I21, enter the formula **=I19+I20**. This formula adds Diane and Glenn's take-home pay for June.

▶ 9. Copy the range **I19:I21**, and then paste the copied formulas into the range **J19:K21**. The summer take-home pay values appear for the months of June through August.

You'll complete the take-home pay values for the remaining school months.

▶ 10. Copy the range **D19:D21**, and then paste it into the range **L19:O21**. The take-home pay for the couple is entered for all twelve months of the year.

Now that you've calculated the monthly take-home pay and expenses for Diane and Glenn, you'll summarize these for the entire year. Diane wants to compare the couple's annual take-home pay to their annual expenses. She also wants to know the average take-home pay and average expenses for a typical month.

Working with Functions

The month-by-month data is too large to see in the workbook window unless you reduce the zoom level, but then the resulting text would be too small to read. Rather than adding another column to this large collection of data, Diane wants to summarize the data at the top of the worksheet. You'll use Excel functions to do these summary calculations.

Summarizing Data | InSight

Statisticians, scientists, and economists often want to reduce a large sample of data into a few easy-to-use statistics. How do they best summarize the data? The most common approach is to average the sample data. You can calculate the average in Excel with the AVERAGE function. However, this is not always the best choice. Averages are susceptible to extremely large or small data values. Imagine calculating the average price of houses on a block that has one mansion and several small homes. The average value is heavily affected by the mansion. When the data includes a few extremely large or extremely small values, it might be best to use the **median**, or middle, value from the sample. You can calculate the median in Excel with the MEDIAN function.

Another approach is to calculate the most common value in the data, otherwise known as the **mode**. The mode is most often used with data that has only a few possible values, such as the number of bedrooms in a house. The most common number of bedrooms per house might provide more relevant information than the average number of bedrooms. You can calculate the mode in Excel using the MODE function.

Understanding Function Syntax

Recall from Tutorial 1 that a function is a named operation that returns a value. Every function has to follow a set of rules, or **syntax**, which specifies how the function should be written. The general syntax of all functions is as follows:

```
FUNCTION(argument1, argument2, ...)
```

In this syntax, *FUNCTION* is the name of the function and *argument1*, *argument2*, and so forth are **arguments**, which are the numbers, text, or cell references used by the function to return a value. Arguments are always separated by a comma.

Not all functions have arguments, and some functions have **optional arguments**, which are not required for the function to return a value, but can be included to provide more control over the returned value. If an optional argument is not included, Excel assumes a default value for it. These tutorials show optional arguments within square brackets along with the argument's default value, as follows:

Tip

Optional arguments are always placed last in the argument list.

```
FUNCTION(argument1, [argument2=value2, ...])
```

In this function, *argument2* is an optional argument and *value2* is the default value used for this argument. As you learn more about individual functions, you will learn which arguments are required and which are optional, and the default values used for optional arguments.

There are hundreds of Excel functions, which are organized into 11 categories. Figure 3-6 describes these different categories.

Figure 3-6 Categories of Excel functions

Category	Contains functions that
Cube	Retrieve data from multidimensional databases involving online analytical processing or OLAP
Database	Retrieve and analyze data stored in databases
Date & Time	Analyze or create date and time values and time intervals
Engineering	Analyze engineering problems
Financial	Have financial applications
Information	Return information about the format, location, or contents of worksheet cells
Logical	Return logical (true-false) values
Lookup & Reference	Look up and return data matching a set of specified conditions from a range
Math & Trig	Have math and trigonometry applications
Statistical	Provide statistical analyses of a set of data
Text	Return text values or evaluate text

You can learn about each function using the Help system. Figure 3-7 describes some of the more common Math, Trig, and Statistical functions that you might often use in your workbooks.

Figure 3-7 Math, Trig, and Statistical functions

Function	Category	Description
AVERAGE(*number1* [, *number2*, *number3*, ...])	Statistical	Calculates the average of a collection of numbers, where *number1*, *number2*, and so forth are either numbers or cell references. Only *number1* is required. For more than one cell reference or to enter numbers directly into the function, use the optional arguments *number2*, *number3*, and so forth.
COUNT(*value1* [, *value2*, *value3*, ...])	Statistical	Counts how many cells in a range contain numbers, where *value1*, *value2*, and so forth are text, numbers, or cell references. Only *value1* is required. For more than one cell reference or to enter numbers directly into the function, use the optional arguments *value2*, *value3*, and so forth.
COUNTA(*value1* [, *value2*, *value3*, ...])	Statistical	Counts how many cells are not empty in ranges *value1*, *value2*, and so forth, or how many numbers are listed within *value1*, *value2*, and so forth.
INT(*number*)	Math & Trig	Displays the integer portion of a number, *number*.
MAX(*number1* [, *number2*, *number3*, ...])	Statistical	Calculates the maximum value of a collection of numbers, where *number1*, *number2*, and so forth are either numbers or cell references.
MEDIAN(*number1* [, *number2*, *number3*, ...])	Statistical	Calculates the median, or middle, value of a collection of numbers, where *number1*, *number2*, and so forth are either numbers or cell references.
MIN(*number1* [, *number2*, *number3*, ...])	Statistical	Calculates the minimum value of a collection of numbers, where *number1*, *number2*, and so forth are either numbers or cell references.
RAND()	Math & Trig	Returns a random number between 0 and 1.
ROUND(*number*, *num_digits*)	Math & Trig	Rounds a number to a specified number of digits, where *number* is the number you want to round and *num_digits* specifies how many digits to which you want to round the number.
SUM(*number1* [, *number2*, *number3*, ...])	Math & Trig	Adds a collection of numbers, where *number1*, *number2*, and so forth are either numbers or cell references.

For example, the AVERAGE function calculates the average value from a collection of numbers. The syntax of the AVERAGE function is as follows:

```
AVERAGE(number1, [number2, number3, ...])
```

In this function, *number1*, *number2*, *number3*, and so forth are either numbers or cell references to numbers. For example, the following function calculates the average of 1, 2, 5, and 8:

```
AVERAGE(1, 2, 5, 8)
```

This function returns the value 4. However, you usually reference values entered in the worksheet. So, if the range A1:A4 contains the values 1, 2, 5, and 8, the following function also returns a value of 4:

```
AVERAGE(A1:A4)
```

Functions can be incorporated as part of larger formulas. For example, consider the following formula:

```
=MAX(A1:A100)/100
```

This formula returns the maximum value from the range A1:A100, and then divides that value by 100. Functions can also be placed inside another function, or **nested**. If a formula contains several functions, Excel starts with the innermost function and then moves outward. For example, the following formula first calculates the average of the values in the range A1:A100 using the AVERAGE function, and then extracts the integer portion of that value using the INT function.

```
=INT(AVERAGE(A1:A100))
```

One challenge of nesting functions is to make sure that you include all of the parentheses. You can check this by counting the number of left parentheses, and making sure that number matches the number of right parentheses. If the numbers don't match, Excel will not accept the formula and offers a suggestion for rewriting the formula so the left and right parentheses do match.

Inserting a Function

Functions are organized in the Function Library group in the Formulas tab on the Ribbon. In the Function Library, you can select a function from a function category or you can open the Insert Function dialog box to search for a particular function.

Inserting a Function | Reference Window

- Click the Formulas tab on the Ribbon.
- To insert a function from a specific category, click the appropriate category button in the Function Library group. To search for a function, click the Insert Function button in the Function Library group, enter a description of the function, and then click the Go button.
- Select the appropriate function from the list of functions.
- Enter the argument values in the Function Arguments dialog box, and then click the OK button.

You'll use the SUM function to add the total take-home pay for the entire year in Diane's proposed budget.

To insert the SUM function:

▶ **1.** Click cell **F9** to select it.

▶ **2.** Click the **Formulas** tab on the Ribbon.

▶ **3.** In the Function Library group on the Formulas tab, click the **Math & Trig** button. A list displays all of the math and trigonometry functions arranged in alphabetical order.

▶ **4.** Scroll down the list, and then click **SUM**. The Function Arguments dialog box opens.

The Function Arguments dialog box lists all of the arguments associated with the SUM function. Required arguments are in bold type; optional arguments are in normal type. Excel tries to "anticipate" the values for the different arguments based on the location of the cell containing the formula and the data contained in other cells of the worksheet. In this case, the range reference F5:F8, which is the range that contains the couple's take-home pay for the summer months and is the range of numbers closest to the cell in which you are entering the SUM function, already appears for the first argument. Because you want to calculate the total take-home pay for the year, you'll replace this range reference with the reference D21:O21.

To enter the argument for the SUM function:

▶ **1.** Click in the worksheet, and then select the range **D21:O21**. The range reference appears as the value of the Number1 argument. See Figure 3-8.

| Figure 3-8 | Function Arguments dialog box |

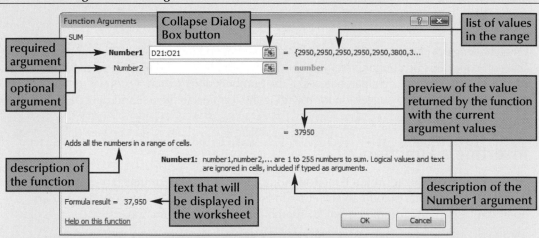

▶ **2.** Click the **OK** button. The formula =SUM(D21:O21) is inserted into cell F9, which displays the value 37,950. This represents the total take-home pay for the year from both Diane and Glenn.

Diane also wants to know how this value compares to the total expenses for the year.

▶ **3.** Click cell **F13**. This is where you want to enter the second SUM function.

▶ **4.** In the Function Library group on the Formulas tab, click the **Math & Trig** button, and then click **SUM**. The Function Arguments dialog box opens. You'll enter the monthly expenses stored in the range D32:O32 for the argument.

> **5.** Select the range **D32:O32** in the worksheet, and then click the **OK** button in the Function Arguments dialog box. The formula =SUM(D32:O32) is inserted in cell F13, which displays the value 35,840. This represents the total projected expenses for the upcoming year. See Figure 3-9.

SUM functions entered   **Figure 3-9**

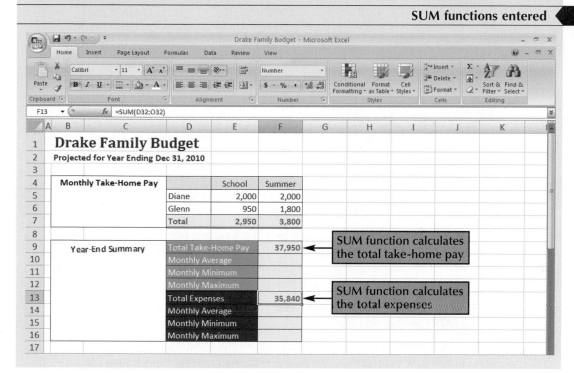

Diane projects that she and Glenn will earn roughly $2,000 more than they will spend throughout the year. It's easier for Diane to plan her budget if she knows how much, on average, the couple takes home and spends each month. You can use the AVERAGE function to do this calculation using the same method you used for the SUM function; but what if you weren't sure of the function's name or its function category? You can use the Insert Function dialog box. The **Insert Function dialog box** organizes all of the functions by category and allows you to search for functions that perform particular calculations.

To insert the AVERAGE function to calculate the average take-home pay:

> **1.** Click cell **F10**.

> **2.** In the Function Library group on the Formulas tab, click the **Insert Function** button. The Insert Function dialog box opens.

> **3.** Type **Calculate an average value** in the Search for a function box, and then click the **Go** button. Functions for calculating an average appear in the Select a function box. See Figure 3-10.

Figure 3-10 **Insert Function dialog box**

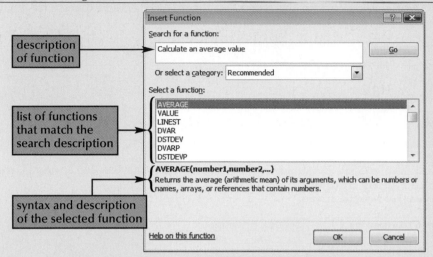

4. Verify that **AVERAGE** is selected in the Select a function box, and then click the **OK** button. The Function Arguments dialog box opens with the arguments for the AVERAGE function. As before, a range reference for cells directly above this cell already appears for the Number1 argument.

5. Select the range reference in the Number1 argument box, and then select the range **D21:O21** in the worksheet.

6. Click the **OK** button. The dialog box closes, and the formula =AVERAGE(D21:O21) is entered in cell F10, displaying the value 3,163, the average take-home pay.

Although the exact average take-home pay is 3,162.50, you see the value 3,163 in the cell because Diane formatted the worksheet to display currency values to the nearest dollar.

How does the couple's average take-home pay compare to their average expenses? To find out, you'll use the AVERAGE function again. Because the function has already been used in your workbook, you can select it from a list of recently used functions.

To calculate the average monthly expenses:

1. Click cell **F14**, and then click the **Insert Function** button fx on the formula bar. The Insert Function dialog box opens.

2. If necessary, click the **Or select a category** arrow, and then click **Most Recently Used**. The most recently used functions, sorted in order of recent use, appear in the Select a function box. The AVERAGE function is at the top followed by the SUM function.

3. Verify that **AVERAGE** is selected in the Select a function box, and then click the **OK** button.

4. Select the range **D32:O32** to insert the range reference D32:O32 in the Number1 box.

5. Click the **OK** button. The formula =AVERAGE(D32:O32) is inserted into cell F14, displaying the value 2,987. This represents the average expenses per month under Diane's budget. See Figure 3-11.

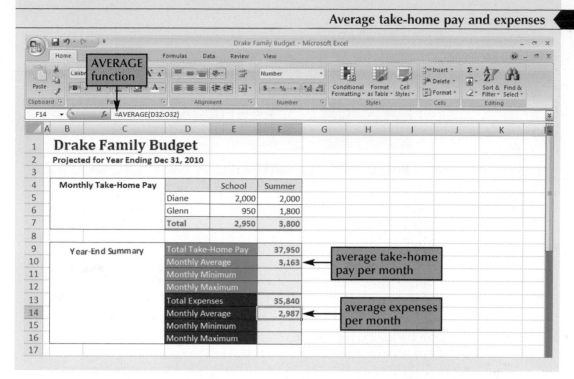

Average take-home pay and expenses | Figure 3-11

From the two averages, Diane sees that the couple will bring in about $200 more than they spend each month. That is not much, so Diane wants to know how much variation is in the budget. What is the most money she could expect to take home during a single month in the upcoming year? What is the least? And what are the largest and smallest values for the monthly expenses? You'll use the MAX and MIN functions to calculate those values.

Typing a Function

After you become more familiar with functions, it is often faster to type the functions directly in cells rather than using the Insert Function dialog box or the Function Library. As you begin to type a function name within a formula, a list of functions that begin with the letters you typed appears. For example, when you type *S*, the list shows all of the functions starting with the letter *S*; when you type *SU,* the list shows only those functions starting with the letters *SU,* and so forth. This helps to ensure that you're entering a legitimate Excel function name.

You'll type the formulas to calculate the minimum monthly take-home pay and expenses under Diane's proposed budget.

To calculate the minimum values for monthly take-home pay and expenses:

▶ **1.** Click cell **F11**. This is the cell in which you want to enter the minimum take-home pay.

▶ **2.** Type **=M**. As you type a formula, a list with function names starting with *M* opens.

▶ **3.** Type **I**. The list shows only those functions starting with *MI*. See Figure 3-12. As soon as the function you want appears in the list, you can double-click its name to enter it in the cell without typing the rest of its name.

Figure 3-12 **Typing a function**

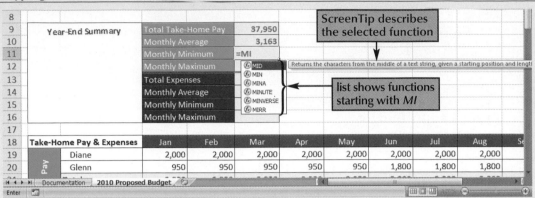

▶ **4.** Double-click **MIN** in the list box. The MIN function with its opening parenthesis is inserted into cell F11 and a ScreenTip shows the syntax for the function. At this point, you can either type in the range reference or select the range with your mouse. To avoid typing errors, it's often better to use your mouse to enter range references.

▶ **5.** Select the range **D21:O21**, type **)**, and then press the **Enter** key. The formula =MIN(D21:O21) is inserted in cell F11, displaying the value 2,950. This is the minimum amount that Diane expects the couple to bring home in a single month for the upcoming year.

Next, you'll calculate the minimum monthly expense projected for the year.

▶ **6.** Click cell **F15**, and then follow Steps 2 through 5 to enter the formula **=MIN(D32:O32)** in cell F15. The cell displays the value 2,265, which is the least amount that Diane expects to spend in a single month in the upcoming year.

The final piece of the year-end summary is the maximum monthly value for both take-home pay and expenses. Maximum values are calculated using the MAX function.

To calculate the maximum values for monthly take-home pay and expenses:

▶ **1.** Click cell **F12**, and then enter the formula **=MAX(D21:O21)**. The value 3,800 appears in cell F12, indicating that the maximum take-home pay the couple can expect in a single month is $3,800.

Trouble? If #NAME? appears in the cell, you probably mistyped the function name. Edit the formula to correct the misspelling.

▶ **2.** Click cell **F16**, and then enter the formula **=MAX(D32:O32)**. The value 5,170 appears in cell F16, indicating that the maximum expenses for a single month are projected to be $5,170. See Figure 3-13.

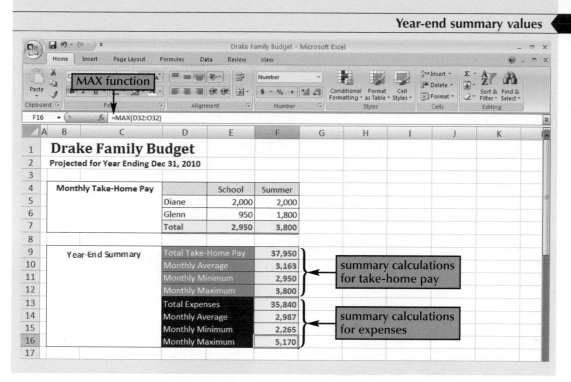

Year-end summary values Figure 3-13

Based on the year-end summary, Diane and Glenn's monthly take-home pay will range from a minimum of $2,950 to a maximum of $3,800 with an average of about $3,163. Monthly expenses, on the other hand, range from a minimum of $2,265 to a maximum of $5,170 with an average of $2,987. Clearly, the Drake family budget does not have a lot of wiggle room.

Diane has just been promoted at work. Her take-home pay will increase from $2,000 per month to $2,500 per month. She wants to know how this affects the year-end summary.

To modify Diane's estimates of her take-home pay:

► 1. In cell E5, enter the value **2500**.

► 2. In cell F5, enter the value **2500**. Figure 3-14 shows the updated calculations for the couple's take-home pay for the entire year as well as the monthly average, minimum, and maximum values.

Figure 3-14 | Revised salary values

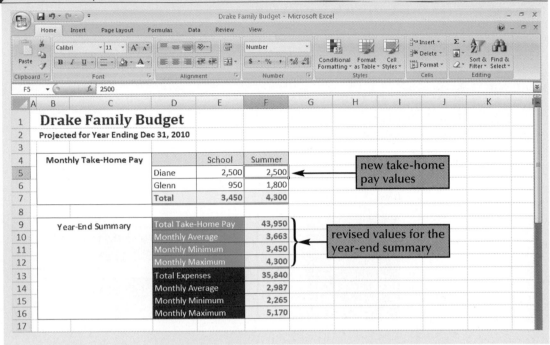

With Diane's new position, the couple's annual take-home pay increases from $37,950 to $43,950 and the monthly average increases from $3,163 to $3,663. The couple's take-home pay should exceed their expenses by an average of $700 per month. The monthly take-home pay now ranges from a minimum of $3,450 up to a maximum of $4,300. The raise has brightened the couple's financial picture quite a bit.

Diane now has a better picture of the family's finances for the upcoming year, and she's more confident about how to manage the couple's budget. She and Glenn hope to save enough for a down payment on a house in a few years. With the promotion, this seems like a real possibility. In the next session, you'll help Diane explore the couple's options in planning for a purchase of a house.

Review | Session 3.1 Quick Check

1. What is the absolute cell reference for cell B21? What are the two mixed references?
2. Cell B10 contains the formula =B1+B2. What formula is entered if this formula is copied and pasted into cell C20?
3. Cell B10 contains the formula =$B1+B$2. What formula is entered if this formula is copied and pasted into cell C20?
4. Cell B10 contains the formula =AVERAGE($A1:$A5). What formula is entered if this formula is copied and pasted into cell C20?
5. What are optional arguments? What happens if you do not include an optional argument in a function?
6. What formula should you enter to add the numbers in the range B1:B10?
7. The range of a set of values is defined as the maximum value minus the minimum value. What formula would you enter to calculate the range of the values in B1:B10?
8. What formula would you enter to calculate the ratio of the maximum value in the range B1:B10 to the minimum value?

Session 3.2

Working with AutoFill

Diane and Glenn hope to purchase a home in the next three years. Currently, the couple has $4,000 in their savings account, and they plan to start putting money into a home savings account. Diane wants to see what impact her proposed budget will have on their savings. To do that, you'll enter the current account information at the top of the worksheet. You'll include the current savings balance and the expected balance at the end of the next year under Diane's proposed budget.

To produce the results Diane wants, you will use a feature known as **AutoFill**, which copies content and formats from a cell or range into an adjacent cell or range. You'll begin by copying the formatting from the Monthly Take-Home Pay section to the range where you'll enter this new Savings section.

To format the range and insert data about the couple's savings account:

▶ 1. If you took a break after the previous session, make sure the Drake Family Budget workbook is open and the 2010 Proposed Budget worksheet is active.

▶ 2. Select the range **B4:F7**, and then, in the Clipboard group on the Home tab, click the **Format Painter** button ![icon] to copy the formatting for the new section.

▶ 3. Select the range **H4:L7** to paste the selected format to this range.

▶ 4. Referring to Figure 3-15, enter the labels and data shown in the range H4:L7. In cell K7, enter a formula to add the values in the range K5:K6. In cell L7, enter a formula to add the values in the range L5:L6.

Initial savings data ◀ Figure 3-15

Diane wants to learn how much the couple could save each month. To find out, you must first determine the couple's monthly net cash flow, which is equal to their take-home pay minus their expenses. You'll start by formatting the cells where you'll enter this data and calculating the net cash flow during the month of January.

To format the range and calculate the net cash flow for January:

▶ 1. Click cell **B18**, and then, in the Clipboard group on the Home tab, click the **Format Painter** button ![icon].

▶ 2. Select the range **B33:C33**. The formatting from cell B18 is pasted into the range, merging the two cells.

▶ **3.** In cell B33, type **Net Cash Flow**, and then right-align the contents of the cell.

▶ **4.** In cell D33, enter the formula **=D21–D32**. This formula subtracts total expenses from total take-home pay for the month of January. The value –1,590 is displayed, indicating a projected shortfall of $1,590 for the month of January. Next, you'll format cell D33 to distinguish net cash flow amount from the other values.

▶ **5.** Click cell **D33**.

▶ **6.** In the Styles group, click the **Cell Styles** button, and then click the **60% – Accent6** style. See Figure 3-16.

| Figure 3-16 | January net cash flow |

18 Take-Home Pay & Expenses	Jan	Feb	Mar	Apr	May	Jun	Jul	Aug	S
19 Diane	2,500	2,500	2,500	2,500	2,500	2,500	2,500	2,500	
20 Glenn	950	950	950	950	950	1,800	1,800	1,800	
21 Total	3,450	3,450	3,450	3,450	3,450	4,300	4,300	4,300	
22 Rent	850	850	850	850	850	850	850	850	
23 Food	650	650	650	650	650	650	650	650	
24 Utilities	225	210	175	165	120	135	145	145	
25 Phone	75	75	75	75	75	75	75	75	
26 Car Payments	175	175	175	175	175	175	175	175	
27 Insurance	125	125	125	125	125	125	125	125	
28 Tuition	1,900	0	0	0	0	900	0	1,900	
29 Books	700	0	0	0	0	300	0	700	
30 Travel	190	120	150	450	120	180	720	400	
31 Miscellaneous	150	150	150	150	150	150	150	150	
32 Total	5,040	2,355	2,350	2,640	2,265	3,540	2,890	5,170	
33 Net Cash Flow	-1,590								
34									
35 Monthly Savings									
36 Starting Balance									

January shows a negative net cash flow

AutoFilling a Formula

You could copy and paste the formula and format from cell D33 into the rest of the row to calculate the net cash flow for the other months, as you've done before, but AutoFill is faster. The small black square in the lower-right corner of a selected cell or range is called the **fill handle**. When you drag the fill handle over an adjacent range, Excel copies the formulas and formats from the original cell into the adjacent range. This process is more efficient than the two-step process of copying and pasting.

| Reference Window | **Copying Formulas and Formats with AutoFill** |

- Select the cell or range that contains the formula or formulas you want to copy.
- Drag the fill handle in the direction you want to copy the formula(s) and then release the mouse button.
- To copy only the formats or only the formulas, click the AutoFill Options button and select the appropriate option.

or

- Select the cell or range that contains the formula or formulas you want to copy.
- In the Editing group on the Home tab, click the Fill button.
- Select the appropriate fill direction and fill type (or click Series, enter the desired fill series options, and then click the OK button).

You'll use AutoFill to fill in the cash flow values for the remaining months of the year.

To copy the formulas and formats using AutoFill:

▶ **1.** Click cell **D33**, if necessary. The fill handle appears in the lower-right corner of the cell.

▶ **2.** Position the pointer over the fill handle until the pointer changes to ✛.

▶ **3.** Drag the fill handle over the range **E33:O33**. A solid outline appears around the selected range as you move the pointer.

▶ **4.** Release the mouse button. The selected range is filled in with the formula and format from cell D33, and the AutoFill Options button appears in the lower-right corner of the selected cells. See Figure 3-17.

Tip

With AutoFill, it's easy to copy formulas into the wrong range; if that happens, click the Undo button and try again.

Formulas and formats copied with AutoFill | **Figure 3-17**

	Mar	Apr	May	Jun	Jul	Aug	Sep	Oct	Nov	Dec
18	Mar	Apr	May	Jun	Jul	Aug	Sep	Oct	Nov	Dec
19	2,500	2,500	2,500	2,500	2,500	2,500	2,500	2,500	2,500	2,500
20	950	950	950	1,800	1,800	1,800	950	950	950	950
21	3,450	3,450	3,450	4,300	4,300	4,300	3,450	3,450	3,450	3,450
22	850	850	850	850	850	850	850	850	850	850
23	650	650	650	650	650	650	650	650	650	650
24	175	165	120	135	145	145	140	140	170	210
25	75	75	75	75	75	75	75	75	75	75
26	175	175	175	175	175	175	175	175	175	175
27	125	125	125	125	125	125	125	125	125	125
28	0	0	0	900	0	1,900	0	0	0	0
29	0	0	0	300	0	700	0	0	0	0
30	150	450	120	180	720	400	130	150	250	300
31	150	150	150	150	150	150	150	150	150	150
32	2,350	2,640	2,265	3,540	2,890	5,170	2,295	2,315	2,445	2,535
33	1,100	810	1,185	760	1,410	-870	1,155	1,135	1,005	915
34										
35										
36										

AutoFill Options button

formula and formats copied to the selected range

fill handle

Ready   Average: 676   Count: 12   Sum: 8,110   120%

▶ **5.** Review the monthly net cash flows to confirm that AutoFill correctly copied the formula into the selected range.

These calculations provide Diane with a better picture of how the couple's net cash flow varies from month to month. Only in January and August do the couple's expenses exceed their take-home pay. In most months, their take-home pay exceeds expenses by at least $1,000, and in July, it exceeds expenses by $1,410.

Using the AutoFill Options Button

By default, AutoFill copies both the formulas and the formats of the original range to the selected range. However, sometimes you might want to copy only the formulas or only the formatting. You can specify what is copied by using the AutoFill Options button that appears after you release the mouse button. As shown in Figure 3-18, clicking this button provides a list of AutoFill options. The Copy Cells option, which is the default, copies both the formulas and the formatting. The Fill Formatting Only option copies the formatting into the selected cells but not any formulas. The Fill Without Formatting option copies the formulas but not the formatting.

AutoFill options | **Figure 3-18**

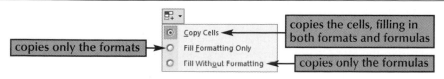

copies only the formats → Fill Formatting Only

Copy Cells ← copies the cells, filling in both formats and formulas

Fill Without Formatting ← copies only the formulas

Filling a Series

AutoFill can also be used to create a series of numbers, dates, or text based on a pattern. To create a series of numbers, you enter the initial values in the series in a selected range and then use AutoFill to complete the series. Figure 3-19 shows how AutoFill can be used to insert the numbers from 1 to 10 in a selected range. You enter the first few numbers in the range A1:A3 to establish the pattern for AutoFill to use. Then, you select the range and drag the fill handle over the cells where you want the pattern continued. In Figure 3-19, the fill handle is dragged over the range A4:A10 and the rest of the series is filled in.

Figure 3-19 **AutoFill extends a numeric sequence**

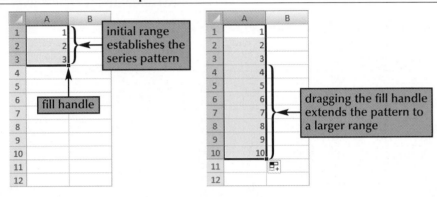

AutoFill can fill in a wide variety of series, including dates and times and text. Figure 3-20 shows examples of some series that AutoFill can generate. In each case, you must provide enough information for AutoFill to identify the pattern. AutoFill can recognize some patterns from only a single value, such as Jan or January to create a series of month abbreviations or names, or Mon or Monday to create a series of the days of the week.

Figure 3-20 **AutoFill applied to different series**

Type	Initial Entry	Extended Series
Values	1, 2, 3	4, 5, 6, ...
	2, 4, 6	8, 10, 12, ...
Dates and Times	Jan	Feb, Mar, Apr, ...
	January	February, March, April, ...
	15-Jan, 15-Feb	15-Mar, 15-Apr, 15-May, ...
	12/30/2010	12/31/2010, 1/1/2011, 1/2/2011, ...
	12/31/2010, 1/31/2011	2/28/2011, 3/31/2011, 4/30/2011, ...
	Mon	Tue, Wed, Thu, ...
	Monday	Tuesday, Wednesday, Thursday, ...
	11:00AM	12:00PM, 1:00PM, 2:00PM, ...
Patterned Text	1st period	2nd period, 3rd period, 4th period, ...
	Region 1	Region 2, Region 3, Region 4, ...
	Quarter 3	Quarter 4, Quarter 1, Quarter 2, ...
	Qtr3	Qtr4, Qtr1, Qtr2, ...

For more complex patterns, you can use the Series dialog box. Enter the first value of the series in a worksheet cell, select the entire range that will contain the series, click the Fill button in the Editing group on the Home tab, and then click Series. The Series dialog box opens. You then choose how a series grows, set how fast the series grows and its stopping value, and decide whether to use existing values in the selected range as the basis for the series trend.

<table>
<tr><td>

Creating a Series with AutoFill

</td><td>| Reference Window</td></tr>
</table>

- Enter the first few values of the series into a range.
- Select the range, and then drag the fill handle of the selected range over the cells you want to fill.

or

- Enter the first few values of the series into a range.
- Select the entire range into which you want to extend the series.
- In the Editing group on the Home tab, click the Fill button, and then click Down, Right, Up, Left, Series, or Justify to set the direction you want to extend the series.

Diane wants to see how the monthly balances in her savings account are affected by the couple's changing expenses and take-home pay. She wants to make sure that the balance doesn't drop too low after months with particularly high expenses—such as January and August when Glenn's tuition payments are due. You'll add data to the worksheet to display the monthly savings balance. Diane already entered titles for the couple's different savings accounts. You'll use AutoFill to enter the month titles.

To use AutoFill to enter a series of months:

1. In cell D35, enter **Jan**. This is the first value in the series. Because Jan is a common abbreviation for January, Excel recognizes it as a month and you don't need to type Feb for the next month in the series.

2. Click cell **D35**, center the text, format it using the **Accent1** cell style, and then add a single border around the cell. This is the formatting you want to use for all the month abbreviations.

3. Position the pointer over the fill handle in cell D35 until the pointer changes to ✛.

4. Drag the fill handle over the range **E35:O35**. As you drag the fill handle, Screen-Tips show the month abbreviations. When you release the mouse button, AutoFill enters the remaining three-letter abbreviations for each month of the year with the formatting you applied to cell D35. See Figure 3-21.

Formatted month titles ◀ Figure 3-21

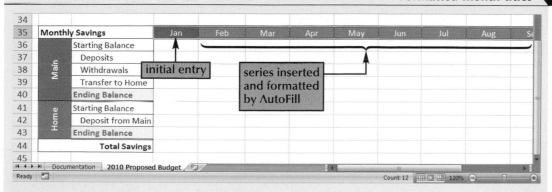

Next, you'll enter formulas to calculate the changing balance in the couple's main savings account and their home savings account. The main savings account balance is determined by four factors: the initial balance, the amount of money they deposit, the amount of money they withdraw, and the amount of money they transfer into their home savings account. The amount Diane and Glenn deposit will always equal their take-home pay, and the amount they withdraw will always equal their expenses. For now, you'll assume that the couple won't transfer any money from their main savings account into their home savings account.

To calculate the initial balances in the savings accounts:

▶ **1.** In cell D36, enter the formula **=$K$5**. The formula uses an absolute reference to set the starting balance in the main savings account (cell D36) equal to the starting balance for the year (cell K5), which is already entered at the top of the worksheet. The absolute reference ensures that the copied formula always refers to the correct cell.

▶ **2.** In cell D37, enter **=D21** to retrieve the couple's take-home pay for January.

▶ **3.** In cell D38, enter **=D32** to retrieve the January expenses. You'll leave cell D39 blank because, at this point, you won't assume that any money will be transferred from the main savings account to the home savings account.

▶ **4.** In cell D40, enter **=D36+D37−D38−D39**. This formula calculates the ending balance for the main savings account, which is equal to the starting balance plus any deposits minus the withdrawals and transfers. Cell D40 displays the value 2,410, representing the balance in the main savings account at the end of January.

▶ **5.** In cell D41, enter the formula **=$K$6**. The formula sets the starting balance for the home savings account equal to the starting balance for the year. Again, you used an absolute reference to ensure that the formula won't change when copied.

▶ **6.** In cell D42, enter the formula **=D39**. Any deposits in the home savings account will be the result of transfers from the main savings account.

▶ **7.** In cell D43, enter the formula **=D41+D42**. The ending balance in the home savings account will be equal to the starting balance plus any deposits.

▶ **8.** In cell D44, enter the formula **=D40+D43**. The total savings is equal to the amount in both accounts at the end of the month.

▶ **9.** Add borders around the cells in the range D36:D43.

▶ **10.** Use the Format Painter to copy the formats from cell D32 into cells D40 and D43, and then use the Format Painter to copy the formats from cell D33 into cell D44. See Figure 3-22.

Figure 3-22 ▶ **Formatted savings account values for January**

	Monthly Savings	Jan	Feb	Mar	Apr	May	Jun	Jul	Aug	S
35	Monthly Savings	Jan	Feb	Mar	Apr	May	Jun	Jul	Aug	S
36	Starting Balance	4,000								
37	Deposits	3,450								
38	Withdrawals	5,040								
39	Transfer to Home									
40	Ending Balance	2,410								
41	Starting Balance	0								
42	Deposit from Main	0								
43	Ending Balance	0								
44	Total Savings	2,410								

January savings

At this point, the couple's projected savings at the end of January will be $2,410, which is $1,590 less than their starting balance of $4,000 at the beginning of the year. The savings formulas for the remaining months are the same as for January except that their starting balances are based on the ending balance of the previous month.

To calculate the remaining balances in the savings accounts:

▶ **1.** Copy the range **D36:D44**, and then paste it into the range **E36:E44**.

▶ **2.** Change the formula in cell E36 to **=D40** so that the February starting balance for the main savings account equals the January ending balance.

▶ **3.** Change the formula in cell E41 to **=D43** so that the starting February balance in the home savings account is equal to the ending January balance.

Next, you'll use AutoFill to copy the February formulas into the remaining months of the year.

▶ **4.** Select the range **E36:E44**, and then drag the fill handle over the range **F36:O44**. All of the formulas and formatting for the rest of the year are filled in. See Figure 3-23.

Savings values for the remaining months ◀ **Figure 3-23**

		Jan	Feb	Mar	Apr	May	Jun	Jul	Aug	Se
35	Monthly Savings									
36	Main — Starting Balance	4,000	2,410	3,505	4,605	5,415	6,600	7,360	8,770	
37	Deposits	3,450	3,450	3,450	3,450	3,450	4,300	4,300	4,300	
38	Withdrawals	5,040	2,355	2,350	2,640	2,265	3,540	2,890	5,170	
39	Transfer to Home									
40	Ending Balance	2,410	3,505	4,605	5,415	6,600	7,360	8,770	7,900	
41	Home — Starting Balance	0	0	0	0	0	0	0	0	
42	Deposit from Main	0	0	0	0	0	0	0	0	
43	Ending Balance	0	0	0	0	0	0	0	0	
44	Total Savings	2,410	3,505	4,605	5,415	6,600	7,360	8,770	7,900	

Documentation | 2010 Proposed Budget

Ready | Average: 3,656 Count: 88 Sum: 321,715 120%

Diane wants to see the ending balances for the two savings accounts without scrolling, so you'll add the ending balances at the top of the worksheet.

▶ **5.** In cell L5, enter the formula **=$O$40**. You used an absolute reference so that the formula won't change if you later copy it to another cell. The ending balance of the main savings account in December—12,110—appears in cell L5.

▶ **6.** In cell L6, enter the formula **=$O$43**. Again, you used an absolute reference to ensure the formula won't change if you later copy it to another cell. The ending balance of the home savings account in December—0—appears in cell L6.

Developing a Savings Plan

Under her current budget projections, Diane expects to have $12,110 in the main savings account at the end of the next year but nothing in the home savings account. Diane wants to transfer some money into the home savings account each month. Because the home savings account is used for longer-term savings, Diane cannot withdraw money from it without penalty. So, she wants to make sure the main savings account always has enough money to meet monthly expenses and any unexpected bills without relying on money from the home savings account.

Diane needs to balance two things in her savings plan: a desire to keep a reasonable amount in the main savings account and the desire to save enough for a future down payment on a home mortgage. To achieve this balance, she needs to determine her overall savings goal and how soon she and Glenn want to meet that goal.

To help Diane determine an overall savings goal, you'll create a new worksheet with calculations for different savings plans. Diane wants to know how much money the couple can save if they put $500 to $1,000 into the home savings account each month for the next three years. You'll create a worksheet that shows the total amount saved in one, two, and three years from deposits starting at $500 that increase in $100 increments through $1,000.

To create the savings plan:

▶ 1. Insert a new worksheet named **Home Savings Plan** at the end of the workbook.

▶ 2. In cell A1, enter **Home Savings Projections**, and then format the title using the **Title** cell style.

▶ 3. Merge and center the range **B3:G3**, enter **Savings Deposit per Month** in the merged cell, and then format the merged cell using the **Heading 2** cell style.

▶ 4. In cell A4, enter **Months**, format the cell in bold.

▶ 5. In cell B4, enter **500**; in cell C4, enter **600**; select the range **B4:C4**; and then drag the fill handle to cell **G4**. The values entered in the series—500, 600, 700, 800, 900, and 1,000—are the different amounts the couple might transfer into their home savings account each month.

▶ 6. In the range A5:A7, enter the values **12**, **24**, and **36**. These monthly values are equal to one year, two years, and three years, respectively. You entered the years in months because Diane and Glenn plan to deposit money into their home savings account each month. So, they would make 12 deposits in one year, they would make 24 deposits in two years, and they would make 36 deposits in three years.

▶ 7. Format the range B4:G4;A5:A7 with the **Input** cell style.

Next, you'll use mixed cell references to calculate the amount of money saved under each plan. The amount saved is equal to the number of months of savings multiplied by the deposit per month.

▶ 8. In cell **B5**, enter **=$A5*B$4**. This formula uses mixed references to calculate the amount of savings generated by saving $500 per month for 12 months. The first mixed reference in the formula, $A5, has a fixed column reference and a relative row reference. When you copy the formula across row 5, the reference to cell A5 remains unchanged. When you copy the formula down column B, the reference to cell A5 changes to cell A6 in row 6 and cell A7 in row 7, which references the correct number of months of savings in the formula. The second mixed cell reference, B$4, has a relative column reference and a fixed row reference. When you copy the formula down column B, the reference to cell B4 remains unchanged. When you copy the formula across row 5, the reference to cell B4 changes to cell C4 in column C, cell D4 in column D, and so forth, which references the correct deposit per month in the formula.

▶ 9. Copy cell **B5** and paste the formula into the range **B5:G7**. The formula results show the projected savings based on different combinations of monthly deposits and lengths of time. Notice that the mixed references in each cell always reference a monthly deposit value from the range B4:G4 and a time length from the range A5:A7. The mixed references enable you to copy and paste the correct formulas quickly.

▶ 10. Format the values in the range B5:G7 using a thousands separator with no digits to the right of the decimal point, and add a single border around each cell in the range. Figure 3-24 shows the completed and formatted values.

Savings from monthly deposits | Figure 3-24

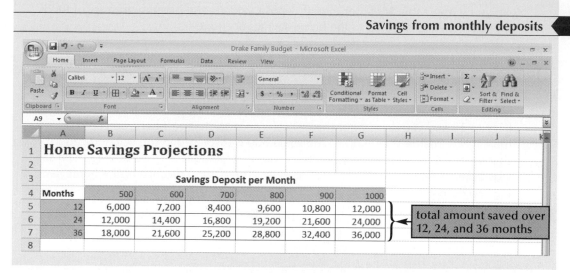

The data shows how increasing the amount that Diane and Glenn save toward their home each month quickly adds up. For example, if they save $800 per month, at the end of three years (36 months), they would have saved $28,800. This is just a little less than the $30,000 they want to save for the down payment. Diane asks you to enter in the budget projections the transfer of $800 from the main savings account to the home savings account each month.

To enter and format the home savings plan section:

▶ **1.** Switch to the **2010 Proposed Budget** worksheet.

▶ **2.** In cell H9, enter **Home Savings Plan**, and then format the cell in bold.

▶ **3.** In cell H10, enter **Monthly Transfer to Home Acct**, and then, in cell K10, enter **800**.

▶ **4.** Merge the range **H10:J10**, left-align the merged cell, and then format the cell using the **20% – Accent6** cell style.

▶ **5.** Add a border around cell H10 and cell K10. See Figure 3-25.

Formatted savings plan | Figure 3-25

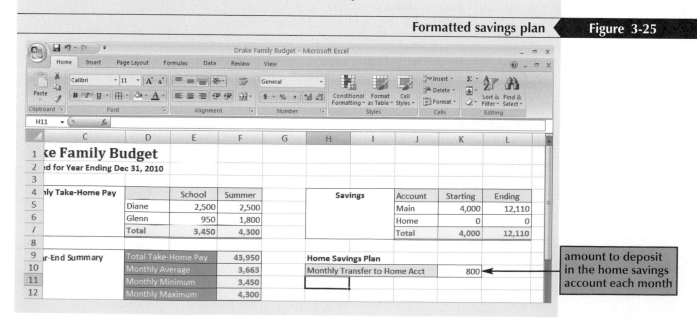

Next, you'll apply this $800 per month deposit value to the monthly transfer of funds from the main savings account to the home savings account.

To project the new savings account balances:

▶ **1.** In cell D39, enter the formula **=$K$10**. You used an absolute value in this formula because the amount to transfer to the home savings account each month is always in cell K10 and you don't want the cell reference to change when you copy the formula to the rest of the months. The value 800 is displayed in the cell, indicating that for the month of January, $800 will be transferred from the couple's main savings account into the home savings account. The ending balance of the home savings account is now $800.

▶ **2.** Copy cell **D39** and paste it into the range **E39:O39**. The value 800 is pasted into the rest of the row, indicating that each month the couple will transfer $800 into the home savings account. See Figure 3-26.

Figure 3-26 **Monthly savings balance**

	Monthly Savings	Jan	Feb	Mar	Apr	May	Jun	Jul	Aug	Se
Main	Starting Balance	4,000	1,610	1,905	2,205	2,215	2,600	2,560	3,170	
	Deposits	3,450	3,450	3,450	3,450	3,450	4,300	4,300	4,300	
	Withdrawals	5,040	2,355	2,350	2,640	2,265	3,540	2,890	5,170	
	Transfer to Home	800	800	800	800	800	800	800	800	
	Ending Balance	1,610	1,905	2,205	2,215	2,600	2,560	3,170	1,500	
Home	Starting Balance	0	800	1,600	2,400	3,200	4,000	4,800	5,600	
	Deposit from Main	800	800	800	800	800	800	800	800	
	Ending Balance	800	1,600	2,400	3,200	4,000	4,800	5,600	6,400	
	Total Savings	2,410	3,505	4,605	5,415	6,600	7,360	8,770	7,900	

amount transferred to the home savings account each month

balance in the home savings account

▶ **3.** Examine the monthly balance in both the main savings account and the home savings account under Diane's proposed savings plan. Notice that the ending balance in the main savings account falls below $2,000 some months.

▶ **4.** Scroll to the top of the worksheet and verify that the value displayed in cell L5 is 2,510 and the value displayed in cell L6 is 9,600.

Under this savings plan, Diane and Glenn will have deposited $9,600 into the home savings account by the end of the year and the balance in their main savings account will be down to $2,510. Although Diane is pleased that $9,600 will be moved into the home savings account in the next year, she's concerned about the amount of money left in the main savings account. Even more troubling are the month-to-month balances in that account. For example, the balance in the main savings account will be $1,500 at the end of August and will remain below $2,000 for several months of the year. Recall that Diane does not want to have a savings plan that will leave the couple with insufficient funds in the main savings account to handle unforeseen expenses.

Part of the problem is that the couple's net cash flow is negative during several months of the year. If they continue to transfer $800 into the home savings account during those months, the main savings account might fall below an acceptable level. Diane wants to modify her savings plan so that money is not transferred into the home savings account during months of negative cash flow. You need a formula that can "choose" whether to transfer the funds. You can build this kind of decision-making capability into a formula through the use of a logical function.

Working with Logical Functions

A **logical function** is a function that works with values that are either true or false. If it seems strange to think of a value as being true or false, consider a statement such as "Today is Monday." If today is Monday, that statement is true or has a true value. If today isn't Monday, the statement has a value of false. In Excel, you usually will not work with statements regarding days of the week (unless you're creating a calendar application), but instead you'll examine statements such as "Is cell A5 equal to 3?" or "Is cell B10 greater than cell C10?"

Using the IF Function

You can use the IF function to evaluate a statement such as "Is cell A5 equal to 3?" The **IF function** is a logical function that returns one value if the statement is true and returns a different value if the statement is false. The syntax of the IF function is as follows:

```
IF(logical_test, value_if_true, [value_if_false])
```

In this function, *logical_test* is a statement that is either true or false, *value_if_true* is the value returned by the IF function if the statement is true, and *value_if_false* is the value returned by the function if the statement is false. Although the *value_if_false* argument is optional, you should usually include this argument so that the IF function covers both possibilities.

The statement in the *logical_test* argument of the IF function always includes a comparison operator. A **comparison operator** is a symbol that indicates the relationship between two values. Figure 3-27 describes the different comparison operators. The most common comparison operator is the equal sign.

Comparison operators　**Figure 3-27**

Operator	Statement	Tests whether
=	A1 = B1	the value in cell A1 *is equal to* the value in cell B1
>	A1 > B1	the value in cell A1 *is greater than* the value in cell B1
<	A1 < B1	the value in cell A1 *is less than* the value in cell B1
>=	A1 >= B1	the value in cell A1 *is greater than or equal to* the value in cell B1
<=	A1 <= B1	the value in cell A1 *is less than or equal to* the value in cell B1
<>	A1 <> B1	the value in cell A1 *is not equal to* the value in cell B1

For example, you might want a formula that compares the values in cells A1 and B1. If they're equal, you want to return a value of 100; if they're not equal, you want to return a value of 50. The IF function to perform this test is as follows:

```
=IF(A1=B1, 100, 50)
```

In many cases, however, you will not use values directly in the IF function. The following formula uses cell references, returning the value of cell C1 if A1 equals B1; otherwise, it returns the value of cell C2.

```
=IF(A1=B1, C1, C2)
```

The IF function also works with text. For example, consider the following formula:

```
=IF(A1="YES", "DONE", "RESTART")
```

This formula tests whether the value of cell A1 is equal to YES. If it is, the formula returns the text DONE; otherwise, it returns the text RESTART. Also, you can nest other functions inside an IF statement. Consider the following formula:

```
=IF(A1="MAXIMUM", MAX(B1:B10), MIN(B1:B10))
```

This function first tests whether cell A1 contains the text MAXIMUM. If it does, the formula uses the MAX function to return the maximum of the values in the range B1:B10. If it doesn't, the formula uses the MIN function to return the minimum of the values in that range.

Diane wants the IF function to test whether the net cash flow for the current month is greater than zero. If it is, the couple has increased their savings and she wants to transfer some of it into the home savings account. On the other hand, if the net cash flow is negative, the couple has not saved any money and Diane doesn't want to transfer any funds to the home savings account. For the month of January, the formula to determine how much money is transferred is as follows:

```
=IF(D33>0, $K$10, 0)
```

Recall that cell D33 contains the net cash flow for the month of January and cell K10 contains the amount of money that Diane wants to transfer when she can. So, this function tests whether the net cash flow for the month of January (cell D33) is positive (greater than zero). If it is, the formula returns $800 (the value in cell K10) as the amount to transfer from the main savings account into the home savings account; otherwise, it returns 0 and no money will be transferred that month. You'll delete the formula currently in cell D39, and then insert this function.

To insert the IF function:

▶ **1.** Right-click cell **D39**, and then click **Clear Contents** on the shortcut menu. The cell's contents are erased.

▶ **2.** In the Function Library group on the Formulas tab, click the **Logical** button, and then click **IF** in the list of logical functions. The Function Arguments dialog box opens.

▶ **3.** Enter **D33>0** in the Logical_test argument box. This tests whether the net cash flow for January is positive (greater than zero).

▶ **4.** Enter **$K$10** in the Value_if_true argument box. If the value in cell D33 is greater than zero (the net cash flow for the month is positive), then the formula returns the value in cell K10, which is the amount of money to transfer from the main savings account into the home savings account. You used an absolute reference because you don't want the cell reference to change when you copy the formula to the other months.

▶ **5.** Enter the value **0** in the Value_if_false argument box. If the value in cell D33 is less than zero (the net cash flow for the month is negative), the formula returns the value 0 and no money will be transferred from the main savings account into the home savings account that month. See Figure 3-28.

Function arguments for the IF function ◄ **Figure 3-28**

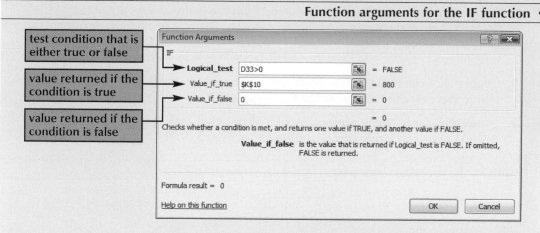

test condition that is either true or false

value returned if the condition is true

value returned if the condition is false

> **6.** Click the **OK** button. A value of 0 is displayed in cell D39. Because the net cash flow for January is −1,590, no money will be transferred from the main savings account into the home savings account. You'll copy this formula into the remaining months of Diane's proposed budget.

> **7.** Click cell **D39**, and then drag the fill handle over the range **E39:O39**. The remaining values are filled in, as shown in Figure 3-29. Examine the monthly balance in both savings accounts.

Amount to transfer to the home savings account each month ◄ **Figure 3-29**

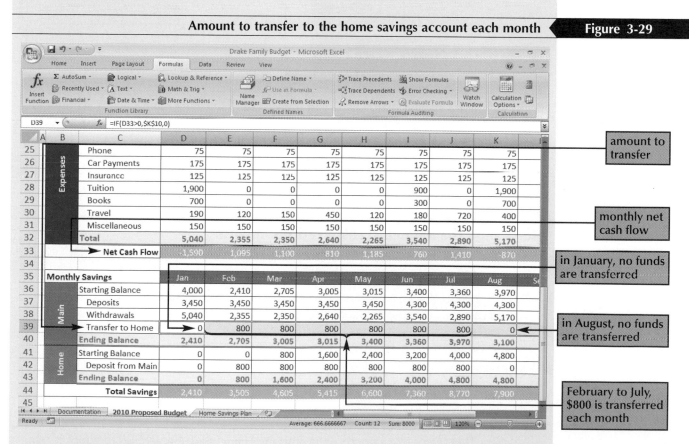

The monthly ending balance in the main savings account remains above $3,000 for most of the year, and $800 is transferred from the main savings account into the home savings account in ten months of the year. Diane wants you to document what the formula results are showing. You'll enter text that clarifies when funds are transferred between accounts in the Home Savings Plan section.

▸ **8.** Double-click cell **H10** to enter editing mode, type an asterisk (*****) at the end of the text in the cell, and then press the **Enter** key.

▸ **9.** In cell H11, enter ***Only during months of positive cash flow**, and then format cell H11 using the **Explanatory** cell style. See Figure 3-30.

Figure 3-30 ▸ Results of the revised savings plan

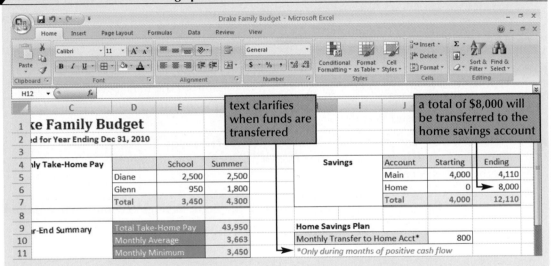

Based on this savings plan, Diane can transfer $800 from the main savings account to the home savings account in all but two months of the year, depositing a total of $8,000 into the home savings account by the end of the year. The main savings account balance stays above $3,000 for most of the year. Diane feels this is adequate, but wants to explore what would happen if she increases the monthly transfer from $800 to $1,000. How would that affect the monthly balance of the main savings account?

To change the amount transferred per month:

▸ **1.** Change the value in cell K10 to **1000**. The total in the home savings account at the end of the year increases to $10,000.

▸ **2.** Scroll down the worksheet and examine how the monthly balance in the main savings account changes throughout the year. Under this scenario, the balance in the main savings account drops to $1,900 in the month of August. This is a little too low for Diane.

▸ **3.** Change the value in cell K10 to **900**. With this savings plan, the couple will save $9,000 toward the purchase of a home.

▸ **4.** Scroll through the worksheet, examining the monthly balances of the two savings accounts. The balance in their savings account stays above $2,500 for most of the year. This seems like a good compromise to Diane, and she decides to adopt it as a model budget for the upcoming year.

Working with Date Functions

Diane's budget is just the start of her financial planning. To be effective, budgets need to be monitored and updated as conditions change. In the upcoming year, Diane plans to use this workbook to enter the actual salaries, expenses, and savings. This will enable her to track how well her projected values match the actual values. Because Diane will be updating the workbook throughout the year, she wants the worksheet to always display the current date so she can tell how far she is into her budget projections. You can accomplish this using a **date function**. Seven of the date functions supported by Excel are described in Figure 3-31. You can use these functions to help with scheduling or to determine on what days of the week certain dates occur.

Date functions ◀ **Figure 3-31**

Function	Description
DATE(*year, month, day*)	Creates a date value for the date represented by the *year*, *month*, and *day* arguments
DAY(*date*)	Extracts the day of the month from the *date* value
MONTH(*date*)	Extracts the month number from the *date* value where 1=January, 2=February, and so forth
YEAR(*date*)	Extracts the year number from the *date* value
WEEKDAY(*date*, [*return_type*])	Calculates the day of the week from the *date* value, where 1=Sunday, 2=Monday, and so forth; to choose a different numbering scheme, set the optional *return_type* value to "1" (1=Sunday, 2=Monday, ...), "2" (1=Monday, 2=Tuesday, ...), or "3" (0=Monday, 1=Tuesday, ...)
NOW( )	Displays the current date and time
TODAY( )	Displays the current date

Perhaps the most commonly used date function is the TODAY function, which returns the current date. The syntax of the TODAY function is as follows:

```
=TODAY()
```

The TODAY function doesn't have any arguments. Neither does the NOW function, which returns both the current date and current time. The values returned by the TODAY and NOW functions are updated automatically whenever you reopen the workbook or enter a new calculation. If you don't want the date and time to change, you must enter the date and time value directly in the cell.

Diane wants the 2010 Proposed Budget workbook to display the current date.

To enter the TODAY function to display the current date:

▶ **1.** In cell J1, enter **Current Date**.

▶ **2.** Merge cells **J1** and **K1**, right-align the merged cell, and then apply the **20% – Accent6** cell style.

▶ **3.** Click cell **L1**. You'll enter the TODAY function in this cell.

▶ **4.** In the Function Library group on the Formulas tab, click the **Date & Time** button, and then click **TODAY** in the date functions list. The Function Arguments dialog box opens, but there are no arguments for the TODAY function.

> **5.** Click the **OK** button. The Function Arguments dialog box closes, and the current date appears in cell L1. See Figure 3-32.

Figure 3-32 **TODAY function displays the current date**

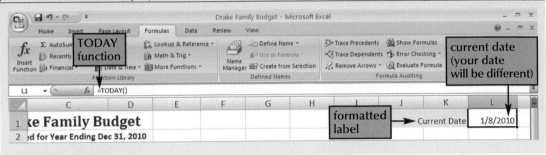

Working with Financial Functions

Diane wants to estimate how much monthly mortgage payments for a house might be. You can use the **PMT function** to calculate the payments for any type of loan.

The PMT function is one of many **financial functions** in Excel that calculate values from loans and investments. Figure 3-33 describes this and some of the other financial functions often used to develop budgets. These financial functions are the same as those widely used in business and accounting to perform various financial calculations, such as depreciation of an asset, the amount of interest paid on an investment, and the present value of an investment.

Figure 3-33 **Financial functions for loans and investments**

Function	Description
FV(*rate, nper, pmt,* [*pv*=0] [,*type*=0])	Returns the future value of an investment, where *rate* is the interest rate per period, *nper* is the total number of periods, *pmt* is the payment in each period, *pv* is the present value of the investment, and *type* indicates whether payments should be made at the end of the period (0) or the beginning of the period (1)
PMT(*rate, nper, pv,* [*fv*=0] [,*type*=0])	Calculates the payments required each period on a loan or investment
IPMT(*rate, per, nper, pv,* [*fv*=0] [,*type*=0])	Calculates the amount of a loan payment devoted to paying the loan interest, where *per* is the number of the payment period
PPMT(*rate, per, nper, pv,* [*fv*=0] [,*type*=0])	Calculates the amount of a loan payment devoted to paying off the principal of a loan, where *per* is the number of the payment period
PV(*rate, nper, pmt,* [*fv*=0] [,*type*=0])	Calculates the present value of a loan or investment based on periodic, constant payments
NPER(*rate, pmt, pv,* [*fv*=0] [,*type*=0])	Calculates the number of periods required to pay off a loan or investment
RATE(*nper, pmt, pv,* [*fv*=0] [,*type*=0])	Calculates the interest rate of a loan or investment based on periodic, constant payments

For expensive items, such as cars and houses, people often borrow money from a bank to make the purchase. Every loan has two main components: the principal and the interest. **Principal** is the amount of money being loaned, and **interest** is the amount charged for lending the money. You can think of interest as a kind of "user fee" because the borrower is paying for the right to use the lender's money for a period of time. The more money borrowed and the longer time for which it's borrowed, the higher the user fee. A few years ago, Diane and Glenn borrowed money to buy a second car and are still repaying the principal and interest on that loan.

Interest is calculated either as simple interest or as compound interest. In **simple interest**, the interest paid is equal to a percentage of principal for each period that the money has been lent. For example, if Diane and Glenn deposit $1,000 in an account that pays simple interest at a rate of 5% per year, they'll receive $50 in interest each year that the money is deposited. More often, interest is calculated as **compound interest** in which the interest paid is calculated on the principal and any previous interest payments that have been added to that principal. For example, the interest payment for a $1,000 deposit at a 5% interest that is compounded every year is $50. If the interest is left in the account, the interest payment for the second year is calculated on $1,050 (the original principal plus the previous year's interest), resulting in an interest payment for the second year of $52.50. With compound interest, the borrower always pays more money to the lender the following year. Most banks and financial institutions use compound interest in their financial transactions.

Using Functions to Manage Personal Finances | InSight

Excel has many financial functions you can use to manage your personal finances. The following list can help you determine which function to use for the most common personal finance problems:

- To determine how much an investment will be worth after a series of monthly payments at some future time, use the FV (future value) function.
- To determine how much you have to spend each month to repay a loan or mortgage within a set period of time, use the PMT (payment) function.
- To determine how much of your monthly loan payment is used to pay the interest, use the IPMT (interest payment) function.
- To determine how much of your monthly loan payment is used for repaying the principal, use the PPMT (principal payment) function.
- To determine the largest loan or mortgage you can afford at present, given a set monthly payment, use the PV (present value) function.
- To determine how long it will take to pay off a loan with constant monthly payments, use the NPER (number of periods) function.

In each case, you usually need to enter the annual interest rate divided by the number of times the interest is compounded during the year. If interest is compounded monthly, divide the annual interest rate by 12; if interest is compounded quarterly, divide the annual rate by 4. You must also convert the length of the loan or investment to the number of interest payments per year. If you will make payments monthly, multiply the number of years of the loan or investment by 12.

Using the PMT Function to Determine a Monthly Loan Payment

You'll use the PMT function to calculate the potential monthly loan payment for Diane and Glenn. For loan or investment calculations, you need to know the following information:

- The annual interest rate
- The payment period, or how often payments are due and interest is compounded (usually monthly for mortgages)

• The length of the loan in terms of the number of payment periods
• The amount being borrowed or invested

In Diane and Glenn's neighborhood, starter homes are selling for about $200,000. If Diane and Glenn can keep to their savings plan, they will have saved $9,000 by the end of the year (as shown in cell L6 in the Proposed Budget 2010 worksheet). If they save this same amount for the next three years, they will have at least $27,000 in their home savings account to put toward the down payment. Based on this, Diane estimates that she and Glenn will need a home loan of about $170,000. To calculate how much it would cost to repay such a loan, you can use the PMT (payment) function. The PMT function has the following syntax:

```
PMT(rate, nper, pv, [fv=0] [type=0])
```

In this function, *rate* is the interest rate for each payment period, *nper* is the total number of payment periods required to pay off the loan, and *pv* is the present value of the loan or the amount that needs to be borrowed. For Diane and Glenn, the present value of the loan is $170,000.

The PMT function has two optional arguments: *fv* and *type*. The *fv* argument is the future value of the loan. Because the intent with most loans is to pay them off completely, the future value is equal to 0 by default. The *type* argument specifies when the interest is charged on the loan, either at the end of the period (*type*=0), which is the default, or at the beginning of the period (*type*=1).

For most loans, the payment period is one month. This means that Diane and Glenn must make a payment on the loan every month, and interest on the loan is compounded every month. The annual interest rate on home loans in Diane and Glenn's area is 6.5%. To determine the interest rate per month, you divide the annual interest rate by 12. For Diane and Glenn, the interest rate each month or payment period is 6.5% divided by 12, or about 0.541% per month.

Diane and Glenn want to pay off their home loan in 20 years, which is a payment period of 240 months (20 years multiplied by 12 payment periods each year). Putting all of this information together, you can calculate the monthly payment for the couple's home loan with the following formula:

```
=PMT(0.065/12, 20*12, 170000)
```

This formula returns a value of −$1,267.47. The value is negative because the payment is considered an expense, or a negative cash flow. If you want to display this value as a positive number in a worksheet, enter a minus symbol directly before the PMT function as follows:

```
=-PMT(0.065/12, 20*12, 170000)
```

Based on these calculations, Diane and Glenn would have to pay the bank $1,267.47 every month for 20 years before the loan and the interest are completely paid. Right now, the couple is spending about $850 per month on rent. So this home loan is a significant increase over their current expenses. Diane asks you to calculate the monthly payment for a home loan of $160,000. You'll make that calculation in another worksheet.

To set up the monthly loan payment calculation:

▶ **1.** Insert a new worksheet named **Loan Analysis** at the end of the workbook.

▶ **2.** In cell A1, enter **Home Loan**, format cell A1 using the **Title** cell style, and then increase the width of column A to **25** characters.

▶ **3.** In the range A3:A9;B3:B8, enter the labels and components of the home loan shown in Figure 3-34. In cell B5, enter **=B3/B4** to calculate the interest rate per period by dividing the annual interest rate by the number of payments per year. In cell B7, enter **=B4*B6** to calculate the number of loan payments per year by multiplying the number of payments per year (12) by the number of years of the loan (20).

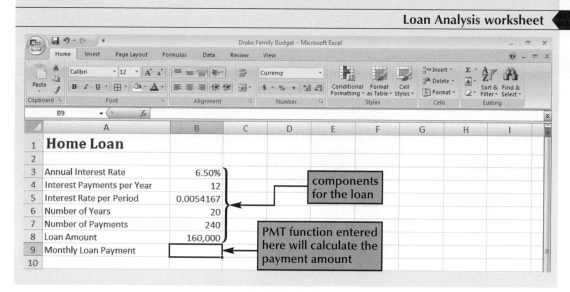

Loan Analysis worksheet ◄ **Figure 3-34**

Next, you'll enter the PMT function to calculate the monthly payment for the $160,000 home loan.

To enter the PMT function to calculate the monthly payment:

▶ **1.** Apply the **Calculation** cell style to cell B9 to distingish the monthly loan payment amount from the loan components.

▶ **2.** In the Function Library group on the Formulas tab, click the **Financial** button, and then click **PMT** in the list of financial functions. The Function Arguments dialog box opens.

▶ **3.** For the Rate argument, enter the cell reference **B5**, which is the cell with the interest rate per payment period.

▶ **4.** For the Nper argument, enter the cell reference **B7**, which is the cell with the total number of payments.

▶ **5.** For the Pv argument enter the cell reference **B8**, which is the cell with the present value of the loan. See Figure 3-35.

Function Arguments dialog box for the PMT function ◄ **Figure 3-35**

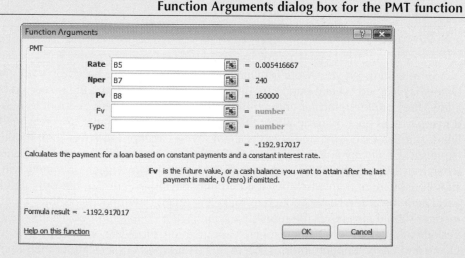

▶ **6.** Click the **OK** button. The value $1,192.92 is displayed in parentheses in cell B9 to indicate a negative currency value.

▶ **7.** Double-click cell **B9**, type – (minus symbol) between = and PMT, and then press the **Enter** key. The value $1,192.92 is displayed as a positive currency value. See Figure 3-36.

Figure 3-36

Monthly payment for a $160,000 loan

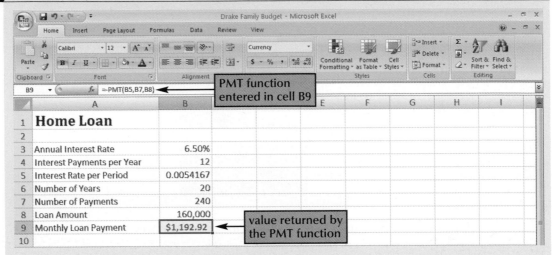

Diane and Glenn would have to pay about $1,193 per month for 20 years to repay a $160,000 loan at 6.5% interest. Diane is interested in other loan possibilities. Because you already set up the worksheet, you can quickly try other scenarios without having to reenter any formulas. Diane wonders whether extending the length of the loan would reduce the monthly payment by a sizeable margin. She asks you to calculate the monthly payment for a 30-year loan.

To calculate other loan options:

▶ **1.** In cell B6, change the value to **30**. The amount of the monthly payment drops to $1,011.31, which is $180 less per month. Next, Diane wants to see the monthly payments for a $150,000 loan with these same conditions.

▶ **2.** In cell B8, change the value to **150,000**. For this smaller home loan, the monthly payment drops even further to $948.10 per month. This is only about $100 more than the couple is currently paying in rent.

▶ **3.** Save your changes to the workbook, and then close it.

You've completed your work on Diane and Glenn's budget. Based on your analysis, Diane has learned several important things. She's discovered that the projected budget allows the couple to transfer enough money to the home savings account to make a down payment on a home in about three years. The savings plan seems reasonable to Diane and leaves enough funds in the main savings account to cover their monthly expenses. Finally, by analyzing some of the possible loan options they might encounter when they buy a home, Diane realizes that the monthly mortgage payments will not be substantially more than what they are currently paying in rent. So, not only will Diane and Glenn be able to save enough to make the initial down payment, their monthly income should also cover the monthly payments. Of course, all budgets must be revised periodically to meet changing expenses and income. However, your work has given Diane and Glenn enough information to make informed choices about their immediate financial future.

Session 3.2 Quick Check | Review

1. How do you use AutoFill to copy a set of cell values, but not the formatting?
2. The first three selected values in a series are 3, 6, and 9. What are the next three values that will be inserted using AutoFill?
3. Cell A5 contains the text Mon. If you select the cell and drag the fill handle over the range A6:A8, what text will be entered into those cells?
4. If cell A3 is greater than cell A4, you want to display the text "OK"; otherwise, you want to display the text string "RETRY". What formula accomplishes this?
5. What formula do you use to display the current date?
6. What formula do you use to display the current date and time?
7. You want to take out a loan for $130,000. The interest on the loan is 5% compounded monthly. You intend to pay back the loan in 20 years. What formula do you enter to calculate the monthly payment required to pay off the loan under those conditions?
8. What financial function do you use to determine how payment periods are required to pay off a loan?

Tutorial Summary | Review

In this tutorial, you learned how to work with Excel functions and formulas. First, you learned about relative, absolute, and mixed cell references and under what conditions you would use each. Then, you looked at function syntax, entered a function using the Insert Function dialog box, and then you entered a function directly into the worksheet to calculate sums, counts, averages, maximums, and minimums. You also searched for a function that matched search criteria. Next, you used AutoFill to quickly copy formulas and formatting and to extend a series of numbers, text, or dates. Then, you used logical functions to return different values based on conditions in the worksheet, and then you entered a date function. Finally, you examined financial functions and used the PMT function to calculate the monthly payments to repay a loan within a set interval of time.

Key Terms

absolute reference	financial function	nested
argument	IF function	optional argument
AutoFill	Insert Function dialog box	PMT function
comparison operator	interest	principal
compound interest	logical function	relative reference
date function	median	simple interest
F4 key	mixed reference	syntax
fill handle	mode	

*Practice the skills you
learned in the tutorial
using the same case
scenario.*

Data File needed for the Review Assignments: Timov.xlsx

Diane and Glenn appreciate the work you did on their budget. Their friends, Sergei and
Ava Timov, ask you to create a similar workbook for their family budget. The Timovs want
to purchase a new home. They are considering two houses with different mortgages. They
want the budget worksheet you create to display the impact of monthly mortgage payments on the couple's cash flow. The couple has already designed the workbook and
entered estimates of their take-home pay and expenses for the upcoming year. They want
you to set up the formulas.

Complete the following:

1. Open the **Timov** workbook located in the Tutorial.03\Review folder included with
   your Data Files, and then save the workbook as **Timov Family Budget** in the same
   folder.
2. In the Documentation sheet, enter your name in cell B3 and the date in cell B4.
3. In the Family Budget worksheet, in the range C17:N17, use AutoFill to enter the
   month names **January** through **December**.
4. In the range C20:N20, calculate the family's take-home pay. In the range C26:N26,
   calculate the monthly expenses. In the range C27:N27, calculate the monthly net
   cash flow (equal to the monthly take-home pay minus the expenses).
5. In cell C6, enter a formula to calculate the sum of Sergei's monthly salary for the
   entire year. In cell D6, calculate Sergei's average take-home pay each month. In cell
   E6, calculate Sergei's maximum monthly take-home pay. In cell F6, calculate Sergei's minimum monthly take-home pay.
6. Select the range C6:F6, and then use AutoFill to copy the formula in the C6:F6 range
   into the C7:F15 range. Use the AutoFill Options button to copy only the formulas
   into the selected range and not both the formulas and formats. (*Hint:* Because you
   haven't yet entered any mortgage payment values, cell D13 will show the value
   #DIV/0!, indicating that Excel cannot calculate the average mortgage payment. You'll
   correct that problem shortly.)
7. In the range J5:J12, enter the following loan and loan conditions of the first mortgage:
   • The loan amount (or value of the principal) is **$315,000**.
   • The annual interest rate is **6.7%**.
   • The interest rate is compounded **12** times a year (or monthly).
   • The mortgage will last **30** years.
   The monthly rate is equal to the annual interest rate divided by how often the interest rate is compounded. The number of payments is equal to the number of years the
   mortgage will last multiplied by 12.
8. In cell J11, enter the PMT function to calculate the monthly payment required to repay
   this loan. The *rate* argument is equal to the monthly rate, the *nper* argument is equal to
   the number of payments, and the *pv* argument is equal to the value of the principal.
9. In cell J11, enter a minus symbol between = and PMT to make the value positive.
10. In the range N5:N12, enter the following loan and loan conditions of the second
    mortgage:
    • The loan amount (or value of the principal) is **$218,000**.
    • The annual interest rate is **6.7%**.
    • The interest rate is compounded **12** times a year (or monthly).
    • The mortgage will last **20** years.

11. In cell N11, enter the PMT function to calculate the monthly payment needed to pay off this loan, and then make the PMT value positive.

12. Sergei and Ava want to be able to view their monthly cash flow under both mortgage possibilities. The mortgage being applied to the budget will be determined by whether 1 or 2 is entered into cell C3. To switch from one mortgage to another, do the following:

   - In cell C25, enter an IF function that tests whether cell C3 equals 1. If it does, display the value from cell J11; otherwise, display the value from cell N11. Use absolute cell references in the formula.
   - Use AutoFill to copy the formula in cell C25 into the range C26:N25.
   - Verify that the values in the range C25:N25 match the monthly payment for the first mortgage condition.

13. In cell C3, edit the value from 1 to **2**. Verify that the monthly payment for the second mortgage appears in the range C25:N25.

14. Sergei and Ava want to maintain an average net cash flow of at least $1,000 per month. Under which mortgage is this achieved?

15. Save and close the workbook, and then submit the finished workbook to your instructor, either in printed or electronic form, as requested.

| Apply | **Case Problem 1** |

Use the skills you learned to create a grading sheet for a chemistry course.

Data File needed for this Case Problem: Chemistry.xlsx

Chemistry 303   Karen Raul is a professor of chemistry at a community college in Shawnee, Kansas. She has started using Excel to calculate the final grade for students in her Chemistry 303 course. The final score is a weighted average of the scores given for three exams and the final exam. Karen wants your help in creating the formulas to calculate the final score and to summarize the class scores on all exams. One way to calculate a weighted average is by multiplying each student's exam score by the weight given to the exam, and then totaling the results. For example, consider the following four exam scores:

- Exam 1 = 84
- Exam 2 = 80
- Exam 3 = 83
- Final Exam = 72

If the first three exams are each given a weight of 20% and the final exam is given a weight of 40%, the weighted average of the four scores is:

84*0.2 + 80*0.2 + 83*0.2 + 72*0.4 = 78.2

Karen already entered the scores for her students and formatted much of the workbook. She wants you to enter the final formulas and highlight the top 10 overall scores in her class. Figure 3-37 shows the worksheet you'll create.

Figure 3-37

	A	B	C	D	E	F	G	H
1	**Chemistry 303**							
2	First Semester Scores							
3	Posted 12/20/2010							
4								
5	Students	36						
6								
7		Exam	Weight	Median	Maximum	Minimum	Range	
8		Exam 1	20%	86.0	99.0	52.0	47.0	
9		Exam 2	20%	80.0	99.0	53.0	46.0	
10		Exam 3	20%	83.0	98.0	50.0	48.0	
11		Final Exam	40%	81.5	99.0	51.0	48.0	
12		Overall	100%	80.5	96.8	55.8	41.0	
13								
14								
15	Student Scores				Top Ten Overall Scores			
16	Student ID	Exam 1	Exam 2	Exam 3	Final Exam	Overall		
17	390-120-2	84.0	80.0	83.0	72.0	78.2		
18	390-267-4	98.0	92.0	91.0	99.0	95.8		
19	390-299-8	54.0	56.0	51.0	65.0	58.2		
20	390-354-3	98.0	95.0	90.0	94.0	94.2		

(Column A, rows 7–12, reads vertically: *Class Summary*)

Complete the following:

1. Open the **Chemistry** workbook located in the Tutorial.03\Case1 folder included with your Data Files, and then save the workbook as **Chemistry 303 Final Scores** in the same folder.

2. In the Documentation sheet, enter your name in cell B3 and enter the date in cell B4.

3. In the First Semester Scores worksheet, in cell F17, enter a formula to calculate the weighted average of the first student's four exams. Use the weights found in the range C8:C11, matching each weight with the corresponding exam score. Use absolute cell references for the four weights.

4. Use AutoFill to copy the formula in cell F17 into the range F18:F52.

5. In cell B5, enter a formula to count the number of final scores in the range F17:F52.

 EXPLORE

6. In cell D8, use the MEDIAN function to calculate the median or middle score for the first exam.

7. In cell E8, calculate the maximum score for the first exam.

8. In cell F8, calculate the minimum score for the first exam.

9. In cell G8, calculate the range of scores for the first exam, which is equal to the difference between the maximum and minimum score.

10. Repeat Steps 6 through 9 for each of the other two exams, the final exam, and the overall weighted score.

11. Use conditional formatting to highlight the top 10 scores in the range F17:F52 in a light red fill with dark red text.

12. Insert a page break at cell A14, repeat the first three rows of the worksheet in any printout, and verify that the worksheet is in portrait orientation.

13. Save and close the workbook, and then submit the finished workbook to your instructor, either in printed or electronic form, as requested.

Apply | **Case Problem 2**

Use the skills you learned to create an order form for a fireworks company.

Data File needed for this Case Problem: Wizard.xlsx

WizardWorks   Andrew Howe owns and operates WizardWorks, an online seller of fireworks based in Franklin, Tennessee. Andrew wants you to help him use Excel to develop an order form for his business. The form needs to contain formulas to calculate the charge for each order. The total charge is based on the quantity and type of items ordered plus the shipping charge and the 5% sales tax. Orders can be shipped using standard 3 to 5 day shipping for $4.99 or overnight for $12.99. Andrew is also offering a 3% discount for orders that exceed $200. Both the shipping option and the discount need to be calculated using formulas based on values entered into the worksheet. Figure 3-38 shows a preview of a sample order.

Figure 3-38

	A	B	C	D	E	F	G
1	**WizardWorks**						
2	250 North Avenue Franklin, Tennessee 37064 Sales: (615) 555-3287 Office: (615) 555-3210						
3							
4	Customer	Kevin Kemper					
5	Date		11/1/2010				
6	Order No.		31528				
7							
8		**Shipping Address**			**Shipping Options**		
9	Address 1	418 Alcorn Lane			Standard	$4.99	
10	Address 2				Overnight	$12.99	
11	City	Greenfield					
12	State	IN			Discount*	3%	
13	Zip	46140			*For orders exceeding $200		
14							
15	Shipping*		overnight				
16	*Enter standard or overnight						
17							
18	Customer Order						
19	Item	Name		Price	Qty	Charge	
20	BF005	Bucket of Fireworks		$42.50	1	$42.50	
21	F128	Nightair Fountain		$9.95	3	$29.85	
22	R315	Mountain Rockets (Box 20)		$49.50	3	$148.50	
23							
24							
25							
26							
27					Subtotal	$220.85	
28					Discount	($6.63)	
29					After Discount	$214.22	
30							
31					5% Sales Tax	$10.71	
32					Shipping	$12.99	overnight
33							
34					TOTAL	**$237.93**	

Complete the following:

1. Open the **Wizard** workbook located in the Tutorial.03\Case2 folder included with your Data Files, and then save the workbook as **WizardWorks Order Form** in the same folder.

2. In the Documentation sheet, enter your name in cell B3 and enter the date in cell B4.

3. In the Order Form worksheet, in cell C4, enter the customer name, **Kevin Kemper**. In cell C6, enter the order number, **31528**. In the range C9:C13, enter the following address:

Address 1:   **418 Alcorn Lane**
City: **Greenfield**
State: **IN**
Zip: **46140**

⊕ **EXPLORE**   4. In cell C5, enter a function that displays the current date.

5. In the range B20:E22, enter the following orders:

Item	Name	Price	Qty
BF005	**Bucket of Fireworks**	**$42.50**	**1**
F128	**Nightair Fountain**	**$9.95**	**3**
R315	**Mountain Rockets (Box 20)**	**$49.50**	**3**

6. In cell C15, enter **overnight** to ship this order overnight.

⊕ **EXPLORE**   7. In cell F20, enter an IF function that tests whether the order quantity in cell E20 is greater than 0 (zero). If it is, return the value of E20 multiplied by D20; otherwise, return no text by entering "". AutoFill this formula into the range F21:F25.

8. In cell F27, calculate the sum of the values in the range F20:F25.

9. In cell F28, enter an IF function that tests whether cell F27 is greater than 200. If it is, return the negative value of F27 multiplied by the discount percentage in cell F12; otherwise, return the value 0 (zero).

10. In cell F29, add the subtotal from cell F27 and the discount value from cell F28.

11. In cell F31, calculate the sales tax by multiplying the after discount value in cell F29 by the sales tax percentage, 0.05.

12. In cell F32, determine the shipping charge by entering an IF function that tests whether cell C15 equals "standard". If it does, return the value in cell F9; otherwise, return the value in cell F10.

13. In cell G32, display the value of cell C15.

14. In cell F34, calculate the total of the after discount value, the sales tax, and the shipping fee.

15. Scale the order form so that it will print on a single page.

16. Reduce the quantity of Mountain Rockets boxes from 3 to **2**, and then verify that the discount is changed to 0 for the order. Change the shipping option from overnight to **standard**, and then verify that the shipping fee is changed to the fee for standard shipping.

17. Save and close the workbook, and then submit the finished workbook to your instructor, either in printed or electronic form, as requested.

| Challenge | **Case Problem 3** |

Explore how to use relative and absolute references and the PMT function to create a loan table.

Data File needed for this Case Problem: Loan.xlsx

Eason Financial Services   Jesse Buchmann is a finance officer at Eason Financial Services in Meridian, Idaho. She works with people who are looking for home mortgages. Most clients want mortgages they can afford, and affordability is determined by the size of the monthly payment. The monthly payment is determined by the interest rate, the total number of payments, and the size of the home loan. Jesse can't change the interest rate, but homebuyers can reduce their monthly payments by increasing the number of years to repay the loan. Jesse wants to give her clients a grid that displays combinations of loan amounts and payment periods so that they can select a loan that best meets their needs and budget. Figure 3-39 shows a preview of the grid that Jesse has in mind.

Figure 3-39

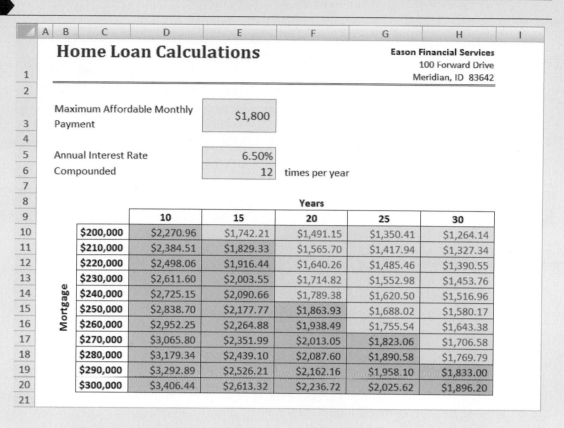

		10	15	20	25	30
				Years		
	$200,000	$2,270.96	$1,742.21	$1,491.15	$1,350.41	$1,264.14
	$210,000	$2,384.51	$1,829.33	$1,565.70	$1,417.94	$1,327.34
	$220,000	$2,498.06	$1,916.44	$1,640.26	$1,485.46	$1,390.55
	$230,000	$2,611.60	$2,003.55	$1,714.82	$1,552.98	$1,453.76
Mortgage	$240,000	$2,725.15	$2,090.66	$1,789.38	$1,620.50	$1,516.96
	$250,000	$2,838.70	$2,177.77	$1,863.93	$1,688.02	$1,580.17
	$260,000	$2,952.25	$2,264.88	$1,938.49	$1,755.54	$1,643.38
	$270,000	$3,065.80	$2,351.99	$2,013.05	$1,823.06	$1,706.58
	$280,000	$3,179.34	$2,439.10	$2,087.60	$1,890.58	$1,769.79
	$290,000	$3,292.89	$2,526.21	$2,162.16	$1,958.10	$1,833.00
	$300,000	$3,406.44	$2,613.32	$2,236.72	$2,025.62	$1,896.20

Jesse already entered much of the layout and formatting for the worksheet containing the loan payment grid. She needs your help in entering the PMT function.

Complete the following:

1. Open the **Loan** workbook located in the Tutorial.03\Case3 folder included with your Data Files, and then save the workbook as **Loan Grid** in the same folder.
2. In the Documentation sheet, enter your name and the date.
3. In the Loan Calculation worksheet, in cell E3, enter a monthly payment of **$2,200**.
4. In cell E5, enter the annual interest rate of **6.5%**. In cell E6, enter **12** to indicate that the interest payment is compounded 12 times a year, or monthly.
5. In the range C10:C20, use AutoFill to enter the currency values **$200,000** through **$300,000** in increments of $10,000. In the range D9:H9, use AutoFill to enter the year values **10** through **30** in increments of 5 years.

⊕ **EXPLORE**
6. In cell D10, use the PMT function to calculate the monthly payment required to repay a **$200,000** loan in **10** years at **6.5%** interest compounded monthly. Use absolute references to cells E5 and E6 to enter the annual interest rate and number of payments per year. Use the mixed references D$9 and $C10 to cells D9 and C10, respectively, to reference the number of years to repay the loan and the loan amount. Place a minus symbol before the PMT function so that the value returned by the function is positive rather than negative.

⊕ **EXPLORE**
7. Using AutoFill, copy the formula in cell D10 into the range D11:H10, and then copy that range of formulas into the range D11:H20. Verify that the values entered in those cells match the values shown in Figure 3-39.

⊕ EXPLORE   8. Conditionally format the range D10:H20 to highlight all of the values in the range that are less than the value in cell E3 in a dark green font on a green fill.

9. Add a second conditional format to the range D10:H20 to highlight all of the values in the range that are greater than the value in cell E3 in a dark red font on a red fill.

⊕ EXPLORE   10. Change the value in cell E3 from $2,200 to **$1,800**. If this represents the maximum affordable monthly payment, use the values in the grid to determine the largest mortgage for payment schedules lasting 15 through 30 years. Can any of the home loan values displayed in the grid be repaid in 10 years at $1,800 per month?

11. Save and close the workbook, and then submit the finished workbook to your instructor, either in printed or electronic form, as requested.

Create	**Case Problem 4**

Create a workbook that automatically grades a driving exam.

Data File needed for this Case Problem: V6.xlsx

V-6 Driving Academy   Sebastian Villanueva owns and operates the V-6 Driving Academy, a driving school located in Pine Hills, Florida. In addition to driving, students must take multiple-choice tests offered by the Florida Department of Motor Vehicles. Students must answer at least 80% of the questions correctly to pass each test. Sebastian has to grade these tests himself. Sebastian realizes that he can save a lot of time if the test questions were in a workbook and Excel totaled the test results. He asks you to help create the workbook.

Sebastian already entered a 20-question test into a workbook. He needs you to format this workbook and insert the necessary functions and formulas to grade a student's answers.

Complete the following:

1. Open the **V6** workbook located in the Tutorial.03\Case4 folder included with your Data Files, and then save the workbook as **V6 Driving Test** in the same folder.

2. In the Documentation sheet, enter your name in cell B3 and enter the date in cell B4.

3. In the Exam1 worksheet, format the questions and possible answers so that the worksheet is easy to read. The format is up to you. At the top of the worksheet, enter a title that describes the exam and then enter a function that returns the current date.

4. Add a section somewhere on the Exam1 worksheet where Sebastian can enter the student's name and answers to each question.

⊕ EXPLORE   5. The answers for the 20 questions are listed below. Use this information to write functions that will grade each answer, giving 1 point for a correct answer and 0 otherwise. Assume that all answers are in lowercase letters; therefore, the function that tests the answer to the first question should check for a "c" rather than a "C".

Question	Answer	Question	Answer	Question	Answer
1	c	8	a	15	b
2	a	9	c	16	b
3	b	10	b	17	b
4	a	11	c	18	b
5	c	12	b	19	b
6	b	13	b	20	c
7	c	14	a		

6. At the top of the worksheet, insert a formula to calculate the total number of correct answers.

7. Insert another formula that divides the total number of correct answers by the total number of exam questions on the worksheet. Display this value as a percentage.

8. Enter a logical function that displays the message "PASS" on the exam if the percentage of correct answers is greater than or equal to 80%; otherwise, the logical function displays the message "FAIL".

Test your worksheet on the following student exams. Which students passed and which failed? What score did each student receive on the exam?

Juan Marquez

Question	Answer	Question	Answer	Question	Answer
1	b	8	a	15	b
2	a	9	c	16	b
3	b	10	b	17	a
4	a	11	c	18	b
5	c	12	c	19	b
6	b	13	b	20	a
7	c	14	a		

Kurt Bessette

Question	Answer	Question	Answer	Question	Answer
1	c	8	b	15	c
2	c	9	c	16	b
3	b	10	b	17	a
4	a	11	c	18	b
5	c	12	a	19	b
6	b	13	b	20	b
7	c	14	a		

Rebecca Pena

Question	Answer	Question	Answer	Question	Answer
1	c	8	a	15	b
2	a	9	c	16	c
3	b	10	a	17	b
4	a	11	c	18	b
5	c	12	b	19	b
6	b	13	b	20	c
7	c	14	a		

9. Save and close the workbook, and then submit the finished workbook to your instructor, either in printed or electronic form, as requested.

Research | Internet Assignments

Use the Internet to find and work with data related to the topics presented in this tutorial.

The purpose of the Internet Assignments is to challenge you to find information on the Internet that you can use to work effectively with this software. The actual assignments are updated and maintained on the Course Technology Web site. Log on to the Internet and use your Web browser to go to the Student Online Companion for New Perspectives Office 2007 at **www.course.com/np/office2007**. Then navigate to the Internet Assignments for this tutorial.

Assess | SAM Assessment and Training

If you have a SAM user profile, you may have access to hands-on instruction, practice, and assessment of the skills covered in this tutorial. Log in to your SAM account (**http://sam2007.course.com**) to launch any assigned training activities or exams that relate to the skills covered in this tutorial.

Review | Quick Check Answers

Session 3.1

1. Absolute cell reference is $B$21. Mixed cell references are $B21 and B$21.
2. =C11+C12
3. =$B11+C$2
4. =AVERAGE($A11:$A15)
5. Optional arguments are not required in a function. If not included, Excel assumes a default value for the argument.
6. =SUM(B1:B10)
7. =MAX(B1:B10)–MIN(B1:B10)
8. =MAX(B1:B10)/MIN(B1:B10)

Session 3.2

1. Drag the fill handle over the selected range, click the AutoFill Options button, and then click Fill Without Formatting.
2. 12, 15, 18
3. Cell A6 displays the text Tue, cell A7 displays Wed, and cell A8 displays Thu.
4. =IF(A3 > A4, "OK", "RETRY")
5. =TODAY()
6. =NOW()
7. =PMT(0.05/12, 12*20, 130000)
8. NPER

Ending Data Files

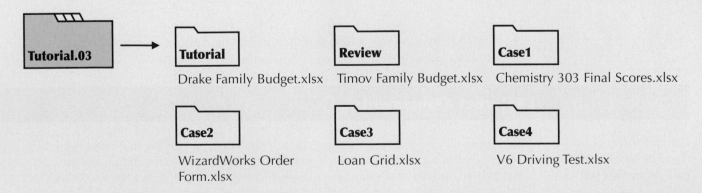

Tutorial.03 →

Tutorial
Drake Family Budget.xlsx

Review
Timov Family Budget.xlsx

Case1
Chemistry 303 Final Scores.xlsx

Case2
WizardWorks Order Form.xlsx

Case3
Loan Grid.xlsx

Case4
V6 Driving Test.xlsx

Reality Check

Excel is valuable to a wide audience of users: from accountants of *Fortune 500* companies to homeowners managing their budgets. An Excel workbook can be complex, recording data from thousands of financial transactions, or it can simply track a few monthly expenses. Everyone who has to balance a budget, track expenses, or project future income can make use of the financial tools in Excel. In this exercise, you'll use Excel to create a sample budget workbook that will contain information of your choice, using Excel skills and features presented in Tutorials 1 through 3. Use the following steps as a guide to completing your workbook.

Note: Please be sure *not* to include any personal information of a sensitive nature in any workbooks you create to be submitted to your instructor for this exercise. Later, you can update the workbooks with such information for your personal use.

1. Create a new workbook for the sample financial data. Use the first worksheet as a documentation sheet that includes your name, the date on which you start creating the workbook, and a brief description of the workbook's purpose.

2. In a second worksheet, enter realistic monthly earnings for each month of the year. Use formulas to calculate the total earnings each month, the average monthly earnings, and the total earnings for the entire year.

3. On the same worksheet, enter realistic personal expenses for each month. Divide the expenses into at least three categories, providing subtotals for each category and a grand total of all the monthly expenses. Calculate the average monthly expenses and total expenses for the year.

4. Calculate the monthly net cash flow (the value of total income minus total expenses).

5. Use the cash flow values to track the savings throughout the year. Use a realistic amount for savings at the beginning of the year. Use the monthly net cash flow values to add or subtract from this value. Project the end-of-year balance in the savings account under your proposed budget.

6. Format the worksheet's contents using appropriate text and number formats. Add colors and line borders to make the content easier to read and interpret. Use cell styles and themes to provide your worksheet with a uniform appearance.

7. Use conditional formatting to automatically highlight negative net cash flow calculated in Step 4.

8. Insert new rows at the top of the worksheet and enter titles that describe the worksheet's contents.

9. Think of a major purchase you might want to make—for example, a car. Determine the amount of the purchase and the current annual interest rate charged by your local bank. Provide a reasonable length of time to repay the loan, such as five years for a car loan or 20 to 30 years for a home loan. Use the PMT function to determine how much you would have to spend each month on the payments for your purchase. Add this information to your monthly budget. If the payment exceeds your budget, reduce the estimated price of the item you're thinking of purchasing until you determine the monthly payment you can afford under the conditions of the loan.

10. Format the worksheets for your printer. Include headers and footers that display the filename of your workbook, the workbook's author, and the date on which the report is printed. If the report extends across several pages, repeat appropriate print titles on all of the pages and include page numbers and the total number of pages on every printed page.

11. Save and close your workbook, and then submit the completed workbook to your instructor, in printed or electronic form, as requested.

Objectives

Session 1.1
- Define the terms field, record, table, relational database, primary key, and foreign key
- Create a blank database
- Identify the components of the Microsoft Access window
- Create and save a table in Datasheet view
- Enter field names and records in a table datasheet
- Open a table using the Navigation Pane

Session 1.2
- Open an Access database
- Copy and paste records from another Access database
- Navigate a table datasheet
- Create and navigate a simple query
- Create and navigate a simple form
- Create, preview, navigate, and print a simple report
- Learn how to manage a database by compacting, backing up, and restoring a database

Creating a Database

Creating a Database to Contain Customer, Contract, and Invoice Data

Case | Belmont Landscapes

Soon after graduating with a degree in Landscape Architecture from nearby Michigan State University, Oren Belmont returned to his hometown of Holland, on the shores of Lake Michigan. There, Oren worked for a local firm that provided basic landscaping services to residential customers. After several years, Oren started his own landscape architecture firm, Belmont Landscapes, which specializes in landscape designs for residential and commercial customers and numerous public agencies.

Belmont Landscapes provides a wide range of services—from site analyses and feasibility studies, to drafting and administering construction documents—for projects of various scales. Oren and his staff depend on computers to help manage all aspects of the firm's operations, including financial and information management. Several months ago the company upgraded to Microsoft Windows and **Microsoft Office Access 2007** (or simply **Access**), a computer program used to enter, maintain, and retrieve related data in a format known as a database. Oren and his staff want to use Access to maintain such data as information about customers, contracts, and invoices. He asks for your help in creating the necessary Access database.

Starting Data Files

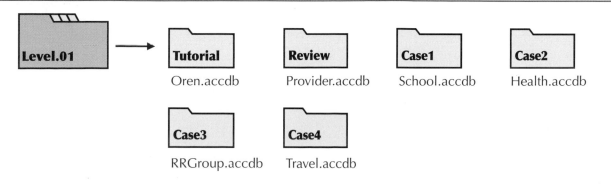

Level.01 → Tutorial — Oren.accdb | Review — Provider.accdb | Case1 — School.accdb | Case2 — Health.accdb

Case3 — RRGroup.accdb | Case4 — Travel.accdb

Session 1.1

Introduction to Database Concepts

Before you begin using Access to create the database for Oren, you need to understand a few key terms and concepts associated with databases.

Organizing Data

Data is a valuable resource to any business. At Belmont Landscapes, for example, important data includes customers' names and addresses and contract amounts and dates. Organizing, storing, maintaining, retrieving, and sorting this type of data are critical activities that enable a business to find and use information effectively. Before storing data on a computer, however, you must organize the data.

Your first step in organizing data is to identify the individual fields. A **field** is a single characteristic or attribute of a person, place, object, event, or idea. For example, some of the many fields that Belmont Landscapes tracks are customer ID, first name, last name, company name, address, phone number, contract amount, contract signing date, and contract type.

Next, you group related fields together into tables. A **table** is a collection of fields that describe a person, place, object, event, or idea. Figure 1-1 shows an example of a Customer table that contains four fields named Customer ID, First Name, Last Name, and Phone.

Figure 1-1 ▶ **Data organization for a table of customers**

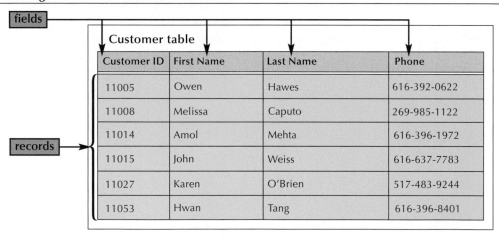

The specific value, or content, of a field is called the **field value**. In Figure 1-1, the first set of field values for Customer ID, First Name, Last Name, and Phone are, respectively: 11005; Owen; Hawes; and 616-392-0622. This set of field values is called a **record**. In the Customer table, the data for each customer is stored as a separate record. Figure 1-1 shows six records; each row of field values is a record.

Databases and Relationships

A collection of related tables is called a **database**, or a **relational database**. In this tutorial, you will create the database for Belmont Landscapes and a table named Contract to store data about contracts. In Tutorial 2, you will create two more tables, named Customer and Invoice, to store related information about customers and their invoices.

As Oren and his staff use the database that you will create, they will need to access information about customers and their contracts. To obtain this information, you must have a way to connect records in the Customer table to records in the Contract table. You connect the records in the separate tables through a **common field** that appears in both tables.

In the sample database shown in Figure 1-2, each record in the Customer table has a field named Customer ID, which is also a field in the Contract table. For example, Owen Hawes is the first customer in the Customer table and has a Customer ID field value of 11005. This same Customer ID field value, 11005, appears in three records in the Contract table. Therefore, Owen Hawes is the customer with these three contracts.

Database relationship between tables for customers and contracts — Figure 1-2

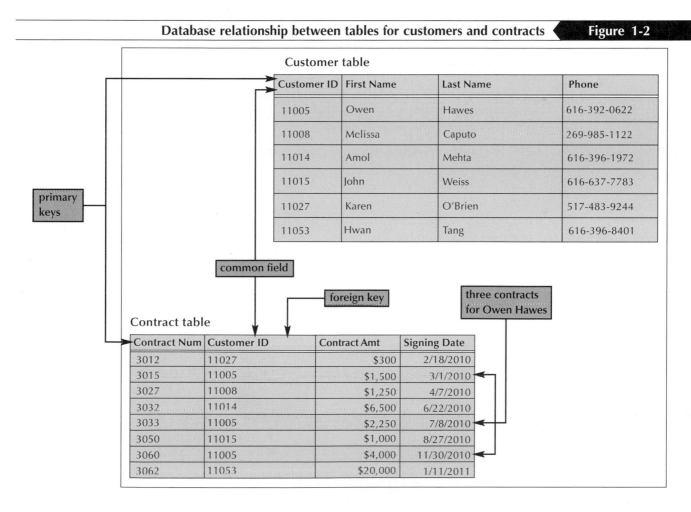

Customer table

Customer ID	First Name	Last Name	Phone
11005	Owen	Hawes	616-392-0622
11008	Melissa	Caputo	269-985-1122
11014	Amol	Mehta	616-396-1972
11015	John	Weiss	616-637-7783
11027	Karen	O'Brien	517-483-9244
11053	Hwan	Tang	616-396-8401

primary keys

common field

foreign key

three contracts for Owen Hawes

Contract table

Contract Num	Customer ID	Contract Amt	Signing Date
3012	11027	$300	2/18/2010
3015	11005	$1,500	3/1/2010
3027	11008	$1,250	4/7/2010
3032	11014	$6,500	6/22/2010
3033	11005	$2,250	7/8/2010
3050	11015	$1,000	8/27/2010
3060	11005	$4,000	11/30/2010
3062	11053	$20,000	1/11/2011

Each Customer ID value in the Customer table must be unique so that you can distinguish one customer from another. These unique Customer ID values also identify each customer's specific contracts in the Contract table. The Customer ID field is referred to as the primary key of the Customer table. A **primary key** is a field, or a collection of fields, whose values uniquely identify each record in a table. No two records can contain the same value for the primary key field. In the Contract table, the Contract Num field is the primary key because Belmont Landscapes assigns each contract a unique contract number.

When you include the primary key from one table as a field in a second table to form a relationship between the two tables, it is called a **foreign key** in the second table, as shown in Figure 1-2. For example, Customer ID is the primary key in the Customer table and a foreign key in the Contract table. Although the primary key Customer ID contains unique values in the Customer table, the same field as a foreign key in the Contract table does not necessarily contain unique values. The Customer ID value 11005, for example, appears three times in the Contract table because Owen Hawes has three contracts. Each foreign key value, however, must match one of the field values for the primary key in the other table. In the example shown in Figure 1-2, each Customer ID value in the Contract table must match a Customer ID value in the Customer table. The two tables are related, enabling users to connect the facts about customers with the facts about their contracts.

Relational Database Management Systems

To manage its databases, a company purchases a database management system. A **database management system (DBMS)** is a software program that lets you create databases and then manipulate data in them. Most of today's database management systems, including Access, are called relational database management systems. In a **relational database management system**, data is organized as a collection of tables. As stated earlier, a relationship between two tables in a relational DBMS is formed through a common field.

A relational DBMS controls the storage of databases on disk and facilitates the creation, manipulation, and reporting of data, as illustrated in Figure 1-3. Specifically, a relational DBMS provides the following functions:

- It allows you to create database structures containing fields, tables, and table relationships.
- It lets you easily add new records, change field values in existing records, and delete records.
- It contains a built-in query language, which lets you obtain immediate answers to the questions you ask about your data.
- It contains a built-in report generator, which lets you produce professional-looking, formatted reports from your data.
- It protects databases through security, control, and recovery facilities.

Figure 1-3 ▶ **Relational database management system**

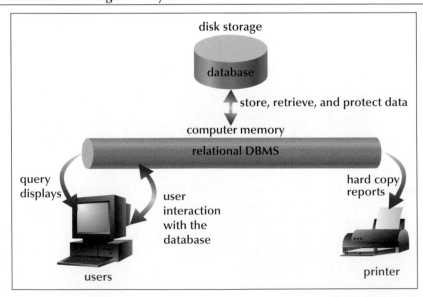

A company such as Belmont Landscapes benefits from a relational DBMS because it allows users working in different groups to share the same data. More than one user can enter data into a database, and more than one user can retrieve and analyze data that other users entered. For example, the database for Belmont Landscapes will contain only one copy of the Contract table, and all employees will use it to meet their specific requests for contract information.

Finally, unlike other software programs, such as spreadsheet programs, a DBMS can handle massive amounts of data and can be used to create relationships among multiple tables. Each Access database, for example, can be up to two gigabytes in size, can contain up to 32,768 objects (tables, queries, forms, and so on), and can have up to 255 people using the database at the same time. For instructional purposes, the databases you will create and work with throughout this text contain a relatively small number of records compared to most databases you would encounter outside the classroom, which likely contain tables with very large numbers of records.

Creating a Database

Now that you've learned some database terms and concepts, you're ready to start Access and create the Belmont database for Oren.

To start Access:

▶ 1. Click the **Start** button 🔵 on the taskbar, click **All Programs**, click **Microsoft Office**, and then click **Microsoft Office Access 2007**. The Getting Started with Microsoft Office Access page opens. See Figure 1-4.

   Trouble? If you don't see the Microsoft Office Access 2007 option on the Microsoft Office submenu, look for it on a different submenu or as an option on the All Programs menu. If you still cannot find the Microsoft Office Access 2007 option, ask your instructor or technical support person for help.

Getting Started with Microsoft Office Access page ◄ **Figure 1-4**

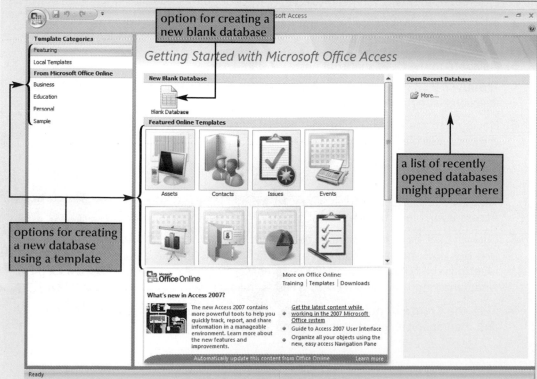

Trouble? If the Microsoft Access program window on your computer is not maximized, click the Maximize button ▭ on the program window title bar.

The Getting Started with Microsoft Office Access page contains options for creating a new database, opening an existing database, or viewing content from Microsoft Office Online. You can create a new database that does not contain any data or objects by using the Blank Database option. If the database you need to create contains objects that match the ones found in common databases, such as ones that store data about contacts or events, you can use a template that Access installs (listed in the "Template Categories" section on the left side of the page) or download a template from Microsoft Office Online (listed in the "Featured Online Templates" section in the middle of the page). A **template** is a predesigned database that includes professionally designed tables, reports, and other database objects that can make it quick and easy for you to create a database.

In this case, the templates provided do not match Oren's needs for the Belmont Landscapes database, so you need to create a new database from scratch. To do this, you will use the Blank Database option on the Getting Started page.

To create the new Belmont database:

▶ 1. Make sure you have created your copy of the Access Data Files, and that your computer can access them.

   Trouble? If you don't have the starting Data Files, you need to get them before you can proceed. Your instructor will either give you the Data Files or ask you to obtain them from a specified location (such as a network drive). In either case, make a backup copy of the Data Files before you start so that you will have the original files available in case you need to start over. If you have any questions about the Data Files, see your instructor or technical support person for assistance.

▶ 2. Click the **Blank Database** option in the center of the page. The right section of the page changes to display options for creating a blank database.

▶ 3. In the File Name text box, select the default name provided by Access, and then type **Belmont**. Next you need to specify the location for the file.

▶ 4. Click the **Browse** button 🗁 to the right of the File Name text box. The File New Database dialog box opens.

▶ 5. Navigate to the drive that contains your Data Files.

   Trouble? If you do not know where your Data Files are located, consult with your instructor about where to save your Data Files.

▶ 6. Navigate to the **Level.01\Tutorial** folder. This is the folder in which you will store the database file you create.

▶ 7. Make sure the "Save as type" text box displays "Microsoft Office Access 2007 Databases."

   Trouble? If your computer is set up to show filename extensions, you will see the Access 2007 filename extension ".accdb" in this text box as well.

▶ 8. Click the **OK** button. You return to the Getting Started page, and the File Name text box now shows the name Belmont.accdb. The filename extension ".accdb" identifies the file as an Access 2007 database. If you do not type the extension when entering the filename, Access adds the extension automatically.

▶ 9. Click the **Create** button. Access creates the new database, saves it to your disk, and then opens an empty table named Table1. See Figure 1-5.

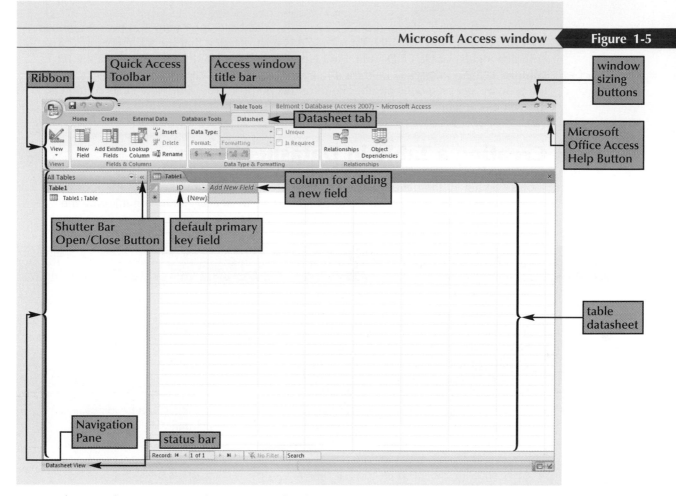

Microsoft Access window — Figure 1-5

Before you begin entering data, you need to become familiar with the components of the Microsoft Access window.

Exploring the Microsoft Access Window

The **Microsoft Access window** (or simply the **Access window**) is the program window that appears when you create a new database or open an existing database. Most of the Access window components—including the title bar, window sizing buttons, Help button, Quick Access Toolbar, Ribbon, tabs, and status bar—are the same as the components in other Microsoft Office 2007 programs.

The new blank table that Access created is displayed in **Datasheet view**, which shows a table's contents as a **datasheet** in rows and columns, similar to a table that you create in Word or an Excel spreadsheet. Each row will be a separate record in the table, and each column will contain the field values for one field in the table. Because you are in Datasheet view, the Datasheet tab is the active tab on the Ribbon. The status bar also indicates the current view.

The **Navigation Pane** is the area on the left side of the window that lists all the objects (tables, reports, and so on) in the database, and it is the main control center for opening and working with database objects. Currently, the Navigation Pane lists only the new table you are in the process of creating, which is named "Table1" by default. You will give the table a more meaningful name as part of creating it. Notice the Shutter Bar Open/Close Button at the top-right of the Navigation Pane (see Figure 1-5). You can use this button to close and open the pane. Depending on the size of your database table, you might want to close the Navigation Pane so that you have more room on the screen to view the table's contents.

When you open tables and other objects in a database, their names appear on tabbed documents. Currently, only the Table1 table is open. Notice that the table contains two columns (fields) labeled "ID" and "Add New Field." By default, Access creates the **ID column** as the primary key field for all new tables. You can choose to keep this field as the primary key or specify another field for this purpose. The **Add New Field column** is the column in which you create the first new field for your table.

Creating a Table in Datasheet View

Tables contain all the data in a database and are the fundamental objects for your work in Access. There are different ways to create a table in Access, including entering the fields and records for a table directly in Datasheet view.

Reference Window	**Creating a Table in Datasheet View**

- Click the Create tab on the Ribbon.
- In the Tables group, click the Table button.
- Accept the default ID primary key field with the AutoNumber data type, or rename the field and change its data type, if necessary.
- Double-click the Add New Field column heading, and then type the name for the field you are adding to the table.
- Press the Tab key or the Enter key.
- Add all the fields to your table by typing the field names in the column headings and pressing the Tab key or the Enter key to move to the next column.
- In the first row below the field names, enter the value for each field in the first record, pressing the Tab key or the Enter key to move from field to field.
- After entering the value for the last field in the first record, press the Tab key or the Enter key to move to the next row, and then enter the values for the next record. Continue this process until you have entered all the records for the table.
- Click the Save button on the Quick Access Toolbar, enter a name for the table, and then click the OK button.

For Belmont Landscapes, Oren needs to track information about the company's contracts with its customers. He asks you to create the Contract table according to the plan shown in Figure 1-6.

Figure 1-6	Plan for the Contract table

Field	Purpose
Contract Num	Unique number assigned to each contract; will serve as the table's primary key
Customer ID	Unique number assigned to each customer; common field that will be a foreign key to connect to the Customer table
Contract Amt	Dollar amount for the full contract
Signing Date	Date on which the customer signed the contract
Contract Type	Brief description of the contract

As shown in Oren's plan, he wants to store data about contracts in five fields, including fields to contain the amount of each contract, when it was signed, and the type of contract. These are the most important aspects of a contract and, therefore, must be tracked. Also, notice that the Contract Num field will be the primary key for the table; each contract at Belmont Landscapes has a unique contract number, so this field is the logical choice for the primary key. Finally, the Customer ID field is needed in the Contract table as a foreign key to tie the information about contracts to customers. The data about customers and their invoices will be stored in separate tables, which you will create in Tutorial 2.

Notice the name of each field in Figure 1-6. You need to name each field, table, and other object in an Access database.

Guidelines for Naming Fields | InSight

Keep the following guidelines in mind when you name fields:

- A field name can consist of up to 64 characters, including letters, numbers, spaces, and special characters, except for a period (.), exclamation mark (!), accent grave (`), and square brackets ([ ]).
- A field name cannot begin with a space.
- Capitalize the first letter of each word in the field name so it is clear which words are part of the name.
- Use concise field names that are easy to remember and reference, and that won't take up a lot of space in the table datasheet.
- Use standard abbreviations, such as Num for Number, Amt for Amount, and Qty for Quantity.
- Give fields descriptive names so that you can easily identify them when you view or edit records.
- Different DBMSs and some organizations have specific rules for naming fields. For example, many experienced database users do not include spaces in field names for ease of use when working with fields and other objects to perform more complex tasks, such as programming.

Renaming the Default Primary Key Field

As noted earlier, Access provides the ID field as a default primary key for a new table you create in Datasheet view. Recall that a primary key is a field, or a collection of fields, whose values uniquely identify each record in a table. However, according to Oren's plan, the Contract Num field should be the primary key for the Contract table. You'll begin by renaming the default ID field to create the Contract Num field.

To rename the ID field to the Contract Num field:

▶ **1.** Right-click the **ID** column heading to display the shortcut menu, and then click **Rename Column**. The column heading ID is selected, so that whatever text you type next will replace it.

▶ **2.** Type **Contract Num** and then press the **Enter** key. The column heading changes to Contract Num and the insertion point moves to the row below the heading. See Figure 1-7.

Trouble? Your instructor might ask you to omit spaces in field names as you create the tables in this book so your table designs will conform to standard field naming conventions. If so, your field names will not match the ones shown in the figures exactly, but this discrepancy will not cause problems.

Figure 1-7 **ID field renamed to Contract Num**

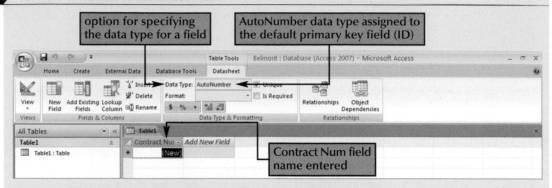

Trouble? If you make a mistake when typing the field name, use the Backspace key to delete characters to the left of the insertion point or the Delete key to delete characters to the right of the insertion point. Then type the correct text. To correct a field name by replacing it entirely, press the Esc key, and then type the correct text.

Trouble? The entire field name "Contract Num" might not be visible on your screen. You'll learn how to resize columns to display the full field names later in this tutorial.

You have renamed the default primary key field, ID, to Contract Num. However, the Contract Num field still maintains the characteristics of the ID field, including its data type. Your next task is to change the data type of this field.

Changing the Data Type of the Default Primary Key Field

Notice the Data Type & Formatting group on the Datasheet tab. One of the options available in this group is the Data Type option (see Figure 1-7). Each field in an Access table must be assigned a data type. The **data type** determines what field values you can enter for the field. In this case, the AutoNumber data type is displayed. Access assigns the AutoNumber data type to the default ID primary key field because the **AutoNumber** data type automatically inserts a unique number in this field for every record. Therefore, it can serve as the primary key for any table you create.

Contract numbers at Belmont Landscapes are specific, four-digit numbers, so the AutoNumber data type is not appropriate for the Contract Num field, which is the new primary key field in the table you are creating. A better choice is the **Text** data type, which allows field values containing letters, digits, and other characters, and which is appropriate for identifying numbers, such as contract numbers, that are never used in calculations. So, Oren asks you to change the data type for the Contract Num field from AutoNumber to Text.

To change the data type for the Contract Num field:

▶ 1. Make sure that the Contract Num column is selected (the column heading should have an orange background).

Trouble? If the background color of the Contract Num column heading is not orange, click the Contract Num column to select it.

▶ 2. In the Data Type & Formatting group on the Datasheet tab, click the **Data Type arrow**, and then click **Text**. The Contract Num field is now a Text field. See Figure 1-8.

Text data type assigned to the Contract Num field | Figure 1-8

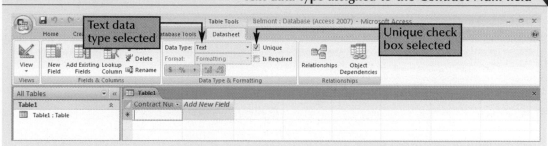

Note the Unique check box in the Data Type & Formatting group. This check box is selected because the Contract Num field assumed the characteristics of the default primary key field, ID, including the fact that each value in the field must be unique. No two records in the Contract table will be allowed to have the same value in the Contract Num field.

With the Contract Num field created and established as the primary key, you can now enter the field names for the rest of the fields in the Contract table. (In Tutorial 2, you'll learn more about the different data types in Access and how to work with them.)

Entering Field Names

When you create a table in Datasheet view, you type the field names as the column headings, and enter the field values for each record in a row. Oren requests that you enter eight records in the Contract table, as shown in Figure 1-9.

Contract table records | Figure 1-9

Contract Num	Customer ID	Contract Amt	Signing Date	Contract Type
3011	11001	$4,000	2/9/2010	Residential landscape plan
3026	11038	$165,000	3/11/2010	Landscape plans for large-scale housing development
3012	11027	$300	2/18/2010	Consultation for backyard, residential
3015	11005	$1,500	3/1/2010	Schematic plan for backyard, residential
3022	11043	$22,000	4/14/2010	Landscape design for two entrances
3017	11012	$2,250	3/1/2010	Peer plan review for town
3023	11070	$39,000	3/22/2010	Renovation of large multifamily housing open space
3021	11040	$28,000	5/3/2010	Landscape plans for multifamily housing site

To enter the rest of the field names for the Contract table:

▶ **1.** Double-click the column heading **Add New Field**. The insertion point replaces the text "Add New Field" in the column heading and is ready for you to type the field name for the second field in the table.

▶ **2.** Type **Customer ID**. Notice that the field name is displayed in italics while you type, signifying this is a new field name you are entering. See Figure 1-10.

Figure 1-10 | **Customer ID field name entered in column heading**

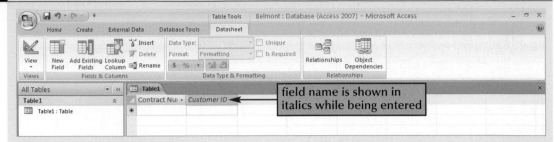

▶ **3.** Press the **Tab** key. The insertion point moves to the next column and is ready for you to enter the next field name.

▶ **4.** Type **Contract Amt** and then press the **Tab** key. Like the Contract Num field name, the Contract Amt field name might not be completely visible. You will resize all the columns to fully display the field names after you finish entering them.

▶ **5.** Type **Signing Date**, press the **Tab** key, type **Contract Type**, and then press the **Tab** key. The datasheet now contains the five fields for the Contract table.

Several of the field names are not completely visible, so you need to resize the datasheet columns.

▶ **6.** Place the pointer on the vertical line between the Contract Num and Customer ID field names until the pointer changes to a ✛ shape.

▶ **7.** Double-click the pointer. The Contract Num column is resized and now displays the full field name.

Trouble? If you click the arrow immediately to the right of the Contract Num column heading by mistake, a menu will open. Simply click the arrow again to close the menu, and then repeat Steps 6 and 7.

▶ **8.** Double-click the ✛ pointer on the vertical line to the right of the Customer ID, Contract Amt, Signing Date, and Contract Type column headings to resize the columns in the datasheet. Your datasheet should now look like the one shown in Figure 1-11.

Figure 1-11 | **Table with field names entered**

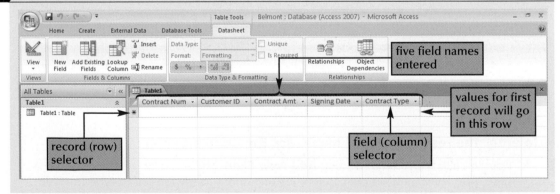

As noted earlier, Datasheet view shows a table's contents in rows (records) and columns (fields). Each column is headed by a field name inside a field selector, and each row has a record selector to its left (see Figure 1-11). Clicking a **field selector** or a **record selector** selects that entire column or row (respectively), which you then can manipulate. A field selector is also called a **column selector**, and a record selector is also called a **row selector**.

With the field names in place, you can now enter the records for the Contract table (see Figure 1-9).

Entering Records

To enter records in a table datasheet, you type the field values below the column headings for the fields. As shown in Figure 1-11, the first record you enter will go in the first row below the field names.

To enter the first record for the Contract table:

▶ **1.** Click in the first row for the Contract Num field, type **3011** (the Contract Num field value for the first record), and then press the **Tab** key. Access adds the field value and moves the insertion point to the right, in the Customer ID column. See Figure 1-12.

First field value entered　　　　**Figure 1-12**

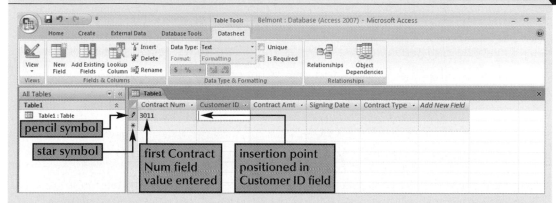

Trouble? If you make a mistake when typing a value, use the Backspace key to delete characters to the left of the insertion point or the Delete key to delete characters to the right of the insertion point. Then type the correct value. To correct a value by replacing it entirely, press the Esc key, and then type the correct value.

Notice the pencil symbol that appears in the row selector for the new record. The **pencil symbol** indicates that the record is being edited. Also notice the star symbol that appears in the row selector for the second row. The **star symbol** identifies the second row as the next row available for a new record.

▶ **2.** Type **11001** (the Customer ID field value for the first record), and then press the **Tab** key. Access enters the field value and moves the insertion point to the Contract Amt column.

▶ **3.** Type **$4,000** (the Contract Amt field value for the first record), and then press the **Tab** key. Notice that Access formats the field value with two decimal places, displaying it as "$4,000.00" even though you did not enter the value this way. You'll learn more about formatting field values later in this text.

Trouble? If Access does not change the value $4,000 to $4,000.00 when you press the Tab key and go to the next field, click the Contract Amt field value, click the Data Type arrow in the Data Type & Formatting group, and then click Currency in the list. Press the Tab key and continue with Step 4.

▶ **4.** Type **2/9/2010** (the Signing Date field value for the first record), and then press the **Tab** key.

Trouble? If your date value is left-aligned in the column after you press the Tab key and go to the next field, instead of right-aligned, click the Signing Date field value, click the Data Type arrow in the Data Type & Formatting group, and then click Date/Time in the list. Press the Tab key and continue with Step 5.

▶ **5.** Type **Residential landscape plan** (the Contract Type field value for the first record), and then press the **Tab** key. The first record is entered into the table, and the insertion point is positioned in the Contract Num field for the second record. The table is now ready for you to enter the second record. See Figure 1-13.

Figure 1-13 | **Datasheet with first record entered**

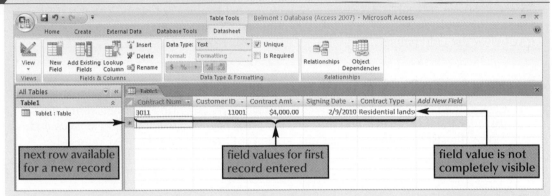

Trouble? Depending on your Windows date setting, your Signing Date field values might be displayed in a different format. This difference will not cause any problems.

Note that the Contract Type field value is not completely displayed. Again, you'll resize the columns, as necessary, after you enter all the data.

InSight | **Understanding How Access Interprets Values Entered**

When you create a table by entering field names and records directly into the table in Datasheet view, Access automatically assigns each field a data type based on the field values you enter. Access also formats the field values accordingly. For example, when you entered the value "$4,000" for the first record in the Contract Amt field, Access interpreted the value as a currency value because you typed a dollar sign and comma in the value. Likewise, when you entered the value "2/9/2010" in the Signing Date field, Access interpreted the value as a date value. After you've entered the first record in this way, Access will continue to format the field values for subsequent records, making data entry easier for you. So, as you continue to enter Contract Amt field values, you don't have to type the dollar sign or comma every time; Access will insert them automatically for you because it "knows" that the Contract Amt field contains currency values. Similarly, as you continue to enter Signing Date field values, you don't have to type the complete year "2010" but can instead type only the final two digits, "10," and Access will automatically insert the full four digits for each year.

As you enter field values in a datasheet, you should verify that Access is assigning them the data type you plan to use. If Access does not correctly interpret the field values you enter, you can easily assign the correct data type using the Data Type option in the Data Type & Formatting group on the Datasheet tab.

Now you can enter the remaining seven records in the Contract table.

To enter the remaining records in the Contract table:

Tip

You can also press the Enter key instead of the Tab key to move from one field to another, and to the next row.

1. Referring to Figure 1-9, enter the values for records 2 through 8, pressing the **Tab** key to move from field to field and to the next row for a new record. Keep in mind that you do not have to type the dollar sign or comma in the Contract Amt values, because Access will add them automatically; also, you can type just the final two digits of the year in the Signing Date values, and Access will display the full four digits in each year value.

Trouble? If you enter a value in the wrong field by mistake, such as entering a Contract Type field value in the Contract Amt field, a menu will open with options for addressing the problem. If this happens, choose the "Enter new value" option on the menu. You'll return to the field with the incorrect value highlighted, which you can then replace by typing the correct value.

To see more of the table datasheet and the full field values, you'll close the Navigation Pane and resize the Contract Type column.

▶ 2. Click the **Shutter Bar Open/Close Button** « at the top of the Navigation Pane. The Navigation Pane closes, and the window displays the complete table datasheet.

▶ 3. Place the pointer on the vertical line to the right of the Contract Type field name until the pointer changes to a ↔ shape, and then double-click the pointer. All the Contract Type field values are now fully displayed. See Figure 1-14.

Datasheet with eight records entered | Figure 1-14

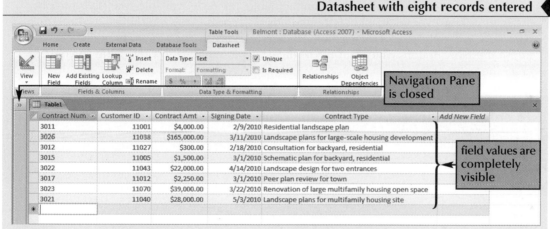

Trouble? If any of the field values on your screen do not match those shown in the figure, you can correct a field value by clicking to position the insertion point in the value, and then using the Backspace key or Delete key to delete incorrect text. Then type the correct text and press the Enter key.

Saving a Table

After you add fields and records to a table, you need to save the table's design. The records you enter are immediately stored in the database as soon as you enter them; however, the table's design—the field names and characteristics of the fields themselves—are not saved until you save the table. When you save a new table for the first time, you should give it a name that best identifies the information it contains. Like a field name, a table name can be up to 64 characters long, including spaces.

Saving a Table | Reference Window

- Click the Save button on the Quick Access Toolbar. The Save As dialog box opens.
- In the Table Name text box, type the name for the table.
- Click the OK button.

Now you need to save the table and give it the name "Contract."

To save and name the Contract table:

► **1.** Click the **Save** button 🔲 on the Quick Access Toolbar. The Save As dialog box opens.

► **2.** With the default name Table1 selected in the Table Name text box, type **Contract**, and then click the **OK** button. The tab for the table now displays the name "Contract," and the Contract table design is saved in the Belmont database.

Tip

You can also choose the Save option from the Office menu to save and name a new table.

Notice that after you saved and named the Contract table, Access reordered the records in the table so that they appear in order by the values in the Contract Num field, because it is the primary key. If you compare your screen to Figure 1-9, which shows the records in the order you entered them, you'll see that the current screen shows the records in order by the Contract Num field values.

Oren asks you to add two more records to the Contract table. When you add a record to an existing table, you must enter the new record in the next row available for a new record; you cannot insert a row between existing records for the new record. In a table with just a few records, such as the Contract table, the next available row is visible on the screen. However, in a table with hundreds of records, you would need to scroll the datasheet to see the next row available. The easiest way to add a new record to a table is to use the New button, which scrolls the datasheet to the next row available so you can enter the new record.

To enter additional records in the Contract table:

► **1.** Click in the first record's Contract Num field value (3011) to make it the current record.

► **2.** Click the **Home** tab on the Ribbon.

► **3.** In the Records group, click the **New** button. The insertion point is positioned in the next row available for a new record, which in this case is row 9. See Figure 1-15.

Figure 1-15 | **Entering a new record**

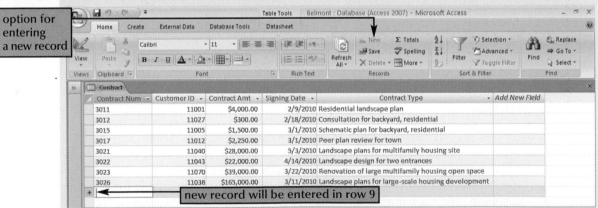

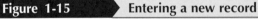

► **4.** With the insertion point in the Contract Num field for the new record, type **3020**, and then press the **Tab** key.

► **5.** Complete the entry of this record by entering each value shown below, pressing the Tab key to move from field to field:

Customer ID = **11055**
Contract Amt = **6500**
Signing Date = **2/19/10**
Contract Type = **Landscape design for restaurant**

▶ **6.** Enter the values for the next new record, as follows:

Contract Num = **3025**
Customer ID = **11083**
Contract Amt = **15500**
Signing Date = **3/25/10**
Contract Type = **Landscape renovation for plaza**

Your datasheet should now look like the one shown in Figure 1-16.

Datasheet with additional records entered ◀ **Figure 1-16**

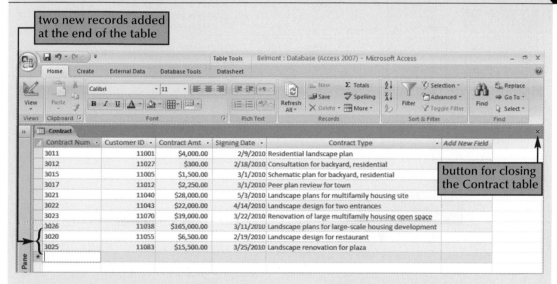

The new records you added appear at the end of the table, and are not in the correct primary key order. For example, Contract Num 3020 should be the fifth record in the table, placed between Contract Num 3017 and Contract Num 3021. When you add records to a table datasheet, they appear at the end of the table. The records are not displayed in primary key order until you close and reopen the table, or switch between views.

▶ **7.** Click the **Close 'Contract'** button ☒ on the table window bar (see Figure 1-16 for the location of this button). The table closes, and the main portion of the Access window is now blank because no database object is currently open.

Opening a Table

Any table you create and save is listed in the Navigation Pane. You open a table, or any Access object (query, form, report), by simply double-clicking the object name in the Navigation Pane. Next, you'll open the Contract table so you can see the order of all the records you've entered.

To open the Contract table:

▶ **1.** On the Navigation Pane, click the **Shutter Bar Open/Close Button** ⟩⟩ to open the pane. Note that the Contract table is listed.

▶ **2.** Double-click **Contract : Table** to open the table in Datasheet view. See Figure 1-17.

Tip

Each record contains a unique Contract Num value because this field is the primary key. Other fields, however, can contain the same value in multiple records; for example, note the two values of 3/1/2010 in the Signing Date field.

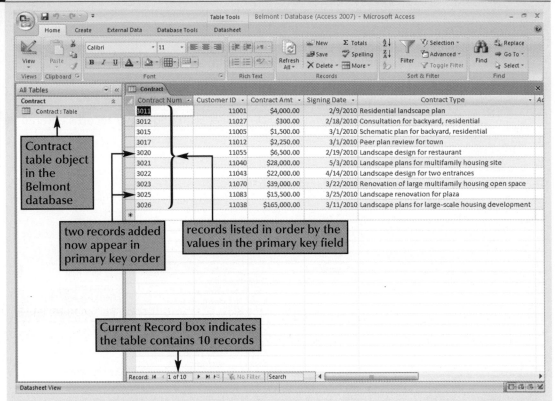

The two records you added, with Contract Num field values of 3020 and 3025, now appear in the correct primary key order. The table now contains a total of 10 records, as indicated by the Current Record box at the bottom of the datasheet. The **Current Record box** displays the number of the current record as well as the total number of records in the table.

Tip

To close an open database without exiting the Access program, click the Office Button, and then click Close Database.

▶ 3. If you are not continuing on to Session 1.2, click the **Close** button ⊠ on the program window title bar. Access closes the Contract table and the Belmont database, and then the Access program closes.

Saving a Database | InSight

Notice the Save button on the Quick Access Toolbar. Unlike the Save buttons in other Office programs, this Save button does not save the active document (database) to your disk. Instead, you use the Save button to save the design of an Access object, such as a table (as you saw earlier), or to save datasheet format changes, such as resizing columns. Access does not have a button or option you can use to save the active database. Similarly, you cannot use the Save As option on the Office menu to save the active database file with a new name, as you can with other Office programs.

Access saves changes to the active database to your disk automatically when you change or add a record or close the database. If your database is stored on a removable medium, such as a USB drive, you should never remove the drive while the database file is open. If you do, Access will encounter problems when it tries to save the database, which might damage the database.

Now that you've become familiar with database concepts and Access, and created the Belmont database and the Contract table, Oren wants you to add more records to the table and work with the data stored in it to create database objects including a query, form, and report. You will complete these tasks in Session 1.2.

Session 1.1 Quick Check | Review

1. A(n) _____ is a single characteristic of a person, place, object, event, or idea.
2. You connect the records in two separate tables through a(n) _____ that appears in both tables.
3. The _____ , whose values uniquely identify each record in a table, is called a(n) _____ when it is placed in a second table to form a relationship between the two tables.
4. The _____ is the area of the Access window that lists all the objects in a database, and it is the main control center for opening and working with database objects.
5. Which field does Access create, by default, as the primary key field for all new datasheets?
6. What does a pencil symbol at the beginning of a record represent? A star symbol?
7. Explain how the saving process in Access is different from saving in other Office programs.

Session 1.2

Copying Records from Another Access Database

When you created the Contract table, you entered records directly into the table datasheet. There are many other ways to enter records in a table, including copying and pasting records from a table in the same database or in a different database. To use this method, however, the tables must have the same structure—that is, the tables must contain the same fields, with the same design and characteristics, in the same order.

Oren has already created a table named Agreement that contains additional records with contract data. The Agreement table is contained in a database named "Oren" located in the Level.01\Tutorial folder included with your Data Files. The Agreement table has the same table structure as the Contract table you created. Your next task is to copy the records from the Agreement table and paste them into your Contract table. To do so, you need to open the Oren database.

Reference Window | **Opening a Database**

- Start Access and display the Getting Started with Microsoft Office Access page.
- Click the More option to display the Open dialog box.
- Navigate to the database file you want to open, and then click the file.
- Click the Open button.

To copy the records from the Agreement table:

▶ 1. If you took a break after the previous session, make sure that the Belmont database is open, and the Contract table is open in Datasheet view.

▶ 2. In the Navigation Pane, click the **Shutter Bar Open/Close Button** « to close the pane (if necessary) and display more of the table datasheet.

   To open a second database, you need to start Access again.

▶ 3. Click the **Start** button 🔵 on the taskbar, click **All Programs**, click **Microsoft Office**, and then click **Microsoft Office Access 2007**. The Getting Started with Microsoft Office Access page opens.

   To open an existing database, you use the More option in the Open Recent Database section on the right side of the page.

▶ 4. Click **More** to display the Open dialog box.

▶ 5. Navigate to the drive that contains your Data Files.

▶ 6. Navigate to the **Level.01\Tutorial** folder, click the database file named **Oren**, and then click the **Open** button. The Oren database opens in a second Access window. Note that the database contains only one object, the Agreement table.

   Trouble? A Security Warning might appear below the Ribbon; this warning cautions you about opening databases that could contain content that might harm your computer. Because the Oren database does not contain objects that could be harmful, you can open it safely. Click the Options button next to the Security Warning. In the dialog box that opens, click the "Enable this content" option button, and then click the OK button.

▶ 7. In the Navigation Pane, double-click **Agreement : Table** to open the Agreement table in Datasheet view. The table contains 55 records and the same five fields, with the same characteristics, as the fields in the Contract table. See Figure 1-18.

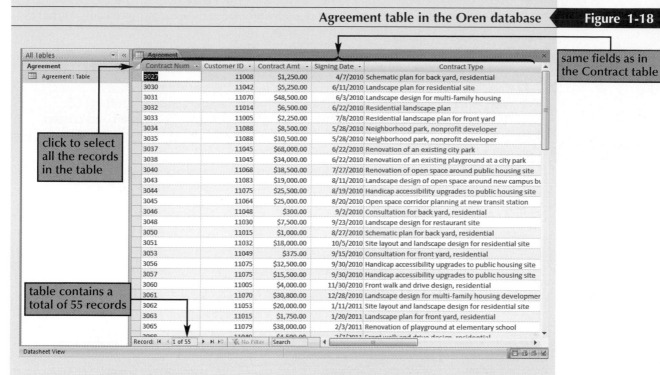

Agreement table in the Oren database — Figure 1-18

Oren wants you to copy all the records in the Agreement table. You can select all the records by clicking the **datasheet selector**, which is the box to the left of the first field name in the table datasheet (see Figure 1-18).

8. Click the datasheet selector to the left of the Contract Num field. Access selects all the records in the table.

9. In the Clipboard group on the Home tab, click the **Copy** button 📄. All the records are copied to the Clipboard.

10. Click the **Close 'Agreement'** button ✕ on the table window bar. A dialog box opens asking if you want to save the data you copied to the Clipboard.

11. Click the **Yes** button in the dialog box. The dialog box closes, and then the table closes.

12. Click the **Close** button ✕ on the Access window title bar to close the Oren database and the second Access program window.

With the records copied to the Clipboard, you can now paste them into the Contract table.

To paste the records into the Contract table:

1. With the Belmont database's Contract table open in Datasheet view, position the pointer on the row selector for row 11, the next row available for a new record, until the pointer changes to a ➡ shape, and then click to select the row.

   Trouble? If you have difficulty displaying the correct pointer shape, click in an empty area of the table datasheet to establish the window as the active window. Then repeat Step 1.

▶ **2.** In the Clipboard group on the Home tab, click the **Paste** button. The pasted records are added to the table, and a dialog box opens asking you to confirm that you want to paste all the records (55 total).

Trouble? If the Paste button isn't active, click the pointer on the row selector for row 11, making sure the entire row is selected, and then repeat Step 2.

▶ **3.** Click the **Yes** button. The dialog box closes, and the pasted records are highlighted. See Figure 1-19. Notice that the table now contains a total of 65 records—10 records that you entered and 55 records that you copied and pasted.

| Figure 1-19 | Contract table after copying and pasting records |

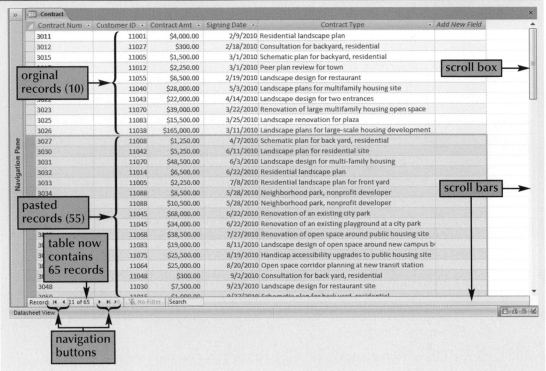

Navigating a Datasheet

The Contract table now contains 65 records, but only some of the records are visible on the screen. To view fields or records not currently visible in the datasheet, you can use the horizontal and vertical scroll bars shown in Figure 1-19 to navigate the data. The **navigation buttons**, also shown in Figure 1-19, provide another way to move vertically through the records. The Current Record box appears between the two sets of navigation buttons and displays the number of the current record as well as the total number of records in the table. Figure 1-20 shows which record becomes the current record when you click each navigation button. Note the New (blank) record button, which works in the same way as the New button on the Home tab you used earlier to enter a new record in the table.

Navigation Button	Record Selected	Navigation Button	Record Selected
⏮	First record	⏭	Last record
◄	Previous record	⏯	New (blank) record
►	Next record		

Oren suggests that you use the various navigation techniques to move through the Contract table and become familiar with its contents.

To navigate the Contract datasheet:

▶ **1.** Click in the first record's Contract Num field value (3011). The Current Record box shows that record 1 is the current record.

▶ **2.** Click the **Next record** navigation button ► . The second record is now highlighted, which identifies it as the current record. Also, notice that the second record's value for the Contract Num field is selected, and the Current Record box displays "2 of 65" to indicate that the second record is the current record.

▶ **3.** Click the **Last record** navigation button ⏭ . The last record in the table, record 65, is now the current record.

▶ **4.** Drag the scroll box in the vertical scroll bar (see Figure 1-19) up to the top of the bar. Notice that record 65 is still the current record, as indicated in the Current Record box. Dragging the scroll box changes the display of the table datasheet, but does not change the current record.

▶ **5.** Drag the scroll box in the vertical scroll bar back down so that you can see the end of the table and the current record (record 65).

▶ **6.** Click the **Previous record** navigation button ◄ . Record 64 is now the current record.

▶ **7.** Click the **First record** navigation button ⏮ . The first record is now the current record.

Tip

You can make a field the current field by clicking anywhere within the column for that field.

The Contract table now contains all the data about the customer contracts for Belmont Landscapes. To better understand how to work with this data, Oren asks you to create simple objects for the other main types of database objects—queries, forms, and reports.

Creating a Simple Query

A **query** is a question you ask about the data stored in a database. In response to a query, Access displays the specific records and fields that answer your question. When you create a query, you tell Access which fields you need and what criteria Access should use to select the records. Then Access displays only the information you want, so you don't have to navigate through the entire database for the information. In the Contract table, for example, Oren might create a query to display only those records for contracts that were signed in a specific month. Even though a query can display table information in a different way, the information still exists in the table as it was originally entered.

Oren wants to focus on the amount of each contract and the contract type. He doesn't want the list to include all the fields in the Contract table (such as Customer ID and Signing Date). To produce this list for Oren, you need to create a query based on the Contract table.

You can design your own queries or use an Access Query Wizard, which guides you through the steps to create a query. The **Simple Query Wizard** allows you to select records and fields quickly, and is an appropriate choice for producing the contract list Oren wants.

To start the Simple Query Wizard:

▶ **1.** Click the **Create** tab on the Ribbon. The Create tab provides options for creating database objects—tables, forms, reports, queries, and so on. See Figure 1-21.

| Figure 1-21 | Create tab on the Ribbon |

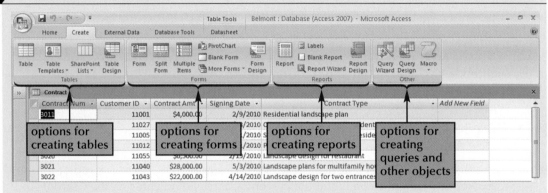

▶ **2.** In the Other group on the Create tab, click the **Query Wizard** button. The New Query dialog box opens.

▶ **3.** Make sure **Simple Query Wizard** is selected, and then click the **OK** button. The first Simple Query Wizard dialog box opens. See Figure 1-22.

| Figure 1-22 | First Simple Query Wizard dialog box |

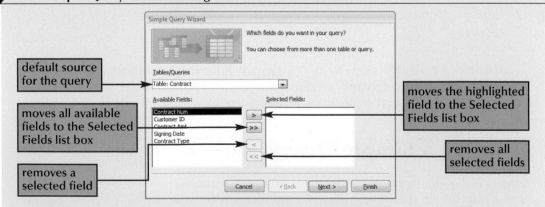

Because the Contract table is the only object in the Belmont database, it is listed in the Tables/Queries box by default. If the database contained more objects, you could click the Tables/Queries arrow and choose another table or a query as the basis for the new query you are creating. The Available Fields list box lists all the fields in the Contract table.

You need to select fields from the Available Fields list box to include them in the query. To select fields one at a time, click a field and then click the $\boxed{>}$ button. The selected field moves from the Available Fields list box on the left to the Selected Fields list box on the right. To select all the fields, click the $\boxed{>>}$ button. If you change your mind or make a mistake, you can remove a field by clicking it in the Selected Fields list box and then clicking the $\boxed{<}$ button. To remove all selected fields, click the $\boxed{<<}$ button.

Each Simple Query Wizard dialog box contains buttons on the bottom that allow you to move to the previous dialog box (Back button), move to the next dialog box (Next button), or cancel the creation process (Cancel button). You can also finish creating the object (Finish button) and accept the wizard's defaults for the remaining options.

Oren wants his list to include data from only the following fields: Contract Num, Contract Amt, and Contract Type. You need to select these fields to include them in the query.

To create the query using the Simple Query Wizard:

▶ 1. Click **Contract Num** in the Available Fields list box to select the field (if necessary), and then click the $\boxed{>}$ button. The Contract Num field moves to the Selected Fields list box.

▶ 2. Repeat Step 1 for the fields **Contract Amt** and **Contract Type**, and then click the **Next** button. The second Simple Query Wizard dialog box opens and asks if you want a detail or summary query. This dialog box opens when the values in one of the fields selected for the query could be used in calculations—in this case, the Contract Amt field. Oren wants to see every field of every record and does not want to perform summary calculations on the Contract Amt field values, so you need to create a detail query.

▶ 3. Make sure the **Detail** option button is selected, and then click the **Next** button. The third, and final, Simple Query Wizard dialog box opens and asks you to choose a name (title) for your query. Access suggests the name "Contract Query" because the query you are creating is based on the Contract table. You'll change the suggested name to "Contract List."

▶ 4. Click at the end of the suggested name, use the **Backspace** key to delete the word "Query," and then type **List**. Now you can view the query results.

▶ 5. Click the **Finish** button to complete the query. Access displays the query results in Datasheet view, on a new tab named "Contract List." A query datasheet is similar to a table datasheet, showing fields in columns and records in rows—but only for those fields and records you want to see, as determined by the query specifications you select.

▶ 6. Place the pointer on the vertical line to the right of the Contract Type field name until the pointer changes to a ⟷ shape, and then double-click the pointer. All the Contract Type field values are now fully displayed. See Figure 1-23.

Tip

You can also double-click a field to move it from the Available Fields list box to the Selected Fields list box.

Figure 1-23 **Query results**

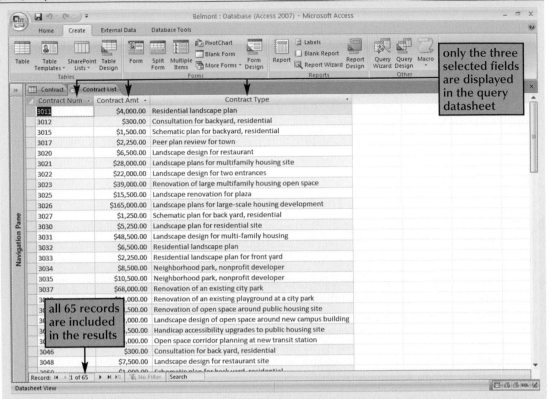

The Contract List query datasheet displays the three selected fields for each record in the Contract table. The fields are shown in the order you selected them in the Simple Query Wizard, from left to right. The records are listed in order by the primary key field, Contract Num. Even though the datasheet displays only the three fields you chose for the query, the Contract table still includes all the fields for all records.

Notice that the navigation buttons are located at the bottom of the window. You navigate a query datasheet in the same way that you navigate a table datasheet.

▶ **7.** Click the **Last record** navigation button ▶|. The last record in the query datasheet is now the current record.

▶ **8.** Click the **Previous record** navigation button ◀. Record 64 in the query datasheet is now the current record.

▶ **9.** Click the **First record** navigation button |◀. The first record is now the current record.

▶ **10.** Click the **Close 'Contract List'** button ✕ on the table window bar. A dialog box opens asking if you want to save the changes to the layout of the query. This dialog box opens because you resized the Contract Type column.

▶ **11.** Click the **Yes** button to save the query layout changes and close the query.

The query results are not stored in the database; however, the query design is stored as part of the database with the name you specified. You can re-create the query results at any time by opening the query again. You'll learn more about creating and working with queries in Tutorial 3.

Next, Oren asks you to create a form for the Contract table so that Belmont Landscapes employees can use the form to enter and work with data in the table easily.

Creating a Simple Form

A **form** is an object you use to enter, edit, and view records in a database. Although you can perform these same functions with tables and queries, forms can present data in many customized and useful ways. In Access, there are many different ways to create a form. You can design your own forms, use the Form Wizard (which guides you through the process of creating a form), or use the Form tool to create a simple form with one mouse click. The **Form tool** creates a form containing all the fields in the table or other database object on which you're basing the form.

Oren wants a form for the Contract table that shows all the fields for one record at a time, with fields listed one below another in a column. This type of form will make it easier for his staff to focus on all the data for a particular contract. You'll use the Form tool to create this form quickly and easily.

To create the form using the Form tool:

► 1. Make sure the Contract table is still open in Datasheet view. The table or other database object you're using as the basis for the form must either be open or selected in the Navigation Pane when you use the Form tool.

   Trouble? If the Contract table is not open, click the Shutter Bar Open/Close Button ⟩⟩ to open the Navigation Pane. Then double-click Contract : Table to open the Contract table in Datasheet view. Click the Shutter Bar Open/Close Button ⟨⟨ again to close the pane.

► 2. In the Forms group on the Create tab, click the **Form** button. The Form tool creates a simple form showing every field in the Contract table and places it on a tab named "Contract." Access assigns the name "Contract" because the form is based on the Contract table. See Figure 1-24.

Form created by the Form tool ◄ **Figure 1-24**

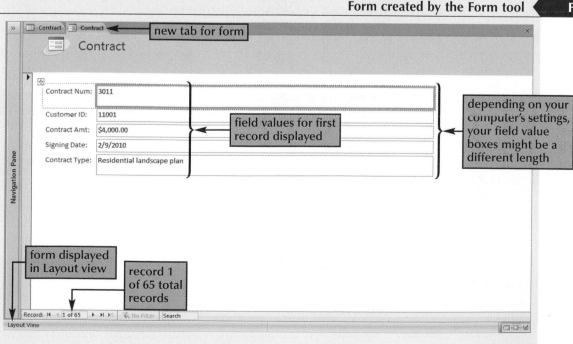

The form displays one record at a time in the Contract table, providing another view of the data that is stored in the table and allowing you to focus on the values for one record. Access displays the field values for the first record in the table and selects the first field value (Contract Num) by placing a border around the value. Each field name appears on a separate line and on the same line as its field value, which appears in a box to the right. Depending on your computer's settings, the field value boxes in your form might be shorter or longer than those shown in the figure. As indicated in the status bar, the form is displayed in Layout view. In **Layout view**, you can make design changes to the form while it is displaying data, so that you can see the effects of the changes you make immediately.

To view and maintain data using a form, you must know how to move from field to field and from record to record. Notice that the form contains navigation buttons, similar to those available in Datasheet view, which you can use to display different records in the form. You'll use these now to navigate the form; then you'll save and close the form.

To navigate, save, and close the form:

▶ 1. Click the **Next record** navigation button ▶. The form now displays the values for the second record in the Contract table.

▶ 2. Click the **Last record** navigation button ▶❙ to move to the last record in the table. The form displays the information for contract number 3110.

▶ 3. Click the **Previous record** navigation button ◀ to move to record 64.

▶ 4. Click the **First record** navigation button ❙◀ to return to the first record in the Contract table.

   Next, you'll save the form with the name "Contract Data" in the Belmont database. Then the form will be available for later use.

▶ 5. Click the **Save** button 🖫 on the Quick Access Toolbar. The Save As dialog box opens.

▶ 6. In the Form Name text box, click at the end of the highlighted word "Contract," press the **spacebar**, type **Data**, and then press the **Enter** key. Access saves the form as Contract Data in the Belmont database and closes the dialog box. The tab containing the form now displays the name "Contract Data."

▶ 7. Click the **Close 'Contract Data'** button ☒ on the form window bar to close the form.

InSight | **Saving Database Objects**

In general, it is best to save a database object—query, form, or report—only if you anticipate using the object frequently or if it is time consuming to create, because these objects use storage space on your disk. For example, a form you create with the Form tool would most likely not be saved, since you can re-create it easily with one mouse click. (However, for the purposes of this text, you need to save the objects you create.)

After attending a staff meeting, Oren returns with another request. He would like to see the information in the Contract table presented in a more readable format. You'll help Oren by creating a report.

Creating a Simple Report

A **report** is a formatted printout (or screen display) of the contents of one or more tables in a database. As with forms, you can design your own reports, use a Report Wizard to guide you through the steps of creating a report, or use the Report tool to create a simple report with one mouse click.

To produce the report for Oren, you'll use the Report tool, which is similar to the Form tool you used earlier to create the Contract Data form. The **Report tool** places all the fields from a selected table (or query) on a report, making it the quickest way to create a report.

To create the report using the Report tool:

▶ **1.** With the Contract table open in Datasheet view, click the **Create** tab on the Ribbon.

▶ **2.** In the Reports group on the Create tab, click the **Report** button. The Report tool creates a simple report showing every field in the Contract table and places it on a tab named "Contract." Again, Access assigns this name because the object you created (the report) is based on the Contract table. See Figure 1-25.

Report created by the Report tool — **Figure 1-25**

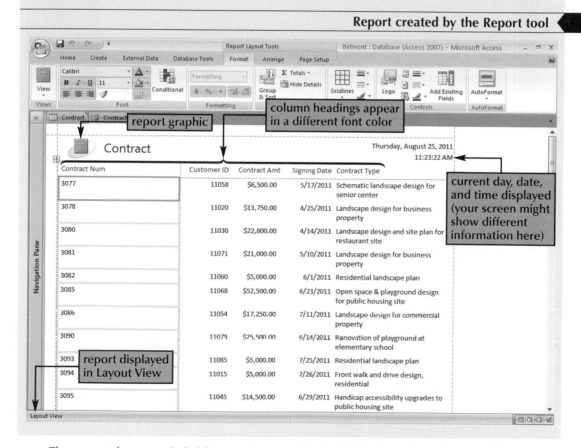

The report shows each field in a column, with the field values for each record in a row, similar to a datasheet. However, the report offers a more visually appealing format for the data, with the column headings in a different color and a line separating them from the records, a graphic of a report at the top left, and the current day, date, and time at the top right. The report is displayed in Layout view, which doesn't show how many pages there are in the report. To see this, you need to switch to Print Preview.

To view the report in Print Preview:

▶ **1.** In the Views group on the Report Layout Tools Format tab, click the **View button arrow**, and then click **Print Preview**. The first page of the report is displayed in Print Preview. See Figure 1-26.

Figure 1-26 | First page of the report in Print Preview

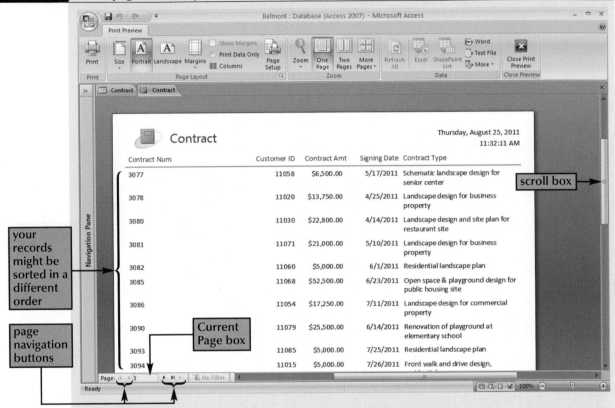

Print Preview shows exactly how the report will look when printed. Notice that Print Preview provides page navigation buttons at the bottom of the window, similar to the navigation buttons you've used to move through records in a table, query, and form.

▶ **2.** Click the **Next Page** navigation button ▶. The second page of the report is displayed in Print Preview.

▶ **3.** Click the **Last Page** navigation button ▶| to move to the last page of the report.

▶ **4.** Drag the scroll box in the vertical scroll bar (see Figure 1-26) down until the bottom of the report page is displayed. The notation "Page 3 of 3" appears at the bottom of the page, indicating that you are on page 3 out of a total of 3 pages in the report. See Figure 1-27.

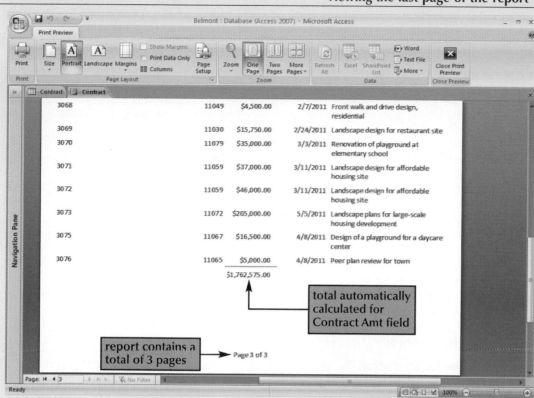

Trouble? Depending on the printer you are using, your report might have more or fewer pages, and some of the pages might be blank. If so, don't worry. Different printers format reports in different ways, sometimes affecting the total number of pages and the number of records printed per page.

Notice the total amount shown at the end of the report for the Contract Amt field. The Report tool calculated this amount and displayed it on the report. Often, you want to include such information as summaries and totals in a report; in this case, the Report tool generated it for you automatically.

5. Click the **First Page** navigation button to return to the first page of the report, and then drag the scroll box in the vertical scroll bar back up so that the top of the report is displayed.

Next you'll save the report as "Contract Details," and then close it.

6. Click the **Save** button on the Quick Access Toolbar. The Save As dialog box opens.

7. In the Report Name text box, click at the end of the highlighted word "Contract," press the **spacebar**, type **Details**, and then press the **Enter** key. Access saves the report as Contract Details in the Belmont database and closes the dialog box. The tab containing the report now displays the name "Contract Details."

Printing a Report

After creating a report, you typically print it to distribute it to others who need to view the report's contents. You use the Print command available from the Office menu to print a report.

Printing a Report

- Open the report in any view, or select the report in the Navigation Pane.
- To print the report with the default print settings, click the Office Button, point to Print, and then click Quick Print.

or

- To display the Print dialog box and select the options you want for printing the report, click the Office Button, point to Print, and then click Print (or, if the report is displayed in Print Preview, click the Print button in the Print group on the Print Preview tab).

Oren asks you to print the entire report, so you'll use the Quick Print option available from the Office Button menu.

Note: To complete the following steps, your computer must be connected to a printer.

To print the report:

▶ 1. Click the **Office Button** 🖱, point to **Print**, and then click **Quick Print**. The report prints with the default print settings.

   Trouble? If your report did not print, make sure that your computer is connected to a printer, and that the printer is turned on and ready to print. Then repeat Step 1.

▶ 2. Click the **Close 'Contract Details'** button ⊠ on the report window bar to close the report.

▶ 3. Click the **Close 'Contract'** button ⊠ on the table window bar to close the Contract table.

You can also use the Print dialog box to print other database objects, such as table and query datasheets. Most often, these objects are used for viewing and entering data, and reports are used for printing the data in a database.

Viewing Objects in the Navigation Pane

The Belmont database now contains four objects—the Contract table, the Contract List query, the Contract Data form, and the Contract Details report. You can view and work with these objects in the Navigation Pane.

To view the objects in the Belmont database:

▶ 1. Click the **Shutter Bar Open/Close Button** 》 on the Navigation Pane to open the pane. See Figure 1-28.

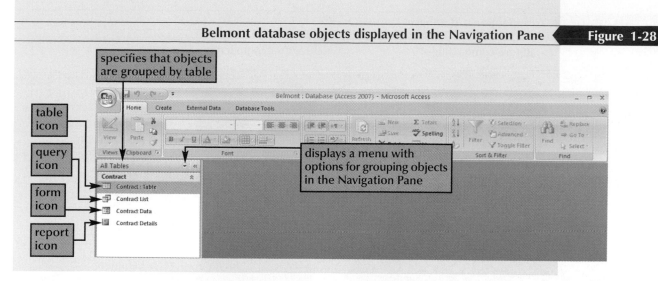

Belmont database objects displayed in the Navigation Pane | Figure 1-28

The Navigation Pane currently displays the default view, **All Tables**, which groups objects according to the tables in the database. Note the bar containing the word "Contract" in the pane; this bar is a heading for the Contract table, which is the only table in the Belmont database. Below the bar, all the objects related to the Contract table, including the table itself, are listed. Each database object—the Contract table, the Contract List query, the Contract Data form, and the Contract Details report—has a unique icon to its left to indicate the type of object. This makes it easy for you to identify the objects and choose which one you want to open and work with.

The arrow on the All Tables bar displays a menu with options for various ways to group and display objects in the Navigation Pane. As you continue to build the Belmont database and add more objects to it in later tutorials, you'll learn how to use the options in this menu.

Managing a Database

One of the main tasks involved in working with database software is managing your databases and the data they contain. By managing your databases, you can ensure that they operate in the most efficient way, that the data they contain is secure, and that you can work with the data effectively. Some of the activities involved in database management include compacting and repairing a database and backing up and restoring a database.

Compacting and Repairing a Database

Whenever you open an Access database and work in it, the size of the database increases. Further, when you delete records and when you delete or replace database objects—such as queries, forms, and reports—the space that had been occupied on the disk by the deleted or replaced records or objects does not automatically become available for other records or objects. To make the space available, you must compact the database. **Compacting** a database rearranges the data and objects in a database to decrease its file size, thereby making more space available on your disk and letting you open and close the database more quickly. Figure 1-29 illustrates the compacting process.

Figure 1-29 Compacting a database

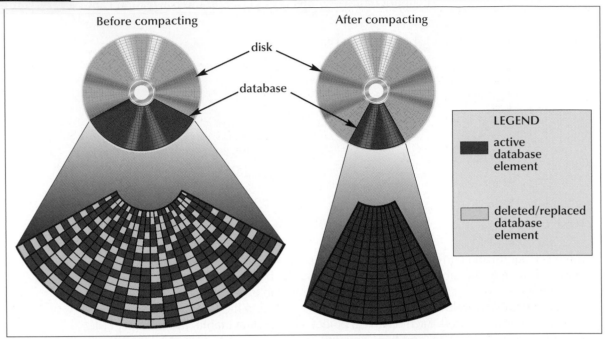

When you compact a database, Access repairs the database at the same time. In many cases, Access detects that a database is damaged when you try to open it and gives you the option to compact and repair it at that time. For example, the data in your database might become damaged, or corrupted, if you exit the Access program suddenly by turning off your computer. If you think your database might be damaged because it is behaving unpredictably, you can use the "Compact and Repair Database" option to fix it.

Reference Window | Compacting and Repairing a Database

- Make sure the database file you want to compact and repair is open.
- Click the Office Button, point to Manage, and then click Compact and Repair Database.

Access also allows you to set an option for your database file so that every time you close the database, it will be compacted automatically. The Compact on Close option is available in the Current Database section of the Access Options dialog box, which you open by clicking the Office Button and then clicking the Access Options button. By default, the Compact on Close option is off.

Next, you'll compact the Belmont database manually using the Compact and Repair Database option. This will make the database a much smaller and more manageable size. After compacting the database, you'll close it.

To compact and repair the Belmont database:

▶ **1.** Click the **Office Button** 🏢, and then point to **Manage**.

   Trouble? Check with your instructor before selecting the option to compact and repair the database. If your instructor tells you not to select this option, click the Exit Access button on the Office menu.

▶ **2.** Click **Compact and Repair Database**. Although nothing visible happens on screen, Access compacts the Belmont database, making it smaller, and repairs it at the same time.

▶ **3.** Click the **Close** button ☒ on the program window title bar. Access closes the Belmont database. Then the Access program window closes.

Backing Up and Restoring a Database

Backing up a database is the process of making a copy of the database file to protect your database against loss or damage. Experienced database users make it a habit to back up a database before they work with it for the first time, keeping the original data intact, and to make frequent backups while continuing to work with a database. Most users back up their databases on tapes, USB drives, recordable CDs or DVDs, or hard disks. Also, it is recommended to store the backup copy in a different location from the original. For example, if the original database is stored on a USB drive, you should not store the backup copy on the same USB drive. If you lose the drive, the original database and its backup copy would both be lost.

The Back Up Database command enables you to back up your database file from within the Access program, while you are working on your database. To use this option, you click the Office Button, point to the Manage option, and then choose Back Up Database. In the resulting Save As dialog box, Access provides a default filename for the backup copy that consists of the same filename as the database you are backing up (for example, "Belmont") plus the current date. This filenaming system makes it easy for you to keep track of your database backups and when they were created.

To restore a backup database file, you simply copy the backup from the drive on which it is stored to your hard drive, or whatever device you use to work in Access, and start working with the restored database file. If the original database file and the backup copy have the same name, restoring the backup copy might replace the original. If you want to save the original file, rename it before you restore the backup copy. To ensure that the restored database has the most current data, you should update the restored database with any changes made to the original between the time it became damaged or lost and the time you created the backup copy. (You will not actually back up the Belmont database in this tutorial.)

With the Contract table in place, you can continue to build the Belmont database so that Oren and his staff members can use it to store, manipulate, and retrieve important data for Belmont Landscapes. In the following tutorials, you'll help Oren complete and maintain the database, and you'll use it to meet the specific information needs of the firm's employees.

Review | **Session 1.2 Quick Check**

1. True or False: You can copy records from any Access database table and paste them in another table.
2. A(n) _____ is a question you ask about the data stored in a database.
3. The quickest way to create a form is to use the _____ .
4. To see the total number of pages in a report and navigate through the report pages, you need to display the report in _____ .
5. In the Navigation Pane, each database object has a unique _____ to its left that identifies the object's type.
6. _____ a database rearranges the data and objects in a database to decrease its file size.
7. _____ a database is the process of making a copy of the database file to protect the database against loss or damage.

Review | **Tutorial Summary**

In this tutorial, you learned the basic concepts associated with databases, including how data is organized in a database and the functions of a relational database management system. You also learned how to create a new blank database, and how to create a table in Datasheet view by entering field names and records. You learned the function of the primary key and its role in the design of a table. To complete the table, you copied and pasted records from another Access database table with the same design. You used the Simple Query Wizard to display only certain fields and their values. Using the Form tool and the Report tool, you learned how to create simple forms and reports quickly in order to view and work with the data stored in a table in different ways. Finally, you were introduced to some of the important tasks involved in managing a database, including compacting and backing up a database.

Key Terms

Access	Datasheet view	query
Access window	field	record
Add New Field column	field selector	record selector
All Tables (view)	field value	relational database
AutoNumber	foreign key	relational database manage-
backing up	form	ment system
column selector	Form tool	report
common field	ID column	Report tool
compacting	Layout view	row selector
Current Record box	Microsoft Access window	Simple Query Wizard
data type	Microsoft Office Access 2007	star symbol
database	navigation buttons	table
database management	Navigation Pane	template
system (DBMS)	pencil symbol	Text (data type)
datasheet	primary key	
datasheet selector	Print Preview	

| Practice | Review Assignments |

Take time to practice the skills you learned in the tutorial using the same case scenario.

Data File needed for the Review Assignments: Provider.accdb

In the Review Assignments, you'll create a new database to contain information about the suppliers that Belmont Landscapes works with on its landscape design projects. Complete the following steps:

1. Create a new blank database named **Supplier**, and save it in the Level.01\Review folder provided with your Data Files.

2. In Datasheet view for the Table1 table, rename the default ID primary key field to **Company ID**. Change the data type of the Company ID field to Text.

3. Add the following 10 fields to the new table in the order shown: **Company Name**, **Product Type**, **Address**, **City**, **State**, **Zip**, **Phone**, **Contact First Name**, **Contact Last Name**, and **Initial Contact Date**. Resize the columns as necessary so that the complete field names are displayed. Save the table as **Company**.

4. Enter the records shown in Figure 1-30 in the Company table. As you enter the field values for the first record, use the Data Type option in the Data Type & Formatting group on the Datasheet tab to confirm that all the fields use the Text data type, except for the Zip field (which should have the Number data type) and the Initial Contact Date field (which should have the Date/Time data type). If necessary, make any changes so the fields have the correct data types.

Figure 1-30

Company ID	Company Name	Product Type	Address	City	State	Zip	Phone	Contact First Name	Contact Last Name	Initial Contact Date
AND225	Anderson OnSite	Site furnishings	200 Lincoln Dr	Kalamazoo	MI	49007	269-337-9266	Matt	Anderson	6/3/2009
HOL292	Holland Nursery	Plants	380 W 20th St	Holland	MI	49424	616-396-9330	Brenda	Ehlert	9/2/2010
BES327	Best Paving	Pavers	780 N Main St	Rockford	MI	49341	616-866-6364	Shirley	Hauser	2/14/2010
MID312	Midwest Lighting	Outdoor lighting	435 Central Dr	Battle Creek	MI	49014	269-979-3970	Weston	Caldwell	5/15/2009
BAC200	Backyard Structures	Play equipment	105 E 8th St	Holland	MI	49423	616-396-3989	Alan	Bastian	4/15/2009

5. Oren created a database named Provider that contains a Business table with supplier data. The Company table you created has the same design as the Business table. Copy all the records from the **Business** table in the **Provider** database (located in the Level.01\Review folder provided with your Data Files) to the end of the Company table in the Supplier database.

6. Resize all the columns in the datasheet so that all the field values are completely displayed, and then save the Company table.

7. Close the Company table, and then use the Navigation Pane to reopen it. Note that the records are displayed in primary key order.

8. Use the Simple Query Wizard to create a query that includes the Company Name, Product Type, Contact First Name, Contact Last Name, and Phone fields (in that order) from the Company table. Name the query **Company List**, and then close the query.

9. Use the Form tool to create a form for the Company table. Save the form as **Company Info**, and then close it.

10. Use the Report tool to create a report based on the Company table. Save the report as **Company Details**, and then close it.
11. Close the Company table, and then compact and repair the Supplier database.
12. Close the Supplier database.

| Apply | **Case Problem 1** |

Use the skills you learned in the tutorial to create a database for a small music school.

Data File needed for this Case Problem: School.accdb

Pine Hill Music School   After giving private piano lessons from her home for several years, Yuka Koyama founded the Pine Hill Music School in Portland, Oregon. Because of her popularity as a music teacher, Yuka attracted top-notch students, and her school quickly established a reputation for excellence. During the past two years, other qualified teachers have joined Yuka to offer instruction in voice, violin, cello, guitar, percussion, and other instruments. As her school continues to grow, Yuka wants to use Access to keep track of information about students, teachers, and contracts. You'll help Yuka create and maintain an Access database to store data about her school. Complete the following:

1. Create a new blank database named **Pinehill**, and save it in the Level.01\Case1 folder provided with your Data Files.
2. In Datasheet view for the Table1 table, rename the default primary key ID field to **Teacher ID**. Change the data type of the Teacher ID field to Text.
3. Add the following five fields to the new table in the order shown: **First Name**, **Last Name**, **Degree**, **School**, and **Hire Date**. Save the table as **Teacher**.
4. Enter the records shown in Figure 1-31 in the Teacher table. As you enter the field values for the first record, use the Data Type option in the Data Type & Formatting group on the Datasheet tab to confirm that all the fields use the Text data type, except for the Hire Date field, which should have the Date/Time data type. If necessary, make any changes so the fields have the correct data types.

Figure 1-31

Teacher ID	First Name	Last Name	Degree	School	Hire Date
13-1100	Yuka	Koyama	MM	Pacific University	1/13/2009
17-1798	Richard	Jacobson	PhD	Pacific University	1/15/2009
55-5310	Annamaria	Romano	BA	Lewis & Clark College	4/21/2009
22-0102	Andre	Dvorak	BM	University of Portland	3/3/2009
34-4506	Marilyn	Schwartz	BM	University of Portland	5/1/2009

5. Yuka created a database named School that contains a Faculty table with teacher data. The Teacher table you created has the same design as the Faculty table. Copy all the records from the **Faculty** table in the **School** database (located in the Level.01\Case1 folder provided with your Data Files) to the end of the Teacher table in the Pinehill database.
6. Resize all the columns in the datasheet so that all the field values are completely displayed, and then save the Teacher table.
7. Close the Teacher table, and then use the Navigation Pane to reopen it. Note that the records are displayed in primary key order.

8. Use the Simple Query Wizard to create a query that includes the First Name, Last Name, and Hire Date fields (in that order) from the Teacher table. Name the query **Start Date**, and then close the query.

9. Use the Form tool to create a form for the Teacher table. Save the form as **Teacher Info**, and then close it.

10. Use the Report tool to create a report based on the Teacher table. Save the report as **Teacher List**, print the report (only if asked by your instructor to do so), and then close it.

11. Close the Teacher table, and then compact and repair the Pinehill database.

12. Close the Pinehill database.

Apply | Case Problem 2

Apply what you learned in the tutorial to create a database for a new business in the health and fitness industry.

Data File needed for this Case Problem: Health.accdb

Parkhurst Health & Fitness Center After many years working in various corporate settings, Martha Parkhurst decided to turn her lifelong interest in health and fitness into a new business venture and opened the Parkhurst Health & Fitness Center in Richmond, Virginia. In addition to providing the usual fitness classes and weight training facilities, the center also offers specialized programs designed to meet the needs of athletes—both young and old—who participate in certain sports or physical activities. Martha's goal in establishing such programs is twofold: to help athletes gain a competitive edge through customized training, and to ensure the health and safety of all participants through proper exercises and physical preparation. Martha wants to use Access to maintain information about the members who have joined the center and the types of programs offered. She needs your help in creating this database. Complete the following:

1. Create a new blank database named **Fitness**, and save it in the Level.01\Case2 folder provided with your Data Files.

2. In Datasheet view for the Table1 table, rename the default primary key ID field to **Program ID**. Change the data type of the Program ID field to Text.

3. Add the following three fields to the new table in the order shown: **Program Type**, **Monthly Fee**, and **Physical Required**. Resize the columns as necessary so that the complete field names are displayed. Save the table as **Program**.

4. Enter the records shown in Figure 1-32 in the Program table. As you enter the field values for the first record, use the Data Type option in the Data Type & Formatting group on the Datasheet tab to confirm that all the fields use the Text data type, except for the Monthly Fee field, which should have the Currency data type. If necessary, make any changes so the fields have the correct data types.

Figure 1-32

Program ID	Program Type	Monthly Fee	Physical Required
201	Junior Full (ages 13-17)	$35.00	Yes
202	Junior Limited (ages 13-17)	$25.00	Yes
203	Young Adult Full (ages 18-25)	$45.00	No
204	Young Adult Limited (ages 18-25)	$30.00	No

5. Martha created a database named Health that contains a Class table with program data. The Program table you created has the same design as the Class table. Copy all the records from the **Class** table in the **Health** database (located in the Level.01\Case2 folder provided with your Data Files) to the end of the Program table in the Fitness database.

6. Resize all the columns in the datasheet so that all the field values are completely displayed, and then save the Program table.

7. Use the Simple Query Wizard to create a query that includes all the fields from the Program table. In the second Simple Query Wizard dialog box, select the Detail option. Resize the columns in the query datasheet so that all the field values are completely displayed, save the query as **Program Data**, and then close the query.

8. Use the Form tool to create a form for the Program table. Save the form as **Program Info**, and then close it.

9. Use the Report tool to create a report based on the Program table. Save the report as **Program List**, print the report (only if asked by your instructor to do so), and then close it.

10. Close the Program table, and then compact and repair the Fitness database.

11. Close the Fitness database.

| Challenge | **Case Problem 3** |

Use what you've learned, and expand your skills, to create a database containing information about an agency that recycles household goods.

Data File needed for this Case Problem: RRGroup.accdb

Rossi Recycling Group   The Rossi Recycling Group is a not-for-profit agency in Salina, Kansas that provides recycled household goods to needy people and families at no charge. Residents of Salina and surrounding communities donate cash and goods, such as appliances, furniture, and tools, to the Rossi Recycling Group. The group's volunteers then coordinate with local human services agencies to distribute the goods to those in need. The Rossi Recycling Group was established by Mary and Tom Rossi, who live on the outskirts of Salina on a small farm. Mary and Tom organize the volunteers to collect the goods and store the collected items in their barn for distribution. Tom wants to create an Access database to keep track of information about donors, their donations, and the human services agencies. Complete the following:

1. Create a new blank database named **Rossi**, and then save it in the Level.01\Case3 folder provided with your Data Files.

2. In Datasheet view for the Table1 table, rename the default primary key ID field to **Donor ID**. Change the data type of the Donor ID field to Text.

3. Add the following four fields to the new table in the order shown: **Title**, **First Name**, **Last Name**, and **Phone**. Resize the columns as necessary so that the complete field names are displayed. Save the table as **Donor**.

4. Enter the records shown in Figure 1-33 in the Donor table. As you enter the field values for the first record, use the Data Type option in the Data Type & Formatting group on the Datasheet tab to confirm that all the fields use the Text data type. If necessary, make any changes so the fields have the correct data types.

Figure 1-33

Donor ID	Title	First Name	Last Name	Phone
36012	Mr.	Joel	Martinson	785-823-9275
36016	Mr.	Doug	Showers	620-793-8477
36001	Mrs.	Janis	Fendrick	785-452-8736
36020	Mrs.	JoAnn	Randolph	785-309-6540
36019	Ms.	Connie	Springen	785-452-1178

5. Tom created a database named RRGroup that contains a Contributors table with data about donors. The Donor table you created has the same design as the Contributors table. Copy all the records from the **Contributors** table in the **RRGroup** database (located in the Level.01\Case3 folder provided with your Data Files) to the end of the Donor table in the Rossi database.

6. Resize all the columns in the datasheet so that all the field values are completely displayed, and then save the Donor table.

7. Close the Donor table, and then use the Navigation Pane to reopen it. Note that the records are displayed in primary key order.

⊕ **EXPLORE** 8. Use the Simple Query Wizard to create a query that includes all the fields in the Donor table *except* the Title field. (*Hint*: Use the ⟩⟩ and ⟨ buttons to select the necessary fields.) Save the query using the name **Donor Phone List**.

⊕ **EXPLORE** 9. The query results are displayed in order by the Donor ID field values. You can specify a different order by sorting the query. Display the Home tab. Then, click the insertion point anywhere within the Last Name column to make it the current field. In the Sort & Filter group on the Home tab, click the Ascending button. The records are now listed in order by the values in the Last Name field. Save and close the query.

⊕ **EXPLORE** 10. Use the Form tool to create a form for the Donor table. In the new form, navigate to record 8, and then print the form *for the current record only*. (*Hint*: You must use the Print dialog box in order to print only the current record. Click the Office Button, point to Print, and then click Print to open the Print dialog box. Click the Selected Record(s) option button and then click the OK button to print the current record.) Save the form as **Donor Info**, and then close it.

11. Use the Report tool to create a report based on the Donor table. Save the report as **Donor List**. Print the report (only if asked by your instructor to do so), and then close it.

12. Close the Donor table, and then compact and repair the Rossi database.

13. Close the Rossi database.

Challenge | **Case Problem 4**

Work with the skills you've learned, and explore some new skills, to create a database for a luxury rental company.

Data File needed for this Case Problem: Travel.accdb

GEM Ultimate Vacations As guests of a friend, Griffin and Emma MacElroy spent two weeks at a magnificent villa in the south of France. This unforgettable experience stayed with them upon returning to their home in a suburb of Chicago, Illinois. As a result, they decided to open their own agency, GEM Ultimate Vacations, which specializes in locating and booking luxury rental properties, primarily in Europe. Recently, Griffin and Emma expanded their business to include properties in Africa as well. From the beginning, Griffin and Emma used computers to help them manage all aspects of their business. They recently installed Access and now would like you to create a database to store information about guests, properties, and reservations. Complete the following:

1. Create a new blank database named **GEM**, and then save it in the Level.01\Case4 folder provided with your Data Files.

2. In Datasheet view for the Table1 table, rename the default primary key ID field to **Guest ID**. Change the data type of the Guest ID field to Text.

3. Add the following eight fields to the new table in the order shown: **Guest First Name**, **Guest Last Name**, **Address**, **City**, **State/Prov**, **Postal Code**, **Country**, and **Phone**. Resize the columns as necessary so that the complete field names are displayed. Save the table as **Guest**.

⊕ EXPLORE 4. Enter the records shown in Figure 1-34 in the Guest table. As you enter the field values for the first record, use the Data Type option in the Data Type & Formatting group on the Datasheet tab to confirm that all the fields use the Text data type, except for the Postal Code field, which should have the Number data type. If necessary, make any changes so the fields have the correct data types. When you type the Postal Code value for the fourth record, Access will open an error menu because you entered letters into a field that is formatted with the Number data type, which stores numbers that will be used in calculations. Because the postal codes will not be used in calculations, choose the option on the menu to convert the data in this column to the Text data type to continue.

Figure 1-34

Guest ID	Guest First Name	Guest Last Name	Address	City	State/Prov	Postal Code	Country	Phone
201	Michael	Miskowsky	153 Summer Ave	Evanston	IL	60201	USA	847-623-0975
203	Tom	Davis	5003 Wilson Blvd	Chicago	IL	60603	USA	312-897-4515
206	Li	Zhu	6509 Great Rd	Gary	IN	46401	USA	219-655-8109
202	Ingrid	Gorman	207 Riverside Dr West	Windsor	ON	N9A 5K4	Canada	519-977-8577
205	Richard	Nelson	34 Settlers Dr	Tinley Park	IL	60477	USA	708-292-4441

5. Emma created a database named Travel that contains a Client table with data about guests. The Guest table you created has the same design as the Client table. Copy all the records from the **Client** table in the **Travel** database (located in the Level.01\Case4 folder provided with your Data Files) to the end of the Guest table in the GEM database.

6. Resize all the columns in the datasheet so that all the field values are completely displayed, and then save the Guest table.

7. Close the Guest table, and then use the Navigation Pane to reopen it. Note that the records are displayed in primary key order.

8. Use the Simple Query Wizard to create a query that includes the following fields from the Guest table, in the order shown: Guest ID, Guest Last Name, Guest First Name, City, and Phone. Name the query **Guest Data**.

⊕ EXPLORE 9. The query results are displayed in order by the Guest ID field values. You can specify a different order by sorting the query. Display the Home tab. Then, click the insertion point anywhere within the Guest Last Name column to make it the current field. In the Sort & Filter group on the Home tab, click the Ascending button. The records are now listed in order by the values in the Guest Last Name field. Save and close the query.

⊕ EXPLORE 10. Use the Form tool to create a form for the Guest table. In the new form, navigate to record 12, and then print the form *for the current record only*. (*Hint*: You must use the Print dialog box in order to print only the current record. Click the Office Button, point to Print, and then click Print to open the Print dialog box. Click the Selected Record(s) option button and then click the OK button to print the current record.) Save the form as **Guest Info**, and then close it.

11. Use the Report tool to create a report based on the Guest table. Save the report as **Guest List**.

⊕ EXPLORE 12. Display the report in Print Preview. Use the Two Pages button in the Zoom group on the Print Preview tab to view both pages of the report at the same time. Use the Landscape button in the Page Layout group to change the orientation of the report to landscape. Print the report (only if asked by your instructor to do so), and then close it.

13. Close the Guest table, and then compact and repair the GEM database.

14. Close the GEM database.

Research | Internet Assignments

Use the Internet to find and work with data related to the topics presented in this tutorial.

The purpose of the Internet Assignments is to challenge you to find information on the Internet that you can use to work effectively with this software. The actual assignments are updated and maintained on the Course Technology Web site. Log on to the Internet and use your Web browser to go to the Student Online Companion for New Perspectives Office 2007 at **www.course.com/np/office2007**. Then navigate to the Internet Assignments for this tutorial.

Assess | SAM Assessment and Training

If you have a SAM user profile, you may have access to hands-on instruction, practice, and assessment of the skills covered in this tutorial. Log in to your SAM account (**http://sam2007.course.com**) to launch any assigned training activities or exams that relate to the skills covered in this tutorial.

Review | Quick Check Answers

Session 1.1

1. field
2. common field
3. primary key; foreign key
4. Navigation Pane
5. ID field
6. the record being edited; the next row available for a new record
7. Access saves changes to the active database to disk automatically, when a record is changed or added and when you close the database. You use the Save button in Access only to save changes to the design of an object, such as a table, or to the format of a datasheet—not to save the database file.

Session 1.2

1. False; to copy and paste records from one table to another, the tables must have the same structure—that is, the tables must contain the same fields, with the same characteristics, in the same order.
2. query
3. Form tool
4. Print Preview
5. icon
6. Compacting
7. Backing up

Ending Data Files

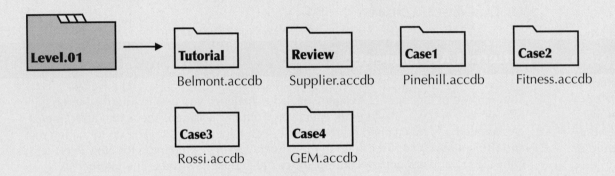

Level.01 → Tutorial — Belmont.accdb

Review — Supplier.accdb

Case1 — Pinehill.accdb

Case2 — Fitness.accdb

Case3 — Rossi.accdb

Case4 — GEM.accdb

Session 2.1
- Learn the guidelines for designing databases and setting field properties
- View and modify field data types and formatting
- Create a table in Design view
- Define fields and specify a table's primary key
- Modify the structure of a table

Session 2.2
- Import data from an Excel worksheet
- Create a table by importing an existing table structure
- Delete, rename, and move fields
- Add data to a table by importing a text file
- Define a relationship between two tables

Building a Database and Defining Table Relationships

Creating the Invoice and Customer Tables

Case | Belmont Landscapes

The Belmont database currently contains one table, the Contract table. Oren also wants to track information about the firm's customers, both residential and commercial, and the invoices sent to customers for services provided by Belmont Landscapes. This information includes such items as each customer's name and address and the invoice amount and invoice date.

In this tutorial, you'll create two new tables in the Belmont database—Invoice and Customer—to contain the data Oren wants to track. You will use two different methods for creating the tables, and learn how to modify the fields. After adding records to the tables, you will define the necessary relationships between the tables in the Belmont database to relate the tables, enabling Oren and his staff to work with the data more efficiently.

Starting Data Files

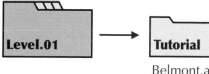

Level.01 →

Tutorial
Belmont.accdb (*cont.*)
Customer.txt
Invoices.xlsx
Sarah.accdb

Review
Goods.xlsx
Supplier.accdb (*cont.*)

Case1
Lessons.xlsx
Music.accdb
Pinehill.accdb (*cont.*)
Student.txt

Case2
Center.xlsx
Fitness.accdb (*cont.*)

Case3
Agency.txt
Gifts.xlsx
Recycle.accdb
Rossi.accdb (*cont.*)

Case4
Bookings.txt
GEM.accdb (*cont.*)
Overseas.accdb

Session 2.1

Guidelines for Designing Databases

A database management system can be a useful tool, but only if you first carefully design the database so that it meets the needs of its users. In database design, you determine the fields, tables, and relationships needed to satisfy the data and processing requirements. When you design a database, you should follow these guidelines:

- **Identify all the fields needed to produce the required information.** For example, Oren needs information about contracts, invoices, and customers. Figure 2-1 shows the fields that satisfy these information requirements.

Figure 2-1 ▶ **Oren's data requirements**

Contract Num	Contract Amt
Customer ID	Signing Date
Company	Invoice Date
First Name	Contract Type
Last Name	Phone
Address	Invoice Paid
City	Invoice Num
State	Invoice Amt
Zip	

- **Organize each piece of data into its smallest useful part.** For example, Oren could store each customer's complete name in one field called Customer Name instead of using two fields called First Name and Last Name, as shown in Figure 2-1. However, doing so would make it more difficult to work with the data. If Oren wanted to view the records in alphabetical order by last name, he wouldn't be able to do so with field values such as "Tom Cotter" and "Ray Yost" stored in a Customer Name field. He could do so with field values such as "Cotter" and "Yost" stored separately in a Last Name field.
- **Group related fields into tables.** For example, Oren grouped the fields related to contracts into the Contract table, which you created in Tutorial 1. The fields related to invoices are grouped into the Invoice table, and the fields related to customers are grouped into the Customer table. Figure 2-2 shows the fields grouped into all three tables for the Belmont database.

Figure 2-2 ▶ **Oren's fields grouped into tables**

Contract table	Invoice table	Customer table
Contract Num	Invoice Num	Customer ID
Customer ID	Contract Num	Company
Contract Amt	Invoice Amt	First Name
Signing Date	Invoice Date	Last Name
Contract Type	Invoice Paid	Phone
		Address
		City
		State
		Zip

- **Determine each table's primary key.** Recall that a primary key uniquely identifies each record in a table. Although a primary key is not mandatory in Access, it's a good idea to include one in each table. Without a primary key, selecting the exact record that you want can be a problem. For some tables, one of the fields, such as a Social Security or credit card number, naturally serves the function of a primary key. For other tables, two or more fields might be needed to function as the primary key. In these cases, the primary key is called a **composite key**. For example, a school grade table would use a combination of student number and course code to serve as the primary key. For a third category of tables, no single field or combination of fields can uniquely identify a record in a table. In these cases, you need to add a field whose sole purpose is to serve as the table's primary key. For Oren's tables, Contract Num is the primary key for the Contract table, Invoice Num is the primary key for the Invoice table, and Customer ID is the primary key for the Customer table.

- **Include a common field in related tables.** You use the common field to connect one table logically with another table. For example, Oren's Contract and Customer tables include the Customer ID field as a common field. Recall that when you include the primary key from one table as a field in a second table to form a relationship, the field is called a foreign key in the second table; therefore, the Customer ID field is a foreign key in the Contract table. With this common field, Oren can find all contracts for a particular customer; he can use the Customer ID value for a customer and search the Contract table for all records with that Customer ID value. Likewise, he can determine which customer has a particular contract by searching the Customer table to find the one record with the same Customer ID value as the corresponding value in the Contract table. Similarly, the Contract Num field is a common field, serving as the primary key in the Contract table and a foreign key in the Invoice table.

- **Avoid data redundancy.** When you store the same data in more than one place, **data redundancy** occurs. With the exception of common fields to connect tables, you should avoid redundancy because it wastes storage space and can cause inconsistencies. An inconsistency would exist, for example, if you type a field value one way in one table and a different way in the same table or in a second table. Figure 2-3, which contains portions of potential data stored in the Customer and Contract tables, shows an example of incorrect database design that has data redundancy in the Contract table. In Figure 2-3, the Company field in the Contract table is redundant, and one value for this field was entered incorrectly, in three different ways.

Figure 2-3   Incorrect database design with data redundancy

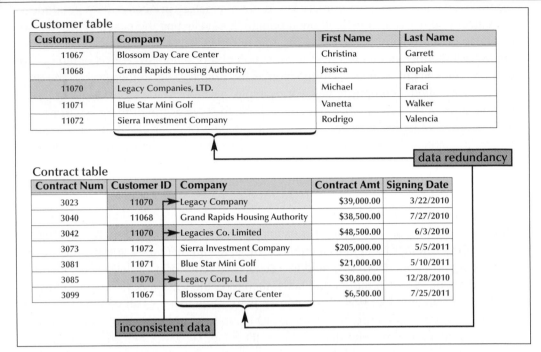

- **Determine the properties of each field.** You need to identify the **properties**, or characteristics, of each field so that the DBMS knows how to store, display, and process the field values. These properties include the field's name, maximum number of characters or digits, description, valid values, and other field characteristics. You will learn more about field properties later in this tutorial.

   The Invoice and Customer tables you need to create will contain the fields shown in Figure 2-2. Before you create these new tables in the Belmont database, you first need to learn some guidelines for setting field properties.

Guidelines for Setting Field Properties

As just noted, the last step of database design is to determine which values to assign to the properties, such as the name and data type, of each field. When you select or enter a value for a property, you **set** the property. Access has rules for naming fields, choosing data types, and setting other properties for fields.

Naming Fields and Objects

You must name each field, table, and other object in an Access database. Access then stores these items in the database, using the names you supply. It's best to choose a field or object name that describes the purpose or contents of the field or object so that later you can easily remember what the name represents. For example, the three tables in the Belmont database will be named Contract, Invoice, and Customer, because these names suggest their contents. Note that a table or query name must be unique within a database. A field name must be unique within a table, but it can be used again in another table. Refer to the "Guidelines for Naming Fields" InSight box in Tutorial 1 for a reminder of these guidelines, which apply to naming all database objects.

Assigning Field Data Types

Each field must have a data type, which is either assigned automatically by Access or specifically by the table designer. The **data type** determines what field values you can enter for the field and what other properties the field will have. For example, the Invoice table will include an Invoice Date field, which will store date values, so you will assign the Date/Time data type to this field. Then Access will allow you to enter and manipulate only dates or times as values in the Invoice Date field.

Figure 2-4 lists the data types available in Access, describes the field values allowed for each data type, explains when you should use each data type, and indicates the field size of each data type.

Data types for fields | Figure 2-4

Data Type	Description	Field Size
Text	Allows field values containing letters, digits, spaces, and special characters. Use for names, addresses, descriptions, and fields containing digits that are not used in calculations.	0 to 255 characters; default is 255
Memo	Allows field values containing letters, digits, spaces, and special characters. Use for long comments and explanations.	1 to 65,535 characters; exact size is determined by entry
Number	Allows positive and negative numbers as field values. Numbers can contain digits, a decimal point, commas, a plus sign, and a minus sign. Use for fields that will be used in calculations, except those involving money.	1 to 15 digits
Date/Time	Allows field values containing valid dates and times from January 1, 100 to December 31, 9999. Dates can be entered in month/day/year format, several other date formats, or a variety of time formats, such as 10:35 PM. You can perform calculations on dates and times, and you can sort them. For example, you can determine the number of days between two dates.	8 bytes
Currency	Allows field values similar to those for the Number data type, but is used for storing monetary values. Unlike calculations with Number data type decimal values, calculations performed with the Currency data type are not subject to round-off error.	Accurate to 15 digits on the left side of the decimal point and to 4 digits on the right side
AutoNumber	Consists of integer values created automatically by Access each time you create a new record. You can specify sequential numbering or random numbering, which guarantees a unique field value, so that such a field can serve as a table's primary key.	9 digits
Yes/No	Limits field values to yes and no, on and off, or true and false. Use for fields that indicate the presence or absence of a condition, such as whether an order has been filled or whether an invoice has been paid.	1 character
OLE Object	Allows field values that are created in other Microsoft Windows programs as objects, such as spreadsheets and word processing documents. These objects can be linked or embedded. Each field value is limited to a single file.	1 gigabyte maximum; exact size depends on object size
Hyperlink	Consists of text used as a hyperlink address, which can have up to four parts: the text that appears in a field or control; the path to a file or page; a location within the file or page; and text displayed as a ScreenTip.	Up to 65,535 characters total for the four parts of the Hyperlink data type
Attachment	Allows field values with one or more attached files, such as images, videos, documents, charts, and other supported files, similar to e-mail attachments. Provides greater flexibility than the OLE Object data type and uses storage space more efficiently.	2 gigabytes maximum; individual attached files cannot exceed 256 MB
Lookup Wizard	Creates a field that lets you look up a value in another table or in a predefined list of values.	Same size as the primary key field used to perform the lookup

Setting Field Sizes

The **Field Size property** defines a field value's maximum storage size for Text, Number, and AutoNumber fields only. The other data types have no Field Size property because their storage size is either a fixed, predetermined amount or is determined automatically by the field value itself, as shown in Figure 2-4. A Text field has a default field size of 255 characters; you can also set its field size by entering a number from 0 to 255. For example, the First Name and Last Name fields in the Customer table will be Text fields with a size of 20 characters and 25 characters, respectively. These field sizes will accommodate the values that will be entered in each of these fields.

InSight		**Understanding the Field Size Property for Number Fields**

When you use the Number data type to define a field, you should set the field's Field Size property based on the largest value that you expect to store in that field. Access processes smaller data sizes faster, using less memory, so you can optimize your database's performance and its storage space by selecting the correct field size for each field. Field Size property settings for Number fields are as follows:

- **Byte:** Stores whole numbers (numbers with no fractions) from 0 to 255 in one byte
- **Integer:** Stores whole numbers from −32,768 to 32,767 in two bytes
- **Long Integer** (default)**:** Stores whole numbers from −2,147,483,648 to 2,147,483,647 in four bytes
- **Single:** Stores positive and negative numbers to precisely seven decimal places and uses four bytes
- **Double:** Stores positive and negative numbers to precisely 15 decimal places and uses eight bytes
- **Replication ID:** Establishes a unique identifier for replication of tables, records, and other objects in databases created using Access 2003 and earlier versions and uses 16 bytes
- **Decimal:** Stores positive and negative numbers to precisely 28 decimal places and uses 12 bytes

For example, it would be wasteful to use the Long Integer field size for a Number field that will store only whole numbers ranging from 0 to 255, because the Long Integer field size uses four bytes of storage space. A better choice would be the Byte field size, which uses one byte of storage space to store the same values.

In Tutorial 1, you created the Belmont database and the Contract table. Access assigned the data types and field formatting for the fields you created in the Contract table based on the data you entered into each field in Datasheet view. Oren suggests that you view the data types and formatting of the fields in the Contract table to determine if you need to modify any of them to better store and format the data they contain.

Viewing and Modifying Field Data Types and Formatting

When you create a table in Datasheet view, such as the Contract table, you enter field (column) headings and field values in the rows below the headings. Access then determines what data type to assign to each field based on the values you enter for the field. If the values entered do not provide enough information for Access to "guess" the data type, the default type assigned is the Text data type.

Now, you'll open the Contract table in the Belmont database to view the data type and formatting for each field in Datasheet view.

To view the data type and formatting of the Contract table's fields:

▶ **1.** Start Access and open the **Belmont** database you created in Tutorial 1. This database file should be located in the Level.01\Tutorial folder provided with your Data Files.

Trouble? If the Security Warning is displayed below the Ribbon, click the Options button next to the Security Warning. In the dialog box that opens, click the "Enable this content" option button, and then click the OK button.

▶ **2.** In the Navigation Pane, double-click **Contract : Table** to open the Contract table in Datasheet view.

▶ **3.** On the Navigation Pane, click the **Shutter Bar Open/Close Button** « to close the pane and view more of the table datasheet.

You can view the data type and some properties for each field using the Datasheet tab.

▶ **4.** Click in the first field value for the **Contract Num** field to make it the current field, and then click the **Datasheet** tab on the Ribbon. The Data Type option in the Data Type & Formatting group indicates that the current field, Contract Num, has the Text data type. In Tutorial 1, you changed the data type for this field to Text after you created this field by renaming the default primary key ID field.

▶ **5.** Press the **Tab** key to move to the Customer ID field and make it the active field. This field has the Number data type. See Figure 2-5.

Data type for the Customer ID field	Figure 2-5

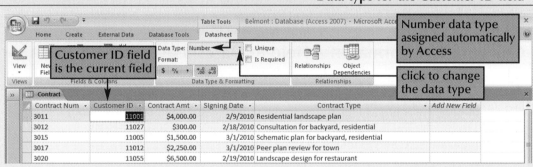

Access automatically assigned the Number data type to the Customer ID field when you created the Contract table in Tutorial 1. Because you entered numeric values in the field, such as 11001, Access determined that the field should be a Number field. However, the Number data type is best used for fields that will be used in mathematical calculations (except those involving money), or for numeric values that require a high degree of accuracy. The Customer ID field values will not be used in calculations; therefore, the Text data type is a better choice for this field.

Changing the Data Type of a Field in Datasheet View

As you learned in Tutorial 1, you can easily change the data type for a field in Datasheet view. Next, you'll change the data type of the Customer ID field to Text.

To change the data type of the Customer ID field:

▶ **1.** Make sure the Customer ID field is still the active field.

▶ **2.** In the Data Type & Formatting group on the Datasheet tab, click the **Data Type arrow**, and then click **Text**. The Customer ID field is now a Text field. See Figure 2-6.

Figure 2-6   **Customer ID field data type changed to Text**

Notice that the values in the Customer ID field now appear left-aligned within their boxes, as opposed to their previous right-aligned format (see Figure 2-5). In Access, values for Text fields are left-aligned, and values for Number, Date/Time, and Currency fields are right-aligned.

The next field in the Contract table, Contract Amt, contains dollar values representing the total amount of each Belmont Landscapes contract. Oren knows that these dollar amounts will never contain cents, because the contracts are drawn up in whole amounts only; therefore, the two decimal places currently shown for the values are unnecessary. Furthermore, Oren feels that the dollar signs clutter the datasheet and are also unnecessary. He asks you to modify the format of the Contract Amt field to remove the dollar signs and decimal places.

Changing the Format of a Field in Datasheet View

The Data Type & Formatting group on the Datasheet tab allows you to modify some formatting for certain field types. When you format a field, you change the way data is displayed, but not the actual values stored in the table. Next, you'll use the options provided to modify the format of the Contract Amt field. You'll also check the format of the Signing Date field and modify it, if necessary.

To modify the format of the Contract Amt and Signing Date fields:

1. With the Customer ID field still active, press the **Tab** key to move to the Contract Amt field. The options in the Data Type & Formatting group indicate that this field has the Currency data type and the Currency format. See Figure 2-7.

Figure 2-7   **Contract Amt field with the Currency data type**

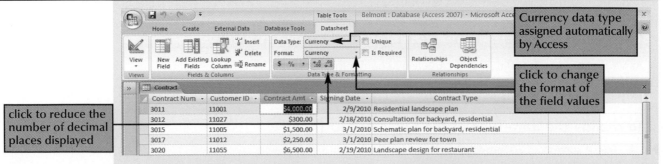

When you first entered the field values for the Contract Amt field in Tutorial 1, you included the dollar sign and commas; therefore, Access determined that this field should have the Currency data type, which is correct. The Currency format specifies that the values appear with dollar signs and two decimal places. You need to change this format to the Standard format, which does not contain dollar signs.

▶ 2. In the Data Type & Formatting group, click the **Format arrow**, and then click **Standard**. The dollar signs are removed, but the two decimal places are still displayed.

▶ 3. In the Data Type & Formatting group, click the **Decrease Decimals** button . Access decreases the decimal places by one, and the values now display only one decimal place.

▶ 4. Click the **Decrease Decimals** button again to remove the second decimal place and the decimal point. The Contract Amt field values are now displayed without dollar signs or decimal places. See Figure 2-8.

Contract Amt field values after modifying the format   **Figure 2-8**

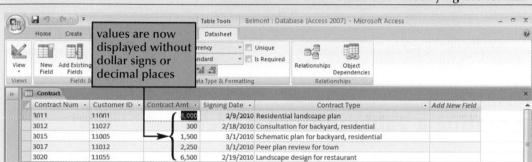

▶ 5. Press the **Tab** key to move to the Signing Date field. The Data Type option shows that this field is a Date/Time field. In Tutorial 1, when you entered date values in this field, Access automatically assigned the Date/Time data type to the field.

By default, Access assigns the General Date format to Date/Time fields. This format includes settings for date or time values, or a combination of date and time values. However, Oren wants only date values to appear in the Signing Date field, so he asks you to specify the Short Date format for the field.

▶ 6. In the Data Type & Formatting group, click the **Format arrow**, and then click **Short Date**. See Figure 2-9.

Signing Date field after modifying the format   **Figure 2-9**

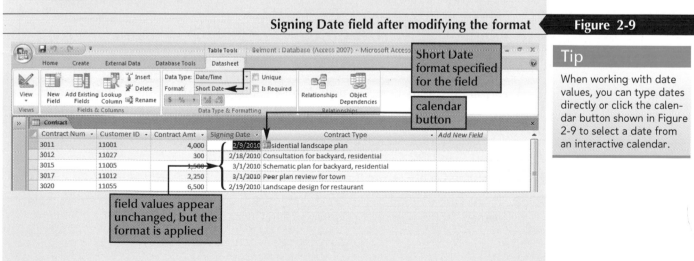

Tip

When working with date values, you can type dates directly or click the calendar button shown in Figure 2-9 to select a date from an interactive calendar.

Although no change is apparent in the worksheet—the Signing Date field values already appear with the Short Date setting (for example, 2/9/2010), as part of the default format—the field now has the Short Date format applied to it. This ensures that only date field values, and not time or date/time values, are allowed in the field.

▶ 7. Press the **Tab** key to move to the Contract Type field. Notice that Access assigned the Text data type to this field, which is correct because this field stores values with fewer than 255 characters.

Each of the three Text fields in this table—Contract Num, Customer ID, and Contract Type—has the default field size of 255. To change the field size, you need to work in Design view. You'll change the field sizes for these fields later in this session, after you learn more about Design view. For now, you can close the Contract table.

To close the Contract table:

▶ 1. Click the **Close 'Contract'** button ☒ on the table window bar.

According to his plan for the Belmont database, Oren wants to track information about the invoices the firm sends to its customers. Next, you'll create the Invoice table for Oren—this time, working directly in Design view.

Creating a Table in Design View

Creating a table in Design view involves entering the field names and defining the properties for the fields, specifying a primary key for the table, and then saving the table structure.

Oren documented the design for the new Invoice table by listing each field's name, data type, size (if applicable), and description, as shown in Figure 2-10.

Figure 2-10 ▷ **Design for the Invoice table**

Field Name	Data Type	Field Size	Description	Other
Invoice Num	Text	4	Primary key	
Contract Num	Text	4	Foreign key	
Invoice Amt	Currency			Format = Currency
				Decimal Places = 2
Invoice Date	Date/Time			Format = mm/dd/yyyy
Invoice Paid	Yes/No			

You will use Oren's design as a guide for creating the Invoice table in the Belmont database.

To begin creating the Invoice table:

▶ 1. Click the **Create** tab on the Ribbon.

▶ 2. In the Tables group on the Create tab, click the **Table Design** button. A new table named Table1 opens in Design view. See Figure 2-11.

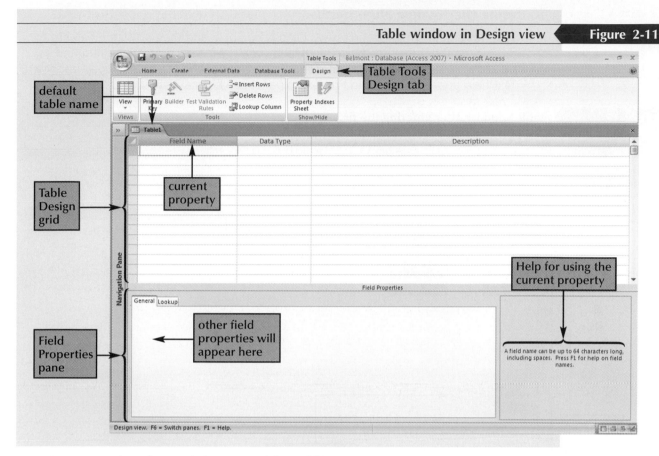

Table window in Design view   Figure 2-11

You use **Design view** to define or modify a table structure or the properties of the fields in a table.

Defining Fields

Initially, the default table name, Table1, appears on the tab for the new table, and the insertion point is located in the first row's Field Name box. After you type the field's name and press the Tab key to move to the Data Type box for the field, the purpose or characteristics of the current property (Field Name, in this case) will appear in the Field Properties pane. You can display more complete Help information about the current property by pressing the **F1 key**.

You enter values for the Field Name, Data Type, and Description field properties in the **Table Design grid**. You select values for all other field properties, most of which are optional, in the **Field Properties pane**. These other properties will appear when you move to the first row's Data Type box.

Defining a Field in Design View | Reference Window

- In the Field Name box, type the name for the field, and then press the Tab key.
- Accept the default Text data type, or click the arrow and select a different data type for the field. Press the Tab key.
- Enter an optional description for the field, if necessary.
- Use the Field Properties pane to type or select other field properties, as appropriate.

The first field you need to define is the Invoice Num field. This field will be the primary key for the Invoice table.

To define the Invoice Num field:

▶ 1. Type **Invoice Num** in the first row's Field Name box, and then press the **Tab** key to advance to the Data Type box. The default data type, Text, appears highlighted in the Data Type box, which now also contains an arrow, and the field properties for a Text field appear in the Field Properties pane. See Figure 2-12.

Figure 2-12	Table window after entering the first field name

Tip

You can also press the Enter key to move from one property to the next in the Table Design grid.

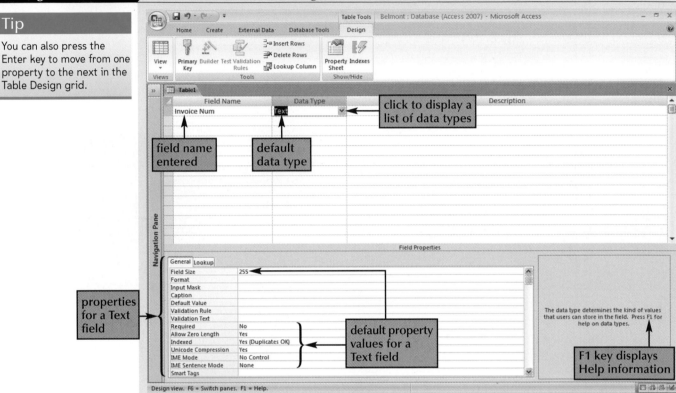

Notice that the right side of the Field Properties pane now provides an explanation for the current property, Data Type. You can display Help information about the current property by pressing the F1 key.

Trouble? If you make a typing error, you can correct it by clicking to position the insertion point, and then using either the Backspace key to delete characters to the left of the insertion point or the Delete key to delete characters to the right of the insertion point. Then type the correct text.

Because the Invoice Num field values will not be used in calculations, you will accept the default Text data type for the field.

▶ 2. Press the **Tab** key to accept Text as the data type and to advance to the Description box.

Next you'll enter the Description property value as "Primary key." You can use the **Description property** to enter an optional description for a field to explain its purpose or usage. A field's Description property can be up to 255 characters long, and its value appears on the status bar when you view the table datasheet. Note that specifying "Primary key" for the Description property does *not* establish the current field as the primary key; you use a button on the Ribbon to specify the primary key in Design view, which you will do later in this session.

▶ 3. Type **Primary key** in the Description box.

Notice the Field Size property for the field. The default setting of 255 for Text fields is displayed. You need to change this number to 4 because all invoice numbers at Belmont Landscapes contain only four digits.

▶ **4.** Double-click the number **255** in the Field Size property box to select it, and then type **4**. The definition of the first field is complete. See Figure 2-13.

Invoice Num field defined ◀ **Figure 2-13**

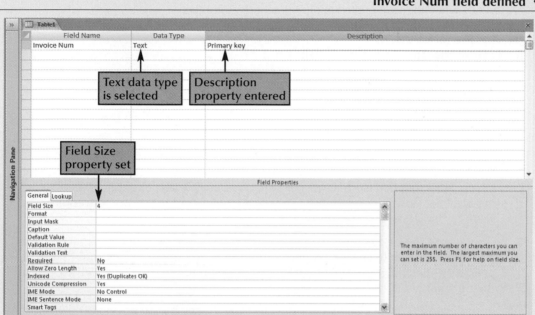

Oren's Invoice table design (Figure 2-10) shows Contract Num as the second field. Because Oren and other staff members want to relate information about invoices to the contract data in the Contract table, the Invoice table must include the Contract Num field, which is the Contract table's primary key. Recall that when you include the primary key from one table as a field in a second table to connect the two tables, the field is a foreign key in the second table. The field must be defined in the same way in both tables.

Next, you will define Contract Num as a Text field with a Field Size of 4. Later in this session, you will change the Field Size of the Contract Num field in the Contract table to 4 so that the field definition is the same in both tables.

To define the Contract Num field:

▶ **1.** In the Table Design grid, click in the second row's Field Name box, type **Contract Num** in the box, and then press the **Tab** key to advance to the Data Type box.

▶ **2.** Press the **Tab** key to accept Text as the field's data type. Because the Contract Num field is a foreign key to the Contract table, you'll enter "Foreign key" in the Description property to help users of the database understand the purpose of this field.

▶ **3.** Type **Foreign key** in the Description box.

Next, you'll change the Field Size property to 4. When defining the fields in a table, you can move between the Table Design grid and the Field Properties pane of the Table window by pressing the **F6** key.

▶ **4.** Press the **F6** key to move to the Field Properties pane. The current entry for the Field Size property, 255, is highlighted.

▶ **5.** Type **4** to set the Field Size property. You have completed the definition of the second field.

The third field in the Invoice table is the Invoice Amt field, which will display currency values, similar to the Contract Amt field in the Contract table. However, for this field, Oren wants the values to appear with two decimal places, because invoice amounts might include cents. He also wants the values to include dollar signs, so that the values will be formatted as currency when they are printed in reports sent to customers.

To define the Invoice Amt field:

▶ **1.** Click in the third row's Field Name box, type **Invoice Amt** in the box, and then press the **Tab** key to advance to the Data Type box.

▶ **2.** Click the **Data Type** arrow, click **Currency** in the list box, and then press the **Tab** key to advance to the Description box.

According to Oren's design (Figure 2-10), you do not need to enter a description for this field. If you've assigned a descriptive field name and the field does not fulfill a special function (such as primary key), you usually do not enter a value for the optional Description property. Invoice Amt is a field that does not require a value for its Description property.

Oren wants the Invoice Amt field values to be displayed with two decimal places, even if he decides to change the format for this field later. The **Decimal Places property** specifies the number of decimal places that are displayed to the right of the decimal point.

Tip

You can display the arrow and the list box simultaneously if you click the right side of a box.

▶ **3.** In the Field Properties pane, click the **Decimal Places** box to position the insertion point there. An arrow appears on the right side of the Decimal Places box. When you position the insertion point or select text in many Access boxes, Access displays an arrow, which you can click to display a list box with options.

▶ **4.** Click the **Decimal Places** arrow, and then click **2** in the list box to specify two decimal places for the Invoice Amt field values. The definition of the third field is now complete. See Figure 2-14.

Figure 2-14 ▶ **Table window after defining the first three fields**

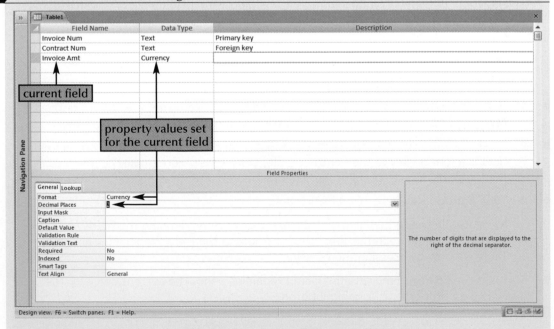

The next field you'll define in the Invoice table is Invoice Date. This field will contain the dates on which invoices are generated for Belmont Landscapes customers. When Belmont Landscapes first draws up contracts with its customers, the firm establishes invoice dates based on the different phases of the projects. For long-term projects with multiple phases, some of these dates are months or years in the future. You'll define the Invoice Date field using the Date/Time data type. Also, according to Oren's design (Figure 2-10), the date values should be displayed in the format mm/dd/yyyy, which is a two-digit month, a two-digit day, and a four-digit year.

To define the Invoice Date field:

1. Click in the fourth row's Field Name box, type **Invoice Date**, and then press the **Tab** key to advance to the Data Type box.

   You can select a value from the Data Type list box as you did for the Invoice Amt field. Alternately, you can type the property value in the box or type just the first character of the property value.

2. Type **d**. The value in the fourth row's Data Type box changes to "date/Time," with the letters "ate/Time" highlighted. See Figure 2-15.

Selecting a value for the Data Type property ◄ Figure 2-15

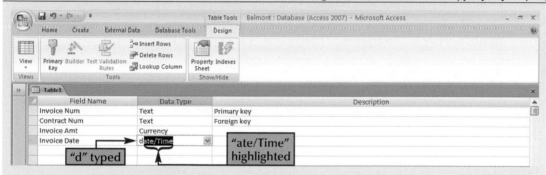

3. Press the **Tab** key to advance to the Description box. Note that Access changes the value for the Data Type property to "Date/Time."

   Oren wants the values in the Invoice Date field to be displayed in a format showing the month, the day, and a four-digit year, as in the following example: 03/11/2010. You use the Format property to control the display of a field value.

4. In the Field Properties pane, click the right side of the **Format** box to display the list of predefined formats for Date/Time fields. As noted in the right side of the Field Properties pane, you can either choose a predefined format or enter a custom format.

   Trouble? If you see an arrow instead of a list of predefined formats, click the arrow to display the list.

   None of the predefined formats matches the exact layout Oren wants for the Invoice Date values. Therefore, you need to create a custom date format. Figure 2-16 shows some of the symbols available for custom date and time formats.

> **Tip**
>
> A complete description of all the custom formats is available in Access Help.

Figure 2-16 **Symbols for some custom date formats**

Symbol	Description
/	date separator
d	day of the month in one or two numeric digits, as needed (1 to 31)
dd	day of the month in two numeric digits (01 to 31)
ddd	first three letters of the weekday (Sun to Sat)
dddd	full name of the weekday (Sunday to Saturday)
w	day of the week (1 to 7)
ww	week of the year (1 to 53)
m	month of the year in one or two numeric digits, as needed (1 to 12)
mm	month of the year in two numeric digits (01 to 12)
mmm	first three letters of the month (Jan to Dec)
mmmm	full name of the month (January to December)
yy	last two digits of the year (01 to 99)
yyyy	full year (0100 to 9999)

Oren wants the dates to be displayed with a two-digit month (mm), a two-digit day (dd), and a four-digit year (yyyy). You'll enter this custom format now.

▶ **5.** Click the **Format** arrow to close the list of predefined formats, and then type **mm/dd/yyyy** in the Format property box. See Figure 2-17.

Figure 2-17 **Specifying the custom date format**

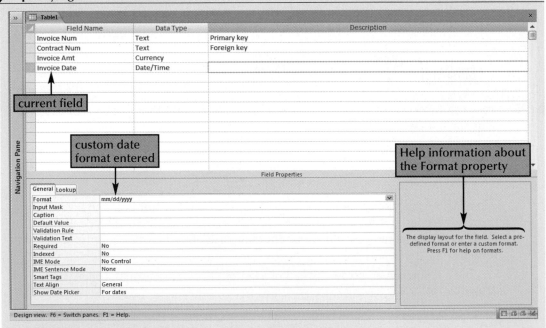

The fifth, and final, field to be defined in the Invoice table is Invoice Paid. This field will be a Yes/No field to indicate the payment status of each invoice record stored in the Invoice table.

To define the Invoice Paid field:

▶ **1.** Click in the fifth row's Field Name box, type **Invoice Paid**, and then press the **Tab** key to advance to the Data Type box.

▶ **2.** Type **y**. Access completes the data type as "yes/No."

▶ **3.** Press the **Tab** key to select the Yes/No data type and move to the Description box.

According to Oren's table design (see Figure 2-10), the Invoice Paid field does not have a description, so you've finished defining the fields for the Invoice table. Next, you need to specify the primary key for the table.

Specifying the Primary Key

As you learned in Tutorial 1, the primary key for a table uniquely identifies each record in a table.

Understanding the Importance of the Primary Key	InSight

Although Access does not require a table to have a primary key, including a primary key offers several advantages:

- A primary key uniquely identifies each record in a table.
- Access does not allow duplicate values in the primary key field. For example, if a record already exists in the Contract table with a Contract Num value of 3020, Access prevents you from adding another record with this same value in the Contract Num field. Preventing duplicate values ensures the uniqueness of the primary key field.
- When a primary key has been specified, Access forces you to enter a value for the primary key field in every record in the table. This is known as **entity integrity**. If you do not enter a value for a field, you have actually given the field a **null value**. You cannot give a null value to the primary key field because entity integrity prevents Access from accepting and processing that record.
- Access stores records on disk as you enter them. You can enter records in any order, but Access displays them by default in order by the field values of the primary key. If you enter records in no specific order, you are ensured that you will later be able to work with them in a more meaningful, primary key sequence.
- Access responds faster to your requests for specific records based on the primary key.

According to Oren's design, you need to specify Invoice Num as the primary key for the Invoice table. You can do so while the table is in Design view.

Specifying a Primary Key in Design View	Reference Window

- In the Table window in Design view, click in the row for the field you've chosen to be the primary key. If the primary key will consist of two or more fields, click the row selector for the first field, press and hold down the Ctrl key, and then click the row selector for each additional primary key field.
- In the Tools group on the Table Tools Design tab, click the Primary Key button.

To specify Invoice Num as the primary key:

▶ **1.** Click in the row for the Invoice Num field to make it the current field.

▶ **2.** In the Tools group on the Table Tools Design tab, click the **Primary Key** button. A key symbol appears in the row selector for the first row, indicating that the Invoice Num field is the table's primary key. See Figure 2-18.

| Figure 2-18 | Invoice Num field selected as the primary key |

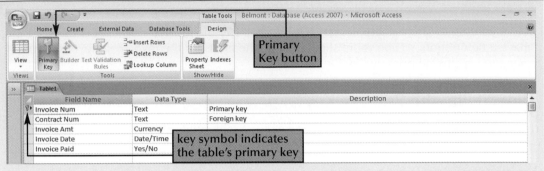

You've defined the fields for the Invoice table and specified its primary key, so you can now save the table structure.

Saving the Table Structure

The last step in creating a table is to name the table and save the table's structure. When you save a table structure, the table is stored in the database file (in this case, the Belmont database file). Once the table is saved, you can use it to enter data in the table. According to Oren's plan, you need to save the table you've defined as "Invoice."

To name and save the Invoice table:

▶ 1. Click the **Save** button 🔲 on the Quick Access Toolbar. The Save As dialog box opens.

▶ 2. Type **Invoice** in the Table Name text box, and then press the **Enter** key. Access saves the table with the name Invoice in the Belmont database. Notice that the tab for the table now displays the name "Invoice" instead of Table1.

Modifying the Structure of an Access Table

Even a well-designed table might need to be modified. Access allows you to modify a table's structure in Design view: you can change the order of fields, add and delete fields, and change field properties.

After meeting with Sarah Fisher, the office manager at Belmont Landscapes, and reviewing the structure of the Invoice table, Oren has changes he wants you to make to the table. First, he wants the Invoice Amt field to be moved so that it appears right before the Invoice Paid field. Then, he wants you to add a new Text field, named Invoice Item, to the table to include information about what the invoice is for, such as schematic landscape plans, construction documents, and so on. Oren would like the Invoice Item field to be inserted between the Invoice Date and Invoice Amt fields.

Moving a Field

To move a field, you use the mouse to drag it to a new location in the Table window in Design view. Next, you'll move the Invoice Amt field so that it is before the Invoice Paid field.

To move the Invoice Amt field:

▶ **1.** Position the pointer on the row selector for the Invoice Amt field until the pointer changes to a ➡ shape.

▶ **2.** Click the **row selector** to select the entire Invoice Amt row.

▶ **3.** Place the pointer on the row selector for the Invoice Amt field, click the ⩗ pointer, and then drag the ⩗ pointer to the row selector for the Invoice Paid field. See Figure 2-19.

Moving the Invoice Amt field in the table structure | Figure 2-19

▶ **4.** Release the mouse button. Access moves the Invoice Amt field between the Invoice Date and Invoice Paid fields in the table structure.

Trouble? If the Invoice Amt field did not move, repeat Steps 1 through 4, making sure you hold down the mouse button during the drag operation.

Adding a Field

Next, you need to add the Invoice Item field to the table structure between the Invoice Date and Invoice Amt fields. To add a new field between existing fields, you must insert a row. You begin by selecting the field that will be below the new field you want to insert.

Adding a Field Between Two Existing Fields | Reference Window

- In the Table window in Design view, select the row for the field above which you want to add a new field.
- In the Tools group on the Table Tools Design tab, click the Insert Rows button.
- Define the new field by entering the field name, data type, optional description, and any property specifications.

To add the Invoice Item field to the Invoice table:

▶ **1.** Click in the Field Name box for the Invoice Amt field. You need to establish this field as the current field so that the row for the new record will be inserted above this field.

▶ **2.** In the Tools group on the Table Tools Design tab, click the **Insert Rows** button. Access adds a new, blank row between the Invoice Date and Invoice Amt fields. The insertion point is positioned in the Field Name box for the new row, ready for you to type the name for the new field. See Figure 2-20.

Figure 2-20 | Table structure after inserting a row

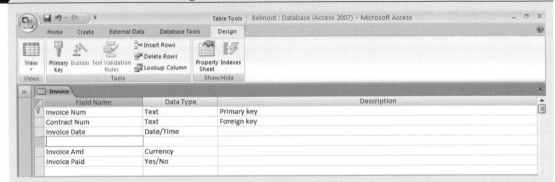

You'll define the Invoice Item field in the new row of the Invoice table. This field will be a Text field with a Field Size of 40.

3. Type **Invoice Item**, press the **Tab** key to move to the Data Type property, and then press the **Tab** key again to accept the default Text data type and to move to the Description property.

4. Press the **F6** key to move to the Field Size property and to select the default field size, and then type **40**. The definition of the new field is complete. See Figure 2-21.

Figure 2-21 | Invoice Item field added to the Invoice table

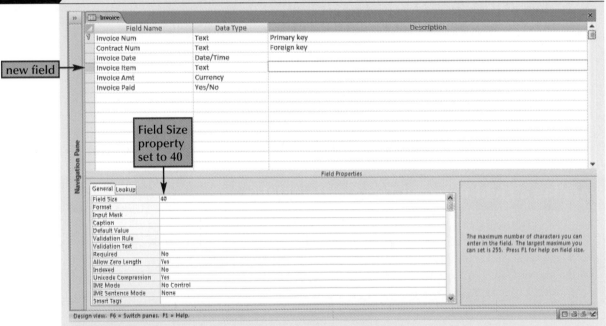

5. Click the **Save** button on the Quick Access Toolbar to save the changes to the Invoice table structure.

Changing Field Properties

With the Invoice table design complete, you can now go back and modify the Field Size property for the three Text fields in the Contract table. Recall that each of these fields still has the default field size of 255, which is too large for the data contained in these fields.

To modify the Field Size property of the Contract table's Text fields:

▶ **1.** Click the **Close 'Invoice'** button ⊠ on the table window bar to close the Invoice table.

▶ **2.** On the Navigation Pane, click the **Shutter Bar Open/Close Button** ⏩ to open the pane. Notice that the Invoice table is listed below the bar containing the word "Invoice." Because the Navigation Pane is set to All Tables view, the pane organizes objects by table and displays each table name in its own bar. See Figure 2-22.

Navigation Pane with two tables ◀ Figure 2-22

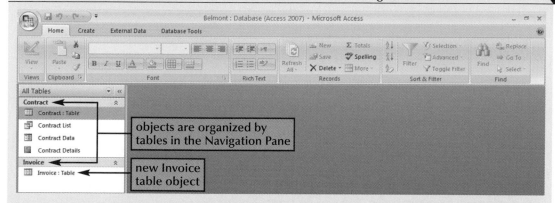

▶ **3.** Double-click **Contract : Table** to open the Contract table in Datasheet view. To change the Field Size property, you need to display the table in Design view.

▶ **4.** In the Views group on the Home tab, click the **View** button. The table is displayed in Design view with the Contract Num field selected. You need to change the Field Size property for this field to 4, because each contract number at Belmont Landscapes consists of four digits.

▶ **5.** Press the **F6** key to move to and select the default setting of 255 for the Field Size property, and then type **4**.

Next you need to set the Customer ID Field Size property to 5, because each Customer ID number at Belmont Landscapes consists of five digits.

▶ **6.** Click in the **Customer ID** Field Name box to make this the active field, press the **F6** key, and then type **5**.

Finally, for the Contract Type field, you will set the Field Size property to 75. This size can accommodate the values for the Contract Type field, some of which are lengthy.

▶ **7.** Click in the **Contract Type** Field Name box, press the **F6** key, and then type **75**. Now you can save the modified table.

▶ **8.** Click the **Save** button 🖫 on the Quick Access Toolbar. A dialog box opens informing you that some data may be lost because you decreased the field sizes. Because you know that all of the values in the Contract Num, Customer ID, and Contract Type fields include fewer characters than the new Field Size properties that you set for each field, you can ignore this message.

▶ **9.** Click the **Yes** button, and then close the Contract table.

▶ **10.** If you are not continuing to Session 2.2, click the **Close** button ⊠ on the program window title bar. Access closes the Belmont database, and then the Access program closes.

You have created the Invoice table and made modifications to its design. In the next session, you'll add records to the Invoice table and create the new Customer table in the Belmont database.

Review | **Session 2.1 Quick Check**

1. What guidelines should you follow when designing a database?
2. What is the purpose of the Data Type property for a field?
3. For which three types of fields can you assign a field size?
4. The default Field Size property setting for a Text field is _____ .
5. In Design view, which key do you press to move from the Table Design grid to the Field Properties pane?
6. A(n) _____ value, which results when you do not enter a value for a field, is not permitted for a primary key.

Session 2.2

Adding Records to a New Table

The Invoice table design is complete. Now, Oren would like you to add records to the table so it will contain the invoice data for Belmont Landscapes. You add records to a table in Datasheet view as you did in Tutorial 1, by typing the field values in the rows below the column headings for the fields. You'll begin by entering the records shown in Figure 2-23.

Figure 2-23 ▶ Records to be added to the Invoice table

Invoice Num	Contract Num	Invoice Date	Invoice Item	Invoice Amt	Invoice Paid
2011	3011	03/23/2010	Schematic Plan	$1,500.00	Yes
2031	3020	04/19/2010	Schematic Plan	$1,500.00	Yes
2073	3023	09/21/2012	Construction Observation	$10,000.00	No
2062	3026	09/12/2011	Permitting	$10,000.00	No

To add the first record to the Invoice table:

▶ 1. If you took a break after the previous session, make sure that the **Belmont** database is open, and the Navigation Pane is open.

▶ 2. In the Navigation Pane, double-click **Invoice : Table** to open the Invoice table in Datasheet view.

▶ 3. Close the Navigation Pane, and then use the ↔ pointer to resize each column so that the field names are completely visible.

▶ 4. In the Invoice Num field, type **2011**, press the **Tab** key, type **3011** in the Contract Num field, and then press the **Tab** key.

Next you need to enter the Invoice Date field value. Recall that you specified a custom date format, mm/dd/yyyy, for this field. You do not need to type each digit; for example, you can type just "3" instead of "03" for the month, and you can type "10" instead of "2010" for the year. Access will display the full value according to the custom date format.

5. Type **3/23/10**, press the **Tab** key, type **Schematic Plan** in the Invoice Item field, and then press the **Tab** key. Notice that Access displays the date "03/23/2010" in the Invoice Date field.

   Next you need to enter the Invoice Amt value for the first record. This is a Currency field with the Currency format and two decimal places specified. Because of the field's set properties, you do not need to type the dollar sign, comma, or zeroes for the decimal places; Access will display these items automatically for you.

6. Type **1500** and then press the **Tab** key. Access displays the value as "$1,500.00."

   The last field in the table, Invoice Paid, is a Yes/No field. Notice the check box displayed in the field. By default, the value for any Yes/No field is "No"; therefore, the check box is initially empty. For Yes/No fields with check boxes, you press the Tab key to leave the check box unchecked, and you press the spacebar to insert a check mark in the check box. For the record you are entering in the Invoice table, the invoice has been paid, so you need to insert a check mark in the check box.

7. Press the **spacebar** to insert a check mark, and then press the **Tab** key. The values for the first record are entered. See Figure 2-24.

First record entered in the Invoice table ◄ **Figure 2-24**

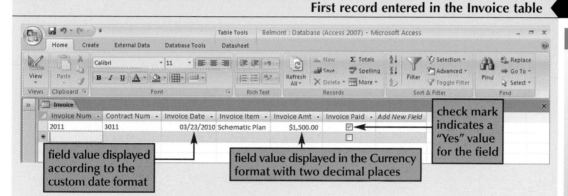

Tip

The spacebar works as a toggle for check boxes in Yes/No fields; you press the spacebar to insert a check mark in an empty check box and to remove an existing check mark. You can also change a check box to select it or deselect it by clicking it with the mouse.

Now you can add the remaining three records. As you do, you'll learn a shortcut for inserting the value from the same field in the previous record.

To add the next three records to the Invoice table:

1. Refer to Figure 2-23 and enter the values for the second record's Invoice Num, Contract Num, and Invoice Date fields.

   Notice the value for the second record's Invoice Item field, "Schematic Plan." This value is the exact same value as this field in the first record. You can quickly insert the value from the same field in the previous record using the **Ctrl + '** (apostrophe) keyboard shortcut.

2. In the Invoice Item field, press the **Ctrl + '** keys. Access inserts the value "Schematic Plan" in the Invoice Item field for the second record.

3. Press the **Tab** key to move to the Invoice Amt field. Again, the value you need to enter for this field—$1,500.00—is the same as the value for this field in the previous record. So, you can use the keyboard shortcut again.

4. In the Invoice Amt field, press the **Ctrl + '** keys. Access inserts the value $1,500.00 in the Invoice Amt field for the second record.

5. Press the **Tab** key to move to the Invoice Paid field, press the **spacebar** to insert a check mark in the check box, and then press the **Tab** key. The second record is entered in the Invoice table.

6. Refer to Figure 2-23 to enter the values for the third and fourth records, using the Ctrl + ' keys to enter the fourth record's Invoice Amt value. Also, for both records, the invoices have not been paid. Therefore, be sure to press the Tab key to leave the Invoice Paid field values unchecked (signifying "No").

7. Resize the columns, as necessary, so that all field values are completely visible. Your table should look like the one in Figure 2-25.

Figure 2-25 | **Invoice table with four records added**

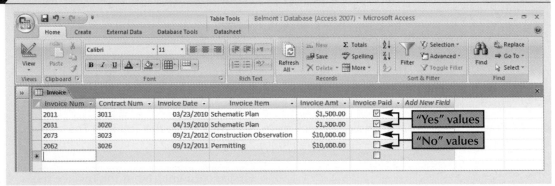

To complete the entry of records in the Invoice table, you'll use a method that allows you to import the data.

Importing Data from an Excel Worksheet

Often, the data you want to add to an Access table exists in another file, such as a Word document or an Excel workbook. You can bring the data from other files into Access in different ways. For example, you can copy and paste the data from an open file, or you can **import** the data, which is a process that allows you to copy the data from a source without having to open the source file.

Oren had been using Excel to track invoice data for Belmont Landscapes and already created a worksheet, named "Invoices," containing this data. You'll import this Excel worksheet into your Invoice table to complete the entry of data in the table. To use the import method, the columns in the Excel worksheet must match the names and data types of the fields in the Access table. The Invoices worksheet contains the following columns: Invoice Num, Contract Num, Invoice Date, Invoice Item, Invoice Amt, and Invoice Paid. These column headings match the fields names in the Invoice table exactly, so you can import the data. Before you import data into a table, you need to close the table.

To import the Invoices worksheet into the Invoice table:

1. Click the **Close 'Invoice'** button ☒ on the table window bar to close the Invoice table. A dialog box opens asking if you want to save the changes to the table layout. This dialog box opens because you resized the table columns.

2. Click the **Yes** button in the dialog box.

3. Click the **External Data** tab on the Ribbon.

4. In the Import group on the External Data tab, click the **Excel** button (with the ScreenTip "Import Excel spreadsheet"). The Get External Data - Excel Spreadsheet dialog box opens. See Figure 2-26.

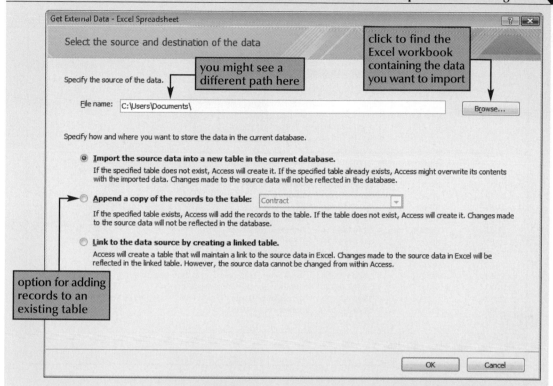

The dialog box provides options for importing the entire worksheet as a new table in the current database, adding the data from the worksheet to an existing table, or linking the data in the worksheet to the table. You need to add, or append, the worksheet data to the Invoice table.

▶ 5. Click the **Browse** button. The File Open dialog box opens. The Excel workbook file is named "Invoices" and is located in the Level.01\Tutorial folder provided with your Data Files.

▶ 6. Navigate to the **Level.01\Tutorial** folder, where your starting Data Files are stored, and then double-click the **Invoices** Excel file. You return to the dialog box.

▶ 7. Click the **Append a copy of the records to the table** option button. The list box to the right of this option becomes active. Next, you need to select the table to which you want to add the data.

▶ 8. Click the **arrow** on the list box, and then click **Invoice**.

▶ 9. Click the **OK** button. The first Import Spreadsheet Wizard dialog box opens. See Figure 2-27.

Figure 2-27 **First Import Spreadsheet Wizard dialog box**

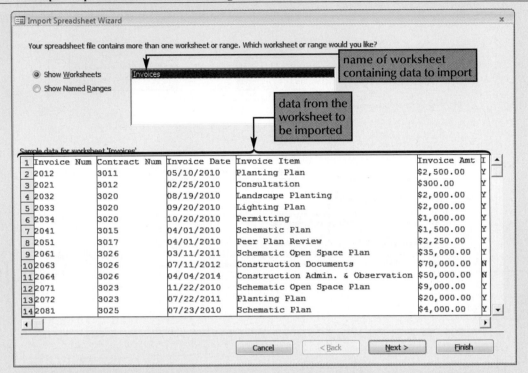

The dialog box shows all the worksheets in the selected Excel workbook. In this case, the Invoices workbook contains only one worksheet, which is also named "Invoices." The bottom section of the dialog box displays some of the data contained in the selected worksheet.

10. Click the **Next** button. The second Import Spreadsheet Wizard dialog box opens and indicates that the column headings from the Invoices worksheet will be used as field names in the table.

11. Click the **Next** button. The third, and final, Import Spreadsheet Wizard dialog box opens. Notice that the Import to Table text box shows that the data from the spreadsheet will be imported into the Invoice table.

12. Click the **Finish** button. A dialog box opens asking if you want to save the import steps. If you needed to repeat this same import procedure many times, it would be a good idea to save the steps for the procedure. However, you don't need to save these steps because you'll be importing the data only this one time. Once the data is in the Access table, Oren will no longer use Excel to track invoice data.

13. Click the **Close** button in the dialog box to close it without saving the steps.

The data from the Invoices worksheet has been added to the Invoice table. Next, you'll open the table to view the new records.

To open the Invoice table and view the imported data:

1. Open the Navigation Pane, and then double-click **Invoice : Table** to open the table in Datasheet view.

2. Resize the Invoice Item column so that all field values are fully displayed. Notice that the table now contains a total of 176 records—four records you entered plus 172 records imported from the Invoices worksheet. The records are displayed in primary key order by the values in the Invoice Num field. See Figure 2-28.

Invoice table after importing data from Excel ◀ Figure 2-28

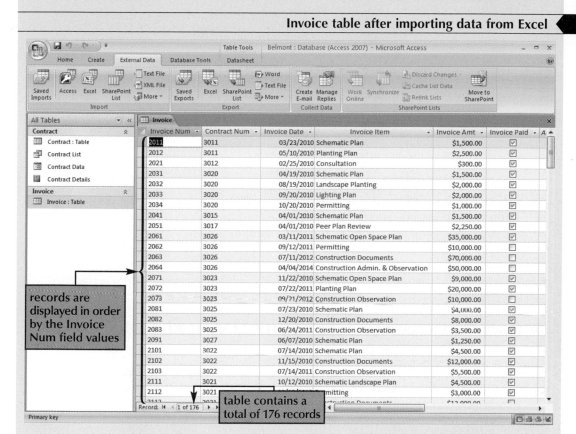

3. Save and close the Invoice table, and then close the Navigation Pane.

Two of the tables—Contract and Invoice—are now complete. According to Oren's plan for the Belmont database, you need to create a third table, named "Customer," to track data about Belmont Landscapes' residential and commercial customers. You'll use a different method to create this table.

Creating a Table by Importing an Existing Table Structure

If another Access database contains a table—or even just the design, or structure, of a table—that you want to include in your database, you can easily import the table and any records it contains or import only the table structure into your database.

Oren documented the design for the new Customer table by listing each field's name, data type, size (if applicable), and description, as shown in Figure 2-29. Note that each field in the Customer table will be a Text field, and the Customer ID field will be the table's primary key.

Figure 2-29 ▶ **Design for the Customer table**

Field Name	Data Type	Field Size	Description
Customer ID	Text	5	Primary key
Company	Text	50	
Last Name	Text	25	Contact's last name
First Name	Text	20	Contact's first name
Phone	Text	14	
Address	Text	35	
City	Text	25	
State	Text	2	
Zip	Text	10	
E-mail Address	Text	50	

Sarah already created an Access database containing a Customer table design. She never entered any records into the table because she wasn't sure if the table design was correct. After reviewing the table design, both Sarah and Oren agree that it contains many of the fields Oren wants to track, but that some changes are needed. Therefore, you can import the table structure in Sarah's database to create the Customer table in the Belmont database, and then modify it to produce the final table structure Oren wants.

To create the Customer table by importing the structure of another table:

▶ **1.** Make sure the **External Data** tab is the active tab on the Ribbon.

▶ **2.** In the Import group, click the **Access** button. The Get External Data - Access Database dialog box opens. This dialog box is similar to the one you used earlier when importing the Excel spreadsheet.

▶ **3.** Click the **Browse** button. The File Open dialog box opens. The Access database file from which you need to import the table structure is named "Sarah" and is located in the Level.01\Tutorial folder provided with your Data Files.

▶ **4.** Navigate to the **Level.01\Tutorial** folder, where your starting Data Files are stored, and then double-click the **Sarah** database file. You return to the dialog box.

▶ **5.** Make sure the **Import tables, queries, forms, reports, macros, and modules into the current database** option button is selected, and then click the **OK** button. The Import Objects dialog box opens. The dialog box contains tabs for importing all the different types of Access database objects—tables, queries, forms, and so on. The Tables tab is the current tab.

▶ **6.** Click the **Options** button in the dialog box to see all the options for importing tables. See Figure 2-30.

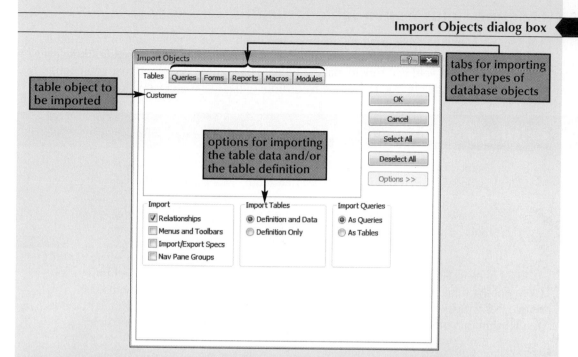

Import Objects dialog box ◄ **Figure 2-30**

Note the Import Tables section of the dialog box, which contains options for importing the definition and data—that is, the structure of the table and any records contained in the table—or the definition only. You need to import only the structure of the Customer table Sarah created.

▶ **7.** On the Tables tab, click **Customer** to select this table.

▶ **8.** In the Import Tables section of the dialog box, click the **Definition Only** option button, and then click the **OK** button. Access creates the Customer table in the Belmont database using the structure of the Customer table in the Sarah database, and opens a dialog box asking if you want to save the import steps.

▶ **9.** Click the **Close** button to close the dialog box without saving the import steps.

▶ **10.** Open the Navigation Pane and note that the Customer table is listed.

▶ **11.** Double-click **Customer : Table** to open the table, and then close the Navigation Pane. See Figure 2-31.

Imported Customer table in Datasheet view ◄ **Figure 2-31**

The Customer table opens in Datasheet view. The table contains no records.

The table structure you imported contains more fields than Oren wants to include in the Customer table (see Figure 2-29). Also, he wants to rename and reorder some of the fields. You'll begin to modify the table structure by deleting fields.

Deleting Fields from a Table Structure

After you've created a table using any method, you might need to delete one or more fields. When you delete a field, you also delete all the values for the field from the table. Therefore, before you delete a field you should make sure that you want to do so and that you choose the correct field to delete. You can delete fields from either Datasheet view or Design view.

Reference Window | **Deleting a Field from a Table Structure**

- In Datasheet view, select the column heading for the field you want to delete.
- In the Fields & Columns group on the Datasheet tab, click the Delete button.
or
- In Design view, click in the Field Name box for the field you want to delete.
- In the Tools group on the Table Tools Design tab, click the Delete Rows button.

Refer back to Figure 2-29. Notice that Oren's design does not specify a Cell Phone field. Oren doesn't think it's necessary to track customers' cell phone numbers because his employees typically contact customers using either their home or business phone numbers. You'll begin to modify the Customer table sturcture by deleting the Cell Phone field.

To delete the Cell Phone field from the table in Datasheet view:

▸ **1.** Click the **Datasheet** tab on the Ribbon.

▸ **2.** Click the **Cell Phone** column heading to select the Cell Phone field.

▸ **3.** In the Fields & Columns group on the Datasheet tab, click the **Delete** button. The Cell Phone field is removed.

You can also delete fields from a table structure in Design view. You'll switch to Design view to delete the rest of the unnecessary fields.

To delete the fields in Design view:

▸ **1.** In the Views group on the Datasheet tab, click the **View** button. The Customer table opens in Design view. See Figure 2-32.

Figure 2-32 **Customer table in Design view**

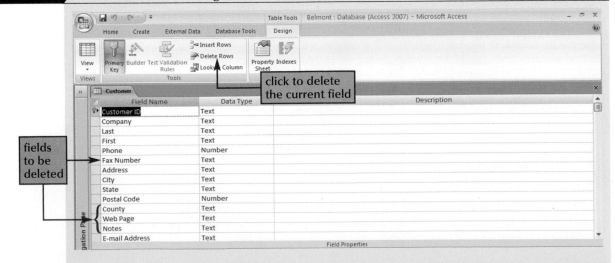

2. Click in the **Fax Number** Field Name box to make it the current field.

3. In the Tools group on the Table Tools Design tab, click the **Delete Rows** button. The Fax Number field is removed from the Customer table structure.

   You'll delete the County, Web Page, and Notes fields next. Instead of deleting these fields individually, you'll use the pointer to select them and then delete them at the same time.

4. Click and hold down the mouse button on the row selector for the **County** field, and then drag the mouse to select the **Web Page** and **Notes** fields.

5. Release the mouse button. The rows for the three fields are selected.

6. In the Tools group on the Table Tools Design tab, click the **Delete Rows** button. See Figure 2-33.

Customer table after deleting fields | Figure 2-33

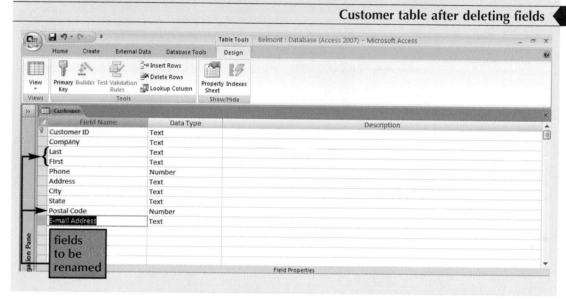

Renaming Fields in Design View

To match Oren's design for the Customer table, you need to rename several fields. In Tutorial 1, you renamed the default primary key field, ID, in Datasheet view. You can also rename fields in Design view by simply editing the names in the Table Design grid.

To rename the fields in Design view:

1. Click to position the insertion point to the right of the word **Last** in the third row's Field Name box, press the **spacebar**, and then type **Name**. The name of the third field is now Last Name.

> **2.** Click to position the insertion point to the right of the word **First** in the fourth row's Field Name box, press the **spacebar**, and then type **Name**. The name of the fourth field is now First Name.
>
> You can also select an entire field name and then type new text to replace it.
>
> **3.** In the ninth field's Field Name box, drag to select the text **Postal Code**, and then type **Zip**. The text you type replaces the original text. See Figure 2-34.

Figure 2-34	Customer table after renaming fields

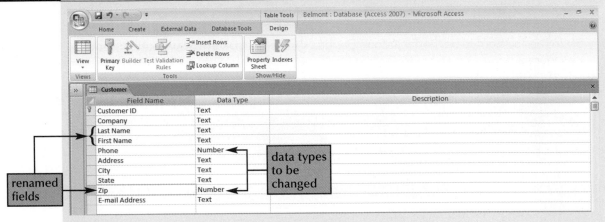

Changing the Data Type for Fields in Design View

According to Oren's plan, all of the fields in the Customer table should be Text fields. The table structure you imported specifies the Number data type for the Phone and the Zip fields. In Tutorial 1, you used an option in Datasheet view to change a field's data type. You can also change the data type for a field in Design view.

To change the data type of the fields in Design view:

> **1.** Click the right side of the **Data Type** box for the Phone field to display the list of data types.
>
> **2.** Click **Text** in the list. The Phone field is now a Text field. Note that, by default, the Field Size property is set to 255. According to Oren's plan, the Phone field should have a Field Size property of 14. You'll make this change next.
>
> **3.** Press the **F6** key to move to and select the default Field Size property, and then type **14**.
>
> **4.** Click the right side of the **Data Type** box for the Zip field, and then click **Text** in the list. The Zip field is now a Text field. According to Oren's plan, you need to change the Field Size property to 10.
>
> **5.** Press the **F6** key to move to and select the default Field Size property, and then type **10**.

Finally, Oren would like descriptions entered for the Customer ID, Last Name, and First Name fields. You'll enter those now.

To enter the Description property values:

▶ **1.** Click in the Description box for the Customer ID field, and then type **Primary key**.

▶ **2.** Press the ↓ key to move to the Description property for the Company field. After you press the ↓ key, a Property Update Options button appears near the Description box for the Company field. When you change a field's property in Design view, you can use this button to update the corresponding property on forms and reports that include the field you've modified. For example, if the Belmont database included a form that contained the Customer ID field, you could choose to **propagate**, or update, the modified Description property in the form by clicking the Property Update Options button, and then choosing the option to make the update everywhere the field is used. The text on the Property Update Options button varies depending on the task; in this case, if you click the button, the option is "Update Status Bar Text everywhere Customer ID is used."

Because the Belmont database does not include any forms or reports that are based on the Customer table, you do not need to update the properties, so you can ignore the button for now.

▶ **3.** Press the ↓ key to move to the Description box for the Last Name field, and then type **Contact's last name**.

▶ **4.** Press the ↓ key to move to the Description box for the First Name field, and then type **Contact's first name**. See Figure 2-35.

Customer table after changing data types and entering descriptions ◀ Figure 2-35

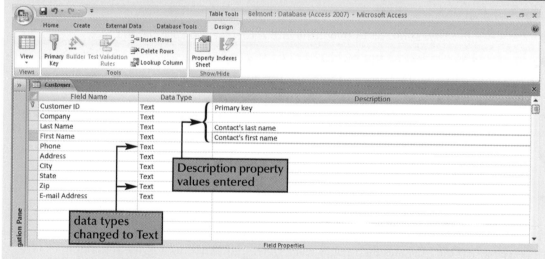

▶ **5.** Click the **Save** button 🔒 on the Quick Access Toolbar to save your changes to the Customer table.

▶ **6.** In the Views group on the Table Tools Design tab, click the **View** button to display the table in Datasheet view. See Figure 2-36.

Figure 2-36 **Modified Customer table in Datasheet view**

After viewing the Customer table datasheet, Oren decides that he would like the First Name field to appear before the Last Name field. Earlier in this tutorial, when you created the Invoice table, you learned how to change the order of fields in Design view. Although you can reorder fields in Datasheet view by dragging a field's column heading to a new location, doing so rearranges only the *display* of the table's fields; the table structure is not changed. To move a field, you must display the table in Design view.

To move the Last Name field to follow the First Name field:

1. In the Views group on the Datasheet tab, click the **View** button. The Customer table opens in Design view.

2. Position the pointer on the row selector for the Last Name field until the pointer changes to a ➡ shape.

3. Click the **row selector** to select the entire row for the Last Name field.

4. Place the pointer on the row selector for the Last Name field, click the ⬚ pointer, and then drag the ⬚ pointer down to the line below the row selector for the First Name field.

5. Release the mouse button. The Last Name field now appears below the First Name field in the table structure.

6. Click the **Save** button 🖫 on the Quick Access Toolbar to save the change to the Customer table design.

7. Display the table in Datasheet view.

With the Customer table design set, you can now enter records in it. You'll begin by entering two records, and then you'll use a different method to add the remaining records.

To add two records to the Customer table:

1. Enter the following values for the fields in the first record (these values are for a residential customer with no company name):

   Customer ID = **11001**
   Company = [do not enter a value; leave blank]
   First Name = **Sharon**
   Last Name = **Maloney**
   Phone = **616-866-3901**
   Address = **49 Blackstone Dr**
   City = **Rockford**

State = **MI**
Zip = **49341**
E-mail Address = **smaloney2@milocal123.com**

▶ **2.** Enter the following values for the fields in the second record, for a commercial customer:

Customer ID = **11012**
Company = **Grand Rapids Engineering Dept.**
First Name = **Anthony**
Last Name = **Rodriguez**
Phone = **616-454-9801**
Address = **225 Summer St**
City = **Grand Rapids**
State = **MI**
Zip = **49503**
E-mail Address = **arod24@gred11.gov**

▶ **3.** Close the Customer table.

Before Belmont Landscapes decided to store data using Access, Sarah managed the company's customer data in a different system. She exported that data into a text file and asks you to import it into the new Customer table. You can import the data contained in this text file to add the remaining records to the Customer table.

Adding Data to a Table by Importing a Text File

There are many ways to import data into an Access database. So far, you've learned how to add data to an Access table by importing an Excel spreadsheet, and you've created a new table by importing the structure of an existing table. You can also import data contained in text files.

To complete the entry of records in the Customer table, you'll import the data contained in Sarah's text file. The file is named Customer.txt and is located in the Level.01\Tutorial folder provided with your Data Files.

To import the data contained in the Customer.txt file:

▶ **1.** Click the **External Data** tab on the Ribbon.

▶ **2.** In the Import group, click the **Text File** button (with the ScreenTip "Import text file"). The Get External Data - Text File dialog box opens. This dialog box is similar to the one you used earlier when importing the Excel spreadsheet and the Access table structure.

▶ **3.** Click the **Browse** button. The File Open dialog box opens.

▶ **4.** Navigate to the **Level.01\Tutorial** folder, where your starting Data Files are stored, and then double-click the **Customer** text file. You return to the dialog box.

▶ **5.** Click the **Append a copy of the records to the table** option button. The list box to the right of this option becomes active. Next, you need to select the table to which you want to add the data.

▶ **6.** Click the **arrow** on the list box, and then click **Customer**.

▶ 7. Click the **OK** button. The first Import Text Wizard dialog box opens. The dialog box indicates that the data to be imported is in a "Delimited" format. A **delimited** text file is one in which fields of data are separated by a character such as a comma or a tab. In this case, the dialog box shows that data is separated by the comma character in the text file.

▶ 8. Make sure the **Delimited** option button is selected in the dialog box, and then click the **Next** button. The second Import Text Wizard dialog box opens. See Figure 2-37.

Figure 2-37 ▶ **Second Import Text Wizard dialog box**

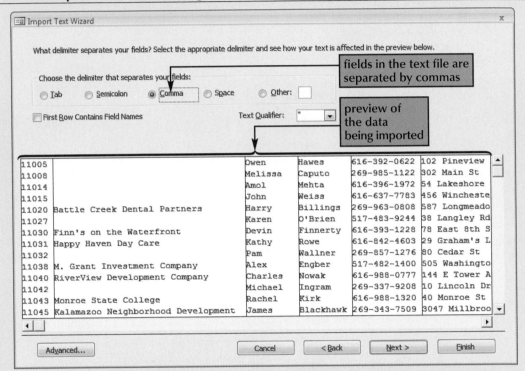

This dialog box asks you to confirm the delimiter character that separates the fields in the text file you're importing. Access detects that the comma character is used in the Customer text file and selects this option. The bottom area of the dialog box gives you a preview of the data you're importing.

▶ 9. Make sure the **Comma** option button is selected, and then click the **Next** button. The third, and final, Import Text Wizard dialog box opens. Notice that the Import to Table text box shows that the data from the text file will be imported into the Customer table.

▶ 10. Click the **Finish** button. A dialog box opens asking if you want to save the import steps. You'll only import the customer data once, so you can close the dialog box without saving the import steps.

▶ 11. Click the **Close** button in the dialog box to close it without saving the import steps.

Oren asks you to open the Customer table in Datasheet view so he can see the results of importing the text file.

To view the Customer table datasheet:

▶ **1.** Open the Navigation Pane, and then double-click **Customer : Table** to open the Customer table in Datasheet view. The Customer table contains a total of 40 records.

▶ **2.** Close the Navigation Pane.

Next, you need to resize all the columns in the datasheet, both to make sure all the field values are fully displayed and to reduce the width of any fields that are wider than the values they contain, such as the Zip field. When you resize a column by double-clicking the pointer on the column dividing line, you are sizing the column to its **best fit**—that is, so the column is just wide enough to display the longest visible value in the column, including the field name.

▶ **3.** Resize all the columns to their best fit, scrolling the table datasheet as necessary. When finished, scroll back to display the first fields in the table. See Figure 2-38.

Customer table after importing data from the text file ◀ **Figure 2-38**

Customer ID	Company	First Name	Last Name	Phone	Address	City	State
11001		Sharon	Maloney	616-866-3901	49 Blackstone Dr	Rockford	MI
11005		Owen	Hawes	616-392-0622	102 Pineview Rd	Holland	MI
11008		Melissa	Caputo	269-985-1122	302 Main St	Saint Joseph	MI
11012	Grand Rapids Engineering Dept.	Anthony	Rodriguez	616-454-9801	225 Summer St	Grand Rapids	MI
11014		Amol	Mehta	616-396-1972	54 Lakeshore Ave	Holland	MI
11015		John	Weiss	616-637-7783	456 Winchester St	South Haven	MI
11020	Battle Creek Dental Partners	Harry	Billings	269-963-0808	587 Longmeadow Rd	Battle Creek	MI
11027		Karen	O'Brien	517-483-9244	38 Langley Rd	Lansing	MI
11030	Finn's on the Waterfront	Devin	Finnerly	616-393-1228	78 East 4th St	Holland	MI
11031	Happy Haven Day Care	Kathy	Rowe	616-842-4603	29 Graham's Ln	Grand Haven	MI
11032		Pam	Wallner	269-857-1276	80 Cedar St	Saugatuck	MI
11038	M. Grant Investment Company	Alex	Engber	517-482-1400	505 Washington Ave	Lansing	MI
11040	RiverView Development Company	Charles	Nowak	616-988-0777	144 E Tower Ave	Grand Rapids	MI
11042		Michael	Ingram	269-337-9208	10 Lincoln Dr	Kalamazoo	MI
11043	Monroe State College	Rachel	Kirk	616-988-1320	40 Monroe St	Grand Rapids	MI
11045	Kalamazoo Neighborhood Development	James	Blackhawk	269-343-7509	3047 Millbrook Ave	Kalamazoo	MI
11048		Olivia	Pappas	616-637-6591	4 N Orchard St	South Haven	MI
11049		Claire	Boucher	269-983-2255	828 Turner St	Saint Joseph	MI
11053		Hwan	Tang	616-396-8401	283 Cottrell St	Holland	MI
11054	Gilded Goose Gift Shop	Taylor	Wilson	616-355-3989	258 Briar Ln	Holland	MI
11055	Fox and Hound Grille	Steve	Gorski	269-979-2004	1440 Beadle Lake Rd	Battle Creek	MI
11058	Cherrywood Senior Center	Lisa	Hall	269-857-1771	77 Forest Hill Rd	Saugatuck	MI
11059	G.R. Neighborhood Development Corp.	Matthew	Fraser	616-392-0015	8045 Jefferson Ave	Grand Rapids	MI
11060		Jerome	Smith	616-949-3862	75 Hillcrest St	East Grand Rapids	MI
11064	Northwest Transit Station	Henry	Goldberg	517-487-4700	2572 Clinton Ave	Lansing	MI
11065	Town of Holland	Amber	Ward	616-392-0402	34 Prospect St	Holland	MI

Record: 1 of 40 No Filter Search

Primary key

Tip

When you resize a column to its best fit, only the visible field values are affected. You must scroll down the datasheet to make sure all field values for the entire column are fully displayed, resizing as you scroll, if necessary.

▶ **4.** Save and close the Customer table, and then open the Navigation Pane.

The Belmont database now contains three tables—Contract, Invoice, and Customer—and the tables contain all the necessary records. Your final task is to complete the database design by defining the necessary relationships between its tables.

Defining Table Relationships

One of the most powerful features of a relational database management system is its ability to define relationships between tables. You use a common field to relate one table to another. The process of relating tables is often called performing a **join**. When you join tables that have a common field, you can extract data from them as if they were one larger table. For example, you can join the Customer and Contract tables by using the Customer ID field in both tables as the common field. Then you can use a query, form, or report to extract selected data from each table, even though the data is contained in two separate tables, as shown in Figure 2-39. In the Customer Contracts query shown in Figure 2-39, the Customer ID, Company, First Name, and Last Name columns are fields from the Customer table, and the Contract Num and Contract Amt columns are fields from the Contract table. The joining of records is based on the common field of Customer ID. The Customer and Contract tables have a type of relationship called a one-to-many relationship.

Figure 2-39 **One-to-many relationship and sample query**

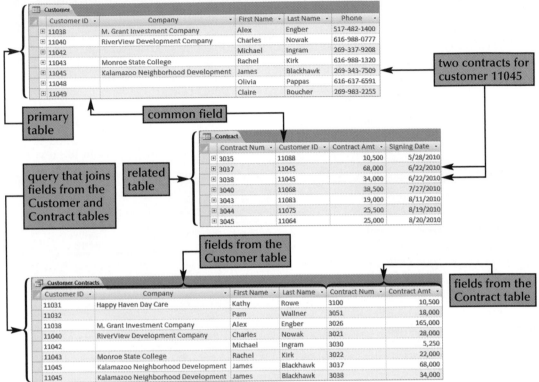

One-to-Many Relationships

A **one-to-many relationship** exists between two tables when one record in the first table matches zero, one, or many records in the second table, and when one record in the second table matches at most one record in the first table. For example, as shown in Figure 2-39, customer 11045 has two contracts in the Contract table. Other customers have one or more contracts. Every contract has a single matching customer.

Access refers to the two tables that form a relationship as the primary table and the related table. The **primary table** is the "one" table in a one-to-many relationship; in Figure 2-39, the Customer table is the primary table because there is only one customer for each contract. The **related table** is the "many" table; in Figure 2-39, the Contract table is the related table because a customer can have zero, one, or many contracts.

Because related data is stored in two tables, inconsistencies between the tables can occur. Consider the following scenarios:

- Oren adds a record to the Contract table for a new customer, Taylor McNulty, using Customer ID 12050. Oren did not first add the new customer's information to the Customer table, so this contract does not have a matching record in the Customer table. The data is inconsistent, and the contract record is considered to be an **orphaned record**.
- Oren changes the Customer ID in the Customer table for Kalamazoo Neighborhood Development from 11045 to 12090. Because there is no customer 11045 in the Customer table, this change creates two orphaned records in the Contract table, and the database is inconsistent.

- Oren deletes the record for Kalamazoo Neighborhood Development, customer 11045, from the Customer table because this customer no longer does business with Belmont Landscapes. The database is again inconsistent; two records for customer 11045 in the Contract table have no matching record in the Customer table.

    You can avoid these problems by specifying referential integrity between tables when you define their relationships.

Referential Integrity

Referential integrity is a set of rules that Access enforces to maintain consistency between related tables when you update data in a database. Specifically, the referential integrity rules are as follows:

- When you add a record to a related table, a matching record must already exist in the primary table, thereby preventing the possibility of orphaned records.
- If you attempt to change the value of the primary key in the primary table, Access prevents this change if matching records exist in a related table. However, if you choose the **cascade updates option**, Access permits the change in value to the primary key and changes the appropriate foreign key values in the related table, thereby eliminating the possibility of inconsistent data.
- When you attempt to delete a record in the primary table, Access prevents the deletion if matching records exist in a related table. However, if you choose the **cascade deletes option**, Access deletes the record in the primary table and also deletes all records in related tables that have matching foreign key values.

Understanding the Cascade Deletes Option	InSight

Although there are advantages to using the cascade deletes option for enforcing referential integrity, its use does present risks as well. You should rarely select the cascade deletes option, because setting this option might cause you to inadvertently delete records you did not intend to delete. It is best to use other methods for deleting records that give you more control over the deletion process.

Now you'll define a one-to-many relationship between the Customer (primary) and Contract (related) tables. You will also define a one-to-many relationship between the Contract (primary) table and the Invoice (related) table.

Defining a Relationship Between Two Tables

When two tables have a common field, you can define a relationship between them in the Relationships window. The **Relationships window** illustrates the relationships among a database's tables. Using this window, you can view or change existing relationships, define new relationships between tables, and rearrange the layout of the tables in the window.

You need to open the Relationships window and define the relationship between the Customer and Contract tables. You'll define a one-to-many relationship between the two tables, with Customer as the primary table and Contract as the related table, and with Customer ID as the common field (the primary key in the Customer table and a foreign key in the Contract table). You'll also define a one-to-many relationship between the Contract and Invoice tables, with Contract as the primary table and Invoice as the related table, and with Contract Num as the common field (the primary key in the Contract table and a foreign key in the Invoice table).

To define the one-to-many relationship between the Customer and Contract tables:

▸ 1. Click the **Database Tools** tab on the Ribbon.

▸ 2. In the Show/Hide group on the Database Tools tab, click the **Relationships** button. The Show Table dialog box opens. See Figure 2-40.

Figure 2-40 ▸ **Show Table dialog box**

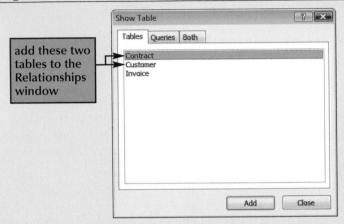

You must add each table participating in a relationship to the Relationships window. Because the Customer table is the primary table in the relationship, you'll add it first.

Tip

You can also double-click a table name in the Show Table dialog box to add it to the Relationships window.

▸ 3. Click **Customer**, and then click the **Add** button. The Customer table is added to the Relationships window.

▸ 4. Click **Contract**, and then click the **Add** button. The Contract table is added to the Relationships window.

▸ 5. Click the **Close** button in the Show Table dialog box to close it.

When you add a table to the Relationships window, the fields in the table appear in a **field list**. So that you can view all the fields and complete field names, you'll resize the Customer table field list.

▸ 6. Use the ⬍ pointer to drag the bottom of the Customer table field list to lengthen it until the vertical scroll bar disappears and all the fields are visible. See Figure 2-41.

Figure 2-41 ▸ **Field list boxes for the two tables**

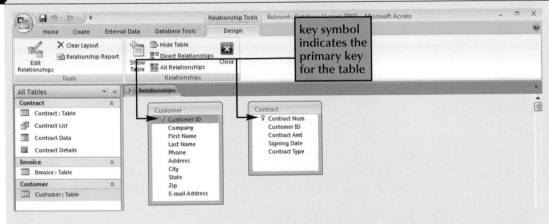

Notice that the key symbol appears next to the Customer ID field in the Customer table field list and next to the Contract Num field in the Contract table field list to indicate that these fields are the primary key fields for their respective tables.

To form the relationship between the two tables, you drag the common field of Customer ID from the primary table to the related table. Then Access opens the Edit Relationships dialog box, in which you select the relationship options for the two tables.

▶ 7. Click **Customer ID** in the Customer field list, and then drag it to **Customer ID** in the Contract field list. When you release the mouse button, the Edit Relationships dialog box opens. See Figure 2-42.

Edit Relationships dialog box　　**Figure 2-42**

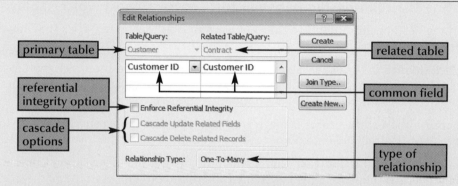

The primary table, related table, and common field appear at the top of the dialog box. The relationship type, One-To-Many, appears at the bottom of the dialog box. When you click the Enforce Referential Integrity check box, the two cascade options become available. If you select the Cascade Update Related Fields option, Access will update the appropriate foreign key values in the related table when you change a primary key value in the primary table. You will not select the Cascade Delete Related Records option, because doing so could cause you to delete records that you do not want to delete; this option is rarely selected.

▶ 8. Click the **Enforce Referential Integrity** check box, and then click the **Cascade Update Related Fields** check box.

▶ 9. Click the **Create** button to define the one-to-many relationship between the two tables and to close the dialog box. The completed relationship appears in the Relationships window. See Figure 2-43.

Defined relationship in the Relationships window　　**Figure 2-43**

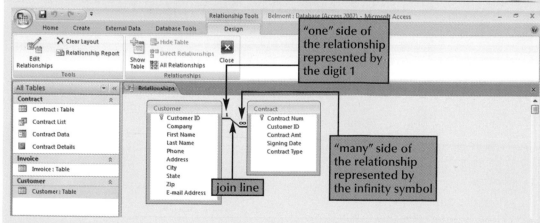

The **join line** connects the Customer ID fields, which are common to the two tables. The common field joins the two tables, which have a one-to-many relationship. The "one" side of the relationship has the digit 1 at its end, and the "many" side of the relationship has the infinity symbol at its end. The two tables are still separate tables, but you can use the data in them as if they were one table.

Now you need to define the one-to-many relationship between the Contract and Invoice tables. In this relationship, Contract is the primary ("one") table because there is at most one contract for each invoice. Invoice is the related ("many") table because there are zero, one, or many invoices set up for each contract, depending on how many project phases are involved for each contract.

To define the relationship between the Contract and Invoice tables:

▶ **1.** In the Relationships group on the Relationship Tools Design tab, click the **Show Table** button. The Show Table dialog box opens.

▶ **2.** Click **Invoice** in the list of tables, click the **Add** button, and then click the **Close** button to close the Show Table dialog box. The Invoice table's field list appears in the Relationships window to the right of the Contract table's field list.

   Because the Contract table is the primary table in this relationship, you need to drag the Contract Num field from the Contract field list to the Invoice field list.

▶ **3.** Click and drag the **Contract Num** field in the Contract field list to the **Contract Num** field in the Invoice field list. When you release the mouse button, the Edit Relationships dialog box opens.

▶ **4.** Click the **Enforce Referential Integrity** check box, and then click the **Cascade Update Related Fields** check box.

▶ **5.** Click the **Create** button to define the one-to-many relationship between the two tables and close the dialog box. The completed relationship appears in the Relationships window. See Figure 2-44.

Figure 2-44 ▶ **Both relationships defined**

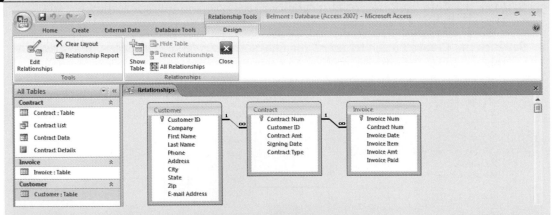

With both relationships defined, you have connected the data among the three tables in the Belmont database.

▶ **6.** Click the **Save** button 🔒 on the Quick Access Toolbar to save the layout in the Relationships window.

▶ **7.** Click the **Close 'Relationships'** button ⊠ on the Relationships tab to close the Relationships window.

▶ **8.** Click the **Office Button** 🏛, point to **Manage**, and then click **Compact and Repair Database**. Access compacts the Belmont database.

▶ **9.** Click the **Close** button ⊠ on the program window title bar. Access closes the Belmont database and then the Access program window closes.

Session 2.2 Quick Check | Review

1. To insert a check mark in an empty check box for a Yes/No field, you press the
   _____ .

2. What is the keyboard shortcut for inserting the value from the same field in the previous record into the current record?

3. _____ data is a process that allows you to copy the data from a source without having to open the source file.

4. What is the effect of deleting a field from a table structure?

5. A(n) _____ text file is one in which fields of data are separated by a character such as a comma or a tab.

6. The _____ is the "one" table in a one-to-many relationship, and the _____ is the "many" table in the relationship.

7. _____ is a set of rules that Access enforces to maintain consistency between related tables when you update data in a database.

Tutorial Summary | Review

In this tutorial, you learned some important guidelines for designing databases and tables and for setting field properties. You put these guidelines into practice by creating two tables—one in Design view, and another by importing the structure of an existing table. You worked in Design view to define fields, set properties, specify a table's primary key, and modify a table's structure. To complete the first table, you imported data from an Excel worksheet into the table. After creating the second table, you deleted, renamed, and moved fields in the table structure. To complete the second table, you imported data from a text file into the table. This tutorial also presented one of the most important database concepts—defining table relationships. You learned how to define a one-to-many relationship between two tables in a database and how to enforce referential integrity as part of the relationship.

Key Terms

best fit	Double	one-to-many relationship
Byte	entity integrity	orphaned record
cascade deletes option	F1 key	primary table
cascade updates option	F6 key	propagate
composite key	field list	properties
Ctrl + '	Field Properties pane	referential integrity
data redundancy	Field Size property	related table
data type	import	Relationships window
Decimal	Integer	Replication ID
Decimal Places property	join	set (a property)
delimited	join line	Single
Description property	Long Integer	Table Design grid
Design view	null value	

| Practice | **Review Assignments** |

Data Files needed for the Review Assignments: Supplier.accdb *(cont. from Tutorial 1)* **and Goods.xlsx**

In addition to tracking information about the suppliers Belmont Landscapes works with, Oren also wants to track information about their products. He asks you to create a new table in the Supplier database by completing the following:

1. Open the **Supplier** database located in the Level.01\Review folder provided with your Data Files, and then open the **Company** table in Design view.
2. Enter **Primary key** for the Company ID field's Description property.
3. Change the Data Type property for the Zip field to Text.
4. Change the Format property for the Initial Contact Date field to Short Date. Do not propagate the field property changes.
5. Change the Field Size property for each Text field in the table, as follows:
   Company ID = **6**
   Company Name = **50**
   Product Type = **40**
   Address = **35**
   City = **25**
   State = **2**
   Zip = **10**
   Phone = **14**
   Contact First Name = **20**
   Contact Last Name = **25**
6. Save and close the Company table. Click the Yes button when a message appears indicating some data might be lost.
7. Create a new table in Design view, using the table design shown in Figure 2-45.

Figure 2-45

Field Name	Data Type	Description	Field Size	Other
Product ID	Text	Primary key	4	
Company ID	Text	Foreign key	6	
Product Type	Text		35	
Price	Currency			Format = Standard Decimal Places = 2
Color	Text		15	
Size	Text		15	
Material	Text		30	
Weight in Lbs	Number		Single	
Discount Offered	Yes/No			

8. Make sure Product ID is specified as the primary key, and then save the table as **Product**.
9. Modify the table structure by adding a new field named **Unit** (Text field, Field Size: 15) between the Price and Color fields. Move the Size field so that it follows the Material field.
10. Enter the records shown in Figure 2-46 in the Product table. When finished, close the Product table.

Figure 2-46

Product ID	Company ID	Product Type	Price	Unit	Color	Material	Size	Weight in Lbs	Discount Offered
5306	GEN359	Pine mulch	23.35	Cubic yard	Dark brown	Softwoods-pine			Y
5013	HOL207	Small bench	712.00	Each	Green	Steel and cast iron	8 x 2 feet	266	N

11. Use the Import Spreadsheet Wizard to add data to the Product table. The data you need to import is contained in the Goods workbook, which is an Excel file located in the Level.01\Review folder provided with your Data Files.
    a. Specify the Goods workbook as the source of the data.
    b. Select the option for appending the data.
    c. Select Product as the table.
    d. In the Import Spreadsheet Wizard dialog boxes, choose the Goods worksheet, make sure Access uses column headings as field names, and import to the Product table. Do not save the import steps.

12. Open the **Product** table and resize all columns to their best fit. Then save and close the Product table.

13. Define a one-to-many relationship between the primary Company table and the related Product table. Select the referential integrity option and the cascade updates option for the relationship.

14. Save the changes to the Relationships window, compact and repair the Supplier database, and then close the database.

Apply	Case Problem 1

Use the skills you learned in the tutorial to create and modify tables containing data for a small music school.

Data Files needed for this Case Problem: Pinehill.accdb (cont. from Tutorial 1), Music.accdb, Lessons.xlsx, and Student.txt

Pine Hill Music School   Yuka Koyama uses the Pinehill database to maintain information about the students, teachers, and contracts for her music school. Yuka asks you to help her build the database by updating one table and creating two new tables. Complete the following:

1. Open the **Pinehill** database located in the Level.01\Case1 folder provided with your Data Files.

2. Open the **Teacher** table, and set field properties as shown in Figure 2-47.

Figure 2-47

Field Name	Data Type	Description	Field Size	Format
Teacher ID	Text	Primary key	7	
First Name	Text		20	
Last Name	Text		25	
Degree	Text		3	
School	Text		50	
Hire Date	Date/Time			Short Date

3. Add a new field as the last field in the Teacher table with the field name **Takes Beginners** and the Yes/No data type.

4. Save the Teacher table. Click the Yes button when a message appears indicating some data might be lost.

5. In the datasheet, resize the Takes Beginners field to best fit, and then specify that the following teachers can take beginners: Schwartz, Romano, Eberle, Norris, Tanaka, Culbertson, and Mueller.

6. Save and close the Teacher table.

7. Yuka created a table named Student in the Music database that is located in the Level.01\Case1 folder provided with your Data Files. Import the structure of the Student table in the Music database into a new table named Student in the Pinehill database. Do not save the import steps.

8. Delete the following fields from the **Student** table: Company, E-mail Address, Business Phone, Fax Number, and Notes.

9. Add two fields to the end of the Student table: **Birth Date** (Date/Time data type) and **Gender** (Text data type).

10. Rename the primary key field, ID, to **Student ID**, and change its data type to Text. Save the Student table.

11. Move the Last Name field so it follows the First Name field.

12. Modify the design of the Student table so that it matches the design in Figure 2-48, including the revised field names. Do not propagate the field property changes.

Figure 2-48

Field Name	Data Type	Description	Field Size
Student ID	Text	Primary key	7
First Name	Text		20
Last Name	Text		25
Address	Text		35
City	Text		25
State	Text		2
Zip	Text		10
Phone	Text		14
Birth Date	Date/Time		Short Date
Gender	Text	F(emale), M(ale)	1

13. Save your changes to the table design, add the records shown in Figure 2-49 to the Student table, and then close the Student table.

Figure 2-49

Student ID	First Name	Last Name	Address	City	State	Zip	Phone	Birth Date	Gender
APP7509	Sam	Applegate	15675 SW Greens Way	Portland	OR	97224	503-968-2245	10/10/1993	M
BAR7544	Andrea	Barreau	7660 SW 135th Ave	Beaverton	OR	97008	503-579-2227	11/28/1996	F

14. Yuka exported the student data that she was maintaining in another computer system to a text file, and she asks you to add this data to the Student table. The data you need to import is contained in the Student text file (located in the Level.01\Case1 folder provided with your Data Files).

   a. Specify the Student text file as the source of the data.

   b. Select the option for appending the data to the table.

   c. Select Student as the table.

   d. In the Import Text Wizard dialog boxes, choose the option to import delimited data, to use a comma delimiter, and to import the data into the Student table. Do not save the import steps.

15. Open the Student table, resize all the columns in the datasheet to their best fit, and then save and close the table.
16. Create a new table in Design view, using the table design shown in Figure 2-50.

Figure 2-50

Field Name	Data Type	Description	Field Size	Other Properties
Contract ID	Text	Primary key	4	
Student ID	Text	Foreign key	7	
Teacher ID	Text	Foreign key	7	
Contract Start Date	Date/Time		Short Date	
Contract End Date	Date/Time		Short Date	
Lesson Type	Text		25	
Lesson Length	Number	30 or 60 minutes	Integer	
Lesson Monthly Cost	Currency			Format: Currency Decimal Places: 0
Monthly Rental Cost	Currency	Monthly rental charge for instrument		Format: Currency Decimal Places: 0

17. Specify Contract ID as the primary key, save the table using the name **Contract**, and then close the table.
18. Use the Import Spreadsheet Wizard to add data to the Contract table. The data you need to import is contained in the Lessons workbook, which is an Excel file located in the Level.01\Case1 folder provided with your Data Files.
    a. Specify the Lessons workbook as the source of the data.
    b. Select the option for appending the data to the table.
    c. Select Contract as the table.
    d. In the Import Spreadsheet Wizard dialog boxes, choose the Sheet1 worksheet, and import to the Contract table. Do not save the import steps.
19. Open the **Contract** table and add the records shown in Figure 2-51. (*Hint*: Use the New button on the Home tab to add a new record.)

Figure 2-51

Contract ID	Student ID	Teacher ID	Contract Start Date	Contract End Date	Lesson Type	Lesson Length	Lesson Monthly Cost	Monthly Rental Cost
3176	VAR7527	91-0178	3/21/2010	3/21/2011	Violin	30	$140	$35
3179	MCE7551	70-4490	6/1/2010	6/1/2011	Guitar	60	$200	$0

20. Resize all the columns in the datasheet to their best fit, and then save and close the Contract table.
21. Define the one-to-many relationships between the database tables as follows: between the primary Student table and the related Contract table, and between the primary Teacher table and the related Contract table. Select the referential integrity option and the cascade updates option for each relationship.
22. Save the changes to the Relationships window, compact and repair the Pinchill database, and then close the database.

Challenge | **Case Problem 2**

Challenge yourself by using the Import Spreadsheet Wizard to create a new table to store data about fitness center members.

Data Files needed for this Case Problem: Fitness.accdb (*cont. from Tutorial 1*) and Center.xlsx

Parkhurst Health & Fitness Center Martha Parkhurst uses the Fitness database to track information about members who join the center and the program in which each member is enrolled. She asks you to help her maintain this database. Complete the following:

1. Open the **Fitness** database located in the Level.01\Case2 folder provided with your Data Files.
2. Open the **Program** table, and change the following field properties:
   Program ID: Type **Primary key** for the description, and change the field size to **3**.
   Monthly Fee: Change the Format property to Standard.
   Physical Required: Change the data type to Yes/No.
3. Save and close the Program table. Click the Yes button when a message appears indicating some data might be lost.

⊕ EXPLORE 4. Use the Import Spreadsheet Wizard to create a table in the Fitness database. As the source of the data, specify the Center workbook, located in the Level.01\Case2 folder provided with your Data Files. Select the option to import the source data into a new table in the current database, and then click the OK button.

⊕ EXPLORE 5. Complete the Import Spreadsheet Wizard as follows:
   a. Select Sheet1 as the worksheet you want to import.
   b. Accept the option specifying that the first row contains column headings.
   c. Accept the field options the wizard suggests, and do not skip any fields.
   d. Choose Member ID as your own primary key.
   e. Import the data to a table named **Member**, and do not save your import steps.

6. Open the **Member** table, and then delete the Initiation Fee Waived field.
7. Modify the design of the Member table so that it matches the design shown in Figure 2-52, including the field names and their order. (*Hint:* For Text fields, delete any formats specified in the Format property boxes.) Do not propagate the field property changes.

Figure 2-52

Field Name	Data Type	Description	Field Size	Other Properties
Member ID	Text	Primary key	4	
Program ID	Text	Foreign key	3	
First Name	Text		18	
Last Name	Text		18	
Street	Text		30	
City	Text		24	
State	Text		2	
Zip	Text		10	
Phone	Text		14	
Date Joined	Date/Time			Format: Short Date
Expiration Date	Date/Time	Date when membership expires		Format: Short Date
Membership Status	Text	Active, Inactive, or On Hold	8	

⊕ EXPLORE

8. Open the Access Help window and enter **default value** as the search text. Select the Help article titled "Set default values for fields or controls," and then select "Set a default value for a table field." Read that section of the Help article, and then scroll down and examine the examples of default values. Set the Default Value property for the Membership Status field to **"Active"** (including the quotation marks). Close the Access Help window.

9. Save the Member table. Click the Yes button when a message appears indicating some data might be lost.

10. Add the records shown in Figure 2-53 to the Member table. (*Hint*: Use the New button on the Home tab to add a new record.)

Figure 2-53

Member ID	Program ID	First Name	Last Name	Street	City	State	Zip	Phone	Date Joined	Expiration Date	Membership Status
1170	210	Ed	Curran	25 Fairway Drive	Bon Air	VA	23235	804-323-6824	6/3/2010	12/3/2010	Active
1172	206	Tung	Lin	40 Green Boulevard	Richmond	VA	23220	804-674-0227	11/16/2010	11/16/2011	Active

11. Resize all the columns in the datasheet to their best fit, and then save and close the table.

12. Define a one-to-many relationship between the primary Program table and the related Member table. Select the referential integrity option and the cascade updates option for this relationship.

13. Save the changes to the Relationships window, compact and repair the Fitness database, and then close the database.

| Apply | **Case Problem 3** |

Use the skills you learned in the tutorial to create and modify tables containing data for a not-for-profit agency that recycles household goods.

Data Files needed for this Case Problem: Agency.txt, Rossi.accdb (*cont. from Tutorial 1*), Gifts.xlsx, and Recycle.accdb

Rossi Recycling Group Tom Rossi uses the Rossi database to maintain information about the donors, agencies, and donations to his not-for-profit agency. Tom asks you to help him maintain the database by updating one table and creating two new ones. Complete the following:

1. Open the **Rossi** database located in the Level.01\Case3 folder provided with your Data Files.

2. Open the **Donor** table. For the Donor ID field, add **Primary key** as the description and set the Field Size property to **5**. Set the Field Size properties for the remaining fields as follows:

   Title: **4**

   First Name: **20**

   Last Name: **25**

   Phone: **14**

3. Save and close the Donor table. Click the Yes button when a message appears indicating some data might be lost.

4. Tom created a table named Agency in the Recycle database that is located in the Level.01\Case3 folder provided with your Data Files. Import the structure of the Agency table in the Recycle database into a new table named Agency in the Rossi database. Do not save the import steps.

5. Delete the following fields from the Agency table: Fax Number, Mobile Phone, E-mail Address, and Notes.
6. Rename the ID field to **Agency ID**, and change its data type to Text. Make sure Agency ID is the primary key.
7. Modify the design of the Agency table so that it matches the design shown in Figure 2-54, including the field names and their order. Do not propagate the field property changes.

Figure 2-54

Field Name	Data Type	Description	Field Size
Agency ID	Text	Primary key	3
Agency Name	Text		40
Contact First Name	Text		20
Contact Last Name	Text		25
Address	Text		30
City	Text		24
State	Text		2
Zip	Text		10
Phone	Text		14

8. Save your changes to the table design, add the records shown in Figure 2-55 to the Agency table, and then close the Agency table.

Figure 2-55

Agency ID	Agency Name	Contact First Name	Contact Last Name	Address	City	State	Zip	Phone
K64	Community Development	Jerri	Clarkson	223 Penn Ave	Salina	KS	67401	785-309-3351
K82	SeniorCare Program	Todd	Groverman	718 N Walnut	McPherson	KS	67460	620-241-3668

9. Tom exported the student data that he was maintaining in another computer system to a text file, and he asks you to add this data to the Agency table. The data you need to import is contained in the Agency text file (located in the Level.01\Case3 folder provided with your Data Files).
   a. Specify the Agency text file as the source of the data.
   b. Select the option for appending the data to the table.
   c. Select Agency as the table.
   d. In the Import Text Wizard dialog boxes, choose the option to import delimited data, to use a comma delimiter, and to import the data into the Agency table. Do not save the import steps.
10. Resize all the columns in the datasheet to their best fit, and then save and close the table.
11. Use Design view to create a table using the table design shown in Figure 2-56.

Figure 2-56

Field Name	Data Type	Description	Field Size	Other Properties
Donation ID	Text	Primary key	4	
Donor ID	Text	Foreign key	5	
Agency ID	Text	Foreign key	3	
Donation Date	Date/Time			Format: Short Date
Donation Description	Text		50	
Donation Value	Currency	Cash amount donated or estimated value of goods donated		Format: Currency Decimal Places: 2
Pickup Required	Yes/No			

12. Specify Donation ID as the primary key, save the table as **Donation**, and then close the table.

13. Use the Import Spreadsheet Wizard to add data to the Donation table. The data you need to import is contained in the Gifts workbook, which is an Excel file located in the Level.01\Case3 folder provided with your Data Files.
    a. Specify the Gifts workbook as the source of the data.
    b. Select the option for appending the data to the table.
    c. Select Donation as the table.
    d. In the Import Spreadsheet Wizard dialog boxes, choose the Sheet1 worksheet, and import to the Donation table. Do not save the import steps.

14. Open the **Donation** table, and add the records shown in Figure 2-57. Whenever possible, use a keyboard shortcut to insert the same value as in the previous record.

Figure 2-57

Donation ID	Donor ID	Agency ID	Donation Date	Donation Description	Donation Value	Pickup Required
2117	36012	K82	2/20/2010	Cash	$50.00	No
2122	36016	N33	3/22/2010	Cash	$35.00	No

15. Resize all the columns in the datasheet to their best fit, and then save and close the table.

16. Define the one-to-many relationships between the database tables as follows: between the primary Donor table and the related Donation table, and between the primary Agency table and the related Donation table. Select the referential integrity option and the cascade updates option for each relationship.

17. Save the changes to the Relationships window, compact and repair the Rossi database, and then close the database.

Challenge | Case Problem 4

Work with the skills you've learned, and explore some new skills, to create a database for a luxury rental company.

Data Files needed for this Case Problem: Bookings.txt, GEM.accdb *(cont. from Tutorial 1),* **and Overseas.accdb**

GEM Ultimate Vacations   Griffin and Emma MacElroy use the GEM database to track the data about the services they provide to the clients who book luxury vacations through their agency. They ask you to help them maintain this database. Complete the following:

1. Open the **GEM** database located in the Level.01\Case4 folder provided with your Data Files.

2. Open the **Guest** table. Add **Primary key** as the description for the Guest ID field and change its Field Size property to **3**. Change the Field Size property for the following fields:

   Guest First Name: **20**

   Guest Last Name: **25**

   Address: **32**

   City: **24**

   State/Prov: **2**

   Postal Code: **10**

   Country: **15**

   Phone: **14**

3. Save and close the Guest table. Click the Yes button when a message appears indicating some data might be lost.

⊕ EXPLORE 4. Open the Access Help window and enter **import table** as the search text. Select the Help article titled "Import or link to data in another Access database," and then select "Import data from another Access database." Read the steps in the "Import the data" section of the Help article. Close the Access Help window, click the External Data tab on the Ribbon, and then click the Access button (with the ScreenTip "Import Access database") in the Import group.

⊕ EXPLORE 5. Import the Rentals table structure and data from the Overseas database into a new table in the GEM database as follows:

   a. As the source of the data, specify the Overseas database, located in the Level.01\Case4 folder provided with your Data Files.

   b. Select the option button to import tables, queries, forms, reports, macros, and modules into the current database, and then click the OK button.

   c. In the Import Objects dialog box, click Rentals, click the Options button, and then make sure that the correct option is selected to import the table's data and structure.

   d. Do not save your import steps.

⊕ EXPLORE 6. Right-click the Rentals table in the Navigation Pane, click Rename on the shortcut menu, and then enter **Property** as the new name for this table.

7. In the Property table, delete the VIP Program field, and then move the Property Type field so that it appears between the Sleeps and Description fields.

8. Make sure that the Property ID field is the table's primary key. Change the data type of the Property ID field to Text with a Field Size property of **4**.

9. Resize all the columns in the datasheet to their best fit, and then save and close the table.

10. Use Design view to create a table using the table design shown in Figure 2-58.

Figure 2-58

Field Name	Data Type	Description	Field Size	Other Properties
Reservation ID	Text	Primary key	3	
Guest ID	Text	Foreign key	3	
Property ID	Text	Foreign key	4	
Start Date	Date/Time			
End Date	Date/Time			
People	Number	Number of people in the party	Integer	
Rental Rate	Currency	Rate per day; includes any discounts or promotions		Format: Currency Decimal Places: 0

11. Specify Reservation ID as the primary key, and then save the table as **Reservation**.

⊕ EXPLORE

12. Open the Access Help window and enter **custom date format** as the search text. Select the Help article titled "Enter a date or time value," and then scroll down and read the "Custom Date/Time format reference" section. Change the Format property of the Start Date and End Date fields to a custom format that displays dates in a format similar to 11/23/10. Save and close the Reservation table, and then close the Access Help window.

13. Griffin exported the reservation data that he was maintaining in another computer system to a text file, and he asks you to add this data to the Reservation table. The data you need to import is contained in the Bookings text file (located in the Level.01\Case4 folder provided with your Data Files).

    a. Specify the Bookings text file as the source of the data.

    b. Select the option for appending the data to the table.

    c. Select Reservation as the table.

    d. In the Import Text Wizard dialog boxes, choose the option to import delimited data, to use a comma delimiter, and to import the data into the Reservation table. Do not save the import steps.

14. Resize all the columns in the datasheet to their best fit, and then save and close the table.

15. Define the one-to-many relationships between the database tables as follows: between the primary Guest table and the related Reservation table, and between the primary Property table and the related Reservation table. Select the referential integrity option and the cascade updates option for each relationship.

16. Save the changes to the Relationships window, compact and repair the GEM database, and then close the database.

Research | Internet Assignments

Use the Internet to find and work with data related to the topics presented in this tutorial.

The purpose of the Internet Assignments is to challenge you to find information on the Internet that you can use to work effectively with this software. The actual assignments are updated and maintained on the Course Technology Web site. Log on to the Internet and use your Web browser to go to the Student Online Companion for New Perspectives Office 2007 at **www.course.com/np/office2007**. Then navigate to the Internet Assignments for this tutorial.

Assess | SAM Assessment and Training

If you have a SAM user profile, you may have access to hands-on instruction, practice, and assessment of the skills covered in this tutorial. Log in to your SAM account (**http://sam2007.course.com**) to launch any assigned training activities or exams that relate to the skills covered in this tutorial.

Review | Quick Check Answers

Session 2.1

1. Identify all the fields needed to produce the required information, organize each piece of data into its smallest useful part, group related fields into tables, determine each table's primary key, include a common field in related tables, avoid data redundancy, and determine the properties of each field.
2. The Data Type property determines what field values you can enter into the field and what other properties the field will have.
3. Text, Number, and AutoNumber fields
4. 255
5. F6
6. null

Session 2.2

1. spacebar
2. Ctrl + '
3. Importing
4. The field and all its values are removed from the table.
5. delimited
6. primary table; related table
7. Referential integrity

Ending Data Files

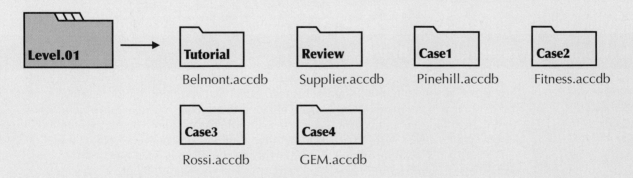

Level.01 →	Tutorial	Review	Case1	Case2
	Belmont.accdb	Supplier.accdb	Pinehill.accdb	Fitness.accdb
	Case3	Case4		
	Rossi.accdb	GEM.accdb		

Objectives

Session 3.1
- Find, modify, and delete records in a table
- Learn how to use the Query window in Design view
- Create, run, and save queries
- Update data using a query datasheet
- Create a query based on multiple tables
- Sort data in a query
- Filter data in a query

Session 3.2
- Specify an exact match condition in a query
- Change the font size and alternating row color in a datasheet
- Use a comparison operator in a query to match a range of values
- Use the And and Or logical operators in queries
- Create and format a calculated field in a query
- Perform calculations in a query using aggregate functions and record group calculations
- Change the display of database objects in the Navigation Pane

Maintaining and Querying a Database

Updating and Retrieving Information About Customers, Contracts, and Invoices

Case | Belmont Landscapes

At a recent meeting, Oren Belmont and his staff discussed the importance of maintaining accurate information about the firm's customers, contracts, and invoices, and regularly monitoring the business activities of Belmont Landscapes. For example, Sarah Fisher and the office staff need to make sure they have up-to-date contact information, such as phone numbers and e-mail addresses, for all the firm's customers. They also must monitor the invoice activity to ensure that invoices are paid on time and in full. Taylor Sico, the marketing manager at Belmont Landscapes, and her marketing staff track customer activity to develop new strategies for promoting the services provided by Belmont Landscapes. In addition, Oren is interested in analyzing other aspects of the business related to contracts and finances. You can satisfy all these informational needs for Belmont Landscapes by updating data in the Belmont database and by creating and using queries that retrieve information from the database.

Starting Data Files

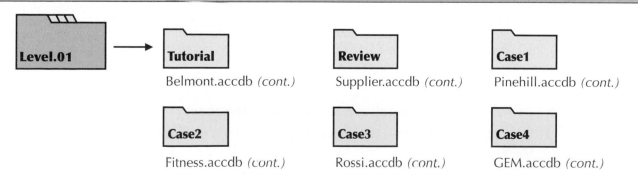

Level.01 → Tutorial
Belmont.accdb *(cont.)*

Review
Supplier.accdb *(cont.)*

Case1
Pinehill.accdb *(cont.)*

Case2
Fitness.accdb *(cont.)*

Case3
Rossi.accdb *(cont.)*

Case4
GEM.accdb *(cont.)*

Session 3.1

Updating a Database

Updating, or **maintaining**, a database is the process of adding, modifying, and deleting records in database tables to keep them current and accurate. After reviewing the data in the Belmont database, Sarah identified some changes that need to be made to the data. She would like you to modify the field values in one record in the Customer table, and then delete a record in the Contract table.

Modifying Records

To modify the field values in a record, you must first make the record the current record. Then you position the insertion point in the field value to make minor changes or select the field value to replace it entirely. In Tutorial 1, you used the mouse with the scroll bars and the navigation buttons to navigate the records in a datasheet. You can also use key-stroke combinations and the F2 key to navigate a datasheet and to select field values. The **F2 key** is a toggle that you use to switch between navigation mode and editing mode:

- In **navigation mode**, Access selects an entire field value. If you type while you are in navigation mode, your typed entry replaces the highlighted field value.
- In **editing mode**, you can insert or delete characters in a field value based on the location of the insertion point.

Figure 3-1 shows some of the navigation mode and editing mode keystroke techniques.

| Figure 3-1 | Navigation mode and editing mode keystroke techniques |

Press	To Move the Selection in Navigation Mode	To Move the Insertion Point in Editing Mode
←	Left one field value at a time	Left one character at a time
→	Right one field value at a time	Right one character at a time
Home	Left to the first field value in the record	To the left of the first character in the field value
End	Right to the last field value in the record	To the right of the last character in the field value
↑ or ↓	Up or down one record at a time	Up or down one record at a time and switch to navigation mode
Tab or Enter	Right one field value at a time	Right one field value at a time and switch to navigation mode
Ctrl+Home	To the first field value in the first record	To the left of the first character in the field value
Ctrl+End	To the last field value in the last record	To the right of the last character in the field value

The Customer table record Sarah wants you to change is for Walker Investment Company, one of Belmont Landscapes' commercial customers. The company recently moved its office from Grand Rapids to Battle Creek, so you need to update the Customer table record with the new address and phone information.

To open the Belmont database and modify the record:

1. Start Access and open the **Belmont** database located in the Level.01\Tutorial folder.

Trouble? If the Security Warning is displayed below the Ribbon, click the Options button next to the Security Warning. In the dialog box that opens, click the "Enable this content" option button, and then click the OK button.

2. Open the **Customer** table in Datasheet view. The first value for the Customer ID field (11001) is highlighted, indicating that the table is in navigation mode.

The record you need to modify is near the end of the table and has a Customer ID field value of 11087.

3. Press the **Ctrl+End** keys. Access displays records from the end of the table and selects the last field value in the last record, record 40. This field value is for the E-mail Address field.

4. Press the **Home** key. The first field value in the last record is now selected. This field value is for the Customer ID field.

5. Press the ↑ key. The Customer ID field value for the previous record (Customer ID 11087) is selected. This record is the one you need to change.

6. Press the **Tab** key four times to move to the Phone field and select its field value, type **269-963-0190**, press the **Tab** key, type **1752 S Main St**, press the **Tab** key, type **Battle Creek**, press the **Tab** key twice, type **49014**, and then press the **Tab** key. The changes to the record are complete. See Figure 3-2.

Table after changing field values in a record ◄ **Figure 3-2**

⊞ Russell	616-940-3380	722 Bee...		...nd Rapids	MI	49506	srussell3@dnd57.org
⊞ Van Dousen	616-392-4629	249 W 11...			MI	49424	jvdousen2@tulips3.com
⊞ Williams	517-337-0990	1003 Alb...		...sing	MI	48823	jwilliams94@hsc7.edu
⊞ DeSantis	616-866-4882	78 Spring St		Rockford	MI	49341	cdesantis9@milocal123.com
⊞ Phillips	616-637-5408	39 Water St		South Haven	MI	49090	ephillips8@milocal123.com
⊞ Belanger	►269-963-0190	1752 S Main St◄		Battle Creek◄	MI	►49014	hbelanger4@wlc88.com
⊞ Kervin	616-454-3327	333 Pearl St		Grand Rapids	MI	49503	skervin3@wcpf47.org

field values changed

Record: I◄ ◄ 39 of 40 ► ►I ►▷ No Filter Search

Datasheet View

7. Close the Customer table.

The next update Sarah asks you to make is to delete a record in the Contract table. The customer who signed Contract Num 3101 owns a chain of small restaurants and had planned to renovate the landscaping at each restaurant site. His plans have changed for one of these sites, and he has cancelled the contract. When you are maintaining database tables, you first need to find the data to change.

Finding Data in a Table

Access provides options you can use to locate specific field values in a table. Instead of scrolling the Contract table datasheet to find the contract that you need to delete—the record for contract number 3101—you can use the Find command to find the record. The **Find command** allows you to search a table or query datasheet, or a form, to locate a specific field value or part of a field value. This feature is particularly useful when searching a table that contains a large number of records.

To search for the record in the Contract table:

1. Open the **Contract** table in Datasheet view. The first field value for the Contract Num field (3011) is selected. You need to search the Contract Num field to find the record containing the Contract Num field value 3101, so the insertion point is already correctly positioned in the field you want to search.

> **2.** In the Find group on the Home tab, click the **Find** button. The Find and Replace dialog box opens. See Figure 3-3.

Figure 3-3   **Find and Replace dialog box**

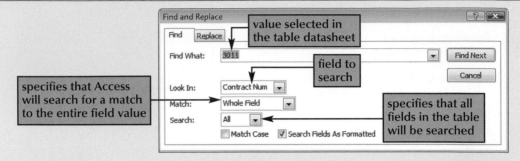

The field value 3011 appears in the Find What text box because this value is selected in the table datasheet. Also, the Contract Num field is displayed in the Look In list box because it is the current field. The Match list box indicates that the Find command will match the whole field value, which is correct for your search. You also can choose to search for only part of a field value, such as when you need to find all contract numbers that start with a certain value. The Search list box indicates that all the records in the table will be searched for the value you want to find. You also can choose to search up or down from the currently selected record.

Trouble? Some of the settings in your dialog box might be different from those shown in Figure 3-3, depending on the last search performed on the computer you're using. If so, change the settings so that they match those in the figure.

> **3.** Make sure the value 3011 is selected in the Find What text box, type **3101** to replace the selected value, and then click the **Find Next** button. Access moves to and selects the field value you specified.

> **4.** Click the **Cancel** button to close the Find and Replace dialog box.

Deleting Records

To delete a record, you need to select the record in Datasheet view, and then delete it using the Delete button in the Records group on the Home tab, or the Delete Record option on the shortcut menu.

Reference Window | **Deleting a Record**

- With the table in Datasheet view, click the row selector for the record you want to delete.
- In the Records group on the Home tab, click the Delete button (or right-click the row selector for the record, and then click Delete Record on the shortcut menu).
- In the dialog box asking you to confirm the deletion, click the Yes button.

Now that you have found the record with Contract Num 3101, you can delete it. To delete a record, you must first select the entire row for the record.

To delete the record:

> **1.** Click the row selector for the record containing the Contract Num field value **3101**, which should still be highlighted. The entire row is selected.

2. In the Records group on the Home tab, click the **Delete** button. A dialog box opens and indicates that you cannot delete the record. The dialog box indicates that the Invoice table contains records that are related to Contract Num 3101 and, therefore, you cannot delete the record in the Contract table. Recall that you defined a one-to-many relationship between the Contract and Invoice tables and enforced referential integrity. When you try to delete a record in the primary table (Contract), Access prevents the deletion if matching records exist in the related table (Invoice). This protection helps to maintain the integrity of the data in the database.

To delete the record in the Contract table, you first must delete the related records in the Invoice table.

3. Click the **OK** button in the dialog box to close it. Notice the plus sign that appears at the beginning of each record in the Contract table. The **plus sign** indicates that the records have related records in another table—in this case, the Invoice table.

4. Scroll the table window down until you see the rest of the records in the table, so that you have room to view the related records for the contract record.

5. Click the **plus sign** next to Contract Num 3101. Access displays the four related records from the Invoice table for this contract. The plus sign changes to a minus sign for the current record when its related records are displayed. See Figure 3-4.

Related records from the Invoice table in the subdatasheet ◄ **Figure 3-4**

The related records from the Invoice table are displayed in a **subdatasheet**. When you first open a table that is the primary table in a one-to-many relationship, the subdatasheet containing the records from the related table is not displayed. You need to click the plus sign, also called the **expand indicator**, to display the related records in the subdatasheet. When the subdatasheet is open you can navigate and update it, just as you can using a table datasheet.

You need to delete the records in the Invoice table that are related to Contract Num 3101 so you can then delete this contract record. The four Invoice table records are for invoices set up to be paid for future phases of the contract, which has now been cancelled. You could open the Invoice table and find the related records. However, an easier way to delete the related records for Contract Num 3101 is to delete them from the subdatasheet. The records will be deleted from the Invoice table automatically.

6. Click and hold the mouse button on the row selector for the first Invoice table record in the subdatasheet, drag the pointer down to select all four records, and then release the mouse button. With the four records selected, you can delete them all at the same time.

▶ **7.** In the Records group on the Home tab, click the **Delete** button. Access opens a dialog box asking you to confirm the deletion of four records. Because the deletion of a record is permanent and cannot be undone, Access prompts you to make sure that you want to delete the records.

▶ **8.** Click the **Yes** button to confirm the deletion and close the dialog box. The records are removed from the Invoice table, and the subdatasheet is now empty.

▶ **9.** Click the **minus sign** next to Contract Num 3101 to close the subdatasheet.

Now that you have deleted all the related records in the Invoice table, you can delete the record for Contract Num 3101. You will use the shortcut menu to delete the record.

▶ **10.** Right-click the row selector for the record for Contract Num **3101**. Access selects the record and displays the shortcut menu.

▶ **11.** Click **Delete Record** on the shortcut menu, and then click the **Yes** button in the dialog box to confirm the deletion. The record is deleted from the table.

▶ **12.** Close the Contract table.

You have finished updating the Belmont database by modifying and deleting records. Next, you'll retrieve specific data from the database to meet various requests for information about Belmont Landscapes.

Introduction to Queries

As you learned in Tutorial 1, a query is a question you ask about data stored in a database. For example, Oren might create a query to find records in the Customer table for only those customers located in a specific city. When you create a query, you tell Access which fields you need and what criteria Access should use to select the records. Access provides powerful query capabilities that allow you to do the following:

• Display selected fields and records from a table.
• Sort records.
• Perform calculations.
• Generate data for forms, reports, and other queries.
• Update data in the tables in a database.
• Find and display data from two or more tables.

Most questions about data are generalized queries in which you specify the fields and records you want Access to select. These common requests for information, such as "Which customers are located in Kalamazoo?" or "How many invoices have been paid?" are called **select queries**. The answer to a select query is returned in the form of a datasheet. The result of a query is also referred to as a **recordset**, because the query produces a set of records that answers your question.

More specialized, technical queries, such as finding duplicate records in a table, are best formulated using a Query Wizard. A **Query Wizard** prompts you for information by asking a series of questions and then creates the appropriate query based on your answers. In Tutorial 1, you used the Simple Query Wizard to display only some of the fields in the Contract table; Access provides other Query Wizards for more complex queries. For common, informational queries, it is easier for you to design your own query than to use a Query Wizard.

Taylor wants you to create a query to display the customer ID, company, first name, last name, city, and e-mail address for each record in the Customer table. Her marketing staff needs this information to complete an e-mail campaign advertising a special promotion being offered to Belmont Landscapes' customers. You'll open the Query window in Design view to create the query for Taylor.

Query Window

You use the Query window in Design view to create a query. In Design view, you specify the data you want to view by constructing a query by example. When you use **query by example (QBE)**, you give Access an example of the information you are requesting. Access then retrieves the information that precisely matches your example.

For Taylor's query, you need to display data from the Customer table.

To open the Query window in Design view:

▶ **1.** Close the Navigation Pane so that more of the workspace is displayed.

▶ **2.** Click the **Create** tab on the Ribbon. Access displays the options for creating different database objects.

▶ **3.** In the Other group on the Create tab, click the **Query Design** button. The Show Table dialog box opens on the Query window in Design view. See Figure 3-5.

Show Table dialog box ◀ **Figure 3-5**

The Show Table dialog box lists all the tables in the Belmont database. You can choose to base a query on one or more tables, on other queries, or on a combination of tables and queries. The query you are creating will retrieve data from the Customer table, so you need to add this table to the Query window.

▶ **4.** Click **Customer** in the Tables list box, click the **Add** button, and then click the **Close** button. Access places the Customer table's field list in the Query window and closes the Show Table dialog box. See Figure 3-6.

Figure 3-6 — **Select query in Design view**

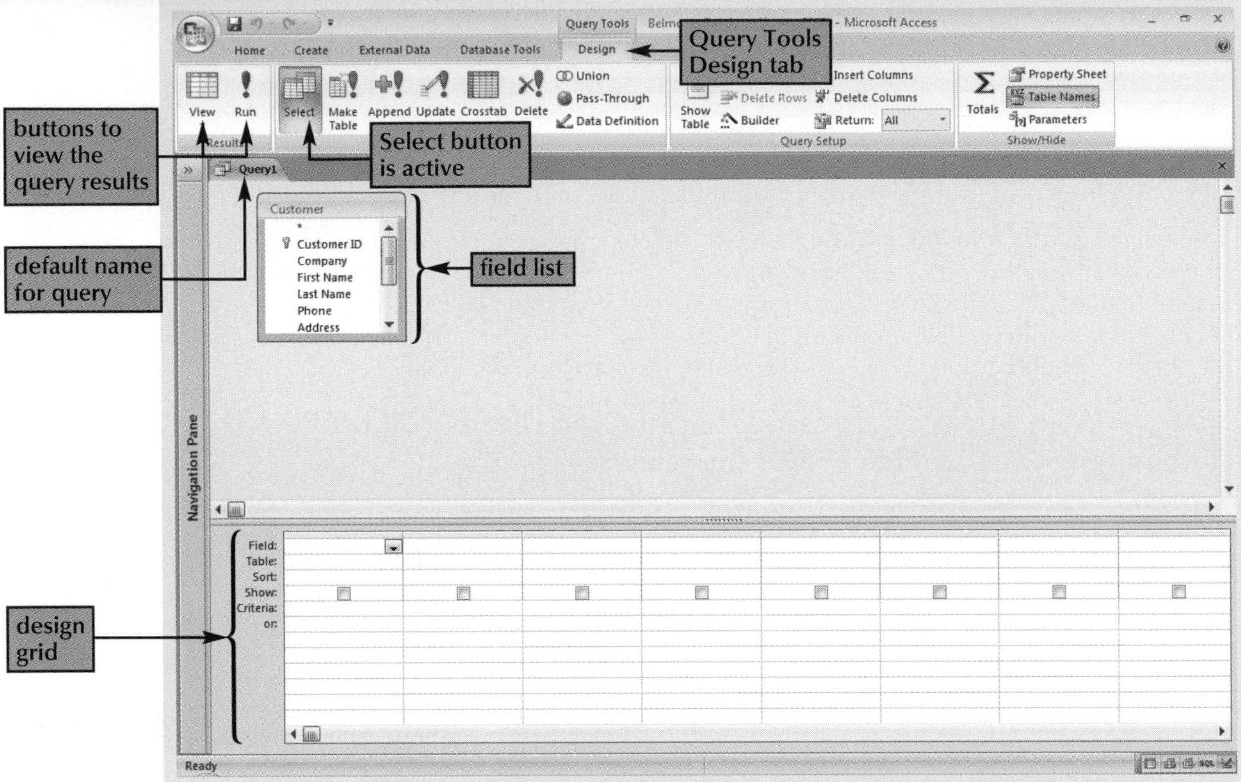

Trouble? If you add the wrong table to the Query window, right-click the bar at the top of the field list containing the table name, and then click Remove Table on the shortcut menu. To add the correct table to the Query window, click the Show Table button in the Query Setup group on the Query Tools Design tab to redisplay the Show Table dialog box, and then repeat Step 4.

In Design view, the Ribbon displays the Query Tools Design tab, with options for creating and running different types of queries. In the Query Type group on the Query Tools Design tab, notice that the Select button is active; this indicates that you are creating a select query, which is the default type of query. The default query name (Query1) is displayed on the tab for the query. You'll change the default query name to a more meaningful one later when you save the query.

The top portion of the Query window in Design view contains the field list (or lists) for the table(s) used in the query, and the bottom portion contains the design grid. Each **field list** contains the fields for the table(s) you are querying. The table name appears at the top of the list box, and the fields are listed in the order in which they appear in the table. Notice that the primary key for the table is identified by the key symbol. You can scroll the field list to see more fields, or you can expand the field list box by dragging its borders to display all the fields and the complete field names. In the **design grid**, you include the fields and record selection criteria for the information you want to see. Each column in the design grid contains specifications about a field you will use in the query. You can choose a single field for your query by double-clicking the field name to place it in the next available design grid column.

Tip

You can also use the mouse to drag a field name from the field list to a column in the design grid.

When you are constructing a query, you can see the query results at any time by clicking the View button or the Run button in the Results group on the Query Tools Design tab. In response, Access displays the query datasheet (or recordset), which contains the set of fields and records that results from answering, or **running**, the query. The order of the fields in the query datasheet is the same as the order of the fields in the design grid.

Comparing Methods for Adding All Fields to the Design Grid		InSight

If the query you are creating includes every field from the specified table, you can use one of the following three methods to transfer all the fields from the field list to the design grid:

- Click and drag each field individually from the field list to the design grid. Use this method if you want the fields in your query to appear in an order that is different from the order in the field list.
- Double-click the asterisk at the top of the field list. Access places the table name followed by a period and an asterisk (as in "Customer.*") in the design grid, which signifies that the order of the fields is the same in the query as it is in the field list. Use this method if you don't need to sort the query or specify conditions for the records you want to select. The advantage of using this method is that you do not need to change the query if you add or delete fields from the underlying table structure. Such changes are reflected automatically in the query.
- Double-click the field list title bar to highlight all the fields, and then click and drag one of the highlighted fields to the design grid. Access places each field in a separate column and arranges the fields in the order in which they appear in the field list. Use this method when you need to sort your query or include record selection criteria.

Now you'll create and run Taylor's query to display selected fields from the Customer table.

Creating and Running a Query

The default table datasheet displays all the fields in the table in the same order as they appear in the table. In contrast, a query datasheet can display selected fields from a table, and the order of the fields can be different from that of the table, enabling those viewing the query results to see only the information they need and in the order they want.

Taylor wants the Customer ID, Company, First Name, Last Name, City, and E-mail Address fields from the Customer table to appear in the query results. You'll add each of these fields to the design grid. First you'll resize the Customer table field list to display all of the fields.

To select the fields for the query, and then run the query:

▶ **1.** Position the pointer on the bottom border of the Customer field list until the pointer changes to a ⬍ shape, and then click and drag the pointer down until the vertical scroll bar in the field list disappears and all fields in the Customer table are displayed.

▶ **2.** In the Customer field list, double-click **Customer ID** to place the field in the design grid's first column Field text box. See Figure 3-7.

Figure 3-7   Field added to the design grid

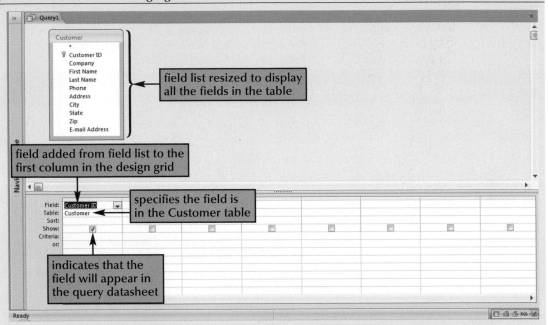

In the design grid's first column, the field name Customer ID appears in the Field text box, the table name Customer appears in the Table text box, and the check mark in the Show check box indicates that the field will be displayed in the datasheet when you run the query. Sometimes you might not want to display a field and its values in the query results. For example, if you are creating a query to list all customers located in Lansing, and you assign the name "Lansing Customers" to the query, you do not need to include the City field value for each record in the query results—the query design only lists customers with the City field value of "Lansing." Even if you choose not to include a field in the display of the query results, you can still use the field as part of the query to select specific records or to specify a particular sequence for the records in the datasheet.

▶ 3. Double-click **Company** in the Customer field list. Access adds this field to the second column in the design grid.

▶ 4. Repeat Step 3 for the **First Name**, **Last Name**, **City**, and **E-mail Address** fields to add these fields to the design grid in that order.

Trouble? If you double-click the wrong field and accidentally add it to the design grid, you can remove the field from the grid. Select the field's column by clicking the pointer ↓ on the field selector, which is the thin bar above the Field text box, for the field you want to delete, and then press the Delete key (or in the Query Setup group on the Query Tools Design tab, click the Delete Columns button).

Having selected the fields for Taylor's query, you can now run the query.

▶ 5. In the Results group on the Query Tools Design tab, click the **Run** button. Access runs the query and displays the results in Datasheet view. See Figure 3-8.

Datasheet displayed after running the query | Figure 3-8

The six fields you added to the design grid appear in the datasheet, and the records are displayed in primary key sequence by Customer ID. Access selected a total of 40 records for display in the datasheet. Taylor asks you to save the query as "Customer E-mail" so that she can easily retrieve the same data again.

▶ **6.** Click the **Save** button 🖫 on the Quick Access toolbar. The Save As dialog box opens.

▶ **7.** Type **Customer E-mail** in the Query Name text box, and then press the **Enter** key. Access saves the query with the specified name in the Belmont database and displays the name on the tab for the query.

Query Datasheet vs. Table Datasheet | InSight

Although a query datasheet looks just like a table datasheet and appears in Datasheet view, a query datasheet is temporary, and its contents are based on the criteria you establish in the design grid. In contrast, a table datasheet shows the permanent data in a table. However, you can update data while viewing a query datasheet, just as you can when working in a table datasheet or form.

When viewing the query results, Taylor noticed that the contact person for the River-View Development Company is incorrect. Charles Nowak recently retired from his position, and she asks you to update the record with the first name, last name, and e-mail address of the new contact.

Updating Data Using a Query

Although a query datasheet is temporary and its contents are based on the criteria in the query design grid, you can update the data in a table using a query datasheet. In this case, Taylor has changes she wants you to make to a record in the Customer table. Instead of making the changes in the table datasheet, you can make them in the Customer E-mail query datasheet because the query is based on the Customer table. The underlying Customer table will be updated with the changes you make.

To update data using the Customer E-mail query datasheet:

▶ **1.** Locate the record with Customer ID 11040, RiverView Development Company (record 13 in the datasheet).

▶ **2.** In the First Name field for this record, double-click **Charles** to select the name, and then type **Susan**.

▶ **3.** Press the **Tab** key to move to and select the value in the Last Name field, and then type **Darcy**.

▶ **4.** Press the **Tab** key twice to move to and select the value in the E-mail Address field, type **sdarcy33@rvdc3.com**, and then press the **Tab** key.

▶ **5.** Close the Customer E-mail query, and then open the Navigation Pane. Note that the Customer E-mail query is listed in the Customer section of the Navigation Pane.

Now you'll check the Customer table to verify that the changes you made in the query datasheet were also made in the Customer table.

▶ **6.** Open the **Customer** table in Datasheet view, and then close the Navigation Pane.

▶ **7.** For the record with Customer ID 11040 (record 13), use the **Tab** key to move through the field values. Notice that the changes you made in the query datasheet to the First Name, Last Name, and E-mail Address field values were made to the record in the Customer table.

▶ **8.** Close the Customer table.

Sarah also wants to view specific information in the Belmont database. She would like to review the contract signing dates and amounts for customers while also viewing certain contact information for the customers. So, she needs to see data from both the Customer table and the Contract table at the same time.

Creating a Multitable Query

A multitable query is a query based on more than one table. If you want to create a query that retrieves data from multiple tables, the tables must have a common field. In Tutorial 2, you established a relationship between the Customer (primary) and Contract (related) tables based on the common Customer ID field that exists in both tables, so you can now create a query to display data from both tables at the same time. Specifically, Sarah wants to view the values in the City, Company, First Name, and Last Name fields from the Customer table and the Signing Date and Contract Amt fields from the Contract table.

To create the query using the Customer and Contract tables:

▶ **1.** Click the **Create** tab on the Ribbon.

▶ **2.** In the Other group on the Create tab, click the **Query Design** button. Access opens the Show Table dialog box. You need to add the Customer and Contract tables to the Query window.

▶ **3.** Click **Customer** in the Tables list box, click the **Add** button, click **Contract**, click the **Add** button, and then click the **Close** button. The Customer and Contract field lists appear in the Query window, and the Show Table dialog box closes.

▶ **4.** Use the ⬍ pointer to resize the Customer field list so that all the fields in the table are displayed.

The one-to-many relationship between the two tables is shown in the Query window, in the same way that Access indicates a relationship between two tables in the Relationships window. Note that the join line is thick at both ends; this signifies that you selected the option to enforce referential integrity. If you had not selected this option, the join line would be thin at both ends and neither the "1" nor the infinity symbol would appear, even though the tables have a one-to-many relationship.

You need to place the City, Company, First Name, and Last Name fields (in that order) from the Customer field list into the design grid, and then place the Signing Date and Contract Amt fields from the Contract field list into the design grid. This is the order in which Sarah wants to view the fields in the query results.

▶ 5. In the Customer field list, double-click **City** to place this field in the design grid's first column Field text box.

▶ 6. Repeat Step 5 to add the **Company**, **First Name**, and **Last Name** fields from the Customer table to the second through fourth columns of the design grid.

▶ 7. Repeat Step 5 to add the **Signing Date** and **Contract Amt** fields (in that order) from the Contract table to the fifth and sixth columns of the design grid. The query specifications are complete, so you can now run the query.

▶ 8. In the Results group on the Query Tools Design tab, click the **Run** button. Access runs the query and displays the results in Datasheet view. See Figure 3-9.

Datasheet for query based on the Customer and Contract tables   ◀ **Figure 3-9**

City	Company	First Name	Last Name	Signing Date	Contract Amt
Rockford		Sharon	Maloney	2/9/2010	4,000
Holland		Owen	Hawes	3/1/2010	1,500
Holland		Owen	Hawes	7/8/2010	2,250
Holland		Owen	Hawes	11/30/2010	4,000
Saint Joseph		Melissa	Caputo	4/7/2010	1,250
Grand Rapids	Grand Rapids Engineering Dept.	Anthony	Rodriguez	3/1/2010	2,250
Holland		Amol	Mehta	6/22/2010	6,500
South Haven		John	Weiss	8/27/2010	1,000
South Haven		John	Weiss	1/20/2011	1,750
South Haven		John	Weiss	7/26/2011	5,000
Battle Creek	Battle Creek Dental Partners	Harry	Billings	4/25/2011	13,750
Lansing		Karen	O'Brien	2/18/2010	300
Holland	Finn's on the Waterfront	Devin	Finnerty	9/23/2010	7,500
Holland	Finn's on the Waterfront	Devin	Finnerty	2/24/2011	15,750
Holland	Finn's on the Waterfront	Devin	Finnerty	4/14/2011	22,800
Grand Haven	Happy Haven Day Care	Kathy	Rowe	8/8/2011	10,500
Saugatuck		Pam	Wallner	10/5/2010	18,000
Lansing	M. Grant Investment Company	Alex	Engber	3/11/2010	165,000
Grand Rapids	RiverView Development Company	Susan	Darcy	5/3/2010	28,000
Kalamazoo		Michael	Ingram	6/11/2010	5,250
Grand Rapids	Monroe State College	Rachel	Kirk	4/14/2010	22,000
Kalamazoo	Kalamazoo Neighborhood Development	James	Blackhawk	6/22/2010	68,000
Kalamazoo	Kalamazoo Neighborhood Development	James	Blackhawk	6/22/2010	34,000
Kalamazoo	Kalamazoo Neighborhood Development	James	Blackhawk	6/29/2011	14,500
Kalamazoo	Kalamazoo Neighborhood Development	James	Blackhawk	8/2/2011	50,000

fields from the Customer table

fields from the Contract table

Record: 1 of 64

Only the six selected fields from the Customer and Contract tables appear in the datasheet. The records are displayed in order according to the values in the Customer ID field, because it is the primary key field in the primary table, even though this field is not included in the query datasheet.

Sarah plans on frequently tracking the data retrieved by the query, so she asks you to save the query as "Customer Contracts."

▶ 9. Click the **Save** button on the Quick Access Toolbar. The Save As dialog box opens.

▶ 10. Type **Customer Contracts** in the Query Name text box, and then press the **Enter** key. Access saves the query and displays its name on the query tab.

Sarah decides she wants the records displayed in alphabetical order by city. Because the query displays data in order by the field values in the Customer ID field, which is the primary key for the Customer table, you need to sort the records by the City field to display the data in the order Sarah wants.

Sorting Data in a Query

Sorting is the process of rearranging records in a specified order or sequence. Sometimes you might need to sort data before displaying or printing it to meet a specific request. For example, Sarah might want to review contract information arranged by the Signing Date field because she needs to know which months are the busiest for Belmont Landscapes in terms of signings. On the other hand, Oren might want to view contract information arranged by the Contract Amt field, because he monitors the financial aspects of the business.

When you sort data in a query, you do not change the sequence of the records in the underlying tables. Only the records in the query datasheet are rearranged according to your specifications.

To sort records, you must select the **sort field**, which is the field used to determine the order of records in the datasheet. In this case, Sarah wants the data sorted by city, so you need to specify City as the sort field. Sort fields can be Text, Number, Date/Time, Currency, AutoNumber, Yes/No, or Lookup Wizard fields, but not Memo, OLE object, Hyperlink, or Attachment fields. You sort records in either ascending (increasing) or descending (decreasing) order. Figure 3-10 shows the results of each type of sort for some of these data types.

Figure 3-10	Sorting results for different data types

Data Type	Ascending Sort Results	Descending Sort Results
Text	A to Z	Z to A
Number	lowest to highest numeric value	highest to lowest numeric value
Date/Time	oldest to most recent date	most recent to oldest date
Currency	lowest to highest numeric value	highest to lowest numeric value
AutoNumber	lowest to highest numeric value	highest to lowest numeric value
Yes/No	yes (check mark in check box) then no values	no then yes values

Access provides several methods for sorting data in a table or query datasheet and in a form. One of the easiest ways is to use the AutoFilter feature for a field.

Using AutoFilter to Sort Data

Tip

You can also use the Ascending and Descending buttons in the Sort & Filter group on the Home tab to quickly sort records based on the currently selected field in a datasheet.

As you've probably noticed when working in Datasheet view for a table or query, each column heading has an arrow to the right of the field name. This arrow gives you access to the **AutoFilter** feature, which enables you to quickly sort and display field values in various ways. When you click this arrow, a menu opens with options for sorting and displaying field values. The first two options on the menu enable you to sort the values in the current field in ascending or descending order. Unless you save the datasheet or form after you've sorted the records, the rearrangement of records is temporary.

Next, you'll use an AutoFilter to sort the Customer Contracts query results by the City field.

To sort the records using an AutoFilter:

▶ 1. Click the arrow on the City column heading to display the AutoFilter menu. See Figure 3-11.

Using AutoFilter to sort records in the datasheet | Figure 3-11

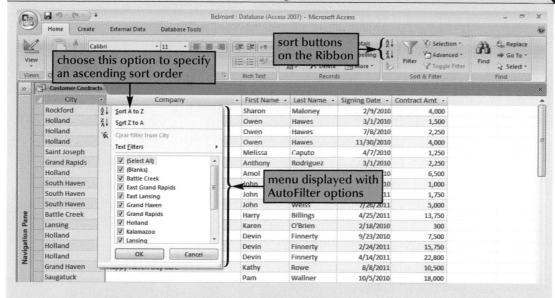

Sarah wants the data sorted in ascending order by the values in the City field, so you need to select the first option in the menu.

▶ 2. Click **Sort A to Z**. The records are rearranged in ascending alphabetical order by city. A small, upward-pointing arrow appears on the right side of the City column heading. This arrow indicates that the values in the field have been sorted in ascending order. If you used the same method to sort the field values in descending order, a small downward-pointing arrow would appear there.

After viewing the query results, Sarah decides that she would also like to see the records arranged by the values in the Contract Amt field, so that she can identify the contracts with the largest amounts. She still wants the records to be arranged by the city field values as well. To produce the results Sarah wants, you need to sort using two fields.

Sorting Multiple Fields in Design View

Sort fields can be unique or nonunique. A sort field is **unique** if the value in the sort field for each record is different. The Customer ID field in the Customer table is an example of a unique sort field because each customer record has a different value in this primary key field. A sort field is **nonunique** if more than one record can have the same value for the sort field. For example, the City field in the Customer table is a nonunique sort field because more than one record can have the same City value.

When the sort field is nonunique, records with the same sort field value are grouped together, but they are not sorted in a specific order within the group. To arrange these grouped records in a specific order, you can specify a **secondary sort field**, which is a second field that determines the order of records that are already sorted by the **primary sort field** (the first sort field specified).

Access lets you select up to 10 different sort fields. When you use the buttons on the Ribbon to sort by more than one field, the sort fields must be in adjacent columns in the datasheet. (Note that you cannot use an AutoFilter to sort on more than one field. This method works for a single field only.) You can specify only one type of sort—either

Tip

The primary sort field is *not* the same as a table's primary key field. A table has at most one primary key, which must be unique, whereas any field in a table can serve as a primary sort field.

ascending or descending—for the selected columns in the datasheet. You highlight the adjacent columns, and Access sorts first by the first column and then by each remaining highlighted column in order from left to right.

Sarah wants the records sorted first by the City field values, as they currently are, and then by the Contract Amt field values. The two fields are in the correct left-to-right order in the query datasheet, but they are not adjacent, so you cannot use the Ascending and Descending buttons on the Ribbon to sort them. You could move the City field to the left of the Contract Amt field in the query datasheet, but both columns would be sorted with the same sort order. This is not what Sarah wants—she wants the City field values sorted in ascending order so that they are in the correct alphabetical order, for ease of reference; and she wants the Contract Amt field values to be sorted in descending order, so that she can focus on the contracts with the largest amounts. To sort the City and Contract Amt fields with different sort orders, you must specify the sort fields in Design view.

In the Query window in Design view, Access first uses the sort field that is leftmost in the design grid. Therefore, you must arrange the fields you want to sort from left to right in the design grid, with the primary sort field being the leftmost. In Design view, multiple sort fields do not have to be adjacent to each other, as they do in Datasheet view; however, they must be in the correct left-to-right order.

Reference Window | Sorting a Query Datasheet

- In the query datasheet, click the arrow on the column heading for the field you want to sort.
- In the menu that opens, click Sort A to Z for an ascending sort, or click Sort Z to A for a descending sort.

or

- In the query datasheet, select the column or adjacent columns on which you want to sort.
- In the Sort & Filter group on the Home tab, click the Ascending button or the Descending button.

or

- In Design view, position the fields serving as sort fields from left to right.
- Click the right side of the Sort text box for the field you want to sort, and then click Ascending or Descending for the sort order.

To achieve the results Sarah wants, you need to modify the query in Design view to specify the sort order for the two fields.

To select the two sort fields in Design view:

Tip

In Design view, the sort fields do not have to be adjacent, and fields that are not sorted can appear between the sort fields.

1. In the Views group on the Home tab, click the **View** button to open the query in Design view. The fields are currently in the correct left-to-right order in the design grid, so you only need to specify the sort order for the two fields.

   First, you need to specify an ascending sort order for the City field. Even though the records are already sorted by the values in this field, you need to modify the query so that this sort order, and the sort order you will specify for the Contract Amt field, are part of the query's design. Any time the query is run, the records will be sorted according to these specifications.

2. Click the right side of the **City Sort** text box to display the arrow and the sort options, and then click **Ascending**. You've selected an ascending sort order for the City field, which will be the primary sort field. The City field is a Text field, and an ascending sort order will display the field values in alphabetical order.

3. Click the right side of the **Contract Amt Sort** text box, click **Descending**, and then click in one of the empty text boxes to the right of the Contract Amt field to deselect the setting. You've selected a descending sort order for the Contract Amt field, which will be the secondary sort field, because it appears to the right of the primary sort field (City) in the design grid. The Contract Amt field is a Currency field, and a descending sort order will display the field values with the highest amounts first. See Figure 3-12.

Selecting two sort fields in Design view | **Figure 3-12**

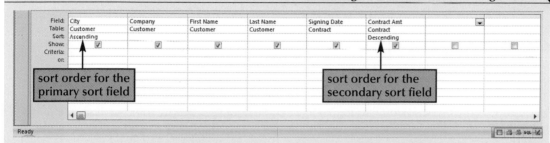

You have finished your query changes, so now you can run the query and then save the modified query with the same query name.

4. In the Results group on the Query Tools Design tab, click the **Run** button. Access runs the query and displays the query datasheet. The records appear in ascending order, based on the values of the City field. Within groups of records with the same City field value, the records appear in descending order by the values of the Contract Amt field. See Figure 3-13.

Datasheet sorted on two fields | **Figure 3-13**

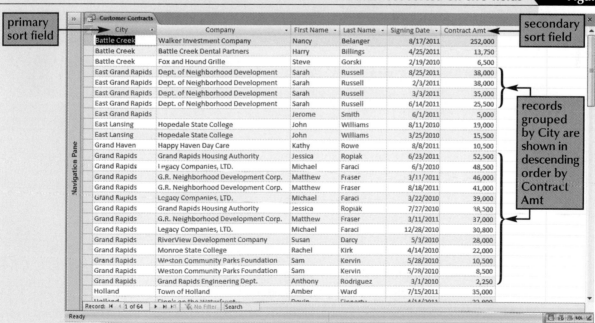

When you save the query, all of your design changes—including the selection of the sort fields—are saved with the query. The next time Sarah runs the query, the records will appear sorted by the primary and secondary sort fields.

5. Click the **Save** button on the Quick Access Toolbar to save the revised Customer Contracts query.

Sarah knows that Belmont Landscapes has seen an increase in business recently for customers located in the city of Grand Rapids. She would like to focus briefly on the information for customers in that city only. Furthermore, she is interested in knowing how many contracts were signed in March, because this month has sometimes been a slow month for Belmont Landscapes in terms of contract signings. Selecting only the records with a City field value of "Grand Rapids" and a Signing Date field value beginning with "3" (for the month of March) is a temporary change that Sarah wants in the datasheet, so you do not need to switch to Design view and change the query. Instead, you can apply a filter.

Filtering Data

A **filter** is a set of restrictions you place on the records in an open datasheet or form to *temporarily* isolate a subset of the records. A filter lets you view different subsets of displayed records so that you can focus on only the data you need. Unless you save a query or form with a filter applied, an applied filter is not available the next time you run the query or open the form.

The simplest technique for filtering records is Filter By Selection. **Filter By Selection** lets you select all or part of a field value in a datasheet or form, and then display only those records that contain the selected value in the field. You can also use the AutoFilter feature to filter records. When you click the arrow on a column heading, the menu that opens provides options for filtering the display based on a field value or the selected part of a field value. Another technique for filtering records is to use **Filter By Form**, which changes your datasheet to display blank fields. Then you can select a value using the arrow that appears when you click any blank field to apply a filter that selects only those records containing that value.

Reference Window | **Using Filter By Selection**

- In the datasheet or form, select part of the field value that will be the basis for the filter; or, if the filter will be based on the entire field value, click anywhere within the field value.
- In the Sort & Filter group on the Home tab, click the Selection button, and then click the type of filter you want to apply.

For Sarah's request, you need to select a City field value of Grand Rapids, and then use Filter By Selection to display only those query records with this value. Then you will filter the records further by selecting only those records with a Signing Date value that begins with "3" (for March).

To display the records using Filter By Selection:

▶ **1.** In the query datasheet, locate the first occurrence of a City field containing the value **Grand Rapids**, and then click anywhere within that field value.

▶ **2.** In the Sort & Filter group on the Home tab, click the **Selection** button. A menu opens with options for the type of filter to apply. See Figure 3-14.

Using Filter By Selection **Figure 3-14**

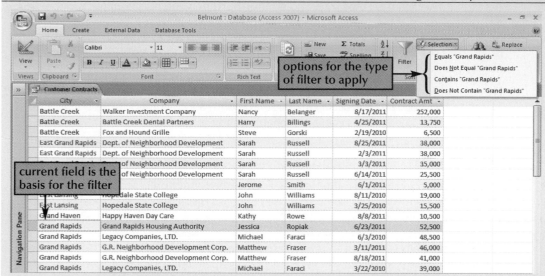

The menu provides options for displaying only those records with a City field value that equals the selected value (in this case, Grand Rapids); does not equal the value; contains the value somewhere within the field; or does not contain the value somewhere within the field. You want to display all the records whose City field value equals Grand Rapids.

▶ **3.** In the Selection menu, click **Equals "Grand Rapids"**. Access displays the filtered results. Only the 13 records that have a City field value of "Grand Rapids" appear in the datasheet. See Figure 3-15.

Datasheet after applying the filter **Figure 3-15**

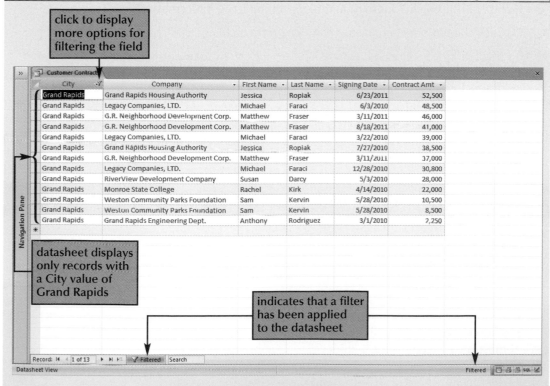

On the status bar, the button labeled "Filtered" to the right of the navigation buttons and the notation "Filtered" both indicate that a filter has been applied to the datasheet. Also, notice that the Toggle Filter button in the Sort & Filter group on the Home tab is active; you can click this button (or the Filtered button next to the navigation buttons) to toggle between the filtered and nonfiltered displays of the query datasheet. The City field also has a filtered icon to the right of the field name; you can click this icon to display additional options for filtering the field.

Next, Sarah wants to view only those records with a Signing Date value in the month of March to focus on the contracts signed in that month for customers located in Grand Rapids. So, you need to apply an additional filter to the datasheet.

▶ **4.** In any Signing Date field value beginning with the number "3" (for the month of March), select only the first digit **3**.

▶ **5.** In the Sort & Filter group on the Home tab, click the **Selection** button. Notice that three filters are available based on your selection: to display only those records with a Signing Date field value that begins with 3; to display only those records with a Signing Date field value that does not begin with 3; or to display only those records with a Signing Date field value that is between two dates. If you choose the between option, a dialog box opens, in which you enter the date values that you want to use.

▶ **6.** Click **Begins With 3** in the Selection menu. The second filter is applied to the query datasheet, which now shows only the four records for customers located in Grand Rapids who signed contracts in the month of March.

Now you can redisplay all the query records by clicking the Toggle Filter button, which you use to switch between the filtered and nonfiltered displays.

▶ **7.** In the Sort & Filter group on the Home tab, click the **Toggle Filter** button. Access redisplays all the records in the query datasheet.

▶ **8.** Close the Customer Contracts query. Access asks if you want to save your changes to the design of the query—in this case, the filtered display, which is still available through the Toggle Filter button. Sarah does not want the query saved with the filter because she doesn't need to view the filtered information on a regular basis.

▶ **9.** Click the **No** button to close the query without saving the changes.

▶ **10.** If you are not continuing to Session 3.2, click the **Close** button ☒ on the program window title bar. Access closes the Belmont database, and then the Access program closes.

The queries you've created will help Belmont Landscapes employees retrieve just the information they want to view. In the next session, you'll continue to create queries to meet their information needs.

Review | **Session 3.1 Quick Check**

1. In Datasheet view, what is the difference between navigation mode and editing mode?
2. What is a select query?
3. Describe the field list and the design grid in the Query window in Design view.
4. How are a table datasheet and a query datasheet similar? How are they different?
5. For a Date/Time field, how do the records appear when sorted in ascending order?
6. True or False: When you define multiple sort fields in Design view, the sort fields must be adjacent to each other.
7. A(n) _____ is a set of restrictions you place on the records in an open datasheet or form to isolate a subset of records temporarily.

Session 3.2

Defining Record Selection Criteria for Queries

Oren wants to display customer and contract information for all customers who live in Holland, Oren's hometown. He is planning to do a special local promotion for Holland customers, because Belmont Landscapes is located there, and Oren wants to increase his firm's presence in the community. For this request, you could create a query to select the correct fields and all records in the Customer and Contract tables, select a City field value of Holland in the query datasheet, and then click the Selection button and choose the appropriate filter option to filter the query results and display the information for only those customers in Holland. However, a faster way of displaying the data Oren needs is to create a query that displays the selected fields and only those records in the Customer and Contract tables that satisfy a condition.

Just as you can display selected fields from a database in a query datasheet, you can display selected records. To tell Access which records you want to select, you must specify a condition as part of the query. A **condition** is a criterion, or rule, that determines which records are selected. To define a condition for a field, you place the condition in the field's Criteria text box in the design grid.

A condition usually consists of an operator, often a comparison operator, and a value. A **comparison operator** asks Access to compare the value in a database field to the condition value and to select all the records for which the relationship is true. For example, the condition >50000 for the Contract Amt field selects all records in the Contract table with Contract Amt field values greater than $50,000. Figure 3-16 shows the Access comparison operators.

Access comparison operators   Figure 3-16

Operator	Meaning	Example
=	equal to (optional; default operator)	="Hall"
<	less than	<#1/1/99#
<=	less than or equal to	<=100
>	greater than	>"C400"
>=	greater than or equal to	>=18.75
<>	not equal to	<>"Hall"
Between ... And ...	between two values (inclusive)	Between 50 And 325
In ()	in a list of values	In ("Hall", "Seeger")
Like	matches a pattern that includes wildcards	Like "706*"

Specifying an Exact Match

For Oren's request, you need to create a query that will display only those records in the Customer table with the value Holland in the City field. This type of condition is called an **exact match** because the value in the specified field must match the condition exactly in order for the record to be included in the query results. You'll create the query in Design view.

To create the query in Design view:

▶ **1.** If you took a break after the previous session, make sure that the Belmont database is open in the Access program window and that the Navigation Pane is closed.

▶ **2.** Click the **Create** tab on the Ribbon.

▶ **3.** In the Other group on the Create tab, click the **Query Design** button. The Show Table dialog box opens. You need to add the Customer and Contract tables to the Query window.

▶ **4.** Click **Customer** in the Tables list box, click the **Add** button, click **Contract**, click the **Add** button, and then click the **Close** button.

▶ **5.** Use the ⇕ pointer to resize the Customer field list so that all the fields are displayed.

▶ **6.** Add the following fields from the Customer table to the design grid in the order shown: **Company**, **First Name**, **Last Name**, **Phone**, **Address**, **City**, and **E-mail Address**.

Oren also wants information from the Contract table included in the query results.

▶ **7.** Add the following fields from the Contract table to the design grid in the order shown: **Contract Num**, **Contract Amt**, **Signing Date**, and **Contract Type**. See Figure 3-17.

Figure 3-17 ▶ **Query in Design view**

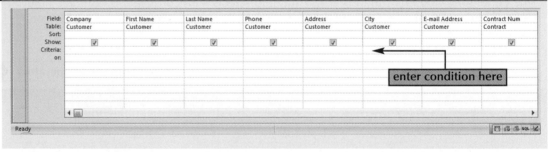

The field lists for the Customer and Contract tables appear in the top portion of the window, and the join line indicating a one-to-many relationship connects the two tables. The fields you selected appear in the design grid; to see all of the fields, you need to scroll to the right using the horizontal scroll bar.

To display the information Oren wants, you need to enter the condition for the City field in its Criteria text box. Oren wants to display only those records with a City field value of Holland.

To enter the exact match condition, and then save and run the query:

▶ **1.** Click the **City Criteria** text box, type **Holland**, and then press the **Enter** key. The condition changes to "Holland".

Access automatically enclosed the condition you typed in quotation marks. You must enclose Text values in quotation marks when using them as selection criteria. If you omit the quotation marks, however, Access will include them automatically.

▶ 2. Click the **Save** button 🖫 on the Quick Access Toolbar to open the Save As dialog box.

▶ 3. Type **Holland Customers** in the Query Name text box, and then press the **Enter** key. Access saves the query with the specified name and displays the name on the query tab.

▶ 4. In the Results group on the Query Tools Design tab, click the **Run** button. Access runs the query and displays the selected field values for only those records with a City field value of Holland. A total of 12 records are selected and displayed in the datasheet. See Figure 3-18.

Datasheet displaying selected fields and records | Figure 3-18

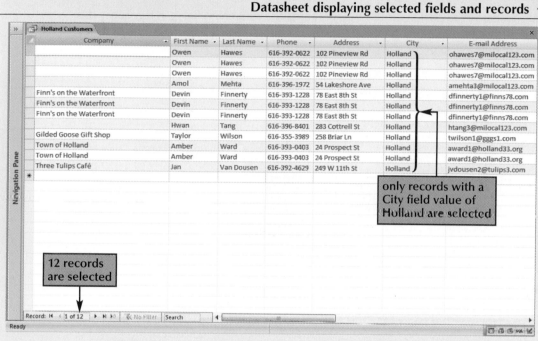

Oren realizes that it's not necessary to include the City field values in the query results. The name of the query, Holland Customers, indicates that the query design includes all customers that are located in Holland, so the City field values are unnecessary and repetitive. Also, he decides that he would prefer the query datasheet to show the fields from the Contract table first, followed by the Customer table fields. You need to modify the query to produce the results Oren wants.

Modifying a Query

After you create a query and view the results, you might need to make changes to the query if the results are not what you expected or want to view. First, Oren asks you to modify the Holland Customers query to remove the City field values from the query results.

To remove the display of the City field values:

▶ 1. In the Views group on the Home tab, click the **View** button. The Holland Customers query opens in Design view.

You need to keep the City field as part of the query design, because it contains the defined condition for the query. You only need to remove the display of the field's values from the query results.

▶ **2.** Click the **City Show** check box to remove the check mark. The query will still find only those records with the value Holland in the City field, but the query results will not display these field values.

Next, you need to change the order of the fields in the query so that the contract information is listed first.

To move the fields from the Contract table before the fields from the Customer table:

▶ **1.** Scroll the design grid to the right until the remaining fields in the query design are visible. You need to move the Contract Num field so it becomes the first field in the query design.

▶ **2.** Position the pointer on the Contract Num field selector until the pointer changes to a ⬇ shape, and then click to select the field. See Figure 3-19.

| Figure 3-19 | Selected Contract Num field |

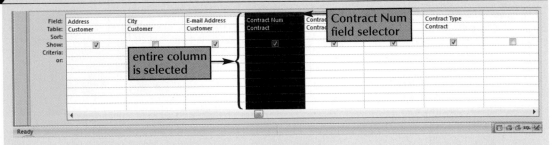

▶ **3.** Position the pointer on the Contract Num field selector, and then click and drag the pointer ⬚ to the left, allowing the design grid to scroll back to the left, until the vertical line to the left of the Company field is highlighted. See Figure 3-20.

| Figure 3-20 | Dragging the field in the design grid |

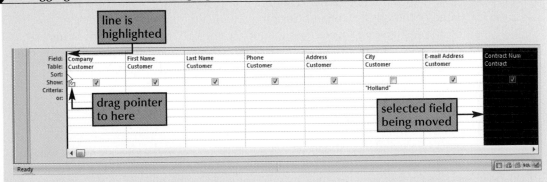

▶ **4.** Release the mouse button. The Contract Num field moves to the left of the Company field.

You can also select and move multiple fields at once.

▶ **5.** Scroll back to the right to view the remaining fields in the design grid. Now you need to select and move the Contract Amt, Signing Date, and Contract Type fields so that they follow the Contract Num field in the query design. To select multiple fields, you simply click and drag the mouse over the field selectors for the fields you want.

6. Click and hold the pointer ↓ on the Contract Amt field selector, drag the pointer to the right to select the Signing Date and Contract Type fields, and then release the mouse button. All three fields are now selected. See Figure 3-21.

Multiple fields selected to be moved ◄ **Figure 3-21**

7. Position the pointer ⌖ anywhere near the top of the three selected fields, and then click and drag the pointer to the left until the vertical line to the right of the Contract Num field is highlighted.

8. Release the mouse button. The four fields from the Contract table are now the first four fields in the query design.

You have finished making the modifications to the query Oren requested, so you can now run the query.

9. In the Results group on the Query Tools Design tab, click the **Run** button. Access displays the results of the modified query. See Figure 3-22.

Results of modified query ◄ **Figure 3-22**

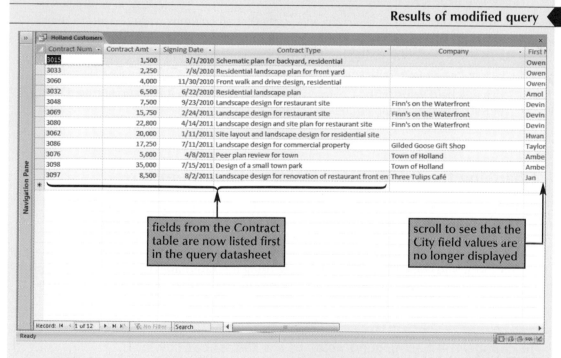

Note that the City field values are no longer displayed in the query results (you need to scroll the datasheet to the right to verify this).

Oren would like to see more fields and records on the screen at one time. He asks you to change the datasheet's font size, and then to resize all the columns to their best fit.

Changing a Datasheet's Appearance

You can change the characteristics of a datasheet, including the font type and size of text in the datasheet, to improve its appearance or readability. As you learned in earlier tutorials, you can also resize the datasheet columns to view more columns on the screen at the same time. You'll change the font size from the default 11 points to 9, and then resize the datasheet columns.

To change the font size and resize the columns in the datasheet:

▶ **1.** In the Font group on the Home tab, click the **Font Size** arrow, and then click **9**. The font size for the entire datasheet changes to 9 points.

Next, you need to resize the columns to their best fit, so that each column is just wide enough to fit the longest value in the column. Instead of resizing each column individually, you'll use the datasheet selector to select all the columns and resize them at the same time.

▶ **2.** Click the **datasheet selector**, which is the box to the left of the Contract Num field name. All the columns in the datasheet are highlighted, indicating they are selected.

▶ **3.** Position the pointer ◀╂▶ at the right edge of any column in the datasheet, and then double-click the pointer. All the columns visible on the screen are resized to their best fit. Because only the visible columns are resized, you must scroll the datasheet to the right to make sure all field values for the entire column are fully displayed, resizing as you scroll, if necessary.

▶ **4.** Scroll the datasheet to the right and verify that all columns were resized to their best fit. If necessary, resize any individual column that might not have been resized to best fit the data it contains.

▶ **5.** Scroll to the left, if necessary, so that the Contract Num field is visible, and then click any field value in the Contract Num column to make it the current field. More columns are now visible in the datasheet.

Changing the Background Color of Datasheet Rows

By default, the rows in a datasheet are displayed with alternating background colors of white and light gray to distinguish one row from another, making it easier to view and read the contents of a datasheet. The default white/gray alternate scheme provides a subtle color difference between the rows. You can change the background color for datasheet rows to something more noticeable using the **Alternate Fill/Back Color button** in the Font group. Oren suggests that you change the row colors of the query datasheet to see the effect of using this feature.

To change the background color of the datasheet rows:

▶ **1.** In the Font group on the Home tab, click the arrow on the **Alternate Fill/Back Color** button ▦ ▾ to display the gallery of color choices. See Figure 3-23.

Gallery of color choices for alternate fill color | Figure 3-23

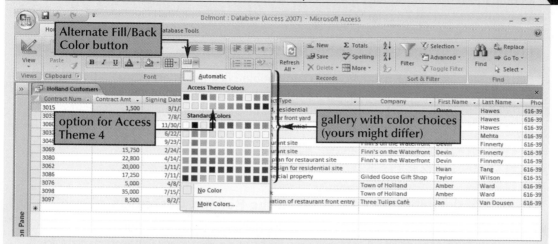

The Access Theme Colors gallery provides colors from Access themes, so that your datasheet's color scheme matches the default used for the Access program. The Standard Colors gallery provides many standard color choices. You might also see a Recent Colors gallery, with colors that you have recently used in a datasheet. On the menu, you could also choose the No Color option, which sets each row's background to white; or the More Colors option, which creates a custom color. You'll use one of the theme colors.

Tip

The name of the color appears in a ScreenTip when you point to a color in the gallery.

▶ **2.** In the Access Theme Colors gallery, click the color box for **Access Theme 4** (second row, fourth color box). The alternating background color is applied to the query datasheet. See Figure 3-24.

Datasheet formatted with new fill color | Figure 3-24

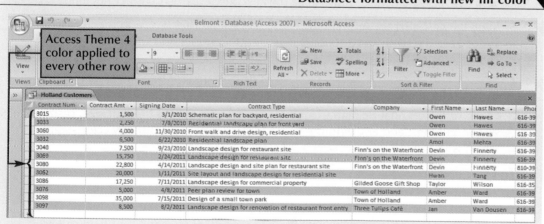

Every other row in the datasheet uses the Access Theme 4 background color. Oren likes how the datasheet looks with this color scheme, so he asks you to save the query.

▶ **3.** Save and close the Holland Customers query.

After viewing the query results, Oren decides that he would like to see the same fields, but only for those records with a Contract Amt field value equal to or greater than $25,000. He is interested to know which Belmont Landscapes customers in all cities and towns have signed the largest contracts, so that he can follow up with these customers personally. To create the query that will produce the results Oren wants, you need to use a comparison operator to match a range of values—in this case, any Contract Amt value greater than or equal to $25,000.

Using a Comparison Operator to Match a Range of Values

Once you create and save a query, you can double-click the query name in the Navigation Pane to run the query again. You can then click the View button to change its design. You can also use an existing query as the basis for creating another query. Because the design of the query you need to create next is similar to the Holland Customers query, you will copy, paste, and rename this query to create the new query. Using this approach keeps the Holland Customers query intact.

To create the new query by copying the Holland Customers query:

▶ 1. Open the Navigation Pane. Note that the Holland Customers query is listed below both the Contract and Customer groups, because the query is based on data from both tables.

You need to use the shortcut menu to copy the Holland Customers query and paste it in the Navigation Pane; then you'll give the copied query a different name. To do so, you could copy either instance of the Holland Customers query in the Navigation Pane.

▶ 2. In the Customer group on the Navigation Pane, right-click **Holland Customers** to select it and display the shortcut menu.

▶ 3. Click **Copy** on the shortcut menu.

▶ 4. Right-click the empty area of the Navigation Pane, and then click **Paste** on the shortcut menu. The Paste As dialog box opens with the text "Copy Of Holland Customers" in the Query Name text box. Because Oren wants the new query to show the contracts with the largest amounts, you'll name the new query "Large Contract Amounts."

▶ 5. Type **Large Contract Amounts** in the Query Name text box, and then press the **Enter** key. The new query appears in both the Contract and Customer groups in the Navigation Pane.

▶ 6. In the Customer group on the Navigation Pane, double-click the **Large Contract Amounts** query to open, or run, the query. Notice that all the design changes you made to the original Holland Customers query—decreasing the font size, resizing all the columns, and applying the new alternating background row color—were saved with the query.

▶ 7. Close the Navigation Pane.

Next, you need to open the query in Design view and modify its design to produce the results Oren wants—to display only those records with Contract Amt field values that are greater than or equal to $25,000.

To modify the design of the new query:

▶ 1. In the Views group on the Home tab, click the **View** button to display the query in Design view.

▶ 2. Click the **Contract Amt Criteria** text box, type **>=25000**, and then press the **Tab** key. See Figure 3-25.

Criteria entered for Contract Amt field   Figure 3-25

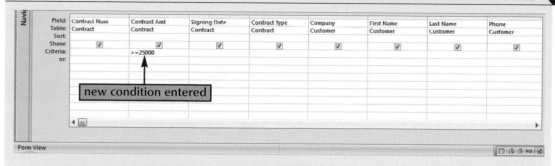

new condition entered

Trouble? If you receive an error message saying that you entered an expression containing invalid syntax, you might have typed a comma in the amount "25000" or a dollar sign. Commas and dollar signs are not allowed in selection criteria. Delete the comma and/or dollar sign from the Contract Amt Criteria box, and then press the Tab key.

The condition specifies that a record will be selected only if its Contract Amt field value is $25,000 or greater. Before you run the query, you need to delete the condition for the City field. Recall that the City field is part of the query, but its values are not displayed in the query results. When you modified the query to remove the City field values from the query results, Access moved the field to the end of the design grid. So, you need to locate the City field, delete its condition, specify that the City field values should be included in the query results, and then move the field back to its original position following the Address field.

▶ 3. Press the **Tab** key eight times until the condition for the City field is highlighted, and then press the **Delete** key. The condition for the City field is removed.

▶ 4. Click the **Show** check box for the City field to insert a check mark so that the field values will be displayed in the query results.

▶ 5. Use the ↧ pointer to select the City field, drag the selected field to the right of the Address field, and then click in an empty box to deselect the City field. See Figure 3-26.

Design grid after moving City field   Figure 3-26

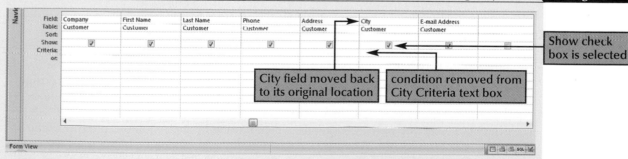

Show check box is selected

City field moved back to its original location

condition removed from City Criteria text box

▶ 6. In the Results group on the Query Tools Design tab, click the **Run** button. Access runs the query and displays the selected fields for only those records with a Contract Amt field value of greater than or equal to $25,000. A total of 23 records are selected. See Figure 3-27.

| Figure 3-27 | Running the modified query |

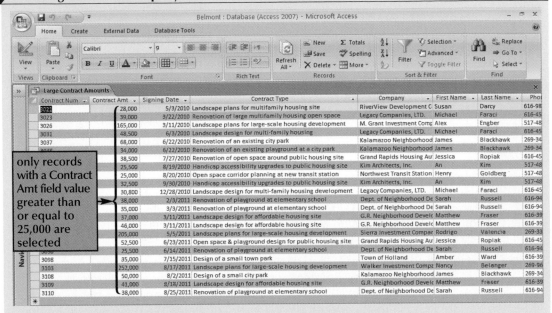

The City field values are also included in the query datasheet; you need to scroll the datasheet to the right to view them.

7. Save and close the Large Contract Amounts query.

Oren recently hired Steve Barry as a new consultant at Belmont Landscapes. Steve will focus primarily on customers located in Lansing. To help Steve prioritize his site visits in Lansing, Oren asks you to provide him with a list of all customers in Lansing who have signed contracts with values greater than $25,000. To produce this list, you need to create a query containing two conditions—one for the city and another for the contract amount.

Defining Multiple Selection Criteria for Queries

Multiple conditions require you to use **logical operators** to combine two or more conditions. When you want a record selected only if two or more conditions are met, you need to use the **And logical operator**. In this case, Oren wants to see only those records with a City field value of Lansing *and* a Contract Amt field value greater than $25,000. If you place conditions in separate fields in the *same* Criteria row of the design grid, all conditions in that row must be met in order for a record to be included in the query results. However, if you place conditions in *different* Criteria rows, a record will be selected if at least one of the conditions is met. If none of the conditions are met, Access does not select the record. When you place conditions in different Criteria rows, you are using the **Or logical operator**. Figure 3-28 illustrates the difference between the And and Or logical operators.

Logical operators And and Or for multiple selection criteria | **Figure 3-28**

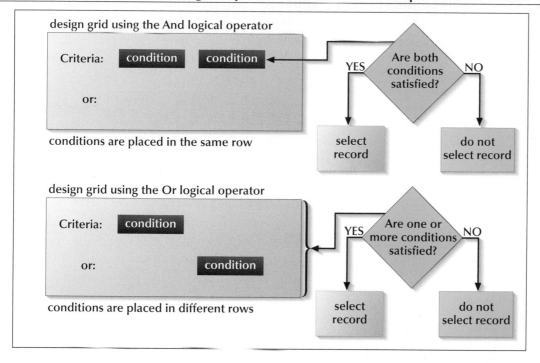

The And Logical Operator

To create the query for Oren, you need to use the And logical operator to show only the records for customers located in Lansing *and* with a contract amount greater than $25,000. You'll create a new query based on both the Customer and Contract tables to produce the necessary results. In the query design, both conditions you specify will appear in the same Criteria row; therefore, the query will select records only if both conditions are met.

To create a new query using the And logical operator:

▶ **1.** Click the **Create** tab on the Ribbon.

▶ **2.** In the Other group on the Create tab, click the **Query Design** button.

▶ **3.** Add the **Customer** and **Contract** tables to the Query window, and then close the Show Table dialog box. Resize the Customer field list to display all the field names.

▶ **4.** Add the following fields from the Customer field list to the design grid in the order shown: **Company**, **First Name**, **Last Name**, **Phone**, and **City**.

▶ **5.** Add the **Contract Amt** and **Signing Date** fields from the Contract table to the design grid.

   Now you need to enter the two conditions for the query.

▶ **6.** Click the **City Criteria** text box, and then type **Lansing**.

▶ **7.** Press the **Tab** key to move to the **Contract Amt Criteria** text box, type **>25000**, and then press the **Tab** key. See Figure 3-29.

| Figure 3-29 | Query to find customers in Lansing with large contracts |

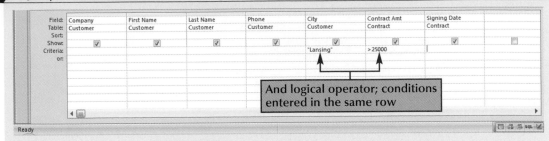

8. Run the query. Access displays only those records that meet both conditions: a City field value of Lansing and a Contract Amt field value greater than $25,000. Three records are selected, for two different customers. See Figure 3-30.

| Figure 3-30 | Results of query using the And logical operator |

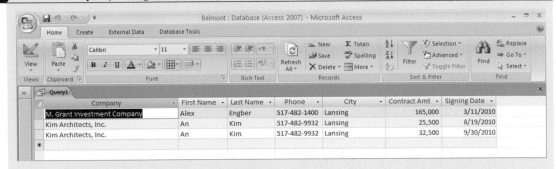

9. Click the **Save** button on the Quick Access Toolbar, and then save the query as **Key Lansing Customers**.

10. Close the query. When Steve begins working at Belmont Landscapes, he can run this query to see which customers in Lansing he should contact first.

Next, Oren and Taylor meet to discuss strategies for increasing business for Belmont Landscapes. They are interested in knowing which customers signed contracts for small amounts—less than $10,000—or which contracts were signed in the first two months of 2011, because business seemed unusually slow during those months. They want to use this information for two reasons: (1) to target specific customers who signed smaller contracts with Belmont Landscapes, to determine if these customers might have additional landscaping needs; and (2) to analyze the number and type of contracts signed during these slow months so they can develop strategies for increasing contract signings in the future. To help with their planning, Oren and Taylor have asked you to produce a list of all contracts with amounts less than $10,000 or that were signed between 1/1/2011 and 3/1/2011. To create this query, you need to use the Or logical operator.

The Or Logical Operator

To create the query that Oren and Taylor requested, your query must select a record when either one of two conditions is satisfied or when both conditions are satisfied. That is, a record is selected if the Contract Amt field value is less than $10,000 *or* if the Signing Date field value is between 1/1/2011 and 3/1/2011 *or* if both conditions are met. You will enter the condition for the Contract Amt field in the Criteria row and the condition for the Signing Date field in the "or" criteria row, thereby using the Or logical operator.

To display the information Oren and Taylor want to view, you'll create a new query containing the First Name, Last Name, Company, and City fields from the Customer table (in that order); and the Contract Amt, Signing Date, and Contract Type fields from the Contract table. Then you'll specify the conditions using the Or logical operator.

To create a new query using the Or logical operator:

▶ 1. Click the **Create** tab on the Ribbon and then, in the Other group, click the **Query Design** button.

2. Add the **Customer** and **Contract** tables to the Query window, close the Show Table dialog box, and then resize the Customer field list.

3. Add the following fields from the Customer table to the design grid in the order shown: **First Name**, **Last Name**, **Company**, and **City**.

4. Add the following fields from the Contract table to the design grid in the order shown: **Contract Amt**, **Signing Date**, and **Contract Type**.

Now you need to specify the first condition, <10000, in the Contract Amt field.

5. Click the **Contract Amt Criteria** text box, type **<10000** and then press the **Tab** key.

Because you want records selected if either of the conditions for the Contract Amt or Signing Date fields is satisfied, you must enter the condition for the Signing Date field in the "or" row of the design grid. To specify the date period for the query, you'll use the Between operator.

6. Press the ↓ key, type **Between 1/1/2011 And 3/1/2011** in the "or" text box for Signing Date, and then press the **Tab** key.

To view the entire condition for the Signing Date field, you'll resize this field's column in the design grid.

7. Place the pointer on the vertical line to the right of the Signing Date field selector until the pointer changes to a ✛ shape, and then double-click to widen the column. The condition in the Signing Date field is now fully displayed. Note that Access automatically places number signs around the date values in the condition to distinguish the date values from the operators. See Figure 3-31.

Query window with the Or logical operator ◄ **Figure 3-31**

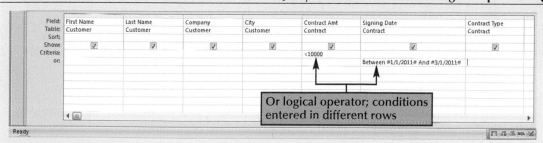

Oren wants the list displayed in descending order by Signing Date, to better analyze the data.

8. Click the right side of the **Signing Date Sort** text box, and then click **Descending**.

▶ **9.** Run the query. Access displays only those records that meet either condition: a Contract Amt field value less than $10,000 or a Signing Date field value between 1/1/2011 and 3/1/2011. Access also selects records that meet both conditions. A total of 29 records are selected. The records in the query datasheet appear in descending order based on the values in the Signing Date field. See Figure 3-32.

Figure 3-32 | **Results of query using the Or logical operator**

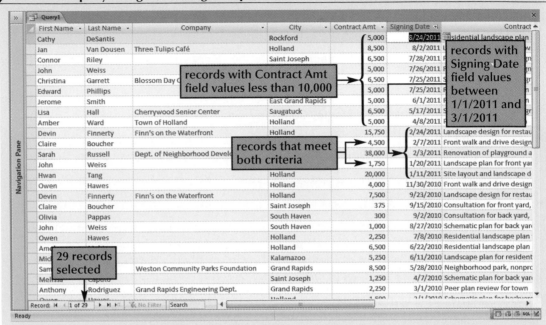

▶ **10.** Save the query as **Small Contracts Or Winter Signings**, and then close it.

InSight | **Understanding the Results of Using And vs. Or**

When you use the And logical operator to define multiple selection criteria in a query, you *narrow* the results produced by the query, because a record must meet more than one condition to be included in the results. When you use the Or logical operator, you *broaden* the results produced by the query, because a record must meet only one of the conditions to be included in the results. This is an important distinction to keep in mind when you include multiple selection criteria in queries, so that the queries you create will produce the results you want.

Next, Oren turns his attention to some financial aspects of his business. He wants to use the Belmont database to perform calculations. He is considering imposing a 3% late fee on unpaid invoices and wants to know exactly what the late fee charges would be, should he decide to institute such a policy in the future. To produce the information for Oren, you need to create a calculated field.

Creating a Calculated Field

In addition to using queries to retrieve, sort, and filter data in a database, you can use a query to perform calculations. To perform a calculation, you define an **expression** containing a combination of database fields, constants, and operators. For numeric expressions, the data types of the database fields must be Number, Currency, or Date/Time; the constants are numbers such as .03 (for the 3% late fee); and the operators can be arithmetic operators (+ − * /) or other specialized operators. In complex expressions, you can enclose calculations in parentheses to indicate which one should be performed first. In expressions without parentheses, Access calculates in the following order of precedence: multiplication and division before addition and subtraction. When operators have equal precedence, Access calculates them in order from left to right.

To perform a calculation in a query, you add a calculated field to the query. A **calculated field** is a field that displays the results of an expression. A calculated field appears in a query datasheet or in a form or report; however, it does not exist in a database. When you run a query that contains a calculated field, Access evaluates the expression defined by the calculated field and displays the resulting value in the query datasheet, form, or report.

To enter an expression for a calculated field, you can type it directly in a Field text box in the design grid. Alternately, you can open the Zoom box or Expression Builder and use either one to enter the expression. The **Zoom box** is a dialog box that you can use to enter text, expressions, or other values. To use the Zoom box, however, you must know all the parts of the expression you want to create. **Expression Builder** is an Access tool that makes it easy for you to create an expression; it contains a box for entering the expression, buttons for common operators, and one or more lists of expression elements, such as table and field names. Unlike a Field text box, which is too small to show an entire expression at one time, the Zoom box and Expression Builder are large enough to display lengthy expressions. In most cases, Expression Builder provides the easiest way to enter expressions, because you don't have to know all the parts of the expression; you can choose the necessary elements from the Expression Builder dialog box.

Tip

If your field names include spaces in the names, as in the fields "First Name" and "Last Name," you must enclose the names in brackets when using them in an expression.

Using Expression Builder | Reference Window

- Open the query in Design view.
- In the design grid, position the insertion point in the Field text box of the field for which you want to create an expression.
- In the Query Setup group on the Query Tools Design tab, click the Builder button.
- Use the expression elements and common operators to build the expression, or type the expression directly.
- Click the OK button.

To produce the information Oren wants, you need to create a new query based on the Invoice table and, in the query, create a calculated field that will multiply each Invoice Amt field value by .03 to calculate the proposed 3% late fee.

To create the new query that will include the calculated field:

▶ **1.** Click the **Create** tab on the Ribbon and then, in the Other group, click the **Query Design** button.

Oren wants to see data from both the Contract and Invoice tables, so you need to add these two tables to the Query window.

▶ **2.** Add the **Contract** and **Invoice** tables to the Query window, and then close the Show Table dialog box. The field lists appear in the Query window, and the one-to-many relationship between the Contract (primary) and Invoice (related) tables is displayed.

▶ **3.** Add the following fields to the design grid in the order given: **Contract Num** and **Contract Amt** from the Contract table; and **Invoice Item**, **Invoice Paid**, and **Invoice Amt** from the Invoice table.

Oren is interested in viewing data for unpaid invoices only, because a late fee would apply only to them, so you need to enter the necessary condition for the Invoice Paid field. Recall that Invoice Paid is a Yes/No field. The condition you need to enter is the word "No" in the Criteria text box for this field, so that Access will retrieve the records for unpaid invoices only.

▶ **4.** In the **Invoice Paid Criteria** text box, type **No** and then press the **Tab** key.

The query name you'll use will indicate that the data is for unpaid invoices, so you don't need to include the Invoice Paid values in the query results.

▶ **5.** Click the **Invoice Paid Show** check box to remove the check mark.

▶ **6.** Save the query with the name **Unpaid Invoices With Late Fees**.

Now you can use the Expression Builder to create the calculated field for the Invoice Amt field.

To create the calculated field:

▶ **1.** Click the blank Field text box to the right of the Invoice Amt field. This field will contain the calculated field values.

▶ **2.** In the Query Setup group on the Query Tools Design tab, click the **Builder** button. The Expression Builder dialog box opens.

The center pane in the dialog box lists the fields from the query so you can include them in the expression. You can use the common operators and expression elements to help you build an expression.

The expression for the calculated field will multiply the Invoice Amt field values by the numeric constant .03 (which represents a 3% late fee). To include a field in the expression, you select the field and then click the Paste button in the dialog box. To include a numeric constant, you simply type the constant in the expression.

▶ **3.** Click **Invoice Amt** in the field list, and then click the **Paste** button in the dialog box. The field name appears in the expression box, within brackets.

To include the multiplication operator in the expression, you click the asterisk (*) button. Note that you do not include spaces between the elements in an expression.

▶ **4.** Click the ***** button in the row of common operators, and then type **.03**. You have finished entering the expression. See Figure 3-33.

Completed expression for the calculated field | Figure 3-33

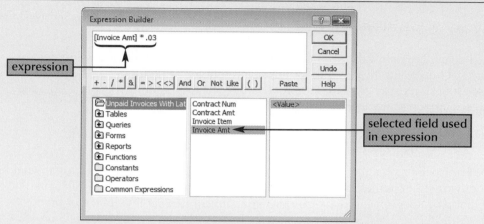

expression

selected field used in expression

Tip

You can also type an expression directly into the expression box, instead of clicking field names, operators, and so on.

▶ **5.** Click the **OK** button. Access closes the Expression Builder dialog box and adds the expression to the design grid in the Field text box for the calculated field.

Next, you need to specify a name for the calculated field as it will appear in the query results.

▶ **6.** Press the **Home** key to position the insertion point to the left of the expression.

You'll enter the name Late Fee, which is descriptive of the field's contents; then you'll run the query. To separate the calculated field name from the expression, you must type a colon between them.

▶ **7.** Type **Late Fee:**. *Make sure you include the colon following the field name.*

▶ **8.** Run the query. Access displays the query datasheet, which contains the specified fields and the calculated field with the name "Late Fee." See Figure 3-34.

Datasheet displaying the calculated field | Figure 3-34

Contract Num ▾	Contract Amt ▾	Invoice Item ▾	Invoice Amt ▾	Late Fee
3026	165,000	Permitting	$10,000.00	300
3026	165,000	Construction Documents	$70,000.00	2100
3026	165,000	Construction Admin. & Observation	$50,000.00	1500
3023	39,000	Construction Observation	$10,000.00	300
3021	28,000	Construction Documents	$12,000.00	360
3021	28,000	Construction Observation	$8,500.00	255
3031	48,500	Layout Plans	$16,000.00	480
3031	48,500	Construction Observation	$9,000.00	270
3037	68,000	Construction Documents	$30,000.00	900
3037	68,000	Construction Admin. & Observation	$15,000.00	450
3038	34,000	Construction Admin. & Observation	$8,000.00	240
3040	38,500	Construction Documents	$18,000.00	540
3040	38,500	Construction Admin. & Observation	$12,000.00	360
3043	19,000	Construction Observation	$3,000.00	90
3044	25,500	Construction Admin. & Observation	$10,000.00	300
3045	25,000	Schematic Plans	$18,000.00	540
3045	25,000	Community Meetings	$7,000.00	210
3048	7,500	Construction Observation	$1,500.00	45
3056	32,500	Construction Documents	$20,000.00	600
3056	32,500	Construction Admin. & Observation	$12,500.00	375
3057	15,500	Construction Observation	$3,500.00	105
3051	18,000	Construction Observation	$3,500.00	105
3061	30,800	Permitting	$3,000.00	90
3061	30,800	Construction Documents	$15,000.00	450
3061	30,800	Construction Observation	$6,800.00	204

specified name for the calculated field

calculated field values

Record: 1 of 100 — No Filter — Search

Ready

> **Trouble?** If the calculated field name does not appear correctly, as shown in Figure 3-34, you might not have included the required colon. Switch to Design view, resize the column in the design grid that contains the calculated field to best fit, and then change your expression to Late Fee: [Invoice Amt]*0.03 and repeat Step 8.

The Late Fee field values are currently displayed without dollar signs and decimal places. Oren wants these values to be displayed in the same format as the Invoice Amt field values, in case he decides to produce a report for customers showing both the invoice amounts and any imposed late fees.

Formatting a Calculated Field

You can specify a particular format for a calculated field, just as you can for any field, by modifying its properties. Next, you'll change the format of the Late Fee calculated field so that all values appear in the Currency format with two decimal places.

To format the calculated field:

▸ **1.** Switch to Design view.

▸ **2.** Right-click the **Late Fee** calculated field in the design grid to open the shortcut menu, and then click **Properties**. The Property Sheet for the calculated field opens on the right side of the window. See Figure 3-35.

Figure 3-35 ▸ **Property Sheet for the calculated field**

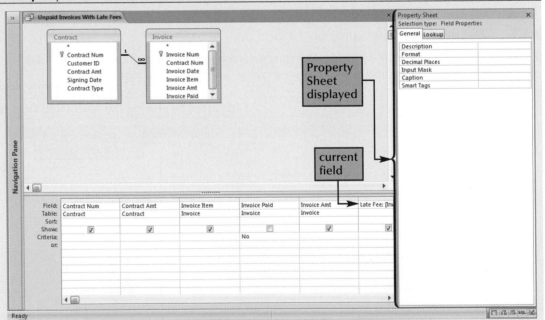

You need to change the Format property to Currency and the Decimal Places property to 2.

▸ **3.** Click the right side of the **Format** text box to display the list of formats, and then click **Currency**.

▸ **4.** Click the right side of the **Decimal Places** text box, and then click **2**.

▶ **5.** Close the Property Sheet for the calculated field, and then run the query. The amounts in the Late Fee calculated field are now displayed with dollar signs and two decimal places.

▶ **6.** Save and close the Unpaid Invoices With Late Fees query.

Creating Calculated Fields | InSight

Values that are produced by calculated fields should not be stored as separate fields in a database table. If you store the results of a calculated field in a table and the data produced by the calculated field becomes outdated, you would have to update the records in the table datasheet with the current data. It is best to create a query that includes a calculated field to perform the calculation you want. Then, every time you open the query, the calculation is performed and the resulting query datasheet reflects the most current data.

Oren wants to prepare a report on a regular basis that includes a summary of information about the contract amounts for Belmont Landscapes. He would like to know the minimum, average, and maximum contract amounts. He asks you to determine these statistics from data in the Contract table.

Using Aggregate Functions

You can calculate statistical information, such as totals and averages, on the records displayed in a table datasheet or selected by a query. To do this, you use the Access aggregate functions. **Aggregate functions** perform arithmetic operations on selected records in a database. Figure 3-36 lists the most frequently used aggregate functions.

Frequently used aggregate functions ◄ Figure 3-36

Aggregate Function	Determines	Data Types Supported
Average	Average of the field values for the selected records	AutoNumber, Currency, Date/Time, Number
Count	Number of records selected	AutoNumber, Currency, Date/Time, Memo, Number, OLE Object, Text, Yes/No
Maximum	Highest field value for the selected records	AutoNumber, Currency, Date/Time, Number, Text
Minimum	Lowest field value for the selected records	AutoNumber, Currency, Date/Time, Number, Text
Sum	Total of the field values for the selected records	AutoNumber, Currency, Date/Time, Number

Working with Aggregate Functions Using the Totals Row

If you want to quickly perform a calculation using an aggregate function in a table or query datasheet, you can use the Totals button on the Home tab. When you click this button, a row labeled "Total" appears at the end of the datasheet. You can then choose one of the aggregate functions for a field in the datasheet, and the results of the calculation will be displayed in the Total row for that field.

Oren is interested to know the total amount of all contracts for the company. You can quickly display this amount using the Sum function in the Total row in the Contract table datasheet.

To display the total amount of all contracts in the Contract table:

▶ 1. Open the Navigation Pane, open the **Contract** table in Datasheet view, and then close the Navigation Pane.

▶ 2. In the Records group on the Home tab, click the **Totals** button. Access adds a row with the label "Total" to the end of the datasheet.

▶ 3. Scroll to the end of the datasheet to view the Total row. You want to display the sum of all the values in the Contract Amt field.

▶ 4. Click the **Contract Amt** field in the Total row. An arrow appears on the left side of the field.

▶ 5. Click the **arrow** to display the menu of aggregate functions. See Figure 3-37.

| Figure 3-37 | Using aggregate functions in the Total row |

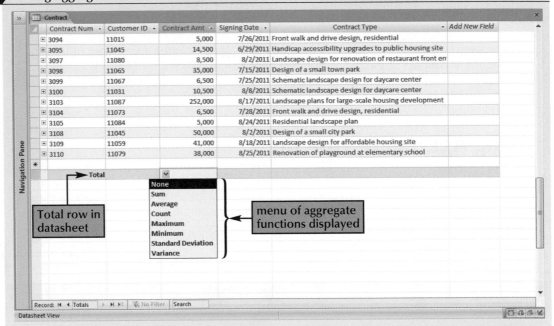

▶ 6. Click **Sum** in the menu. Access adds all the values in the Contract Amt field and displays the total 1,753,075 in the Total row for the field.

Oren doesn't want to change the Contract table to always display this total. You can remove the Total row by clicking the Totals button again; this button works as a toggle to switch between the display of the Total row and the results of any calculations in the row, and the display of the datasheet without this row.

▶ 7. In the Records group on the Home tab, click the **Totals** button. Access removes the Total row from the datasheet.

▶ 8. Close the Contract table without saving the changes.

For Oren's report, he wants to know the minimum, average, and maximum contract amounts for the company. To produce this information for Oren, you need to use aggregate functions in a query.

Creating Queries with Aggregate Functions

Aggregate functions operate on the records that meet a query's selection criteria. You specify an aggregate function for a specific field, and the appropriate operation applies to that field's values for the selected records.

To display the minimum, average, and maximum of all the contract amounts in the Contract table, you will use the Minimum, Average, and Maximum aggregate functions for the Contract Amt field.

To calculate the minimum, average, and maximum of all contract amounts:

1. Create a new query in Design view, add the **Contract** table to the Query window, and then close the Show Table dialog box.

   To perform the three calculations on the Contract Amt field, you need to add the field to the design grid three times.

2. Double-click **Contract Amt** in the Contract field list three times to add three copies of the field to the design grid.

   You need to select an aggregate function for each Contract Amt field. When you click the Totals button in the Show/Hide group on the Query Tools Design tab, a row labeled "Total" is added to the design grid. The Total row provides a list of the aggregate functions that you can select.

3. In the Show/Hide group on the Query Tools Design tab, click the **Totals** button. A new row labeled "Total" appears between the Table and Sort rows in the design grid. The default entry for each field in the Total row is the Group By operator, which you will learn about later in this tutorial. See Figure 3-38.

Total row inserted in the design grid — Figure 3-38

In the Total row, you specify the aggregate function you want to use for a field.

4. Click the right side of the first column's **Total** text box, and then click **Min**. This field will calculate the minimum amount of all the Contract Amt field values.

   When you run the query, Access automatically will assign a datasheet column name of "MinOfContract Amt" for this field. You can change the datasheet column name to a more descriptive or readable name by entering the name you want in the Field text box. However, you must also keep the field name Contract Amt in the Field text box, because it identifies the field whose values will be calculated. The Field text box will contain the datasheet column name you specify followed by the field name (Contract Amt) with a colon separating the two names.

▶ **5.** Click to the left of Contract Amt in the first column's Field text box, and then type **Minimum Contract Amt:**. *Be sure that you type the colon following the name.*

▶ **6.** Click the right side of the second column's **Total** text box, and then click **Avg**. This field will calculate the average of all the Contract Amt field values.

▶ **7.** Click to the left of Contract Amt in the second column's Field text box, and then type **Average Contract Amt:**.

▶ **8.** Click the right side of the third column's **Total** text box, and then click **Max**. This field will calculate the maximum amount of all the Contract Amt field values.

▶ **9.** Click to the left of Contract Amt in the third column's Field text box, and then type **Maximum Contract Amt:**.

▶ **10.** Run the query. Access displays one record containing the three aggregate function values. The single row of summary statistics represents calculations based on all the records selected for the query—in this case, all 64 records in the Contract table.

▶ **11.** Resize all columns to their best fit so that the column names are fully displayed, and then click the field value in the first column. See Figure 3-39.

Figure 3-39 ▶ **Result of the query using aggregate functions**

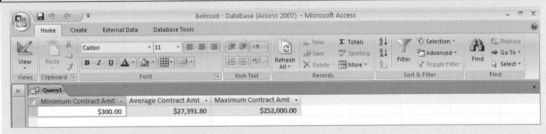

▶ **12.** Save the query as **Contract Amt Statistics**.

Oren also wants his report to include the same contract amount statistics (minimum, average, and maximum) grouped by city.

Using Record Group Calculations

In addition to calculating statistical information on all or selected records in selected tables, you can calculate statistics for groups of records. For example, you can determine the number of customers in each city or the average contract amount by city.

To create a query for Oren's latest request, you can modify the current query by adding the City field and assigning the Group By operator to it. The **Group By operator** divides the selected records into groups based on the values in the specified field. Those records with the same value for the field are grouped together, and the datasheet displays one record for each group. Aggregate functions, which appear in the other columns of the design grid, provide statistical information for each group.

You need to modify the current query to add the Group By operator to the City field from the Customer table. This will display the statistical information grouped by city for all the records in the query datasheet. To create the new query, you will save the Contract Amt Statistics query with a new name, keeping the original query intact, and then modify the new query.

To create a new query with the Group By operator:

1. Display the **Contract Amt Statistics** query in Design view.

2. Click the **Office Button** ⚫, point to **Save As**, and then click **Save Object As**. The Save As dialog box opens, indicating that you are saving a copy of the Contract Amt Statistics query as a new query.

3. Type **Contract Amt Statistics By City** to replace the highlighted name, and then press the **Enter** key. The new query is saved with the name you specified.

   You need to add the City field to the query. This field is in the Customer table. To include another table in an existing query, you open the Show Table dialog box.

4. In the Query Setup group on the Query Tools Design tab, click the **Show Table** button to open the Show Table dialog box.

5. Add the **Customer** table to the Query window, close the Show Table dialog box, and then resize the Customer field list.

6. Drag the **City** field from the Customer field list to the first column in the design grid. When you release the mouse button, the City field appears in the design grid's first column, and the existing fields shift to the right. Group By, the default option in the Total row, appears for the City field.

7. Run the query. Access displays 12 records—one for each City group. Each record contains the City field value for the group and the three aggregate function values. The summary statistics represent calculations based on the 64 records in the Contract table. See Figure 3-40.

Aggregate functions grouped by City   **Figure 3-40**

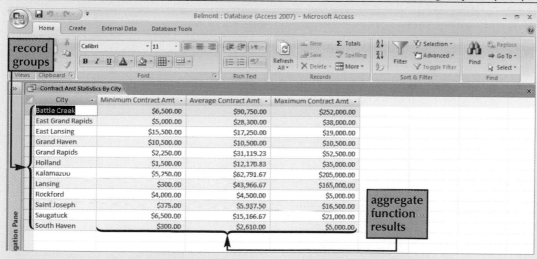

8. Save and close the query.

9. Open the Navigation Pane.

You have created and saved many queries in the Belmont database. The Navigation Pane provides options for opening and managing the queries you've created, as well as the other objects in the database, such as tables, forms, and reports.

Working with the Navigation Pane

As noted in Tutorial 1, the Navigation Pane is the main area for working with the objects in a database. As you continue to create objects in your database, you might want to display and work with them in different ways. The Navigation Pane provides options for grouping database objects in various ways to suit your needs. For example, you might want to view only the queries created for a certain table or all the query objects in the database.

The Navigation Pane divides database objects into categories, and each category contain groups. The groups contain one or more objects. The default category is **Tables and Related Views**, which arranges objects by tables, and the default group is **All Tables**, which includes all tables in the database in the list. You can also choose to display the objects for a specific table only.

The default group name, All Tables, appears at the top of the Navigation Pane. Currently, each table in the Belmont database—Contract, Invoice, and Customer—is displayed in a bar, and the objects related to each table are listed below the table name. Some objects appear more than once. As noted earlier, when an object is based on more than one table, that object appears in the group for each table. For example, the Holland Customers query is based on both the Contract and Customer tables, so it is listed in the group for both tables.

To group objects differently, you can select another category by using the Navigation Pane menu. You'll try this next.

Tip

You can hide the display of a group's objects by clicking the bar for the group; click the bar again to expand the group and display its objects.

To group objects differently in the Navigation Pane:

▶ 1. At the top of the Navigation Pane, click the **All Tables** bar. A menu is displayed for choosing different categories and groups. See Figure 3-41.

Figure 3-41   Navigation Pane menu

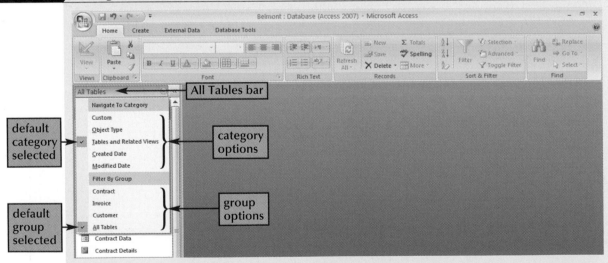

The top section of the menu provides the options for choosing a different category. The Tables and Related Views category has a check mark next to it, signifying that it is the currently selected category. The lower section of the menu provides options for choosing a different group; these options might change depending on the selected category.

▶ **2.** In the top section of the menu, click **Object Type**. The Navigation Pane is now grouped into categories of object types—tables, queries, forms, and reports. See Figure 3-42.

Database objects grouped by type in the Navigation Pane ◀ **Figure 3-42**

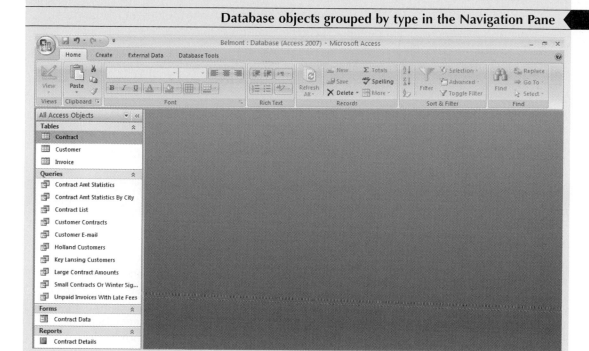

Trouble? If your Navigation Pane doesn't show all the object types, click the bar at the top of the pane to open the Navigation Pane menu, and then click All Access Objects.

You can also select a different group for a category display.

▶ **3.** Click the **All Access Objects** bar to display the Navigation Pane menu, and then click **Queries**. The Navigation Pane now shows only the query objects in the database.

▶ **4.** Click the **Queries** bar, and then click **Tables and Related Views** to return to the default display of the Navigation Pane.

▶ **5.** Compact and repair the Belmont database, and then close Access.

The default Tables and Related Views category is a predefined category. You can also create custom categories to group objects in the way that best suits how you want to manage your database objects. As you continue to build a database and the list of objects grows, creating a custom category can help you to work more efficiently with the objects in the database.

The queries you've created and saved will help Oren, Taylor, Sarah, and others to monitor and analyze the business activity of Belmont Landscapes and its customers. Now any staff member can run the queries at any time, modify them as needed, or use them as the basis for designing new queries to meet additional information requirements.

Review | **Session 3.2 Quick Check**

1. A(n) _____ is a criterion, or rule, that determines which records are selected for a query datasheet.
2. In the design grid, where do you place the conditions for two different fields when you use the And logical operator? The Or logical operator?
3. To perform a calculation in a query, you define a(n) _____ containing a combination of database fields, constants, and operators.
4. How does a calculated field differ from a table field?
5. What is an aggregate function?
6. The _____ operator divides selected records into groups based on the values in a field.
7. What is the default category for the display of objects in the Navigation Pane?

Review | **Tutorial Summary**

In this tutorial, you learned how to maintain a database by finding specific data, modifying values in records, and deleting records. You also learned how to create queries in Design view, based on one or more tables, and how to run and save queries. You learned different methods for sorting and filtering data to view records in a particular order. Using record selection criteria, you specified an exact match in a query, used a comparison operator to match a range of values, and used the And and Or logical operators to meet various requests for data retrieval. You also created a calculated field in the Expression Builder dialog box to display the results of an expression in a query, and you used aggregate functions and the Group By operator to calculate and display statistical information in a query. Finally, you learned how to change the display and grouping of database objects in the Navigation Pane.

Key Terms

aggregate function	Expression Builder	query by example (QBE)
All Tables	F2 key	Query Wizard
Alternate Fill/Back Color button	field list	recordset
	filter	run (a query)
And logical operator	Filter By Form	secondary sort field
AutoFilter	Filter By Selection	select query
calculated field	Find command	sort
comparison operator	Group By operator	sort field
condition	logical operator	subdatasheet
datasheet selector	maintain (a database)	Tables and Related Views
design grid	navigation mode	unique sort field
editing mode	nonunique sort field	update (a database)
exact match	Or logical operator	Zoom box
expand indicator	plus sign	
expression	primary sort field	

Practice		Review Assignments

Build on what you learned in the tutorial by practicing those skills using the same case scenario.

Data File needed for the Review Assignments: Supplier.accdb *(cont. from Tutorial 2)*

Oren asks you to update some information in the Supplier database and also to retrieve specific information from the database. Complete the following:

1. Open the **Supplier** database located in the Level.01\Review folder provided with your Data Files.

2. Open the **Company** table, and then change the following field values for the record with the Company ID MID312: Address to **2250 E Riverview St**, Phone to **269-979-0700**, Contact First Name to **Aimee**, and Contact Last Name to **Gigandet**. Close the table.

3. Open the **Product** table, find the record with Product ID 5318, and then delete the record. Close the table.

4. Create a query based on the Company table. Include the following fields, in the order shown, in the query: Company Name, Contact First Name, Contact Last Name, Phone, and Initial Contact Date. Sort the query in ascending order based on the Company Name. Save the query as **Contact List**, and then run the query.

5. Use the Contact List query datasheet to update the Company table by changing the Phone field value for Genesis Garden Center to **616-456-1783**.

6. Change the alternate background color for the rows in the Contact List query datasheet to Light Label Text, and then save and close the query.

7. Use Design view to create a query based on the Company and Product tables. Select the Company Name and City fields from the Company table, and the Product Type, Price, Unit, and Discount Offered fields from the Product table. Sort the query results in descending order based on the Price. Select only those records with a City field value of Holland, but do not display the City field values in the query results. Save the query as **Holland Companies**, and then run the query. Resize all columns in the datasheet, if necessary, and then save and close the query.

8. Use Design view to create a query that lists all products that cost more than $5,000 and are not eligible for a discount. Display the following fields from the Product table in the query results: Product ID, Product Type, Price, Unit, and Weight in Lbs. (*Hint*: The Discount Offered field is a Yes/No field that should not appear in the query results.) Save the query as **High Prices No Discount**, run the query, and then close it.

9. Use Design view to create a query that lists companies located in Grand Rapids or products that cost less than $1,000. Include the Company Name, City, Contact First Name, and Contact Last Name fields from the Company table; and the Product Type, Price, and Discount Offered fields from the Product table. Save the query as **Grand Rapids Or Low Prices**, run the query, and then close it.

10. Use Design view to create a query that lists only those products that are eligible for a discount, along with a 5% discount amount based on the current price. Include the following fields from the Product table in the query: Product ID, Product Type, and Price. (*Hint:* The Discount Offered field is a Yes/No field that should not appear in the query results.) Display the discount in a calculated field named **Discount** that determines a 5% discount based on the Price field values. Display the results in descending order by Price. Save the query as **Prices With Discount Amounts**, and then run the query.

11. Modify the format of the Discount field in the Prices With Discount Amounts query so that it uses the Standard format and two decimal places. Run the query, resize all columns in the datasheet to best fit, and then save and close the query.

12. Create a query that calculates the lowest, highest, and average prices for all products using the field names **Lowest Price**, **Highest Price**, and **Average Price**, respectively. Run the query, resize all columns in the datasheet to best fit, save the query as **Price Statistics**, and then close it.

13. In the Navigation Pane, copy the Price Statistics query, and then rename the copied query as **Price Statistics By Company**.

14. Modify the Price Statistics By Company query so that the records are grouped by the Company Name field in the Company table. Company Name should appear as the first field in the query datasheet. Save and run the query, and then close it.

15. Change the Navigation Pane so that it displays all objects grouped by object type.

16. Compact and repair the Supplier database, and then close it.

| Apply | **Case Problem 1** |

Use the skills you learned in the tutorial to update records and create queries in a database for a small music school.

Data File needed for this Case Problem: Pinehill.accdb *(cont. from Tutorial 2)*

Pine Hill Music School After reviewing the Pinehill database, Yuka Koyama wants to modify some records and then view specific information about the students, teachers, and contracts for her music school. She asks you to update and then query the Pinehill database to perform these tasks. Complete the following:

1. Open the **Pinehill** database located in the Level.01\Case1 folder provided with your Data Files.

2. In the **Teacher** table, change the following information for the record with Teacher ID 55-5310: Degree is **BM** and Hire Date is **3/12/2009**. Close the table.

3. In the **Student** table, find the record with the Student ID HAV7535, and then delete the related record in the subdatasheet for this student. Delete the record for Student ID HAV7535, and then close the Student table.

4. Create a query based on the Student table that includes the Last Name, First Name, and Phone fields, in that order. Save the query as **Student Phone List**, and then run the query.

5. In the results of the Student Phone List query, change the phone number for Andrea Barreau to **503-579-2277**. Close the query.

6. Use Design view to create a query based on the Teacher and Contract tables. Display the Last Name field from the Teacher table, and the Student ID, Contract End Date, Lesson Type, Lesson Length, and Lesson Monthly Cost fields, in that order, from the Contract table. Sort in ascending order first on the teacher's last name, and then in ascending order by the Student ID. Save the query as **Lessons By Teacher**, and then run it.

7. Use the Office Button to save the Lessons By Teacher query as **Current Lessons**.

8. Modify the Current Lessons query to display all contracts that end on or after 7/1/2010. Save your changes, and then run the query.

9. Save the Current Lessons query as **Current Guitar Lessons**.

10. Modify the Current Guitar Lessons query to display only those records for guitar lesson contracts that end on or after 7/1/2010. Do not include the Lesson Type field values in the query results. Run and save the query.

11. In the Current Guitar Lessons query datasheet, calculate the total monthly amount for current guitar lessons.

12. Change the alternate background color for the rows in the Current Guitar Lessons query datasheet to Light Label Text and the font size to 12. Resize all columns in the datasheet to fit the data, and then save and close the query.

13. Change the Navigation Pane so that it displays all objects grouped by object type.

14. Compact and repair the Pinehill database, and then close it.

| Create | **Case Problem 2** |

Follow the steps provided and use the figures as guides to create queries for a health and fitness center.

Data File needed for this Case Problem: Fitness.accdb (*cont. from Tutorial 2*)

Parkhurst Health & Fitness Center   Martha Parkhurst needs to change a few records in the Fitness database, and analyze the records for members enrolled in different programs at the fitness center. To help her perform these tasks, you'll update the Fitness database and create queries to answer her questions. Complete the following:

1. Open the **Fitness** database located in the Level.01\Case2 folder provided with your Data Files.

2. In the **Member** table, find the record for Member ID 1158, and then change the Street value to **89 Mockingbird Lane** and the Phone to **804-751-1847**. Close the table.

3. In the **Program** table, find the record for Program ID 205. In the subdatasheet, delete the related record from the Member table. Then delete the record for Program ID 205 in the Program table. Close the table.

4. Use Design view to create a query that lists members who are required to have physical examinations. In the query results, display the First Name, Last Name, and Date Joined fields from the Member table, and the Monthly Fee field from the Program table. Sort the records in descending order by the Date Joined. Select records only for members required to take a physical. (*Hint:* The Physical Required field is a Yes/No field.) Save the query as **Physicals Needed**, and then run the query.

5. Use the Physicals Needed query datasheet to update the Member table by changing the Date Joined value for Ed Curran to **10/18/2010**.

6. Use the Physicals Needed query datasheet to display the total Monthly Fee for the selected members. Save and close the query.

7. Use Design view to create a query that lists the Member ID, First Name, Last Name, Date Joined, Program Type, and Monthly Fee fields for members who joined the fitness center between June 1 and June 30, 2010. Save the query as **June Members**, run the query, and then close it.

8. Create and save the query to produce the results shown in Figure 3-43. Close the query when you are finished.

Figure 3-43

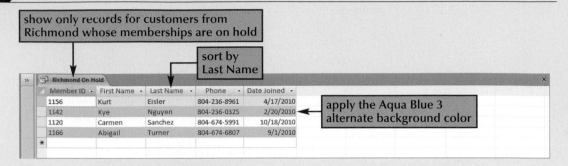

EXPLORE 9. Create and save the query to produce the results shown in Figure 3-44. Close the query when you are finished.

Figure 3-44

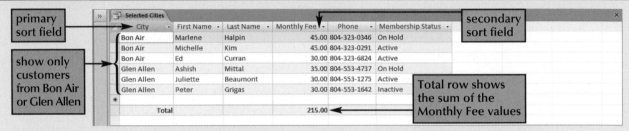

EXPLORE 10. Create and save the query to produce results that display statistics for the Monthly Fee field, as shown in Figure 3-45. Close the query when you are finished.

Figure 3-45

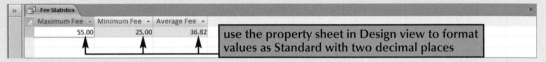

11. In the Navigation Pane, copy the Fee Statistics query and rename the copied query as **Fee Statistics By City**.
12. Modify the Fee Statistics By City query to display the same statistics grouped by City, with City appearing as the first field. (*Hint*: Add the Member table to the query.) Run the query, and then save and close it.
13. Change the Navigation Pane so that it displays all objects grouped by object type.
14. Compact and repair the Fitness database, and then close it.

Challenge | **Case Problem 3**

Work with the skills you've learned, and explore some new skills, to create queries for a not-for-profit agency that recycles household goods.

Data File needed for this Case Problem: Rossi.accdb *(cont. from Tutorial 2)*

Rossi Recycling Group   Tom Rossi needs to modify some records in the Rossi database, and then he wants to find specific information about the donors, agencies, and donations to his not-for-profit agency. Tom asks you to help him update the database and create queries. Complete the following:

1. Open the **Rossi** database located in the Level.01\Case3 folder provided with your Data Files.

2. In the **Donor** table, delete the record with a Donor ID of 36065. (*Hint:* Delete the related record first.) Close the table.

3. Create a query based on the Agency table that includes the Agency Name, Contact First Name, Contact Last Name, and City fields, in that order. Save the query as **Agencies By City**, and then run it.

4. Modify the Agencies By City query so that it sorts records in ascending order first by City and then by Agency Name. Save and run the query.

5. In the Agencies By City query datasheet, change the contact for the Community Development agency to **Beth Dayton**. Close the query.

6. Use Design view to create a query that displays the Donor ID, First Name, Last Name, Donation Description, and Donation Value for all donations over $50. Sort the query in ascending order by Donation Value. Save the query as **Large Donations**, and then run the query.

7. Save the Large Donations query as **Large Cash Donations**.

⊕ **EXPLORE**   8. Modify the Large Cash Donations query to display only those records with donations valuing more than $50 in cash. Use the query datasheet to calculate the average large cash donation. Save and close the query.

9. Use Design view to create a query that displays the Agency ID, Donation ID, Donation Date, and Donation Description fields. Save the query as **Senior Donations**, and then run the query.

10. Filter the results of the Senior Donations query datasheet to display records for all donations to the SeniorCare Program (Agency ID K82).

⊕ **EXPLORE**   11. Format the datasheet of the Senior Donations query so that it does not display gridlines, uses an alternate background color for rows of Green 2, and displays a font size of 12. (*Hint*: Use the Gridlines button on the Home tab to select a gridlines option.) Resize the columns to display the complete field names and values. Save your changes.

12. Save the Senior Donations query as **Computer Or Youth Donations**.

13. Modify the Computer Or Youth Donations query to display donations of computer equipment or those to the After School Youth agency (Agency ID Y68). Sort the records in ascending order first by Donation Description and then by Agency ID. Run, save, and then close the query.

⊕ **EXPLORE**   14. Use Design view to create a query that displays the Donor ID, Agency Name, Donation Description, and Donation Value fields for all donations that require a pickup. (*Hint:* The Pickup Required field is a Yes/No field.) Create a calculated field named **Net Donation** that displays the results of subtracting $8.75 from the Donation Value field values. Display the results in ascending order by Donation Value. Save the query as **Donations After Pickup Charge**, and then run it. Modify the query to format the calculated field as Currency with two Decimal Places. Run the query and resize the columns in the datasheet to their best fit. Save and close the query.

⊕ **EXPLORE**   15. Use the **Donation** table to display the sum, average, and count of the Donation Value field for all donations. Then complete the following:

a. Specify column names of **Total Donations**, **Average Donation**, and **Number of Donations**.

b. Save the query as **Donation Statistics**, and then run it.

c. Modify the field properties so that the values in the Total Donations and Average Donation columns display two decimal places and the Standard format. Run the query and resize the columns in the datasheet to their best fit. Save and close the query.

d. In the Navigation Pane, create a copy of the Donation Statistics query named **Donation Statistics By Agency**.

e. Modify the Donation Statistics By Agency query to display the sum, average, and count of the Donation Value field for all donations grouped by Agency Name, with Agency Name appearing as the first field. (*Hint*: Add the Agency table to the query.) Sort the records in descending order by Total Donations. Save, run, and then close the query.

16. Change the Navigation Pane so that it displays only queries. (*Hint:* Display the objects by type, and then select Queries in the Filter by Group section of the Navigation Pane menu.)

17. Compact and repair the Rossi database, and then close it.

Challenge | Case Problem 4

Work with the skills you've learned, and explore some new skills, to create queries for a luxury rental company.

Data File needed for this Case Problem: GEM.accdb *(cont. from Tutorial 2)*

GEM Ultimate Vacations   Griffin and Emma MacElroy want to modify some records, and then analyze data about their clients and the luxury properties they rent. You offer to help them update and query the GEM database. Complete the following:

1. Open the **GEM** database located in the Level.01\Case4 folder provided with your Data Files.

2. In the **Guest** table, delete the record with a Guest ID of 224, and then close the table.

3. Create a query based on the Property table that includes the Property Name, Location, Country, Nightly Rate, and Property Type fields, in that order. Sort in ascending order based on the Nightly Rate field values. Save the query as **Properties By Rate**, and then run the query.

⊕ EXPLORE   4. In the results of the Properties By Rate query, change the nightly rate for the Hartfield Country Manor property to $2,500, and then use the datasheet to display the number of properties and the average nightly rate. Save and close the query.

5. Create a query that displays the Guest Last Name, City, State/Prov, Reservation ID, Start Date, and End Date fields. Save the query as **Guest Trip Dates**, and then run the query. Change the alternate background color of the rows in the query datasheet to Access Theme 2. In Datasheet view, use an AutoFilter to sort the query results from oldest to newest Start Date. Save and close the query.

6. Create a query that displays the Guest Last Name, City, Reservation ID, People, Start Date, and End Date fields for all guests from Illinois (IL). Sort the query in ascending order by City. Save the query as **Illinois Guests**, run it, and then close the query.

⊕ EXPLORE   7. Create a query that displays the Guest Last Name, City, Reservation ID, Start Date, and Property ID fields for all guests who are not from Illinois or who are renting a property starting in the month of June 2010. Sort the query in descending order by Start Date. Save the query as **Out Of State Or June**, and then run the query.

8. Save the Out Of State Or June query as **Out Of State And June**.

9. Modify the Out Of State And June query to select all clients who are not from Illinois and who are renting a property beginning in the month of June 2010. Sort the query in ascending order by Start Date. Run the query, and then save and close it.

10. Create a query that displays the Reservation ID, Start Date, End Date, Property ID, Property Name, People, and Rental Rate fields for all reservations. Add a field to the query named **Cost Per Person** that displays the results of dividing the Rental Rate field values by the People field values. Display the results in descending order by Cost Per Person. Save the query as **Rental Cost** and then run it. Modify the query by setting the following properties for the Cost Per Person field: Format set to Currency and Decimal Places set to 2. Run the query, resize all datasheet columns to their best fit, and then save your changes.

11. Save the Rental Cost query as **Top Rental Cost**.

⊕EXPLORE 12. Open the Access Help window and use **top values query** as the search text. Select the Help article titled "Find the records with the top or bottom values in a group or field," and then read the "Find the records that contain top or bottom values" section. Close the Access Help window. Modify the Top Rental Cost query in Design view to display only the top five values for the Cost Per Person field. (*Hint:* Use the Return list box in the Query Setup group on the Query Tools Design tab.) Save, run, and then close the query.

⊕EXPLORE 13. Use the Reservation table to determine the minimum, average, and maximum Rental Rate values for all reservations. Then complete the following:

　　a. Specify column names of **Lowest Rate**, **Average Rate**, and **Highest Rate**.

　　b. Save the query as **Rate Statistics**, and then run the query.

　　c. In Design view, use the property sheet for each column to format the results with the Standard format and two decimal places.

　　d. Run the query, resize all the datasheet columns to their best fit, save your changes, and then close the query.

　　e. Create a copy of the Rate Statistics query named **Rate Statistics By Country**.

　　f. Revise the Rate Statistics By Country query to display the rate statistics grouped by Country of the property, with Country appearing as the first field. Save your changes and then run and close the query.

14. Change the view of the Navigation Pane to show all Access objects grouped by object type.

15. Compact and repair the GEM database, and then close it.

Research | **Internet Assignments**

Use the Internet to find and work with data related to the topics presented in this tutorial.

The purpose of the Internet Assignments is to challenge you to find information on the Internet that you can use to work effectively with this software. The actual assignments are updated and maintained on the Course Technology Web site. Log on to the Internet and use your Web browser to go to the Student Online Companion for New Perspectives Office 2007 at **www.course.com/np/office2007**. Then navigate to the Internet Assignments for this tutorial.

Assess | **SAM Assessment and Training**

If you have a SAM user profile, you may have access to hands-on instruction, practice, and assessment of the skills covered in this tutorial. Log in to your SAM account (**http://sam2007.course.com**) to launch any assigned training activities or exams that relate to the skills covered in this tutorial.

Session 3.1

1. In navigation mode, the entire field value is selected, and anything you type replaces the field value; in editing mode, you can insert or delete characters in a field value based on the location of the insertion point.

2. A select query is a general query in which you specify the fields and records you want Access to select.

3. The field list contains the table name at the top of the list box and the table's fields listed in the order in which they appear in the table; the design grid displays columns that contain specifications about a field you will use in the query.

4. A table datasheet and a query datasheet look the same, appearing in Datasheet view, and can be used to update data in a database. A table datasheet shows the permanent data in a table, whereas a query datasheet is temporary and its contents are based on the criteria you establish in the design grid.

5. oldest to most recent date

6. False

7. filter

Session 3.2

1. condition

2. in the same Criteria row; in different Criteria rows

3. expression

4. A calculated field appears in a query datasheet, form, or report but does not exist in a database, as does a table field.

5. a function that performs an arithmetic operation on selected records in a database

6. Group By

7. Tables and Related Views

Ending Data Files

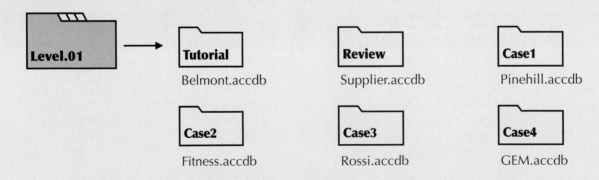

Level.01 →

Tutorial
Belmont.accdb

Review
Supplier.accdb

Case1
Pinehill.accdb

Case2
Fitness.accdb

Case3
Rossi.accdb

Case4
GEM.accdb

Reality Check

The Microsoft Access program is widely used in corporations to track business data, but it can also be a valuable tool to use to track data in your personal life. For example, you might want to create an Access database to track information about items in a personal collection, such as CDs, DVDs, or books; items related to a hobby, such as coin or stamp collecting, travel, or family history; or items related to sports teams, theater clubs, or other organizations to which you might belong. In this exercise, you'll use Access to create a database that will contain information of your choice, using the Access skills and features presented in Tutorials 1 through 3.

Using Templates

The Access program includes templates for creating databases and tables. A **database template** is a database containing predefined tables, queries, forms, and reports. A **table template** is a template containing predefined fields. Using a database or table template can save you time and effort in the creation process. For example, if the fields available in one of the table templates Access offers are similar to the data you want to track, you can use the table template to quickly create a table with the fields and field properties already created and set for you. You can then modify the table, as necessary, to suit your needs. Before you begin to create your own database, review the following steps for using database and table templates.

To create a database using a database template:

1. On the Getting Started with Microsoft Office Access page, click the appropriate link in the Template Categories pane; or click a link in the From Microsoft Office Online pane; or click one of the templates in the Featured Online Templates section in the middle of the page.
2. Specify the name for your database and a location in which to save the database file.
3. Click the Create button (or the Download button if you are using an Office Online template).
4. Use the resulting database objects to enter, modify, or delete data or database objects.

To create a table using a table template:

1. With your database file open, click the Create tab on the Ribbon.
2. In the Tables group, click the Table Templates button. A gallery opens listing the different table templates provided with Access.
3. Click the template you want to use.
4. Modify the resulting table as needed, by adding or deleting fields, changing field properties, and so on.

You can decide to use a database and/or table template for the following exercise if the templates fit the data you want to track. Note, however, that you still need to create the additional database objects indicated in the following steps—tables, queries, forms, and reports—to complete the exercise successfully.

Note: Please be sure *not* to include any personal information of a sensitive nature in the database you create to be submitted to your instructor for this exercise. Later on, you can update the data in your database with such information for your own personal use.

1. Create a new Access database to contain personal data you want to track.
2. Create two or three tables in the database that can be joined through one-to-many relationships.
3. Define the properties for each field in each table. Make sure you include a mix of data types for the fields (for example, do not include only Text fields in each table).
4. Specify a primary key for each table.
5. Define the necessary one-to-many relationships between the tables in the database with referential integrity enforced.
6. Enter 20 to 30 records in each table. If appropriate, you can import the data for a table from another source, such as an Excel spreadsheet or a text file.
7. Create 5 to 10 queries based on single tables and multiple tables. Be sure that some of the queries you create include some or all of the following: exact match conditions, comparison operators, and logical operators.
8. For some of the queries, use various sorting and filtering techniques to display the query results in various ways. Save these queries with the sort and/or filter applied.
9. If possible, and depending on the data you are tracking, create at least one calculated field in one of the queries.
10. If possible, and depending on the data you are tracking, use aggregate functions to produce summary statistics based on the data in at least one of your tables.
11. Create a simple form for each table in your database.
12. Create a simple report based on each table in your database.
13. Submit your completed database to your instructor as requested. Include printouts of any database objects, such as reports, if required.

Creating a Presentation

Presenting Information About a Recreational Timeshare Company

Case | Share-My-Toys, Inc.

After Sandra Corwin graduated from Idaho State University with a degree in business administration, she worked for a large company, Anaconda Kayaks and Canoes, in Redding, California. After several years, she decided to return to her home town of Montpelier, Idaho, and start her own business. Montpelier is located near Bear Lake and other recreational areas in southeastern Idaho and western Wyoming, and Sandra grew up participating in camping, hiking, snowmobiling, boating, and other water sports. During that time, she noticed that her family often borrowed outdoor recreational equipment from family and friends, but now, because of the population increase in the area and the rise in equipment costs, many people don't have access to the equipment to do the activities that she enjoyed as a youth.

With these ideas in mind and her experience in the outdoor equipment industry, Sandra started the company Share-My-Toys, Inc., which specializes in selling timeshares for recreational equipment, including ski boats, wave runners, snowmobiles, recreational vehicles (RVs), and all-terrain vehicles (ATVs). The company would allow everyone, even those of modest means or few family members in the area, to have access to a wide range of outdoor activities.

In this tutorial, you'll first examine a presentation that Sandra created for potential members. Viewing this file will help you to become familiar with **Microsoft Office PowerPoint 2007** (or simply **PowerPoint**). You'll then create a presentation for Sandra that describes her business plan for Share-My-Toys to banks and potential investors. The presentation you create will be based on content that PowerPoint suggests by using a template. You'll modify the text in the presentation, and you'll add and delete slides. You'll check the spelling of the presentation, and then you'll view the completed slide show. Finally, you'll save the slide show and print handouts.

Starting Data Files

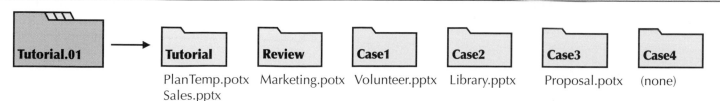

Tutorial.01	→	Tutorial	Review	Case1	Case2	Case3	Case4
		PlanTemp.potx Sales.pptx	Marketing.potx	Volunteer.pptx	Library.pptx	Proposal.potx	(none)

Session 1.1

What Is PowerPoint?

PowerPoint is a powerful presentation graphics program that provides everything you need to produce an effective presentation in the form of on-screen slides, a slide presentation on a Web site, or black-and-white or color overheads. You might have already seen your instructors use PowerPoint presentations to enhance their classroom lectures.

Using PowerPoint, you can prepare each component of a presentation: individual slides, speaker notes, an outline, and audience handouts. The presentation you'll create for Sandra will include slides, notes, and handouts.

To start PowerPoint:

1. Click the **Start** button 🔵 on the taskbar, click **All Programs**, click **Microsoft Office**, and then click **Microsoft Office PowerPoint 2007**. PowerPoint starts and the PowerPoint window opens. See Figure 1-1.

   Trouble? If you don't see Microsoft Office PowerPoint 2007 on the Microsoft Office submenu, look for it on a different submenu or on the All Programs menu. If you still cannot find it, ask your instructor or technical support person for help.

Figure 1-1 ▶ **Blank PowerPoint window**

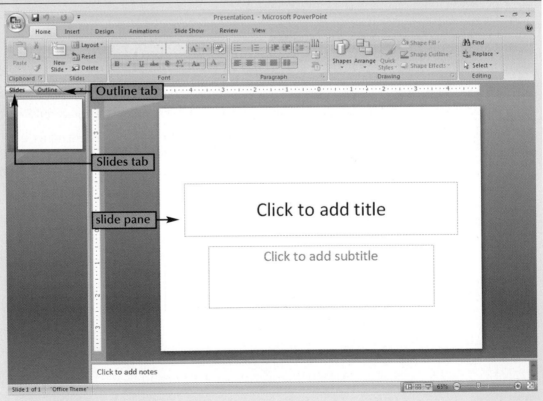

Opening an Existing PowerPoint Presentation

Before you prepare the presentation on Share-My-Toys, Sandra suggests that you view an existing presentation that she recently prepared so that you can see examples of PowerPoint features. When you examine the presentation, you'll learn about some PowerPoint capabilities that can help make your presentations more interesting and effective. You'll open the presentation now.

To open the existing presentation:

▶ **1.** Make sure you have access to the Data Files in the Tutorial.01 folder.

Trouble? If you don't have the starting Data Files, you need to get them before you can proceed. Your instructor will either give you the Data Files or ask you to obtain them from a specified location (such as a network drive). In either case, make a backup copy of your Data Files before you start so that you will have the original files available in case you need to start over. If you have any questions about the Data Files, see your instructor or technical support person for assistance.

▶ **2.** In the upper-left corner of the PowerPoint window, click the **Office Button** . A menu of commands appears.

▶ **3.** Click **Open** to display the Open dialog box.

▶ **4.** Expand the Folders list, if necessary, and then navigate to the **Tutorial.01\Tutorial** folder included with your Data Files.

▶ **5.** Click **Sales**, and then click the **Open** button to display Sandra's presentation. The presentation opens in Normal view. See Figure 1-2. Notice, on the left side of the status bar, that you are on the first slide of a presentation that contains nine slides.

PowerPoint window with presentation | Figure 1-2

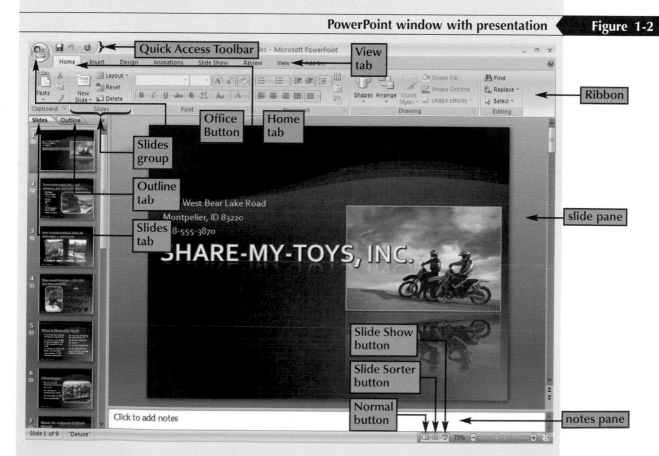

Trouble? If you see filename extensions on your screen (such as ".pptx" appended to "Sales" in the filename), don't be concerned; they won't affect your work.

Switching Views and Navigating a Presentation

The PowerPoint window contains features common to all Windows programs, as well as features specific to PowerPoint. One obvious difference between the PowerPoint window and other Office programs is that the PowerPoint window is divided into sections. The large section in the center of the screen is the slide pane. The **slide pane** shows the current slide as it will look during your slide show. When you type text or insert graphics on your slide, you'll mainly use the slide pane. Just below the slide pane is the notes pane. The **notes pane** contains notes (also called speaker notes) for the presenter; for example, the notes pane might contain specific points to cover or phrases to say during the presentation. During a slide show, the audience does not see the contents of the notes pane.

To the left of the slide pane, you can see another pane that contains two tabs, the Slides tab and the Outline tab. The **Slides tab** is on top when you first start PowerPoint. It shows a column of numbered slide **thumbnails** (miniature images) so you can see a visual representation of several slides at once. You can use the Slides tab to jump quickly to another slide in the slide pane by clicking the desired slide. The **Outline tab** shows an outline of the titles and text of each slide of your presentation.

At the lower right of the PowerPoint window, on the status bar to the left of the Zoom slider, are three buttons you can use to switch views: the Normal button 🔲 , the Slide Sorter button 🔠 , and the Slide Show button 🖵 . These three buttons allow you to change the way you view a presentation. PowerPoint is currently in Normal view. **Normal view** is best for working with the content of the slides. You can see how the text and graphics look on each individual slide, and you can examine the outline of the entire presentation. When you switch to **Slide Sorter view**, the pane that contains the Slides and Outline tabs disappears from view and all the slides appear as thumbnails. Slide Sorter view is an easy way to reorder the slides or set special features for your slide show. **Slide Show view** is the view in which you run the slide show presentation and the slide fills the entire screen. The View tab on the Ribbon also contains buttons for Normal, Slide Sorter, and Slide Show views, as well as for other views of the PowerPoint presentation, including Notes Page view.

Next, you'll examine Normal and Slide Sorter views. PowerPoint is currently in Normal view with Slide 1 in the slide pane.

To examine the presentation in Normal and Slide Sorter views:

▶ **1.** In the pane that contains the Slides tab, click the **Slide 2** thumbnail. Slide 2 appears in the slide pane.

▶ **2.** Click the **Next Slide** button ⬇ at the bottom of the vertical scroll bar on the right side of the slide pane. Slide 3 appears in the slide pane.

▶ **3.** Drag the scroll box in the slide pane vertical scroll bar down to the bottom of the scroll bar. Notice the ScreenTip that appears as you drag. It identifies the slide number and the title of the slide at the current position.

▶ **4.** In the pane that contains the Slides and Outline tabs, click the **Outline** tab. The text outline of the slides appears in the Outline tab.

▶ **5.** Drag the scroll box in the vertical scroll bar of the Outline tab up to the top of the scroll bar, and then, in the Outline tab, click the **slide icon** ▭ next to Slide 3. Slide 3 again appears in the slide pane.

▶ **6.** In the pane that contains the Slides and Outline tabs, click the **Slides** tab. The Outline tab disappears behind the Slides tab.

▶ **7.** On the status bar, to the left of the Zoom slider, click the **Slide Sorter** button 🔠. Slide Sorter view appears, and Slide 3 has a colored frame around it to indicate that it is the current slide.

▶ **8.** Position the pointer over the **Slide 2** thumbnail. A colored frame appears around Slide 2.

▶ **9.** Click the **Slide 2** thumbnail to make it the current slide. The colored frame disappears from Slide 3 and stays around Slide 2.

▶ **10.** Double-click the **Slide 1** thumbnail. The view switches back to Normal view and Slide 1 appears in the slide pane. You could also have clicked the Normal button on the status bar to switch back to Normal view.

Now that you're familiar with the PowerPoint window, you're ready to view Sandra's presentation. You'll do this in Slide Show view.

Viewing a Presentation in Slide Show View

Slide Show view is the view you use when you present an on-screen presentation to an audience. When you click the Slide Show button on the status bar, the slide show starts beginning with the current slide (the slide currently in the slide pane in Normal view or the selected slide in Slide Sorter view). When you click the Slide Show button on the View tab on the Ribbon or press the F5 key, the slide show starts at the beginning of the presentation—at Slide 1—even if Slide 1 is not the current slide. In a slide show, the slides fill the screen; no toolbars or other Windows elements are visible on the screen.

In Slide Show view, you move from one slide to the next by pressing the Spacebar, clicking the left mouse button, or pressing the → key. In addition, PowerPoint provides a method for jumping from one slide to any other slide in the presentation during the slide show: You can right-click anywhere on the screen, point to Go to Slide on the shortcut menu, and then, in the list that appears, click one of the slide titles to jump to that slide.

When you prepare a slide show, you can add special effects to the show. For example, you can add **slide transitions**, the manner in which a new slide appears on the screen during a slide show. You can also add **animations** to the elements on the slide; that is, a text or graphic object on the slide can appear on the slide in a special way or have a sound effect associated with it. A special type of animation is **progressive disclosure**, a technique in which each element on a slide appears one at a time after the slide background appears. Animations draw the audience's attention to the particular item on the screen.

You can also add a footer on the slides. A **footer** is a word or phrase that appears at the bottom of each slide in the presentation.

You want to see how Sandra's presentation will appear when she shows it in Slide Show view to a potential Share-My-Toys member. You'll then have a better understanding of how Sandra used PowerPoint features to make her presentation informative and interesting.

To view the presentation in Slide Show view:

▶ **1.** On the status bar, to the left of the Zoom slider, click the **Slide Show** button 🖵. The slide show begins by filling the entire viewing area of the screen with Slide 1 of Sandra's presentation. When you click the Slide Show button on the status bar, the slide show starts from the current slide. Watch as the slide title moves across the screen from left to right and right to left, the address block moves down the screen, and the picture of dirt bikers moves up the screen.

Tip

To start the slide show from the first slide no matter what the current slide is, click the View tab on the Ribbon, and then, in the Presentation Views group, click the Slide Show button, or press the F5 key.

As you view this first slide, you can already see some of the types of elements that PowerPoint allows you to place on a slide: text in different styles, sizes, and colors; graphics; and a background design. You also saw an example of an animation when you watched the slide title scroll across the screen and other elements move onto the screen. You can also see other special effects: text shadows, text reflection, and photo reflection.

▶ **2.** Press the **Spacebar**. The slide show goes from Slide 1 to Slide 2. See Figure 1-3. Notice that during the transition from Slide 1 to Slide 2, Slide 2 appeared as if it were a wheel with four spokes spinning onto the screen.

Figure 1-3 ▷ **Slide 2 in Slide Show view**

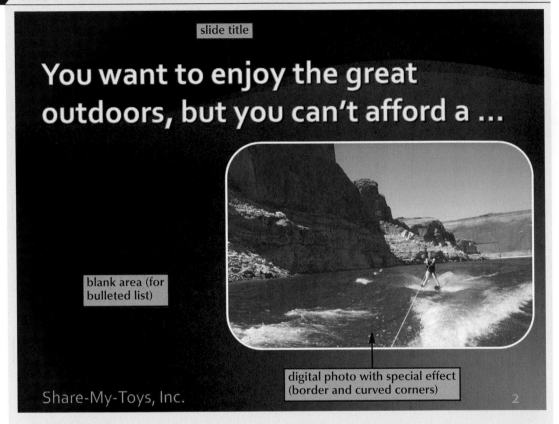

Trouble? If you missed the transition from Slide 1 to Slide 2, or if you want to see it again, press the ← key twice to redisplay Slide 1, and then press the Spacebar to go to Slide 2 again.

Notice in Figure 1-3 that Slide 2 displays (1) a colored background that varies in color across various sections of the slide, (2) a title in large, pale yellow text with a black **drop shadow** (a thin shadow on one side of the characters), (3) a photograph with a white border and curved corners of a woman on water skis, and (4) a blank area to the left of the photo. A bulleted list will appear in the blank area after you press the Spacebar. Also note that the slide number appears in the lower-right corner of the slide.

▶ **3.** Press the **Spacebar**. The bulleted list moves onto the slide. Now you can see 10 items—the list of recreational equipment available through Share-My-Toys, Inc. They "flew" onto the screen in progressive disclosure—one item at a time—without your having to press the Spacebar to reveal each item.

4. Click the left mouse button. Slide 3 appears on screen. During the transition from Slide 2 to Slide 3, you again see a spinning wheel with four spokes that covers up one slide and reveals the next slide. After the slide appears on the screen, you see two photographs slowly move onto the slide, a houseboat from the left and a kayak from the right. These photos each have three PowerPoint special effects applied to them: They are positioned at an angle, have beveled edges, and show reflections below them. PowerPoint supports many special effects for pictures that you insert into a presentation.

5. Press the **Spacebar** to go to Slide 4. A picture of a woman in a boat and the slide title appear on screen, followed by the twirling text "Share-My-Toys." This is an example of custom animation.

6. Proceed to the next slide by clicking the left mouse button or pressing the **Spacebar**. The title of Slide 5 appears on the screen, with a large blank area below the title. You can't see any of the items of the bulleted list yet, but through progressive disclosure, you'll display the bulleted items one at a time.

7. Press the **Spacebar**. A bulleted item flies onto the slide from the bottom of the screen. Notice that the bullet itself is a red diamond and the text is white.

8. Press the **Spacebar** again. The next bulleted item appears on the slide. As this item appears, the previous item dims. Dimming the previous bulleted items helps focus the audience's attention on the current bulleted item.

9. Press the **Spacebar** four more times, reading the bulleted text as it appears on the screen, and a fifth time to dim the final bulleted item. Notice that this bulleted list is a two-column list.

> **Tip**
>
> To end a slide show before you reach the last slide, press the Esc key

Using Conservative Animations in Formal Presentations | InSight

Flashy or flamboyant animations are acceptable for informal, fun-oriented presentations but would not be appropriate in a formal business, technical, or educational presentation. These types of presentations should be more conservative. When you are creating a formal presentation, it's best not to include superfluous animations that might detract from your message.

So far, you've seen several important PowerPoint features: slide transitions, progressive disclosure, animations, and special photographic effects. Now you'll finish the presentation and see more special effects, including custom animations, simple drawings, and a chart.

To continue viewing the slide show:

1. Press the **Spacebar** to go to Slide 6, and then press the **Spacebar** three more times to reveal the three bulleted list items in progressive disclosure. This time, the items are not dimmed as others appear on the slide.

2. Advance to Slide 7, where you see first the slide title and then a chart appear on the slide. PowerPoint has powerful features that allow you to add a wide variety of different types of charts and apply special effects to them.

3. Press the **Spacebar** to go to Slide 8. Here, you see the title and a simple drawing of a face in the middle of the slide. PowerPoint drawing tools let you draw simple pictures and diagrams for your presentations. This slide also demonstrates other drawing objects and animations. After you press the Spacebar in the next step to reveal the rest of the objects on this slide, watch the eyes of the face as you read the items in the flow diagram.

4. Press the **Spacebar** to initiate the animation of the flow diagram.

Trouble? If you want to watch the animations again, press the ← key, and then press the Spacebar to animate the diagram.

5. Press the **Spacebar** to move to Slide 9, the final slide, and then press the **Spacebar** again. A black, nearly blank slide appears with small text at the top identifying the end of the presentation.

6. Press the **Spacebar** one more time to exit Slide Show view and return to the view from which you started the slide show, in this case, Normal view.

7. In the upper-left corner of the window, click the **Office Button** 🏢, and then click **Close**.

As you can see from this slide show, PowerPoint has many powerful features. You'll learn how to use many of these features in your own presentations as you work through these tutorials.

You're now ready to create a presentation for Sandra, which she plans to give to bankers and potential investors. The presentation will include the business plan for Share-My-Toys. Before you begin, however, you need to plan the presentation.

Planning a Presentation

Planning a presentation before you create it improves the quality of your presentation, makes your presentation more effective and enjoyable, and, in the long run, saves you time and effort. As you plan your presentation, you should answer several questions: What is my purpose or objective for this presentation? What type of presentation is needed? Who is the audience? What information does that audience need? What is the physical location of my presentation? What is the best format for presenting the information contained in this presentation, given its location?

In planning your presentation, you should determine the following aspects:

- **Purpose of the presentation**: To acquire loans and investment funds for Share-My-Toys
- **Type of presentation**: Business plan (a summary of the operational and financial objectives of a business, including detailed plans and budgets showing how the objectives will be realized)
- **Audience for the presentation**: Local banks and potential investors
- **Audience needs**: To understand the mission, objectives, budgets, marketing, resources, and so forth, for Share-My-Toys
- **Location of the presentation**: Small conference room
- **Format**: Oral presentation accompanied by an electronic slide show of 6 to 8 slides

You have carefully planned your presentation. Now you'll use a PowerPoint template to create it.

Using Templates

PowerPoint helps you quickly create effective presentations by using a **template**, a PowerPoint file that contains the colors, background format, font styles, and accent colors for a presentation. Templates can also contain sample text. After you start creating a presentation with a given template, you can make changes to the design features and the text of the template. As you will see, each slide in a template has a predetermined way of organizing the objects on a slide.

When you create a presentation from a template, you can use a template that you or someone else designed, or you can use a template that you download from Microsoft Office Online. In this tutorial, you'll use a template that Sandra created while she worked for Anaconda Kayaks and Canoes in California. The slides in templates usually have existing text. The purpose of this text is to guide you in selecting and inserting the proper text content into your presentation. You'll now open the template.

Selecting a Template from Microsoft Office Online | InSight

To find many more templates, it's a good idea to look on Microsoft Office Online, which provides a variety of template categories to help you select the correct template for your presentation needs, including agendas, award certificates, calendars, design, reports, resumés, schedules, and so forth. After you select a category, you can examine and download different templates to see which you like the most. You can also view user ratings of the various templates, based on the feedback from hundreds, and, in some cases, even thousands, of users.

To use a template in starting a presentation:

▶ **1.** Click the **Office Button** 🔘, and then click **New**. The New Presentation dialog box opens. See Figure 1-4. You'll now select the template that Sandra created.

New Presentation dialog box ◀ **Figure 1-4**

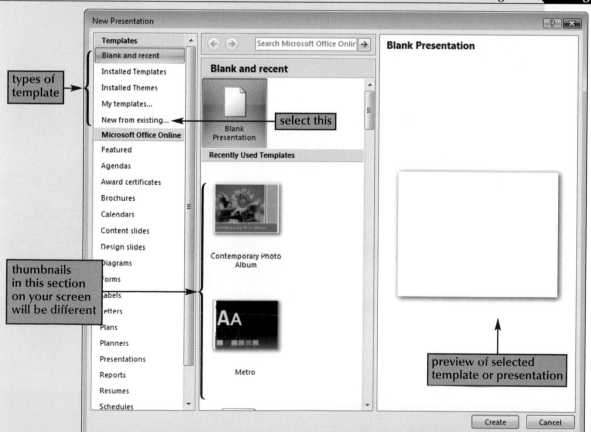

2. In the pane on the left side of the New Presentation dialog box, click **New from existing** in the list under Templates. The New from Existing Presentation dialog box opens.

3. Navigate to the **Tutorial.01\Tutorial** folder included with your Data Files.

4. Double-click **PlanTemp**.

The Business plan presentation template contains text on the slides to help you insert your business plan information. See Figure 1-5. PlanTemp is a PowerPoint template file, not a presentation file, but when you click New from existing in the New Presentation dialog box, you are allowed to choose from all PowerPoint files in the current folder. Notice that the filename in the title bar is "Presentation2" instead of the name of the file you opened "PlanTemp." This indicates that this is the second presentation of your current session, but that you opened a template or another presentation as a template.

Trouble? If the number in the filename on the title bar is a number other than 2 (such as "Presentation3"), don't worry about it. It just means that you have opened or created more than two presentations during this session.

Figure 1-5 **PowerPoint window with business plan presentation**

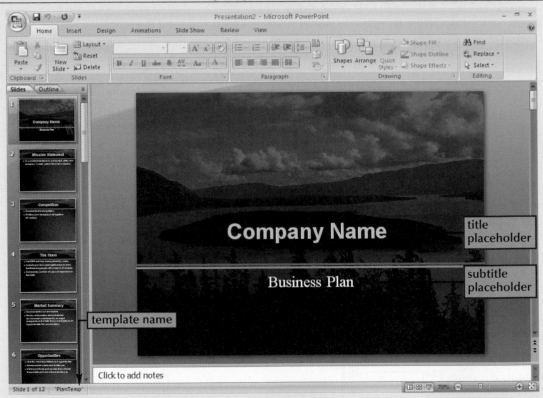

You have successfully started a new presentation using the template. You'll now save the presentation to your disk.

To save and name the presentation:

1. On the Quick Access Toolbar, click the **Save** button 🖫 . The Save As dialog box opens.

▶ 2. Expand the Folders list, if necessary, and then navigate to the **Tutorial.01\Tutorial** folder included with your Data Files, if necessary.

▶ 3. In the File name text box, click immediately after Company Name, the default file-name, press the **Backspace** key enough times to delete the default filename, and then type **Business Plan**.

▶ 4. At the bottom of the dialog box, click the **Save** button. PowerPoint saves the presentation as Business Plan and displays that name in the title bar of the PowerPoint window.

In the next session, you'll edit the text of Sandra's template, as well as create notes.

Session 1.1 Quick Check | Review

1. Describe the components of a PowerPoint presentation.
2. Name and describe the three panes in the PowerPoint window in Normal view.
3. Define or describe the following:
   a. slide pane
   b. progressive disclosure
   c. slide transition
   d. template
   e. layout
4. What are some of the questions that you should answer when planning a presentation?
5. Describe the purpose of the existing text in a template.
6. Describe Slide Show view.

Session 1.2

Modifying a Presentation

Now that you've started a presentation using a template with existing text, you're ready to edit the words in the presentation to fit Sandra's specific needs. You'll keep the presentation design, which includes the dark blue background and the size and color of the text.

The template includes the title slide, as well as other slides, with suggested text located in placeholders. A **placeholder** is a region of a slide, or a location in an outline, reserved for inserting text or graphics. To edit the template outline to fit Sandra's needs, you must insert text or objects into the placeholders one at a time. Text placeholders are a special kind of **text box**, which is an object that contains text. You can edit and format text in a text box or you can manipulate the text box as a whole. When you manipulate the text box as a whole, the text box is treated as an object, something that can be manipulated or resized as a unit.

When the text box is **active**, you can add or revise the text in it and the box appears with dashed lines and sizing handles around the text. **Sizing handles** are small circles and squares that appear at each corner and on each side of the active box that you can drag to make a text box or other object larger or smaller on the slide. When the entire text box is selected as a single object, you can apply effects to all of the text inside it and the text box appears as a solid line with sizing handles.

Many of the slides in your presentation for Share-My-Toys contain bulleted lists. A **bulleted list** is a list of "paragraphs" (words, phrases, sentences, or paragraphs) with a special character (dot, dash, circle, box, star, or other character) to the left of each paragraph. A **bulleted item** is one paragraph in a bulleted list. Bullets can appear at different outline levels. A **first-level bullet** is a main paragraph in a bulleted list; a **second-level bullet**—sometimes called a **subbullet**—is a bullet beneath (and indented from) a first-level bullet. Using bulleted lists reminds both the speaker and the audience of the main points of the presentation. In addition to bulleted lists, PowerPoint also supports numbered lists. A **numbered list** is a list of paragraphs that are numbered consecutively on the slide.

When you edit the text on the slides, keep in mind that the bulleted lists aren't meant to be the complete presentation; instead, they should emphasize the key points to the audience and remind the speaker of the points to emphasize. In all your presentations, you should follow the **6 x 6 rule** as much as possible: Keep each bulleted item to no more than six words, and don't include more than six bulleted items on a slide. This is, however, just a general guideline. You'll sometimes have slides with seven or eight bulleted items, and sometimes have items with more than six words. Never sacrifice clarity and purpose for brevity.

InSight | **Creating Effective Text Presentations**

- Think of your text presentation as a visual map of your oral presentation. Show your organization by using overviews, making headings larger than subheadings, and including bulleted lists to highlight key points and numbered steps to show sequences.
- Follow the 6 × 6 rule: Use six or fewer items per screen, and use phrases of six or fewer words. Omit unnecessary articles, pronouns, and adjectives.
- Keep phrases parallel. For example, if one bulleted item starts with a verb (such as "Summarize"), all the other bulleted items should start with a verb (such as "Include," "List," or "Review"). Or, if one bulleted list is a complete sentence, all the items should be complete sentences.
- Make sure your text is appropriate for your purpose and audience.

Sandra reviewed the presentation template with its existing text, and she has several suggestions to customize it for the presentation she wants you to create. First, she wants you to replace the placeholder text with information about Share-My-Toys. She also wants you to delete unnecessary slides and change the order of the slides in the presentation. You'll start by editing the text on the slides.

Editing Slides

Most of the slides in the presentation contain two placeholder text boxes. The slide **title text** is a text box at the top of the slide that gives the title of the information on that slide; the slide **content** is a large box in which you type a bulleted or numbered list or insert some other kind of object. In this presentation, you'll modify or create title text in some of the slides and modify the content text in all the slides that you keep in the presentation.

To edit the template text to fit Sandra's needs, you must select text in each of the placeholders, and then replace that text with other text. You'll now begin to edit and replace the text to fit Sandra's presentation. The first text you'll change is the title placeholder on the first (title) slide.

To edit and replace text in the first slide:

▶ **1.** If you took a break after the previous session, make sure PowerPoint is running, and then open the presentation **Business Plan** located in the Tutorial.01\Tutorial folder included with your Data Files. Slide 1 appears in the slide pane and the Slides tab is on top in the pane on the left.

   Trouble? If the Slides tab isn't on top in the pane on the left, click it to make the entire tab appear.

▶ **2.** Position the pointer over the title text (currently "Company Name") in the slide pane so that the pointer changes to I, and then drag it across the text to select it. See Figure 1-6. The text box becomes active, as indicated by the dashed lines around the box and the sizing handles at each corner and on each side of the text box, and the text becomes highlighted, as indicated by the gray box around it. The Mini toolbar appears because you used the mouse to select the text.

Selecting placeholder text   **Figure 1-6**

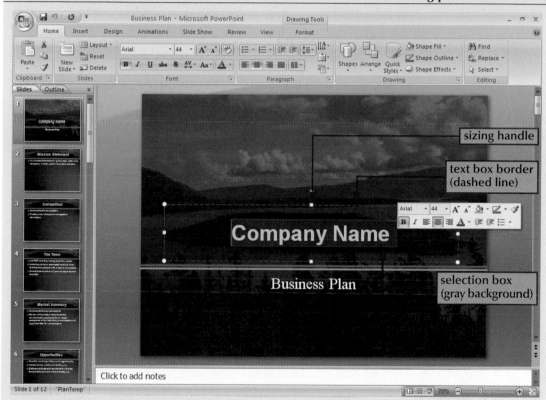

▶ **3.** Type **Share-My-Toys**. As soon as you start to type, the selected text disappears, and the typed text appears in its place. Now the title slide has the title Sandra wants for your presentation.

▶ **4.** Select the subtitle text ("Business Plan"), and then type your first and last name (so your instructor can identify you as the author of this presentation), and then click anywhere else on the slide to make the text box inactive. The dashed lines and sizing handles around the text box disappear. See Figure 1-7. (The figures in this book will show the name Sandra Corwin.)

Figure 1-7 ▶ Slide 1 after replacing placeholders with user text

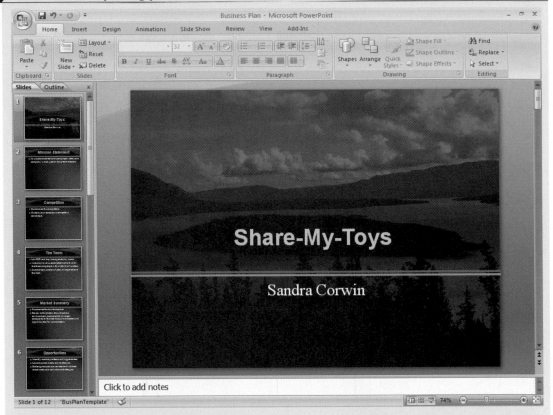

Trouble? If PowerPoint marks your name with a red wavy underline, this indicates that the word is not found in the PowerPoint dictionary. Ignore the wavy line for now; you'll learn how to deal with this later in this tutorial.

You'll now edit Slides 2 through 12 by replacing the placeholder text and adding new text, and by deleting slides that don't apply to your presentation. You'll edit text not only in the slide pane but also in the Outline tab.

To edit the text in the slides:

▶ 1. At the bottom of the vertical scroll bar in the slide pane, click the **Next Slide** button ⬇. Slide 2 appears in the slide pane.

▶ 2. Drag across the text in the bulleted item to select all the text in that item.

Now you're ready to type the Share-My-Toys mission statement.

▶ 3. Type **Share-My-Toys is a start-up company that sells timeshares of recreational equipment for outdoor activities in southeastern Idaho and western Wyoming.** (including the period).

▶ 4. Click in a blank space in the slide pane, just outside the edge of the slide, to make the text box inactive.

Trouble? If you clicked somewhere on the slide and selected another object (the other text box), click another place on the slide, preferably just outside the edge of the text box, to deselect all items.

Now you're going to edit the text in the Outline tab.

To edit the text using the Outline tab:

1. Click the **Next Slide** button ⬇ to go to Slide 3.

2. In the pane that contains the Slides and Outline tabs, click the **Outline** tab. In the Outline tab, you can see the text on each of the slides, but not the slide design. The Slide 3 slide icon is highlighted because Slide 3 is the current slide.

3. In the Outline tab, drag to select the text **Summarize the competition.**, located just below the title of Slide 3. The text is highlighted with a light-blue background.

4. Type **Southeastern Idaho has several recreational equipment rental companies but no timeshare companies.** (including the period). Notice that as you type, the text changes on the slide in the slide pane as well as in the Outline tab where you are typing.

5. In the Outline tab, select the text of the second bulleted paragraph ("Outline your company's competitive advantage.").

6. Type **SMT has a wider range and greater inventory of equipment.** (including the period).

With the insertion point at the end of the second bulleted item, you're ready to create additional bulleted items.

To create additional bulleted items:

1. With the insertion point blinking at the end of the last bulleted item (after the period) in the Outline tab, press the **Enter** key. PowerPoint creates a new bullet and leaves the insertion point to the right of the bullet, waiting for you to type the text.

2. Type **Timeshare gives members ownership.** (including the period), and then press the **Enter** key.

3. To the right of the new bullet, type **Membership fees provide needed business capital.** (including the period), and press the **Enter** key.

   Now you'll switch back to typing in the slide pane.

4. In the slide pane, click just below the last bulleted item. The new bullet you inserted in the Outline tab comes into view, and the insertion point is blinking to the right of it.

5. Type **Members get more use of equipment for less money.** (including the period). Notice that as you typed, PowerPoint automatically adjusts the size of the text in the slide pane so that the bulleted text fits within the text box on the slide.

6. Click a blank area of the slide to deselect the bulleted list text box. The completed Slide 3 should look like Figure 1-8.

Figure 1-8

Completed Slide 3

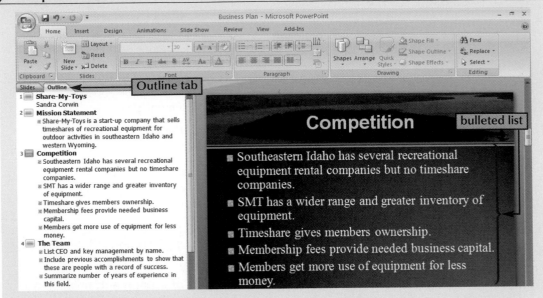

You're now ready to edit the text on another slide and create subbullets.

To create subbullets:

▶ **1.** Click the **Next Slide** button ⬇ to move to Slide 4.

▶ **2.** Select all the text (all three bulleted items) in the slide pane, and then type **Sandra Corwin, CEO** (with no period). Now you want to add subbullets to provide information about Sandra, in addition to the fact that she is the company CEO (chief executive officer).

▶ **3.** Press the **Enter** key to insert a new bullet, and then press the **Tab** key. The new bullet changes to a subbullet. In the design used in this presentation, subbullets are a gold-colored filled circle.

▶ **4.** Type **B.S., Business Administration, Idaho State University**, and then press the **Enter** key. As you can see, PowerPoint automatically creates a new bullet at the same level as the previous bullet (in this case, the second-level), not a first-level bullet. You're now ready to type the next item to describe Sandra's qualifications.

▶ **5.** Type **Product Manager, Anaconda Kayaks and Canoes, Redding, CA, 6 years**, and then press the **Enter** key to display another subbullet.

Next you want to input information about Ernesto Candelaria, the chief financial officer (CFO) for Share-My-Toys. Because this information is not related to the previous first-level bullet, it should not be listed as a subbullet under that first-level bullet.

▶ **6.** In the Paragraph group on the Home tab, click the **Decrease List Level** button 🔲. The bullet is converted from a second-level to a first-level bullet.

▶ **7.** Type **Ernesto Candelaria, CFO**, and then press the **Enter** key. Now you want to provide information about Ernesto, so you will convert this first-level bullet to a second-level bullet.

▶ **8.** In the Paragraph group on the Home tab, click the **Increase List Level** button 🔲.

9. Type **M.S., Accountancy, University of Montana**, and then press the **Enter** key.

10. Type **CPA for KPMG Accounting Firm, 12 years**, and then press the **Enter** key.

11. Type **Private CPA, Montpelier, ID, 7 years**, then click a blank area of the slide.

   You have completed editing Slide 4. See Figure 1-9.

Completed Slide 4 | **Figure 1-9**

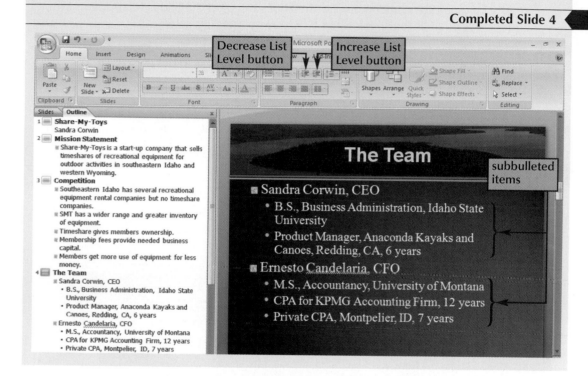

Sandra suggests that you delete Slides 5 ("Market Summary"), 6 ("Opportunities"), and 7 ("Business Concept") because she is trying to keep the presentation short and because the Market Summary slide implies the desired business opportunities and gives the basic business concept. Besides, she plans to have a handout for her audience with a market summary and other business ideas.

Deleting Slides

When creating a presentation, you'll often delete slides. A template might provide slides that you don't think are necessary, or you might create slides that you no longer want. Keep in mind that after you delete a slide, you can recover it by immediately clicking the Undo button on the Quick Access Toolbar.

Deleting Slides | Reference Window

- In Normal view, go to the slide you want to delete so it appears in the slide pane, and then click the Delete button in the Slides group on the Home tab.

or

- Click the desired slide thumbnail in the Slides tab, click the slide icon in the Outline tab, or in Slide Sorter view, select the slides you want to delete, and then press the Delete key.

To delete slides 5 through 7:

▶ 1. Go to Slide 5, and then, in the Slides group on the Home tab, click the **Delete** button. Slide 5 disappears and what was Slide 6 becomes Slide 5 and appears in the slide pane. You'll delete this Slide 5 using a different method.

▶ 2. In the pane that contains the Slides and Outline tab, click the **Slides** tab to display it. The Outline tab is hidden behind the Slides tab, and the Slides tab appears with thumbnails of all of the slides. Slide 5 ("Opportunities") is selected.

▶ 3. With Slide 5 selected in the Slides tab, press the **Delete** key. The "Opportunities" slide is deleted and the new Slide 5 ("Business Concept") appears in the slide pane.

▶ 4. Delete Slide 5 ("Business Concept"). The new Slide 5 becomes the "Goals and Objectives" slide.

▶ 5. Select all the bulleted text in the new Slide 5 and replace it with the text shown in Figure 1-10.

Figure 1-10	Completed new Slide 5

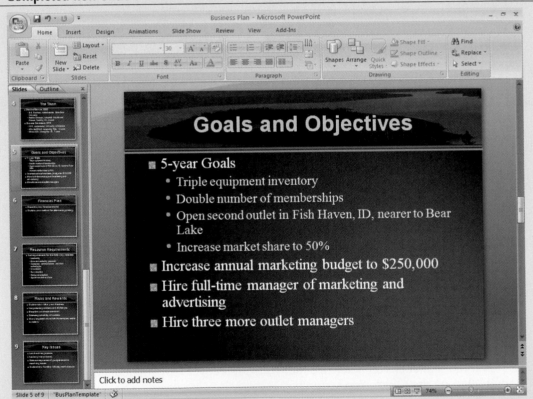

Now Sandra wants you to delete Slides 6 ("Financial Plan") and 7 ("Resource Requirements").

▶ 6. In the Slides tab, click **Slide 6** to select it, press and hold the **Shift** key, click **Slide 7** in the Slides tab, and then release the **Shift** key. Slides 6 and 7 are both selected in the Slides tab.

▶ 7. In the Slides group on the Home tab, click the **Delete** button. The two slides disappear, leaving a total of seven slides in the presentation.

Now you'll finish editing the presentation and save your work.

▶ **8.** Replace the text on Slide 6 ("Risks and Rewards") with the text shown in Figure 1-11.

Completed Slide 6 ◀ **Figure 1-11**

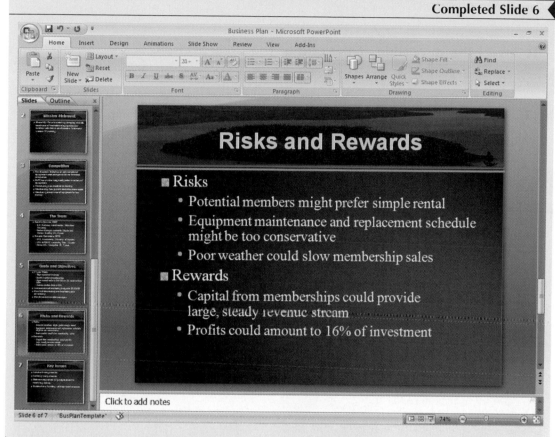

▶ **9.** Delete Slide 7 ("Key Issues").

▶ **10.** On the Quick Access Toolbar, click the **Save** button 🖫 to save the presentation.

Sandra reviews your presentation and wants you to add a slide at the end of the presentation stating what action she wants the audience to take as a result of your presentation.

Adding a New Slide and Choosing a Layout

Sandra suggests that you add a new slide at the end of the presentation with contact information for Share-My-Toys. When you add a new slide, PowerPoint formats the slide using a **layout**, which is a predetermined way of organizing the objects on a slide including placeholders for title text and other objects (bulleted lists, photographs, clip art, charts, and so forth). PowerPoint supports nine built-in layouts, including Title Slide (placeholders for a title and a subtitle, usually used as the first slide in a presentation); Title and Content (the default slide layout, with a title and a bulleted list or other object placeholder); Two Content (same as Title and Text, but with two side-by-side columns for text or other objects); and Title Only (includes only one placeholder, for the slide title). A content placeholder can contain not only a bulleted list, but can also contain a table, graph, chart, clip-art picture, photograph, or some other graphic object.

When you insert a new slide, it appears after the current slide, with the default layout, Title and Content. To use a different layout, you click the Layout button in the Slides group on the Home tab. You'll now insert a new slide at the end of your presentation with the contact information.

To insert the new slide at the end of the presentation:

▶ 1. Because you want to add a slide after Slide 6, make sure Slide 6 is still in the slide pane.

▶ 2. In the Slides group on the Home tab, click the **New Slide** button. A new Slide 7 appears in the slide pane with the default layout (Title and Content) applied. See Figure 1-12.

| Figure 1-12 | A new slide with the Title and Content placeholders |

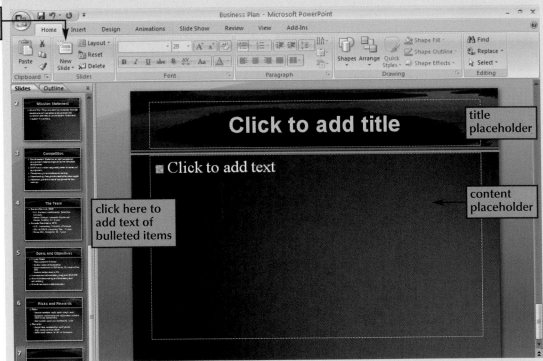

Trouble? If a gallery of choices appeared when you clicked the New Slide button, you clicked the arrow under the button instead of clicking the button itself. Click anywhere in the slide pane to close the menu, and then repeat Step 2, this time being careful to click the icon on the button, above the words "New Slide."

The Title and Text layout was applied to the new slide because the previous slides contain only bulleted lists. You'll accept the default layout for this slide. The new slide contains a blank title text placeholder, which means that you don't need to select the text on the slide to replace it with your text. After you enter your text, the dotted line outlining the edge of the text box will disappear.

▶ 3. Click anywhere in the title text placeholder in the slide pane, where it says "Click to add title." The title placeholder instructions ("Click to add title") disappear and the insertion point blinks at the left of the title text box.

▶ 4. Type **How to Conntact Share-My-Toys** (with no period). Make sure you type "Conntact" with two *n*s in the middle. You'll correct this misspelling later.

5. Click to the right of the bullet in the content placeholder. The placeholder text ("Click to add text") disappears, and the insertion point appears just to the right of the bullet.

6. Type **There are three ways too contact us.** (including the period). Make sure you type the incorrect word "too" instead of the correct word "to." You'll correct this problem later.

7. Press the **Enter** key, type **Call Sandra Corwin, CEO, at 208-555-3870, ext. 110**, and then press the **Enter** key.

8. Type **Or call Ernesto Candelaria, CFO, at ext. 210**, and then press the **Enter** key.

9. Type **Or visit our Web site at www.share-my-toys.com**, and then press the **Spacebar**.

When you press the Spacebar after typing the Web site address, PowerPoint automatically changes the Web site address (the URL) to a link. It formats the link by changing its color and underlining it. When you run the slide show, you can click this link to jump to that Web site if you are connected to the Internet. The URL is split between two lines. You can force it to start on a new line without inserting a new bullet by pressing the Shift and Enter keys at the same time.

10. Click immediately before the "www", press and hold the Shift key, and then press the Enter key. The line is broken in front of the URL and the entire URL appears on its own line.

11. On the Quick Access Toolbar, click the **Save** button 🖫 to save the changes to your presentation.

Contact Information in a Printed Presentation | InSight

In a business presentation, the printed presentation should always include contact information so that audience members know how to contact the presenter. The information should include all the ways that someone might want to contact the presenter: the presenter's name, office phone number, cell phone number, e-mail addresses, mailing address, and company Web site. If the presenter is not the only contact person at the company, or not the best contact person, include information about other people—sales representatives, marketing personnel, accountants, or other employees.

You have inserted a new slide at the end of the presentation and added text to the slide. Next you'll create a new slide by promoting text from an existing slide in the Outline tab.

Promoting, Demoting, and Moving Outline Text

You can modify the text of a slide in the Outline tab as well as in the slide pane. Working in the Outline tab gives you more flexibility because you can see the outline of the entire presentation, not only the single slide currently in the slide pane. Working in the Outline tab also allows you to easily move text from one slide to another or to create a new slide by promoting bulleted items from a slide so that they become the title and content on a new slide.

To **promote** an item means to raise the outline level of that item, for example, to change a bulleted item into a slide title or to change a second-level bullet into a first-level bullet. When you promote an item, you are changing the outline level from a higher number to a lower number. A slide title is at the first outline level, a bulleted item is at the second outline level, and a subbullet is at the third outline level. To **demote** an item means to decrease the outline level (but to increase the level number)—for example, to change a slide title into a bulleted item on the previous slide or to change a first-level bullet into a second-level bullet. You'll begin by promoting a bulleted item to a slide title, thus creating a new slide.

To create a new slide by promoting outline text:

▶ **1.** In the pane that contains the Slides and Outline tab, click the **Outline** tab. The outline of the presentation appears.

Now you're ready to promote outline text. Sandra wants you to divide Slide 5 ("Goals and Objectives") into two slides, one for "Goals" and the other for "Objectives."

▶ **2.** In the Outline tab, move the pointer over the bullet to the left of the "5-year Goals" bullet in Slide 5 so that the pointer becomes ⊕, and then click the bullet. The text for that bullet and all its subbullets is selected.

Trouble? If you can't see Slide 5 in the Outline tab, drag the scroll box in the Outline tab up until you can see Slide 5.

Now you'll promote the selected text so that it becomes the title text and first-level bullets on a new slide.

▶ **3.** Click the **Decrease List Level** button ◀≣ in the Paragraph group. PowerPoint promotes the selected text one level. Because the bullet you selected was a first-level bullet, the first-level bullet is promoted to a slide title on a new Slide 6, and the second-level bullets become first-level bullets on the new slide. See Figure 1-13. Remember, when you promote text, the outline list level number *decreases*—in this case, from 2 to 1—so you click the Decrease List Level button to decrease the level number.

Figure 1-13 ▶ **New Slide 6 after promoting text**

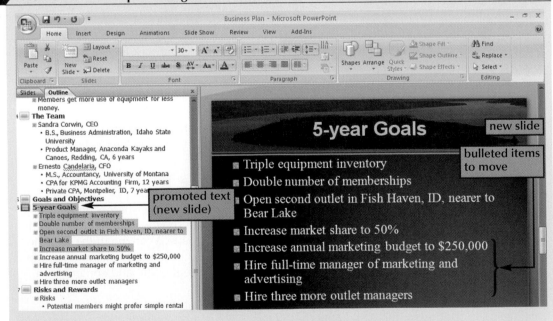

Now you'll edit text and move a bulleted item from Slide 6 to Slide 5.

4. In the Outline tab, click to the left of "Objectives" in the slide title of Slide 5, and then press the **Backspace** key as many times as necessary to delete "Goals and."

5. In the Outline tab in the title of Slide 6, change "year" to "Year".

6. In the Outline tab, point to the bullet icon to the left of "Increase market share to 50%" in Slide 6, press and hold down the left mouse button, and then drag the bullet and its text up until the horizontal line is below the slide title "Objectives," as shown in Figure 1-14.

Tip

To select bulleted items or objects that are not adjacent to one another, press and hold the Ctrl key instead of the Shift key while clicking.

Moving a slide in Slide Sorter view | Figure 1-14

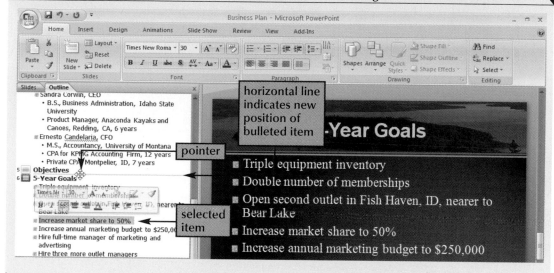

7. Using the same procedure as in Step 6, drag the last three bulleted items in Slide 6 onto slide 5.

Sandra looks at your presentation. It meets Sandra's goal for a short presentation of seven to eight slides, but she suggests that you move the current Slide 5 ("Objectives") after Slide 6 ("5-Year Goals"). You could make this change in the Outline tab by dragging the slide icon for Slide 5 above the slide icon for Slide 7. Instead, you'll move the slide in Slide Sorter view.

Moving Slides in Slide Sorter View

In Slide Sorter view, PowerPoint displays all the slides as thumbnails, so that several slides can appear on the screen at once. This view not only provides you with a good overview of your presentation, but also allows you to easily change the order of the slides and modify the slides in other ways.

To move Slide 5:

1. On the status bar, click the **Slide Sorter** button 🔡 . You now see your presentation in Slide Sorter view. A thick colored frame appears around Slide 5, indicating that the slide is selected.

2. Point to **Slide 5**, and then drag Slide 5 so that the vertical line position marker appears on the left side of Slide 7, as shown in Figure 1-15.

Figure 1-15 Moving a slide in Slide Sorter view

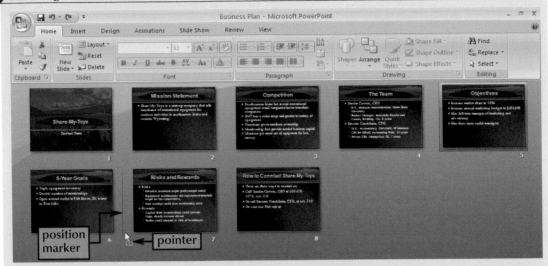

> **3.** Release the mouse button. The old Slide 5 is now Slide 6.
>
> **4.** On the status bar, click the **Normal** button 🔲 to return to Normal view, and then in the pane that contains the Outline and Slides tab, click the Slides tab.

Your next task is to check the spelling of the text in your presentation.

Checking the Spelling in a Presentation

Before you print or present a slide show, you should always perform a final check of the spelling of all the slides in your presentation. This helps to ensure that your presentation is accurate and professional looking.

PowerPoint performs two types of spell check. The standard type is when PowerPoint finds a word that's not in its dictionary. The word is then underlined with a red wavy line in the slide pane. The other type is called **contextual spelling**, which checks the context in which a word is used, and marks it with a red wavy line even though the word is in the dictionary. For example, if you type "their" when you mean "there" (or vice versa), or type "too" when you mean "to" (or vice versa), PowerPoint might flag the error. Of course, a computer program can't be 100 percent correct in determining the correct context, especially in bulleted items that are incomplete sentences, so you still have to carefully proofread your presentation.

When you right-click a word marked with the red wavy line, PowerPoint displays suggestions for alternate spellings as well as commands for ignoring the misspelled word or opening the Spelling dialog box. You can also click the Spelling button in the Proofing group on the Review tab on the Ribbon to check the spelling in the entire presentation. You'll now check the spelling in the Share-My-Toys presentation.

To check the spelling in the presentation:

> **1.** Click the **Office Button** 📄, click the **PowerPoint Options** button, click **Proofing** in the left pane, make sure the **Use contextual spelling** check box is selected, and then click the **OK** button.
>
> **2.** Go to **Slide 8**. The spelling check always starts from the current slide.

3. Click the **Review** tab on the Ribbon. The Ribbon changes to display the commands available for reviewing and correcting your presentation.

4. In the Proofing group on the Review tab, click the **Spelling** button. The Spelling dialog box opens. The word you purposely mistyped earlier, "Conntact," is highlighted in the slide pane and listed in the Spelling dialog box in the Not in Dictionary text box. Two suggested spellings appear in the Suggestions list box, and the selected word in the Suggestions list box appears in the Change to text box. See Figure 1-16.

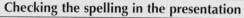

Checking the spelling in the presentation | Figure 1-16

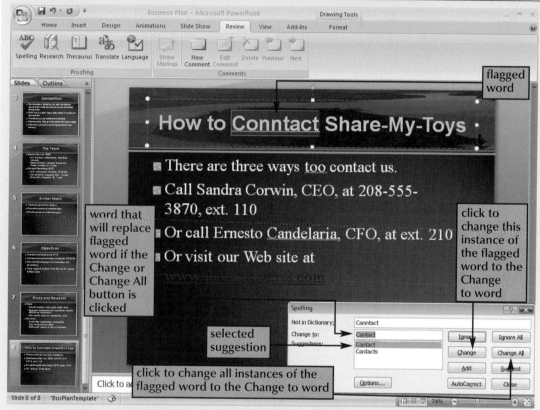

5. With "Contact" selected in the Suggestions list box and listed in the Change to text box, click the **Change** button in the Spelling dialog box. If you knew that you misspelled that word throughout your presentation, you could click the Change All button to change all of the instances of the misspelling in the presentation to the corrected spelling.

The word is corrected, and the next word in the presentation that PowerPoint flags is "too" in the first bulleted item. This word is in PowerPoint's dictionary, but it is contextually misspelled.

6. With "to" selected in the Suggestions list box and in the Change to text box, click the **Change** button. The correct word appears on the slide.

Next, PowerPoint stops at the word "Candelaria." This word, however, is not misspelled; it is a surname.

Trouble? If PowerPoint doesn't flag "Candelaria," someone might have added it to the PowerPoint dictionary. Read Step 7 but don't do anything, and then continue with Step 8.

7. Click the **Ignore All** button. The word is not changed on the slide. If you wanted to ignore only this instance of that word in the presentation, you could click the Ignore button instead of the Ignore All button.

PowerPoint continues checking the presentation for misspelled words. When it reaches the final slide, it cycles back to the first slide and continues searching until it reaches the slide prior to the one you started checking. When it doesn't find any other words that aren't in the PowerPoint dictionary, a dialog box opens telling you that the spelling check is complete.

Trouble? If another word in the presentation is flagged as misspelled, select the correct spelling in the Suggestions list, and then click the Change button. If your name on Slide 1 is flagged, click the Ignore button.

▶ 8. In the dialog box, click the **OK** button. The dialog box closes.

▶ 9. On the Quick Access Toolbar, click the **Save** button 🔲 to save the changes to your presentation.

After you check the spelling, you should always reread your presentation; the spell checker, even with the contextual spelling feature, doesn't catch every instance of a mis-used word.

Sandra is pleased with how you have edited your presentation slides, but she thinks the word "large" in Slide 7 might not be precise enough. She asks you to find an appropriate replacement word.

Using the Research Task Pane

PowerPoint enables you to search online services or Internet sites for additional help in creating a presentation. Using these resources helps you make your presentations more professional. For example, you could look up specific words in a thesaurus. A **thesaurus** contains a list of words and their synonyms, antonyms, and other related words. Using a thesaurus is a good way to add variety to the words you use or to choose more precise words. You could also look up information in online dictionaries, encyclopedias, news services, libraries, and business sites.

You access the Research task pane by clicking the Review tab on the Ribbon, and then clicking either the Research or the Thesaurus button in the Proofing group. When you click the Research button, the search is executed in all available sources. When you click the Thesaurus button, the search is automatically restricted to just the thesaurus.

You'll begin by using the thesaurus. You'll now look for synonyms for "large."

To do research using the thesaurus:

Tip

To expand a search in the Research task pane, click the arrow in the box below the Search for text box, and then in the list, click another source or category.

▶ 1. Go to **Slide 7**, and then, in the slide pane, in the first subbullet under "Rewards," click anywhere in the word "large." The thesaurus lets you completely select the word or simply position the insertion point anywhere within the word.

▶ 2. In the Proofing group on the Review tab, click the **Thesaurus** button. PowerPoint selects the word "large," and the Research task pane opens with the word "large" in the Search for text box and Thesaurus: English (U.S.) listed in the box under the Search for text box. Below that, the task pane displays synonyms for "large" found in the built-in thesaurus.

▶ 3. In the list of synonyms, below the bold entry "sizeable (adj.)," position the pointer over the word **significant**. A box appears around the term, and an arrow appears at the right end of the box.

▶ 4. Click the arrow in the box. A menu opens, as shown in Figure 1-17.

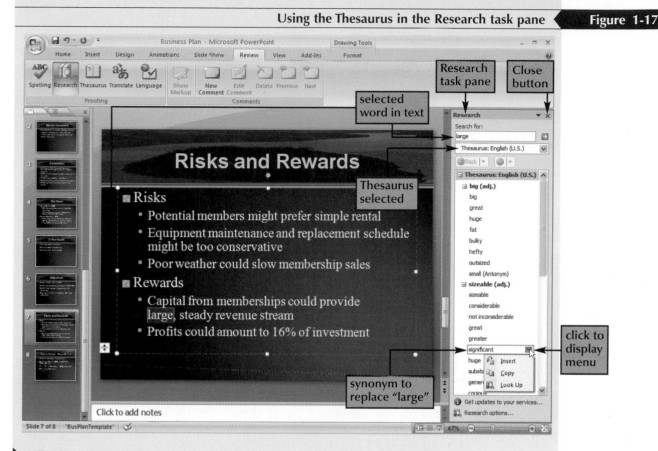

Using the Thesaurus in the Research task pane | Figure 1-17

▶ **5.** Click **Insert**. The word "significant" replaces "large" on the slide.

▶ **6.** In the task pane title bar, click the **Close** button ☒. The Research task pane closes.

When you show the presentation to Sandra, she is satisfied. Now you're ready to create notes for Sandra's presentation to help her remember important points during the slide show.

Creating Speaker Notes

Notes (also called **speaker notes**) help the speaker remember what to say when a particular slide appears during the presentation. They appear in the notes pane below the slide pane in Normal view; they do not appear during the slide show. You can also print notes pages with a picture of and notes about each slide.

You'll create notes for only a few of the slides in the presentation. For example, Sandra wants to remember the names of the Share-My-Toys' competitors when she displays Slide 3. You'll create a note reminding her to mention the names of the competitors.

To create notes:

▶ **1.** Go to **Slide 3**. The notes pane currently contains placeholder text.

▶ **2.** Click in the notes pane, and then type **Rental companies include A-1 Recreation Rentals, Boats4Rent, and Camping Gear To Go**. See Figure 1-18.

Figure 1-18 ▶ Notes on Slide 3

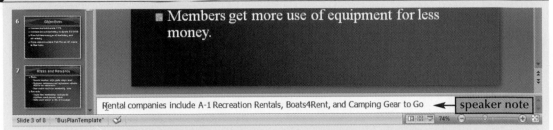

Now Sandra wants you to add a note on Slide 6 to remind her to give the audience a handout on marketing plans.

▶ 3. Go to **Slide 6**, click in the notes pane, and then type **Pass out marketing plan handouts**.

▶ 4. Save the changes to the presentation.

Before Sandra gives her presentation, she'll print the notes of the presentation so she'll have them available during her presentations. You can now view the completed presentation to make sure that it is accurate, informative, and visually pleasing.

To view the slide show:

▶ 1. Click the **View** tab on the Ribbon, and then, in the Presentation Views group, click the **Slide Show** button. The slide show starts from Slide 1.

▶ 2. Proceed through the slide show as you did earlier, clicking the left mouse button or pressing the Spacebar or the right arrow key to advance from one slide to the next.

▶ 3. If you see a problem on one of your slides, press the **Esc** key to leave the slide show and display the current slide on the screen in Normal view, fix the problem on the slide, save your changes, and then click the **Slide Show** button 🖵 on the status bar to resume the slide show from the current slide.

▶ 4. When you reach the end of your slide show, press the **Spacebar** to move to the blank screen, and then press the **Spacebar** again to return to Normal view.

You're now ready to preview and print your presentation.

Previewing and Printing a Presentation

Before you give your presentation, you might want to print it. PowerPoint provides several printing options. For example, you can print the slides in color using a color printer; print in grayscale or pure black and white using a black-and-white printer; or print the notes pages (the speaker notes printed below a picture of the corresponding slide). You can also print handouts with 2, 3, 4, 6, or 9 slides per page. **Handouts** are printouts of the slides themselves; these can be arranged with several slides printed on a page. Some presenters like to give the audience handouts so that they can more easily take notes during the presentation. Finally, you can also format and then print the presentation onto overhead transparency film (available in most office supply stores).

If you're going to print your presentation on a black-and-white printer, you should first preview the presentation to make sure the text will be legible. You also need to make sure that any graphics on the background do not make it difficult to read the text on the slides. You'll use Print Preview to see the slides as they will appear when they are printed.

To preview the presentation and hide background graphics:

▶ **1.** Click the **Office Button** 🔵, and then point to the **Print** button. The pane on the right side of the menu changes to include print options.

▶ **2.** In the pane on the right of the menu, click **Print Preview**. The Preview window appears, displaying Slide 1. Notice that the only tab on the Ribbon is the Print Preview tab.

▶ **3.** In the Print group on the Print Preview tab, click the **Options** button, point to **Color/Grayscale**, and then click **Grayscale**. The current slide is displayed in grayscale. See Figure 1-19. As you can see, the text is illegible in grayscale. You'll now fix that problem in preparation to print your presentation in black and white.

Print Preview window showing Slide 1 in grayscale | **Figure 1-19**

▶ **4.** In the Preview group on the Print Preview tab, click the **Close Print Preview** button to return to Normal view.

▶ **5.** On the status bar, click the **Slide Sorter** button 🔳, click **Slide 1**, if necessary, press and hold the **Shift** key, and then click **Slide 8**. All the slides are selected.

▶ **6.** Click the **Design** tab on the Ribbon, and then, in the Background group, click the **Hide Background Graphics** check box. The background images and lines on the slides disappear.

Now you're ready to return to Print Preview and continue to view how your presentation will look when you print it.

To preview and print your presentation:

▶ **1.** Return to Print Preview and set the Options to Grayscale as you did previously. Now you can read the text of your presentation.

▶ **2.** In the Preview group on the Print Preview tab, click the **Next Page** button. Slide 2 appears in the Print Preview window.

Next you will change the option to print handouts.

▶ **3.** In the Page Setup group on the Print Preview tab, click the **Print What** arrow, and then click **Handouts (4 Slides Per Page)**. The preview changes to display four slides on a page.

▶ **4.** In the Print group on the Print Preview tab, click the **Print** button. The Print dialog box opens. See Figure 1-20.

Figure 1-20 ▶ **Print dialog box**

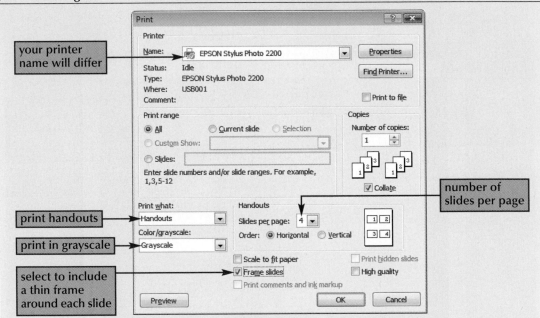

your printer name will differ

print handouts

print in grayscale

select to include a thin frame around each slide

number of slides per page

▶ **5.** Compare your dialog box to the one shown in Figure 1-20, make any necessary changes, and then click the **OK** button to print the handouts on two pages. The Print dialog box closes, and the slides print as handouts, four slides per page.

Now you're ready to print the notes.

▶ **6.** In the Page Setup group on the Print Preview tab, click the **Print What** arrow, and then click **Notes Pages**. The current slide is displayed as a notes page, with the slide on the top and space for notes on the bottom.

▶ **7.** Drag the scroll box on the vertical scroll bar down until the ScreenTip identifies the current slide as Page 3 of 8. This is one of the slides to which you added notes.

▶ **8.** In the Print group, click the **Print** button to open the Print dialog box again.

▶ **9.** In the Print range section of the Print dialog box, click the **Slides** option button, click in the text box to the right of the Slides option button, and then type **3,6** (with no space before or after the comma). These are the only slides with notes on them, so you do not need to print all eight slides as notes pages.

▶ **10.** Click the **OK** button to print the notes. Slides 3 and 6 print on two pieces of paper as notes pages.

▶ **11.** In the Preview group, click the **Close Print Preview** button. The view returns to Slide Sorter view. In Slide Sorter view, the slides appear on the screen in several rows, depending on the current zoom percentage shown next to the Zoom slider (located in the lower-right corner of the PowerPoint window) and on the resolution and size of your monitor.

▶ **12.** On the Zoom slider, drag the slider tab to the right, until the zoom is about 90%. See Figure 1-21.

Completed presentation in Slide Sorter view **Figure 1-21**

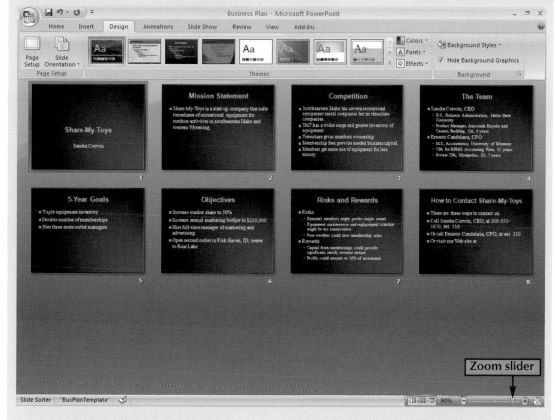

Trouble? If all the slides are not visible on your monitor after setting the Zoom to 90%, drag the Zoom slider to the left until you can see all of the slides.

▶ **13.** Compare your printed handouts (with their four slides per page) with the slides shown in Slide Sorter view.

▶ **14.** Save the presentation in Slide Sorter view. When Sandra opens the presentation, it will appear in Slide Sorter view.

▶ **15.** In the upper-right corner of the PowerPoint window, click the **Close** button X on the title bar.

You have created a presentation using a template, edited it according to Sandra's wishes, and created and printed notes and handouts. Sandra thanks you for your help; she believes that your work will enable her to make an effective presentation to banks and potential investors.

| Review | **Session 1.2 Quick Check** |

1. Explain how to do the following in the Outline tab:
   a. move text up
   b. delete a slide
   c. change a first-level bullet to a second-level bullet
2. What does it mean to promote a bulleted item in the Outline tab? To demote a bulleted item?
3. Explain a benefit of using the Outline tab rather than the slide pane.
4. What is the thesaurus?
5. What are notes? How do you create them?
6. Describe contextual spell checking.
7. Why is it beneficial to preview a presentation before printing it?

| Review | **Tutorial Summary** |

In this tutorial, you learned how to plan and create a PowerPoint presentation by modifying template slides. You learned how to edit the text in both the Outline tab and the slide pane; add a new slide and choose a slide layout; delete slides; and promote, demote, and move text in your outline. You also learned how to check the spelling in your presentation, create speaker notes, and preview and print your presentation.

Key Terms

6 × 6 rule	layout	slide pane
active	Normal view	Slide Show view
animation	note (speaker note)	Slide Sorter view
bulleted item	notes pane	slide transitions
bulleted list	numbered list	Slides tab
content	Outline tab	subbullet
contextual spelling	placeholder	template
demote	PowerPoint	text box
drop shadow	progressive disclosure	thesaurus
first-level bullet	promote	thumbnail
footer	second-level bullet	title text
handout	sizing handle	

Practice	**Review Assignments**

Practice the skills you learned in the tutorial using the same case scenario.

Data File needed for the Review Assignments: Marketing.potx

Calista Dymock, the new director of marketing at Share-My-Toys, asks you to prepare a PowerPoint presentation explaining the new marketing strategy. She recommends that you start with an existing template prepared by Sandra Corwin in her previous job. Your job is to edit the presentation according to Calista's instructions. Complete the following steps:

1. Start a new PowerPoint presentation using the existing template **Marketing** located in the Tutorial.01\Review folder where your Data Files are located, and then save the presentation as **Marketing Plan** in the Tutorial.01\Review folder.

2. In Slide 1, replace the text "[Product or Service Name]" with **Share-My-Toys Membership**, and then change the "[Your Name]" subtitle to your name.

3. Go to Slide 2, and then replace all the content text with the following first-level bulleted items: **Current memberships: 218**, **Maximum memberships: 800**, and **Current members live in:**.

4. Below "Current members live in," add the following second-level bulleted items: **Montpelier, ID**, **Soda Springs, ID**, and **Fish Haven, ID**.

5. Below the three second-level bullets, add the following first-level bulleted item: **Additional target locations**, and below that, the following second-level bulleted items: **Preston, ID**, **Logan, UT**, and **Afton, WY**.

6. Go to Slide 3 ("Product Definition"), replace the bulleted item with **Membership in Share-My-Toys provides the following services:**, and then below that, insert the subbullets **Unlimited use of equipment** and **Free service, maintenance, and replacement of equipment**.

7. Below the subbullets, add the first-level item **Membership lasts for three years**.

8. Go to Slide 4 ("Competition"), and then replace the bulleted text with the following first-level bulleted items: **Retail recreational equipment stores** and **Recreational equipment rental companies**.

9. Delete Slide 5 ("Positioning"), and then on the new Slide 5, change the title "Communication Strategies" to **Overcoming Disadvantages**, and replace the first-level bulleted items with **Institute low-interest monthly payment program**, and **Open distribution centers in more cities**.

10. Go to Slide 6 ("Public Relations"), and then replace the content text with the first-level bulleted items **Hold public ATV and dirt-bike safety courses** and **Participate in local outdoorsman radio talk shows**.

11. Go to Slide 7 ("Advertising"), and then replace the bulleted items with the first-level bulleted items: **Local radio**, **Local TV**, **Local newspapers**, and **Advertisement mailers**.

12. Go to Slide 8 ("Success Metrics"), and then replace the bulleted items with the first-level bulleted items **Sell 200 memberships per year**, **Maintain high customer satisfaction**, **Develop indirect earnings**, **Interest on membership monthly payment program**, **Sales of used, out-of-date equipment**.

13. Go to Slide 2 and add **Explain how often equipment will need to be replaced.** as a note, and then go to Slide 3 and add **Explain that we must set a maximum number of memberships to ensure that members get the equipment they want.** as a note.

14. Delete Slide 9, leaving eight slides in the presentation.

15. Switch to Slide Sorter view, move Slide 7 ("Advertising") before Slide 6 ("Public Relations"), and then move Slide 8 ("Success Metrics") to become the new Slide 2.

16. Double-click Slide 3 ("Market Summary") to switch to Normal view, and then click the Outline tab in the pane on the left.

17. In the Outline tab, click the bullet icon next to "Additional target locations," and then, in the Paragraph group on the Home tab, click the Decrease List Level button so that it becomes a new slide. In the new slide title, change the "t" in "target" and the "l" in "locations" to uppercase so that the title words are capitalized.

18. In the Outline tab, in Slide 3, drag the "Maximum Members: 800" bullet up so it becomes the first bulleted item.

19. In the Outline tab, in Slide 2 ("Success Metrics"), select the final two bulleted items, and then demote them so they become subbullets under "Develop indirect earnings."

20. Use the spelling checker, along with your own proofreading to check spelling in the presentation. Change misspelled words and ignore flagged words that are spelled correctly.

21. Go to Slide 9 and then use the thesaurus to replace the word "hold" with an appropriate synonym.

22. View the presentation in Slide Show view. Look carefully at each slide and check the content. If you see any errors of formatting problems, press the Esc key to end the slide show, fix the error, and then start the slide show again.

23. Switch to Slide Sorter view, adjust the zoom so that the thumbnails are maximum size yet still all visible at once on the screen, and then save the presentation using the default filename.

24. Preview the presentation in grayscale, and then print the presentation in grayscale as handouts, four slides per page.

25. Print Slides 2 and 3 as notes pages in grayscale, and then close the file.

| Apply | **Case Problem 1** |

Apply the skills you learned in this tutorial to modify a presentation for a pharmaceutical research lab.

Data File needed for this Case Problem: Volunteer.pptx

Department of Social Services, Yosemite Regional Hospital Mercedes Cirillo is head of Volunteer Services at Yosemite Regional Hospital in Wawona, CA. One of her jobs is to recruit and train hospital volunteers. Volunteer positions include Family Surgical Liaison, Family Waiting Area Liaison, Hospitality and Escort Volunteer, Volunteer Information Ambassador, Book Cart and Special Requests Volunteer, Flower Shop Assistant, and Pastoral Care Volunteer. Mercedes wants to give a PowerPoint presentation to individuals, couples, church groups, and service organizations on opportunities and requirements for volunteer service at the hospital. She has a rough draft of a presentation and asks you to help her revise the presentation. Complete the following steps:

1. Start PowerPoint and open the file **Volunteer** located in the Tutorial.01\Case1 folder with your Data Files.

2. Click the Office Button, click Save As, and then save the presentation using the filename **Hospital Volunteers** in the Tutorial.01\Case1 folder.

3. In Slide 1, change the name "Mercedes Cirillo" to your name.

4. Delete Slide 3.

5. In Slide Sorter view, move Slide 5 so it becomes Slide 3.

6. In Normal view, in Slide 2, add a new bulleted item to the end of the bulleted list, with the text **Volunteers work in almost all departments within the hospital.**

7. In the notes pane of Slide 2, add the speaker note, **Departments that don't have volunteers include Food Services, Medical Research, Security, Custodial Services, and others.**

8. In Slide 3, after the second bulleted item ("Select a desired volunteer position"), insert the bulleted item **Pick up application form from Volunteer Services office.**

⊕ EXPLORE

9. In Slide 3, AutoFit the text to the placeholder so that the last bulleted item isn't too close to the bottom of the slide. To do this, make sure the insertion point is in the main text box (the bulleted list), click the AutoFit Options button that appears to the left of the new bulleted item, and then, on the menu that opens, click the AutoFit Text to Placeholder option button.

10. In the notes pane of Slide 3, add the speaker note, **Announce that I have application forms with me.**

11. In Slide 4, use the Outline tab to move the bulleted items "Book Cart Volunteer" and "Special Requests Volunteer" down below "Gift Shop Assistant" (but above "Pastoral Care Volunteer").

12. In Slide 5, click the insertion point in the Outline tab just before the phrase "4 hours per week," and press the Enter key to make that phrase a new bullet.

13. Demote the phrases "4 hours per week" and "3-month commitment" to second-level bullets under "Minimum volunteer time."

14. After Slide 5, insert a new Slide 6.

15. In Slide 6, insert the title text **Before You Decide to Volunteer**, and then insert the following first-level bulleted items: **Understand the time commitment to do a particular job.**; **Base your decision on your interests, skills, and schedule.**; **Know HIPA laws regarding confidentiality.**; and **Be willing to learn and to give and receive feedback.**

16. Check the spelling throughout the presentation, including contextual spelling. Change misspelled words to the correct spelling, and ignore any words (such as proper names) that are spelled correctly but are not in the built-in dictionary.

17. Read each slide, proofreading for spelling errors that the spelling checker didn't detect. Notice that, on Slide 2, the word "weak" should be "week." Contextual spelling failed to detect this error, probably because the bulleted items are not complete sentences. Make that change and correct any other spelling errors you find.

18. View the presentation in Slide Show view.

19. Preview the presentation in grayscale. Remove the background graphics if necessary. Save your changes.

20. Print the presentation in grayscale as handouts with four slides per page.

21. Print notes pages for Slides 2 and 3 (the only ones that have speaker notes).

22. Close the file.

Apply | Case Problem 2

Apply the skills you learned to modify an existing presentation.

Data File needed for this Case Problem: Library.pptx

Carriage Path Public Library   Davion McGechie is head of the Office of Community Outreach Services for the Carriage Path Public Library in Milford, Connecticut. Davion and his staff coordinate outreach services and develop programs in communities throughout the Long Island Sound. These services and programs depend on a large volunteer staff. Davion wants you to help him create a PowerPoint presentation to train his staff. Complete the following steps:

1. Open the file **Library** in the Case2 folder in the Tutorial.01 folder of your Data Files, and then save it back to the same folder using the filename **Library Outreach**.

2. In Slide 1, replace the subtitle placeholder ("Davion McGechie, Director") with your name.

3. In Slide 2, add the speaker's note **Mention that community groups include ethnic neighborhood councils, religious organizations, and civic groups.**

4. Add a fourth bulleted item to Slide 2: **To implement outreach programs in the surrounding communities**.

5. Move the second bulleted item in Slide 2 ("To provide staff training") so that it becomes the last bulleted item.

6. In Slide 3, make "Four central libraries with in-depth collections" and "Six neighborhood branch libraries" second-level bulleted items below the first bullet.

7. Promote the bulleted item "Special Events & Programs" and its subbullets so that they become a new slide.

⊕**EXPLORE**   8. In the Slides tab, drag Slide 6 ("Branch Libraries") above Slide 5.

9. Add a new slide at the end (Slide 8) with the title **Volunteer Opportunities**.

10. On Slide 8, create three bulleted items with the first line **Literacy Instructors**, the second line **Computer Instructors**, and the third line **Children's Hour Story Tellers**.

11. Under the third bullet, add the subbullets **After-school story hour** and **Bookmobile story hour**.

⊕**EXPLORE**   12. Click the word "Instructors" in the first bulleted item, and then use the thesaurus to select a synonym. (*Hint*: The thesaurus can't find a synonym for a plural word, so click the Related Word "instructor" in the Research task pane to look up a synonym for the singular form of the word.) Make sure you pluralize the replacement word, if necessary.

13. Check the spelling in the presentation. Correct any spelling errors and ignore any words that are spelled correctly.

14. View the presentation in Slide Show view.

15. Save the presentation using its default filename.

16. Preview the presentation in grayscale, and then print the presentation in grayscale as handouts with four slides per page.

17. Print Slide 2 as a notes page.

18. Close the file.

| Create | **Case Problem 3** |

Create a new presentation about a marketing company by using and expanding on the skills you learned in this tutorial.

Data File needed for this Case Problem: Proposal.potx

AfterShow, Inc. Karla Brown is president of AfterShow, Inc., a company that markets specialized merchandise to attendees at trade shows, training seminars, and other large business events. For example, after a recent trade show of the American Automobile Manufacturers, AfterShow mailed advertisement flyers and made phone calls to the trade show participants to sell them art pieces (mostly bronze sculptures) depicting antique automobiles. In another case, after a large business seminar in which the keynote speakers were famous business leaders and athletes, AfterShow contacted participants in an effort to sell them autographed books written by the speakers. Karla asked you to create a presentation to be given to event organizers in an effort to work with those organizers in developing an after-show market and profit-sharing program. The slides in your complete presentation should look like the slides in Figure 1-22. The following instructions will help you in creating the slide show. Read all the steps before you start creating your presentation.

Figure 1-22

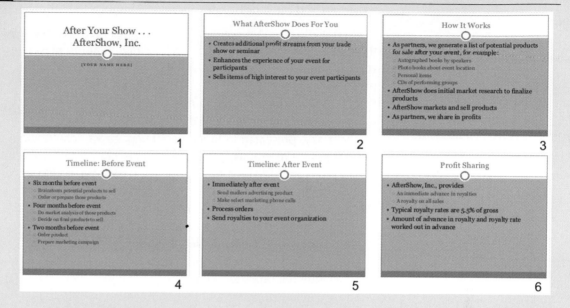

Complete the following steps:

1. Create a new presentation based on the template **Proposal** located in the Tutorial.01\Case3 folder included with your Data Files.
2. Save the file as **AfterShow** to the same folder.
3. After starting the presentation with the "Proposal" template, add slides, titles, and bulleted text as you learned in this tutorial.
4. In Slide 1, replace the placeholder "[Your name here]" with your name.
5. Promote and demote text as needed to produce the bulleted lists.
6. Delete any unnecessary slides.
7. Read through your presentation and make sure your ideas are presented clearly. Consider using the thesaurus to find words to enliven your presentation.
8. Check the spelling, including contextual spelling, in the final presentation, and examine the slides in Slide Show view.
9. Save the completed presentation using the default name and location.
10. Preview the presentation in grayscale, and delete the background objects, if necessary, to make the text legible.
11. Print the final presentation in grayscale as handouts with six slides per page.

Research | **Case Problem 4**

Use the Internet to research MP3 players and use PowerPoint's Help system to find out how to format text.

There are no Data Files needed for this Case Problem.

Review of a Portable Digital Audio Player   Your assignment is to prepare a review of a portable digital audio player (for example, an MP3 player) for presentation to the class. If you are not familiar with what portable digital audio players are, you might want to search the Internet or talk to other students for an explanation of what they are, how they work, and why so many people like them. You should then search the Internet for information or reviews about various brands and models of digital audio players. Alternatively, if you own a portable digital audio player, you could search the Internet for information about your player. You should organize your information into a PowerPoint presentation, with at least six slides. (Your instructor might also assign you to give an oral presentation based on your PowerPoint file.) Complete the following steps:

1. Go to Google.com, Yahoo.com, or some other Web site that allows you to search the Web, and search using such terms as **digital audio player review** or **MP3 player review**. You should read about various brands of players to get an idea of the most popular sellers.

2. Select one brand and model of digital audio player; search the Internet for more information and reviews about that player.

⊕ **EXPLORE**   3. Create a new presentation based on a template you can download from Microsoft Office Online. To do this, make sure you are connected to the Internet, open the New Presentation dialog box, on the left, under Microsoft Office Online, click Presentations, and then in the pane in the middle of the dialog box, click the Business link. Scroll down the list in the pane in the middle of the dialog box until you find the template titled "Product overview presentation" with an orange background and a wide pale blue stripe on the left, click it, and then click the Download button. In the dialog box that opens asking you to validate your copy of Microsoft Office, click the Continue button. After the template downloads and opens, the PowerPoint Help window opens with information about the template. Read this, and then click the Close button in the Help window title bar.

4. Save the presentation in the Tutorial.01\Case4 folder included with your Data Files, using the filename **Review**.

5. Replace the title placeholder text "Product Name" with the brand and model of your selected digital audio player. For example, the title might be something like "Apple iPod" or "Creative Zen Micro Photo 4GB MP3 Player."

6. Replace the subtitle text "Insert Product Photograph Here" with your full name. You won't include a photograph of your selected digital audio player. You can also ignore the little box labeled "Your Logo Here."

7. In Slide 2 ("Overview"), include basic information about the digital audio players in the bulleted list. The information might include brand name, model name or number, capacity (for example, 128 MB or 256 MB), retail price, and street price.

8. In Slide 3 ("Features & Benefits"), delete part of the title so it just says "Features." Replace the bulleted list placeholder text with specific features such as number of tunes the player holds, total playing time, expansion slots, battery life, auxiliary features (for example, pictures, calendar, videos), and so forth.

9. Delete Slide 4 ("Applications").

10. In what is now Slide 4 ("Specifications"), list technical specifications (for example, size, weight, interface).

11. In Slide 5 ("Pricing"), give the manufacturer's suggested retail price (MSRP) and examples of online or in-store prices (for example, from Buy.com, Amazon.com, and Circuit City).

12. Delete Slide 6.

13. Create at least three new slides, using the topics **Ease of Use**, **Desktop Computer Software**, and **Reviewers' Comments**. (Feel free to change the wording of these titles.)

⊕ **EXPLORE**   14. Use the Research task pane (click the Review tab and then, in the Proofing group, click the Research button) to find additional information about the topic of the digital audio player you've chosen. (*Hint*: In the Research task pane, type the phrase **digital audio player** into the Search for text box, make sure your computer is connected to the Internet, and then select All Research Sites in the box below the Search for text box.) You might or might not find anything useful about digital audio players.

15. Create a slide titled **Summary and Recommendations** as the final slide in your presentation, giving your overall impression of the player and your recommendation for whether the player is worth buying.

16. View the presentation on the Outline tab. If necessary, change the order of the bulleted items on the slides, or change the order of the slides.

◈ EXPLORE 17. If there are any slides with more than about six or seven bulleted items, split the slide in two. If there are any slides in which the text extends below the bulleted list text box, fix the problem. (*Hint*: In either case, click to place the insertion point in the body text box, click the AutoFit Options that appears near the lower-left corner of the text box, and then click the appropriate command on the menu.)

18. Go through all the slides, correcting problems of case (capitalization), punctuation, number of bulleted items per slide, and number of lines per bulleted item.

19. Check the spelling of your presentation.

20. View the presentation in Slide Show view. If you see any typographical errors or other problems, stop the slide show, correct the problems, and then continue the slide show. If you find slides that aren't necessary, delete them.

21. Preview the presentation in grayscale, and then print the presentation in grayscale as handouts with four slides per page. Print speaker notes if you created any, and then close the file.

Research | **Internet Assignments**

Go to the Web to find information you can use to create presentations.

The purpose of the Internet Assignments is to challenge you to find information on the Internet that you can use to work effectively with this software. The actual assignments are updated and maintained on the Course Technology Web site. Log on to the Internet and use your Web browser to go to the Student Online Companion for New Perspectives Office 2007 at **www.course.com/np/office2007**. Then navigate to the Internet Assignments for this tutorial.

Assess | **SAM Assessment and Training**

If you have a SAM user profile, you may have access to hands-on instruction, practice, and assessment of the skills covered in this tutorial. Log in to your SAM account (**http://sam2007.course.com**) to launch any assigned training activities or exams that relate to the skills covered in this tutorial.

Review | **Quick Check Answers**

Session 1.1

1. A presentation's components can consist of individual slides, speaker notes, an outline, and audience handouts.

2. The slide pane shows the slide as it will look during your slide show. The notes pane contains speaker notes. The third pane, to the left of the slide pane, contains two tabs: The Outline tab shows an outline of your presentation; the Slides tab displays thumbnails of each slide.

3. (a) shows the current slide as it will look during your slide show; (b) a feature that causes each element on a slide to appear one at a time; (c) the manner in which a new slide appears on the screen during a slide show; (d) a file that contains the colors and format of the background and the font style of the titles, accents, and sample text; (e) a predetermined way of organizing the objects on a slide

4. What is my purpose or objective? What type of presentation is needed? Who is my audience? What is the physical location of my presentation? What is the best format for my presentation?

5. The existing text provides a guide in selecting and inserting the proper text content into your presentation.

6. The view you use to present an on-screen presentation to an audience.

Session 1.2

1. (a) Click a slide or bullet icon, and then drag the selected item up. (b) Right-click the slide icon of the slide to be deleted, and then click Delete Slide on the shortcut menu. (c) In the Outline tab, click the slide or bullet icon, and then click the Decrease List Level button.

2. Promote means to decrease the level (for example, from level two to level one) of an outline item; demote means to increase the level of an outline item.

3. In the Outline tab, you can see the text of several slides at once, which makes it easier to work with text. In the slide pane, you can see the design and layout of the slide.

4. The thesaurus is a list of words and their synonyms, antonyms, and other related words.

5. Notes are notes for the presenter. They appear in the notes pane in Normal view or you can print notes pages, which contain a picture of and notes about each slide.

6. A feature in which spelling is checked in the context of how the words are used.

7. By previewing your presentation, you make sure that the slides are satisfactory, and that the presentation is legible in grayscale if you use a monochrome printer.

Ending Data Files

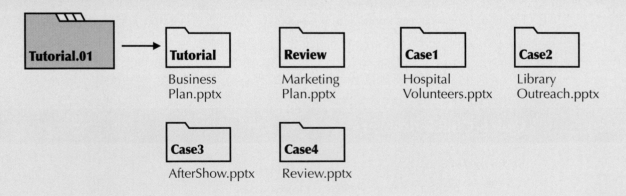

Reality Check

If you're like most people, you enjoy a hobby or have a special interest that you do for recreation. Is your special interest quilting, guitar playing, scrapbooking, or playing computer games? Do you enjoy rock climbing, backpacking, boating, snowmobiling, or another outdoor activity? Do you regularly attend concerts, visit museums, or go to the theater? Whatever your hobby or activity, other people might be interested in hearing about it. If you are asked by a group to explain your hobby, you might want to use a PowerPoint presentation to outline the major points. In this exercise, you'll use PowerPoint to create a presentation about your hobby or special interest, using the PowerPoint skills and features presented in Tutorial 1.

Note: Please be sure *not* to include any personal information of a sensitive nature in the presentation you create to be submitted to your instructor for this exercise. Later on, you can update the presentation with such information for your own personal use.

1. Start a new PowerPoint presentation using a template of your choice. Choose a template that is close to your type of presentation (giving general information). Don't worry if the text from the template doesn't apply, because you can delete or modify it.

2. On Slide 1, make the presentation title the same as the title of your hobby or special activity. Add your name as a subtitle.

3. Create new slides with titles such as "Getting Started with _____ " (where the blank is the name of your special activity), "Books and Magazines," "Web Sites on _____ ," "National Organizations," "Local Organizations," "Needed Equipment," "Needed Supplies," "Costs of Getting Started," and so forth.

4. Create one or more slides relating to your personal experiences, such as projects you've completed, activities you've engaged in, or trips you've taken.

5. On each slide, create a bulleted list to explain the details of the information you want to present.

6. Add speaker notes to some of the slides to help you in giving your presentation.

7. Check the spelling, including contextual spelling, of your presentation. Proofread your presentation. Use the thesaurus if you think you could find a better word to substitute for any of your original words.

8. Save the presentation.

9. Submit the completed presentation to your instructor in printed or electronic form, as requested.

Objectives

Session 1
- Start and exit Outlook
- Explore the Outlook window
- Navigate between Outlook components
- Create and send e-mail messages
- Create and edit contact information

Session 2
- Read and respond to e-mail messages
- Attach files to e-mail messages
- File, sort, save, and archive messages

Communicating with Outlook 2007

Sending and Receiving E-mail Messages

Case | Take Home Cooking

Cassie Reynolds noticed that her friends and neighbors were often too busy with work, school, and other activities to find the time to shop and cook nutritious meals throughout the week. She founded Take Home Cooking a few years ago to provide a way for people to prepare a week's worth of healthy meals using local and organic ingredients without the added time of menu planning and shopping. Cassie plans a week's worth of complete meals, from soup and salad through dessert, and then shops for the necessary supplies. Customers come to her professional kitchen, select which meals they want for the week, and then follow the simple instructions to prepare the meals using the provided supplies. Cassie is on hand to offer suggestions and help solve any problems that arise. Customers pack their completed dishes in take-away containers that they can use to reheat their meals at home. To coordinate all the activities involved in running Take Home Cooking, Cassie relies on **Microsoft Office Outlook 2007**, or **Outlook**, an information management and communication program.

You will use Outlook to help Cassie with the variety of tasks she performs. In this tutorial, you'll explore the Outlook window and its components. You'll use e-mail to send information about the upcoming week's menu options. You'll set up contact information for customers. You'll receive, read, and respond to e-mail messages. Finally, you'll organize messages by filing, sorting, and archiving them.

Starting Data Files

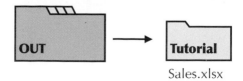

Sales.xlsx

Organic.docx

Freida Cohn.vcf   (none)

Session 1

Exploring Outlook

Outlook is a powerful information manager. You can use Outlook to perform a wide range of communication and organizational tasks, such as sending, receiving, and organizing e-mail; organizing contact information; scheduling appointments, events, and meetings; creating a to-do list and delegating tasks; and writing notes.

Outlook has six main components. The **Mail** component is a message/communication tool for receiving, sending, storing, and managing e-mail. The three mail folders you will use the most often are the Inbox folder, which stores messages you have received; the Outbox folder, which stores messages you have written but not sent; and the Sent Items folder, which stores copies of messages you have sent. You also can create other folders to save and organize e-mail you've received and written. The **Calendar** component is a scheduling tool for planning appointments, events, and meetings. The **Contacts** component is an address book for compiling postal addresses, phone numbers, e-mail and Web addresses, and other personal and business information about people and businesses with whom you communicate. The **Tasks** component is a to-do list for organizing and tracking items you need to complete or delegate. The **Notes** component is a notepad for jotting down ideas and thoughts that you can group, sort, and categorize. The **Journal** component is a diary for recording your activities, such as time spent talking on the phone, sending an e-mail message, or working on a document. As you work with these components, you create items such as e-mail messages, appointments, contacts, tasks, notes, and journal entries. An **item** is the basic element that holds information in Outlook, similar to a file in other programs. Items are organized into **folders**. Unlike folders in Windows Explorer, Outlook folders are available only from within Outlook.

Starting Outlook

You start Outlook the same way as any other program—using the Start menu. If Outlook is the default e-mail program on your computer, you can also click the E-mail link in the pinned items list at the top of the Start menu to start the program.

To start Outlook:

▶ 1. Click the **Start** button ⊕ on the taskbar, click **All Programs**, click **Microsoft Office**, and then click **Microsoft Office Outlook 2007**. After a short pause, the Outlook program window appears.

Trouble? If you don't see the Microsoft Office Outlook 2007 option in the Microsoft Office folder, look for it in a different folder or as an option on the All Programs menu, or click the E-mail Microsoft Office Outlook option at the top of the Start menu. If you still can't find the Microsoft Office Outlook 2007 option, ask your instructor or technical support person for help.

Trouble? If the Outlook 2007 Startup dialog box opens to guide you through the process of configuring Outlook, click the Next button, enter the information requested (for more information, refer to the "Setting up an Outlook e-mail account" steps), and then continue with Step 2.

Trouble? If a dialog box opens, asking whether you want your RSS Feeds in Outlook to be synchronized with the Common Feed List, click the No button unless your instructor or technical support person instructs you otherwise.

Trouble? If a dialog box opens, asking whether you want to make Outlook the default program for Mail, Calendar, and Contacts, click the No button.

Trouble? If a dialog box opens, asking whether you want to AutoArchive your old items now, click the No button.

▶ **2.** If necessary, click the **Maximize** button ▭. Figure 1 shows the maximized Outlook window.

Outlook window ◄ **Figure 1**

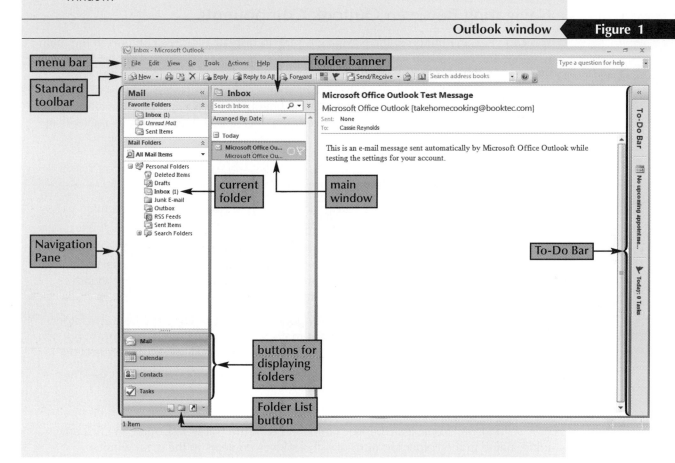

The Outlook window contains some elements that might be familiar to you from other Office programs, such as Word or Excel. Other elements are specific to Outlook, including:

- **Navigation Pane.** A central tool for accessing the Outlook folders. You can reduce the Navigation Pane to a vertical bar along the left side of the Outlook window, leaving more space for the main window.

- **Folder List.** A hierarchy of the Outlook folders you can display in the Navigation Pane that you use to store and organize items; also provides a way to navigate among the Outlook folders. The Folder List is not shown in Figure 1; you'll work with it later in this tutorial.

- **Folder banner.** A bar at the top of the main window that displays the name of the open folder.

- **Main window.** The display of items stored in the selected folder; may be divided into panes. For example, the center pane of the Inbox main window displays a list of e-mail messages in the Inbox, and the right pane displays the contents of the selected e-mail message.

- **To-Do Bar.** A vertical bar on the right side of the window that shows a summary of your current appointments and tasks. In Figure 1, the minimized To-Do Bar lists no upcoming appointments and zero tasks to complete for the day. You can expand the To-Do Bar to see this month's calendar, a list of appointments for the day, and your task list. Or, you can close it.

No matter which component is active, these elements of the Outlook window work in the same way. You can use the View menu to display or hide any of these elements, depending on your needs and preferences.

Navigating Between Outlook Components

You can click any button in the Navigation Pane to display a folder's contents in the main window. The Navigation Pane contains buttons for the most commonly used Outlook folders—Mail, Calendar, Contacts, Tasks, Notes—as well as buttons to open the Folder List and Shortcuts. Depending on the size of your monitor, the Notes, Folder List, and Shortcuts buttons might appear as icons at the bottom of the Navigation Pane rather than as bars with the name of the pane displayed. You click a button to display its contents in the Navigation Pane.

To use the Navigation Pane:

▶ **1.** Click the **Mail** button in the Navigation Pane. The Inbox appears in the main window. If the Mail button was already selected, your view does not change.

▶ **2.** Click the **Calendar** button in the Navigation Pane to switch to the Calendar folder, and then click the **Day** button at the top of the main window, if necessary. The daily planner and task list appear in the main window, and the current month's calendar appears at the top of the Navigation Pane.

▶ **3.** Click the **Contacts** button in the Navigation Pane to switch to the Contacts folder. The list of contacts is displayed in the main window; yours might be empty, but you still see letter buttons along the right side that you use to scroll the contacts list.

▶ **4.** Click the **Tasks** button in the Navigation Pane to switch to the Tasks folder. The tasks list appears in the main window.

A second way to navigate between folders is with the Folder List. You can click any folder name in the Folder List to display the folder's contents in the main window.

To navigate with the Folder List:

▶ **1.** Click the **Folder List** button 🖿 in the Navigation Pane. The Folder List appears in the Navigation Pane with the All Folders group expanded to display icons for each of the folders in Outlook.

▶ **2.** Click **Calendar** in the All Outlook Items group in the Folder List. The Calendar appears in the main window and the current month's calendar appears at the top of the Navigation Pane right above the All Folders group.

▶ **3.** Click **Inbox** in the All Folders group in the Navigation Pane. The Inbox folder appears in the main window. If you have messages in your Inbox, the content of the selected message might appear in the Reading Pane to the right of or below the main window. See Figure 2.

Folder List — Figure 2

click to minimize the Navigation Pane

click to expand the To-Do Bar

All Folders group in the Folder List

Creating and Sending E-mail Messages

The main window currently displays the contents of the Inbox folder, where you receive, create, and send e-mail. **E-mail**, the electronic transfer of messages between computers, is a simple and inexpensive way to communicate with friends around the corner, family across the country, and colleagues in the same building or around the world. The messages you send are delivered immediately and stored until recipients can read those messages at their convenience. Cassie uses e-mail to correspond with her customers and suppliers because it is fast, convenient, and inexpensive. In addition, it saves her the cost of paper, ink or toner, and other supplies.

Before you can send and receive e-mail messages with Outlook, you must have access to an e-mail server or Internet service provider (ISP), an e-mail address, and a password. An **e-mail address** is a user ID and a host name separated by @. A **user ID** (or user name or account name) is a unique name that identifies you to your mail server. A user name can include upper and lowercase letters, numbers, and periods; although symbols are allowed, you should avoid them because some ISPs may not accept them. The **host name** consists of the name of your ISP's computer on the Internet plus its domain or level. For example, in the e-mail address "cassie@takehomecooking.com," "cassie" is the user ID and "takehomecooking.com" is the host name. Although many people might use the same host, each user ID is unique, enabling the host to distinguish one user from another. A **password** is a private code that you enter to access your account. (In this tutorial, you will use your own e-mail address to send all messages.)

If you haven't already set up an Outlook e-mail account, you'll need to do so now by completing the following steps.

To set up an Outlook e-mail account:

▶ 1. Click **Tools** on the menu bar, and then click **Account Settings**. The Account Settings dialog box opens with tabs for each type of account you might need to create in Outlook. You'll create an e-mail account.

▶ 2. On the E-mail tab, click the **New** button. The Add New E-mail Account wizard opens. The first step is to choose your e-mail service—most e-mail accounts fit into the first group.

Trouble? If the Auto Account Setup dialog box opens, continue with Step 4.

▶ **3.** Select the type of server you will use to access your e-mail, and then click the **Next** button. The wizard opens the Auto Account Setup dialog box, depending on the type of server you selected. Figure 3 shows the options when the Microsoft Exchange, POP3, IMAP, and HTTP option is selected as the e-mail service.

| Figure 3 | Add New E-mail Account wizard |

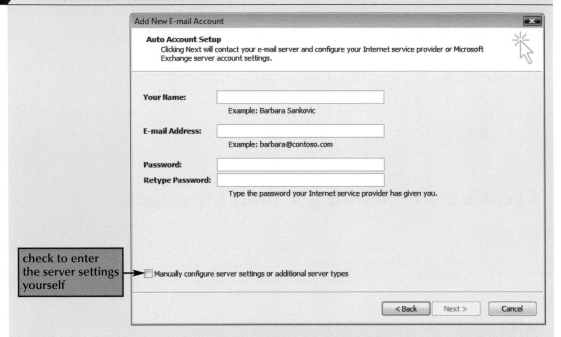

check to enter the server settings yourself

▶ **4.** Enter the requested information in the dialog box, and then click the **Next** button. Outlook connects to your e-mail account to determine the rest of the server settings needed to configure your e-mail account.

Trouble? If you are unsure what information to enter in the Internet E-mail Settings dialog box or if Outlook was unable to configure your server settings, ask your instructor or technical support person for help.

▶ **5.** Click the **Finish** button to confirm that Outlook has successfully set up your e-mail account.

▶ **6.** Click the **Close** button in the Account Settings dialog box.

Choosing a Message Format

Outlook can send and receive messages in three formats: HTML, Rich Text, and plain text. Although you specify one of these formats as the default for your messages, you can always switch formats for an individual message. HTML provides the most formatting features and options (text formatting, numbering, bullets, alignment, horizontal lines, backgrounds, HTML styles, and Web pages). Rich Text provides some formatting options (text formatting, bullets, and alignment). With both HTML and Rich Text, some recipients will not be able to see the formatting if their e-mail software is not set up to handle formatted messages. Plain text messages include no formatting, and the recipient specifies which font is used for the message.

When you reply to a message, Outlook uses the same format in which the message was created, unless you specify otherwise. For example, if you reply to a message sent to you in plain text, Outlook sends the response in plain text.

You'll set the message format to HTML so you can customize your messages.

To choose HTML as the default message format:

▶ **1.** Click **Tools** on the menu bar, and then click **Options**. The Options dialog box opens.

▶ **2.** Click the **Mail Format** tab.

▶ **3.** If necessary, click the **Compose in this message format** arrow, and then click **HTML**. See Figure 4.

Mail Format tab in the Options dialog box   Figure 4

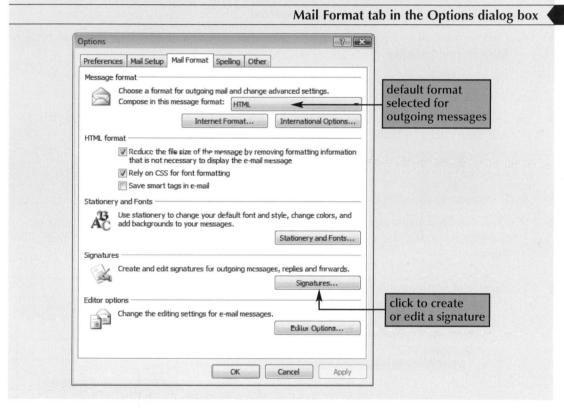

Outlook uses the HTML format each time you create a message, unless you select a different format for that message. Because you selected HTML as the message format, you can customize your messages with a formatted signature. You'll do that before closing the Options dialog box.

Adding a Signature

A **signature** is text that is automatically added to every e-mail message you send. A signature can contain any text you want. For example, you might create a signature with your name, job title, company name, and phone number. Take Home Cooking might create a signature containing a paragraph that describes what the company offers. You can create more than one signature for an e-mail account. If you have more than one e-mail account, you can create different signatures for each e-mail account you have set up. Although you can attach a signature to a message in any format, the HTML and Rich Text formats enable you to apply font and paragraph formatting. You'll show Cassie how to create a simple signature containing your name.

Note that the figures in this book show the name Cassie Reynolds, whose e-mail address is takehomecooking@booktec.com.

To create a formatted signature:

▶ 1. On the Mail Format tab in the Options dialog box, click the **Signatures** button. The Signatures and Stationery dialog box opens with the E-mail Signature tab displayed.

▶ 2. Click the **New** button. The New Signature dialog box opens.

▶ 3. Type **Take Home Cooking** in the Type a name for this signature box, and then click the **OK** button. The signature name is selected in the Select signature to edit box.

▶ 4. Click in the Edit signature box, type your name, press the **Enter** key, and then type **Take Home Cooking**.

   Next, you'll change the format of part of the signature. You can change the font, size, style, color, and alignment of the text in the signature.

▶ 5. Select **Take Home Cooking**, click **Arial** in the Font list, click the **Bold** button **B**, and then click the **Italic** button **I**. The selected text is reformatted.

   You'll add your signature to new messages you create, but not to messages you respond to.

▶ 6. If necessary, click the **E-mail account** arrow, and then click your e-mail address.

▶ 7. Click the **New Messages** arrow, and then click **Take Home Cooking** (the name of the signature you just set up). Leave the Replies/forwards box set to (none). See Figure 5.

| **Figure 5** | **Signatures and Stationery dialog box** |

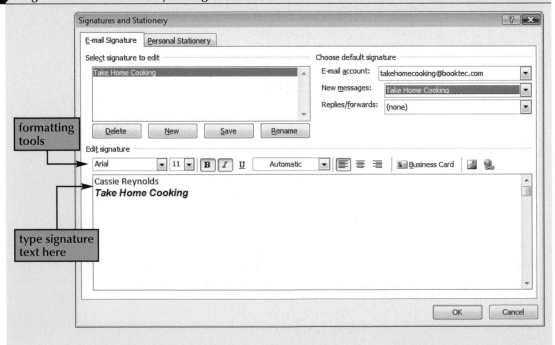

▶ **8.** Click the **OK** button. The Signatures and Stationery dialog box closes and the Options dialog box reappears.

▶ **9.** Click the **OK** button. The Options dialog box closes.

Using Stationery or Themes

Stationery and themes are a way to quickly distinguish your HTML messages with a pre-set design. **Stationery** is an HTML file that includes complementary background colors, images, or patterns. A **theme** includes complementary backgrounds as well as other design elements such as fonts, bullets, colors, and effects. Stationery and themes increase the size of the outgoing message. To add stationery or a theme to a message, you click Actions on the menu bar, point to New Mail Message Using, and then click More Stationery to open the Theme or Stationery dialog box and select the one you want to use. Previously selected stationeries and themes appear above the More Stationery command. To add the same stationery or theme to all your outgoing messages, you can click the Stationery and Fonts button on the Mail Format tab of the Options dialog box, and then click the Theme button on the Personal Stationery tab of the Signatures and Stationery dialog box to open the Theme or Stationery dialog box. You also can create your own stationery. Stationery uses HTML message format, so recipients whose e-mail programs don't read HTML e-mail won't see the stationery, but they will still be able to read the message text.

Creating an E-mail Message

An e-mail message looks similar to a memo, with header lines for Date, To, From, Cc, and Subject, followed by the body of the message. Outlook fills in the Date line with the date on which you send the message and the From line with your name or e-mail address; these lines are not visible in the window in which you create your e-mail message. You complete the other lines. The To line lists the e-mail addresses of one or more recipients. The Cc line lists the e-mail addresses of anyone who will receive a courtesy copy of the message. An optional Bcc line lists the e-mail addresses of anyone who will receive a blind courtesy copy of the message; Bcc recipients are not visible to each other or to the To and Cc recipients. The Subject line provides a quick overview of the message topic, similar to a headline. The main part of the e-mail is the message body.

E-mail, like other types of communication, is governed by its own customs of behavior, called **netiquette** (short for Internet etiquette), which helps prevent miscommunication. As you write and send e-mail messages, keep in mind the following guidelines:

- **Think before you send.** Your words can have a lasting impact. Be sure they convey the thoughts you intend and want others to attribute to you. Your name and e-mail address are attached to every message that you send, and your message can be forwarded swiftly to others.
- **Be concise.** The recipient should be able to read and understand your message quickly.
- **Use standard capitalization.** Excessive use of uppercase is considered shouting, and exclusive use of lowercase is incorrect; both are difficult to read.
- **Check spelling and grammar.** Create and maintain a professional image by using standard spelling and grammar. What you say is just as important as how you say it.
- **Avoid sarcasm.** Without vocal intonations and body language, a recipient may read your words with emotions or feelings you didn't intend. You can use punctuation marks and other characters to create **emoticons**—also called **smileys**—such as :-), to convey the intent of your words. (Tilt your head to the left to look at the emoticon sideways to see the "face"—in this case, a smile.) To learn additional emoticons, search the Web for emoticon or smiley dictionaries.
- **Don't send confidential information.** E-mail is not private; once you send a message, you lose control over where it may go and who might read it. Also, employers and schools usually can legally access their employees' and students' e-mail messages, even after a message is deleted from an Inbox.

The adage "Act in haste; repent in leisure" is particularly apt for writing e-mail. For more e-mail netiquette guidelines, search the Web for e-mail etiquette or netiquette Web sites.

Reference Window | **Creating an E-mail Message**

- Click the New button arrow on the Standard toolbar, and then click Mail Message.
- Type recipient e-mail address(es) in the To box (separate by semicolons).
- Type recipient e-mail address(es) in the Cc box and the Bcc box, as needed.
- Type a topic in the Subject box, and then type the message body.
- Format the message as needed.
- Click the Send button.

You'll create an e-mail message. Although you would usually send messages to other people, you will send messages to yourself in this tutorial so you can practice sending and receiving messages.

To create an e-mail message:

▶ 1. Click the **New button arrow** on the Standard toolbar. A list of new items you can create in Outlook appears. Because a Mail folder is the current folder, Mail Message appears at the top of the list, and is the default if you simply click the New button.

▶ 2. Press the **Esc** key twice to close the New button list and deselect the button, and then position the pointer over the **New** button on the Standard toolbar. A ScreenTip identifies this button as the New Mail Message button. Another clue is the icon next to the word New on the button, which is an open envelope and a piece of paper. The New button's icon changes, depending on which Outlook folder is active.

3. Click the **New** button on the Standard toolbar. A Message window opens with the blinking insertion point in the To box. Your signature appears in the **message body**, where the content of your message appears; you'll type your message above the signature. The title bar indicates that this is an Untitled Message.

4. In the To box, type your e-mail address.

5. Press the **Tab** key twice to move to the Subject box. You skipped the Cc box because you aren't sending a courtesy copy of this e-mail to anyone.

   Trouble? If the insertion point is not in the Subject box, then the Bcc box is displayed. Press the Tab key again to move to the Subject box, and then continue with Step 6.

6. Type **This Week's Order** in the Subject box, and then press the **Tab** key. The insertion point moves to the message body just above the signature. As soon as you move the insertion point out of the Subject box, the title bar shows the subject of the message.

7. Type **Please include 40 pounds of Yukon Gold potatoes in this week's order.** (including the period), press the **Enter** key twice, and then type **Thank you.** (including the period).

Tip

To send an e-mail message to multiple recipients, type a comma or semicolon between each address.

You don't need to type your name because you included it as part of the signature. Before sending your message, however, you want to add some text formatting. You have access to the standard text formatting features available in all the Office programs. For example, you can set bold, underline, and italics; change the font, font size, and font color; align and indent text; create a bulleted or numbered list; and even apply paragraph styles. People whose e-mail programs cannot read formatted e-mail will still be able to read your messages in plain text.

To format text in the message body:

1. Select **40 pounds of Yukon Gold potatoes** in the message body. You'll make this text bold and orange.

2. In the Basic Text group on the Message tab, click the **Bold** button **B** . The text changes to boldface.

3. In the Basic Text group, click the **Font Color button arrow** **A·** , and then click the **Orange, Accent 6** color (the last color in the first row in the Theme Colors section of the Font Color gallery). The text changes to orange.

4. Press the **Down Arrow** key to deselect the text and move the insertion point to the next line.

Keep the following guidelines in mind to create effective, professional messages:

- **One topic per e-mail.** A distinct conversation thread makes it simpler to find messages related to a topic.
- **Short, descriptive subject line.** A clear subject quickly tells recipients the main point of a message (and reminds you when they reply). Also, some people decide whether to read a message based on its subject line.
- **Concise, complete message.** An effective message conveys information quickly and fully, so the entire contents appear in the Reading Pane. People receive many messages each day, and tend to save poorly written or meandering messages to deal with later.
- **Format to enhance rather than decorate.** Recipients may see a message that looks very different from the one you sent with variations in colors or fonts. Add emphasis with bold, italic, and other basic formatting as needed. Use white or a light colored background with black or a dark colored text. Choose common fonts and sizes, such as 10 or 12 pt Arial and Times New Roman.
- **Use an attachment for complex content.** If you want to send a more elaborately formatted message, an attached Word document or PDF file might be a better option.

Next, you'll add icons to the message indicating its importance.

Setting the Importance and Sensitivity Levels

You can add icons that appear in the message pane of the Inbox to provide clues to the recipient about the importance and sensitivity of the message. You can specify an importance level of High ⚑ or Low ⬇ or leave the message set at the default Normal importance level. High importance tells the recipient that the message needs prompt attention, whereas a Low importance tells the recipient that the message can wait for a response. Use the importance level appropriately. If you send all messages with a High importance, recipients will learn to disregard the status.

You'll change the message importance level to High.

To change the message importance level to High:

▶ 1. In the Options group on the Message tab, click the **High Importance** button ⚑. The button remains selected to indicate the importance level you selected for the message. See Figure 6.

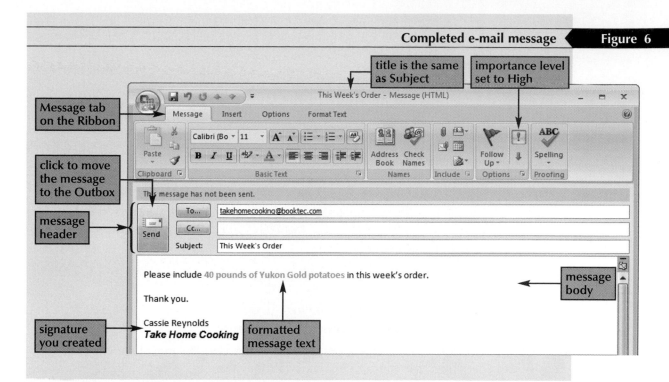

Completed e-mail message | Figure 6

You can also change the normal sensitivity level for the message to Personal, Private, or Confidential. This is another way to help recipients determine the content of a message before reading it. To set the sensitivity level, in the Options group on the Message tab, click the dialog box launcher to open the Message Options dialog box, click the Sensitivity arrow, and then select the sensitivity level you want for the message. You'll leave the sensitivity set to Normal for this message.

Sending E-mail

You can set up Outlook in various ways for sending messages. Your messages can be sent immediately (assuming your computer is connected to your e-mail server), or they can remain in the Outbox until you click the Send/Receive button. You also can set up a schedule for Outlook to automatically send and receive messages at regular intervals that you specify (such as every 15 minutes or every few hours).

If you are working **offline** (not connected to your e-mail server) or change the default setup, any messages you write remain in the Outbox until you choose to send them. You select how messages are sent in the Options dialog box. You'll set these options now.

To change your message delivery options:

▶ **1.** Click the **Inbox - Microsoft Outlook** button on the taskbar to return to the Inbox.

▶ **2.** Click **Tools** on the menu bar, click **Options** to open the Options dialog box, and then click the **Mail Setup** tab.

▶ **3.** In the Send/Receive section, click the **Send immediately when connected** check box to remove the check mark, if necessary. Outlook will store your completed messages in the Outbox until you choose to send them rather than immediately delivering them to your e-mail server.

▶ **4.** Click the **OK** button.

When you click the Send button in the Message window, the message will move to the Outbox. You must then click the Send/Receive button on the Standard toolbar to check for and deliver new messages.

To send the completed message to the Outbox:

▶ **1.** Click the **This Week's Order - Message** button on the taskbar to return to your message.

▶ **2.** Click the **Send** button in the message header area. The Message window closes and the message moves to the Outbox. You return to the Outlook window.

The Outbox folder name in the All Folders group in the Folder List changes to boldface and is followed by [1], which indicates the folder contains one outgoing message. You can send and receive e-mail from any folder; you'll switch to the Outbox to deliver this message.

To switch to the Outbox and send the message:

▶ **1.** Click **Outbox** in the All Folders group in the Folder List. The message in the Outbox folder appears in the Outbox window. See Figure 7.

Figure 7 | **Message in the Outbox**

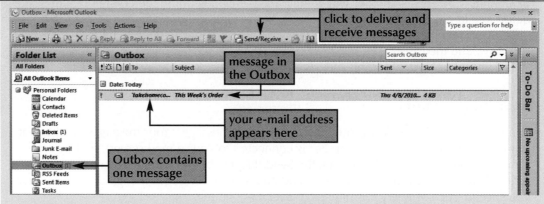

▶ **2.** On the Standard toolbar, click the **Send/Receive button arrow**, and then click **Send All**. All messages in the Outbox are sent. The Outlook Send/Receive Progress dialog box remains open until the message is sent. After the message is sent, the Outbox is empty and the boldface and [1] have disappeared.

Trouble? If you are not already connected to the Internet, connect now.

Trouble? If Outlook requests a password, you need to enter your password before you can send and receive your messages. Type your password, and then click the OK button.

A copy of the message is stored in the Sent Items folder, which provides a record of all the messages you sent. The time your e-mail takes to arrive at its destination varies, depending on the size of the message, the speed of your Internet connection, and the number of other users on the Internet.

Organizing Contact Information

The Contacts folder is an address book where you store information about the people and businesses with whom you communicate. Each person or organization is called a **contact**. You can store business-related information about each contact, including job title, phone and fax numbers, postal and Web addresses, and e-mail addresses, as well as more personal information, such as birthdays, anniversaries, and spouse and children's names.

Each piece of information you enter about a contact is called a **field**. For example, a complete contact name, such as Mr. Javier L. Brown, Jr., is comprised of a Title field, First field, Middle field, Last field, and Suffix field. The field's name, or label, identifies what information is stored in that field. You can use fields to sort, group, or look up contacts by any part of the name.

Creating Contacts

Cassie stores information about Take Home Cooking suppliers and customers in the Contacts folder. Cassie asks you to create new contacts for several suppliers. You can start a new contact from any folder by clicking the New button arrow on the Standard toolbar, and then clicking New Contact. Instead, you'll switch to the Contacts folder.

To create a contact:

▶ 1. Click **Contacts** in the All Folders group in the Folder List to display the Contacts folder. The icon on the New button changes to reflect the most likely item you'll want to create from this folder—in this case, a new contact.

▶ 2. On the Standard toolbar, click the **New** button. A Contact window opens, displaying text boxes in which to enter the contact information.

▶ 3. Maximize the Contact window, if necessary.

Contact information is entered on two pages. The General page stores the most pertinent information about a contact, including the contact's name, job title and company, phone numbers, and addresses. The Details page contains less frequently needed information, such as the names of the contact's manager, assistant, and spouse, as well as the contact's birthday, anniversary, and nickname.

Creating a Contact | Reference Window

- Click the New button arrow on the Standard toolbar, and then click Contact.
- On the General page, enter the contact's name, job title, company, mailing address, phone numbers, e-mail addresses, and Web site (click the down arrow to select other address, number, or e-mail options).
- In the Show group on the Contact tab, click the Details button, and then enter other business or personal data as needed.
- In the Actions group on the Contact tab, click the Save & New button to create another contact or click the Save & Close button if this is the last contact.
- If the Duplicate Contact Detected dialog box opens, select whether to add the contact anyway or merge with existing contact, and then click the OK button.

You'll enter the first contact's name and company.

To enter the first contact's name and company:

▶ 1. Type **Mr. Javier L. Brown, Jr.** in the Full Name text box, and then press the **Enter** key. The insertion point moves to the Company box, and the contact name appears, last name first, in the File as box. By default, Outlook organizes contacts by their last names. The contact's name also appears at the top of the business card and in the title bar of the Contact window.

▶ 2. Click the **Full Name** button. The Check Full Name dialog box opens. Although you entered the contact name in one box, Outlook stores each part of the name as a separate field. See Figure 8.

Figure 8 ▶ Check Full Name dialog box

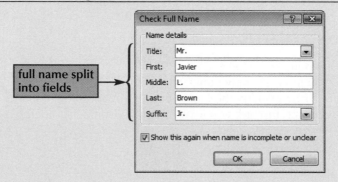

full name split into fields

▶ 3. Click the **Cancel** button to close the dialog box without making any changes. If Outlook cannot distinguish the parts of a name, the Check Full Name dialog box opens so you can correct the fields.

▶ 4. Click in the **Company** box, and then type **Green Grocer Produce**.

▶ 5. Press the **Tab** key to move to the Job title box, and then type **Customer Rep**.

Next, you'll enter the contact's phone numbers. You can enter as many as 19 numbers per contact. No matter how you enter the numbers—with or without spaces, hyphens, or parentheses—Outlook formats them consistently in the format (415) 555-3928.

To enter the contact's phone numbers, mailing address, and e-mail address:

▶ 1. Click in the **Business** box in the Phone numbers section. Clicking the Business button opens the Check Phone Number dialog box, which is similar in function and appearance to the Check Full Name dialog box.

▶ 2. Type **415 555 9753**, and then press the **Tab** key. Outlook formats the phone number with parentheses around the area code and a hyphen after the prefix, even though you didn't type them.

Trouble? If the Location Information dialog box opens, enter the appropriate information about your location, and then click the OK button. If the Phone and Modem Options dialog box opens, click the Cancel button.

Next to each phone number box is an arrow button you can click to change the name of the phone field. Although you can display only four phone fields at a time, you can enter information in all the fields, using any or all of the four available phone number boxes.

▶ 3. Click the **Home arrow button** ⊡ to display the phone number field labels, click **Assistant** to change the field label, and then type **415-555-9752** for the phone number of Javier's assistant.

You'll switch to the Details page to enter the name of Javier's assistant, and then return to the General page to enter the fax number, postal address, and e-mail address.

▶ 4. In the Show group on the Contact tab, click the **Details** button, click in the Assistant's name box, and then type **Jean Ash**.

▶ 5. In the Show group, click the **General** button to return to the General page, and then type **415-555-6441** as the Business Fax number.

▶ 6. In the Addresses section on the General page, click in the **Business** box, type **12 Haymarket Blvd.**, press the **Enter** key, and then type **San Francisco, CA 94102**. You could verify that Outlook recorded the address in the correct fields by clicking the Business button, but you don't need to do so for a simple address.

As soon as you start typing the address, a check mark appears in the This is the mailing address check box. Outlook sets the first address you enter for a contact as the mailing address. You could enter additional addresses for Home and Other, and specify any one of them as the mailing address.

▶ 7. Click in the **E-mail** box, type your e-mail address, and then press the **Tab** key to move the insertion point to the Display as box. The e-mail address you typed becomes underlined, and the contact's name appears in the Display as box with your e-mail in parentheses after the name. The Display as box shows how the e-mail address will appear in the To box of e-mail messages. Although you can enter any text you like in the Display as box, you'll leave the default. See Figure 9.

Completed Contact window for Javier L. Brown, Jr. ◀ Figure 9

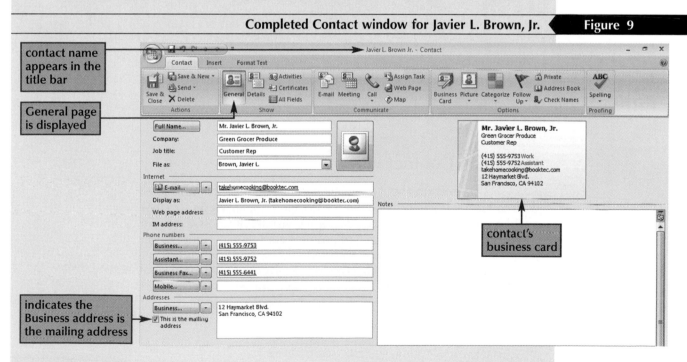

Trouble? If only the e-mail address appears in the Display as box, you need to edit the display as name. Type "Javier L. Brown, Jr. (" to insert the contact's name and an opening parenthesis, press the Right Arrow key to move the insertion point to the end of the Display as box, and then type ")" to insert the closing parenthesis.

In most cases, each contact would have a unique e-mail address to which you would send e-mail messages. You have completed the contact information for Javier. You can close his Contact window and open a new Contact window in the same step.

To create additional contacts:

1. In the Actions group on the Contact tab, click the **Save & New** button to save Javier's contact information and open a new Contact window.

2. Enter the following information: full name **Julia Shang**, company **Foods Naturally**, job title **Manager**, your e-mail address, business phone **415-555-1224**, business fax **415-555-4331**, and business address **19 Hillcrest Way, Novato, CA 94132**.

3. In the Actions group, click the **Save & New** button. Outlook detects that another contact already has the same e-mail address as Julia Shang and opens the Duplicate Contact Detected dialog box.

4. Click the **Add new contact** option button, and then click the **Add** button.

5. Enter the following contact information: full name **Kelley Ming**, company **Ming Nuts Company**, your e-mail address, business phone **415-555-9797**, and business address **2932 Post Street, San Francisco, CA 94110**.

6. In the Actions group, click the **Save & New** button, add Kelley Ming as a new contact, and then enter the following contact information: full name **Cassie Reynolds**, company **Take Home Cooking**, and your e-mail address.

7. In the Actions group, click the **Save & Close** button, and then add Cassie Reynolds as a new contact to save her contact information and return to the Contacts folder. The business cards for the four contacts you added appear in the Contacts main window, sorted alphabetically by last name.

Switching Contact Views

All of the information about a contact is called a **contact card**. There are a variety of ways to look at the information in the Contacts folder. **Views** specify how information in a folder is organized and which details are visible. Business Cards view displays the names and addresses in a standard business card format. Address Cards view displays names and addresses in blocks. Detailed Address Cards view displays additional information in this same format. Phone List view displays details about your contacts, such as name, company, and telephone numbers, in columns. Each Outlook folder has a set of standard views from which you can choose. You'll change the Contacts folder view to Detailed Address Cards.

To change the Contacts view:

▶ **1.** Click the **Contacts** button in the Navigation Pane, and then, in the Current View group, if necessary, click the **Business Cards** option button. The My Contacts group appears at the top of the Navigation Pane with the Contacts folder selected. The Current View group appears below the My Contacts group, and it lists all the available standard views for the Contacts folder. Business Cards displays each contact's name, company name, job title, up to four phone numbers, e-mail address, and mailing address. See Figure 10.

Contacts in Business Cards view ◀ **Figure 10**

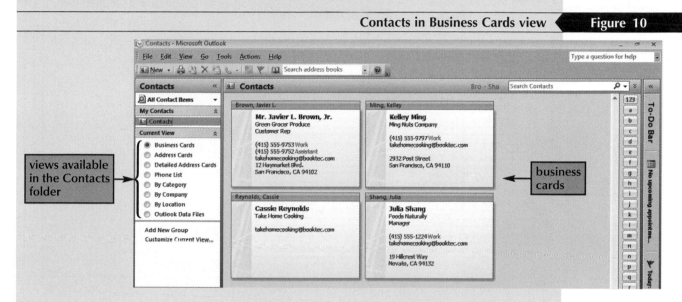

▶ **2.** In the Current View group, click the **Detailed Address Cards** option button. Detailed Address Cards view displays more contact information in the main window than the Business Cards or Address Cards view. See Figure 11.

Figure 11 **Contacts in Detailed Address Cards view**

Tip

You can widen the column and the cards by dragging the vertical line to the right of a column of business cards.

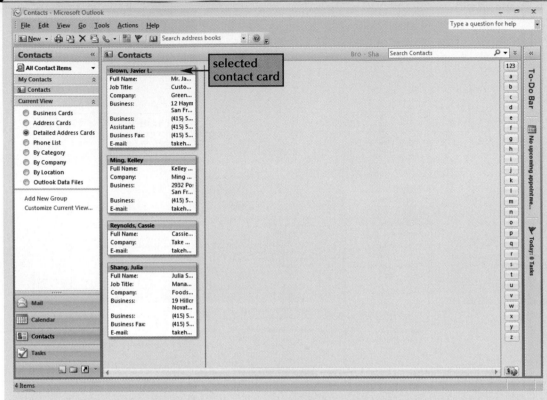

In the Business Cards, Address Cards, and Detailed Address Cards views, Outlook organizes your contacts in the main window in alphabetical order by last name, as specified in the File as box. When you have many contacts, you find a certain contact quickly by typing their name in the Search Contacts box in the folder banner and clicking the Search button. You can also click the letter button along the right side of the main window that corresponds to the first letter of a contact's last name, and then use the scroll bar at the bottom of the window to display that contact.

Editing Contacts

Many aspects of a contact's information may change over time. A person or company might move to a new street address or be assigned a new area code. A person might change jobs. You might discover that you entered information incorrectly. Rather than deleting the card and starting over, you can update the existing contact card as needed. You can double-click the contact to open its Contact window, and then edit the information as needed. You can also make the change directly in the Contacts folder main window in Address Cards view or Detailed Address Cards view. No matter how many changes you need to make to a contact's information, the contact card remains neat and organized.

Cassie tells you that the zip code for Foods Naturally is actually 94947. You'll make this correction directly in the Detailed Address Cards view.

To edit Julia Shang's contact card:

▶ **1.** In the Contacts window, point to the vertical bar to the right column of contact cards until the pointer changes to ↔, and then drag the **vertical bar** right until the cards are wide enough to display all the address text.

▶ **2.** Click the **S** button along the right side of the Contacts main window to select Julia Shang's contact card.

   Trouble? If your contacts list has additional contacts, the first contact beginning with "s" will be selected. Scroll until you can see Julia Shang's contact card.

▶ **3.** Click the address portion of Julia Shang's contact card to position the insertion point anywhere within the address.

▶ **4.** Use the arrow keys to move the insertion point between the 4 and 1 in the zip code.

▶ **5.** Press the **Delete** key three times to erase the incorrect digits, and then type **947**.

▶ **6.** Click anywhere outside Julia Shang's contact card. Outlook saves the change.

Sending Contact Information by E-mail

If you ever need to send some of your contacts to others, you can do so quickly by forwarding the contact information. When you forward contact information as an Outlook contact card, it includes the same data contained in your Contacts folder. If you forward the Outlook contact card, the recipient must use Outlook in order to be able to read the card. Not only are you sending the most complete information, but the recipient can also quickly drag the contact into his or her own Contacts folder. To forward a contact card, right-click the contact in the Contacts folder, and then click Send as Business Card on the shortcut menu or point to Send Full Contact and then click In Internet Format (vCard) or In Outlook Format. A new Message window opens with the contact included as an attachment to the message in the format you specified.

If you are not sure whether the recipient uses Outlook, you can send contact information as a vCard. A **vCard** is a file that contains a contact's personal information, such as the name, mailing address, phone numbers, and e-mail address. The vCard files are compatible with other popular communication and information management programs. You can also use vCards to exchange contact information with handheld personal digital assistants (PDAs).

When you receive a forwarded contact card, you can add the contact information directly to your Contacts folder without retyping the information. Just drag the contact card from the message to the Contacts folder, and the new contact card is created.

Creating and Modifying Distribution Lists

Sometimes you need to repeatedly send one e-mail message—such as a weekly progress report or company updates—to the same group of people. Rather than selecting the names one by one from the Contacts list, you can create a distribution list. A **distribution list** is a group of people to whom you frequently send the same messages, such as all suppliers. A distribution list saves time and ensures that you don't inadvertently omit someone. You can create multiple distribution lists to meet your needs, and individuals can be included in more than one distribution list.

Reference Window | **Creating a Distribution List**

- Click the New button arrow on the Standard toolbar, and then click Distribution List.
- In the Members group on the Distribution List tab, click the Select Members button.
- Click the Address Book arrow, and then click Contacts.
- Double-click the names you want to add to the distribution list, and then click the OK button.
- Click in the Name text box, and then type a contact name for the distribution list.
- In the Actions group on the Distribution List tab, click the Save & Close button.

Cassie asks you to create a distribution list to all Take Home Cooking suppliers as she frequently needs to send the same information to all of them.

To create a distribution list:

1. Click the **New button arrow** on the Standard toolbar, and then click **Distribution List**. A Distribution List window opens.

2. Type **Suppliers** in the Name box, and then press the **Tab** key. This is the contact name for the distribution list.

3. In the Members group on the Distribution tab, click the **Select Members** button. The Select Members: Contacts dialog box opens.

4. If necessary, click the **Address Book** arrow, and then click **Contacts**. A contact appears once for each e-mail address and fax number.

   You'll move the three suppliers into the distribution list.

5. Double-click the top **Julia Shang** entry (the one with her e-mail address) to move the contact to the Members box. Double-clicking the name is the same as clicking the name and then clicking the Members button.

6. Double-click the **Kelley Ming** entry and the top **Javier L. Brown, Jr.** entry to select them as members of the distribution list. See Figure 12.

Figure 12 | Select Members: Contacts dialog box

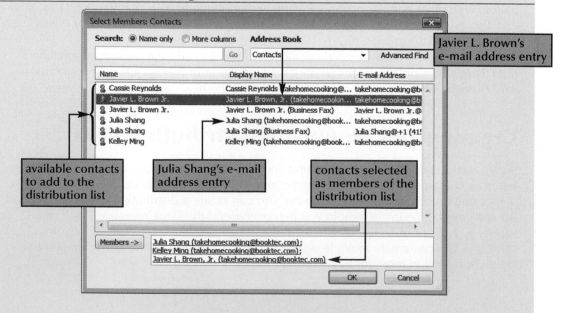

▶ **7.** Click the **OK** button. The three suppliers appear as members of the Suppliers distribution list. See Figure 13.

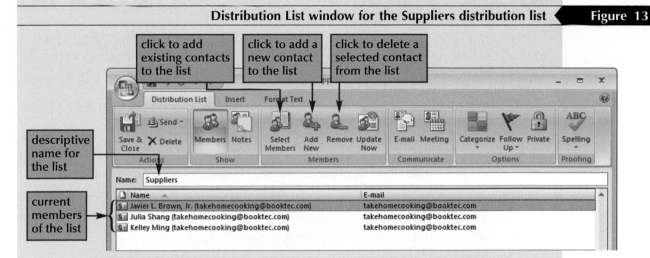

Distribution List window for the Suppliers distribution list | Figure 13

click to add existing contacts to the list

click to add a new contact to the list

click to delete a selected contact from the list

descriptive name for the list

current members of the list

Name: Suppliers

Name	E-mail
Javier L. Brown, Jr. (takehomecooking@booktec.com)	takehomecooking@booktec.com
Julia Shang (takehomecooking@booktec.com)	takehomecooking@booktec.com
Kelley Ming (takehomecooking@booktec.com)	takehomecooking@booktec.com

▶ **8.** In the Actions group on the Distribution List tab, click the **Save & Close** button. The distribution list appears in the Contacts folder filed under Suppliers, the name of the distribution list. The group icon in the upper-right corner of the contact card indicates that this is a distribution list rather than a one-person contact.

You can use the Suppliers distribution list contact just as you would any one-person contact.

Modifying a Distribution List

At times, you'll need to update a distribution list. You may need to delete a contact from the distribution list or add a new contact to the distribution list. You do this by double-clicking the distribution list contact in the Contacts folder to open its Distribution List window, and then, in the Members group on the Distribution tab, click the Select Members button to add other contacts to the list or click the Remove button to delete a selected contact from the list. Removing a contact from a distribution list only deletes the contact from the distribution list; the individual's contact card remains intact in the Contacts folder. If you need to update the information for an existing contact, you do so in the individual's contact card. If you find that you no longer need a distribution list, you delete it just like an individual contact.

If you regularly communicate with a group of people, distribution lists can be very handy. For example, you can create distribution lists for the members of a club, sports team, volunteer group, and so forth. However, sending identical messages to the group is likely to get them tagged as spam. Also, many ISPs limit how many messages you can send each day or week in an attempt to stop spam. Check with your ISP to find out what message limits they have as well as to let them know of your plans to do bulk mailings.

Session 1 Quick Check | Review

1. Describe the purposes of the Inbox and the Outbox.
2. Define e-mail and list two benefits of using it.
3. What is a signature?
4. List five types of contact information that you can store in Outlook.
5. Explain the purpose of a distribution list.

Session 2

Receiving E-mail

You check for new e-mail messages by clicking the Send/Receive button on the Standard toolbar. Outlook connects to your e-mail server, if necessary, sends any messages in the Outbox, and receives any incoming messages that have arrived since you last checked. New messages are delivered into the Inbox.

You'll switch to the Inbox and download the message you sent yourself earlier.

To receive e-mail:

▶ **1.** If you took a break after the previous session, make sure Outlook is running.

▶ **2.** Click the **Mail** button in the Navigation Pane, and then, in the Mail Folders group, click **Inbox**.

▶ **3.** On the Standard toolbar, click the **Send/Receive** button.

Trouble? If you are not already connected to the Internet, connect now.

▶ **4.** Watch for the new message to appear in the Inbox. The number of unread messages in the Inbox appears within parentheses next to the Inbox folder name in the Navigation Pane. See Figure 14. Your Inbox might contain additional e-mail messages.

Figure 14 ▶ **Received messages in the Inbox**

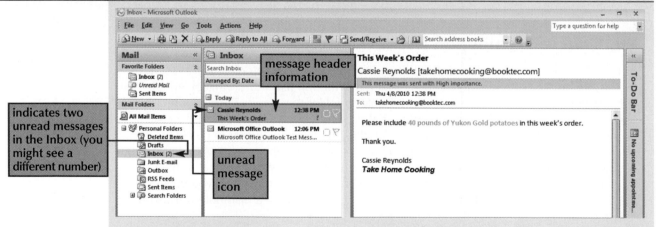

Trouble? If no messages appear, your e-mail server might not have received the message yet. Wait a few minutes, and then repeat Steps 3 and 4.

After a message arrives, you can read it. The Inbox folder is divided into two panes. The Inbox main window displays a list of e-mail messages that you have received, along with information about the message. The **message header** includes the sender's name, the message subject, and the date the message was received, as well as icons that indicate the message's status (such as the message's importance level and whether the message has been read). The **Reading Pane** displays the content of the selected message in a memo format. The subject, the sender, importance level, and all the recipients (except Bcc recipients) appear at the top of the memo. You can resize the panes by dragging the border between the Inbox main window and the Reading Pane left or right.

To read a message:

▶ **1.** Click the **This Week's Order** message in the Inbox main window to display its contents in the Reading Pane. In a moment, the mail icon changes from unread ☑ to read ☑, and the message no longer appears in boldface.

Trouble? If the Reading Pane does not appear on your screen or if it appears on the bottom of the screen, click View on the menu bar, point to Reading Pane, and then click Right.

Trouble? If the mail icon in the Inbox main window does not change to indicate that the message has been read, click Tools on the menu bar, click Options, click the Other tab, click the Reading Pane button, click the Mark item as read when selection changes check box to check it, and then click the OK button twice.

▶ **2.** Read the message in the Reading Pane. Because Outlook can view HTML messages, the formatting added to the message is visible.

Trouble? If you don't see the HTML formatting, your mail server may not display the HTML formatting in e-mail messages. Continue with the tutorial.

You can also open a message in its own window by double-clicking the message header in the Inbox pane. After you read a message, you have several options—you can leave the message in the Inbox and deal with it later, reply to the message, forward the message to others, print it, file it, or delete it.

Replying to and Forwarding Messages

Many messages you receive require some sort of response—for example, confirmation you received the information, the answer to a question, or sending the message to another person. The quickest way to respond to messages is to use the Reply, Reply to All, and Forward features. **Reply** responds to the sender, and **Reply to All** responds to the sender and all recipients (including any Bcc recipients); Outlook inserts the e-mail addresses into the appropriate boxes. **Forward** sends a copy of the message to one or more recipients you specify; you enter the e-mail addresses in the To or Cc box. With both Reply and Forward, the original message is included for reference, separated from your new message by a line and the original message header information. By default, new text you type is added at the top of the message body, above the original message. This makes it simpler for recipients to read your message because they don't have to scroll through the original message to find the new text.

You'll reply to the This Week's Order message. Typically, you respond to someone other than yourself.

To reply to the This Week's Order message:

▶ **1.** Make sure that the **This Week's Order** message is selected in the Inbox main window, and then, on the Standard toolbar, click the **Reply** button. A Message window opens with the receiver's name and e-mail address in the To box (in this case, your name and address) and RE: (short for Regarding) inserted at the beginning of the Subject line. The body of the original message appears in the message body pane below a divider line, and the insertion point is blinking above the message, ready for you to type your reply.

▶ **2.** If necessary, click in the message area, and then type **Your order has been updated. Thank you.**, press the **Enter** key twice, and then type your name (remember that your signature is not added for replies). Your reply message appears in blue because you selected HTML format.

Trouble? Depending on how your computer is configured, you might not see the HTML formatting.

▶ **3.** Click the **Send** button to move the message to the Outbox. The icon next to the message header in the Inbox main window changes to 🔄 to indicate you have replied to this message.

Next, you'll forward the message to Julia Shang, the manager at Foods Naturally. Because Julia's contact information is in the Contacts folder, you can address the message to her quickly.

To forward a message:

▶ **1.** Make sure that the **This Week's Order** message is selected in the Inbox main window, and then, on the Standard toolbar, click the **Forward** button. This time, the insertion point is in the empty To box and FW: (for Forward) precedes the Subject line.

▶ **2.** Type **Julia Shang** in the To box.

▶ **3.** Click at the top of the message body, above the forwarded message, and then type **Please update the Take Home Cooking account.** (including the period).

▶ **4.** Click the **Send** button to move the message to the Outbox. The Check Names dialog box opens because Julia Shang has multiple contact information—an e-mail address and a fax number.

▶ **5.** Click the top **Julia Shang**, the entry with her e-mail address, and then click the **OK** button. The icon next to the message header in the Inbox main window changes to 🔄 to indicate that this message has been forwarded.

▶ **6.** On the Standard toolbar, click the **Send/Receive** button, if necessary, to send the messages to your mail server.

Printing Messages

Cassie asks you to print the message for future reference. Although e-mail eliminates the need for paper messages, sometimes you'll want a printed copy of a message to file or distribute, or to read when you're away from your computer. You can use the Print button on the Standard toolbar to print a selected message with the default settings, or you can use the Print command on the File menu to open the Print dialog box, where you can verify and change settings before you print. All default print styles include the print date, user name, and page number in the footer. You'll use the Print dialog box to verify the settings and then print the This Week's Order message.

To verify settings and print the message:

▶ **1.** If necessary, select the **This Week's Order** message in the Inbox main window.

▶ **2.** Click **File** on the menu bar, and then click **Print**. The Print dialog box opens.

▶ **3.** Make sure that the correct printer appears in the Name box.

Trouble? If you're not sure which printer to use, ask your instructor or technical support person for assistance.

4. If necessary, click **Memo Style** in the Print style section to select it.

   Memo style prints the contents of the selected item—in this case, the e-mail message. Table Style prints the view of the selected folder—in this case, the Inbox folder. Other Outlook folders have different print style options.

▶ 5. Click the **OK** button. The message prints.

Working with Attachments

In your work at Take Home Cooking, you'll often want to send information that is stored in a variety of files on your computer. Some of this information could be typed into an e-mail message, but the original file might be long with complex formatting that is inappropriate for e-mail. Also, many kinds of files (such as photos and spreadsheets) cannot be inserted into e-mail messages. Instead, you can send files as attachments.

An **attachment** is a file that you send with an e-mail message. Attachments can be any type of file, including documents (such as a Word document, Excel workbook, or Power-Point slide presentation), images, sounds, and programs. For example, you might send an attachment containing Take Home Cooking's latest sales figures to Cassie for her review. Recipients can then save and open the file; the recipient must have the original program or a program that can read that file type. For example, if Cassie receives a Lotus 1-2-3 spreadsheet, she can open and save it with Excel.

> **Tip**
>
> Many ISPs don't accept messages with attachments that exceed a certain size or in file formats commonly used to spread viruses. You may not be notified that the recipient didn't receive your message.

To attach a file to the e-mail:

1. With the Inbox folder selected, on the Standard toolbar, click the **New** button to open a Message window.

2. Click the **To** button. The Select Names: Contacts dialog box opens.

   Trouble? If the Select Names dialog box shows a different folder, you need to change the Address Book. Click the Address Book arrow, and then click Contacts.

▶ 3. Click **Cassie Reynolds** in the list of contacts, and then click the **To** button at the bottom of the dialog box. Cassie's name is added to the To list.

4. Click the **OK** button.

5. In the Subject box, type **Latest Sales**.

6. In the message body area, type **The attached Excel workbook contains the latest sales figures. It looks like we're on track.** (including the period).

7. In the Include group on the Message tab, click the **Attach File** button 🔘 . The Insert File dialog box opens; it functions like the Open dialog box.

8. Navigate to the **OUT\Tutorial** folder included with your Data Files.

   Trouble? If you don't have the Outlook Data Files, you need to get them before you can proceed. Your instructor will either give you the Data Files or ask you to obtain them from a specified location (such as a network drive). In either case, be sure that you make a backup copy of your Data Files before you start using them, so that the original files will be available on your copied disk in case you need to start over because of an error or problem. If you have any questions about the Data Files, see your instructor or technical support person for assistance.

▶ 9. Double-click **Sales** in the file list. The file is attached to your e-mail message, and the Insert File dialog box closes. See Figure 15. The message is ready to send.

Figure 15 | **Message created with an attached file**

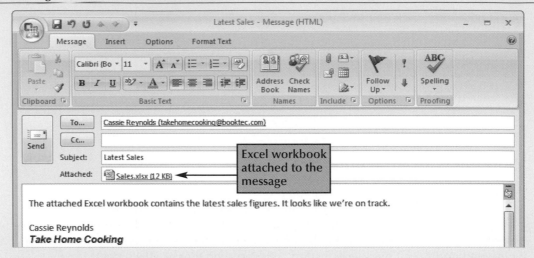

> **10.** Click the **Send** button, and then, on the Inbox Standard toolbar, click the **Send/ Receive** button to send the message to your mail server and receive the two messages you sent earlier.

A message with an attachment may take a bit longer to send because it's larger than an e-mail message without an attachment. Messages with attached files display a paper clip icon in the message header. If the appropriate program is installed on your computer, you can open the attached file from the message itself. You can also save the attachment to your computer and then open, edit, and move it like any other file on your computer. You can reply to or forward any message with an attachment, but the attachment is included only in the forwarded message because you rarely, if ever, want to return the same file to the sender. After you receive the message with the attachment, you'll save the attachment and then view it from within the message.

To save and view the message attachment:

> **1.** If the Latest Sales message (with the attachment) is not already in your Inbox, click the **Send/Receive** button on the Standard toolbar. It might take a bit longer than usual to download the message with the attachment.

> **2.** Click the **Latest Sales** message in the Inbox main window to view the message in the Reading Pane. The attachment file icon and name appear in the Reading Pane.

> **3.** Right-click the attached file **Sales.xlsx** in the Reading Pane, and then click **Save As** on the shortcut menu. The Save Attachment dialog box opens, where you can select the location to save the attachment.

> **4.** Navigate to the **OUT\Tutorial** folder included with your Data Files.

> **5.** Change the filename to **First Quarter Sales**, and then click the **Save** button to save the attached file. You can work with this file just as you would any other file on disk.

You can also view the attached file in the Reading Pane.

> **6.** Click **Sales.xlsx** in the Reading Pane. The Reading Pane displays a warning that you should only open attachments from trustworthy sources.

Tip

You can double-click a message in the Inbox main window to open the message in its own window if you don't want to use the Reading Pane.

Trouble? If the Excel file appears in the Reading Pane without first displaying the warning, this message has been turned off for your computer. Continue with Step 8.

▶ **7.** Click the **Preview file** button. The attached file appears in the Reading Pane, so you can view its contents. See Figure 16.

Message in Inbox with an attached file | **Figure 16**

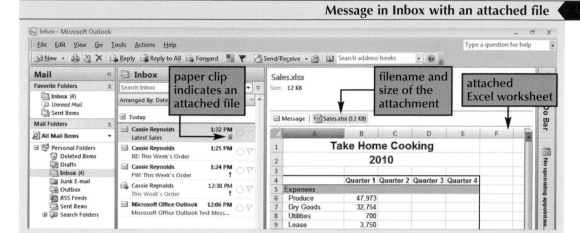

▶ **8.** Review the sales figures, and then click the **Message** button in the Reading Pane. The e-mail message appears in the Reading Pane.

Flagging and Color Coding Messages

Some messages you receive require a specific response or action. Although the subject should be informative and the message can provide explicit instructions, often a more obvious reminder would better draw attention to messages that require action. A **flag** is an icon that appears in the message header to indicate the item has been added as a task; text appears in the Reading Pane with a reminder of the start date and deadline. To add a flag, click the flag icon in a message header, click Add Reminder to open the Custom dialog box, then choose preset flag text or enter your own text, and select a specific due date or enter descriptive words such as "tomorrow" that Outlook converts to the correct date. Outlook will then display a reminder about the flag at the appropriate time. You can also choose six preset **color categories** or add others to better organize or rank your messages.

You'll flag the message to Julia Shang to review the sales figures by tomorrow and add it to the green color category.

To color code and flag Julia Shang's message:

▶ **1.** In the Inbox main window, in the Latest Sales message header, right-click the **color category** icon ☐, and then click **Green Category** in the list of available colors on the shortcut menu. The Rename Category dialog box opens. You can choose to enter a descriptive category name or keep the default name.

Trouble? If the Rename Category dialog box doesn't open, you need to use the Color Categories dialog box. Right-click the color category icon, and then click All Categories on the shortcut menu. In the Color Categories dialog box, click Green Category in the Name list, click the Rename button, type Sales as the new name, press the Enter key to change the name, and then click the OK button.

▶ **2.** Type **Sales** in the Name box, and then click the **Yes** button. The Latest Sales message's color category icon is green in the Inbox main window.

Next, you'll add the flag to the message.

▶ **3.** In the Latest Sales message header, right-click the **flag** icon 🏳, and then click **Add Reminder**. The Custom dialog box opens. See Figure 17.

Figure 17 ▶ **Flag for Follow Up dialog box**

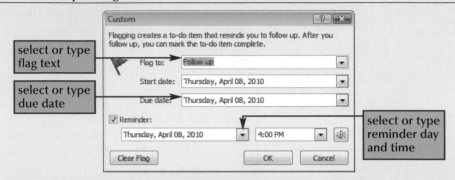

You want to set the flag message to Review and add a due date for tomorrow.

▶ **4.** Click the **Flag to** arrow to display the preset flag options, and then click **Review**.

▶ **5.** Click the **Due date** arrow to open a calendar showing this month with today's date highlighted, and then click the date for the next workday. A reminder is set for the next workday.

▶ **6.** Click the **OK** button. The Custom dialog box closes. The Follow up banner in the Reading Pane changes to reflect the selections you made. See Figure 18.

Figure 18 ▶ **Message with color category and flag**

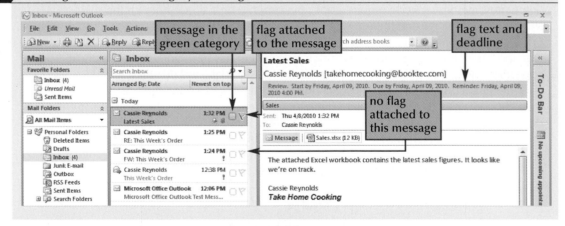

After you have performed the requested action, you can mark the flag completed by right-clicking the flag icon in the message header, and then clicking Mark Complete on the shortcut menu.

Organizing and Managing Messages

So far, all the messages you received are stored in the Inbox folder. As you can readily see, messages can collect quickly in your Inbox. Even if you respond to each message as it arrives, all the original messages still remain in your Inbox. Some messages you'll want to file and store, just as you would file and store paper memos in a file cabinet. Other messages you'll want to delete.

Creating a Folder

The Folder List acts like an electronic file cabinet. You should create a logical folder structure in which to store your messages. For example, Cassie might create subfolders named "Customers" and "Suppliers" within the Inbox folder. You can create folders at the same level as the default folders, such as Inbox, Outbox, and Sent Messages, or you can create subfolders within these main folders. For now, you'll create one subfolder in the Inbox folder, named "Suppliers."

To create a Suppliers subfolder in the Inbox:

1. In the Mail Folders group in the Navigation Pane, right-click **Inbox**, and then click **New Folder** on the shortcut menu. The Create New Folder dialog box opens.

2. Type **Suppliers** in the Name box.

3. If necessary, click the **Folder contains** button, and then click **Mail and Post Items**. You can also create subfolders to store other items, such as contacts, notes, tasks, and so forth.

4. Click **Inbox** in the Select where to place the folder list box if it is not already selected.

5. Click the **OK** button. The new folder appears indented below the Inbox folder in the Mail Folders group in the Navigation Pane.

   Trouble? If you don't see the Suppliers folder, the Inbox list is collapsed. Click the plus sign button next to Inbox.

Filing Messages

One method for keeping messages organized and the Inbox uncluttered is to move a message out of the Inbox as soon as you have dealt with it. This leaves the Inbox filled only with messages you still need to deal with. To file a message, you can drag selected messages from one folder to another or use the Move to Folder button on the Standard toolbar. You'll file messages related to Take Home Cooking suppliers in the new subfolder.

To file the Latest Sales message:

1. In the Inbox main window, select the **Latest Sales** message. It is the first message that you will move.

2. Drag the Latest Sales message to the **Suppliers** subfolder in the Mail Folders group in the Navigation Pane.

3. When the pointer is over the Suppliers subfolder and the Suppliers subfolder is highlighted, release the mouse button to move the message from the Inbox into the Suppliers subfolder.

You want to move all messages related to Take Home Cooking into the subfolder. You could continue to move each message individually, but it is faster to move all of them at once.

To file the remaining Take Home Cooking messages:

1. Click the **This Week's Order** message in the Inbox main window, the first message you want to file.

Tip

Use the Ctrl key to select
nonadjacent messages, and
the Shift key to select a
range of adjacent messages.

▶ **2.** Press and hold the **Ctrl** key and click the remaining two This Week's Order messages ("RE: This Week's Order" and "FW: This Week's Order") in the Inbox main
window.

▶ **3.** Release the **Ctrl** key. The three messages are selected.

▶ **4.** Drag the three selected messages from the Inbox main window into the **Suppliers**
subfolder.

The Inbox is now empty of messages related to Take Home Cooking. However, the
sales figures e-mail does not belong in the Suppliers folder. You'll create a new folder
named "Sales" to file that e-mail.

To create a Sales subfolder:

▶ **1.** Right-click the **Inbox** folder banner, and then click **New Folder**. The Create New
Folder dialog box opens.

▶ **2.** Type **Sales** in the Name box, and then verify that **Mail and Post Items** appears in
the Folder contains box.

▶ **3.** Click **Inbox** in the Select where to place the folder list box if it's not already
selected, and then click the **OK** button. The Sales subfolder appears indented
below the Inbox folder in the Mail Folders group in the Navigation Pane.

Creating Rules

You'll use a rule to move the sales figures message to the Sales folder. Rather than manually filing messages, you can create rules that specify how Outlook should process and
organize them. For example, you can use rules to move messages to a folder based on
their subjects, flag messages about a particular topic, or forward messages to a person or
a distribution list.

Each **rule** includes three parts: the conditions that determine if a message is to be
acted on, the actions that should be applied to qualifying messages, and any exceptions
that remove a message from the qualifying group. For example, a rule might state that all
messages you receive from Julia Shang (condition) are moved to the Suppliers folder
(action) except for ones marked as High importance (exception). Outlook can apply rules
to incoming, outgoing, or stored messages.

You can create a simple rule from common conditions and actions in the Create Rule
dialog box, or use the Rules Wizard, a feature that steps you through the rule-writing
process, to write more complex rules that also include exceptions. As you build a rule,
you continue to refine the sentence that describes the conditions, actions, and
exceptions.

If you are using Outlook with Exchange Server, you must be online to create rules.

You want to create a rule to move all sales messages related to the Sales folder. A message must be selected in order for the Create Rule button to be available. You can select
any message to create a rule. Note that the information from the selected message automatically appears as conditions in the Create Rule dialog box.

To create the rule to move all sales messages to the Sales folder:

▶ 1. In the Navigation Pane, click the **Suppliers** folder, and then click the **Latest Sales** message.

▶ 2. On the Standard toolbar, click the **Create Rule** button 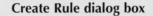. The Create Rule dialog box opens.

▶ 3. Click the **Subject contains** check box to insert a check mark. The Subject text box already contains the subject from the selected message, so you do not need to replace this text.

▶ 4. Click the **Move the item to folder** check box. The Rules and Alerts dialog box opens.

▶ 5. In the Choose a folder list, click the Inbox **plus sign** button ⊞ if necessary, click **Sales**, and then click the **OK** button. The conditions and actions for this rule are set. See Figure 19.

Create Rule dialog box ◀ Figure 19

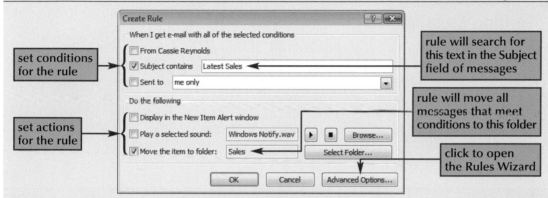

▶ 6. Click the **OK** button. The Success dialog box opens, indicating that the rule "Latest Sales" has been created. You want to run the rule on the message in the Inbox folder.

Trouble? If a dialog box opens and displays the message, "This rule is a client-only rule, and will process only if Outlook is running," then you are set up to run Outlook with Exchange. This message appears because Outlook has determined that the rule requires access to your computer to run. Click the OK button. Outlook saves the rule and adds "(client only)" after the name of the rule in the Rules and Alerts dialog box to remind you that your computer must be logged onto Exchange for the rule to be run.

▶ 7. Uncheck the **Run this rule now on messages already in the current folder** check box, if necessary, and then click the **OK** button.

Next, you'll run the rule.

To run the Latest Sales rule:

▶ 1. Click **Tools** on the menu bar, and then click **Rules and Alerts**. The Rules and Alerts dialog box opens.

▶ 2. On the E-mail Rules tab, click the **Run Rules Now button**. The Run Rules Now dialog box opens.

▶ **3.** Click the **Latest Sales** check box to insert a check mark, read the rule description, and then click the **Run Now** button. The rule runs on the messages in the Inbox folder and the Latest Sales message is moved to the Sales folder.

▶ **4.** Click the **Close** button in the Run Rules Now dialog box, and then click the **OK** button in the Rules and Alerts dialog box.

▶ **5.** In the Mail Folders group in the Navigation Pane, click the **Sales** folder to confirm the Latest Sales message was moved.

Rearranging Messages

As your folder structure becomes more complex and you have more stored messages, it might become difficult to locate a specific message you filed. Finding, using Search Folders, sorting, and changing views provide different ways to organize your messages.

Finding Messages

Rather than searching through multiple folders, you can have Instant Search find the desired message (or any other Outlook item). The Instant Search pane is available below the folder banner in all the main Outlook folders. You select the folder you want to search and then enter search text in the Instant Search box. As you type, items with that search text appear in the main window with the search text highlighted. Attachments are also searched, but the search text is not highlighted in them. To narrow your search, you can click the Expand Query Builder button, and then enter additional criteria. Items that meet the more focused search appear in the main window.

Reference Window	**Finding Messages**

- Open the folder you want to search.
- Type the search text in the Instant Search box.
- To narrow your search, you can click the Expand Query Builder button, and then enter additional criteria.

You'll use Instant Search to look for replies to the This Week's Order message in the Suppliers folder.

To find replies to the This Week's Order message:

▶ **1.** In the Mail Folders group in the Navigation Pane, click the **Suppliers** subfolder to display its contents in the main window.

▶ **2.** Type **RE: This Week's Order** in the Search box below the folder banner, and then click the **Search** button 🔍 , if necessary. The one message that contains "RE: This Week's Order" appears in the main window, and "1" appears in the status bar. See Figure 20.

Instant Search results | Figure 20

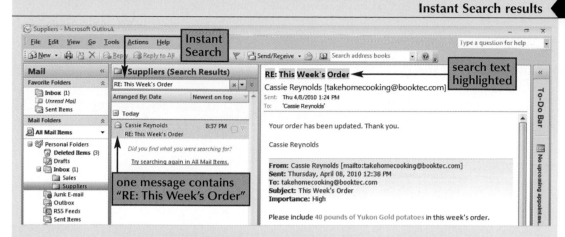

3. Click the **Clear Search** button ☒ in the Instant Search box. All messages in the Suppliers folder reappear in the main window.

Using Search Folders

Another way to find specific messages is with Search Folders. **Search Folders** are folders that display any e-mail messages that match specific search criteria. Any messages that meet the Search Folder's criteria are displayed in that Search Folder but remain stored in their current Outlook folders. This enables you to open one folder to view similar messages, but store them in other folders with a logical filing system. Outlook has several preset Search Folders. For example, the Categorized Mail Search Folder displays messages grouped by their color categories, the Large Mail Search Folder displays any messages larger than 100 KB, and the Unread Mail Search Folder displays all messages that have an unread icon. A message can appear in more than one Search Folder. For example, a message in the blue category that is 200 KB and marked as unread will appear in at least three Search Folders: Categorized, Large Mail, and Unread Mail. You can use the existing Search Folders, customize them to better fit your needs, or create your own Search Folders.

If you delete a Search Folder, the messages that were displayed in that folder are not deleted because they are actually stored in other Outlook folders. However, if you delete an individual message from within a Search Folder, the message is also deleted from its storage folder.

You'll use Search Folders to look for categorized messages and unread messages.

To view the Categorized Mail and Unread Mail Search Folders:

1. In the Mail Folders group in the Navigation Pane, click the **plus sign** button ⊞ next to Search Folders to display three Search Folders—Categorized Mail, Large Mail, and Unread Mail.

   Trouble? If a minus sign button appears next to Search Folders instead of the plus sign button, the folder is already expanded. Continue with Step 2.

> **2.** Click the **Categorized Mail** Search Folder. One message appears in the main window under the green group heading "Sales." See Figure 21. If you had more than one message categorized and used different colors, the messages would appear in different groups.

| Figure 21 | Categorized Mail Search Folder |

Tip

To add a Search Folder, right-click Search Folders in the Mail Folders group in the Navigation Pane, click New Search Folders, select the Search Folder you want to add, and then click the OK button.

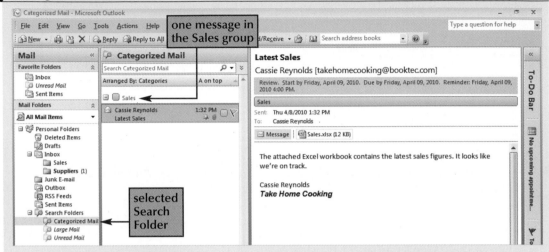

> **3.** Click the **Unread Mail** Search Folder. The contents of the Unread Mail Search Folder appear in the main window. Any messages you haven't yet read are listed.

Switching Views and Arrangements

Another way to manage messages is to change the view or arrangement. You are already familiar with views, which specify how items in a folder are organized and which details are visible. Each Outlook folder has a set of standard views from which you can choose. **Arrangements** are a predefined organization of how items in a view are displayed. Views and arrangements enable you to see the same items in a folder in different ways.

To switch views and arrangements of the Suppliers folder:

> **1.** In the Mail Folders group in the Navigation Pane, click **Suppliers** to display the contents of this folder in the main window.

> **2.** Click **View** on the menu bar, point to **Current View** to display the list of default views, and then click **Messages**. This is the default view, so the folder view in the main window probably didn't change. All the messages appear in the folder arranged according to the date they were received.

> **3.** Click **View** on the menu bar, point to **Arrange By** to display the list of default arrangements, and then click **Conversation**. All the messages appear in the main window grouped according to their Subjects.

> **4.** Click the **Arranged By** column header to display the list of default arrangements, and then click **Importance**. All the messages appear in the main window arranged according to their importance levels, in this case High or Normal. Each level (High, Low, or Normal) becomes a heading for a different group. The other arrangements display the e-mail messages in different ways.

Sorting Messages

Sorting is a way to arrange items in a specific order—either ascending or descending. **Ascending order** arranges messages alphabetically from A to Z, chronologically from earliest to latest, or numerically from lowest to highest. **Descending order** arranges messages in reverse alphabetical, chronological, or numerical order. By default, all messages are sorted in descending order by their Received date and time. You can, however, change the field by which messages are sorted; for example, you might sort e-mail messages alphabetically by sender. Alternatively, you can sort messages by multiple fields; for example, you might sort e-mail messages alphabetically by sender and then by subject. The simplest way to change the sort order is to click a column heading in the folder pane. You would press the Shift key as you click the second sort column.

To sort messages in the Suppliers folder by importance level:

▶ **1.** In the Suppliers main window, click the **High on top** column heading. The Importance sort order changes to ascending, as indicated by the up arrow icon in the column heading. See Figure 22.

Messages sorted in ascending order by importance   **Figure 22**

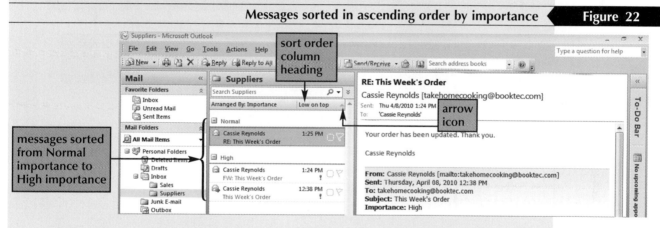

Trouble? If you don't see "on top" as part of the column heading, your main window is too narrow to display the entire column label. Click High to change the sort order to ascending by importance.

Trouble? If there is only a Low on top column heading and the arrow icon points up, then the sort order is already ascending. Continue with Step 2.

▶ **2.** In the main window, click the **Low on top** column heading. The Importance sort order returns to descending, as indicated by the down arrow icon in the column heading.

▶ **3.** In the main window, click the **Arranged By** column heading, and then click **Date**.

You can sort messages in any view except Message Timeline view.

Coloring Messages

Sometimes you'll want messages that you send to a certain person or that you receive from a certain person to stand out from all the other messages. A simple way to do this is to create a rule to change the color of the message headers in the Inbox for those messages. You choose to change all messages to or from a particular person to a color you select. You can also select a color for any messages that are sent only to you. You can set up both these rules in the Organize pane, which also provides another way to move items from one Outlook folder to another and to switch views.

To change the color of messages from you:

▶ **1.** Click **Tools** on the menu bar, and then click **Organize**. The Ways to Organize Suppliers pane opens at the top of the main window.

▶ **2.** Click the **Using Colors** link. The options for setting colors for specific messages appear in the pane. You'll use the first sentence.

▶ **3.** If necessary, click the left arrow, and then click **from**.

▶ **4.** If necessary, click in the middle box, and then type your name.

▶ **5.** If necessary, click the right arrow, and then click **Red**. The rule is complete.

▶ **6.** Click the **Apply Color** button. The rule is applied to the messages in the current folder, and the message headers in the Suppliers folder for messages you sent change to red. See Figure 23.

Figure 23	Organize pane

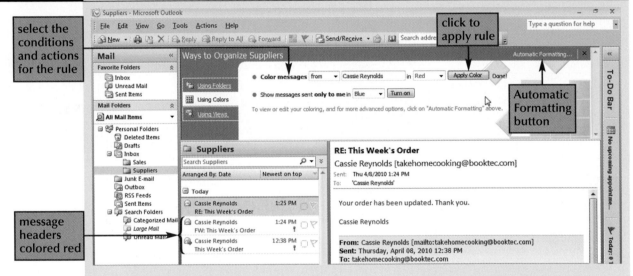

▶ **7.** In the Ways to Organize Suppliers pane, click the **Automatic Formatting** button. The Automatic Formatting dialog box opens.

▶ **8.** In the Rules for this view box, click **Mail received from** your name to select the rule, click the **Delete** button to delete the selected rule, and then click the **OK** button. All the message headers in the Suppliers folder return to the default black.

▶ **9.** Click **Tools** on the menu bar, and then click **Organize**. The Ways to Organize Suppliers pane closes.

You can use different colors to highlight messages to or from different people at one time.

Storing Messages

After a time, you may not need immediate access to the messages you have compiled in the Outlook folders. You can store messages by saving them in other file formats or by archiving them.

Saving Messages

You can use the Save As command to save messages and other Outlook items in other file formats so that you can save them on your hard drive or removable storage device (such as a USB flash drive) just as you save other files, and then delete them from Outlook. You can open such messages with other programs. For example, you can save an e-mail message as a Text Only (.txt) file that most word processing programs can read. You can also save HTML messages as HTML (.htm) files to preserve their original formatting.

Tip

To save a message as a Word document, select and copy the message, paste it into an open document, and then save the document from Word.

To save the This Week's Order message as a text file:

1. In the main window, click the **This Week's Order** message to select it.

2. Click **File** on the menu bar, and then click **Save As**. The Save As dialog box opens, with the message's subject in the File name box.

3. Change the Save in location to the **OUT\Tutorial** folder included with your Data Files.

4. Click the **Save as type** button to display the available file formats from which you can choose, and then click **Text Only** to select that file format.

5. Click the **Save** button. The message is saved as a text file.

Understanding Save As File Formats | InSight

- Outlook Template, Outlook Message Format, Outlook Message Format – Unicode are Outlook formats that can be read only by Outlook. These formats limit your options in sharing the saved files you save.
- Text Only saves the message as plain text but loses any formatting and images. Most word processing programs can read this format. Select this format when you want to save the content of a message without its formatting or images.
- HTML saves the message with all its formatting but stores images in a subfolder. Most Web browsers can read this format. Select this format when you want to save a message's content as well as its formatting and images.
- MHT is a Microsoft format that saves the message with all its formatting and images into a single file that Internet Explorer and most desktop search programs can read. Select this format if you want to consolidate the file and know that you and others with whom you want to share the file have a program that can read this format.

Archiving Mail Messages

Eventually, even the messages in your subfolders can become too numerous to manage easily. More often than not, you don't need immediate access to the older messages. Rather than reviewing your filed messages and moving older ones to a storage file, you can archive them. When you **archive** a folder, you transfer messages or other items stored in a folder (such as an attachment in the e-mail folder) to a personal folder file when the items have reached the age you specify. A **personal folders file** is a special storage file with a .pst extension that contains folders, messages, forms, and files; it can be viewed only in Outlook. Outlook calculates the age of an e-mail message from the date the message was sent or received, whichever is later.

When you create an archive, your existing folder structure from Outlook is recreated in the archive file and all the messages are moved from Outlook into the archive file. If you want to archive only a subfolder, the entire folder structure is still recreated in the archive file; however, only the messages from the selected subfolder are moved into the archive file. For example, if you archive the Suppliers folder, the archive file will include both the Inbox and the Suppliers subfolder, but only the messages in the Suppliers sub-folder will be moved. Any messages in the Inbox remain in the Outlook Inbox. All folders remain in place within Outlook after archiving—even empty ones.

You can manually archive a folder at any time, such as when you finish a project or event. You specify which folders to archive, the age of items to archive, and the name and location of the archive file.

To manually archive a folder:

▶ 1. Click **File** on the menu bar, and then click **Archive**. The Archive dialog box opens.

▶ 2. If necessary, click the **Archive this folder and all subfolders** option button.

▶ 3. If necessary, click the **plus sign** button ⊞ next to Inbox to display the subfolders, and then click the **Suppliers** folder.

▶ 4. Type **tomorrow** in the Archive items older than box, and then press the **Tab** key. Outlook will move any files dated with today's date or earlier to the archive file.

▶ 5. Click the **Browse** button. The Open Personal Folders dialog box opens.

▶ 6. Change the Save in location to the **OUT\Tutorial** folder included with your Data Files, type **Suppliers Archive** as the filename, and then click the **OK** button.

▶ 7. Click the **OK** button in the Archive dialog box.

▶ 8. Click the **Yes** button to confirm that you want to archive all the items in the folder. All the messages in the Suppliers folder are moved into the archive file you specified. The empty Suppliers folder remains in the folder structure.

▶ 9. Repeat Steps 1 through 8 to create an archive for the **Sales** folder named **Sales Archive**.

The archive folders are open and displayed in the Folder List. You can access items in your archive files several ways: open the file using the Open command on the File menu and then drag the items you need to a current folder; add the archive file to your profile; or restore all the items in the archive file by using the Import and Export command on the File menu. If you don't need access to the archive folders, you can close them.

To close archive folders:

▶ 1. In the Navigation Pane, scroll down to see the two archive folders at the end of the list.

▶ 2. In the Folder List, right-click the top **Archive Folders**, and then click **Close "Archive Folders."** The folder closes.

▶ 3. In the Folder List, right-click the remaining **Archive Folders**, and then click **Close "Archive Folders."** The folder closes.

Archived folders let you keep the contents of your folders manageable and current while providing the security of knowing older information is available if you need access to the information.

Deleting Items and Exiting Outlook

After you finish working with Outlook, you should exit the program. Unlike other programs, you don't need to save or close any files. Before you exit, however, you'll delete the rule and each of the items you created in this tutorial. Deleted items are moved into the Deleted Items folder. This folder acts like the Recycle Bin in Windows. Items you delete stay in this folder until you empty it.

To delete the rule, items you created, and your signature:

1. Click **Tools** on the menu bar, and then click **Rules and Alerts**. The Rules and Alerts dialog box opens with the E-mail Rules tab active.

2. Click **Latest Sales** in the Rule (applied in the order shown) box to select the rule, and then click the **Delete** button on the toolbar at the top of the tab.

3. Click the **Yes** button to confirm the deletion, and then click the **OK** button to close the Rules and Alerts dialog box. The rule is deleted.

4. In the Navigation Pane, in the Mail Folders group, click the **Suppliers** folder.

5. On the Standard toolbar, click the **Delete** button ⊠, and then click the **Yes** button to confirm that the folder and all of its messages should be moved to the Deleted Items folder.

6. In the Folder List, click the **Sales** folder, click the **Delete** button ⊠ on the Standard toolbar, and then click the **Yes** button to confirm that the folder and all of its messages should be moved to the Deleted Items folder.

7. In the Favorite Folders group, click the **Sent Items** folder, click the first message you sent in this tutorial, press and hold the **Ctrl** key as you click each additional message you sent in this tutorial, release the **Ctrl** key, and then click the **Delete** button ⊠ on the Standard toolbar. The messages move to the Deleted Items folder.

8. In the Navigation Pane, click the **Contacts** button, press and hold the **Ctrl** key as you click each of the four contacts and one distribution list contact you created in this tutorial, release the **Ctrl** key, and then press the **Delete** key. The contacts you created for this tutorial are deleted.

9. In the Navigation Pane, click the **Folder List** button 🖿.

10. In the All Folders group, right-click the **Deleted Items** folder, click **Empty "Deleted Items" Folder** on the shortcut menu, and then click the **Yes** button to confirm the deletion. The folder empties and the items are permanently deleted.

11. Click **Tools** on the menu bar, click **Options** to open the Options dialog box, and then click the **Mail Format** tab.

12. Click the **Signatures** button, click **Take Home Cooking** in the Select signature to edit box, and then click the **Delete** button.

13. Click the **Yes** button to confirm that you want to delete this signature.

14. Click the **OK** button in the Signatures and Stationery dialog box, and then click the **OK** button in the Options dialog box.

Review | Session 2 Quick Check

1. Explain the difference between Reply and Reply to All.
2. True or False? You can save a file attached to a message, but you cannot open the attachment from within Outlook.
3. How do you move an e-mail message from the Inbox to a subfolder?
4. What is a Search Folder?
5. What is the purpose of a rule?
6. What does it mean to archive a folder?

Review | Tutorial Summary

In this tutorial, you learned about the Outlook components, started Outlook, viewed its window elements, and navigated between components. You created and sent e-mail messages. You created and organized a contact list and created a distribution group. You received, read, replied to, forwarded, and printed e-mail messages. Then you added and read attachments to e-mail messages. You organized messages in subfolders by filing them manually and using a rule to move them. You rearranged messages by changing a folder's view and arrangement, and sorting the messages. Finally, you saved messages in other formats, archived messages within a folder, and then deleted items you created.

Key Terms

archive
arrangement
ascending order
attachment
Calendar
color category
contact
contact card
Contacts
descending order
distribution list
e-mail
e-mail address
emoticon
field
flag
folder

folder banner
Folder List
Forward
host name
item
Journal
Mail
main window
message body
message header
Microsoft Office Outlook
   2007 (Outlook)
Navigation Pane
netiquette
Notes
offline

password
personal folders file
Reading Pane
Reply
Reply to All
rule
Search Folder
signature
smiley
sort
stationery
Tasks
theme
user ID
vCard
view

Practice	**Review Assignments**

Practice the skills you learned in the tutorial.

Data File needed for the Review Assignments: Organic.docx

Cassie Reynolds asks you to help her with customer communication for Take Home Cooking. Complete the following:

1. Create a signature that uses your name and **Cooking Representative** as your title. Apply the signature to new messages and replies and forwards.

2. Create a new e-mail message addressed to your e-mail address with the subject **Welcome New Cook** and the message **Welcome to Take Home Cooking. We're sure you'll enjoy cooking healthy meals with us. We do the hard part—the planning, the shopping, and all the clean up—and leave the fun part for you—cooking.**

3. Format the text of your e-mail in 12-point Times New Roman.

4. Send the e-mail to the Outbox and then to your mail server.

5. Create a contact card for **Cassie Reynolds** at **Take Home Cooking** with a fictional business mailing address and business phone number; use your e-mail address.

6. Create contact cards for the following three customers at their home addresses, using your e-mail address. (*Hint:* Click the arrow button in the address section, and then click Home.)

   - **Alex Runyon, 384 Leavenworth Street, San Francisco, CA 94103, 415-555-1232**
   - **Mai Ching, 1938 Grant Avenue, San Francisco, CA 94110, 415-555-0907**
   - **Perry Walker, 2938 Golden Gate Avenue, San Francisco, CA 94124, 415-555-6497**

7. Create a distribution list named **Customers** that includes Mai Ching, Alex Runyon, and Perry Walker.

8. Edit Mai Ching's contact card to change the address to **1938 Presidio Street**.

9. Create an e-mail message addressed to **Cassie Reynolds** with **Organic Ingredients** as the subject and **Do you use any organic foods in your recipes?** as the message body. Send the e-mail to the Outbox and then to your mail server.

10. Download your new messages. If the Organic Ingredients message hasn't arrived, wait a few minutes and try again.

11. Reply to the Organic Ingredients message with the text: **Take Home Cooking provides all organic ingredients for our recipes. In addition, we are committed to using foods that are locally grown and in season. The attached file explains our philosophy.**

12. Attach the **Organic** document located in the OUT\Review folder included with your Data Files to the file, and then send the message to your Outbox.

13. Forward the Organic Ingredients message to Cassie Reynolds with the message: **Let's add this information to our Web site.** Mark the message as High importance. Send the message to the Outbox.

14. Send all messages in your Outbox to your mail server.

15. Create a new folder named **Customers** that contains Mail and Post Items placed in the Inbox folder.

16. Create a rule to move messages you receive from yourself to the Customers folder. Run the rule now.

17. Download your messages, and verify that the Welcome New Cook message and the three Organic Ingredients messages were filed in the Customers subfolder.

18. Add a blue color category to the Organic Ingredients message.

19. Find the three messages in the Customers folder that contain the word **organic**.

20. Save each of the messages that were found in HTML format to the OUT\Review folder included with your Data Files (if your server does not support HTML, save the messages in Text Only format).

21. Save the attachment in the RE: Organic Ingredients message as **Organic Philosophy** in the OUT\Review folder included with your Data Files.

22. Print the RE: Organic Ingredients message and its attachment. (*Hint:* In the Print dialog box, check the Print attached files check box.)

23. Archive all the messages in the Customers folder to the OUT\Review folder included with your Data Files, using the filename **Cooking Archive**. Close the archive folder.

24. Delete each Outlook item you created, the signature, the rule, the subfolder, the messages in the Sent Items folder, and the contacts, and then empty the Deleted Items folder.

| Apply | **Case Problem 1** |

Apply what you learned in the tutorial to send and respond to e-mail messages for a car sharing company.

Data File needed for this Case Problem: Frieda Cohn.vcf

AutoLink   For urban dwellers who drive fewer than 10,000 miles per year, car sharing is a popular alternative to owning a car. AutoLink, a car sharing company founded by Mitchell Scott in 2001, has cars located throughout Philadelphia's neighborhoods, close to members' homes and workplaces. Members reserve cars by the hour and pay a small fee in addition to their annual dues. You'll use Outlook to send e-mail to some of AutoLink's members. Complete the following:

1. Display the Contacts folder, and then create the following new contacts, using the Save & New button to create each new contact:

   - Full name **Joe Weiss**; company name **Ace Home Care**; job title **Nurse**; your e-mail address; mobile phone **215-555-8712**; home mailing address **17 University Ave., Philadelphia PA 19287**; spouse's name **Eva Lorenson**

   - Full name **Ann Morell**; company name **A Plus Insurance**; job title **Agent**; your e-mail address; business phone **215-555-3100**; home phone **215-555-3101**; home mailing address **2949 Broad St., Philadelphia PA 19157**; spouse's name **Charley Boyd**

   - Full name **Walt Camden**; your e-mail address; home phone **215-555-6741**; home mailing address **841 Carpenter St., Philadelphia PA 19157**

   - Full name **Michael Lang**; job title **Student**; your e-mail address; home phone **215-555-8715**; mobile phone **215-555-2145**; home mailing address **78 Carpenter St., Philadelphia PA 19109**; nickname **Mike**

   - Full name **Mitchell Scott**; company name **AutoLink**; job title **President**; your e-mail address; business phone **215-555-9797**; business fax **215-555-9701**; pager **215-555-2157**; business mailing address **2932 12th St., Philadelphia PA 19102**

2. View the contacts as Detailed Address Cards in the Contacts main window.

3. Edit Ann Morell's contact card to add **215-555-6110** as her mobile phone number.

4. Create a distribution list called **AutoLink Members** that includes all members with an e-mail address; do not include Mitchell Scott.

✦ **EXPLORE**

5. Send Mitchell Scott's contact information as a vCard. Right-click Mitchell Scott's contact card, point to Send Full Contact, and then click In Internet Format. A Message window opens with the contact card included as an attachment. Send the message to the AutoLink Members distribution list, use **FW: Mitchell Scott's Contact Info** as the Subject, and include the message **Attached is the contact information for Mitchell Scott, president of AutoLink. If you have questions or comments about AutoLink, please contact him directly.** followed by your name on a separate line.

6. Send a new e-mail message to Mitchell Scott with the subject **Frieda Cohn's contact** and no message; attach the vCard file **Frieda Cohn** located in the OUT\Case1 folder included with your Data Files.

✦ **EXPLORE**

7. Download your messages, select the Frieda Cohn's contact message, drag the vCard attachment icon from the Reading Pane to the Contacts folder in the Navigation Pane, and then save and close the new contact card.

8. Create a new folder named **AutoLink** that contains Mail and Post Items placed in the Inbox folder.

9. Find all messages in the Inbox related to the subject **contact**.

10. Save the two messages you found as HTML files in the OUT\Case1 folder included with your Data Files, and then file them in the AutoLink folder.

11. Archive the AutoLink subfolder as **AutoLink Archive** in the OUT\Case1 folder included with your Data Files. Close the archive.

12. Delete the AutoLink folder, the two messages in the Sent Items folder, and the six contacts and one distribution list, and then empty the Deleted Items folder.

Challenge | Case Problem 2

Extend what you've learned to create e-mail information about club members.

There are no Data Files needed for this Case Problem.

40 Lanes Emily Rose owns 40 Lanes, a bowling alley that hosts a bowling league on Tuesday evenings and Saturday mornings. Emily has collected a list of customers who have expressed interest in joining the bowling league. She is planning a party at the alley where these potential league members can meet and create a new team. Complete the following:

1. Create contact cards for five potential bowling league members. Include their names, addresses, phone numbers, and e-mail addresses. Enter your e-mail address for each contact. Create a contact card for Emily Rose that includes her name, company name, and your e-mail address.

2. Create a distribution list named **Potential Members** that includes the contact cards of all the potential bowling league members.

3. Edit three contacts to include one item of personal information, such as a birthday or spouse's name.

✦ **EXPLORE**

4. Create an e-mail message using stationery for the party invitation. With the Inbox selected, click Actions on the menu bar, point to New Mail Message Using, click More Stationery, select the stationery you want, and then click the OK button. Address the invitation to the Potential Members distribution list. Type an appropriate subject.

5. Enter an appropriate message for the invitation; be sure to include the day, time, and place of the party. Format the message text appropriately. Send the message to the Outbox and then to your mail server.

6. Create a new folder named **Bowling** that contains Mail and Post Items placed in the Inbox folder, and then move the invitation e-mail into the subfolder.

7. Switch to the Contacts folder, and then change the view to Detailed Address Cards.

8. Create a new folder named **Team** that contains Contact Items placed in the Contacts folder, and then move the contact cards you created for this Case Problem into it. (*Hint:* Make sure you change the Folder contains box to Contact Items in the Create New Folder dialog box.)

⊕ EXPLORE   9. Export your contact list. Click File on the menu bar, and then click Import and Export. Click Export to a file, and then click the Next button. Click Microsoft Access 97-2003, and then click the Next button. If necessary, click the plus button next to Contacts to display the Teams subfolder, select the subfolder, and then click the Next button. Use the Browse button to save the file as **Bowling List** to the OUT\Case2 folder included with your Data Files. Click the Next button, and then click the Finish button. The contact list is exported as an Access database.

10. Download your message, and then save it as an HTML file in the OUT\Case2 folder included with your Data Files. (You might receive only one message because you used the same e-mail addresses for all your contacts.)

11. Archive the messages in the Bowling subfolder as **Bowling Archive** in the OUT\Case2 folder included with your Data Files.

⊕ EXPLORE   12. Expand the Archive folder files, and then copy the Teams subfolder to the archive. Click the Teams subfolder, press and hold the Ctrl key as you drag the folder to the archive file, and then release the Ctrl key. Close the archive file.

13. Delete the rule you created, the Bowling subfolder, the Teams subfolder with the contacts you created, and the messages in the Sent Items folder, and then empty the Deleted Items folder.

Review | Quick Check Answers

Session 1

1. The Inbox stores e-mail messages you have received; the Outbox stores e-mail messages you have written but not yet sent.
2. The electronic transfer of messages between computers on the Internet. It's an inexpensive way to communicate with others who are nearby or far away. You can send and read messages at your convenience.
3. Text that is automatically added to every e-mail message you send, such as your name, job title, and company name.
4. a contact's name, job title, company name and address, phone and fax numbers, as well as personal information such as birthdays, anniversaries, and children's names
5. Creates a contact card for a group of people to whom you frequently send the same messages; a distribution list saves time and ensures that you don't inadvertently omit someone.

Session 2

1. Reply responds to only the sender of the e-mail message; Reply to All responds to the sender and any other recipients of the e-mail message.
2. False
3. Drag the message from the Inbox pane to the subfolder in the Folder List.
4. a folder that displays any e-mail messages that match specific search criteria; messages are stored in their current Outlook folder.
5. specifies how Outlook should process and organize your e-mail messages
6. moves items you selected from Outlook into a personal folder file

Ending Data Files

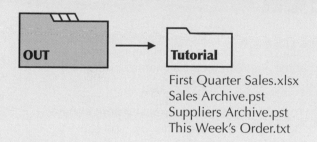

OUT → **Tutorial**

First Quarter Sales.xlsx
Sales Archive.pst
Suppliers Archive.pst
This Week's Order.txt

Review

Cooking Archive.pst
FW Organic Ingredients.htm
Organic Ingredients.htm
Organic Philosophy.docx
RE Organic Ingredients.htm

Case1

AutoLink Archive.pst
Frieda Cohn's contact.htm
FW Mitchell Scott's Contact Info.htm

Case2

Bowling Archive.pst
Bowling List.mdb
Join a New Bowling Team.htm

Reality Check

Outlook is a great way to organize all your e-mails and contacts for business, school, and personal use. To make it even more functional, you can create signatures, rules, and an organization system that fits your personal work style and needs.

Note: Please be sure *not* to include any personal information of a sensitive nature in the files you create to be submitted to your instructor for this exercise. Later on, you can update your data in Outlook with such information for your own personal use.

1. Start Outlook, and set up your e-mail account, if needed.
2. Create at least one signature that includes your name and other information you consider important to include. Format the signature appropriately.
3. Create at least five contacts with names, e-mail addresses, and at least two other pieces of information.
4. Create a distribution list that includes at least three contacts; use an appropriate name to identify the distribution list, such as Family or Friends.
5. Write an e-mail message to send to your distribution list. You can send an appropriate holiday message, life update, or your upcoming vacation schedule.
6. Format the e-mail appropriately.
7. Attach a relevant file, such as a picture or travel itinerary. Send the message.
8. Reply to any responses you receive to your e-mail.
9. Create folders in which to organize your e-mail messages logically.
10. File your messages in your folder.
11. Create a rule that colors messages from one or more contacts in a specific color. For example, you could color all messages from your family in red.
12. Submit your completed messages and contact information to your instructor as requested. Include printouts of any items, if required.

Glossary/Index

distribution lists, OUT 21–23

exiting, OUT 41

finding messages, OUT 34–36

navigating between components, OUT 4–5

Outlook window, OUT 3–4

sorting messages, OUT 37

starting, OUT 2–3

storing messages, OUT 38–40

switching views and arrangements, OUT 36

Microsoft Office Power Point 2007 A presentation graphics program you use to create a presentation in the form of on-screen slides, a slide presentation in a Web site, or black-and-white or color overheads; the slides can contain text, charts, and pictures. OFF 2, PPT 1, PPT 2

starting, PPT 2

Microsoft Office Word 2007 A word-processing program you use to create text documents. OFF 2, WD 1

Microsoft Windows Vista The most recent version of the Windows operating system. WIN 2

desktop elements, WIN 3

starting, WIN 2–4

turning off, WIN 39–40

MIN function, EX 122

Mini toolbar A toolbar that appears next to the pointer whenever you select text and contains buttons for the most commonly used formatting commands, such as font, font size, styles, color, alignment, and indents that may appear in different groups or tabs on the Ribbon. OFF 15–16

Minimum function, AC 137

minus sign (–), AC 104, EX 28

mistake. *See* error correction

mixed reference Cell reference that contains both relative and absolute references, for example, B$4. EX 118–120

mode The most common value in data. EX 121

MONTH function, EX 145

most frequently used programs list A list of programs on the Start menu you have opened recently. WIN 9, WIN 10

mouse A pointing device that has a rolling ball on its underside and two or more buttons for clicking commands; you control the movement of the pointer by moving the entire mouse around on your desk. WIN 5

entering cell references in formulas, EX 30

with scroll wheel, WIN 25

move a file To remove a file from its current location and place it in a new location. FM 12–13

moving

bullets, PPT 16

cell ranges, EX 24–25

fields in tables, AC 62–63

insertion point, WD 18–19

slides, in Slide Sorter view, PPT 23–24

text. *See* moving text

worksheets, EX 36

moving text

cutting or copying and pasting, WD 57–61

dragging and dropping, WD 54–57

multiple lines, selecting, WD 30

multiple paragraphs, selecting, WD 30

multiple recipients, sending e-mail messages, OUT 11

multiplication operator (*), EX 28

multitable query, AC 110–111

multitask To work on more than one task at a time and to switch quickly between projects. WIN 12–16

closing programs from taskbar, WIN 16

switching between programs, WIN 14–16

N

Name box The box located on the far left of the Formula bar in which the cell reference to the active cell is also displayed. EX 5

naming files, FM 14–15

navigate To move from one location to another on the computer, such as from one window to another.

Computer window, WIN 27–31, WIN 34

to data files, FM 8–10

between Outlook components, OUT 4

presentations, PPT 4–5

Windows Explorer, WIN 33–35

worksheets, EX 6–7

navigation buttons A set of buttons found at the bottom of a table datasheet or form that you use to move through the records in the table. AC 22–23

navigation mode The mode in which Access selects an entire field value, and your typed entry replaces the highlighted field value. AC 100

Navigation Pane (Access) The area on the left of the program window that lists all the objects in the database. AC 7, AC 142–143

Navigation Pane (Outlook) A central tool for accessing Outlook folders, or files and folders on your computer or network, that contains buttons to access additional panes within the Navigation Pane. OUT 3

nested Functions or other parts of a formula placed inside another function. EX 123

netiquette Short for Internet etiquette; customs of behavior for communicating by e-mail. OUT 10

nonadjacent range Cell range that is comprised of two or more separate adjacent ranges. EX 21

selecting, EX 22

nonprinting characters Symbols that can appear on the screen but are not visible on the printed page. WD 8–9

nontheme font In Excel, a font that can be used no matter what theme the workbook has. EX 59

nonunique sort field A sort field for which more than one record can have the same value. AC 113

Normal view (Excel) The view that renders the workbook and worksheets for the computer screen. EX 41

Normal view (PowerPoint) A view designed for working with slide content that shows how text and graphics look on each slide. PPT 4

not equal to operator (<>), EX 141

note Information on the slide for the presenter; also called a speaker note. PPT 27–28

Notes An Outlook folder in which you can jot down ideas and thoughts that you can group, sort, and categorize. OUT 2

notes pane The area of the PowerPoint window that contains speaker notes. PPT 4

notification area, WIN 3

NOW function, EX 145

NPER function, EX 146

null value The value that results from not entering a value for a field; a null value is not permitted for a primary key. AC 61

number data A numerical value that can be used in a mathematical calculation. EX 9

entering in cells, EX 13–15

formatting in worksheets, EX 65–66

Number data type, AC 49

Field Size property, AC 50

numbered list A list of paragraphs that are numbered consecutively. PPT 12

Numbering Library A panel in the Numbering menu that contains a variety of numbered list formats. WD 76–77

O

object Anything that can be manipulated independently as a whole, such as a chart, table, picture, video, or sound clip. OFF 15

object in a database

grouping in Navigation pane, AC 142–143

naming, AC 48

Select All button, Excel, EX 4, EX 5

select query A query in which you specify the fields and records you want Access to select, and the results are returned in the form of a datasheet. AC 104

selection bar The blank space in the left margin area of the Document window. WD 29

selection criteria for queries. *See* record selection criteria

sending e-mail, OUT 13–14

sensitivity, e-mail messages, OUT 12, OUT 13

sentence, selecting, WD 30

series, filling with AutoFill, EX 134–137

serif font A font that includes small horizontal lines (called serifs) at the tops and bottoms of letters. EX 59

set (a property) To select or enter a property for a field. AC 48

shared printer, WD 35

sharing styles and themes, EX 80

sheet. *See* chart sheet; worksheet

sheet tab The area at the bottom of a worksheet that identifies the worksheet; clicking a sheet tab makes the worksheet active. EX 4, EX 5

sheet tab scrolling button, Excel, EX 4, EX 5

shortcut A special type of file that serves as a direct link to another location that your computer can access, such as a folder, a document in a file, a program, a Windows tool, or a Web site. WIN 30

shortcut menu A list of commands directly related to the object that you right-clicked. OFF 17, WIN 8

Show/Hide ** button, Word window, WD 8, WD 47

sidebar, WIN 3

signature Text that is automatically added to every e-mail message you send. OUT 7–9

simple interest The type of interest in which the interest paid is equal to a percentage of principal for each period that the money has been lent. EX 147

Simple Query Wizard An Access wizard that lets you quickly select the records and fields for a query. AC 24–26

Single A Field Size property that stores positive and negative numbers to precisely seven decimal places and uses four bytes. AC 50

6 x 6 rule In PowerPoint, a rule for keeping each bulleted item to no more than six words and including no more than six bulleted items on a slide. PPT 12

sizing button, OFF 6, WIN 17

sizing handle A circle or square on the border of a selected object, such as a graphic, that you can drag to change the object's size. PPT 11

slash (/), division operator, EX 28

slide

content, PPT 12

creating by promoting outline text, PPT 22–23

deleting, PPT 17–19

editing. *See* editing slides

first, starting show from, PPT 5

moving in Slide Sorter view, PPT 23–24

new, adding, PPT 19–21

slide pane The area of the PowerPoint window that shows the current slide as it will look during the slide show. PPT 4

Slide Show view A PowerPoint view that displays the slide show presentation and fills the entire screen. PPT 4, PPT 5–8

Slide Sorter view A PowerPoint view that hides the Slides and Outline tabs and displays slides as thumbnails. PPT 4–5, PPT 31

moving slides, PPT 23–24

slide transition The manner in which a new slide appears on the screen during a slide show. PPT 5

Slides tab The area of the PowerPoint window that shows a column of numbered slide thumbnails so that you can *see* a visual representation of several slides at once. PPT 4

smiley. *See* emoticon

sort (Access) To rearrange records in a specified order or sequence. AC 112–115

AutoFilter, AC 112–113

sorting multiple fields in Design view, AC 113–115

sort (Outlook) To arrange items in a specific order-either ascending or descending. OUT 37

sort field The field used to determine the order of records in a datasheet. AC 112

primary, AC 113

secondary, AC 113

spacebar as toggle bar for Yes/No field, AC 67

speaker note. *See* note

spell checking, PPT 24–26

Spelling and Grammar checker A feature that checks a document against Word's built-in dictionary and a set of grammar rules. WD 50–52

spelling checker A feature that checks the words in a document against the program's built-in dictionary and helps you avoid typographical errors. EX 39–40, WD 21–24

spreadsheet A tool used in business for budgeting, inventory management, and decision making for analyzing and reporting information. EX 2–3

Standard Buttons toolbar, exploring files and folders, FM 6

standard color A color that is always available regardless of the workbook's theme. EX 60

star symbol The symbol that appears in a row selector to indicate that the row is the next one available for a new record. AC 13

Start button, WIN 3

Start menu A menu that provides access to programs, documents, and much more. WIN 6, WIN 9–12

Start Search box A text box on the Start menu that helps you quickly find anything stored on your computer, including programs, documents, pictures, music, videos, Web pages, and e-mail messages. WIN 9, WIN 10

starting

Office programs, OFF 3–5

Outlook, OUT 2–3

PowerPoint, PPT 2

stationery Background colors, images, or patterns for e-mail messages. OUT 9

Statistical functions, EX 122

status bar An area at the bottom of the program window that contains information about the open file or the current task on which you are working. WIN 17

getting information, OFF 7–8

Office programs, OFF 6

style A saved collection of formatting options—number formats, text alignment, font sizes and colors, borders, and background fills—that can be applied to cells in a worksheet. EX 76–78

applying, EX 77–78

sharing, EX 80

table. *See* table style

sub-bullet. *See* second-level bullet

subdatasheet A datasheet that displays the records related to the current record. AC 103

subfolder A folder contained within another folder. FM 3, FM 10, WIN 49

submenu A list of choices that extend from a main menu. WIN 5

subtraction operator (–), EX 28

SUM function, EX 122, EX 124–125

Sum function, AC 137

switching

between programs and files, OFF 5, WIN 14–16

views, OFF 8, PPT 4–5

syntax Rules that specify how a function should be written; the general syntax of all Excel functions is FUNCTION(argument1, argument2, . . .). EX 121–123

user name A unique name that identifies you to Windows Vista; also the name that you enter or have been assigned when your e-mail account is being set up. WIN 2

V

value, interpretation in Access, AC 14

vCard A file that contains a contact's personal information, such as the contact's name, mailing address, phone numbers and e-mail address; compatible with popular communication and information management programs and PDAs. OUT 21

vertical scroll bar, Excel, EX 4, EX 5

view. *See also specific views*
 changing, WIN 31–33
 switching, OFF 8, PPT 4–5

view (Outlook) Specifies how information in a folder is organized and which details are visible. OUT 18
 switching, OUT 36

view button, Word window, WD 5

view shortcut
 Excel, EX 4, EX 5
 Office programs, OFF 6

viewing
 attachments to e-mail messages, OUT 28–29
 presentations in Slide Show view, PPT 5–8

W

WEEKDAY function, EX 145

Welcome Center window, WIN 3

what-if analysis An approach using an electronic spreadsheet in which you change one or more of the values in the worksheet and then examine the recalculated values to determine the effect of the change. EX 2

window A rectangular area of the screen that contains a program, text, graphics, or data. WIN 4. *See also specific windows*
 manipulating, WIN 18–21
 resizing, OFF 6–7, WIN 21

window element, common, OFF 6–10

window title, WIN 17

Windows Basics category, Windows Help and Support, WIN 37

Windows Explorer A tool that shows the files, folders, and drives on your computer, making it easy to navigate, or move from one location to another within the file hierarchy. FM 5, FM 7–8
 exploring files and folders, FM 5–6, FM 7–8
 navigating with, WIN 33–35

Windows Vista. *See* Microsoft Windows Vista

Word. *See* Microsoft Office Word 2007

word, selecting, WD 30

Word window, WD 3–5
 displaying nonprinting characters, WD 8–9
 displaying rulers, WD 7–8
 elements, WD 4–5
 font and font size, WD 9
 Home tab, WD 8
 Print Layout view, WD 6–7
 Zoom setting, WD 9–11

word wrap Automatic line breaking. WD 13

workbook The file in which Excel stores an electronic spreadsheet. EX 4, OFF 2
 effective, EX 8
 formatting, EX 58. *See also* formatting worksheet cells; formatting worksheets
 planning, EX 8–9
 saving, EX 21

workbook window Window in which a workbook is displayed; also called worksheet window. EX 4, EX 5

worksheet Each workbook is made up of individual worksheets, or sheets containing formulas, functions, values, text, and graphics. EX 4, EX 35–46
 changing view, EX 41–42
 copying, EX 36
 deleting, EX 35
 editing, EX 36–40
 finding and replacing items, EX 38–39

formatting. *See* formatting worksheet cells; formatting worksheets
formulas. *See* formulas
functions. *See* functions
 inserting, EX 35
 moving, EX 36
 navigating, EX 6–7
 page orientation, EX 42–43
 previewing, EX 40–43
 printing, EX 43
 redoing actions, EX 38
 renaming, EX 35–36
 scrolling, EX 7
 spell checking, EX 39–40
 undoing actions, EX 37–38

workspace, WIN 17
 Office programs, OFF 6
 resizing, OFF 6–7
 zooming, OFF 8–10

Y

YEAR function, EX 145

Yes/No data type, AC 49

Yes/No field, spacebar as toggle bar, AC 67

Z

zoom To magnify or shrink your view of a window. OFF 8
 workspace, OFF 8–10

Zoom box A large text box you can use to enter text, expressions, or other values when working with queries. AC 133

zoom control
 Excel, EX 4, EX 5
 Office programs, OFF 6

Zoom level A setting that controls a document's on-screen magnification. WD 9–11
 viewing margin, WD 65

Task Reference

TASK	PAGE #	RECOMMENDED METHOD
Absolute reference, change to relative	EX 119	*See* Reference Window: Entering Relative, Absolute, and Mixed References
Access, start	AC 5	Click 🔵, click All Programs, click Microsoft Office, click Microsoft Office Access 2007
Action, redo	EX 38, WD 20	Click ↻
Action, undo	EX 38, WD 20	Click ↺
Actions, redo several	EX 38	Click ↻ ▾, select the action(s) to redo
Actions, undo several	EX 38	Click ↺ ▾, select the action(s) to undo
Aggregate functions, use in a datasheet	AC 138	Open table or query in Datasheet view, in Records group on Home tab click Totals button, click Total field row, click function
Aggregate functions, use in a query	AC 139	Display the query in Design view, click Totals button in the Show/Hide group on the Query Tools Design tab
Archive folder, close	OUT 40	Right-click 📎 Archive Folder in Folder List, click Close "Archive Folder"
Arrangement, switch	OUT 36	Click View, point to Arrange By, click desired arrangement
Attachment, add to e-mail	OUT 27	In Message window, click 📎, select file location, double-click file to insert
Attachment, save	OUT 28	Right-click 📎 in Reading Pane or Message window, click Save As, select save location, enter filename, click Save
Attachment, view	OUT 28	Click 📎 in Reading Pane, click Preview file
AutoFill, copy formulas	EX 132	*See* Reference Window: Copying Formulas and Formats with AutoFill
AutoFill, create series	EX 135	*See* Reference Window: Creating a Series with AutoFill
AutoCorrect, set options	WD 21	Click 📋, click Word Options, click Proofing, click AutoCorrect Options
AutoSum, apply	EX 33	Click cell, in Editing group on Home tab click Σ, click AutoSum function
Background color, apply	EX 61	Select range, in Font group on Home tab click 🎨 ▾, click color
Boldface, add to text	WD 78	Select text, in Font group on Home tab click **B**
Border, create	EX 71	Select range, in Font group on Home tab click ⊞ ▾, click border
Bullets, add to paragraph	WD 74	Select paragraph, in Paragraph group on Home tab click ☰
Calculated field, add to a query	AC 133	*See* Reference Window: Using Expression Builder
Cell, clear contents of	EX 20	Right-click cell, click Clear Contents
Cell, edit	EX 37	Double-click cell, enter changes
Cell reference, change	EX 119	*See* Reference Window: Entering Relative, Absolute, and Mixed References
Cells, delete	EX 20	Select range, click Delete button in Cells group on Home tab
Cells, insert	EX 19	*See* Reference Window: Inserting a Column or Row
Cells, merge and center	EX 70	Select adjacent cells, in Alignment group on Home tab click ▦
Clipboard, use to cut, copy, and paste	WD 57	*See* Reference Window: Cutting (or Copying) and Pasting Text
Clipboard task pane, open	WD 57	In Clipboard group on Home tab, click Clipboard

TASK	PAGE #	RECOMMENDED METHOD
Column, change width	EX 16	*See* Reference Window: Changing the Column Width or Row Height
Column, insert	EX 19	*See* Reference Window: Inserting a Column or Row
Column, resize width in a datasheet	AC 12	Double-click ↔ on the right border of the column heading
Column, select	EX 19	Click column heading; to select a range of columns, click the first column heading in the range, hold down Shift and click the last column heading
Compressed files, extract	FM 18	Right-click compressed folder, click Extract All, select location, click Extract
Compressed folder, create	FM 17	Right-click a blank area of a folder window, point to New, click Compressed (zipped) Folder
Computer, open	WIN 22	Click 🏁, click Computer
Conditional format, apply	EX 87	*See* Reference Window: Applying Conditional Formats (Data Bars and Highlights)
Contact, create	OUT 15	*See* Reference Window: Creating a Contact
Contact, edit	OUT 21	In Contacts window, switch to Address Cards or Detailed Address Cards view, click in contact card, edit text as usual, click outside contact card
Contact, forward by e-mail	OUT 21	Right-click contact card in Contacts folder, click Send as Business Card
Contacts view, change	OUT 19	Click Contacts button in Navigation Pane, click option button in Current View pane
Database, compact and repair	AC 34	*See* Reference Window: Compacting and Repairing a Database
Database, compact on close	AC 34	Click 🏁, click Access Options, click Current Database, click Compact on Close
Database, create a blank	AC 6	Start Access, click Blank Database, type the database name, select the drive and folder, click OK, click Create
Database, open	AC 20	*See* Reference Window: Opening a Database
Datasheet view for tables, switch to	AC 77	In the Views group on the Table Tools Design tab, click View button
Date, insert current	EX 145	Insert TODAY() or NOW() function
Date, insert with AutoComplete	WD 25	Start typing date, press Enter
Dates, fill in using AutoFill	EX 135	*See* Reference Window: Creating a Series with AutoFill
Deleted Items folder, empty	OUT 41	Right-click Deleted Items folder in All Folders pane in Navigation Pane, click Empty "Deleted Items" Folder, click Yes
Design view, switch to	AC 65	In Views group on Home tab, click View button arrow, click Design View
Distribution list, create	OUT 22	*See* Reference Window: Creating a Distribution List
Distribution list, modify	OUT 23	Double-click distribution list contact in Contacts folder, click Select Members to add more contacts, click Remove to delete selected contact
Document, open	WD 46	Click 🏁, click Open, select drive and folder, click filename, click Open
Document, open new	WD 5–6	Click 🏁, click New
Document, preview	WD 34	Click 🏁, point to Print, click Print Preview
Document, save with same name	WD 17	On Quick Access Toolbar, click 💾
E-mail account, set up new account	OUT 5	Click Tools, click Account Settings, on E-mail tab, click New, follow wizard to Add a new e-mail account
E-mail message, create	OUT 10	*See* Reference Window: Creating an E-mail Message

TASK	PAGE #	RECOMMENDED METHOD
E-mail message, format	OUT 11	Select text, click appropriate buttons on Message tab
E-mail message, forward	OUT 26	Select message, click Forward button on Standard toolbar in Inbox, enter recipient e-mail address(es), type message, click Send button
E-mail message, open	OUT 25	Double-click message in Inbox main window
E-mail message, print	OUT 26	Select message in Inbox main window, click File, click Print, verify printer, select print style, click OK
E-mail message, read	OUT 25	Click message in Inbox main window, read message in Reading Pane
E-mail message, reply	OUT 25	Select message, click Reply button on Standard toolbar in Inbox, type reply message, click Send button
E-mail message, send to Outbox	OUT 14	Click Send button in message header
E-mail message, set importance	OUT 12	Click 📍 or ⬇ in Options group on Message tab
E-mail message, set sensitivity	OUT 13	In Options group on Message tab, click dialog box launcher to open Message Options dialog box, click Sensitivity arrow, select a sensitivity level
E-mail messages, send from Outbox	OUT 14	Switch to Outbox folder, click Send/Receive button on Standard toolbar
E-mail, receive	OUT 24	Switch to Mail folder, click Send/Receive button on Standard toolbar
Envelope, create	WD 36	*See* Reference Window: Creating an Envelope
Excel, start	EX 3	Click 🏁, click All Programs, click Microsoft Office, click Microsoft Office Excel 2007
Field, add to a table	AC 63	*See* Reference Window: Adding a Field Between Two Existing Fields
Field, define in a table	AC 55	*See* Reference Window: Defining a Field in Design View
Field, delete from a table	AC 74	*See* Reference Window: Deleting a Field from a Table Structure
Field, move to a new location in a table	AC 78	Display the table in Design view, click the field's row selector, drag the field with the pointer
Field property change, update	AC 77	Click 🖋, select option for updating field property
File, close	OFF 21	Click 🏁, click Close
File, copy	FM 14	*See* Reference Window: Copying a File or Folder
File, delete	FM 16	Right-click the file, click Delete
File, move	FM 12	*See* Reference Window: Moving a File or Folder
File, open	OFF 22	*See* Reference Window: Opening an Existing File or Creating a New File
File, print	OFF 27	*See* Reference Window: Printing a File
File, rename	FM 16	Right-click the file, click Rename, type the new name, press Enter
File, save	OFF 18	*See* Reference Window: Saving a File
File, switch between open	OFF 5	Click the taskbar button for the file you want to make active
Files, compress	FM 17	Drag files into a compressed folder
Files, sort by file detail	WIN 26	Click the column heading for the file detail
Files, view as large icons	WIN 25–26	Click the Views button arrow, click Large Icons
Files, view details	WIN 26	Click the Views button arrow, click Details
Filter By Selection, activate	AC 116	*See* Reference Window: Using Filter By Selection
Flag, add reminder to message in Inbox	OUT 30	Right-click flag icon in message header in Inbox main window, click Add Reminder, select or type a message in Flag to list, select due date in left Due by list, select due time in right Due by list, click OK

TASK	PAGE #	RECOMMENDED METHOD
Flag, add to message in Inbox	OUT 29	Right-click flag icon in message header in Inbox main window, click desired flag color
Flag, mark complete	OUT 30	Right-click flag icon, click Mark Complete
Folder List, display	OUT 4	Click 📁 in Navigation Pane
Folder List, use	OUT 4	Click folder in Folder List pane; click ➕ to see nested folders
Folder or drive contents, view in Windows Explorer	FM 7–8	Click ▷
Folder, copy	FM 14	See Reference Window: Copying a File or Folder
Folder, create	FM 11	See Reference Window: Creating a Folder
Folder, create	OUT 31	Right-click folder in Navigation Pane, click New Folder, type folder name, select items you want to store in Folder contains list, select folder location, click OK
Folder, move	FM 12	See Reference Window: Moving a File or Folder
Folder, open	WIN 28	Double-click the folder
Folder, rename	FM 16	Right-click the folder, click Rename, type the new name, press Enter
Font, change color	EX 61	In Font group on Home tab, click 🅰 ▾, click color
Font, change size	EX 60	In Font group on Home tab, click Font Size arrow, click point size
Font, change style	EX 60	In Font group on Home tab, click 𝐁, click 𝐼, or click U̲
Font, change typeface	EX 59, WD 81	In Font group on Home tab, click Font arrow, click font
Font size, change	WD 82	In Font group on Home tab, click Font Size arrow, click point size
Format, apply Accounting Style, Percent Style, or Comma Style	EX 65–66	In Font group on Home tab, click \$, click % or click ❟
Format, copy	WD 73	See Reference Window: Using the Format Painter
Format, copy using Format Painter	EX 75	Select range, in Clipboard group on Home tab click 🖌, click range
Format, decrease decimal places	EX 66	In Number group on Home tab, click ⬚
Format, find and replace	EX 38	In Editing group on Home tab, click Find & Select, click Replace
Format, increase decimal places	EX 66	In Number group on Home tab, click ⬚
Format Cells dialog box, open	EX 72	In Number group on Home tab, click Dialog Box Launcher
Formula, copy	EX 24	See Reference Window: Moving or Copying a Cell or Range
Formula, copy using the fill handle	EX 132	See Reference Window: Copying Formulas and Formats with AutoFill
Formula, enter	EX 29	See Reference Window: Entering a Formula
Formulas, view	EX 44	Click ⊞, press Ctrl+`
Forwarded contact card, add to Contacts folder	OUT 21	Drag contact card attachment from Message window to Contacts folder
Function, insert	EX 123	See Reference Window: Inserting a Function
Grayscale, preview presentation in	PPT 29	Click Print Preview tab, click Options button in Print group, point to Color/Grayscale, click Grayscale
Handouts, print	PPT 30	Click Print Preview tab, click Print What arrow in Page Setup group, click Handouts (4 Slides Per Page), click Print button
Header/footer, create	EX 99	In Page Layout view, click header or footer section, type text or click button in Header & Footer Elements group on Design tab

TASK	PAGE #	RECOMMENDED METHOD
Help, display basic topics	WIN 30	In Help and Support, click 🔹, click Windows Basics
Help, display table of contents	WIN 30	In Help and Support, click 🔹, click Table of Contents
Help, find topic	WIN 31	In Help and Support, click in the Search Help box, type word or phrase, click 🔎
Help, start	WIN 28–29	Click ⊕, click Help and Support
Help task pane, use	OFF 24	*See* Reference Window: Getting Help
Italics, add to text	WD 79	Select text, in Font group on Home tab click I
Items, delete	OUT 41	Click item, click ✖, click Yes if necessary
Items, select multiple	OUT 41	Click first item, press and hold Ctrl key, click additional items, release Ctrl key
Line spacing, change	WD 32	Select text to change, in Paragraph group on Home tab click spacing option
List box, scroll	WIN 19	Click list box arrow to display the list of options; click the scroll down or up arrow; or drag the scroll box
Margins, change	WD 65	*See* Reference Window: Changing Margins for a Document
Menu command, select	WIN 5–6	Click the command on the menu; for submenus, point to a command on the menu
Message format, choose	OUT 7	Click Tools, click Options, click Mail Format tab, select HTML in the Compose in this message format list, click OK
Messages, archive manually	OUT 40	Click File, click Archive, click Archive this folder and all subfolders option button, click folder to archive, type date in Archive items older than text box, click Browse, select save in location, click OK, click OK, click Yes
Messages, color	OUT 38	Click Tools, click Organize, click Using Colors link, set options, click Apply Color
Messages, file	OUT 31	Select message or messages in main window, drag to appropriate folder or subfolder
Messages, find	OUT 34	*See* Reference Window: Finding Messages
Messages, save	OUT 39	Select the message, click File, click Save As, select location, enter filename, click Save as type, select the file format, click Save
Messages, sort	OUT 37	Click column heading
Messages, sort by two or more columns	OUT 37	Click column heading, hold down Shift, click additional column headings, release Shift
Navigation Pane, use	OUT 4	Click button in Navigation Pane, click folder if necessary
Nonprinting characters, show	WD 8	In Paragraph group on Home tab, click ¶
Notes, create	PPT 27	Click in the Notes pane, type text
Notes, print	PPT 30	Click Print Preview tab, click Print What arrow in Page Setup group, click Notes Pages, click Print
Numbering, add to paragraphs	WD 76	Select paragraphs, in Paragraph group on Home tab click ☷
Object, open	AC 17	Double-click object in Navigation Pane
Object, save	AC 16	Click 💾, type the object name, click OK
Office program, start	OFF 3	*See* Reference Window: Starting Office Programs

TASK	PAGE #	RECOMMENDED METHOD
Outline text, promote	PPT 22	Click Outline tab, click paragraph, in Paragraph group on Home tab click
Page, change orientation	EX 96	Click Page Layout tab, click Orientation button in Page Setup group, choose orientation type
Page, view width	WD 10	Click Zoom level, click Page width, click OK
Page break preview, switch to	EX 96	Click
Page break, set	EX 97	See Reference Window: Setting and Removing Page Breaks
Paragraph, decrease indent	WD 72	In Paragraph group on Home tab, click
Paragraph, increase indent	WD 72	In Paragraph group on Home tab, click
PowerPoint, exit	PPT 31	Click
PowerPoint, start	PPT 2	Click , click All Programs, click Microsoft Office, click Microsoft Office PowerPoint 2007
Presentation, close	PPT 8	Click , click Close
Presentation, open	PPT 3	Click , click Open, navigate to folder, click filename, click Open
Presentation, print	PPT 30	Click Print Preview tab, click Print in Print group, select options, click OK
Primary key, specify	AC 61	See Reference Window: Specifying a Primary Key in Design View
Print area, define	EX 96	Select range, click Page Layout tab, click Print Area button in Page Setup group, click Set Print Area
Print layout view, change to	WD 7	Click
Program, close	WIN 11	Click or click
Program, close inactive	WIN 13	Right-click program button on taskbar, click Close
Program, Office, exit	OFF 28	Click on the title bar
Program, start	WIN 9	See Reference Window: Starting a Program
Program, switch to another	WIN 12–13	Click the program button on the taskbar
Programs, Office, open	OFF 3	See Reference Window: Starting Office Programs
Programs, switch between open	OFF 5	Click the taskbar button for the program you want to make active
Property sheet, open	AC 136	Right-click the object or control, click Properties
Query datasheet, sort	AC 114	See Reference Window: Sorting a Query Datasheet
Query, define	AC 120	Click Create tab, click Query Design button in Other group
Query, run	AC 121	Double-click query in Navigation Pane or, in Results group on Query Tools Design tab, click Run button
Query results, sort	AC 114	See Reference Window: Sorting a Query Datasheet
Range, copy	EX 24	See Reference Window: Moving or Copying a Cell or Range
Range, move	EX 24	See Reference Window: Moving or Copying a Cell or Range
Range, select adjacent	EX 22	See Reference Window: Selecting Cell Ranges
Range, select nonadjacent	EX 22	See Reference Window: Selecting Cell Ranges
Record, add a new one	AC 16	In Records group on Home tab, click New button
Record, delete	AC 102	See Reference Window: Deleting a Record
Record, move to first	AC 23	Click
Record, move to last	AC 23	Click

TASK	PAGE #	RECOMMENDED METHOD
Record, move to next	AC 23	Click ▶
Record, move to previous	AC 23	Click ◀
Records, redisplay all after filter	AC 118	In Sort & Filter group on Home tab, click Toggle Filter button
Recycle Bin, view contents of	WIN 6	Double-click Recycle Bin icon
Relative reference, change to absolute	EX 119	*See* Reference Window: Entering Relative, Absolute, and Mixed References
Report, print all	AC 32	*See* Reference Window: Printing a Report
Row, change height	EX 16	*See* Reference Window: Changing the Column Width or Row Height
Row, delete	EX 27	*See* Reference Window: Inserting or Deleting a Cell Range
Row, hide	EX 95	In Cells group on Home tab, click Format button, point to Hide & Unhide, click Hide Rows
Row, insert	EX 19	*See* Reference Window: Inserting a Column or Row
Row, select	EX 19	Click row heading; to select a range of rows, click the first row heading in the range, hold down Shift and click the last row in the range
Row, unhide	EX 95	Select rows above and below hidden rows, in Cells group on Home tab click Format button, point to Hide & Unhide, click Unhide Rows
Rows, repeat in printout	EX 98	Click Page Layout tab, click Print Titles button in Page Setup group, click Rows to repeat at top
Rule, create simple	OUT 33	Click Create Rule button on Standard toolbar, select conditions and set their values, select actions and set their values, click OK
Rule, delete	OUT 41	Click Tools, click Rules and Alerts, click rule in Rule list box, click Delete, click Yes, click OK
Rulers, display	WD 7	*See* Reference Window: Displaying the Rulers
ScreenTip, view	WIN 4–5	Position ↕ pointer over an object
Search Folder, display new	OUT 36	Right-click Search Folders in All Mail Folders pane in Navigation Pane, click New Search Folder, click desired Search Folder, click OK
Search Folder, use preset	OUT 35	Click ➕ next to Search Folders in All Mail Folders pane in Navigation Pane, click a search folder
Shortcut menu, open	WIN 7	Right-click an object
Signature, create new	OUT 8	Click Tools, click Options, click Mail Format tab, click Signatures, click New, enter a name for signature, click OK, type signature text, add font and paragraph formatting as needed, click OK
Signature, delete	OUT 41	Click Tools, click Options, click Mail Format tab, click Signatures, click signature in Signature list box, click Delete, click Yes, click OK, click OK
Signature, select for e-mail account	OUT 8	Click Tools, click Options, click Mail Format tab, select e-mail account name in Choose default signature list, select signature in Signature for new messages list, select signature in Signature for replies and forwards list, click OK
Slide, add new	PPT 20	In Slides group on Home tab, click New Slide button
Slide, delete	PPT 17	*See* Reference Window: Deleting Slides
Slide, go to next	PPT 4	Click ⯯

TASK	PAGE #	RECOMMENDED METHOD
Slide, move	PPT 23	Click ⊞, drag slide to new position
Slide Show, view	PPT 5	Click 🖵
Slide Sorter View, switch to	PPT 5	Click ⊞
Sort, specify ascending in datasheet	AC 113	Click column heading arrow, click Sort A to Z
Sort, specify descending in datasheet	AC 113	Click column heading arrow, click Sort Z to A
Speaker Notes, create	PPT 27	Click in the Notes Pane, type text
Spelling, check in presentation	PPT 25	Click Review tab, click Spelling in Proofing group
Spelling, check in worksheet	EX 40	Click Review tab, click Spelling in Proofing group
Spelling, correct individual word	WD 23	Right-click misspelled word (as indicated by a wavy red line), click correctly spelled word
Spelling and grammar, check	WD 50	See Reference Window: Checking a Document for Spelling and Grammar Errors
Start menu, open	WIN 5	Click 🔘
Stationery, create an e-mail message with	OUT 9	In Inbox, click Actions, point to New Mail Message Using, click More Stationery, select desired stationery, click OK
Style, apply	EX 77	See Reference Window: Applying Styles
Table, create in a database in Datasheet View	AC 8	See Reference Window: Creating a Table in Datasheet View
Table, open in a database	AC 17	Double-click table in Navigation Pane
Table, save in a database	AC 15	See Reference Window: Saving a Table
Text, align	WD 69–71	Select text, click, 📄, 📄, 📄, or 📄 on Mini toolbar
Text, align within a cell	EX 68	In Alignment group on Home tab, click 📄, click 📄, or click 📄
Text, copy and paste	WD 57	See Reference Window: Cutting (or Copying) and Pasting Text
Text, delete	WD 52	Press Backspace to delete character to left of insertion point; press Delete to delete character to the right; press Ctrl+Backspace to delete to beginning of word; press Ctrl+Delete to delete to end of word
Text, enter into cell	EX 10	Click the cell, type text entry, press Enter
Text, enter multiple lines in a cell	EX 12	See Reference Window: Entering Multiple Lines of Text Within a Cell
Text, find and replace	WD 62	See Reference Window: Finding and Replacing Text
Text, increase or decrease indent of	EX 68	In Alignment group on Home tab, click 📄 or 📄
Text, move by drag and drop	WD 54	See Reference Window: Dragging and Dropping Text
Text, select entire document	WD 30	Press Ctrl and click in selection bar
Text, select multiple adjacent lines	WD 30	Click and drag in selection bar
Text, select multiple nonadjacent lines	WD 30	Select text, press and hold Ctrl, select additional lines of text
Text, select multiple paragraphs	WD 30	Click and drag in selection bar
Thesaurus, use in PowerPoint	PPT 26	Click Review tab, click Thesaurus button in Proofing group
View, switch	OUT 36	Click View, point to Current View, click desired view
Window, close	OFF 6, WIN 6	Click ✕ or click ✕

TASK	PAGE #	RECOMMENDED METHOD
Window, maximize	OFF 7, WIN 15	Click ⬚ or click ⬚
Window, minimize	OFF 7, WIN 15	Click ⬚ or click ▬
Window, move	WIN 15	Drag the title bar
Window, resize	WIN 16	Drag a corner or edge of the window
Window, restore	OFF 7, WIN 15	Click ⬚ or click ⬚
Windows Explorer, start	FM 7, WIN 27	Click 🅦, click All Programs, click Accessories, click Windows Explorer
Windows Vista, shut down	WIN 32	Click 🅦, click ▶, click Shut Down
Windows Vista, start	WIN 2	Turn on the computer
Word, start	WD 3	Click 🅦, click All Programs, click Microsoft Office, click Microsoft Office Word 2007
Workbook, preview	EX 43	Click 🄱, click Print, click Print Preview
Workbook, print	EX 43	Click 🄱, click Print, click Print
Workbook, save	EX 21	On Quick Access Toolbar, click 💾
Worksheet, add background image	EX 63	Click Page Layout tab, click Background button in Page Setup group, click image file, click Insert
Worksheet, delete	EX 35	Right-click sheet tab, click Delete
Worksheet, insert	EX 35	Click 🗐
Worksheet, move	EX 36	Drag sheet tab to new location
Worksheet, rename	EX 36	Double-click sheet tab, type new name, press Enter
Worksheets, move between	EX 7	Click sheet tab; or click a tab scrolling button and then click the sheet tab
Workspace, zoom	OFF 8	*See* Reference Window: Zooming the Workspace
Zoom setting, change	WD 10	Drag Zoom slider